HARRY JOHNSON

Harry Johnson (1923–1977) was such a striking figure in economics that Nobel Laureate James Tobin designated the third quarter of the twentieth century as the age of Johnson. Johnson played a leading role in the development and extension of the Heckscher–Ohlin model of international trade, wrote fundamental articles on the balance of payments, and later developed the monetary approach to the balance of payments. Within monetary economics, he was also a seminal figure who, in a series of surveys, identified and explained the links between the ideas of the major postwar innovators. His discussion of the issues that would benefit from further work set the profession's agenda for a generation. Johnson was the consummate editor of his generation; he was managing editor of the *Review of Economic Studies* and editor of the *Journal of Political Economy* (twice), the *Manchester School*, and *Economica*. Trained at Toronto, Cambridge, and Harvard, he taught at Cambridge (1949–1956), Manchester (1956–1959), Chicago (1959–1977), the London School of Economics (1966–1974), and Geneva (1976–1977). This book chronicles his intellectual development and his contributions to economics, economic education, and, particularly in Canada and Britain, the discussion of economic policy.

D. E. Moggridge has been Professor of Economics at the University of Toronto since 1974. He previously served as a Research Fellow and Fellow of Clare College, Cambridge, from 1967 to 1975. Professor Moggridge was invited by the Royal Economics Society in 1969 to be an editor of *The Collected Writings of John Maynard Keynes*, thirty volumes of which appeared between 1970 and 1989. His coeditor of the volumes was Elizabeth Johnson, wife of the subject of this book. Professor Moggridge is also the author of *British Monetary Policy, 1924–1931* (Cambridge University Press, 1992); *Keynes* (1993); and *Maynard Keynes: An Economist's Biography* (1992). He also coedited with Susan Howson *The Wartime Diaries of Lionel Robbins and James Meade, 1943–45* (1990) and *The Cabinet Office Diary of James Meade, 1944–46* (1990). Professor Moggridge served as president of the History of Economics Society in 1988–1989 and has also served as review editor of *History of Political Economy* since 1998.

General Editor: Craufurd D. Goodwin, *Duke University*

This series contains original works that challenge and enlighten historians of economics. For the profession as a whole, it promotes better understanding of the origin and content of modern economics.

Other Books in the Series

William J. Barber, *Designs within Disorder: Franklin D. Roosevelt, the Economists, and the Shaping of American Economic Policy, 1933–1945*

William J. Barber, *From New Era to New Deal: Herbert Hoover, the Economists, and American Economic Policy, 1921–1933*

Timothy Davis, *Ricardo's Macroeconomics: Money, Trade Cycles, and Growth*

Jerry Evensky, *Adam Smith's Moral Philosophy: A Historical and Contemporary Perspective on Markets, Law, Ethics, and Culture*

M. June Flanders, *International Monetary Economics, 1870–1960: Between the Classical and the New Classical*

J. Daniel Hammond, *Theory and Measurement: Causality Issues in Milton Friedman's Monetary Economics*

Lars Jonung (ed.), *The Stockholm School of Economics Revisited*

Kyn Kim, *Equilibrium Business Cycle Theory in Historical Perspective*

Gerald M. Koot, *English Historical Economics, 1870–1926: The Rise of Economic History and Mercantilism*

David Laidler, *Fabricating the Keynesian Revolution: Studies of the Inter-War Literature on Money, the Cycle, and Unemployment*

Odd Langholm, *The Legacy of Scholasticism in Economic Thought: Antecedents of Choice and Power*

Harro Maas, *William Stanley Jevons and the Making of Modern Economics*

Philip Mirowski, *More Heat Than Light: Economics as Social Physics, Physics as Nature's Economics*

Philip Mirowski (ed.), *Nature Images in Economic Thought: "Markets Read in Tooth and Claw"*

Mary S. Morgan, *The History of Econometric Ideas*

Takashi Negishi, *Economic Theories in a Non-Walrasian Tradition*

Heath Pearson, *Origins of Law and Economics: The Economists' New Science of Law, 1830–1930*

Malcolm Rutherford, *Institutions in Economics: The Old and the New Institutionalism*

Esther-Mirjam Sent, *The Evolving Rationality of Rational Expectations: An Assessment of Thomas Sargent's Achievements*

Yuichi Shionoya, *Schumpeter and the Idea of Social Science*

Juan Gabriel Valdes, *Pinochet's Economists: The Chicago School of Economics in Chile*

Karen I. Vaughn, *Austrian Economics in America: The Migration of a Tradition*

E. Roy Weintraub, *Stabilizing Dynamics: Constructing Economic Knowledge*

Harry Johnson

A Life in Economics

D. E. MOGGRIDGE
University of Toronto

CAMBRIDGE
UNIVERSITY PRESS

CAMBRIDGE UNIVERSITY PRESS
Cambridge, New York, Melbourne, Madrid, Cape Town, Singapore, São Paulo, Delhi

Cambridge University Press
32 Avenue of the Americas, New York, NY 10013-2473, USA

www.cambridge.org
Information on this title: www.cambridge.org/9780521874823

First published 2008

Printed in the United States of America

A catalog record for this publication is available from the British Library.

Library of Congress Cataloging in Publication Data

Moggridge, D. E. (Donald Edward), 1943–
Harry Johnson : a life in economics / D. E. Moggridge.
p.   cm. – (Historical perspectives on modern economics)
Includes bibliographical references and index.
ISBN 978-0-521-87482-3 (hardback)
1. Johnson, Harry G. (Harry Gordon), 1923–1977.   2. Economists – Canada – Biography.
3. Economics – Canada – History – 20th century.   I. Title.   II. Series.
HB121.J65M64   2008
330.15–dc22
[B]   2007014002

ISBN   978-0-521-87482-3 hardback

Contents

Contents

Photographs and Drawings

1. Harry's parents at Spruce Ridges – New Year's 1946 (Elizabeth Simpson)

2. Harry Johnson senior at Mitch Hepburn's birthday party at Hepburn's farm in Elgin County – 12 August 1938 (Harry senior is second from the left in the back row; in the middle of the second row are Eve Hepburn, Peter Hepburn, Mitch and Patsy Hepburn; second from the right in the front row is Maurice Duplesis, the premier of Quebec) (Elizabeth Simpson)

3. Harry at St. George's School – 1926 (Harry is on the left at the back) (Blatz Papers)

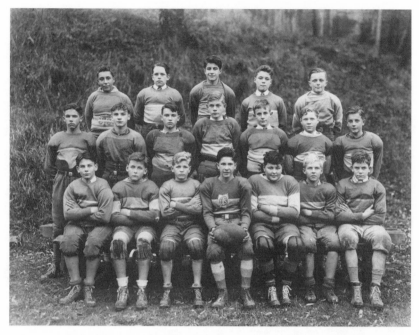

4. Harry with the UTS 100-lb rugby team – 1936 (Harry is third from the right in the front row; Harry Parkinson is second from the left in the back row) (Elizabeth Simpson)

5. Harry in 1944 (Elizabeth Simpson)

8. Harry at LSE – late 1960s (Elizabeth Simpson)

9. Harry and Liz with Zvi Griliches and his wife – late 1972 (Elizabeth Simpson)

10. The Octograph – 1973 (Roger Vaughan)

11. Harry carving at the Konstanz Seminar – June 1973 (Elizabeth Simpson)

12. Harry in London – January 1976 (Elizabeth Simpson)

13. Harry in Tokyo – October 1976 (Elizabeth Simpson)

HARRY JOHNSON

Introduction

Harry Johnson . . . bestrode our discipline like a Colossus.

A Nobel Prize? He was the people's choice within the profession. Though selection committees stress quantum innovations, sooner or later they would surely have rewarded the massive incremental and synthetic advancement of knowledge that Johnson achieved.

Tobin 1978, 443, 457

During the past two decades Harry Johnson . . . towered above the rank and file of economists, not only in contributions to international economics but more importantly . . . he stood large and alone among economists as a wide-ranging social critic who was constantly extending the boundaries of economics.

He more than anyone else took up the tremendous task of clearing the tangled thicket of half-truths in economics. A phrase from Saul Bellow tells it all, " . . . to live, to breathe, to be, we must get clear of the rubbish and the cliches."

Schultz, Harry G. Johnson Memorial Meeting, 3

Thus two Nobel laureates, James Tobin and T. W. Schultz, remembered Harry Johnson after his death in 1977. He was not the best known living Canadian-born economist; John Kenneth Galbraith occupied that position. But Harry, as he was known throughout the profession, was certainly the best known Canadian-citizen economist. Outside the profession, except in Canada and Great Britain, where he was a public intellectual, he was relatively unknown.

During his brief professional career, cut short by a stroke in 1973 and his death in 1977 just over two weeks before his 54th birthday, Harry Johnson played a dominant role in two areas of economics. In the development of trade theory in the Heckscher–Ohlin tradition, he made fundamental contributions to the theory of tariffs and to the formal theory of trade and growth. He also began to move beyond Heckscher–Ohlin to the "new trade theory" now associated with Paul Krugman and others. In monetary and international monetary economics, he was almost as seminal a figure.

1

In classic surveys of the literature, he identified and explained the links between the ideas of the major postwar innovators in monetary theory and, in his discussion of issues that would benefit from further research, set the profession's agenda for a generation. He was the founding contributor to the monetary approach to the balance of payments. He creatively extended economic analysis to encompass new phenomena – opulence, economic nationalism, science policy, and the organisation and working of institutions of higher education.

He was the most peripatetic economist of his generation, speeding ideas around the world. He was a missionary for what he called scientific economics and played an important role in raising professional standards and improving professional training in Canada and Britain. As a major figure in turning economics into an international enterprise, he knew everybody.

Moreover, his skills were recognised early and exploited. In June 1949 he was invited to join the Advisory Board of Editors of the *Review of Economic Studies*. Two years later he became Assistant Editor. His editorial career would include editorships of the *Journal of Political Economy* (twice), the *Manchester School*, and *Economica*, as well as a watching brief on the *Journal of International Economics*. He was the best editor of his generation. With his encyclopedic knowledge of the literature and the profession, he could guide authors in fruitful directions and place their contributions in the context of contemporary developments in the discipline. Here his constant travelling, conference-going, and networking played a crucial role. He was on to trends before they appeared in print. He once remarked that if he had relied on libraries or publication he would be at least two years behind where he was and thus be obsolete (see discussion in Chapter 12).

His contemporaries recognised his skills as an expositor. Almost all of the organisers of the leading lectures in economics welcomed his participation – the Wicksell (Sweden), the de Vries (Netherlands), the Stamp (Great Britain), the Ely (United States), the Innis (Canada), the Jahnsson (Finland), the Horowitz (Israel) – not to mention hundreds of seminars and local lectures. His knowledge of the literature made him the ideal person to provide the concluding remarks at conferences. He made lecture tours of Australia and New Zealand. In the last eleven months of his travels, although he had never fully recovered from his earlier stroke, he visited fifteen countries.

His contemporaries honoured him with honorary degrees (seven); fellowships (the American Academy of Arts and Sciences, the British Academy, the Royal Society of Canada, and the Econometric Society); prizes (including the Innis-Gérin medal of the Royal Society of Canada, the Bernhard Harms Prize of the University of Kiel, and the Prix Mondial Messin Habif of the University of Geneva); and, because he was also competent, professional society offices – the Canadian Political Science Association, the British Association of University Teachers of Economics, and Section F of the British Association for the Advancement of Science. If he had lived longer, he would probably have served as president of the American Economic Association. He had been considered as a possible president of the Royal Economic Society well before he died, but he had been thought too controversial with his zeal for reform and too "difficult" (British Library of Political and Economic Science, Royal Economic Society Archives, RES4/4/4, E. A. G. Robinson to Charles Carter, 11 February 1970). He had been nominated for the Nobel Prize in economics but whether he would have received it had he lived is more debatable.[1]

All his achievements occurred in a professional life that lasted just over twenty-eight years. He produced over five hundred academic papers and fifteen books or pamphlets, as well as numerous edited collections. He left institutions behind him – the "study group" in the social sciences in Britain; the before-the-beginning-of-term crash course in mathematics and statistics that starts graduate programmes in economics. And he was read: His colleagues and graduate students eagerly awaited his latest surveys of the state of the art. In the last six years of his life, with an average of 249 citations per year, he was the second most-cited international economist after Paul Samuelson.

Harry's active academic life spanned important years in the history of economics. In trade theory, it was the period when the Heckscher–Ohlin model was elaborated and filled out and when "new" theories of trade made their appearance. In monetary economics, Keynesianism rose to dominance before fading in the face of monetarism. The latter was part of a broader trend that brought back a liberal tradition in economic theory and policy that seemed to have fallen victim to two world wars and a depression. As a student at Toronto, Cambridge, and Harvard and a faculty member at St. Francis Xavier and Cambridge, Harry started a man of the left, favourably disposed to the economic and social reform and the political and economic views of the Cambridge Keynesians. In 1952 Dennis Robertson saw him becoming "the first manager of Branch X of the United Bank of the British (? or Canadian) Soviet Socialist Republic" (see discussion in Chapter 6). Yet, and not just after his move to Chicago, he was at the centre of the liberalising

---

[1] Both James Tobin and Gottfried Haberler thought he would have received it had he lived (Tobin 1978, 457; Hoover Institution, Haberler Papers, Box 18, Haberler to E. Johnson, 23 May 1977).

movement – to which he made substantial contributions both as a theorist and as a commentator on contemporary policy developments and evolving institutions. A classic example of this was his making the case for a free trade agreement with the United States in September 1960 to a meeting of liberally minded Canadians concerned with the rejuvenation of the Liberal Party of Canada. He was "too liberal for the Liberals" (see discussion in Chapter 9). But such an agreement came into force in 1989 – in part the result of his nurturing Canadian opinion. His views about the regulation of financial institutions provide another example. These views, derided by Robertson in 1952, were far removed from his advocacy of competition in British banking in the late 1960s and early 1970s.

The purpose of this book is to trace Harry Johnson's intellectual biography and his contributions to the discipline of economics. Its first source is his publications: His bibliography runs to fifty-three printed pages of the *Journal of Political Economy* (Longawa 1984). The second source is the memoirs and assessments of his contemporaries and his students. His papers and those of his contemporaries, which are scattered in archives on both sides of the Atlantic, including institutional archives, are the third source.

Harry himself also left behind a substantial amount of autobiographical material. The earliest fragment, "Analysis of Rooming House Group," provided the basis for a graduate term paper at the University of Toronto in 1946–7 (Box 31, Toombs Human Relations Industry). His 1969 Autobiographical Notes, which unlike "Harry Johnson's Contributions to Economics: An Evaluation by Himself" of February 1974 (Box 31, Manuscripts 1973–4) was listed in his bibliography (Longawa 1984, 703), accompanied the creation of a repository for his published works at Lakehead University in Thunder Bay, Ontario. The first of the published autobiographical sketches, "Cambridge in the 1950s: Memoirs of an Economist" (1974), was prepared for a pair of talks given by Harry and his wife Elizabeth at Amherst College on 19 February 1973. The second, "Cambridge as an Academic Environment in the Early 1930s: A Reconstruction from the Late 1940s" (1977), was an attempt, as he put it, to answer the question: "What, then, was Cambridge like as an environment for economic discussion and research in the period of the writing of *The General Theory?*" (1978a, 84) for a conference devoted to those years of creation for Keynes. These two papers were collected together with other pieces on Cambridge and Keynes in *The Shadow of Keynes* (1978e). One of the origins for the 1974 Self-Evaluation was the stimulation provided by a colleague at the Graduate Institute of International Studies in Geneva. Gerard Curzon told Harry that his name had been suggested for a Nobel Prize in economics and remarked that the only person who could do justice to the range of his interests was Harry himself. Harry responded with a thirty-two page evaluation written in the third person, attaching a brief curriculum vitae and a bibliography classed by type of publication. There were probably other influences. Harry's stroke in October 1973 and his resignation from his chair at the London School of Economics (LSE) in 1974 shook him deeply and caused him to reevaluate his past. During August and September 1974, while he was clearing up his affairs in London, he wrote four memoirs: one covering his life to 1943 and concentrates on his undergraduate education at the University of Toronto (1974 Memoir I); another focuses on his year (1943–4) as the one-man economics department at St. Francis Xavier University at Antigonish, Nova Scotia (1974 Memoir II); and two deal with his years at LSE (1974 Memoirs III and IV). These memoirs were probably also an outlet for his restless energy. Before his stroke, a major outlet for this energy, other than work and travel, had been the carving of small figures or puzzles in wood. He had started this as a boy but took it up again seriously as an adult when he stopped smoking in 1956. Although he was ambidextrous, he carved with his dominant left hand. The stroke affected his left side and forced him to find substitutes. He tried working with his other hand with a vise attached to his desk. For a time he tried animal silhouettes made with an electric saw and Elmer's glue. He also tried small figures in plasticine. In these circumstances, memoir-writing became a form of therapy. In the end, travel became the best therapy – and he pursued it more assiduously in the last year of his life than ever before. But autobiography kept intruding, as in his tribute and reminiscence of "Ruth Cohen: A Neglected Contributor to Contemporary Capital Theory," which appeared in *The Shadow of Keynes*, and in his last published paper, "Networks of Economists and International Monetary Reform" (1982), which was a reflection on two such networks in which he had participated.

At the heart of any autobiography is the subject's memory, which may be supplemented by diaries, correspondence, and other external evidence. Psychologists and others have been concerned with the character of memory for decades given the importance of memory in many walks of life and the consequences of memory loss. Although the first experiments with what psychologists now refer to as autobiographical memory date from 1879, the serious study of such memory dates from the 1980s.[2] Nonetheless there were

---

[2] For a good collection of essays on autobiographical memory with an historical dimension that stretches from the nineteenth century to the present, see Draaisma (2004).

studies of other types of memory. For example, in a classic study by F. C. Bartlett, *Remembering* (1932), which included experiments using a native American folktale, "The War of the Ghosts," adapted from a translation by Franz Boas, the following experimental results emerged.

1. It appears that accuracy of reproduction, in a literal sense, is the rare exception. . . .
2. In a chain of reproductions obtained from a single individual, the general form or outline is remarkably persistent. . . .
4. With frequent reproduction the form and items of remembered detail very quickly become strengthened and thereafter suffer little change.
5. With infrequent reproduction, omission of detail, simplification of events and structure, and transformation of items into more familiar detail may go on almost indefinitely, or so long as unaided recall is possible.
6. . . . [I]n long-distance remembering, elaboration becomes more common in some cases; and there may be increasing importation, or invention. . . .
8. Detail is outstanding when it fits in with a subject's pre-formed interests and tendencies. It is then remembered, though often transformed and it tends to take a progressively earlier place in successive reproductions. . . .
10. In all successive rememberings, rationalisation, the reduction of material to a form which can be readily and 'satisfyingly' dealt with is very prominent. (93–4)

The recent studies of autobiographical memory suggest that as the memory has to deal with more complex situations it becomes less accurate. The construction of autobiographical memories from their various components will also be "guided by the person's goals at the time of retrieval, as well as by the goals at the time of encoding [the components, so that] changes in what is remembered should be expected" (Rubin 1996, 4). The presence of specific details may convince individuals that the remembered event occurred, even when there is evidence that it did not (5). High levels of emotional stress increase accurate recall, while depression leads to the recall of general rather than specific events (10).

A central process in the working memory constructs and maintains autobiographical memories, which are stored in the long-term memory. The knowledge is indexed by "personally meaningful and self-relevant themes" (Conway 1996, 72). These themes, which are central to psychoanalysis, may be period-specific (e.g., to transitions such as university or the achievement of specific possible selves). But such knowledge is selectively encoded so memories are never "complete."

Events that do not impinge upon the current themes, plans and goals of the self, and that do not correspond to existing autobiographical knowledge structures, may simply not be encoded in long-term memory. Thus event knowledge is only incompletely retained and events themselves are only retained to the extent that they are self-relevant and/or compatible with the relevant pre-existing long-term knowledge. (87–8)

Memories are not complete, but they are not necessarily inaccurate. They are likely to be fairly accurate if only because if autobiographical memory exists to provide some record of past selves, one needs records of relevant episodes such as the attainment of particular goals. C. R. Barclay believes

most autobiographical memories are true but inaccurate. What is remembered in particular does not reflect the way some event really happened. These errors . . . may be mediated by an accurate "self-portrait" because not just any "memory" is acceptable as one's own. The sense of familiarity created by an event is associated with a judgment that the event is true to what most likely occurred and consistent with what should have happened. (1986, 97)

References to events such as leaving university leads us to another characteristic of autobiographical memories, their concentration – what Draaisma calls "the reminiscence effect" (2004, 193). Investigators in study after study have found that the density of memories is "humped" with a peak in early adulthood. The young adulthood hump is stable across cultures and characterises all kinds of memories – movies, songs, styles of clothing, members of sports teams (Rubin, Rahall, and Poon 1998). It is robust and "cannot be expunged completely even under extreme pathological conditions" (Draasima 2004, 193). The same hump appears for autobiographically consequential memories. Of course, there are several possible explanations. The simplest is that significant first times occur more frequently during early adulthood.

During our youth and early adult years events occur that shape our personality, determine our identity and guide the course of our life. Accidental encounters, a book that made a great impression on us, a penetrating talk that made us suddenly realize what we wanted to do with our life – we are at our most responsive to that sort of event during those years. The [reminiscence] effect contrives that someone, once in his life, recalls the events that have turned him into what he now is . . . [but] the narrator tries to make them look more or less coherent. (195)

Economists are no exception to this tendency to judge from a study of twenty-four article-length autobiographies (Weintraub 2005).

Harry's memoirs did not always concentrate on the years of young adulthood, which as he was born in 1923 would take him to his early years in

Manchester after 1956. That is not surprising: He was still in middle age when he wrote the memoirs. His 1969 Autobiographical Notes come closest to the general pattern with the first seven pages being concerned with his family and his education, the next two with his years in Cambridge and the last seven to his subsequent career. In contrast, his 1974 Self-Evaluation devotes only three pages to his student days, three to his years in Cambridge and then eleven to Chicago from 1959 to 1966 and eleven to the Chicago/LSE years. But if one takes the full range of the memoirs, Harry is typical.

Harry's memoirs, generally speaking, are internally consistent. They are, however, not always accurate on such things as the details of particular courses at Toronto or particular details of teaching arrangements at Cambridge. Their level of accuracy is, moreover, questionable over several events that Harry made much of: the importance of the liquidity preference versus loanable funds debate in Cambridge immediately after the war; his own choice of fields of specialisation in the 1940s; his experience with a Harvard doctoral dissertation, which he abandoned in the early 1950s; his 1958 decision to leave the University of Manchester; his involvement in discussions of Canadian economic policy after his arrival in Chicago in 1959; his "policy" in Chicago "of avoiding conflict with senior economists – specifically Milton Friedman" (1974 Self Evaluation, 16); and his relationships with his colleagues, both senior and junior, at LSE.

The memoirs have a common characteristic that reflects Harry's definition of himself. He always tended to see himself as an outsider. This probably made some sense as a 9-year-old city-bred, privately educated student in a two-room local public school in Scarborough in 1932–3; as a socially unsophisticated and immature 16-year-old undergraduate entering the University of Toronto in 1939; as a 20-year-old Toronto Protestant professor of economics at the Scots-Catholic St. Francis Xavier University in Antigonish, Nova Scotia, in 1943; or as a newly arrived student in Cambridge in October 1945. But it looked odder the longer he stayed in Cambridge, as he became a fellow of King's College and an Apostle. It looked even odder when he returned to England in 1966 as Lionel Robbins's successor at LSE. Nonetheless, perhaps because he retained his Chicago connection, he continued to behave as a social anthropologist examining the behaviour of some exotic tribe to many of whose rituals he was admitted by virtue of office. In some cases, this led to peculiar results.

Inevitably, I have used Harry's memoirs often. Wherever possible, I have tried to check them against other material. But that has not always been possible. The reader should treat the autobiographical evidence as being at best the same quality as more conventional documentary evidence.

In the course of working on this biography I have incurred innumerable debts. The longest standing are to Ed Safarian, the colleague who first raised the idea of a intellectual biography, and Harry's widow, Elizabeth Simpson, my former coeditor of the *Collected Writings of John Maynard Keynes*, who assisted my passage in innumerable ways. The Donner Canadian Foundation generously agreed to finance the project and were patient when periods of academic administration slowed things down. Then there are my debts to archivists and librarians. The most important here are Dan Meyer of the University of Chicago who informed me of an agreement among research libraries for the lending of archives that made it possible for the Johnson Papers to migrate to Canada and to Richard Landon, the director of the Thomas Fisher Rare Book Library at the University of Toronto, who provided them with a home and me with research space and the support of Luba Frastacky. Thanks here are also due to the University of Toronto Press in the form of Ron Schoeffel, who took the papers across the border on the regular runs between the Press's warehouses in Toronto and Buffalo. Thanks are also due to archivists at the British Library of Political and Economic Science; the U.K. National Archives at Kew; Cambridge University Library; the Hoover Institution at Stanford University; the Houghton Library at Harvard University; Jesus College, Cambridge; the Modern Archive Centre at King's College, Cambridge; the Perkins Library at Duke University; the Public Archives of Canada; the Regenstein Library at the University of Chicago; St. Francis Xavier University; the Thomas Fisher Rare Book Library at the University of Toronto; the University of Toronto Archives; University of Toronto Schools; and the Wren Library at Trinity College, Cambridge. I also thank the Director of the London School of Economics for making Harry's Personal File available, Christopher Johnson for allowing me to use and quote from Lionel Robbins's Papers, the Provost and Scholars of King's College, Cambridge for permission to quote material in the Kahn and Kaldor Papers, Elizabeth Simpson for permission to quote from Harry's published and unpublished writings, Richard Landon for permission to reproduce a photograph of Harry from the Blatz Papers, Roger Vaughan for permission to reproduce "The Octograph," and Donald Winch for easing my way into certain parts of the Royal Economic Society Archives. In the course of my work, I received research assistance from Megan MacGarvie, Kathy Rasmussen, and the late Shauna Saunders. I would also like to thank George Altmeyer, Mark Blaug, James Cameron, Dennis Coppock, Hugh Corbett,

Max Corden, Meghnad Desai, Christopher Foster, the late Milton Friedman, Geoff Harcourt, Al Harberger, Jack Johnston, David Laidler, Allan MacEachan, R. M. MacIntosh, Joseph MacNeil, Alvin Marty, the late Don Patinkin, Will Peters, Ed Safarian, Aubrey Silberston, and participants at the Harry Johnson Remembrance and Appreciation Session organised by Larry Moss for the History of Economics Society Meeting at Vancouver in July 2000 for information and help over various details. I enjoyed helpful discussions with Dan Hammond and participants at the 2005 History of Economics Society meetings at Tacoma, as well as those attending the 2005 British History of Economic Thought Conference at Exeter, on a paper on the evolution of Harry's macroeconomics and his attitudes to Keynes. When this volume was in draft, *History of Political Economy*'s 2006 Conference on Lifewriting and the History of Economic Thought allowed me to exchange ideas with fellow practitioners. Finally, I thank those who have read and commented on various drafts: Sue Howson, who spent the summer of 2004 on what I came to call "persecution," going through my draft with a very fine toothed comb; Elizabeth Simpson, who spent the summer of 2005 applying her experienced editorial skills to the manuscript; Roger Backhouse; David Laidler; and Ed Safarian.

In the pages that follow, I have used the now normal convention of referring to published work by author and date. In Harry's case, I have also used short forms for his published books and collections of articles. The short forms are as follows:

ATT – *Aspects of the Theory of Tariffs* (1971)

CQ – *The Canadian Quandary: Economic Problems and Policies* (1963; 2nd ed. 1977; 3rd ed. 2006)

E&S – *On Economics and Society* (1975)

EPLDC – *Economic Policies Towards Less Developed Countries* (1967)

EME – *Essays in Monetary Economics* (1967)

FEME – *Further Essays in Monetary Economics* (1973)

IMC – *Inflation and the Monetarist Controversy* (1972)

ITEG – *International Trade and Economic Growth; Studies in Pure Theory* (1958)

MABP – *The Monetary Approach to the Balance of Payments* (ed. with Jacob Frenkel) (1975)

MMT – *Macroeconomics and Monetary Theory* (1971)

MTEG – *Money, Trade and Economic Growth: Survey Lectures in Economic Theory* (1962)

SEME – *Selected Essays in Monetary Economics* (1978)

Shadow – The Shadow of Keynes: Understanding Keynes, Cambridge, and Keynesian Economics (with Elizabeth Johnson) (1978)
WEC – The World Economy of the Cross roads (1965)

References to Harry's papers in the Regenstein Library at the University of Chicago are referred to simply by box number, file title. References to other papers include source information and the named individual or institution.

ONE

Toronto

Harry Gordon Johnson was born on 26 May 1923 at Victoria Memorial Hospital in Toronto. He was the first child of Henry Herbert Gordon Johnson, who was also known as Harry, and Frances Lily Muat. Harry senior had been born in 1891, one of six children of a master plumber who had come to Canada from southern Ireland. Frances Muat's father had come from Scotland at age 19, served in the Governor General's Guards in the North-West Rebellion, and eventually spent twenty-six years as a travelling salesman for H. J. Heinz. He became president and secretary of the Canadian Grocers Association. Frances had two sisters. Harry senior was educated at Jarvis and Riverdale Collegiate Institutes in Toronto and entered the University of Toronto in 1910 as a student of engineering. He did not go past his second year. Frances, who had been educated at Jarvis Collegiate and Westminster College also entered the University of Toronto in 1910 as a student at University College.[1] She graduated in 1914 and proceeded to the University's Faculty of Education as a general student in 1914–15 before beginning her teaching career at Souris, Manitoba, where she taught English, history, and modern languages. After a year, however, she returned to Toronto to marry Harry senior, who had become a journalist, initially with the Toronto *World*, then with the *Mail and Empire* and the *Globe*, where he rose to be city editor. At the time of Harry's birth, Harry senior was city editor of the *Toronto Star* under Harry Hindmarsh. "*Star* city editors were the hardest working in the business, and it was a rare man who stood the pace for more than three or four years" (Harkness 1963, 156). Harry senior lasted seven years in

---

[1] University education was rare at the time: As late as 1948 of 100 pupils entering elementary school in Ontario only 4 would enter university. Women were less likely to enter than men: in 1913–14 only 27.2 percent of University of Toronto undergraduate were female. The percentage in 1950–1 was the same (Gidney 1999, Figure 1; McKillop 1994, 556).

the job before he returned to the editorial department of the *Globe* in 1928. However, he did not remain there long, for in April 1929 he was appointed secretary of the Ontario Liberal Association.

At the time of Harry's birth, Toronto was a city of just over 520,000. It would number almost 670,000 in 1941.[2] The city was the central focus of Anglophone Canadian culture, and it was vying to replace Montreal as Canada's premier economic metropolis. It was the capital and economic and cultural centre of the province of Ontario. In the 1920s, Toronto was very much an Anglo-Celtic Protestant place: In the 1921 census 85.3 percent of the population listed their ethnic origin in the British Isles; 33.2 percent were like Harry senior Anglican, with the Methodists, Presbyterians, Congregationalists, and Baptists accounting for another 42.5 percent. Catholics accounted for 12.4 percent of the population and 6.6 percent was listed as Jewish (Lemon 1985, Appendix Tables VIII and IX). Although Ulster Protestants were a small part of the whole, Toronto's politics were dominated by the Orange order, where the Glorious 12th was less a manifestation of triumphalism as an occasion for social festivities. Indeed the order had taken on a distinctly Canadian identity, where the myths remained Irish but English, Scots, and German Protestants were represented. It was so dominant that the first non-Protestant, non-Orange-order-member mayor was not elected until 1954.

In a world where there were separate organisations for provincial and federal political parties, the Toronto of Harry's youth was dominated by the Conservatives: Federally the city returned one Liberal in 1921 and 1930 and none in 1925 and 1926. At the time Harry senior became secretary, the provincial Liberal Party was in disarray: It had been out of office since 1905 and had gone through six leaders while losing seven elections. In the last Ontario election in 1926, it had nominated candidates in fewer than half the province's 112 ridings and won 21 seats. In October 1929 it would nominate only 87 candidates and won 13 seats only one of which was urban and none of which was francophone. "The Ontario provincial Liberal Party was not much more than a rural Protestant splinter group, narrowly based on a dozen primarily dry ridings" (McKenty 1967, 30–1). Its relations with the federal party were poor: "Mackenzie King [the federal Liberal leader] treated his provincial cousins as though they were carriers of the plague" (Oliver 1975, 136). King refused to campaign for the provincial party and in 1929 refused to provide financial support. Johnson's appointment outraged many federal

---

[2] The metropolitan area (now the city of Toronto) had a population of 611,000 in 1921 and 900,000 in 1941 (Lemon 1985, Appendix Table I). Now it is 2.5 million.

Liberals. One wrote to King that "those who knew Johnson 'state that in their opinion he does not possess one qualification to fit him as an organiser' and that not even King's 'bitterest political enemy' could have devised a scheme more certain to bring political disaster at the next election" (Saywell 1991, 45). Just six months later, Senator Hayden told King that Johnson "seems to be an excellent man and for the first time in years there is hope of doing something in Ontario" (45). Just what that "something" was is unclear, but the form it took was another matter.

The Ontario Liberals called a leadership convention in Toronto for 16 December 1930. W. E. Sinclair who had led the party in the elections of 1926 and 1929 had never been elected by the Ontario Liberal Association, only by his legislature caucus. One possible contender for the position was the 34-year-old federal Member of Parliament (M.P.) for Elgin West since 1926, Mitchell Hepburn, "Mitch" to his friends and foes alike. He was a powerful speaker and charming personality with boundless energy. He had a charming wife and looked an attractive candidate. However he had a downside in a fondness for women, scotch, and roué friends. As Harry senior told Norman Lambert, formerly his federal Liberal counterpart in 1934, "If you hear anything break regarding Hepburn & women you'll know it is probably true"(McKenty 1967, 181). "I have a little Scotch in me," Hepburn would say with a grin, "sometimes more, sometimes less" (Saywell 1991, 121). "Words came easily, sometimes too easily if he had been drinking, and any audience, large or small started the adrenalin flowing" (125). As a result of this reputation, his candidacy was opposed by the *Globe*, the *Star*, the older generation of Ontario Liberals, and Mackenzie King, who tried to stop him but couldn't manage to find an alternative candidate. As a result Hepburn was elected leader. But the party wasn't out of the woods yet: Hepburn was still a federal M.P. and remained one until 1934, when he won a seat in the Ontario legislature. Fund-raising remained difficult, and the Johnson family felt the difficulty directly: In the summer of 1931 both the office rent and Harry Johnson senior's salary were overdue, and the same was true in November 1932 (105, 106). Even with the government's unpopularity, the Liberals still began the 1934 election campaign on a shoe-string, but the tide turned: "One day when they were at a restaurant in either Kingston or Belleville, Harry Johnson raced in with a cheque – 'We're in, the breweries have come through.'" (149 n.23). By that stage Johnson had the organisational infrastructure in place and relations with the federal Liberal organisation in Ontario stabilised. The 1934 provincial election gave the Liberals 71 of the Legislature's now 90 seats but only 6 of 13 in Toronto.

Hepburn would remain in office until 1942, and the Liberals, in power until 1943. Harry senior retired from provincial politics in 1943 after a cerebral haemorrhage. He then worked in public relations for Algoma Steel, but worked for the federal Liberals from early 1945.

While his father was establishing his political reputation and fostering the revival of the Liberals in Ontario, Harry was acquiring his basic education, and his mother was acquiring an important new career. For a time, the two overlapped as the child study movement came to Toronto.

The first child study laboratory in North America emerged at the State University of Iowa in 1910. Later in the decade and in the early 1920s, the movement spread to California, Minnesota, Harvard, Yale, and Columbia. It also spread to Canada in the 1920s with schools at the University of Toronto and McGill, both funded by the Laura Spellman Rockefeller Memorial Foundation. The McGill scheme collapsed in 1930; the Toronto one survives to this day. The Toronto scheme was an outgrowth of World War I. The Hart House Muscle Function Re-education Programme of 1916–19 existed to rehabilitate wounded soldiers.[3] It revealed that rehabilitation was much more successful if the patients were increasingly independent members of the programme – if they were participant learners mastering the present situation and meeting later problems with confidence. The idea was to take this experience over to the education of children. They would be younger, the tasks would be simpler, but the motivation would be the same with the emphasis on self-direction and progressive achievement. In the education scheme, the important element was learning; content was secondary.

Learning is defined simply but dynamically as the response whereby the child seeks to meet his needs within his environment. Thus understood, success in any learning situation becomes the experience of satisfaction following effort, and what behaviour the child learns will depend on what brings satisfaction. The responsibility of the adult is to make provision for successful learning throughout the child's day.…

In St. George's School, from the beginning the routines of the nursery school day were considered to hold a prominent place in the child's learning experience. (Millichamp and Fletcher 1951, 29)

The Toronto school, which later grew into and became a part of the larger Institute of Child Study, had as its founding director William Blatz, a psychologist who had been involved in the Hart House Programme. The scheme had the full support of the university's newly independent Department of Psychology, as well as the School of Hygiene. St. George's School was to be a

---

[3] Hart House was the men's student union at the University of Toronto.

centre for research and training focused on the understanding of, education of, and care of young children. At the heart of Blatz's vision was security.

Security was for him a state of mind characterised by serenity, which grew out of trust in one's ability to deal with the future. He said it is a state of mind which accompanies a willingness to accept the consequences of one's decisions. He argued that security was acquired through early experience. Initially children needed to develop dependent security, a feeling of complete trust in their caretakers. This gave them the courage to be brave, accept insecurity, explore, learn and develop trust in themselves (independent security). Blatz's plan for child guidance was aimed at emancipation and the development of responsibility. It emphasised the importance of gradually increasing the child's freedom to make decisions independently, to experience consequences, both the successes and failures, and acquire effective ways of coping with the consequences. (Wright 1984, 1–2)

St. George's School demanded parent cooperation and involvement. From the beginning there were parent education study groups. Initial participation in such groups was optional, but within two years it became a condition of admission. Blatz set out their importance.

While the child can be studied to advantage in the Nursery School it is also realised that such an environment can only approximate to home conditions. Thus there is a large fraction of the life of the child which is left untouched. To this part of the child's life the parents and particularly the mother hold the key. Mothers have therefore been organised into groups in the Parent Education division to discuss the problems which they meet in handling children at home. Several enquiries are being carried out with the cooperation of these mothers, and it is hoped that in this way information can be collected which will be of use not only for themselves but also for others. By study, discussion and reading of the literature of child study, the mothers in those groups are working to make themselves more intelligent in the guidance of their children's lives. The Nursery School division and the Parent Education division are thus complementary in their aim to arrive at as complete an understanding as possible of the life of the pre-school child and the work of the two staffs is being correlated to this end. (University of Toronto, Thomas Fisher Rare Book Library, Blatz Papers, Box 17, Folder 6, "The St. George's School for Child Study," May 1926)

An important part of Parent Education was record-keeping. Over time it became even more so, as the Nursery School began collecting records from birth. Such record-keeping then became a condition of admission to the school as well. With the addition of regular follow-ups for students who had graduated, the school developed longitudinal data sets that followed individuals to age twenty-four. According to one observer, these records "read like a who's who of prominent people in contemporary Toronto" (Wright 1983, 7). As one of the first students, Harry Johnson is not in those records. In 1928, as a condition of admission, Blatz also demanded that parents abjure corporal punishment. Blatz's "forceful personality and flair for publicity convinced progressive middle-class parents to support Toronto's school" (Strong-Boag 1982, 169).

Early Education

St. George's School opened on 28 January 1926 in a house at 47 St. George Street. Harry was one of the first pupils (his brother Robert followed him). He would later credit the school for his "quite exceptional powers of concentration, retention, speed reading and analysis" (Rosenbluth 2001, 606). Frances joined the Parent Education group in February 1926. Other members included the wives of young university professors such as Harold Innis, W. P. M. Kennedy, and H. W. Kemp of the Department of Political Economy. By November 1926 Frances was leading the group of mothers with children at the school and by June 1927 she was spending 16 hours a week as a parent education leader, helping to spread the school's message and training others. She also contributed publicity in the form of an article, 'Where a Child Can be a Child', in the issue of *Chatelaine*, the leading Canadian women's magazine, for March 1928. In the issue for June 1929, she reviewed Blatz's monograph (with E. A. Bott) *Parents and the Pre-School Child*. By then she was in the MA programme of the Department of Psychology and received her degree in 1930 for her thesis "A Genetic Theory of Distraction in Young Children". By then she was also listed as a member of staff of the St. George School for Child Study. She became an instructor in 1931, where she remained for another thirty years, although she was seconded to the provincial government to direct the training programme for parent education after World War II.

Harry remained at St. George's until June 1927. At the time of Harry's birth, his parents lived at 97 Manor Road, just south of Eglington Avenue and east of Yonge Street. At the time of Harry senior's move back to the *Globe* the family, which included a second son, Robert, born in 1925, had moved to 64 Castlefield Avenue, north of Eglington and just west of Yonge, where Frances's recently widowed mother lived. From there Harry, now six, entered St. Clement's School, a nearby private girls' school in North Toronto which accepted – and still accepts – boys in the early grades. The students are known as Clementines. The Johnsons remained on Castlefield until the end of 1930 when the family bought a ninety-four-acre farm near Wexford, a crossroads community in Scarborough Township east of Toronto, which then had a population of 20,000, having grown by 76 percent over the previous decade

(Lemon 1985, Appendix Table II). Scarborough was even more Anglo-Celtic (91.7 percent), if marginally less Protestant, than Toronto.[4] Frances named the farm Spruce Ridges. From the outside, the concrete block farmhouse was dismal (see Plate 1), but over the years Frances made it attractive and comfortable. She ran the house and the farm. Once circumstances allowed, she had an English cook, Mark, and one other servant. She also made it into a dairy farm with a herd of pedigree Ayrshire cattle. But this was later. Initially they were "land-poor." Harry later remembered the penury lasting five years. The family's position was not helped by depression prices for farm outputs and the uncertainty of Harry senior's income.[5] As for his father, Harry remembered

his idea of farming was striding around in jodhpurs on Saturday morning in the summer and ordering the field hand to hitch up the team and pull the car out of snowbanks or ferry us to it by sleigh in the snowy weather – also breaking in the occasional colt, till one broke some of his ribs instead. (1974 Memoir I, 6)

The move to the country had important implications for Harry. As he remained at St. Clement's, he was a city boy in the country – moreover, he was an unusual city boy because he was attending a girls' school. When the family's financial circumstances changed in mid-depression, Harry left St. Clement's in 1933 for Section School #8 at Hough's Corners, a little east of the present intersection of Eglinton Avenue and Birchmount. Built in 1863 and in use until 1958, the school had two rooms for all eight grades. It was presided over by "an old Scotsman" Mr. MacQuarrie who was assisted by a young woman teacher.

I can remember walking the lonely mile and a half to and from the country school where we were forced to go in the financially worst year, with patches on our pants and no money ever in our pockets; my father trying to comfort me in some emotional crisis with a single penny he fished with difficulty from his pocket. (8)

He also remembered having to fight from time to time and being "brilliantly superior to my class mates in my ability to stand up before the whole class and take a hard strapping without blubbering... [from] Mr. MacQuarrie, whose Scottish rectitude obliged him to strap me as well as my tormenters, though he knew full well how the fights started"(8).

---

[4] Now part of the city of Toronto, it has a population of 600,000 of whom 55 percent are foreign born and 59 percent non-white.
[5] The regularity of Frances's $800 per annum from the St. George School would have made all the difference.

His time at SS #8 lasted one year. During that year, although he was only 10 and some of his contemporaries were as old as 16, he came first in the school in the high school entrance examination. That result brought "an unexpected present" from his father – "fifty cents to spend any way I wanted" (8). That examination result also took him back to the city, this time to University of Toronto Schools (UTS), which had been founded in 1910 as a part of the Faculty of Education of the university with its staff not only teaching the boys but also playing an important role in the education of the prospective high school teachers enrolled in the faculty.[6] The school was academically exclusive and places, allocated by competitive examination, were not easy to come by.

Entering UTS at age eleven, Harry was three years younger than most of his contemporaries. The long, daily journey to and from Spruce Ridges with his parents, and eventually also his younger brother, meant that he had little time for visiting and roughing with his peers. Moreover, because working on the farm occupied his summers, he lost the chance of the summer-cottage socialising and other group activities that many of his middle-class UTS contemporaries engaged in. One summer he did go to camp where he had managed a two-week canoe trip in the Gatineau (1974 Memoir II, 2). Attending UTS also meant that he had little opportunity for contact with girls of his own age. Not surprisingly, he was extremely shy with them – so shy that the one formal dance at UTS was "too fearsome for me to choose to go to" (1974 Memoir I, 5). His shyness was not helped by the fact that he was "repulsively and puppy-ishly fat and knew it" (1974 Memoir I, 6). *The Twig*,[7] the UTS magazine, began a piece of doggerel in 1934: "Imagine Harry Johnson/Weighing only ninety pounds/If Parky wasn't such an egg/They'd kick him from the grounds." "Parky" was Harry Parkinson, the longest standing of the "only three fairly close" friends he later reported from his years at UTS.[8] The other two were J. (Jack) W. Grant, also of UTS, with whom he formed "a friendship based on the collection and telling of dirty jokes," and Joe Nastourni, the son of a market gardener and "the only boy my age within walking distance of the farm" (1974 Memoir I, 12).

At UTS, Harry won scholarships in 1937 for chemistry and physics, in 1938 for general proficiency, and in 1939 university entrance scholarships for chemistry, physics, algebra, and geometry, as well as general proficiency.

---

[6] The original plan had included a similar practice school for girls, but the money ran out. Hence the word "schools" in the name. Girls were not admitted to UTS until 1973.

[7] A play on the University of Toronto motto "velut arbor aevo."

[8] *The Twig* for 1938 reported Parkinson's motto as "be different" and his hobbies as including "swing music, poetry, Harry Johnson and old cars."

He also had an athletic career, which he said later could be "most charitably described as 'undistinguished'" '(Jesus College Archives, H. G. Johnson File, 1949 curriculum vitae), reaching the school finals in boxing and wrestling, playing inside lineman on a 100-pound rugby team that won four of its six games, and taking part in hockey and basketball. As was usual at the time, he was also a member of the school's cadet corps. The 1937 issue of *The Twig* reports him as losing the election for Form Captain of IV-B, in a clever account of the election where he was leader of the "Preservatives" – the other two parties being the "Fibbers-all" and the "C. C. F." (Coeducation Can't Fail) – and contains a piece of doggerel by Harry honouring his successful opponent. When he left UTS, *The Twig* for 1939 reported:

Harry has started early in his law career. Last summer he worked in a law office. This year he entered Political Science and he intends to graduate from Osgoode Hall. Harry took part in many activities during his five years at the school but we recall him foremost as a mighty wrestler at the annual Assault-At-Arms.[9]

In the years Harry was at UTS, the family became reasonably affluent. They began to run two cars. They could now afford help in the house and on the farm, as well as bone china in the cupboard. In 1938 Frances and Harry senior travelled to Europe. The trip included a royal garden party in London. Their growing affluence could not be ostentatiously displayed "for political reasons" but

the farm was really a brilliant investment of my father's in his political career. Ownership of a farm de-classes one, enabling one to be either rich or poor depending on whether one emphasises the standard of living or the cost of living that way, according to choice and custom; and it is an excellent way of disguising and burying windfalls. But to my mother and us boys the concept was too subtle, and the farm always appeared as a hostage to fortune. (1974 Memoir I, 9)

There was also the "liability" of his father's association with Mitch Hepburn.

Hepburn the rumbustious onion-farmer was anathema to both the solid traditional landed aristocracy of Ontario created by British policy to keep Canada safe from the revolutionary ideas of the revolting American colonials, and the solid English and Scottish industrial and banking family monopolists of Toronto and Hamilton. And Hepburn the politician who won an election on the slogan 'Keep the C. I. O. out of Ontario' was anathema to the Toronto intellectuals, particularly on the University staff, who with characteristic colonial intellectual dependency imported from England the identification of Hepburn with Hitlerite fascism and from the United States the idea that the C. I. O.'s industrial alternative to craft unionism represented a new wave of radical socialism. (9–10)

[9] The annual championships in boxing, wrestling, fencing, and gymnastics.

There was one other inheritance from his parents as Harry later recalled.

> I had a latent conflict between my mother's and my father's social outlooks on my hands. My mother . . . had a strong Scottish respect for the established order in general and for university trained and employed people in particular. My father . . . he had an Irish sense of the comicality of people who take themselves too seriously, and a politician's sense that the university is just another pressure group that overestimates its social worth. My mother's values and determination made me a determined and persistent scholar and a believer in the university's values; but my father's occasional serious warnings against the dangers of being 'taken up' by university intellectuals and used for their own purposes kept me careful and my own man where my mother's faith and respect would have betrayed me. To paraphrase an old saying about Hungarians (which has a lot of folk truth in it), 'if you have an intellectual for a friend you don't need an enemy.' My mother taught me to be an honest scholar; but my father taught me how to stay that way. I could have been a Professor at Toronto, or Cambridge, or Harvard, depending on when I chose to drop out of scholarship into academic politics, if I had followed my mother's beliefs and sometimes explicit advice; but my father's understanding of politics and universities made me alert to invitations to sell out, and aware of how little I was really being offered for what I would have to sell. I learned two things from my father, that I think are now basic constituents of my professional personality for good or bad. One . . . was to be tolerant and flexible in relations with other people, even though you know they are trying to put something over on you or put you down; but if they really try to put something over on you, make sure that they get their noses bloodied. The other was the core of his philosophy as a politician; always be careful about giving your word; but if you give it, keep it; because your word is the only thing you've got to live by, and if you betray other peoples' confidence in it you are finished. Fortunately for me, a peace-loving type, an academic career produces more occasions for proving the goodness of your word than for proving your capacity to deal out bloody noses. (9–10)

University

It had been assumed by his parents that Harry and his brother would both enter the professions. In Harry's case this meant the law; in his brother's, medicine. At the time, there were two ways into the legal profession in Ontario: You could article yourself in a law firm for seven years and go to lectures for the bar admission examinations at Osgoode Hall, which was controlled by the Law Society of Upper Canada, or you could go to university (where you were not obliged to take a law course) and be excused the equivalent years of articles. With the law in mind, from the summer of 1939, Harry began working for Ward Wright, a UTS alumnus and friend of his father who was a partner in Wright and McMillan, corporate lawyers on King Street in the financial district. Harry consulted Wright about university courses. He was told that the University of Toronto's law course was not very useful in that it would only gain exemption from an examination in Roman law at Osgoode Hall. He was advised to avoid "like the plague" the three-year pass arts degree and the General Honours course, for "they taught you little and their examinations did not require you to know even that little" (3). The best degree course Wright advised would be Commerce and Finance, modelled on the programme developed by the university's first professor of Political Economy, W. J. Ashley, at the University of Birmingham after he had left Toronto. However, Commerce and Finance was not an Honours course and Harry would not be able to use his scholarships there. Thus he ended up in Political Science and Economics, an Honours course, which offered the same economics material and substituted political science for accounting.

Harry also had to choose a college. There were four alternatives – St. Michael's (Roman Catholic), Trinity (Anglican), University (secular), and Victoria (United Church).[10] He became a member of Victoria, where each year he took his compulsory pass course in religious knowledge and any courses in English, French, or German. Harry senior's Anglicanism might have taken his son to Trinity except that it was too establishment and Victoria's scholarships were more generous.

Honours courses were four-year degree programmes wherein students had to pass every single Honours course (both term work and final examination counted separately) in every year or forfeit the whole year.[11] Successful students were ranked in order of merit each year. Honours course students were taught separately from those in the pass or general programmes so that they could be taught more carefully and thoroughly. Upper-level Honours courses often served as courses for the few graduate students in many departments. In those days, when the university had few graduate students, the teaching of honours students was regarded as the principal business of a department.[12] The programme in political science and economics shared a common first year with modern history and the other social sciences. Thereafter students specialised, and in the third and fourth years they did nothing other than honours courses in political science and economics.

[10] The United Church of Canada was born in 1925 from a merger of the Congregationalists, the Methodists, and two-thirds of the Presbyterians.
[11] Any student who forfeited a year twice was ineligible to reenroll in any university in Ontario.
[12] For example, there were twenty-three graduate students in Political Economy in 1938. The department had produced a total of seven PhDs in economics and political science, three in 1938. One economics PhD had been granted in 1912 on the basis of publications to James Mavor, the head of the department who did not have a university degree. The department produced only two more PhDs between 1938 and 1948 (Mills and Dombra 1968, 39–40, 130).

Only in the fourth year did the students have any choice in courses in their specialty.

The Department of Political Economy was home for Harry's programme. It also housed Commerce and Finance. The department lived at 273 Bloor Street West in what until 1930 had been McMaster University and is now the Royal Conservatory of Music. It contained a large lecture hall – the former McMaster Chapel – classrooms, a library, and a reading room. Although known as the Economics Building, it also contained the Departments of Chemistry and Social Science; later when it emerged from the Department of Political Economy, the Department of Geography found itself at the back in what had once been student dormitories. Political Economy occupied the first two floors at the front of the building, which had been reconditioned (including the installation of electric lights) before the department moved in for the 1933–4 session. The upper two floors at the front remained derelict until after World War II, when they found use with minimal refurbishment.

The department Harry entered in September 1939 had fewer than twenty faculty members. Of the "economists," certainly the most distinguished was Harold Innis, an economic historian of Canada whose interests were broadening to include world technological and cultural history. Others who were or would become significant figures in Canadian economics included Vincent Bladen, a specialist in industrial organisation with a strong interest in the history of economics, and Donald MacGregor, a statistician and early contributor to national accounting in Canada. Among the political scientists were Robert MacGregor Dawson, soon to be the dominant figure in Canadian political science, and two younger figures, the political theorist C. B. Macpherson and the student of comparative Commonwealth government Alexander Brady. There were also individuals of less moment such as Virginius Frank Coe, a Chicago PhD under Jacob Viner who reviewed The *General Theory* critically for the *Canadian Forum* and whose wartime service would take him to be Harry Dexter White's assistant in the U.S. Treasury and eventually to residence in the People's Republic of China. Coe did not teach Harry, but Wynne Plumptre, a former student of Keynes's, who took Dennis Robertson's side in the post–*General Theory* debates before disappearing into the Ottawa bureaucracy, did. At the time, nobody amongst the economists was regarded as a "theorist":[13] excluding the economic historians, all the economists were regarded as applied economists – which was regarded as

---

[13] The first theorist was G. A. Elliot, a specialist in international trade, who arrived as a full professor from Alberta in 1946. Interestingly, Harry did not take his course.

a perfectly satisfactory arrangement in a department whose main business was undergraduate education.

Between the end of the Grade 13 provincial secondary school examinations in June and the beginning of Harry's first-year classes on 27 September, World War II broke out. Initially it meant relatively little to students' programmes of study. The most noticeable early effect was the increased popularity of the Canadian Officers' Training Corps (COTC), whose syllabus had provided training for officer posts in the nonpermanent, active militia. At Toronto the COTC's normal strength was 300; at the beginning of the 1939 academic year, 1,800 enrolled, of whom 1,300 were undergraduates. With the war, lecture courses in Military Studies were treated as equivalent to Religious Knowledge, which had been compulsory in the denominational colleges and had a secular equivalent at University College. Prewar COTC candidates took a two-year course. Lectures and drill occupied six hours a week. Initially, all took the same training regardless of future speciality [artillery, engineers, signals, infantry (rifles), infantry (machine gun), ordinance, service corps, medical corps, dental corps]: a course of drill, rifle exercises, organisation and administration, military law, and map reading. Candidates trained three times a week, at first in civilian clothes but, later in uniform. An examination was held at the end of March. After the first year, specialist training began. In addition to regular drill and classes, candidates were also expected to go into camp at Niagara-on-the-Lake for a fortnight after the end of the academic year. Harry's first camp was 10–23 June 1940. Ernest Sirluck, later a Professor of English at Chicago when Harry was in economics, remembered his first camp:

Immediately following convocation the COTC went . . . for a two-week camp which was to complete one year's training. The weakness of the directing staff and the amateurishness of the whole enterprise were even more evident than in the part time training during the school year. It was not surprising – Canada's small Permanent Force and trained reserve were needed as a core for the active forces and the COTC had to depend for its cadre on a few "retreads" from the First World War and some younger people who knew little more about the army than we did – but it was discouraging. When they had exhausted their meagre stock of obsolete lectures and tactical exercises and didn't know what to do with us they sent us on route marches or to the rifle ranges or the drill square, from which we returned little wiser in the arts of battle or command. (1996, 80)

And Sirluck's first camp was a year after Harry's first! It seems to have improved in 1942 (91). Harry's academic transcript from Toronto noted that he did four years of COTC and took four courses in Military Studies.

In June 1940, Parliament passed the National Resources Mobilisation Act, under which all able-bodied single men and childless widowers between 21 and 45 were required to register and 800,000 proved eligible for home defence.[14] Students, particularly scientists, were encouraged to continue their education, but they had to agree to compulsory military training while attending classes. Students between 18 and 21 who were physically fit were also obliged to undergo military training. If successful academically, students would not be called up for active war service until they had completed their course of study. But there was a bit of an incentive: From early 1942 at Queen's and Toronto, students who passed their COTC examinations were given a 3 mark bonus in each academic course (McKillop 1994, 535). Amendments in 1942 to the National War Students Regulations required that universities report students who failed a term or a year course to the federal government so that they would be subject to immediate call-up. In January 1943 the federal government announced that certain designated categories of students would be exempt from conscription – medicine, dentistry, engineering. But "any others would be afforded this status if they placed in the top half of the class at final examinations" (535).

Not only did the campus become more military, it also became more serious. Normal extracurricular activities were curtailed. Hart House, the men's union, suspended its debates; the medical society cancelled Daffy-dil, its annual review; the Senior Intercollegiate Rugby Union (Canadian football) cancelled its seasons from 1940–1, a move followed by most other sports; dances were not banned but they became less frequent with decorations austere and dress less extravagant. But student societies still flourished, and *Varsity* the undergraduate student newspaper kept publishing. Harry would be a reporter in his third year. Not surprisingly, he was also a member of the University Liberal Club and its president in his third and fourth years.

Although compulsory military training rather than the 1914–18 encouragement to enlist kept university enrolments up, it increased the pressures on university departments as faculty members departed for war work or military service. In the Department of Political Economy, H. R. Kemp and Frank Coe went off to Ottawa and Washington, never to return; Wynne Plumptre moved to Ottawa where he stayed until 1965; while J. F. Parkinson and C. B. Macpherson left for a time. However, they didn't all go immediately, so Harry did manage classes with Plumptre, Parkinson, and Macpherson.

---

[14] Until the end of 1944, those called up under the National Resources Mobilisation Act could not be sent overseas without their consent.

University meant new friends. Of the UTS collection of friends, only Harry Parkinson went on to University of Toronto, but he went to Trinity and took the law course and, according to Harry, "developed into a typical Toronto 'sharpie', with an old car and a rapid succession of girl friends, both activities beyond my immature years" (1974 Memoir I, 12). At Victoria Harry made his first young-adult friends: Jimmy Weld, Charles Scott, and Blyth Young, all from Ottawa. They soon named themselves "little sigma," thus spoofing the St. George Street fraternity life of Trinity and University College students on the western edge of the campus. All three, like Harry, had strong mothers "caring of and ambitious for their children." Jimmy's father was a senior civil servant spending the war in Washington, Charlie's was a high-class grocer, and Blyth's, the chief reporter of Hansard. For Harry they had the attraction "of the different society and social ideas of Ottawa, which enabled me to escape from my doubtfully legitimate and restricted position in Toronto" (1974 Memoir I, 15). Through his new friends he met girls from Ottawa, including, in his second year, Elizabeth Serson, a student at University College and his future wife. Harry and his friends did a certain amount of partying at Spruce Ridges at the beginning of the year and after the Christmas vacation. Harry remembered that "Charlie Scott once remarked, with token ambiguity, that the meals my mother laid on for us 'help to ease the way into boarding-house life'" (14). Blyth and Jimmy became civil servants; Charlie, an Ottawa lawyer.

Harry also made new friends in the department, which was easier each year because the students moved through the same courses together, and classes, after the first year, were both small and increasingly taught in the department, which was physically isolated from the rest of the university. One new friend was Meyer Bucovetsky from Timmins in northern Ontario, one of the two other 16-year-olds in the class.[15] With Meyer "the contemporary conventions of institutionalised anti-semitism in Ontario prevented us from being more than classroom acquaintances . . . [but] I got to know him better, and with real trust and affection, at Cambridge after the war"(4– 5). Meyer and Harry were keen rivals at examination time. After Toronto and Cambridge, Meyer went back into the family clothing store in Timmins but later returned to Toronto to do a PhD and became a member of the Toronto Political Economy Department in 1967. According to Harry, "Apart from Weld and Bucovetsky . . . my closest friend came to be W. R. (Wild Bill) Dymond," who was also a member of Victoria and a *Varsity* reporter. Dymond did graduate work in Toronto after the war before going

---

[15] The other was Miss D. M. Grimshaw from Trinity.

into the federal Department of Labour, where he became research director. Harry also mentions Geoffrey Hobbs, who had been known as Johnson at UTS, an Anglophile who had gone to Trinity and who ended up at Sun Life in Montreal; Bill Robinson from Victoria who followed his father into law in Brampton, a small town just northwest of Toronto; and Jack Coleman, also from Victoria, who went on to do a PhD in labour economics at Chicago before teaching at MIT and Carnegie Institute of Technology and, eventually, becoming president of Haverford College.

Others joined the course, and the small number with first-class honours, along the way. William Merritt, who arrived after spending two years at the University of Manitoba, was a statistician who tried teaching the subject but ended up with Phillips, the electronics firm. Then there was John Dales, "probably the most original mind in our group," who had been a banker in the 1930s before starting off in Commerce and Finance. Dales went on to Harvard for a PhD in economic history and taught at McGill before returning to Toronto in 1954. According to Harry, later "he was by all odds the best journal editor I have ever known (with the possible exception of Bernard Haley)[16] because he took the job with appropriate seriousness and cared deeply and personally about the truth and importance of what he published" (1974 Memoir I, 17). Finally, there was Gideon Rosenbluth, a German refugee who had been at the London School of Economics for a year before being interned as an enemy alien and moved to Canada; he was eventually released for university studies in the fall of 1941. Rosenbluth was a Marxist whose beliefs "dated from a period when it was a respectable social and political philosophy . . . he had culture and knew a lot of economics we didn't know, especially that connected with the Keynesian revolution" (1974 Memoir I, 18). After graduating from Toronto, Rosenbluth went to the Dominion Bureau of Statistics before taking a PhD at Columbia and enjoying a successful academic career at Queen's University in Kingston, Ontario, and the University of British Columbia. Rosenbluth later remembered that as an undergraduate

Harry had great physical strength, a competitive spirit and, paradoxically perhaps, a shortage of self confidence. He was always overweight, and his sport was wrestling. He would work hard, drink hard, and never seemed to relax. (2001, 606)

The two of them later founded an undergraduate political economy club, which they induced Bill Dymond to join.

---

[16] Editor of the *American Economic Review* 1952–62.

Undergraduate Economist

For Harry's undergraduate career, over and above the usual regulations and calendar materials, we have Harry's own 1974 memoir, supplemented by his "Autobiographical Notes" of 1969 and Gideon Rosenbluth's memoir, as well as Harry's own reading lists, notes from lectures, reading notes, and essays. His student notes are incomplete: There is nothing from his first year and only one economics and one political science course from his second year. His notes are complete for all courses in economics and political science starting in the third year. His memoir ignores the pass language courses of his first two years and is occasionally thin on details.

As well as a pass course in French and Military Studies, Harry's first year courses included a second pass course in English. The instructor was Kathleen Coburn, the first modern editor of Coleridge. "The course, like most minor options, bored her as much as it bored us" (1974 Memoir I, 21). Then there was an Honours course in "Ancient History, where the lecturer, Professor Woodside, . . . concentrated on Greek philosophy and made its study both interesting and for us unaccountably civilised" (4).

Social Psychology was taught by a colleague of my mother's, Bill Ketchum, and went about as far as an academic could go at the time in a first year general course in raising questions about the structure of Canadian society – indirectly, it is true, and largely by making us think about concepts developed in Europe and the United States for the objective discussion of social phenomena (not, however, including social class, which was a dirty word in the psychology department and the university generally). (19)

Then there were the Honours courses offered by the Department of Political Economy. There was Robert MacGregor Dawson's Canadian Government, "a mixture of unmemorable facts and a few memorable anecdotes" (19).[17] Harry thought, however, that "perhaps because of intense exposure through my father to the seamy side of Canadian politics, I never found academic political science intellectually attractive" (20). Introductory economics was taught by Vincent Bladen, who had come to Toronto direct from Balliol College, Oxford, in 1920. He continued teaching in the university until his death in November 1981. In 1978 he published his memoirs *Bladen on Bladen* where Harry made several appearances.

---

[17] According to Norman Ward, also a student at Toronto in the 1940s, Dawson was "a brilliant rhetorical speaker in class, full of anecdotes, which he told well, and occasional jokes" (Spafford 2000, 121).

Bladen's course was a mixture of elementary diagram-less principles, and problems of Canadian economic policy that he had actually been concerned with in his career, especially 'Combines Policy'; it ultimately became the famous 'Green Book'.[18] Most of my colleagues didn't care for Bladen's rather fruity English accent, somewhat bumbling Oxford style of lecturing, and mundane theoretical simplicity and descriptive tedium of course content. But it made me an economic theorist. The course included a section on a simple model of a vegetable-growing peasant economy, and gave us a class exercise in analysing the effect of a technical improvement in cabbage production. I somehow got interested in the effects on the number of cabbage farmers and discovered for myself the concept of elasticity of demand. Further when class-time came around, I was chosen to read my paper, and was dumb-struck with nervousness; Bladen gently told me that I might as well make the most of what I'd got, because it was all I'd got. That lesson grew on me slowly but steadily. (21)

At the end of the year, except in English, his marks were all As.

In the summer, he returned to Wright and McMillan, this time at the increased pay of five dollars a week.[19]

At those wages I actually saved some money in a bank account for college, as well as seeing a fair bit of the day and night life of downtown Toronto. But the work was both unexciting and uninteresting – it was primarily a corporation law firm, and aside from helping on the occasional rape case or Lake shipping suit (Great Lakes maritime law being the specialty of one of the pleasanter partners), I and another student devoted most of the limited amount of the time the firm needed us to the collection of small debts for a coal company client. (The trick was to keep the correspondence threatening legal action going until the irrevocable final ultimatum could be reasonably dated for the day after one had left the firm till next summer.) Otherwise, we stretched lunch hour as far as possible to play snooker in the various basement pool halls nearby, and on good days volunteered to walk legal documents around to distant firms, courts and the land registry office to save the firm time and postage, and made up for arriving back at the office late by leaving early. In addition, I read nearly everything available from the local public library. (2)

Of Harry's second year, as before we know nothing of his pass French course and his Military Studies. Nor do we know anything from him of his Political Science course, "The Government of Great Britain and the British Dominions," taught by Alexander Brady.[20] All we know about Honours History 2c, "British and Colonial 1485–1763," was that it was "taught

---

[18] *An Introduction to Political Economy* (1941). The author was introduced to economics with the red third edition of 1956.

[19] It had been two dollars in 1939 and would rise to eight dollars in 1941. At the time, student lawyers normally paid for the privilege of being in a firm.

[20] In his memoir in place of Brady's course, Harry mistakenly transplanted his course in political theory with C. B. Macpherson from his third to his second year.

by an embittered and crusty war-blinded Scot." The individual, Donald
McDougall had been blinded during World War I, after which he had won a
Rhodes scholarship and a first from Oxford. His scholarship on the English
seventeenth century and his annual review articles on British and Commonwealth history in the *Canadian Historical Review* had made him "a leading
student" of those subjects (McNaught 1999, 25).

But there were three Honours courses in economics.

One was A. F. W. Plumptre's theory course based on Marshall's Principles. Plumptre
had spent a period at Cambridge, where he was on the Robertson side against
Keynes, in the course of preparation of his excellent study of *Central Banking in
the British Dominions* (1940). He was a small man with a famous Toronto city
government mother,[21] and a reedy Toronto-English accent that provoked student
contempt – he made a practice in the first two weeks of the year of expelling an
arbitrarily picked student from the class for excessive talking, to impress the need
for disciplined behaviour on the others; but he was a first class Marshallian theorist
(in his last lecture he would even admit that Keynes had something to add to the
master's work) and taught principles superbly. He wrote about this time a very good
book on wartime management of the Canadian economy making the point that
only gradually dawned on American economists, that price and even wage control
was perfectly feasible for the industrial sector but that the agricultural sector, with
its atomistic organisation and high substitutability between markets was the weak
link in any control system.[22] (1974 Memoir I, 22)

Then there was Donald MacGregor's course in statistics. MacGregor could
not "keep command of a class.... It was the only university class I have
ever seen in which the students threw chalk at the teacher as soon as he
turned his back to write on the blackboard." Harry did well (his transcript
records a mark of 97), "but it didn't excite me" (1974 Memoir I, 23).[23]
Finally, there was Lorne Morgan's course on British and European economic
history.

Morgan, a squat, bull-chested red-head, had gone to the University of California
after the first world war and there learned the secret of acquiring a Ph.D. and pursuing a teaching career without really trying. It consisted of making very careful
well-organised notes on a minimum of important books, and memorising them.

---

[21] Adelaide Plumptre was a city alderman.

[22] Plumptre (1941).

[23] He recorded at this point in his 1974 Memoir: "I had altogether three good courses in
statistics – MacGregor at Toronto, Charles Carter at Cambridge, and Crum and Frickey at
Harvard – and none of them turned me on. I missed the econometric revolution (and also
the mathematical theory one), and I never had time thereafter to do more than study the
cookbook and learn to make the conventional remarks about the fragrance of the spices
used and the skill of the chef. I comfort myself with the thought that, lacking the technique,
I have had to use my brains instead. Most people have to."

His real interests were in left-wing politics and workers' education. He later acquired local fame with a pamphlet entitled *The Permanent War or Homo the Sap* (1943) a tongue-in-cheek proposal on Keynesian lines for a permanent war between Canada and Mexico to provide full employment, taken up in all seriousness by a local businessman with an advertising budget larger than his cranial capacity. . . . We were fascinated by Morgan in the second year; but by the time we reached fourth year, those of us who attended it found his course on European fascism disappointingly banal.[24] Morgan's second year course was memorable for me for only one reason: in the course of the year there appeared as his teaching assistant an Austrian refugee, Karl Helleiner, who was a really impressive scholar of medieval history, commanding many European languages and a vast knowledge of historical sources.[25] (23–24a)

Harry's notes for Morgan's economic history course suggest minimal reading as compared with his other courses, and there is no trace of an essay. At the end of the year, he was top of the class with straight As and the Alexander Mackenzie Scholarship in Political Science and Economics.

In the course of his second year, Harry met Elizabeth Serson, a first year student in English Language and Literature at University College. Harry recalled the occasion in October 1976:

In 1940, there used to be a little restaurant, formerly the first floor of a house, on Hoskin Avenue just opposite St. George Street.[26] A year of Hart House lunchtime sterile efficiency had palled on us sophomores, who were willing to swap worse food for more select company. One day, a group of us were eating the twenty-five cent *table d'hôte*, when a girl approached whom some of my friends knew. It turned out she was a fledgling reporter for *The Varsity*, sent out to survey the neighbouring student eateries. My friends began to tell her about the attractions of the restaurant, and were waxing enthusiastic about the quality for the price of the food. In the midst of this I forked the crust off my rhubarb pie, and found a large living worm in the rhubarb. I reported the information without comment. But it was enough to kill the conversation, and the *Varsity* story. I wouldn't remember it except that the reporter eventually became my wife. (Note dated 19 October 1976 printed in the *University of Toronto Graduate* 1977)

There was another summer at Wright and McMillan, which "made the law seem increasingly unattractive" (1969 Autobiographical Notes, 2), before starting his third year where except for Military Studies all his courses would be Honours courses in either Political Science or Economics. Comparative

[24] Harry did not take this course for credit.
[25] Helleiner remained in Toronto for the rest of his distinguished career.
[26] The description suggests that it was on Harbord, the continuation of Hoskin west of St. George, as all the Hoskin corners were occupied with more substantial buildings. The place remained until the 1960s when it was known as Mac's. It was then demolished when the Robarts Library was built.

Government and Institutions was jointly taught by Robert MacGregor Dawson, who covered American government, and C. B. Macpherson, who covered municipal politics for the United States, Britain, and Canada. Harry
remembered it as "some sort of split course of which the memorable half
was MacPherson [sic] on municipal government . . . [who] made the subject interesting by linking it up with political theory" (1994 Memoir I, 28).
There was also Macpherson's course in Political Theory

concentrating on Hobbes, Locke and Rousseau. . . . Macpherson had been a student
of Harold Laski at the L. S. E. at the beginning of the 1930s, and kept alive Laski's
enthusiastic discovery (via Marx) that economic interests are decisive for democratic
politics and the viability of democracy itself. He was an exciting teacher . . . and one
who . . . remained interesting and an intellectual force to be reckoned with. (24)

In economics there was "[H. A.] Logan's competent but uninspiring (to
me) course in labour economics and social security" the only trace of which
survives in this fragment of a sentence. There was also

a course on money and banking taught by a young Harvard Hansenian Keynesian called Roger Anderson. Anderson gave a well organised course, finishing with
an innocuous dose of Keynesian interest theory. But Toronto under Innis and his
generation was not and never became sympathetic to Keynesianism and Anderson
eventually drifted downtown to the financial community and then off to the operating end of the I. M. F. – taking with him the most beautiful political science lecturer
I've ever seen.[27] (27–8)

Anderson's course began with an institutional description of the Canadian
banking system. It then turned to more theoretical matters with a discussion
of monetary theory followed by a discussion of industrial fluctuations, which
went as far as "savings-investment analysis" in its seven lectures, before
moving on to international economics. The course concluded with a brief
discussion of monetary and fiscal policy. Harry's reading notes were strongly
institutional, but he did read D. H. Robertson's *Money*, Alvin Hansen's
Fiscal Policy and Business Cycles, and selected chapters of Keynes's *General
Theory* (8, 10, 11, 12, 13, 15, and 22) and chapters 9 and 10 and Part II of
Haberler's *Prosperity and Depression*. His only surviving essay for the course
was "Outline the main types of business done by the Canadian chartered
banks. How far do you think that these banks, led by the central bank, can
influence business conditions in Canada by altering their interest rates and
credit policies?" for which he received an A.

   Then there was Harold Innis, from whom Harry would eventually take
four courses, at last managing to get an A on his final pair as a graduate

[27] Miss R. L. Savage.

student. Born a farmer's son in southwestern Ontario, Innis had been educated at McMaster University in Toronto and – after service in the artillery
on the Western front and a serious wound at Vimy Ridge – the University
of Chicago where he completed his PhD on the history of the Canadian
Pacific Railway in 1920, the year he joined the Toronto Political Economy
Department. He became a full professor in 1936 and head of the department in 1937. By then he had transformed the study of Canadian economic
history by concentrating on the role of export staples in shaping the economic, political, and social life of Canada. Best known for his *The Fur Trade
in Canada* (1930) and *The Cod Fisheries: The History of an International
Economy* (1940), he turned his attention in the 1940s to the role of media of
communication on society and thus influenced Marshall McLuhan and the
field of media studies. During this time he accumulated positions of power
and influence in Canadian academic life – dean of the graduate school at
Toronto, president of the Royal Society of Canada, head of the Social Science
Research Council of Canada, and chief Canadian adviser to both the Rockefeller Foundation and the Carnegie Endowment for International Peace.
He gained international recognition as Stamp Memorial Lecturer in the
University of London (1948), Beit Lecturer at Oxford (1948), president of
the Economic History Association (1942–3) and, in the last year of his life
(1952), president of the American Economic Association. Harry came to
regard Innis as the greatest economic theorist Canada has ever produced,[28]

comparable in his way to the Americans Frank Knight and Irving Fisher, and in
some ways very similar to Frank Knight and the earlier Chicago economist Thorsten
Veblen and my later Chicago colleague T. W. Schultz. All four came to economics off
the farm ... and all four came from minority but respected ethnic groups,[29] both
factors being important in making a man think independently about the nature of
his society. (1974 Memoir I, 24–5)

As a teacher, Innis left a lot to be desired. He

was an extremely difficult teacher. He made no effort to be interesting – though
occasionally gave us an anecdote that amused him; and his courses, like his early
books, presented masses of uninteresting facts of unexplained and unestimable relevance – like the trade stores of a Hudson's Bay factor, the food stores and equipment

---

[28] In his introductory remarks as chair at the first Innis Lecture of the Canadian Economics
Association in June 1975, he elaborated on this point saying that he was "using for this
purpose my own standards of theoretical originality, which stresses the discernment of
causal connections between and among socially and economically significant phenomena"
[Box 34, Writing 1975(2)].

[29] Here Harry must be referring to the four American economists, as the Innis family being
English and his mother Scots hardly made him a member of a minority ethnic group in
Ontario.

of a cod-fishing boat, and the number of miles of rail laid each year by the Canadian Pacific Railway between one even now obscure little Canadian whistle-stop town and its equally obscure neighbours to the west. Only at the end would come a severely condensed summary of the world-historic themes to which the facts were supposed to be relevant – imperfect competition among drainage basins in giving Americans better access to the market of Canada than the Canadians had, the superiority of British West Indian rum over French brandy in creating brand loyalty among the Indians and permitting the British to take Canada from France, the influence of the triangular trade in codfish, rum and furs in shaping North American democracy and so forth.[30] Worst of all Innis always set his examinations not on the course he gave that year, but on the problems the course had given him to work on for next year's course.

It was only later, when I was a graduate student of his and mature enough to try really to understand some of his ideas, that I came to comprehend the pattern of his scholarly career. . . .

In the meantime we struggled with the fur-trading and the cod-fishing history in preparation for the final year course on railways, wheat, gold and other non-ferrous metals and newsprint, much baffled over the relevance of imperfect competition to the fur trade and over the relevance of liquidity preference to gold exporting (Innis used economic concepts like Humpty-Dumpty used English words). (25–7)

With Bs in Economic History and Political Theory to offset his As in Labour Economics, Money and Banking, and Comparative Politics, in 1942 Harry fell to third place behind Bucovetsky and Rosenbluth.

As he was "restive with the law firm," in his third university summer Harry took a construction labourer's job at the munitions plant run by General Engineering on Eglington Avenue East.[31] It was "an 8 to 6-except-Saturdays, boring job shovelling dirt," which paid fifty cents an hour with overtime only after the full fifty-hour week had been completed. He relieved the boredom by learning to touch type for an hour before walking the two and a half miles to work. He left his summer job early to study for a special prize in Canadian economic history. In the process he enjoyed reading W. A. Mackintosh's *The*

---

[30] Harry's memoir echoed Donald Creighton's characterisation of Innis's writing: "His style was difficult, highly condensed, extremely elliptical, and not infrequently obscure. Long, none too obviously relevant quotations and big chunks of statistics were inserted, in a solidly unassimilated form, in the middle of his text. The steps that led him from the immense detail of his evidence to the grand, sweeping generalisations of his conclusion were often most imperfectly indicated; and there were huge excrescences in the material and gaps and discontinuities in the argument which might only too easily bewilder and exasperate a reader" (1957, 101).

[31] "I never forgave my father for turning down on my behalf and without asking me an offer of a lucrative job on the Alcan Highway." Also known as the Alaska Highway, this originally military road runs from Dawson Creek, British Columbia, to Fairbanks, Alaska.

Economic Background to Dominion-Provincial Relations (1939).[32] In the end John Dales won first prize, and Harry was left with the Second Maurice Cody Scholarship (in Economic History) worth $200, or a month's wages at the munitions plant.

Fourth year classes began on 23 September 1942. On 4 October, Humphrey Mitchell the federal minister of labour, approached Ontario and Quebec university presidents with a problem: a shortage of farm labour threatened the loss of a substantial portion of a bumper wheat crop and would the universities grant leaves of absence to students in arts, commerce, and law – courses "not directly concerned with war work" (Gibson 1983, 203). They were offered a minimum of four dollars a day and board, with free transport west and return transport provided at no more than ten dollars if they returned after 31 October. At the University of Toronto, applications opened on 7 October. As of 4 P.M., according to *Varsity* the undergraduate newspaper (8 October), there were 304 applicants. Eventually, a Toronto contingent of 279 left Toronto's Union Station in two trains of colonist cars on 10 October. Four hundred volunteers from Western and Queen's were with them. Harry travelled with the Victoria and Trinity contingents on the Canadian Pacific train. The trains left "in the loudest, gayest, most college-like atmosphere Toronto has witnessed since the hey-day of inter-collegiate football" (*Varsity*, 13 October). The Toronto students were supplied with box lunches packed by female undergraduates, which, according to *Varsity* (13 October), contained 1,797 sandwiches, 1,000 apples, 1,200 doughnuts, 1,296 pieces of celery, and canned goods. The CPR train also had a dining car. The train arrived in Winnipeg on Canadian Thanksgiving[33] and reached Regina the next day the 13th.

Harry, for whom "the taste for new experiences had bitten into my spirit," and Dick Wottom, the son of one of his father's former newspaper colleagues who had spent the summer at the munitions plant, ended up in Ernfold Saskatchewan, "a coffee-shop cross-roads" just west of Moose Jaw with a family called Beech who farmed 2,700 acres.[34]

It was my first exposure to completely commercial agriculture: aside from a few barnyard eggs, all the food was brought in. The life was incredibly hard if you weren't used to it: up at 4 A.M., harness your team, ride them out to the wheat-field a mile or two off, eat breakfast in the dark and stay out harvesting until it was dark

[32] Appendix 3 to the *Report* of the Royal Commission on Dominion-Provincial Relations (the Rowell-Sirois Report).
[33] The second Monday in October.
[34] The family was probably called Beach, for a family of that name still farms at Ernfold.

again – one man one wagon, three wagons for the threshing machine, fill your wagon full enough to take your turn at the machine, with Wottom as spike pitcher to all three wagons – with four meals including breakfast delivered to the field and a final one after you got home with the team. Fortunately the Beeches were religious and didn't work on Sunday. On Saturday night we could bath in a bucket of boiling water, if we felt the need of it (Wottom and I used a bucket between us) and go to the local dance – a piano, a fiddle, played respectively by an old lady and a young girl, and a fast crowd of young people sufficient for more than one and less than two square-dance sets. . . .

Towards the end of the second week it began to rain, and Wottom and I decided to use the time off and blow our accumulated pay on a visit to Banff in the Rockies: fifteen hours by bus each way, starting at 1 A.M. Saturday morning and arriving back at 5 A.M. Monday morning. It was worth it. When we got back, we found that we student harvesters had been recalled – some of them took two weeks to fight through the temptations of being a one day's wonder at the western universities – back to eastern civilisation. (1974 Memoir I, 28–30)

On their return the harvesters were given special instruction for three weeks from 9 November to bring them back up to speed and the examiners of their finals were instructed to give them special consideration when considering the results (*Varsity*, 9 November 1942). Harry also had a substantial back-up of lecture notes taken by others.

Harry's discussion of his fourth year was brief:

The courses . . . consisted compulsorily of instalment two of Innis, instalment two of Brady on modern political philosophy and instalment two of Bladen, on the history of economic thought – which I recall as consisting of a large block of time devoted to Adam Smith, his favourite, rather less to Malthus and still less to Ricardo, and an introduction to Chamberlin's *Monopolistic Competition*. As options I took J. F. Parkinson on international economics – he was good on a Canadian floating exchange rate and speculative capital movements and in that course I wrote a paper re-inventing Joan Robinson's essay on the foreign exchanges, and arguing that the elasticities were likely to be high enough to increase the incomes of Canadian wheat producers (our major equivalent of industrial unemployment) – and C. A. Ashley on corporate finance. . . . His corporate finance course was based largely on novels and business biographies, which in his view captured the essence of big business but in our view made the course a snap. (1974 Memoir I, 31–3)

Harry's reading lists, lecture and reading notes give a few more details. The Political Theory course was effectively a continuation of his third-year course covering such figures as Marx, Engels, John Stuart Mill, Graham Wallas, Harold Laski, and E. H. Carr. The Bladen course was actually called Economic Theory. It had a substantial historical dimension so that Harry did end up reading Smith and Malthus. But in addition to Chamberlin he read Frank Knight's *Risk, Uncertainty and Profit* (1921) and Book I of

J. R. Hicks's *Value and Capital* (1939). As for the lectures, not only did they cover Smith to Mill, but they even went so far as to concern themselves with Oskar Lange's "The Rate of Interest and the Optimum Propensity to Consume" (1938). All in all Bladen's course was idiosyncratic but interesting.[35] Parkinson's international economics course concentrated on trade theory and commercial policy. There were discussions of international monetary arrangements and the transfer problem using Taussig, Viner, and Ohlin, but the content was generally institutional with little formal international monetary economics. The essay, which replicated the results of Joan Robinson's "The Foreign Exchanges" was "In what circumstances might a policy of exchange depreciation be expected to raise the incomes of exporters proportionately? In what circumstances would this be unlikely? What other objections could be offered to such a policy?" Harry's mark was an A—.

Despite Bs from Innis and Brady, Harry finished the year at the top of his class. The other firsts were all friends: John Dales, Meyer Bucovetsky, Gideon Rosenbluth, William Dymond, William Merritt, and Jimmy Weld. Harry won the gold medal presented by Victoria to its best student in Political Science and Economics.

By the time he graduated, Harry recorded later,

I was acutely conscious, as a result of comments by Brady and Bladen on papers I wrote that year, and observation of my fellow students, that I was a first-class scholar of economics but not as yet an economist capable of using and advancing the subject.... I had decided against the law and military service didn't appeal to me, in spite of my at the time radical views on politics.... I found the prospect unattractive, especially after four years' exposure to the colonial-British military mind.... My only escape, being certified A1 physically in spite of a left shoulder scarred and impaired by septic arthritis in childhood, was graduate study which I had not previously contemplated, so I registered for a Toronto M. A. for the next year. (1974 Memoir I, 34–5)

For the summer of 1943, Harry became a temporary wartime civil servant in Ottawa. He lived with Donald Rowat, another Political Science and Economics graduate, in a ramshackle cottage at Britannia Bay on the Ottawa River and cycled ten miles to work and back most days. He had hoped for a

[35] After a visit to St. Andrews, Harry sent Bladen an Adam Smith tie, saying, "I thought of sending it to you because, up there, they have a strong political economy and history of thought tradition. I was reminded of your lectures on Adam Smith, and particularly of your kindness in repeating them for those of us who went out West harvesting in the autumn of 1942" (University of Toronto Archives, Blanden Papers, B74–0073, to Vincent Bladen, 2 November 1970).

post at the National Film Board but ended up instead at the Wartime Prices and Trade Board

with a miserable job compiling statistics on the shortage of women's underwear, a shortage evident to the eye on the hot streets of Ottawa and easily explained by the price control in conjunction with material scarcity and the relatively high profit margins on children's underwear. I laboured away daily at a little desk in a large office . . . collating reports of production by tiny enterprises whose monthly production was measured in single numbers of dozens or two figures of pairs. . . . The product of my summer's labours, and probably my only net positive contribution to the Canadian war effort, was two pie charts, showing that there was indeed a shortage of women's underwear on the production side. In the long run I probably contributed more positively to Canadian Government by my determination never to take another civil service job. (36)

TWO

Antigonish

Harry was staying in Ottawa between the end of his summer as a civil servant and the start of his Toronto MA programme when events in eastern Canada irrevocably changed his career – and set him firmly on the road to becoming a professional economist. St. Francis Xavier University (known as St. F. X.) in Antigonish, Nova Scotia, suddenly found itself without an economist when one member of the department, Egbert Munzer, a former Minister of Economics in Weimar Germany, resigned to take up a post at the University of Toronto (where he taught until he went to Laval University in Quebec City in 1946) and the other member, the Reverend Joseph A. MacDonald, suffered a nervous breakdown. As a result, Daniel J. MacDonald, the President of St. F. X., wrote to Harry:

In conversation with Dr. Innis of Toronto University a few days ago he recommended you as a teacher of economics and is willing to give you whatever releases you need. Please tell me as soon as possible on what terms you would be willing to come here to teach for the coming year. (St. F. X. Archives, RG5/10/20648, 8 September 1943)

Harry was attracted. He was

on the one hand terrified by the prospect of having to motivate my own studies and on the other deeply bitten by geographical and social *wanderlust* and anxious to test my own ability to meet bigger challenges than had been my prospect thus far. (1974 Memoir II, 2)

He replied on 13 September from 58 Willard Avenue in Ottawa, Elizabeth Serson's house, that he would be glad to come for the academic year if Innis could arrange his release at the Toronto end and if St. F. X. could make the necessary arrangements with National Selective Service, who had given him an indefinite exemption as a graduate student. He stated that his present salary in Ottawa was $1,841 per annum, including a cost-of living bonus; that

39

he would not consider coming for less if he was a full-time teacher; and that he assumed that St. F. X. would be responsible for his travel expenses (St. F. X. Archives, RG5/11/20649). When he got back to Toronto on 17 September, he found that he had been called by the National Selective Service for a medical reexamination on 20 September. If, as expected, he was found fit for military service, St. F. X. would have to arrange a deferral of his draft call. If that was refused "I shall of course volunteer for Active Service with the Army" (St. F. X. Archives, RG5/11/20650, HGJ to D. J. MacDonald, 17 September). In the same letter he also told of his COTC experience at Toronto and offered to help with the COTC in Antigonish. The medical examination put him in category A1, and he was required to appear for an interview on Friday 24 September. The result was a deferment. He had intended to leave Toronto on 25 September and arrive in Antigonish two days later. He was delayed waiting for his deferment and did not arrive in Antigonish until late in the evening on 4 October, more than a week after the start of classes. He met the dean, the Reverend Patrick Joseph Nicholson, the next morning.

St. Francis Xavier University, founded at Arichat on Cape Breton Island in 1853, had moved to the mainland in 1865. The university served the Catholic Highland Scots of eastern Nova Scotia – the diocese of Arichat, which followed the university to the mainland in 1880, had a population of nearly 106,000 in 1851 of whom 67 percent were Scots (Cameron 1996, 5–6). The university received the power to grant degrees from the colony of Nova Scotia in 1866. This was important at the time as there was a worry that Canadian Confederation, which was imminent, would freeze the denominational educational arrangements in the new Dominion where the rights to denominational schools for Protestants and Catholics were protected under the British North America Act.[1] In 1881 provincial support for denominational education at the university level ended in Nova Scotia (it had disappeared in Ontario in 1868). In 1883 Mount Bernard College for Women was established. It formally affiliated with St. F. X. in 1894 when the first degrees for women were awarded – the first at any Catholic college in North America. Four years earlier, the university had started awarding master's degrees. In 1899 it added a Faculty of Applied Science, or engineering, which initially offered a two-year course, later extended to a three-year diploma.

---

[1] At the same time, Catholic colleges in Toronto, Ottawa, Windsor, and Kingston attempted to obtain charters, but only the College of Ottawa and St. Michael's College in Toronto were successful (McKillop 1994, 35).

In 1939–40, the university had 359 students, the majority of whom were in Arts and Science.[2] All but six of the students were Catholics. A third were from outside the diocese of Antigonish. The faculty numbered thirty-one. By the time Harry arrived, student numbers had risen towards five hundred. Not only did higher wartime incomes mean that more people could afford to attend university, but the Wartime Bureau of Technical Personnel attempted to encourage students in the sciences to stay (Cameron 1996, 253, 261). Approximately two-thirds of the students were in residence, most of them in the town, which even when students and faculty were in residence had a total population of less than a thousand. Harry remembered: "[T]he town had about three blocks of sparse and ramshackle main street buildings, including one movie theatre that could do all its business on one day a week" (1974 Memoir II, 3).

As well as seeing Dean Nicholson on 5 October, Harry had to arrange his accommodation on his first full day in town. He was to live at what was referred to as "the Professor's," a term that mystified him because he found himself in a household of three elderly ladies in West Street, across from the university. The mystery was dispelled in two stages. MacDonalds were so common that surnames were never used and were replaced by an identifying descriptor. The ladies' father, Ronald, had been professor of Geology at St. F. X. This descriptive practice became clearer when he met his large elementary class: it had eight MacDonalds, five MacGillivrays, and three MacIsaacs. The three MacDonald daughters in West Street were Louise, "a nurse with a well-founded contempt for men" who had served with the army in World War I and then made her professional career in Massachusetts before retirement; Margaret, who had stayed in Antigonish to look after her father; and Anne Marie, who was secretary to the local Member of Parliament.[3] Harry's accommodation consisted of a small bedroom and the professor's large study, which was rather cheerless in winter.

Professing Economics

Harry spent a lot of time in the study that winter, partially because there was little in the way of alternative entertainment in Antigonish but mainly because he had many lectures to prepare. His teaching load consisted

---

[2] Small size was not unusual in the Nova Scotia university world. In 1941 the five universities in the province had a total population of 1,964 undergraduates and 60 graduate students, who were taught by 192 full-time teachers [Leacy (ed.) 1983, series W369, 372, and 478].

[3] A fourth daughter had married and settled in New England.

of five courses: Principles of Economics, the introductory course, with
H. A. Logan and M. K. Inman's *A Social Approach to Economics* (1939) as the
text; Principles of Economics for Advanced Students, where he used Chamberlin's *Theory of Monopolistic Competition* and Hansen's *Fiscal Policy and
Business Cycles* (supplemented by Haberler's *Prosperity and Depression*, part
I and selected sections of Keynes's *General Theory*) as his texts; Statistical
Methods; Corporation and Public Finance; and a Senior Seminar. Classroom hours came to 13 per week. The course with one term of public and
one of corporation finance was eliminated quite quickly as there were only
two or three students and a half-year course in economics for engineers was
substituted. We have Harry's notes only for the advanced principles course.

The day before he started his advanced course on 12 October he wrote to
Innis, asking for advice on the finance and statistics courses. He reported that
"[t]he atmosphere here is very friendly, although perhaps too aggressively
co-operative" and concluded "I believe that I shall enjoy my work here very
much" [University of Toronto Archives, Innis Papers, B72-0025/003/(03)].
His first lecture was a bit of a trial: He ran out of material after half an
hour (MacEachen 1997, 19; Box 44, Economic Theory Advanced, Notes).
His next letter to Innis showed him learning.

I have had some difficulty in getting into the swing of things here largely because
the system of education is entirely different. The average student is more average
and less student than I am accustomed to, and the technique is to make him (or
her) attend the lectures of which there are three a week in each course, by taking
attendance and giving frequent quizzes, as well as essays. So far, I have avoided taking
attendance in my senior classes, although this is somewhat of an Indian gift because
they daren't skip a lecture on Chamberlin to save their souls.

I must have created an impression on their minds. I did not find out till after my
first lecture on Chamberlin that they have about as much grounding in economic
theory as a Toronto student has, if he finishes Professor Bladen's class and reads a
book for himself on the milder uses of curves. Consequently, my feat of running
through the complete theory of pure competition, with diagrams, in one lecture
took them by surprise and filled their hearts with apprehension. Since then I have
had to spend two lectures going over the use of diagrams, right from the demand
curve up. I created a similar awesome impression in my course in elementary theory,
by assigning them an essay in economic history, to be limited to two thousand words.
I do not believe that they have ever conceived before that an essay could take more
than a few hundred.

This three lecture a week system threw me completely, the first few days. At the
rate at which I started off my lectures, I would have been through Chamberlin,
Hansen, Keynes, and Haberler by the end of November. I was giving about as much
content in all three as was given at Toronto. Since then I have started to take lectures
in sociology, and have come to the conclusion that I could give that course in a
week; owing to the lower level of the background students have here, plus the fact
that you have three or perhaps even four years, as well as pre-medical and science

students all in one class, lectures have very little content and much explanation. I have tried to adjust myself to that situation by elaborating more upon my material, and presenting it very slowly. In my senior classes, of course I go a little more rapidly, and of course go much deeper into the subject. [University of Toronto Archives, Innis Papers, B72-0025/003(03), to Harold Innis, 21 October 1943]

But the faculty had been "very helpful indeed, in providing good advice and making me feel welcome here."

Harry's lecture notes show him honing his teaching skills. He became careful, as he would for the rest of his career, in writing out in some detail the material he wanted to cover – in the second term he was typing out his notes. In that term he involved his students more (and reduced his lecturing requirements) by covering the practical aspects of business cycles in a series of fourteen Saturday-morning sessions at each of which a student read a paper that was subsequently turned in for a mark and then distributed to the rest of the class. In his introductory course, he reported to Innis:

I have been trying some interesting experiments. . . . I attempted a true-false test as a part of an examination on price theory, which didn't work out too well; and also an oral examination, which was very interesting as an experiment, and effective as an examination. The time required is offset by the saving in the interpretation and judgment of written papers. [University of Toronto Archives, Innis Papers, B72-0025/003(03), 15 April 1944]

In his advanced course, most of the presentation was fairly straightforward. In the case of Chamberlin, he worked through the book using chapter-by-chapter reading notes. In the business cycle material, he was relatively nontechnical until towards the end he took them carefully through a Robertsonian savings/investment model and put it through its paces, before proceeding with a Keynesian analysis of the same phenomenon, in both cases sticking closely to Hansen. There was more emphasis on the mathematics of income determination and the determination of investment than on the theory of the rate of interest. The course concluded with a well-organised final examination.

He also got to know his students.

The introductory students were a pretty formless and gormless lot: it was not their fault, though it took me time to appreciate the educational privileges I had had, that most of them came from the mining towns, the fishing villages, and the niggardly farms of the Cape Breton Island region to the north, from houses that typically had one book (the Bible) and took in one slim, very local newspaper, much of which was apt to be written in Gaelic. (1974 Memoir II, 19)

He came to appreciate the important role of the teacher, providing guidance, strength, and simple help, and he gradually became more sympathetic towards his students. He later regarded it as a benefit that his first two experiences of teaching, at St. F. X. and later at Toronto

left no tracks visible to my subsequent colleagues, and further to have had after each year a period of further study, maturation and reflection on my past mistakes, so that by the time I really started my professional teaching career . . . I had more or less succeeded in objectifying my professional personality and detaching it from my personal self and its worries (the process started by Bladen).[4] (1974 Memoir II, 20)

However, "even much later when his reputation was well established, you could literally see him break out in a sweat before going in to give a lecture or seminar" (Rosenbluth 2001, 607).

He got to know the senior students better, partly because "they have more distinct personalities, potentialities and plans" and probably because they were his own age – or in some cases a year or two older. Amongst the most impressive he later recalled Ainsley Kerr, "a very intelligent 'all rounder' from Ottawa, who carried much of the student activity of the place on his shoulders." He would become a journalist on the Ottawa *Journal* for a time before going into the cooperative movement. Then there was Alan MacEachen from Inverness, Nova Scotia, "a very bright but lazy . . . person with a political career in mind – at that time, like all Canadian young intellectuals, in the C.C.F."[5] With Harry's encouragement and financial support, he went on to graduate work at Toronto and then at Chicago and the Massachusetts Institute of Technology. He returned to St. F. X. as Professor of Economics in 1946 and was briefly head of the Department of Economics before going into politics as a Liberal, getting elected in 1953 and holding a succession of ministerial posts from 1963 including minister of finance and minister of foreign affairs (twice). The third was Joseph MacNeil from Sydney on Cape Breton,

an unpolished but serious and thoughtful boy who taught me a lot about applied economics inadvertently by remarking that national union wage demands had eliminated a lot of local jobs for the benefit of "Upper Canadian" union members, and producing a good paper arguing sensibly that the two bakeries in his little town did not constitute a case of the wastes of monopolistic competition. (1974 Memoir II, 21–2)

MacNeil entered the priesthood and became director of extension at St. F. X. in 1961. In 1968 he became bishop of St. John, New Brunswick. In 1973 he became archbishop of Edmonton, a post he held until 1999.

[4] See discussion in Chapter 1.
[5] The socialist Co-operative Commonwealth Federation, which later became the New Democratic Party.

Harry also mentioned a few young women – most of them not economists. Theresa McLeod had already embarked on a career in children's broadcasting. Three came from outside the area: Norma Thompson from Charlottetown in Prince Edward Island, in his Advanced Economics class who was "one of a type of very competent North American young women who always frightened me in my youth and subsequently came to seem to me to represent a great waste of female talent on punctilious management of trivia"; "a tall, willowy, spoiled blonde . . . presumably destined to become some affluent man's expensively ornamented other half"; and "Irene Gotto, whose father was reputed to be a bootlegger in Montreal."[6] She was "smart, flexible and 'cool.'" Harry liked her very much and she became his

girl friend for the time being to the extent that a movie once a week, a coffee shop and long country walks in a damp and snowbound climate permitted any infringement of the adolescent innocence that permeated the place. . . . I saw her once, after I came back from Cambridge to Toronto, but by then things were very different for me. (1974 Memoir II, 22–3)

Outside the classroom, Harry adjusted to the university and the town. The professor's daughters invited him in "rarely and stiffly." However he made good friends with the next door neighbours: Cecil MacLean, the professor of French with a Sorbonne doctorate; his wife Marion; and her freshman sister. Marion had been a rural school teacher and was "a very solid, sensible and understanding woman – and pleasantly attractive in both looks and manners." Harry learned a lot from the MacLeans about the town and its hinterland (1974 Memoir II, 8). Then there was John Atwood, who had come as a lecturer in political science at the same time as Harry but with "a wry stick of an English wife and a brilliant little daughter." Atwood had graduated in law from Dalhousie in 1928 but never practised law. Instead he had a variegated career as a statistician at the Vancouver Stock Exchange, department manager for Dunn & Bradstreet and for Associated Credit Bureau of Canada in Vancouver ("incidentally becoming partners with the madam of a brothel in the ownership of a race-horse"), and school teacher on an Indian reserve. While at St. F. X., Atwood was taking some courses.

[A]s a lapsed Catholic he plied me with descriptions of the seamier side of Catholic practice which, by their contrast with the general simple goodness I found among the priests and nuns I worked with, served mainly to inoculate me against the kind

---

[6] In her final year, the St. F. X. calendar listed her as coming from Montreal but a year earlier she was listed as coming from New Waterford, Nova Scotia.

of blind anti-Catholic prejudice that was part of my Toronto boyhood. . . . John was also the only colleague I dared to drink with – not that there was much opportunity for drinking, with the legal ration being restricted to a 26 ouncer of rye or a dozen quarts of New Brunswick Moosehead Ale or a dozen tins of Nova Scotian hard cider per month.[7] (9–10)

After his stint at St. F. X., Atwood did not go back to school teaching on a reserve. Instead he joined the Nova Scotia Department of Industry. When Harry came back from war in 1946, he saw Atwood in Halifax, and Atwood drove him to Toronto. Later Atwood went to Chicago, and when Harry ended up there, they would meet occasionally for dinner. By then, Atwood

was between his third and fourth wives on his way down hill back on the credit investigator game – 'one less wife or one less drink might have made all the difference', one of the many bosses who fired him once told him. . . . He . . . ended up confined physically to a shabby apartment and financially to an inflation-eroding pittance of a social security check. We used to see him occasionally when we were in Chicago, bringing him south for a good meal and a long chat (which he wanted more) and loading him up before we took him home with all the food and liquor we could decently describe as leftovers. (10)

Harry met most other members of the staff at meals in the Refectory, there being no self-catering facilities at "the Professor's" and no meal service there, and "there was no restaurant good enough to eat at regularly in a town that size – unless [you] were a Cantonese" (12). The Refectory offered five meals a day: breakfast, lunch, Scottish tea, dinner, and a 10 P.M. raid on the refrigerator. Harry got into the habit of having steak for breakfast, when it was available, both before and after his 8 A.M. class. The diet, which was of high quality, was supplemented by gifts from present and former parishioners of the priests. As a result, Harry's weight on his five foot ten inch frame "rose steadily from the relatively trim 159 pounds of my Ottawa bicycling summer to the 196 pounds from which the Army had to reduce it." The regular company in the Refectory, who often stayed on for bridge, included Clive Nunn, the manager of the university's radio station CJFX; Doug McGillivray, its announcer who had a passion for doing the play-by-play for hockey games; and a run of priests associated with St. F. X. – Doc Hughie (Hugh Joseph Somers), professor of history; William Patrick Fogarty, professor of engineering; George Louis Kane, professor of English;

[7] But smuggled West Indian rum and bootleg liquor were also available. For almost all of his period at St. F. X., Harry was under the legal drinking age.

Daniel MacCormack, professor of commerce; Dr. Hugh MacPherson from the Extension Department; and Moses Coady, the director of extension. Of Coady, Harry remembered:

I got off to a very bad start with him, badly overbidding at bridge and carrying him as my partner away down on my first evening there – I never dared to play again. He was a commanding presence, with an apt and sometimes salty turn of phrase.[8] (15)

Harry's contacts with townspeople were very limited. He later recalled:

I only got to know one of the townspeople, and him I did my best to un-know after my first evening with him. He was the local grocer, reputed to be the father of half the kids on the isolated farms located round about, whose farm-wives his delivery truck served with provisions and he, the driver, with other physical comforts. He was married . . . the wedding having been a hasty and unexpected *fait accompli*; before that, I found out later, he had shared a house with a young man called Oscar, whom the Professors described innocently as 'a really beautiful young man', until the army found other uses for Oscar. I found out more, and more quickly, about the meaning of his life than I wanted to, when he took me to his grocery store after hours, offered me biscuits, complained about the price of the pack I chose, and launched an unsuccessful homosexual assault which he completed solo in the manner of Onan (though not for the same reason). He got me out with him only once more, with the line of a phone call from a self-styled beautiful blonde who claimed to have seen me often and been smitten, and insisted on inviting me to a party that night. The party turned out to be in the home of a local bigwig whose wife was having the gang in while her respected public-figure husband was away on business; the party was all nasty adulterous fun and games and dodging the damp and dirty digits of the delicatessen-dealer, though there were some lighter moments of innocent necking with the teen-age daughter of the house. I heard from John Atwood years later that he had had a similar experience with the grocer. (1974 Memoir II, 10–11)

The Antigonish Movement

The extension movement at St. F. X., or the Antigonish Movement as it was later known, had at its roots a number of factors, but the key motivation was a desire to improve social and working conditions for the farmers, fishermen, and workers in the mines and mills of eastern Nova Scotia. After 1918, greater competition in industry, stagnation in the fisheries, and

---

[8] "I let myself bid up to six no trumps and Father Coady as my partner told me off when, inevitably, I went down two tricks." (Box 39, HGJ to Alexander Laidlaw, 8 June 1971).

absolute decline in agriculture produced a period of crisis. The population of Antigonish County, St. F. X.'s home district, fell from 16,114 in 1891 to 11,518 in 1921 and 10,073 in 1931. In the 1920s, almost 150,000 people, among them many of the more skilled and productive members of society, left the Maritimes (Cameron 1996, 166, 211). Added to these economic worries were the concerns of the Scottish Catholic Society of Canada, which had been founded in 1919 to promote Catholicism amongst the Scots, to preserve their traditions and to advance their educational and social standing. In 1928 the Society pledged to raise $100,000 over five years to educate farmers and workers in cooperation and self-help. At the same time a series of diocesan rural conferences held at St. F. X. addressed social problems and promoted a reform agenda in the diocese. The university had dabbled in extension before the 1920s. Dr. Hugh MacPherson, manager of the college farm, who also advised and assisted local farmers using his experience at the Nova Scotia Department of Agriculture, had become interested in agricultural cooperation. Dr. Jimmy Tompkins,[9] the vice-rector, had heard accounts of American extension in Wisconsin, found out about Workers Educational Association programmes in Britain that were breaking new ground, and examined experience in western Canada. Early in 1918 he began "For the People" a weekly column in the local paper, *The Casket*, and recruited other columnists for his reform movement. In 1920 he wrote a pamphlet, *Knowledge for the People*, an extended argument for St. F. X.'s involvement in the extension movement; he was also a major force behind the diocesan conferences mentioned earlier. Between 17 January and 12 March 1921 his ideas were tried out at the first people's school. Fifty-two adults registered for the school, which offered courses in English, economics, mathematics, public speaking, and agriculture. A second school held at Antigonish in 1922 attracted even more students. Two more were held at Glace Bay in 1923 and 1924. Although the movement lost Tompkins in December 1922 when he was sacked as vice-rector and exiled to the parish of Canso for his outspoken support of a scheme for Maritime university federation, the pressure for an extension programme persisted. The 1927–8 MacLean Royal Commission on the Fishery, before which Coady appeared, recommended an expansion of adult education in May 1928. Its recommendations provided fodder for the October 1928 Rural and Industrial Conference. Representatives of the Alumni Association appeared before the Board of Governors of the university demanding action and on 27 November the board approved the establishment of a Department of Extension

---

[9] Tompkins was Coady's cousin.

and appointed Coady as director. They also granted him leave from January 1929 to study extension work elsewhere in Canada and in the United States.

Coady spent several months touring and talking extension, but, he claimed, "found no institution which had started anything really useful." The Maritimes would have "to work out their own salvation" with St. F. X. helping though schools, libraries, broadcasting, and economic organisations (Cameron 1996, 217). Then another opportunity arose; the federal Department of Fisheries asked Coady to organise the fishermen of eastern Canada. The assignment, which lasted from September 1929 to June 1930 and resulted in the formation of the United Maritime Fishermen with 168 locals, gave Coady more knowledge of regional problems, more experience of community organisation, and, perhaps most important, more contacts and an enhanced reputation. But in the fall of 1930, the business of organising the Department of Extension began in earnest. St. F. X., the Scottish Catholic Society, and the Carnegie Corporation provided financial support. The extension programme worked through economic cooperation, with the key tool being the community's study club embodying the notions of self-help, cooperation in learning, study and self-improvement. The clubs, normally organised after a mass meeting in the area concerned, helped farmers and fishermen to understand the background and characteristics of their plight and to think of solutions. At St. F. X. all of this activity came together in the annual Rural and Industrial Conference, in the production of study materials and the organisation of travelling libraries and the mounting of short (four to six week) courses for community leaders. And the movement spread. By the fall of 1932, there were 207 study clubs, 8 lobster factory coops, and 9 credit unions. By 1940, with 30,000 people involved in study clubs, there were 382 credit unions, 39 fishing cooperatives, 42 stores, and 20 other varieties of coops in the Maritimes. By then, the Department of Extension had 11 full-time and 7 part-time workers, and through the department a federally sponsored fisheries programme employed another 15 in the field (Cameron 1996, 226). Finally as part of the extension movement CJFX went on the air in March 1943.

Harry found all of this quite exciting. He reacted in two ways: by trying to understand it and by taking part in it. The process of trying to understand the movement resulted in his first publication. He went to a course of lectures given by Daniel MacCormack, which included discussion of the principles of the movement. Harry also discussed the principles with others, notably Catherine ("Tot") Sears in the Department of Extension. But to go from lectures and conversations to a publication required motivation and a venue. Harry's stretched back to Toronto.

> In my late high school and early college days, I had a girl-friend whose father I respected greatly, and the family had moved to Wolfville, Nova Scotia, where he was in charge of price control and she was going to Acadia University. So I hitch-hiked down there a few times for Friday and Saturday nights. . . . On one of those week-ends I met Acadia's Professor of Economics, a man called Mosher. . . . He invited me to give a lecture the next time I came. . . . When I [next] reached Acadia, Mosher had forgotten me completely, despite a letter I'd sent him to confirm the date [29 April 1944], and I had a scratch collection of puzzled students to listen for only half of the planned time. Once back in Antigonish, I circulated the lecture, and Father Coady decided to publish it for the Extension Department. (1974 Memoir II, 15–16)

The fourteen-page pamphlet both pleased and embarrassed Harry. He was naturally pleased by the publication, and he would have been impressed if he had known that Coady had used his distillation of the movement's principles in his statement to the Royal Commission on the Taxation of Co-operatives in 1945 (MacEachen 1997, 19). Later he would be somewhat embarrassed that much of the work was really Father MacCormack's. He would become even more embarrassed when two graduate students at the Coady International Institute at St. F. X. reported that his was the first published presentation of the principles of the movement and asked him how he had got them from Coady (Box 36, Bede Onuoha to HGJ, 17 January 1964; HGJ to Onuoha, 29 January 1964).[10]

The pamphlet began by outlining "The Maritime Problem":

> The problem of the Maritimes is to a large extent the problem of the large monopolistic or semi-monopolistic (i.e. monopolistically competitive) corporation. Legislative control has been attempted in the past but has largely proved ineffective; moreover, it has been more than offset by the legislative favours the corporations have been able to obtain, particularly in the form of tariffs. The only effective check on these super-corporations is for the people to go into business for themselves both to secure to themselves the profits made on their own business, and by their competition to exercise control over the activities of the companies. Co-operation, not legislation, is the most direct route to the control of the modern corporation. (1944, 4–5)

It then provided a brief history of the movement, the guiding principles that had evolved during that history, the techniques used, and examples of fields where cooperation had been successful. The famous six principles were as follows: "the primacy of the individual," "social reform must come through

---

[10] This had also been pointed out to Harry by Doris Boyle, who taught sociology at St. F. X., when Alexander Laidlaw's *Campus and the Community* appeared in 1961 (Box 56, Doris Boyle to HGJ, 7 November 1961; HGJ to Doris Boyle, 28 November 1961).

education," "education must begin with the economic," "education must be through group action," "effective social reform involves fundamental changes in social and economic institutions," and "the ultimate objective of the movement is a full and abundant life for everyone in the community" (1944, 6–9). The lecture concluded with a discussion of free enterprise versus socialism which ended:

Co-operation, The People's Way

For co-operation is the people's way into big business. The masses cannot hope to get into big business as individual producers; they have neither the resources nor the capacity for that; but by co-operating as consumers, they can on the one hand retain the advantages of free enterprise, and on the other they can, by their competition, force the corporations into the service of the people. Consumers' co-operation is in fact the people's free enterprise; it is the democratic way of carrying on big business. And if socialism does come, to the extent that the people have been educated by economic co-operation, they will be able to exercise effective democratic control over their government.

Co-operation, then, is the effective way to preserve the advantages of free enterprise. More than that, co-operation may provide a dynamic principle on which a better post-war world may be based. We cannot build a better world solely on a philosophy of social security and "full employment"; such a philosophy is negative, lacking the power to motivate human development, and those who insist on "security" as the only post-war aim are Quislings to social progress.[11] Social and economic security are essentials; but if our civilisation is to advance, socially and economically, it must find some dynamic idea, some new principle to motivate men to action. "Free enterprise" no longer commands the loyalty of men: perhaps co-operation will provide the explosive idea for the new world of the common man. (1944, 14)

His practical involvement in the Movement was associated with two individuals.

Alex MacIntyre, a senior extension worker and former communist organiser I got to know, asked me to prepare a scheme for strikers' benefits and retirement benefits for co-operative workers. I was interested, because I had been reading the [British] Beveridge Report [on Social Insurance, 1942] and the Canadian Marsh Report [1943] rushed out to defend the Liberal Party's claim to liberalism. I soon realised that the actuarial calculation for a pension plan was beyond me, but I produced a strikers' benefit plan. It was accepted, after a change insisted on by the co-op managers recognising their right to full pay during strikes in place of my Beveridge-inspired flat rate of $7.00 a week; and I am told it is still in operation (except, I presume, for the $7.00 rate). MacIntyre expressed tremendous admiration; but

[11] V. Quisling was a Norwegian officer and diplomat who collaborated with the Germans in 1940 and afterwards.

co-operative gratitude produced only a cheque for \$44.00 for what had been about a month's hard work.[12] (1974 Memoir II, 17)

The second individual was Tot Sears of the Extension Department. During the fall of 1943, Harry had taken to visiting coops in the surrounding countryside and on Cape Breton. Later he learned to operate a movie projector, and he went with Tot to visit coop gatherings in remote villages, sometimes by car, sometimes by sleigh. He reported one visit to Innis, who had been a member of the 1934 Nova Scotia Royal Commission on the effect of federal fiscal and trade policies on the provincial economy and had attended the 1938 Rural and Industrial Conference at St. F. X., which had included a preconference tour of some of the movement's projects such as the cooperative housing project then under construction at Reserve Mines.

I have just returned from a visit to Cape Breton, where I spent much of my time visiting co-operatives. I paid a visit to Father Tompkins, to whom I gave your regards. A rift has developed between Dr. Tompkins and the Extension Department in the last few years: Dr. Tompkins stresses the provision of libraries for the people as a means of education, and condemns the Extension Department for its concentration on economic co-operation and the study club technique. I was quite impressed by the Reserve Housing Project and by the Credit Union developed in New Waterford. [University of Toronto Archives, Innis Papers, B72-0025/003(03), HGJ to H. A. Innis, 15 April 1944]

Tompkins had become parish priest at Reserve Mines in 1935 (Welton 2001, 115, 118–19). Harry's last expedition with Tot was to Sydney. They started off at mid-afternoon and arrived safely; however, they got stuck in a ditch on the way back and had two flat tyres on the way to catch the ferry at the Canso Gut. As a result, Harry got back to Antigonish for his final Advanced Economic Theory examination on 16 May 1944 exhausted. "I fell asleep proctoring it" (1974 Memoir II, 26).

Harry's other professional first, in addition to advising the co-ops, was unpaid – submitting

a memorandum on the Maritime university system I did for my old teacher, temporarily a one-man commission, Robert MacGregor Dawson. Something like eighteen institutions (really undergraduate colleges) for a population of 750,000 was clearly too many; and the religious and ethnic divisions among the New Brunswick herring shuckers and the Nova Scotia apple pickers and the Prince Edward Island spud islanders that had created the few hundred-student-sized universities with their Arts and Divinity offerings should, I thought, be submerged into a more compact federated system. Father Jimmy Tompkins, founder of the co-operative movement,

[12] Of course if one looked at Harry's recommendation, it was quite generous.

had I knew been 'banished' from St. F. X. president [sic] to parish priest for voicing the same thought in the 1920's, but I believed, wrongly, that times had changed. They hadn't, and Dawson understood why though I didn't; but the Maritime universities began eventually to prosper, at least temporarily, in the 1950's and 1960's, with the new western world belief in universal college education as the key to economic growth. For myself, I now realise, thinking in preparation for that memorandum shaped my view on graduate level education in economics when I began to consult on that problem for the Province of Ontario nearly thirty years later.[13] (17–18)

Harry's Antigonish experience was important in other ways than he remembered in 1974. When, just over a year after leaving St. F. X., he applied for a Rhodes Scholarship, he expressed a strong interest in adult education as a result of his recent experience, an interest strengthened by his current employment in Army education. His application concluded:

After I complete my studies, I intend to return to the teaching of economics in my own country, preferably in one of the smaller universities. In that way I feel I shall be making the best use of my capacities.

I should prefer to teach in a small university for two chief reasons. First, I believe that the small university has a definite educational role, especially in the fostering of community spirit and responsibility among students, but it is often handicapped in playing its role by the drain of talent to the large Universities of Canada and the United States, a handicap that can only be offset by a movement of trained men into the smaller institutions. Secondly, a position in a small university would permit closer contact with the non-university community, facilitate a greater integration of my work with community life, and perhaps allow me to develop my interest in adult education mentioned earlier. (Box 44, Rhodes Scholarship Application, 1945)

It also ensured, as he told a convocation audience at St. F. X. twenty-one years later, that the experience was a part of breaking away from the standards of his origins.

I originated as a White Anglo-Saxon Protestant . . . and beyond that, and more deplorably a Torontonian, indoctrinated with prejudice against Catholics, Jews, French-Canadians, Englishmen, Americans, and coloured people of all sorts. When I came to St. Francis Xavier, I learned my first real lesson about society: that the Catholic church in Nova Scotia was more sincerely concerned about the problem of poverty and human betterment than the Church and the culture in which I had been brought up, and that it had been concerned enough to develop an action programme that really produced results.

Without that breaking away,

I would have been a Toronto lawyer, and I would probably have gone into politics, and become a proponent of the regionally self-serving and narrowly nationalistic

---

[13] This topic is discussed in more detail in Chapter 11.

policies . . . of this country. (St. F. X. Archives, RG 30-4/22/11–12, "The Progressive Society," 13 May 1965)

The term at St. F. X. ended on 24 May 1944. Harry headed home via the meetings of the Canadian Political Science Association, which were held in Montreal on 1 and 2 June. There he met up with Gideon Rosenbluth and his fiancée. Rosenbluth later remembered:

From there we hitchhiked west together and after that our paths began to diverge both geographically and ideologically. I had my last glimpse of Harry the radical late at night, as my fiancée and I stood by the side of the highway in Prescott, Ontario and waved good-bye to Harry riding off to Toronto in a furniture van.[14] (2001, 610)

[14] Prescott with its bridge across the St. Lawrence had good road connections with Ottawa where Rosenbluth was then employed at the Dominion Bureau of Statistics.

THREE

England

On his return to Toronto, Harry had a few weeks' leisure before he enlisted in the army on 27 July 1944. With his COTC experience, he could have taken his chances as an officer cadet, but he chose to enter as a private, as he had said he would do the previous September. He did his basic training at Cornwall in eastern Ontario and his advanced infantry (machine gun) training at Camp Borden, which sprawled across sandy hills fifty miles north of Toronto. After training he was shipped overseas from Halifax by fast liner and arrived in England on 18 March 1945. En route to England, he developed sinusitis with the result that he spent almost a month in hospital and was then declared unfit for overseas service as an infantryman on 18 April. He thus remained at the Canadian centre at Aldershot to be a clerk in the orderly room of the Chaudières Regiment. There, he reported to Innis, he was "having a fair time . . . living with men who have been in the army for five or six years, so that I hear many interesting stories of black market activities and rackets by which soldiers are able to live beyond their income (it being virtually impossible to live within it)" [University of Toronto Archives, Innis Papers, B72-0025/003(03), 29 April 1945]. After almost a month in the orderly room, he was transferred to the 13th Canadian Education Section at Canadian Military Headquarters (CMHQ) in London. The Education Section occupied the basement of the Sun Life Building in Cockspur Street next to Canada House. On 12 June 1945, he became an acting corporal, his highest military rank.

London

CMHQ at the time consisted of 616 officers, 2,712 other ranks, and 745 civilians; the education section was small – only 55 officers and 126 other ranks (Stacey, 1966, 200). Staff at CMHQ were "on subsistence" – "paid an allowance and found their own places to live." As a result, Harry later reported to Allan MacEachen, "I had a sociological summer in 1945, in a slummy section of London (all I could afford on the money the army gave me)" (MacEachen Papers, 12 September 1946). He ended up in a rooming house on the margins of West Kensington. His experience there became the basis of a paper for F. C. Toombs's seminar on Human Relations in Industry during Harry's MA year in Toronto in 1946–7 (Box 54, Toombs, Human Relations in Industry, "Analysis of Rooming House Group").

The house was owned by Ken Watts who also operated a small business in photographic prints and dealt in the black market in a number of other items. Ken's assistant Lennie, aged twenty-three, also lived in the house and shared a room with him. The house was looked after by Molly, aged twenty-eight, who lived in a small room on the second floor. The third floor was occupied by a woman in her late thirties who had been a tenant under a previous landlord and thus had security of tenure independent of the wishes of the current incumbent. The remaining three doubles were occupied by Canadian soldiers, Harry and Frank from the Education Section of CMHQ, two Catering Corps privates nicknamed Don, and transients referred to the house by the Knights of Columbus canteen. Ken was "extremely ambitious; a failure in several occupations, he was very anxious to succeed in his photography business." Lennie "was really Ken's mistress," even though it was clear that Lennie preferred a merchant seaman called Jack who had previously lived in the house. Ken's relationship with Lennie was insecure, and he regularly showered Lennie with gifts beyond his means. Ken's other major relationship was with Molly, with whom he had "long serious conversations on . . . topics which Lennie was not intelligent enough to discuss." Molly cooked and cleaned in return for her room, and she had invested £30 in the photography business. Ken also had a shared interest with Frank in photography and in making money through sharp practice. Ken talked with Harry about general matters, "particularly the social problems of homosexuality, and once or twice took him pub-crawling along Dene [sic] Street with Lennie and Molly to introduce him to homosexual society." But Harry felt some contempt from Ken "on account of his negative attitudes and indecisiveness." Frank was "a French-Canadian, an uneducated and rather vain man" who had owned a photographic equipment store in Montreal before joining the Army. He had come to the Education Section at the same time as Harry, but their relationship became increasingly strained as Frank "felt extremely inferior and insecure in company with the younger man's superior education." The insecurity led to attempts to dominate Harry's spare time – to keep him to an arrangement that they speak French every day and to complain at his failure to go out drinking together in the evening. Harry reacted by withdrawing into a circle of outside acquaintances, which didn't help the relationship. Frank had also taken Molly as a mistress, but the relationship was unstable, partly because Harry developed a close friendship with Molly. According to Harry, the "friendship originated in curiosity to know the psychology of an apparent nymphomaniac, and grew into a fairly intimate sharing of ideas and reactions . . . [and] long conversations about psychology (especially her own problems)." She also provided him with tea and laundry services, for which he reciprocated with cigarettes and chocolate bars.

At the time Harry reported himself as feeling "a sense of shame over his whole environmental situation (a shame aggravated by his acquaintance with university people in London)." He recorded "his general depression about his army rank and the work he was doing." When Molly eventually took a housekeeping job elsewhere in London and left the house, he moved out.

One of Harry's "university people in London" was Frederick Norman, professor of German at King's College, London, since 1937, who was spending his war in the Foreign Office. Harry's contact with Norman was through his daughter Jean who had been an undergraduate at University College, Toronto, between 1942 and 1944. The Normans lived at Bletchley in Buckinghamshire, where Harry would later stay during at least part of one Cambridge vacation. Frederick Norman, as one of Harry's referees for his Rhodes Scholarship application, reported on him as follows:

I would say that in the many conversations that I have had with Mr. Johnson on general matters, I have been most favourably impressed by the extent of his general knowledge of economic problems and their political repercussions, the ready fluency with which he is able to draw on his knowledge and develop coherent arguments from it, and the intelligence and invariable courtesy with which he has frequently been able to expound matters to someone very much his senior. His comments, enlivened by humour and wit, are never – as they unfortunately are with so many graduates – dryly textbook and are always stamped with his own personality and outlook.

Mr. Johnson is without doubt the most intelligent of the Canadians it has been my privilege to welcome to my house during the war. He has become a real friend of the family, and his personal charm, quick responsiveness and general vivacity, coupled with his alive and alert intelligence, have made him welcome and will continue to do so whenever he can come. (Box 44, Letter to Rhodes Scholarship Selection Committee, 12 September 1945)

By the time he was applying for the Rhodes, the next step in Harry's career was becoming clearer. With the end of the war in Europe and a prospective shortage of shipping space to repatriate its forces overseas, it was necessary to keep the troops still in England or on the Continent occupied. The Canadian government initially planned to set up a series of Khaki Colleges in England and perhaps on the Continent that would teach courses laid down by Canadian universities and administer centrally set examinations on the University of London model. When Harry first heard of the scheme, he told Innis that he hoped to be able to become an instructor in economics in one of these. However, he also told Innis that he hoped to stay in England for postgraduate work and asked for his advice [University of Toronto Archives, Innis Papers, B72-0025/003(03), to H. A. Innis, 29 April 1945]. The Khaki College scheme floundered, but when a successor Khaki University scheme emerged in Britain (Oliver 1998, 40), Harry found that he could go to Cambridge where the authorities found him a place at Jesus College. Initially the arrangement was to be for one term. Accordingly, Harry reported to the Porter's Lodge at Jesus on 6 October 1945 and settled into rooms in Chapel Court.

Cambridge Undergraduate

Despite being the college of T. R. Malthus, Jesus had a long tradition of not electing economists to its fellowship. Thus for supervisions, where students discussed their weekly essay for an hour with a faculty member, Harry was farmed out to Maurice Dobb, a lecturer in economics in the faculty since 1922, but as an avowed communist, he did not become a college fellow until elected by Trinity in 1948. Later Dobb became a reader in economics and a Fellow of the British Academy, as well as an historian of economics of some distinction. Harry's closest new friend was another Jesus economist reading Part II of the Economics Tripos that year, Aubrey Silberston, who had just returned from the a German prisoner-of-war camp where he had been teaching himself economics.

For the University of Cambridge, 1945–6 was a transitional year. Student numbers were higher than during the war, but the real influx of veterans would come the next year. Among the faculty in economics, Richard Kahn, Brian Reddaway, and Austin Robinson had not yet returned from their "wartime" Civil Service duties. Maynard Keynes who was still alive and advising the new chancellor of the exchequer, Hugh Dalton, was in Washington negotiating for postwar financial assistance from the United States. Dennis Robertson, who had left Cambridge for the London School of Economics at the end of 1938, joined the Treasury in the summer of 1939 and been elected professor of political economy in succession to A. C. Pigou in February 1944, was, after almost a year of catching up on the literature, giving his first lectures since the spring of 1939. He had decided as professor, to offer a set of lectures on economic principles twice a week in all three terms. He would eventually publish his revised notes as *Lectures on Economic Principles* in three volumes between 1957 and 1959. There had been some new appointments since 1939, such as the Quaker statistician Charles Carter, but the large infusion of new postwar blood had yet to come. The relative shortage of teachers meant that A. C. Pigou was drawn back in from retirement to supervise undergraduates, something that he had not done since being elected Alfred Marshall's successor as professor of political economy in 1908.

Once Harry was in Cambridge and his abilities and preferences became known, his college and the Faculty of Economics quickly took the necessary steps to move him from Khaki University to the position of a regular Affiliated Student who had graduated from another university and was a candidate for a Cambridge BA. Because of his earlier degree, he would normally be excused one of the three years of residence required for the Cambridge degree. Then, because of his wartime service, Harry, like other undergraduates who had served in the war, was excused another year's residence with the result that he could sit the examinations for Part II of the Economic Tripos in June 1946. Under the rules, as an Affiliated Student, he would be asked to sit five papers, or examinations at the end of the year: Subjects for an Essay, Economic Principles, Industry, Labour, and Money. But, although Cambridge was quick in doing its part of the business, "The army," as he told Innis on 31 December 1945, "true to style, is not prepared to give me a definite decision on whether I shall be allowed to stay or not" [University of Toronto Archives, Innis Papers, B72-0025/004(03)]. Eventually he was allowed to stay and was discharged from the army in England on 12 April 1946.

The Cambridge examination system differed from Toronto's. Final examinations did not take place in every year of an undergraduate's course. Rather students in economics were required to sit two sets of examinations, Parts I and II of the Tripos, in three years – one at the end of their first year and one at the end of their third – for which they received a single mark. As well, the final examinations were not set by those who had lectured that year on particular subjects. Instead, a set syllabus provided guidance as to the material covered upon which a Board of Examiners, including examiners from outside Cambridge, could set questions. To prepare for these examinations, students could go to the lectures organised and offered by the faculty to cover parts of the syllabus, write weekly supervision essays whose topics were designed to cover the syllabus, and read. The emphasis was on supervisions, which were regarded as compulsory. The system effectively made lectures optional: students went if they or their advisers thought they would be useful. Unlike Toronto's, Cambridge lectures were formal affairs, very often carefully written out and delivered with varying degrees of skill. As the course for Part II normally covered two years, Harry's lectures would contain an admixture of people taking Part II in 1946 and 1947. Harry's cohort included Aubrey Silberston and I. G. Patel (later director of the London School of Economics), while the next year would include Norman Macrae (later editor of *The Economist*), Robin Marris (later a Fellow of King's and professor at Birkbeck College, London), Robert Nield (later a professor in Cambridge), Eric Russell (later a professor at Adelaide), Brian Rose (who went on to a career at the International Monetary Fund), Dorothy Barnard (later as Dorothy Wedderburn a distinguished sociologist at Imperial College, London), and P. Lesley Cook (later an industrial organisation specialist in the Department of Applied Economics at Cambridge). There were also some people who were not taking the exam such as Kenneth Berrill (later bursar of St. Catherine's College and King's College and chief economic adviser to the Treasury) and Harry's fellow members of Khaki College, including Meyer Bucovetsky who went to Gerald Shove in King's for supervision during his single term in Cambridge.

Not only was the educational regime different from Harry's past experience, but the classes were larger. Harry's Toronto cohort in political science and economics had been fifteen, although the presence of commerce students in his economics classes would have made them larger. His Part II cohort in 1946 numbered thirty-two and that of 1947 even larger. Added to them were also the ex- or semi-ex-servicemen from Khaki College or similar American schemes that added over 160 students to the Cambridge total in the autumn of 1945.

For Harry's activities, we have a good record of reading notes, lecture notes, and some supervision essays. We also have the supervision reports that Dobb wrote each term for his Jesus Tutor. His lectures are listed in Table 3.1. His level of involvement varied with the course. For Rostas, we only have notes from the first lecture; for Brogan, Postan, Shove, Kirkaldy, and Cohen on Reconversion, we have lecture notes but no immediately associated reading notes; for the rest we have some lecture notes and some reading

Table 3.1. *Cambridge Lectures, 1945–1946*

Lecturer	Michaelmas	Lent	Easter
D. H. Robertson	Economic Principles	Economic Principles	Money and Economic Fluctuations
Joan Robinson	Money	Problems of Foreign Trade	Determination of Profit Margins
		International Exchange	
M. H. Dobb		Problems of a Collectivist Economy	
J. W. F. Rowe	Industry		
H. W Kirkaldy	Industrial Relations		
R. Cohen		Problems of Reconversion Monopoly	
M. Postan	English Economic History in the Nineteenth Century		
L. Rostas		Public Finance	
C. Guillebaud	Labour and the State		
C. F. Carter		Theory of Statistics	
D. Brogan	Political Theory 1776–1914	American New Deal	
G. Shove		Classical Theory of Value and Distribution	Classical Theory of Value and Distribution

notes. As well, there are a number of files of reading notes by themselves for Marshall's *Principles of Economics* and *Industry and Trade*, Robertson's *Essays in Monetary Theory*, Pigou's *Economics of Welfare*, and Beveridge's *Full Employment in a Free Society*. His course reading notes included Joan Robinson's *The Economics of Imperfect Competition*, *An Introduction to the Theory of Employment*, *Essays on the Theory of Employment*, and *An Essay on Marxian Economics*, John Strachey's *A Programme for Progress*, and Michal Kalecki's *Essays in the Theory of Economic Fluctuations*.

From his supervisions, only a selection of his essays survives.[1] The topics included (Box 34, Writings 1975, part 3, essays do not survive for topics with an asterisk):

It is sometimes suggested that a boom is brought to an early end by a rise in the rate of interest checking investment, while others have suggested that it is due to an increase in capital equipment or a failure of consumption to expand. Discuss.

The relation between the equilibrium firm and the optimum firm under conditions of increasing returns.

Railway rates – joint supply.

Describe the changes in the location of British industries during the years 1918–1939. Do you regard the trends of that period as likely to continue after the war?

Is it true that the schemes for the regulation of prices and output in the British coal industry have resulted in inefficient mines being supported at the expense of efficient. If so, would it be sufficient to condemn the schemes as unsound?

Discuss the main criticisms to be made of the existing structure and organisation of the British cotton industry.

Outline the main provisions of the National Insurance Bill, pointing out any differences between it and the Coalition White Paper and the Beveridge Plan. In what way do you think its provisions might be improved on?

A wages council is established in an industry in which widely different wage rates prevail in different establishments in that industry, both in the same locality and in different localities. What factors should determine (a) the initial minimum rates of wages fixed (b) whether there should be differentials as between districts?

Discuss the way in which the quantity theory of money may be criticised as an explanation of the forces governing the general level of prices.

* Examine recent tendencies in British trade unionism. How do you think these will be changed after the war.

---

[1] Normally he would have written about twenty essays, but as Harry found his original supervision partner uncongenial, he arranged to have fewer supervisions but be supervised alone (*Shadow*, 130).

* "Full employment does not mean there is no unemployment" (Beveridge). Of what levels and what orders of magnitude would you expect unemployment to be in a postwar Britain with a successful policy of "Full Employment"?

His essays were written to a high standard – much higher than those he had written two years before at Toronto. Occasionally he seemed less than enthusiastic in dealing with British institutions. On the other hand, he was not unwilling to tackle institutional matters as shown by his choice of final examination questions, which is discussed in more detail later.

He had also started his reading programme into Dobb's own writings, which would carry over into the next year. His 1945–6 reading notes – all on the distinctive, low-quality, paper he used in Cambridge – covered *Wages* (1928), *Capitalist Enterprise and Social Progress* (1925), *Political Economy and Capitalism* (1937), "A Sceptical View of the Theory of Wages" (*Economic Journal*, 1929), and "Economic Theory and the Problem of a Socialist Economy" (*Economic Journal*, 1933).

He obviously impressed Dobb, whose supervision reports to his Tutor in Jesus ran as follows:

[Michaelmas 1945] Johnson is very promising and I very much hope that he will be allowed to stay here for the whole year. He already has a fair grasp and a deep knowledge of economics; and evidently has a very good mind, mature and original. . . . he has alpha quality in his make-up. An unusually stimulating student to teach.

[Lent 1946] Johnson . . . continues to show ability and competence of a high order. . . . He certainly has alpha touches; but while he is sure-footed and very competent, he may possibly lack that touch of originality necessary for a consistently first class performance.

[Easter 1946] . . . Competent and original in his thought . . . he has had a difficulty in covering the whole field in the time at his disposal. But he certainly has elements of α-quality in him. (Jesus College Archives, H. G. Johnson File)

Where there is some ambiguity in the record is over the liquidity-preference/loanable funds debate between Dennis Robertson and the younger Keynesians, which would wrack Cambridge in the late 1940s and provide Harry with a very useful publication in the *Review of Economic Studies* in 1952. Harry's memoirs of Cambridge are full of the debate (see, for example, *Shadow*, 141–5). However, other memories, such as Aubrey Silberston's, suggest that Harry was remembering a later period:

I discovered that Harry already knew a lot of economics, having taken what I think was a full undergraduate course at the University of Toronto. He hadn't, however, done much Keynesian economics, which was very much a Cambridge specialty then, its diffusion as an undergraduate subject having been delayed by the war. I vividly remember walking around the College playing fields with Harry for an hour or more trying to sort out the Keynesian theory of liquidity preference. There was little attempt at critical appraisal. We were simply trying to understand what was then a novel and difficult theory, with few or none of the elementary textbooks that later become available. We did not become fully aware of Dennis Robertson's criticisms of Keynes' theory until late in the year, because Robertson discussed these issues only in the final term. (1978, 2)

Silberston's supervisor, by the way, was Joan Robinson.

Much of Silberston's recollection is consistent with the facts on the ground in Cambridge. Joan Robinson's lectures on money were really not about monetary theory but rather about employment theory and policy. The rate of interest was the subject of one lecture on 9 November 1945, where, to judge from Harry's notes, loanable funds were touched on in passing. Robertson's Easter term lectures on "The Theory of Money and Economic Fluctuations" provided the criticism, but, of course, they had not been given before 1946. One therefore suspects that the reaction in Joan's lectures and in supervisions came in Michaelmas 1946 when she tried to inoculate students against Robertson.[2] Moreover, even in the "Money" paper, there was no examination question where a knowledge of the controversy was of any use to a candidate. Harry did, of course, read Robertson's *Essays in Monetary Theory*, but he bought the book in a 1946 reprinting during his visit in the summer of 1947 (copy in the author's possession). All of this is more consistent with Silberston's memory than Harry's later recollections.

Harry's reactions to his teachers varied. He was fascinated by Maurice Dobb as an intellectual figure and appears to have enjoyed him as a person. As previously noted, Harry read several of Dobb's books and papers while in Cambridge. When he was back in Toronto, Harry embarked on a larger-scale study of Dobb and his thought for which Dobb provided off-prints and comments. Dobb was a good supervisor. He was not a good lecturer, however: Though well prepared, having written his lectures out in detail in advance, "He used to read these things in a flat monotone, and I went to these lectures out of a sense of duty, which was certainly required" (*Shadow*, 129). In a country that had just elected its first majority Labour government in a landslide, the topic of Dobb's lectures, problems of a collectivist economy, was, in principle, attractive. At first the class had between forty-five and fifty members, but it soon dwindled to a rump consisting of Harry and

---

[2] For partial confirmation see Robertson Papers C8/1, Robertson to Joan Robinson, 20 May and 3 November 1946.

economist members of the Communist Party as Dobb reworked the "social-ist calculation debate" of the 1930s which had involved, among others, Dobb, Oskar Lange, Friedrich Hayek, and H. D. Dickinson. But another economist who laboriously wrote his lectures out in full each year beforehand, was a different matter.

> And then Robertson came in and talked. They were brilliant lectures, but you had to know at least enough economics for a Ph.D. before you could understand them. In his youth he had been quite an eminent amateur actor, and his delivery was beautiful. (129)

He found M. M. Postan "inaudible," which was rather surprising to later generations. Joan Robinson aroused mixed feelings. As Harry told Innis, "she lectures in a monologue and has a rambling way which confuses her English students." He also found the lectures "quite polemical" and "polit-ical" [University of Toronto Archives, Innis, Papers, B72-0025/004(05), HGJ to H. A. Innis, 27 October and 31 December 1945]. Later, however, he recalled

> [t]he only exciting lecturer was Joan Robinson: and this, again, was a bit of a surprise. We had had female lecturers at Toronto who appeared nicely dressed and perfumed and wearing skirts and other kinds of recognisable sex symbols. But we all assembled for Joan Robinson's lecture – and in strode this rather mousey-looking woman, wearing a sort of blouse and vest combination on top and a pair of slacks down below and sandals. She proceeded to put an elbow on the lectern, peered out at us and started off in a rather flat monotone "well, it's very difficult these days to lecture on economic theory because now we have both socialist countries and capitalist countries. . . . " Everyone thought "Gosh, what a wonderful new idea!"[3] (*Shadow*, 130)

However, he was generally unimpressed by the lecturing: "I think they are at present a little bored with things: the lectures I've been taking are not very stimulating" [University of Toronto Archives, Innis Papers, B72-0025/004(05); HGJ to H. A. Innis, 31 December 1945]. In his letters to Innis he explicitly compared Toronto to Cambridge, not treating the latter favourably. Indeed, from the end of December, he hoped to be in Toronto for the next academic year, and on 18 January 1946 he accepted a position at Toronto at a salary of $1,800.

As previously mentioned, Keynes was not teaching in the autumn of 1945 and winter of 1946: He was in the Treasury until his death on Easter

---

[3] Harry's lecture notes run as follows: "Problem not one but two systems, each complicated by special local & hist'l factors, therefore must treat everything as a special hist'l case, much more difficult" (Box 44, Joan Robinson Money Lectures, Michaelmas 1945, 1).

Sunday 1946. Nonetheless, as Harry told Innis on 27 October 1945, "The theory lectures seem shadowed by the spirit of Keynes, with everyone paying lip-service to the principal of effective demand" [Innis Papers, B72-0025/004(05)] However the "shadow" came to Cambridge and his path crossed Harry's.

When he took the professorship, Robertson, with Keynes's permission revived the Political Economy Club in the autumn of 1945 (Keynes Papers, RES/12, Robertson to Keynes, 14 January 1945). Keynes had founded the club in 1909. Membership was by invitation, normally on the basis of Tripos performance and the recommendation of a director of studies. The usual practice was for an undergraduate member to provide the paper for discussion, but contributions could come from senior members. Keynes had talked several times over the years, and outsiders visiting Keynes often spoke. After the paper, undergraduates commented on it from the hearth rug in front of the coal fire, the order of their comments being determined by lot, as was the practice of the Apostles, the famous "secret" Cambridge society of which Harry would later become a member (see discussion in Chapter 5).

Harry did not have any Tripos results to become a member of the club, but his brilliance became known to Robertson, probably through Maurice Dobb, although Aubrey Silberston credits Joan Robinson (Silberston 1978, 3). His membership began in the Lent Term of 1946. On 4 January, Robertson asked Keynes if he wished to say anything about the Anglo-American Loan Agreement concluded in December 1945 or related matters either in a public lecture "or more intimately at (say) the Pol. Econ. Club" (King's College, Cambridge, Keynes Papers, UA/56). Keynes accepted. He was going to be in Cambridge to receive an honorary degree on 31 January and the club met 2 February.

The basis for Keynes's talk was a paper, "The Balance of Payments of the United States," which would appear in the *Economic Journal* for June 1946. That paper had its origins in the recent Anglo-American Loan negotiations: Once it was clear that a loan rather than a grant-in-aid from the United States would be available to Britain, the question of the terms of repayment became of some importance, as did their balance-of-payments implications. On 25 October Keynes sent to London a paper, "Will the Dollar Be Scarce," which he had prepared with the assistance of Frederic Harmer and David McCurrach. After the Loan Agreement (and the Articles of Agreement of the International Monetary Fund and World Bank) were through Parliament, while Keynes was resting at Tilton, his country house, he decided to work the paper up into a journal article. He told R. F. Harrod, the editor of the *Economic Journal*, of his intention on 4 January, completed a draft by 25 January, and received Treasury approval for it on 2 February. In his discussion of the prospective American balance-of-payments position, he concluded that "the chances of the dollar becoming dangerously scarce in the next five to ten years are not very high" (Moggridge (ed.) 1979b, 444). There followed a series of paragraphs that echoed his defence of the Loan Agreement in the House of Lords on 18 December. "In the long run much more fundamental forces may be at work which may ultimately transcend ephemeral statistics." He continued:

I find myself moved, not for the first time, to remind contemporary economists that the classical teaching embodied some permanent truths of great significance, which we are liable to-day to overlook because we associate them with other doctrines which we cannot now accept without much qualification. There are in these matters deep undercurrents at work, natural forces, one can call them, or even the invisible hand, which are operating towards equilibrium. If it were not, we could not have got on even so well as we have for many decades.

The United States was becoming a high-cost country, which would help restore equilibrium in normal circumstances. The "Proposals for Consideration by an International Conference on Trade and Employment," published simultaneously with the Loan Agreement were designed to allow "the classical medicine to do its work."[4]

It shows how much modernist stuff gone wrong and turned sour and silly, is circulating in our system, also incongruously mixed, it seems, with age-old poisons, that we should have given so doubtful a welcome to this magnificent objective approach which a few years ago we should have regarded as offering incredible promise of a better scheme of things.

Bretton Woods (that is the International Monetary Fund and International Bank for Reconstruction and Development whose articles of agreement emerged from the UN conference at Bretton Woods in July 1944) would speed the operation of the classical medicine in less painful ways. Between them, Bretton Woods and the Washington Proposals "marry the use of the necessary expedients to the wholesome long-run doctrine" and were "an attempt to use what we have learned from modern experience and modern analysis, not to defeat, but to implement the wisdom of Adam Smith" (Moggridge (ed.) 1979b, 444–5). Strong words, made even stronger in Cambridge to judge from Keynes's own speaking notes (Moggridge 1992,

---

[4] The result of the proposals was the General Agreement on Tariffs and Trade (GATT) of 1947.

824) and Harry's notes from the occasion, later used by Harrod (with due acknowledgement) in his *Life of John Maynard Keynes* (1951, 620).

Harry later remembered the occasion:

> Keynes sat there in an armchair with his legs slumped out in front of him – and he had very long legs.... He had some notes on the table beside him, but he never seemed to use them. He gave us a very elegant talk, beautifully constructed, every sentence a piece of good English prose and every paragraph condensed – just a wonderful performance. But it was in the discussion afterwards that I learned so much from him. (*Shadow*, 133)

It was Harry's luck, at his first meeting of the club, to open the discussion.

> I got up and struggled through a rather lame argument. It was to the effect that given the availability of lots of farm labour in the United States, it would take some time before the pressure of demand for industrial products would force up the level of wages because labour could be drawn from the farms. I was not really convinced of this myself, particularly after having listened to Keynes. But he was very kind, and he picked up the point and made something of it. But I noticed that this is what he did. One of the secrets of his charm was that he would go out of his way to make something flattering out of what a student had said.... On the other hand when a faculty member got up – ... and at that time Joan Robinson stood up and attempted to argue with him – he simply cut their heads off.[5] (*Shadow*, 133)

The winter was cold and miserable. Coal was in short supply; so Harry studied in his army greatcoat, trying to type with gloves on (*Shadow*, 128; Elizabeth Simpson, 26 July 2005). Later in life Harry also remembered drinking beer and arguing about politics in Cambridge. He was "highly impressed with the real intellectual freedom in England, which did me a lot of good in sorting out some ideas I have" (MacEachen Papers, to Allan MacEachen, 12 September 1946). He was a member of the University Labour Club and contributed to its *Cambridge Labour Review* a review of James Burnham's *The Managerial Revolution* in the Lent Term (Vol. 4, No. 3) and a commentary on two articles on Canada – Geoffrey Ashe's "The Spy Scandal" and Robin Marris's "The Rise of the C.C.F." – in the Easter Term (Vol. 5, No. 2). He joined the Marshall Society, the undergraduate economics club, was elected to its committee and played an important role in drafting a report on Tripos reform, which went to the Faculty Board in the autumn of 1946. Like most such discussions, nothing came of them. He also took part in an Anglo-American discussion group for which he produced a paper on U.S.

---

[5] Later Harry remembered: "I happened to meet Robertson a day or two after this, and I expressed my tremendous appreciation both for the invitation and for the paper itself. He said to me, 'Ah, but you missed something that used to be there – the impishness of his mind'" (*Shadow*, 134).

exports in the Michaelmas Term and one on American reconversion during the Lent Term.

During the Easter vacation, Harry, I. G. Patel, and Robin Marris repaired to a flat rented by Robin's parents in Seaview on the Isle of Wight, and I. G. taught them how to cook curry. In the village, they found a local grocer who had survived the war with a full stock of dried raw curry ingredients and herbs kept in tiny drawers. The butcher had steak, and for the first time I. G. was introduced to eating meat (King's College 2006, 68).

However, the Tripos examinations loomed. They were not as stressful as Harry's memoir suggested.[6] Examiners' names (including the external's) were published well in advance, and the system of double-marking papers (with provisions for third readers if differences persisted) made it unlikely that students' examination scripts got as caught up in the faculty's internal wars as he suggested.[7]

As a part of the preparations for exams, the "Johnson group" came into being. About half a dozen students met weekly in Aubrey Silberston's room in Jesus to discuss past examination questions and to sort out the best possible answers.

Harry was our leader, so to speak. He knew much more than anyone else and was clearly the best economist among us, but he didn't have the sort of overpowering stature that came later. (Silberston 1978, 3)

Then came the examinations. The schedule was brutally short. They started with Economic Principles at 9 A.M. on Monday, 3 June and finished with the Labour paper, which was over by noon on Wednesday, 5 June. Except for the Essay paper on Tuesday afternoon, where Harry wrote on "New Towns," he was expected to write five essay-type answers in three hours. The questions that he answered varied. Some, most notably the Industry and Labour papers, required some local knowledge. A full list is appended to this chapter.

The results were available just over two weeks later: Harry had got his first class degree – indeed, it was better than that, as Joan Robinson reported:

---

[6] The memoirs are misleading in other places. For example, he suggests that Robertson in the 1930s had gone to the London School of Economics because "[h]e had been prevented from receiving what he (and many others) considered was the final reward of a serious academic career, namely the professorship at Cambridge" (*Shadow*, 139). This ignores the fact that A. C. Pigou, the incumbent, had not retired. When he reached 65 in 1943, he duly retired, and Robertson was appointed professor. Again he says on page 88 (*Shadow*) that Gerald Shove, a fellow of King's since 1925, did not have a university post, when he had been a university lecturer since 1923 and was appointed reader in 1945.

[7] In the author's experience this was so even in the late 1960s and early 1970s when the internal wars over capital theory and its implications for standard economic theory were at their height.

I gather you fairly bowled the Part II examiners – altho' there's an unusual number of 1^{sts} yours was clearly the best. Of course you have had more experience than the others – but it isn't by any means every lecturer in economics who'd get a first in our Tripos.

I want to thank you for all you did for the chaps. Your discussion group did far more for them than any of the official teaching.

It was nice of you to give time to them. . . .

I was very glad Silberston collared a first – he was one who owed a lot to your help. (Box 44, Cambridge University Papers, 22 June 1946)

The previous day Harry had received a letter from Nicholas Kaldor, the external examiner from the London School of Economics (LSE) who "was much impressed by your consistently high standard [in the Tripos] and the way you presented your arguments," offering to put his name forward for a vacant lectureship at LSE, which he did (Box 44, Cambridge University Papers, 21 June 1946; Robbins Papers, Staff, File I, 1945–50, Kaldor to Robbins, 26 and 29 June 1946). Jesus College offered him a Research Studentship of £60 per annum if he would stay on. But Harry was determined to return to Toronto for further study, even refusing the offer of a professorship of Commerce at Dalhousie University in Halifax. He told Innis: "On the basis of this year's experience I should say that Toronto's standards compare very favourably with those of Cambridge: but that may be a biased view" [University of Toronto Archives, Innis Papers, B72-0025/004(05), 25 June 1946]. He then took a month-long external course at the University of Rennes. As he told Allan MacEachen:

It was wonderful: freedom complete, mainly the army's money, and good people to mix with. If you ever get the chance, go to Europe: problems disappear, at least temporarily. (MacEachen Papers, 12 September 1946)

Back in England, he attended the Fabian Summer School at Ferndon in Surrey, before he sailed for Halifax in late August. There he was met by John Atwood, who drove him to Toronto.

APPENDIX: TRIPOS EXAMINATION QUESTIONS ANSWERED BY HGJ

Economic Principles – 3.6.46 – 9–12

3. "The prejudices of some political writers against shopkeepers and tradesmen are entirely without foundation. So far is it from being necessary either to tax them or to restrict their numbers, they can

never be multiplied so as to hurt the public, though they may be so as to hurt one another." (Adam Smith). Discuss.

4. Discuss the role which varying expectations regarding the future play in the causation of business cycles.

8. What reasons, if any, are there for doubting whether the long-term rate of interest will ever fall below about 2%?

9. "It is wages which determine the standard of life, not the standard of life which determines wages." Discuss.

10. What room, if any, is there for the concept of marginal utility in explaining the forces governing the exchange value of money in terms of commodities?

Industry – 3.6.46 – 1:30 – 4:30

1. Describe the problems in any industry in which a Government "working party" has been or might be appointed, and summarise the advice which you as an economist would give if you were called as a witness.

2. "Government bulk buying and trading through organised produce markets are not mutually exclusive alternatives. They can and should supplement each other." Discuss this statement generally, and in particular with reference to the recent Government decision not to re-open the Liverpool Cotton Exchange.

3. Why has industrial combination in Great Britain developed in such varied forms?

5. "Price regulation alone is inadequate to secure stability in the primary industries: output must be regulated too." What support does the history of artificial control schemes in the inter-war period give to this dictum as a guide to policy?

7. "Output per man hour in manufacturing industries is a very inadequate criterion of relative industrial efficiency in Great Britain and the United States." Discuss.

Money – 4.6.46 – 9–12

2. It has been emphatically stated by different authorities that the Bretton Woods Agreement (a) does, (b) does not, imply a return to the Gold Standard. How far do you accept either view?

4. Can you suggest circumstances in which a system of bilateral trading would lead to a greater aggregate volume of international trade than

a system of multilateral trading? Explain how far you regard your answer as relevant to the problems confronting the United Kingdom at the present day.

7. Describe and account for the main changes which have occurred since 1914 in the composition of the assets of the English joint-stock banks. Do you expect these changes to be reversed to any considerable extent in the future?

8. "The old-fashioned policy of using public works as a make-weight for the fluctuations in private capital outlay would, even if it were successful, result merely in stabilising the amount of unemployment, not in reducing the total amount of unemployment over time." Is this, in your view, a valid criticism of the policy in question.

11. Examine the view that general movements in money wage rates can only affect the level of employment through affecting the rate of interest.

Labour – 5.6.46 – 9–12

1. "The self-adjusting character of industry has been profoundly changed by the development of a system of social security." Elucidate and discuss.

3. Examine some of the ways in which differences in the method of wage-payment may influence the effect of improvements in the technique and methods of production upon the earnings of labour and upon costs of production.

5. What are the economic and social arguments for and against the legal establishment in Great Britain of a universal 5 day week of 40 working hours.

9. "Full employment in peace time is not practicable without a national wage policy." What do you understand by a "national wage policy" in this context?

10. It has been said that collective bargaining involves a "false standardisation" of the price of labour, with consequent injury to the national output. Examine this contention. (Box 44, Cambridge University Papers)

FOUR

North American Postgraduate

Toronto Instructor

The University of Toronto, where classes began on 24 September 1946, was a very different institution from the one Harry had left for Antigonish just three years earlier. In 1943 total enrolment had been under 7,000; in 1946 it was 17,173, up from 12,515 the previous year. Of the 17,173, no fewer than 8,723 were veterans. In the Department of Political Economy, undergraduate enrolments had grown from 1,534 – of whom 35 were taking more than three courses in the fourth year of Political Science and Economics or Commerce and Finance – to 6,787 – of whom 101 were taking more than three fourth-year courses. Part of the expansion was in the service course for engineers, where enrolments went from 300 to 2,160.[1] Enrolment in economics would peak at 8,800 in 1947–8. Graduate school enrolment had also exploded – and the graduate students were needed as teaching assistants, whose numbers had risen in the department from six to forty-eight. Although the department's faculty had grown since 1943 from twenty-one to forty-four, the long-term, full-time staff had only risen to replace wartime losses. All the expansion in numbers had occurred in the ranks of lecturer and instructor (Harry's rank). Instructors were virtually unknown before the war, but they numbered four in 1943–4 and fifteen in 1946–7. There would be only three in that rank in 1951–2 (Drummond 1983, 97).

With increased numbers of students and faculty, the department's building on Bloor Street was bulging at the seams. The third and fourth floors, unused since the University of Toronto had taken over the building in 1930 were opened up, unrenovated, for the new junior faculty with two

[1] The figures for 1943–4 and 1946–7 are from the Annual Report of the President, 1943–4 and 1946–7 and University of Toronto Monthly, November 1946, 35.

or more sharing an office, with the elevator still derelict and with only one telephone per floor. There was no accommodation for the graduate students. The instructors, who were more than one-third of the department, even though they did less than one-third of the teaching, were not, according to Harry, "voting members," although in a department unused to voting on anything, then and now, it is not clear what enfranchisement would have brought. Harry later described the experience as "a pretty sordid one" (1969 Autobiographical Notes, 6).

Innis's management of the department did little to ease the situation. As Harry later recalled:

Communication was difficult and almost non-existent. One saw the Department Head briefly on appointment, to discuss teaching duties, and any difficulties one was foolish enough to raise, and once at one of two Sunday tea parties he offered to junior staff later in the year, one for sheep possibly on their way down from the fourth floor to the ground floor, and one for goats definitely on their way down from the fourth floor to the exit door. Apart from that, one saw him only by appointment under strain, usually for advice or a reference in connection with a possible job for next year; his stock response to an implicit request for reassurance was "Well we wouldn't want to stand in your way."

As a result,

The ethos of the fourth floor was one of gossip, rumour and sometimes panic, of needlessly hard and unfocussed work, and of conviction that one was not good enough to be a scholar, that if one were one would not produce anything for hopeless years ahead, and that if one did produce something it would be read only by a handful of other scholars, all of whom would be devastatingly critical. No wonder so many used the exit! (*Shadow*, 86)

A colleague described the slightly later "conditions" at 273 Bloor Street West "where the chill 'always belittlin' hand of past and present Baptistism[2] was constantly present to cramp the soul" as

absorption in the self; gloom, introversion, protestant ethic rampant; denigration; withdrawal into private worlds; administrative anarchy; back-stabbing; log-rolling; nepotism; cliquism; neurotic primae donnae; student discontent; ulcers. (Drummond 1983, 86–7) .

In this scheme of things Harry played two roles. As an instructor he taught a section of Economics 2c, the Honours course Introduction to Economic Theory, which met Wednesday at 5, Thursday at 4, and Saturday at 11. The other two sections were taught by Norman Ryder, later a distinguished

---

[2] McMaster University, the original occupant of the building, had been a Baptist foundation.

sociologist,[3] and W. C. Hood, a graduate of Mount Allison University in New Brunswick who had come to Toronto for a PhD after two years teaching at the University of Saskatchewan. After a postdoctoral fellowship at the Cowles Commission at the University of Chicago (1949–50), Hood had a distinguished career in the department before departing in 1968 for the Department of Finance in Ottawa and ultimately the Research Department of the International Monetary Fund. In his second period in the department, as research director of the Royal Commission on Banking and Finance, he would employ Harry (see discussion in Chapter 10). The text for Economics 2c was Kenneth Boulding's *Economic Analysis* (1941 ed.) for which Hood and Johnson, after correspondence with the author, provided "the outline of an approach to the theory of the firm which is more in keeping with the orthodox treatment" (Box 20, Economics 2c, Notes on the Theory of the Firm in a Perfectly Competitive Economy).

Harry's other role was that of graduate student. At the time, only three English-speaking universities in Canada (Toronto, McGill, and Queen's) attempted to offer staff and facilities for doctoral work and then only in some areas. Toronto had the largest graduate school in the country. Over the decade 1935–44 the number of graduate students averaged 530, and the university produced on average 33 PhDs and 90 Masters degrees a year (Brebner 1945, 47). But it was only a beginning, and as J. B. Brebner put it in his 1945 survey:

It has taken a generation for Toronto's graduate school to grow from local aspirations to conscious efforts to serve the nation as a whole on a broad front of scholarship, and there are many American and European universities which comfortably outrank it. (44)

For his programme, Harry was taking four courses: one in economic history, a seminar in economic history, a seminar in the theory of employment, and a seminar in human relations in industry. We have already encountered traces of the last seminar in Harry's analysis of his London living arrangements. It was taught by Farrell Toombs and "was a pedagogical disaster but a lot of intellectual fun for everyone except Toombs who ... [wound] up psycho-analysing himself in a series of rather embarrassing seminars" (1969 Autobiographical Notes, 6). In addition to "Analysis of a Rooming House Group," Harry produced for the seminar a joint paper with Gordon Greenaway, Herbert Shepard, and a sociologist, Jessica Lambert, on "The Dynamic Relationship between Technology and Social Values." This collaboration necessitated more than one session at the King Cole Room at the Park Plaza

---

[3] Sociology did not separate from Political Economy until 1963.

hotel, the beer parlour nearest to the department. Harry's papers suggest that he had some interest in Jessica. As for his share in the enterprise, he seems to have provided the section on Marx. For the seminar, Harry also provided drafts and a final version of an interview with Paul Fox, a Victoria contemporary and fellow instructor who later became a senior member of the department. The subject of the interview was the selection interviews for the Rhodes Scholarships in the fall of 1945, the results of which the two of them agreed had been determined by the length of the candidates' military service.

The economic history course was Innis's fourth year Honours course that Harry had taken in 1942–3. It had changed with Innis's thinking to become less North American economic history than a history of certain aspects of Western culture. Harry wrote essays on "The Influence of the Newsprint Industry on Public Opinion" and "The Implications of the Electrical (Radio) Industry for Public Opinion." As for the graduate economic history seminar, S. D. Clark, a former student and young colleague later recalled:

The seminar sessions seldom varied in format. Papers were prepared and presented by various students in turn. Vigorous discussion ensued. Yet throughout Innis said little. There was no expounding on his part; no effort to present, certainly in any systematic manner, his ideas. A pointed remark now and then constituted what appeared to be his total contribution to the discussion. It was, however, his very presence that made participation in the seminar a unique intellectual experience. Every student in the seminar felt called upon to put forward his or her best. It was here that the graduate student learned what was involved in the essence of scholarship. (1981, 28–9, quoted in part in Watson 2006, 403)

For this seminar Harry did two papers on the ideas of economists. One was Maurice Dobb; the other, Léon Walras. Harry took advantage of his recently honed French to read the relevant Walras texts. For the Dobb paper, he had the advantage of personal knowledge and contact: His subject provided him with copies of pamphlets and offprints, as well as a copy of *Studies in the Development of Capitalism* in advance of its publication in North America. Dobb also provided Harry with his reaction to the piece.

I was very flattered to be made the subject of a paper – which has never happened to me before to my knowledge – and such a long paper too. My debt to you is considerable. I was interested to find that you found so much to say about my 23 year old Ph.D. thesis,[4] and made such an original story out of it. I always tell people nowadays (if they ever hear of it) not to read it. But perhaps it is true that one's most naive early work contains more fresh ideas than one's more polished later work with which one is more self-satisfied.

[4] *Capitalist Enterprise and Social Progress*, London: Routledge, 1925.

Incidentally the only omission I can find in your imposing bibliography at the end was my 1939 E. J. article on 'Saving and Investment in a Socialist Economy." (Box 44, Dobb: Problems of a Collectivist Economy, 2 July 1947)

With respect to the seminar on the Theory of Employment and International Trade, Harry, "working over some memories" in 1974, told Hood that it 'was probably what got me into the field' (Box 52, Correspondence 1972–7, C-G, 22 February 1974).[5] Harry's papers contain Hood's typed summary of lectures for 26 September; 3, 10, 17, and 24 October; 13, 20, and 27 March; and 3 April. There are also Harry's own reading notes for 26 September to 24 October, plus notes of discussions of Keynes and Pigou compared and Haberler's International Aspects of Business Cycles, all led by Hood. Finally there are a series of typed reports "Employment and International Trade – the Harrod Approach"; "Machlup's Contribution to the Theory of International Capital Movements"; "Metzler's Contribution to the Theory of Trade and Employment"; "The Meaning and Measurement of International Equilibrium"; "The International Aspects of Full Employment"; "Oscar Lange Price Flexibility and Employment"; and "Monopolistic Competition and International Trade and Its Relation to Domestic Employment." Harry himself wrote the papers on Machlup and Lange. Here Harry was working on classic materials then at the frontier of his field and doing so carefully and critically. Given Hood's 1948 Toronto PhD dissertation was "Some Aspects of the Theory of Employment and International Trade" (Mills and Dombra 1968, 48), the coverage of the course is understandable.

English Summer

While he was at Toronto, Harry was somewhat homesick for Cambridge. Letters from Maurice Dobb kept him informed of developments there.

This is quite a lively student year here; although the severe weather combined with the coal crisis is adding to the rigors of this term. The death of Keynes, however, added to other factors, is causing the tide in the world of academic economics to set in the conservative direction as far as Cambridge is concerned.[6] (Box 44, Dobb: Problems of Collectivist Economy, 13 February 1947)

The counter-reformation (as Joan Robinson terms it) is gathering momentum here, and as regards L.S.E. has practically conquered (they've made a number of new

---

[5] He also noted that "I'm still struggling with Metzler."

[6] It was the coldest February in 200 years, and there was continuous snow cover from 22 January to 13 March. In these conditions, difficulties in moving coal resulted in restrictions on domestic and industrial electricity use from 9 February.

appointments, all of a Rightish tendency bar one; and Kaldor has left to join Myrdal at Geneva on the European Econ. Commission).[7] Still things are not quite so bad, I imagine, as in the States, and we're not quite a colony of U.S.A. yet. (Box 44, Dobb: Problems of Collectivist Economy, 3 July 1947)

By the time Harry would have received Dobb's second letter, he was in England, having worked his way over to Manchester on a cattle boat. His first destination was London, where he stayed several weeks with Aubrey Silberston and his wife Dorothy in a flat at the top of a large house at 28 Bryanston Square in Marylebone. The neighbourhood had been pretty badly bombed and "whole sections of surrounding buildings had been shorn away so that you could see how staircases led up from floor to naked floor" (Elizabeth Simpson, 26 June 2005). Aubrey Silberston remembered him:

He was cheerful, witty in a quiet way, helpful, and a delight to have around. He was unsure of himself, however, and pretty vulnerable personally. Nor was he yet very confident as an academic. . . . He was at that time, to use his sort of language, a really "sweet guy." (Silberston 1978, 5)

During his time in London, Harry worked in the British Library of Political and Economic Science at LSE.[8] He visited Cambridge and worked in the Marshall Library of Economics. He observed the evolving economic situation as Britain, obliged under the terms of the Anglo-American Loan Agreement of December 1945 to make sterling convertible from 15 July 1947, suffered its first postwar balance-of-payments crisis. In the early stages, as he told Innis:

I attended the Royal Economic Society meeting three weeks ago, to hear Henderson and a man called Paish condemn the Chancellor's budget.[9] Academic opinion is swinging away from the cheap money policy as such [see discussion in Chapters 5 and 6], to the failure of the government to achieve a sufficiently large budgetary surplus to equate saving and investment and reduce inflationary tendencies which are making it very difficult to balance production between more and less essential industries. The basic problem is of course an absence of planning as distinct from wishful thinking, the persistence of British liberalism as a basic postulate of international relations, and the unwillingness of public opinion, especially among trade unionists, to accept the implications of economic receivership. . . .

---

[7] He had, however, not yet resigned from LSE.
[8] As Harry had paid £10 for a Life Membership of the Royal Economic Society in October 1946, he could use the Library (receipt dated 4 October in Box 44).
[9] The meeting was held on 3 July at LSE. After the meeting there was a discussion of Cheap Money and the Budget introduced, according to the notice of meeting, by H. D. Henderson and Nicholas Kaldor. Hubert Henderson was Drummond Professor of Economics at Oxford, while Frank Paish was at LSE.

An economic crisis is approaching rapidly. Austin Robinson has been taken into the economic planning commission, and has taken with him two friends of mine,[10] so that I hope to get some inside information on this two-years-late body. I have already looked at their four-year draft plan, which does not seem much of an improvement over the [Economic Survey] White Paper [of February 1947]. [University of Toronto Archives, Innis Papers, B72-0025/006(061), HGJ to Innis, 21 July 1947]

What Harry did not tell Innis was that he had been encouraged to join Berrill and Marris in assisting Austin Robinson, but had declined. And although he mentioned to Innis that he had seen Dennis Robertson during his Cambridge visit and that they had discussed the advantages of the smaller newspapers resulting from a cut in the newsprint ration, he did not say that he had seen Robertson at I. G. Patel's recommendation and that Robertson had asked if he would be interested in a post in Cambridge. "I was overjoyed, and he said that he would write to me at Harvard" (1969 Autobiographical Notes, 6).

But before he could get back to Cambridge, Harry had to get on at Harvard where he had been accepted as a graduate student from September 1947. He had a Harvard fellowship that covered tuition and gave him $500 a year, and, of course, he received $60 per month from the Department of Veterans Affairs under the Veterans' Rehabilitation Act, which he had preserved by registering as a graduate student in 1946–7 (Lemieux and Card 2001, 320).

Harvard

Like other North American universities, the Harvard Harry joined in September 1947 was awash with graduate students. Those whose careers had been interrupted by the war resumed their studies; at the same time large numbers of veterans took advantage of government assistance to continue their education. The Department of Economics (and the university) had decided to admit more students, but the attractiveness of economics meant that the department did not need to reduce standards. Classes were large, often thirty to fifty students as compared with the prewar ten. Some classes had more than fifty.

The faculty was not significantly different from that of the prewar. In the 1930s the Harvard department had not hired any of its graduates into the permanent faculty. It had added to its strength by hiring Alvin Hansen, Gottfried Haberler, Wassily Leontief, Joseph Schumpeter, and Sumner Slichter. Prior to that, with the exceptions of William Leonard Crum and Edwin

---

[10] Robin Marris and Kenneth Berrill.

Frickey, who had come to Cambridge to join the Harvard Economic Service (which collapsed in 1931), all the other members of the permanent faculty had Harvard PhDs. Some of these, such as the economic historian A. P. Usher, Edward Chamberlin of *Monopolistic Competition* fame, Edward S. Mason and John Henry Williams were distinguished. Some were nonentities. H. H. Burbank ("Burbie"), the chair, was "a negligible quantity as a scholar and economist," "a disappointed reactionary" who for Paul Samuelson at least "stood for everything in scholarly life for which I had utter contempt and abhorrence" (Mason 1982, 413; Samuelson 1977, 162). According to John Kenneth Galbraith,

He was engaged in a failing struggle to protect Harvard from alien intellectual influences, although he did not much care for the domestic sort either.... It was known in the department of economics that it had been some years since Burbank had read a book. (1981, 46–7)

O. H. (Nat) Taylor was a competent, if uninspiring, historian of economics. The serious weakness in the department was in the teaching of mathematical economics. E. B. Wilson of the School of Public Health provided a course, but there was no local appointment for some time to come. The position was sufficiently serious between the wars that Schumpeter, who had never taken a course in mathematics, taught a course in 1933 and 1934 before passing it over to "the more competent hands of Leontief" (Mason 1982, 422; Allen 1991, II, 3; Swedeberg 1991, 116–17). Nonetheless, in 1946 Schumpeter and Crum produced a textbook – *Rudimentary Mathematics for Economists and Statisticians*.

Haberler, Hansen, Leontief, and Schumpeter opened the Harvard department to theoretical developments elsewhere, particularly in continental Europe. They also strengthened the teaching in basic economic theory. The department had some strength in that area already in the person of Edward Chamberlin, but his teaching and research interests were very narrow:

He had found a lifework in elaborating the theory of monopolistic competition, answering his numerous critics, and differentiating his product from that of his rivals. As the title of his second book suggests,[11] he considered himself to be engaged in developing a more general theory of value. As a scholar Chamberlin was a "lone wolf" whose work owed remarkably little to the literature of the 1920s on increasing returns.[12] He was not much interested in developments in areas of economics other than his own. (Mason 1982, 423)

[11] *Towards a More General Theory of Value* (1967).
[12] One should remember that Allyn Young supervised Chamberlin's dissertation and Frank Knight also taught him before he went to Harvard. See Samuelson (1967, 106). See also

Scholarship in the Harvard department was not collaborative. As Mason noted:

[T]here appears to be a large difference between the working habits of economists at Harvard and at Cambridge, England.... [A]t Cambridge (and perhaps also at Chicago) production frequently arises out of group discussion from which the author emerges, if not as an interpreter of group opinion, at least as one whose ideas have been shaped and re-shaped by the give and take of discussion. Research at Harvard has not usually had the benefit of this process. (Mason 1982, 424–5)

Of the scholars who would influence Harry at Harvard, perhaps the most intellectually isolated by 1947 was Joseph Schumpeter. He arrived permanently at Harvard from Bonn in 1932.[13] Although in the 1930s he had been at the centre of a group of younger faculty – Chamberlin, Seymour Harris, Leontief, Mason, and later Haberler – who met frequently to present papers and discuss economic problems, usually over and after a good meal, Schumpeter was disinterested in his senior colleagues. Even before the war, Schumpeter's circle shrank: He fell out with Chamberlin because he "tried to walk a tightrope between Chamberlin's work and that of Joan Robinson" (Allen 1991, II, 64). The war shattered other links. Schumpeter believed that war should be avoided at all costs because it would destroy the European economy and European culture. He saw the Nazis, whom he did not regard as permanent, as a bulwark against the Soviet Union. He "feared the consequences of war for all the world more than he feared German hegemony in Europe and Japanese advances in Asia" (Allen 1991, II, 91). As a consequence, he was out of sympathy with British prewar policy. After September 1939, he favoured American neutrality and a negotiated settlement. When the United States entered the war, his pro-German position was only slightly altered, and he remained unsparing in his criticisms of Roosevelt, the British, and the policy of unconditional surrender. As late as 1944, he told his friends that Germany and Japan might *not* lose the war (Allen 1991, II, 155). Nor were these views privately held; as a result, he alienated colleagues and made himself the subject of the attentions of the FBI. With the end of the war, his isolation was reduced somewhat because he had more contact with Leontief and Haberler, but he was unable to rejoin the community as he had in the 1930s. He also lost his links to the younger faculty and graduate students. The graduate students were in a hurry to get on with their degrees, and although he was president of the American Economic Association from

Blitch (1995, 118–19) for evidence that Young had discussed monopolistic competition extensively in class before Chamberlin put pen to paper.

[13] He had visited Harvard in 1927–8 and 1930.

December 1947, he was regarded as being in a backwater in the world of the new economics and the interventionist state. He was something out of the past – "someone who could say 'marginal utility' in seventeen languages" (Swedberg 1991, 168).

A second important figure was Alvin Hansen, then the leading exponent of the "new economics" in the United States.[14] Hansen had come to Harvard from the University of Minnesota in 1937. Prior to his arrival, his main interest had been in business cycles.

> He had been markedly unsympathetic to strands of doctrine shaped in the 1920s that anticipated a number of the policy conclusions of the *General Theory*.... The early Hansen had also been critical of Keynes's theoretical contributions. He took sharp issue with the formulation in the *Treatise on Money* and his first reading of the *General Theory* was generally negative. (Barber 1987, 191)

Hansen's conversion to Keynesianism was significant in that he was one of the very few older economists who responded positively to the *General Theory* – he was 50 years old when the book appeared. His initially negative reviews had appeared in the *Yale Review* and the *Journal of Political Economy* (JPE) (1936a, 1936b).[15] Hansen was a participant in the discussions of Haberler's *Prosperity and Depression* in Geneva between 29 June and 2 July 1936,[16] where, not surprisingly, he did not take a very Keynesian position.

> For example, he stressed the ups and downs of profits as the essential characteristics of the business cycle, while Bertil Ohlin and I argued in terms of expansions and contractions of output and employment. (Haberler 1976, 10)

The change in view seems to have occurred during his first year at Harvard. By November Barber could record: "Hansen was near the point of embracing the Keynesian account of income determination, but he was not yet all the way there" (1987, 201). However, he was closer in April 1938 with "Pump Priming, New and Old," the latest piece included in *Full Recovery or Stagnation* (1938) with its revised *JPE* review of the *General Theory*. This dating is consistent with memories of participants in the first of the fiscal

---

[14] This does not mean that Hansen didn't have colleagues who were also exponents of the new views, most notably Seymour Harris who acted as a tireless publicist in *The New Economics: Keynes' Influence on Theory and Public Policy* (1947) and his biography *John Maynard Keynes: Economist and Policy-Maker* (1955).

[15] After his change of view, Hansen reprinted the second review with significant alterations to reflect his new intellectual position.

[16] The discussions did not occur in September as Haberler (1976, 10) states. There was a September meeting in Geneva that Haberler attended, but that was in 1937 and concerned Tinbergen's early econometric work on business cycles.

policy seminars he held with John Henry Williams for twenty years (Salant 1976, 15, note 3). Certainly from 1938 Hansen was the senior scholar of American Keynesianism.[17]

Williams was one of American Keynesianism's strongest critics. A student of Frank Taussig, Williams had written his dissertation on the international adjustment mechanism in pre-1914 Argentina (Williams 1920) – one of three empirical studies of the adjustment mechanism by Taussig students, the other two being Jacob Viner on Canada and Harry Dexter White on France. After brief stints at Princeton and Northwestern, Williams returned to Harvard in 1922, where he remained until his retirement. He was probably the best teacher in the department in the 1920s, although he would have faced competition from Allyn Young until 1927 and played a big role in the study of money and banking and international economics. Williams also had strong ties to the financial community. He was economic adviser to the Federal Reserve Bank of New York (1933–56) and a vice president of the Bank (1936–47). When Lucius Littauer gave Harvard $2 million in 1935 for a graduate school of public administration, it was agreed after some discussion that it should concentrate on public policy. Williams became the first dean. One of his first appointments was Hansen.

> Hansen was active and persistent in looking for positive programs that would make the economy work better, and he had definite views as to what should be done. . . . Williams was much more the skeptic and cautious critic. His skepticism extended to a number of policies that Hansen strongly advocated. It was clear to the students that they disagreed, but relations between them . . . were excellent. (Salant 1976, 21)

They didn't snipe at each other outside the seminar either: "their courtesy, civility and friendship persisted" (Samuelson 1976, 31).

Wassily Leontief, a Russian emigré, had come to the department in 1931 from Germany where he had studied in Berlin and worked at Kiel. He made valuable contributions to the theory of international trade in the 1930s, but he became most famous for his development of input–output analysis. This appeared in book form in his *The Structure of the American Economy,*

---

[17] Perry Mehrling (1997, 130–6) questions the notion of a "conversion" arguing that Hansen "was never really an orthodox neoclassical economist," that his "apparent Keynesianism" was a feature of his thought in the early 1930s and "owes . . . practically nothing to Keynes." However, despite the twists and turns of Mehrling's argument – notably that Keynes's "Economic Consequences of a Declining Population" "opened Hansen's mind to the possibility that Keynes might have more to offer than first appeared, and that Keynes might be less stuck in neo-classical orthodoxy than first appeared" – the emphasis is still on a change of mind.

1919–1929: An Empirical Application of Equilibrium Analysis (1941), which was concerned with the industrial interrelationships between inputs and outputs across the whole economy. This prodigious feat of theorising and statistical calculation won him a Nobel Memorial Prize in 1973. One of the offshoots of this analysis was a study of the structure of American foreign trade, which suggested, counterintuitively, that American exports could be characterised as labour-intensive. The so-called Leontief paradox would keep trade theorists busy during much of Harry's career as an economist.[18]

Gottfried Haberler came to Harvard permanently in 1936 from Vienna. By that stage, he had two major accomplishments behind him. In 1933 he had published *Der internationale Handel: Theorie der weltwirtschaftlichen Zusammenhünge sowie Darstellung und Analyse der Aussenhandelspolitik* (*The Theory of International Trade with Its Applications to Commercial Policy* English translation 1936), which transformed the so-called classical theory of international trade by considering the implications of abandoning the labour theory of value. With Haberler's modifications, trade theory could handle multifactor technologies and heterogeneous labour inputs. Along with the contemporaneous work of Eli Heckscher and Bertil Ohlin it provided one of the springboards for the modern theory of international trade. Haberler's second accomplishment before coming to Harvard began in 1933 when, after D. H. Robertson had declined the offer, the League of Nations asked him to survey the existing state of business cycle theory. The result was *Prosperity and Depression: A Theoretical Analysis of Cyclical Movements* (1937), whose first edition "nicely record[s] in amber the pre-*General Theory* state of the art" (Samuelson 1996, 1682). Subsequent editions in 1938 and 1941 provide a wonderful guide to the various debates surrounding the *General Theory*, a guide that Keynes himself called "scrupulously fair" [Moggridge (ed.) 1979a, 274]. As Keynes put it in an anonymous review of the second edition in the *Economic Journal* for September 1939,

Professor Haberler threads his way through complicated controversies with great skill, and his *resumé* is much enriched by very full (and extremely up-to-date) references to the relevant periodical literature. [Moggridge (ed.) 1979a, 275]

These were some of the major figures who were present at Harvard when Harry arrived. He had encountered several before, both as a student and a teacher. Harvard was well endowed with younger faculty and graduate

---

[18] Leontief is one of four economists having articles in both volumes of the American Economic Association's readings relating to international economics. The other three are Haberler, Metzler, and Samuelson.

students. Among the latter, he already knew John Dales, Herbert Shepard, and Stefan Stykolt from Toronto and I. G. Patel from Cambridge, but there were also Anthony Scott, G. M. Meier, Robert Solow, and Thomas Schelling. James Duesenberry and James Tobin were then junior teaching fellows in the department.

The preliminary stage of a Harvard PhD involved course-work and an oral "general examination," normally taken at the end of the second year in residence. Harry intended to offer economic theory, money and banking, international trade, and economic history for his generals. The courses for which reading lists, reading notes, and some lecture notes survive are set out in Table 4.1. In addition to the courses listed, Harry sampled some summer courses in 1948. He started with David McCord Wright on international trade,

but he was so awful I switched to a reading course under him. I amused myself by working very carefully through Marshall's writings, and discovered that his analysis changed greatly between the *Pure Theory* and *Money, Credit and Commerce*; I never got round to writing this up as I intended. (1969 Autobiographical Notes, 7)

He also started learning mathematics in a small group using R. G. D. Allen's *Mathematics for Economists*, a process which he continued the next summer in the original Cambridge.

Harry did well in all his courses, gaining an A in every case bar one, when he got an A+ from Hansen for Money and Banking in the fall of 1947.[19] He seems to have run into difficulties only in Leontief's course during his first term where an essay on "The Douglas Cross-Section Production Function – A Scatter Diagram Analysis" earned him a B, the first such mark since his courses in Economic History and Political Theory in his fourth year at Toronto.

Judging by the surviving materials, his most influential teachers were Haberler, Hansen, Leontief, Schumpeter, and Williams. Schumpeter's History of Economic Analysis course, and his encouragement, gave Harry his first two professional journal publications – "'An Error in Ricardo's Exposition of His Theory of Rent" (1948) and "Demand for Commodities Is Not Demand for Labour" (1949). The Ricardo error he later found out from Piero Sraffa had been discovered previously by Edwin Cannan and reported in his *History of the Theories of Production and Distribution in English Political Economy* (1893/1917). Cannan's book was "particularly recommended"

[19] Schumpeter said he would have given Harry an A+ in the History of Economic Analysis in the Winter term of 1948 had that grade not been abolished by a faculty vote (postcard dated 2 May 1948 in Box 26).

Table 4.1. *Harry Johnson's Harvard Courses*

Fall 1947	Winter 1948
101a Economic Theory (Chamberlin)	101b Economic Theory (Chamberlin)
102a Economic Theory (Leontief)	102B Economic Theory (Leontief)
141a Money and Banking (Hansen)	141b Money and Banking (Williams)
121a Statistics (Crum)	121b Statistics (Frickey)
143a International Trade (Haberler)	143b International Trade (Haberler)
133a Economic History (Usher)	133b Economic History (Usher)
	113b History of Economic Analysis (Schumpeter)

Fall 1948
202a Economic Theory (Leontief)
203a Economic Theory (Schumpeter)
241a Money and Banking (Hansen)
145a Business Cycles (Hansen)
246a Economic History (Usher)
242 International Monetary Organisation
   and Policy (Williams)
244 Seminar of the European Recovery
   Program (Harris)

in Schumpeter's reading list among "works dealing with the history of individual doctrines or persons" (Box 44).

That taught me two lessons: one about the scholarship of Cambridge, and the other about the scholarship of Joseph Schumpeter, who had got me to write up and publish the note. On balance I far prefer Schumpeter's style: if one does not know the literature, and a young man can prove an error one has not noticed, it is better to encourage him than to assume that he must be wrong; better still, of course, to check the literature to guard against unnecessary originality in the establishment of errors. (*Shadow*, 94–5)

Schumpeter fascinated and stimulated Harry. He went back to him in the fall of 1948 for Economics 203a whose "primary object . . . is to train students in the art of conceptualising the salient features of the economic process." He later wrote of Harvard:

Schumpeter was the only truly cultured and intellectually interested man there and he had a wide streak of charlatanism; and the other professors and students had considerable contempt for him, whether for the one reason or the other one could not be sure. (1974 Memoir I, 17)

In the same memoir, he mentioned being "culture-shocked and appalled by the graduate school mass mill and the cultural narrowness and superficiality of most of the professors" (17). His initial reactions were, as in Cambridge, negative. Just over two weeks after he arrived, he wrote Innis:

By and large the Graduate School here seems organized much more on German than on British lines, with concentration on reading vast numbers of more or less shoddy text-books (with emphasis on the Professor's own, particularly if expensive). The quality of the lecturing is poor – as a rough and ready generalization:

Harberler takes much too long to come to an elementary point, and rambles in an annoying fashion

Usher presents economic history like a bed-time story – 'what the baron said to the tenant' sort of thing. He is also addicted to using the Marxist interpretation of history as a whipping boy

Hansen is fairly clear and straightforward but often repeats himself from lecture to lecture

Crum is bored

Chamberlin seems played out and also seems to know it. He lectures in an irritating high-school fashion, to the contempt of his class, who have frequently made him appear foolish. Burbank told me 'he can't help riding the same old horse'

Leontief is a keen brain and an excellent teacher – the only one who doesn't seem to be serving time here.

The classes are very large – every one has had to be moved to a larger room – and the students ask questions almost incessantly, which makes things even harder. The questions are often put as a demonstration of superiority, rather than for information. The competitive spirit is keen. This is a trade school slavishly subservient to the written tradition. [University of Toronto Archives, Innis Papers, B72-0025/006(06), 8 October 1947]

After two months, he was still unhappy. He wrote Dennis Robertson:

My experience at Harvard has been rather disappointing. There are several hundred graduate students in Economics, and this, with the lecture system, prevents one from learning much from the Professors. The lectures themselves are not too good, but like Patel I am constrained to attend. However, there are some very good younger men here, and the system does have advantages of its own, which I would appreciate more if I was an American. (Box 44, Cambridge University Correspondence, 3 December 1947)

The major advantage of the Harvard graduate system was that it gave students a sense of the literature. Preparing for generals required one to know the literature in a fairly comprehensive manner – with the result that, as in Cambridge, Harry formed a group.

Johnson's previous exposure to economics at Cambridge and Toronto, not to mention his amazing quickness, retentive memory, and inexhaustible energy, quickly identified him as one of the leading graduate students. Rarely was he to be found without a straggling band of contemporaries, all anxious to get his help with difficult courses, try out new ideas, or challenge his interpretation of what was being handed down by the faculty. . . . Hansen's famous reading list was absorbed by Johnson and a small group of fellow students whom he organised to make sure no gem in the exploding literature went undetected. (Reuber and Scott 1977, 671–2)

Elizabeth Simpson remembered "how intensely these students and others talked when they got together in our apartment at the end of the day" (26 July 2005).

From his reading notes, it is clear that he was not stimulated by Chamberlin, for he read relatively little for either segment of his course: It was "out-of-date and fussy . . . but one had to master monopolistic competition theory and the differences between it and imperfect competition theory in case he appeared at one's Generals" (1969 Autobiographical Notes, 7). Even later he reported Chamberlin's as "the most extreme example of forcing students to immerse themselves in the details of a controversial scholastic literature I have ever encountered" (*Shadow*, 153). In contrast he found Haberler's course "excellent" (1969 Autobiographical Notes, 7) complementing the courses he had already had from Parkinson and Hood. Hansen's version of Keynesian economics was also stimulating.

Harry's choice of subjects for his generals had the advantage of substantial spillovers between lecture courses. Haberler's international trade lectures followed the organisation of his 1933/6 book and covered the monetary aspects of the subject (the balance of payments and international adjustment) before turning to the pure theory of trade and policy issues involving both trade and payments. Williams's half of money and banking covered not only the employment policy discussions in Britain and the United States but also the discussion of contemporary international economic issues – the Anglo-American Loan Agreement of 1945 and its subsequent unravelling, as well as the postwar international monetary plans and their realisation in the International Monetary Fund. Harry used Williams's thirty-nine-page reading list for International Monetary Organisation and Policy, which included trade theory, as a checklist of books and articles he had read and noted. He used the reading notes from this course as the core to which he attached others after he left Harvard, something that he did with no other course. As a result, the notes contain reports on, among others, Lloyd Metzler's "Tariffs, the Terms of Trade and the Distribution of Income" (1949) and S. S. Alexander's "Effect of Devaluation on the Trade Balance" (1952). Hansen's Money and Banking had him reading not only about the practical nuts and bolts of American monetary management but also the classics – Marshall, Wicksell, Hayek, Hawtrey, and Keynes, as well as his post-1936 interpreters such as Lerner, Modigliani, Tobin, and, of course, Hansen. Leontief's course took him through basic price theory, as well as, in the second term, capital theory, interest theory, and, what would become a major preoccupation of some theorists in the next two decades, the growth theory associated with Harrod and Domar.

All in all, Harry was becoming systematically very well read in economics – something that would remain his trademark. As Jan Graaff put it in 1961:

> I now see exactly what Joan Robinson meant when she said (in reply to my remark that I'd spent the afternoon looking through the journals in the Marshall Library to see what had been happening in the last 10 years) "Why don't you get on Harry Johnson's circulation list – that will keep you up to date." (Box 31, Correspondence to 1963, D–G, from J. Graaff, 29 May)

On his arrival in London after finishing his generals at Harvard, Harry met Aubrey Silberston whom he hadn't seen for over a year. Aubrey remembered that

> [p]ersonally he was not very different: a little more assured and mature perhaps, but as nice as ever. However, as an economist he had altered dramatically. He *knew* so much. He had apparently read everything and remembered everything. He was a walking bibliography.... [I]t seemed to have been Harvard that made the big difference. (1978, 6)

Silberston's reunion with Harry was at the end the story that had started in the summer of 1947 when I. G. Patel had suggested that Harry see Dennis Robertson who had asked him if he would be interested in a job in Cambridge. The next stage came in November 1947, when Robertson renewed contact. The faculty was expanding its complement of lecturers, and this would open up some assistant lectureships. Some colleges were "nibbling at the idea of creating Fellowships in the subject," although Jesus was "*not* among those who are on the possible nibble," as Robertson had ascertained from the Master E. M. W. Tillyard (Box 44, Cambridge University Correspondence, Robertson to HGJ, 12 November 1947). Harry replied immediately

> I wish to assure you that I am definitely interested in any prospect of employment at Cambridge. My two months at Harvard have, if anything, reinforced my opinion in this respect – in spite of the material comforts of life on this side of the Atlantic.

The only problem was the date. Robertson had suggested 1 October 1948. Harry continued

> The requirements for a Ph.D. here, as you likely know, include not only two years of course work but also a General oral examination which covers a much broader field. I am fairly sure of being excused a year of the former, although Professor Burbank has

refused to commit himself until I complete the first year; but I should like sufficient time to prepare adequately for the Generals, and had planned to present myself shortly before next Christmas. Accordingly I should prefer to delay my prospective return to Cambridge until January 1949, or later. (Box 44, Cambridge University Correspondence, 3 December 1947)

There matters stood until 9 February 1948 when Robertson as chair of the Faculty Board formally offered Harry a job. It would be an assistant lectureship paying £600 per annum (£500 if resident in a college). The position was for three years in the first instance, renewable for a further two. "But," Robertson continued, "it would be my hope and expectation, though I can make no promises, that on or before the expiry of the five years you would be promoted to a full University lectureship."[20] Coupled with the university offer was the offer of a college assistant lectureship at Jesus, paying £320.[21] His duties would begin with the beginning of the Lent Term on 12 January 1949, when he would be expected to give two lectures a week.

Harry accepted Robertson's offer on 21 February, reporting that he had made arrangements to take his generals in November. As for teaching, he continued:

Concerning possible lectures, I am at present most interested in the history of economic thought, and in particular in examining the development of economic theory in order to elucidate the nature of economic problems, and the application of economic concepts in solving them. I am hesitant about suggesting this subject, however, since I am fully aware that a proper presentation of it requires many more years of research and experience than I should be able to bring to it; and I should appreciate any alternative suggestions you might make. For my 'generals' I am preparing to present money and banking, international trade, economic theory and economic history, which will serve as some indication of the fields in which I shall be qualified on my arrival in Cambridge. Moreover, the preparation of lectures on any subject related to these fields would probably be more of a help than a hindrance in meeting the Harvard requirements. (Box 44, Cambridge University Correspondence)

Robertson replied on 4 March that the death of Gerald Shove had led the faculty to withdraw history of economic thought "rather than have it dealt with perfunctorily by anybody who wasn't really keen on it" and suggested money as the likely subject. Thus when the 1948–9 lecture list appeared, Harry was down for money and banking for both the Lent and the Easter

[20] The salary scale for the latter was £750 per annum rising over 15 years to £1,050.

[21] At the existing exchange rate, this brought his income to just over $3,700 – compared with the $2,000 starting salary for a lecturer at Toronto, where the floor for full professors was only $5,500 (Drummond 1983, 87)!

terms. The history of economic thought as a possible subject for teaching or research was never mentioned again until Harry's post-1973 periods of reminiscence.

In his December 1947 letter to Robertson, Harry revealed that he planned to marry "sometime next year." His fianceé was Elizabeth Scott Serson, the daughter of H. V. Serson of Ottawa and Campbell River, British Columbia. Harry had met Liz, who was a year behind him at Toronto and reading English, through the group of Ottawa friends mentioned in Chapter 1. Both had worked on *Varsity*, where Liz was assistant news editor in her fourth year. They had sporadically kept in touch after graduation, while Liz worked for a year as a reporter for the Ottawa *Journal* before going off to the Columbia School of Journalism in 1945–6 and returning to the *Journal*.

They had planned a small wedding, but Liz's parents, who were then in British Columbia, had the responsibility for organising it. When they couldn't come east for the spring date, Harry's mother offered to take over. She planned a big meet-the-engaged-couple party at Spruce Ridges before the wedding. Harry and Liz wouldn't have it. They eloped and were married in Cambridge, Massachusetts, on 28 May 1948. According to Liz,

[t]wo days after our Cambridge town hall wedding, we hitch-hiked to Toronto, arriving in the clothes we stood up in. (We had sent our respectable clothes with the Dales, whose car broke down on the way.) It was a most successful party with political big-wigs and cronies, farming neighbours, child study types, Johnson and Muat family connections hobnobbing together. (Elizabeth Simpson, 26 July 2005)

They settled in a "too-small apartment" (Elizabeth Johnson to Dorothy Silberston, 29 September 1948) at 48 Boylston Street as Harry worked towards his generals. Eventually he got a date for them, 12 November. Initially Harry and Liz had planned to sail for England on 8 December, but they moved the date to allow them time to see both families and to collect and pack their dispersed belongings – not to mention see friends. Harry began to grow tired of studying. He wished the examinations would come sooner, even though he was cramming two years' work into thirteen months (Silberston Papers, Elizabeth Johnson to Aubrey and Dorothy Silberston, 21 October 1948). When the examinations results came, Harry was graded "Excellent."

Harry and Liz sailed on the S.S. *Britannic* from New York on 15 December. Arriving in London, they stayed in the flat in Bryanston Square where Harry had stayed with the Silberstons during his 1947 visit. Sheila and Kim Ferguson, both economists, had inherited it from the Silberstons who had moved to Wimbledon. As the Fergusons were away in the north with Sheila's parents over Christmas, the Johnsons had the place to themselves. They were overwhelmed: The Fergusons had left them their meat and other rations for two weeks. It was miserably cold "but you could warm up by taking a very hot bath in a large tub fuelled by shillings on the gas meter" (Elizabeth Simpson, 26 July 2005). Finally they got to Cambridge where, after a short period in a Jesus College student lodging house on Maid's Causeway where the landlady and her family gave them a warm welcome, they moved into a Jesus College–owned flat, 3 Park Lodge in Park Terrace, described by Pevsner as "the largest domestic composition at Cambridge" and "especially worth-while," which faced Parker's Piece, a large tree-lined common space (Pevsner 1970, 252). They would spend the next seven years there.

FIVE

Cambridge Don

Although he had an assistant lectureship at Jesus, Harry did not have a college fellowship during his first year in Cambridge. This meant that he did not have a college room in which to work or see students and he did not have regular day-to-day contact with other senior members of the college. He could dine regularly but not bring in guests. Nor did he have a room in the Faculty of Economics, which did not have its own building with offices until the 1960s. Thus, he worked from Flat 3, Park Lodge.

Cambridge economics in the 1940s and 1950s was so organised that, as Charles Carter later put it, "You had to manufacture occasions for discussions with other members of the Faculty" (Tribe 1997, 147). Since 1935 the faculty had space in Downing Street (a five-minute walk from Park Lodge) for the Marshall Library, a room for classes and lectures and Marshall Society meetings, an office for the Royal Economic Society, and a faculty administrative office with one secretary. The Department of Applied Economics, which was directed by Richard Stone, had space in a temporary building in the courtyard. Most lectures were held in the Mill Lane lecture rooms (another five minutes' walk further away) or, if space was available, in the colleges. One met one's colleagues on a day-to-day basis by chance. There were few other opportunities: The faculty met for annual elections to the Faculty Board and its committees and had two sherry parties, one early in the Michaelmas term and one at the end of the annual Marshall Lectures. There were, however, seminars organised by the Department of Applied Economics, which, in addition to its own research staff, attracted a bevy of distinguished economists to Cambridge for short periods, to supplement research students' seminars and the occasional visitor. But the Department 'was pretty much an island unto itself, detached from college life and ignored by the regular faculty' (Tobin 1978, 451). There was also the so-called secret seminar, of which more later. One might meet colleagues at the Political

93

Economy Club, which Harry attended with some regularity, "thus lessening the intellectual and psychological isolation of Sir Dennis [Robertson] in his later years" (Bhagwati 1998, 485) and providing some contact with the young; such meetings were hardly occasions for intellectual discussion with colleagues. One might meet colleagues on committees for setting examination papers, organising the lecture list, or politicking over appointments. Nor was there much contact with colleagues with college rooms. Leaving aside the possible influence of Pigou's long reign as professor – he was a bachelor and after World War I "a distinct misogynist and misanthrope" (*Shadow*, 93), there were several other factors inhibiting contact. Most colleges had at best one economist.[1] Timetables were crowded during Full Term with lectures (2 hours per week) and supervisions (8 to 12 hours per week). The former were morning events, the latter late afternoon ones, with games (for the students) and committees (for the dons) filling up the time in between; the chances of finding a colleague free were not high. Moreover, there was an emphasis on the privacy of one's college room: "one opened them for one's pupils and a few college familiars and cronies, but casual dropping in by colleagues was unwelcome on the one side and known to be presumptuous on the other" (*Shadow*, 93). Harry was, according to Aubrey Silberston, particularly fierce in defending his privacy once he had a college room in King's.

Harry did not always have all the time in the world for me when I chose to drop in. I was, however, struck by how offensive he could be on occasions, and was hurt by it. With a British academic similarly placed (if ever there was one!) you might expect something like – "I'm terribly sorry, I am a bit tied up now. Can we find a time when we are both free?" Harry on the other hand would open his door, look loweringly at you, say curtly "I'm busy!", and close the door in your face. After one or two such experiences I stopped calling on him. (1978, 9)

Harry also mentioned the absence of automobiles as discouraging contact (*Shadow*, 96), but he must have forgotten the geography of central Cambridge, which made driving inefficient.

Harry made known his unhappiness at not having a college fellowship. It would appear that the Master of Jesus, E. M. W. Tillyard, attempted to remedy the situation, but matters moved slowly, perhaps because Harry had offended some fellows with his striped T-shirts and by not having his son, Ragnar, born in June 1949, baptised (Silberston 1978, 7).[2] A. L. Percival, his tutor at

---

[1]   The exceptions were King's with four; Trinity with three; and St. John's and Gonville and Caius with two in 1949.

[2]   As Joan Robinson later remarked: "Harry seems a very keen atheist. What a complicated character he is" (King's College, Cambridge, Kahn Papers, 13/90/5, Joan Robinson to

Jesus, later remembered him as "a man of very simple tastes and interests outside the complexities of his work" but also remarked on "his collection of quaint and ingenious wooden figures which he had carved himself" (Jesus College Archives, H. G. Johnson File, to Kildare Dobbs, 26 September 1962). As a result, when the Berry-Ramsey Fellowship in King's was advertised in October 1949 with a deadline for applications of 1 November and the College Council had not come to a conclusion on 28 October (Box 44, Correspondence 1949–56, from E. M. W. Tillyard, 29 October 1949), Harry applied to King's. His referees were Dennis Robertson, Joan Robinson, and Alvin Hansen. In his application Harry set out his programme of research.

The applicant is at present engaged in research into postwar British monetary policy, with special reference to the 'cheaper money' policy of Chancellor [of the Exchequer, Hugh] Dalton [in 1946–7]. It is intended to complete this study within the next eighteen months. . . .

If elected to the Berry-Ramsey Fellowship, the applicant proposes to complete this research and to undertake a study of the mathematical theory of saving and investment, with the intention of working out an analysis of the problems of economic growth in which the consumption standards of the community are assumed to be rising over time, in some definite relationship to the level and rate of change of current income, rather than fixed at the beginning of the period over which the analysis extends. (Box 44, Correspondence 1949–56, to the Provost of King's, 29 October 1949)

On 18 February 1950, eleven days after he had been promoted to a university lectureship in economics, Harry learned that he had won the competition for the King's fellowship. He was admitted the following Wednesday, 22 February. In terms of economics, he had struck it rich: King's was Keynes's college; its other fellows in economics were A. C. Pigou, Richard Kahn, Richard Stone, and Nicholas Kaldor, and Joan Robinson was "virtually an unofficial fellow" (and later made an honorary fellow) (Silberston 1978, 7). King's gave him a fine set of rooms on H staircase in the eighteenth-century Gibbs Building next to the Chapel. Robertson's comment when Harry told him was "one in the ear for Jesus" (Silberston Papers, to Aubrey Silberston, February 1950).

The election to King's put Harry clearly in the Keynesian camp that revolved around Kahn, Kaldor, and Joan Robinson. It also confirmed him as a member of the "secret seminar" that met every Tuesday during the Michaelmas and Lent terms in Richard Kahn's rooms in King's.

Richard Kahn, 2 December 1955). It is interesting that she didn't find this out until attending a meeting of the Humanist Society almost six years after Harry's arrival in Cambridge.

The description 'secret seminar' was a violent misnomer: its existence was known to all, and non-invitation to attend was deliberately used to snub those who lacked the correct Keynesian qualifications and/or political orientation, even though their theoretical abilities were indisputably at least equal to the group's average. (*Shadow*, 143)

It had been started in 1949 and continued in existence until at least the late 1960s. Its members included Jan Graaff, Joan Robinson, the four King's Keynesians (although Stone didn't come often), Piero Sraffa (who rarely came), Ruth Cohen, Brian Reddaway, Robin Matthews, and Kenneth Berrill. Later members included Richard Goodwin, Aubrey Silberston, and Robin Marris. Those excluded included Dennis Robertson, Alan Prest, Peter Bauer, Stanley Dennison, and Ronald Henderson, and later Michael Farrell and Malcolm Fisher. The standard practice was for one of the members to read a paper and, after refreshments provided by Kahn, for the paper to be discussed. The papers reflected the interests of the members, although later, according to Harry, the seminar "increasingly became a forum for the advanced testing of the technical analysis of Joan Robinson's *The Accumulation of Capital*"(1956) (*Shadow*, 143). Also, over time, the seminar became more like the typical Cambridge seminar, about which Robert Solow once remarked, consisted of Joan Robinson talking for 75 percent of the time and Nicky Kaldor talking for 75 percent of the time. According to Silberston:

Harry was no lightweight in the secret seminar, but he didn't stand out, as did Jan Graaff, for example. He was a mature economist, but by the standards of the seminar he was just beginning. . . . Indeed, when I said after one or two meetings how terrified I felt, Harry implied that even he had felt that way at first. "These people have been at it all their lives. You can't expect to know what it's all about as early as this." (1978, 11)

With his election to King's, Harry settled into his Cambridge routine of lecturing, college teaching, and supervision. He sharply cut back his teaching for Jesus to two to three hours in 1950–1 and gave it up completely the next year, only taking on the occasional exceptional student such as Samuel Brittan, later the financial journalist, in the Lent term of 1955. Brittan recalled Harry as "a genuine prodigy – on the surface flashy and Americanized – and not the feared personality he later became. He was the supervisor from whom I probably derived most benefit" (2000, 273). (Brittan's other supervisors were Peter Bauer, Milton Friedman, and Joan Robinson.) In 1950–1 Harry also acted as lector in economics for Trinity with a stipend of £120 per annum for four hours a week of supervisions (Box 44, Correspondence 1949–56, from R. M. Rattenbury, 27 July 1950). The centre of his undergraduate supervising was King's, which had a number of vintage years: in 1952 King's had five of the six firsts in Part II of the Tripos plus the top II-1.[3] King's also brought him more contact with graduate students, in particular John Young, Alvin Marty, Tom Asimakopolis, Conrad Blyth, Stephen Kaliski, Daniel Ellsberg, and Geoffrey Harcourt – to mention only members of the college.

The fall of 1949 brought two Canadians of Harry's age to Cambridge. One of them was Stefan Stykolt whom Harry had first met when both were undergraduates at Toronto. Stykolt had gone directly to Harvard in 1946, and it was only when Harry went there in 1947 that they got to know each other well. By that stage Stykolt was having marital problems and he did not do as well in his generals as he should have. During his first year at Trinity College, Cambridge, he was on his own and spent his first few months living with Harry and Liz.

He was a lively house-guest, and always an interesting conversationalist. His opinions were original, and frequently expressed in the salty language that so often shocked his more timid fellow Torontonians; his mind ranged widely over economics, politics, philosophy and literature, and his capacity to compress some fairly complicated and well thought out idea or judgment into a pithy sentence or two was a constant delight. [Stankiewicz (ed.) 1964, 37]

The only difficulties he caused followed from his passion for warmth and his habit "of singing over and over a few old songs that had somehow captured his imagination" (37–8). He spent his first year toying with a thesis on British capital exports to Canada before he lost interest; he spent his second year reading extensively in economics and settled on a topic only after he returned to teach at Toronto in 1951.

Through Stykolt, Harry met R. M. MacIntosh, a McGill PhD candidate working on his thesis on cheap money and the British housing boom in the 1930s. An early draft of part of it became an article in the *Economic Journal* for March 1951. MacIntosh gave this as a paper to the Oxford–Cambridge–London graduate seminar, which met in Oxford in February 1950. The seminar had been founded in 1933 to bridge the intellectual gaps between the three centres and had recently been revived, partly through Harry's influence. Harry drove MacIntosh over in fog in a borrowed car and, on the appointed day, "sat in the front row and machine-gunned every critic" (communication from R. M. MacIntosh, 10 May 2003). MacIntosh, upon

---

[3] He compared that year with his own Part II year in Cambridge and his experience at Chicago in the early 1970s with Jacob Frenkel, Rudiger Dornbusch, Manuel Guitian, Michael Mussa, Russell Boyer, Rachael McCulloch, and Douglas Purvis (1974 Memoir I, 15).

returning to Canada in 1950, taught at Bishop's University in Quebec for three years before becoming a successful banker. He and Harry would meet whenever Harry was in Toronto – often with Stykolt making up a threesome. Their paths would also cross when Harry (partly at their instigation) became involved in discussions of Canadian economic policy (see discussion in Chapter 9).

New friends were made outside Cambridge. Paul Samuelson remembered visiting LSE where William Baumol was a lecturer and Frank Hahn a graduate student.

At Will and Hilda Baumol's London lodgings Frank Hahn introduced Harry, who had come from Cambridge to address a seminar of lively LSE prodigies. At no time was Harry without a cigarette; before one burned out, he left it glued to his lip while lighting another; a third of the time he kept two going. (2001, 604)

Ralph Turvey, another junior member of LSE staff, reported to Baumol: "I stayed last weekend with Jan [Graaff], & had a very pleasant time. . . . He and I had a long evening with Harry Johnson whom I find very likeable and extremely bright"(Duke University, Baumol Papers, 8 December 1950) Harry became a regular attendee at seminars at LSE where he made contact with the younger economists.

Other acquaintances from the past returned to Cambridge. Kenneth Berrill, who had gone off to Whitehall to plan with Austin Robinson in 1947, became a university lecturer in 1949. Aubrey Silberston returned in 1950 as a research fellow of St. Catherine's College. There were new members of the faculty such as Frank Thistlethwaite, a fellow of St. John's, who came to teach economic history in 1950. With their wives they formed a comfortable community, supplementing that of their own college communities. On some occasions, there would be a Canadian import, square dancing:

Harry was the caller. . . . I have the most vivid memories of a large Harry dressed in a Canadian checked shirt, calling the dances and skipping vigorously round the room, sweating profusely all the while. He organised us, corrected us, bullied us, and generally drove us along. They were wonderful evenings. (Silberston 1978, 8)

Unfortunately some of these relationships soured later. Harry and Aubrey Silberston drifted apart after the latter was hurt by Harry's tendency to lash out and be offensive (9–10).

Although Cambridge life could be interesting and stimulating, it also had a certain drabness. Unlike London and other towns and cities, Cambridge had not been badly bombed. Bombs had fallen on only twenty-two occasions (about 1,000 incendiary and 118 high explosive bombs in total), and twenty-nine people had been killed (Gray and Brittain 1979, 206; Roach

1959, 283). Moreover, most bombs had fallen near the railway, which was away from the city centre, and no university or college building had suffered severe damage. Rather, as Andrew Gow put it in June 1945, "The wartime visitors to Cambridge, though not to my knowledge responsible for any loss of life, have done far more damage to College property than the bombs, both by turning it inside out for their own convenience and by setting it on fire" (1945, 255). For as well as playing host to the London School of Economics, Bedford College, the School of Oriental and African Studies, and St. Bartholomew's Medical School, the colleges provided space for Royal Air Force training, the hordes of civil servants who arrived when Cambridge became a regional government centre and various Dominion, Colonial, and American educational courses for the troops. At the same time the buildings were being used more heavily than previously, and it became impossible to carry out routine maintenance. With shortages of materials and manpower, resources were controlled by the university and the state. Between 1945 and 1948, for example, the exemption limits for building licences was £20 (Dow 1965, 150). Thus one college had to apply to the Ministry of Works for permission to repaint (Twigg, 1987, 361). As a result, most repair and restoration had to wait until the 1950s. There were similar restrictions on householders. The limits were later raised, but with houses they were £100 until 1953, while for schools they fluctuated between £200 and £1,000. The drabness extended to public transport, which was very badly run down.

And then there was rationing, which immensely complicated day-to-day life, given the need to be registered with one retailer for the basic ration (goods rationed on points could be used in any shop). By the end of 1948, bread and jam had been derationed, but among foodstuffs, the following rations remained (date of abolition in parentheses): bacon (July 1954), cheese (May 1954), cooked gammon and ham (October 1952), fats, including butter (May 1954), meat (July 1954), milk (May 1950), processed foods subject to points rationing (May 1950), soap (December 1950), sugar (September 1953), sweets and chocolates (February 1953), tea (October 1952). The food ration would provide a nutritionally adequate diet, but quality was not always good, and the results were not always appealing. Moreover, rationing was only part of the problem. Queues were "endemic"; in an April 1947 Gallup poll, 46 percent of those polled reported queuing in the previous week, mostly for food, with most reporting 1–2½ hours and only 20 percent reporting less than an hour (Zweiniger-Bargielowska 2000, 95).

Nor were foodstuffs the only goods subject to rationing. Coal was rationed until 1958; petrol, until May 1950 with the basic ration from March 1948 set at 90 miles per month. Most clothing and furniture rationing ended during 1948–9, but the end of rationing did not mean that supplies were adequate, particularly as stocks of both clothing and furniture became more dilapidated as time passed (Zweiniger-Bargielowska 2000, 122–4). The same gap between supplies and demand existed with miscellaneous consumers' goods that had never been rationed – crockery, glassware and hardware, anything containing rubber, prams, combs, toothbrushes, toilet paper, and the like (95–6).

Of course, Harry and Liz were somewhat protected by their relatively late entry into the system. Moreover, before coming they had made enquiries of the British Information Service and the Silberstons and others as to the availability and price of various goods (Silberston Papers, Elizabeth Johnson to Dorothy Silberston, 29 September 1948; to Dorothy and Aubrey Silberston, 21 October 1948). The emphasis was particularly on household goods (kitchen gadgets, domestic linen, furniture, and refrigerators, although Liz had to be reminded by Dorothy about washing machines). In the end, they decided "to try and travel as light as possible and save on freight" (Silberston Papers, to Dorothy and Aubrey Silberston, 21 October 1948). Doubtless that decision was influenced not only by their means but also by their expectations, which might have been shaped by the Canadian experience after 1945, which had been more austere than the American; many household goods, particularly durables, were very hard to get until the early 1950s and even then tended to come in older prewar models (Parr 1999, Chapters 1 and 3). Thus, they came forewarned and somewhat prepared and with stocks of clothing probably in far better shape than their British contemporaries. Moreover, their families overseas could relieve some strains. But, fresh from student life, their expectations were small, and it was all a novelty, an adventure. Liz shopped and queued at the co-op in the nearby Kite. They "saved their meat rations for special occasions, like entertaining overseas visitors." They also shared. Liz remembers that

for a time Ruth Cohen loaned us her car – and the Kaldors loaned us their cast-off refrigerator. And we loaned the Annans our baby carriage. Jane Thistlethwaite loaned her Hoover and I often took my washing to her Bendix. (26 June 2005)

To judge by Liz's own later washing machine, by 1951 they also managed to work the local system quite effectively (see discussion later in this Chapter).

Teacher

As noted previously, when he was appointed, Harry suggested that he lecture in money and banking and international trade. The faculty put him down for money and banking for both the Lent and Easter terms of 1949, but this was changed so that he did sixteen lectures on money and banking in Lent and five on the pure theory of international trade in the Easter term. Thereafter his money and banking (expanded to thirty-two lectures in 1949–50) and advanced theory of international trade lectures remained staples, to which he added classes with the national income machine (Lent 1953), lectures on international monetary institutions (carved out of his money and banking lectures in 1953–4), and international monetary theory (1954–5), as well as a class on money taught jointly with Joan Robinson and Richard Kahn. In 1954–5 and 1955–6 Harry gave eighteen lectures in international monetary economics at LSE when A. C. L. Day went off on secondment to the Economic Section in the Treasury.

Jagdish Bhagwati, who took Part II in 1956, later remembered Harry's lectures:

His lectures on the theory of international trade attracted a large audience of under-graduates, graduate students and visiting scholars – I remember being introduced, after a class, to Lorie Tarshis [then teaching at Stanford]. Harry spoke rapidly from a text and handed out sheets of mathematical derivations and diagrams mimeographed in two tones of red and blue on a machine reputedly at the Department of Applied Economics. In virtually eight, tightly packed lectures, we were treated to a remarkably succinct review of the principal dimensions of trade theory. It was fascinating, and in fact seduced me into trade theory permanently, but it left us all somewhat breathless. (1998, 484)

The lectures did not always go down well. In 1951 Pigou wrote Harry:

I was asking an undergraduate the other day how he was getting on with economics. In the course of the talk he said that your lectures were very difficult to hear further than the second row. This is the sort of thing that I think one ought to pass on, because undergraduates are unlikely to tell it themselves to a lecturer but, of course, he would want to know. So I hope you won't think this note intrusive. (Box 44, Correspondence, 1949–56)

Nor did Harry's compressed Cambridge style favouring content over expla-nation go down well at LSE. At the end of his first term of standing in for A. C. L. Day, James Meade wrote to him:

I do hope you will excuse me if I pass on to you the information that a number of our students are finding the lectures rather difficult. I think that they are frightened by the algebra and find the accompanying non-mathematical exposition too rapid. The problem of covering the ground is a frightful one; but personally I feel that it is better to omit certain parts of the subject from lectures if thereby one can drive the rest of it into the heads of some of the weaker brethren. I hope you will forgive me raising these points, but I felt it best to pass them on for what they are worth. (Box 43, London Lectures, Cambridge IMT, 14 December 1954)

Harry followed the Robertson model of writing very full notes beforehand, notes in some cases typed up afterwards and reused. Harry also worried about outcomes – whether he had gone too fast, what he had left out, what he would do next year. Sometimes he would sketch out a "Forecast of Contents" or "Intentions" against which he would contrast the lectures as actually delivered. He could be a fierce critic of himself: "deadly dull stuff & I'm going very slowly – more than a lecture behind – *must rewrite*," "obscure at points," "should have gone further – there was no climax at the end," "needs redoing next year to see if I still believe it," "lousy – got to middle of p. 4," "slow and halting, due to poor preparation." Harry's first money and banking lectures inevitably betrayed their graduate-student roots; nine of the sixteen lectures were on American banking, with parts of two lectures devoted to nineteenth-century historical experience. When he gave the lectures again in Michaelmas 1949, he did not reach American experience until lecture 14.

Harry's involvement in teaching with the National Income Machine probably needs some explanation.[4] The machine which is better known as the Phillips machine is a hydraulic model of the British economy measuring 7 feet × 5 feet × 3 feet, in which the circular flow of income and expenditure is represented by coloured water flowing in clear plastic tubes. The machine was developed in 1949 by A. W. H. (Bill) Phillips, later famous among macroeconomists for the Phillips curve, who demonstrated it in Lionel Robbins's graduate seminar at LSE on 29 November 1949. The School financed a second model, which arrived on 12 October 1950 – the day that Phillips, who had published in the August 1950 *Economica* a description of the machine, which was the first application of dynamic control theory in economics, was offered an assistant lectureship at the School. By this stage, Phillips, who had a pass degree in sociology, was James Meade's doctoral student. He finished his thesis in 1953, became a reader in 1954 and Tooke Professor of Economic Science and Statistics in 1958.

When the second LSE machine was completed, the manufacturers White-Ellerton produced them for others: The School acquired another one in 1952 so that James Meade could use it with the second to teach international macroeconomics. Others were bought by Oxford, Cambridge, Birmingham, Manchester, and Melbourne.

The Cambridge faculty acquired its machine in April 1951. Harry was given control of access and the responsibility of making proposals for using the machine in the faculty's teaching programme. He was also asked to

[4] What follows depends heavily on Barr (2000).

demonstrate the machine to undergraduate and graduate students during the Easter term of 1951 (Box 44, Correspondence 1949–56, from Ruth Cohen, 1 May 1951). Phillips came to Cambridge to discuss the machine with Richard Stone. He dined in King's and went back to 3 Park Lodge to talk shop with Harry. According to Liz,

they walked in on my frustration with the washer. I met a slight-statured, quiet man who modestly asked if he could help. He tried something with a screwdriver ... and went back to talking economics. (E. Johnson 2000, 23)

Liz also remembered:

The trouble with the Phillips Machine was its inflationary tendencies – the national income demonstrated a strong propensity to overflow.... Harry was frequently called out to deal with the monetary crisis in the shape of a pink cascade pouring down the stairway from the Department of Applied Economics. (2000, 23)

In North America, A. P. Lerner was excited by the machine and became Phillips's American agent and sold machines calibrated in dollars to Roosevelt College in Chicago, Harvard, and the Ford Motor Company. Harry used his Cambridge experience with the machine to provide a possible "puff" for Lerner's American sales efforts

Where the machine has been useful, even in the restricted circumstances of its use here, has been in teaching students the essentials of stock and flow relations in monetary theory, and in giving them an appreciation of the many variables that have to be considered in monetary theory, even in the most aggregative treatment. It has also been helpful in teaching them to think for themselves – that is, we keep asking them what the result of a certain change will be, and if they are wrong we can show them conclusively what they have forgotten to consider. (Box 44, Correspondence 1949–56, from A. P. Lerner, 21 May 1952)

Harry also, unsuccessfully tried to convince Vincent Bladen that the Toronto Department of Political Economy needed one for its teaching.[5]

The machine at LSE fell into disuse from the mid-1950s. The Cambridge one lasted until 1964–5 when A. B. Atkinson remembers a course on The National Income Machine. Harry would later be involved in an effort to restore one of the LSE machines – an effort which resulted in a restored machine going on permanent display in the Science Museum in South Kensington in 1995 (Barr, 2000). The Cambridge machine, restored in 1995,

---

[5] Bladen reported to Harry on 13 March 1953, "The machine is better than I thought – the unpredictable leak makes it a much better model" (Box 40). However, the departmental history does not mention a machine, and W. C. Hood, a long-standing macroeconomist member of the department has no memory of one being purchased.

now resides in the Meade Room in the Economics Faculty in Sidgwick Avenue, where the author saw it in operation during the Fiftieth Anniversary Celebrations of the Department of Applied Economics in December 1995.

Journal Editor

Other academic jobs came Harry's way. On 20 June 1949 the Advisory Board of Editors of the *Review of Economic Studies* agreed to invite Harry to become a member. The *Review* had been founded in 1933 by three graduate students, Abba Lerner, Paul Sweezy, and Ursula Webb (later Hicks) to publish the work of younger economists and as a result was christened "the children's newspaper" by the older generation in Cambridge. The other Cambridge members when Harry joined were Nicholas Kaldor, Jan Graaff, and Ruth Cohen.

The duties are to advise and assist in editing articles in your particular field, & assist with finding good articles – either by supplying them yourself or making other people write them. (Box 44, Correspondence 1949–56, from Ursula Hicks, 21 June 1949)

Later, Hicks added to the duties "someone who can wheedle articles out of Nicky [Kaldor] in reasonable time, otherwise quite useless to get him to help in the vetting. This seems more necessary than 'standing up' to him in any theoretical sense" (Box 32, *Review of Economic Studies*, 22 May 1952). When Harry joined the board, Graeme Dorrance of LSE was assistant editor and Paul Samuelson was the American editor. In the summer of 1951, with Dorrance's impending departure for the International Monetary Fund, Harry became assistant editor and later assistant managing editor. He remained associated with the *Review* until after his departure for Chicago in 1959, despite the long-standing convention of the journal, broken only by Nicholas Kaldor, that academic promotions, such as Harry's Manchester chair or even a readership, ended one's tenure on the board.[6]

Harry was an influential and successful editor. He made it his business to know what was going on in the profession and to use that knowledge to nurture aspiring authors and improve their output. Richard Lipsey provides two examples from his early years at LSE.

---

[6] His last listing as assistant managing editor was in the issue for June 1961. In the next issue, he was listed as one of the American editors, where the convention regarding promotion did not apply. He remained on the masthead until July 1966.

During my first year on the staff [1955–6] two sequences of events stand out. The first began one morning when I was in my room reading an article by Andrew Ozga on customs unions [1955]. Kelvin Lancaster came in for the usual morning gossip. I said to him in high excitement, "You know these guys are all discovering the same kind of theorem in different guises." Kelvin replied that ever since he had read Samuelson's *Foundations [of Economic Analysis]* (1947), he had wondered why people put such stress on fulfilling selected optimum conditions when all of them could never be fulfilled. I went to the common room for coffee and, as luck would have it, I bumped into Harry Johnson and explained our great insight to him. "Publish immediately" was his advice. Kelvin worked out the general proof and I worked on my customs union example and the literature survey. Harry played an important role in arguing that if the article was to have the impact it deserved, we should do an exhaustive survey of the literature. He suggested several articles of which we were unaware and helped us write an article which had world wide impact rather than going unnoticed as it might have done if less care had been spent on it.

The article was "The General Theory of the Second-Best" (1956).[7] Lipsey continued with a second example.

The second sequence began [again in 1955–6] when I ran into Harry in the senior common room and he reminded me of a point I had made to him about trade diversion and welfare some 12 months previously. He asked, "Had I done anything about publishing it?" "No", said I. "Well", said Harry, "I have had a similar article submitted to the *Review of Economic Studies* and I advise you to publish your idea quickly." I wrote it up in a few days and submitted it to *Economica* the LSE house journal [1957]. It was published about the same time as the *Review of Economic Studies* published the same point in an article by Hans Gehrels [1957]. (2000, 120; Lipsey has further examples in 2001, 612–13)

Lipsey also remembered Harry encouraging others.

The most memorable of which I have direct experience is the famous Rybczynski Theorem. I recall being at a party at which Tad Rybczynski, who was a fellow graduate student, told Harry about the result he had obtained in the course of working on this thesis. I remember Harry's excitement and the enormous pressure he put on a skeptical Tad arguing that the result was important enough to warrant immediate publication. If Harry had not intervened, I am not sure that Tad would ever have

---

[7] Harry had different memories of at least parts of the process. He raised them in a discussion of his own originality with Max Corden in 1972: "[T]he idea was Lipsey's. (It was really mine, but I had enough ideas to keep my professional head above water, whereas Lipsey was in some doubt on that question.)" (Box 51, Correspondence 1971–7, C–G, 30 July 1972). His second, amplifying comment came in a letter to an unhappy Chicago graduate student in 1973: "Second-best theory was a big vogue in the late 50's and early sixties (I happen to have been around London when it started, and suggested to Lipsey both the general proposition and that he should write an article about it)" (Box 41, Chicago School, to Gary Ericksen, 8 August).

published it (Rybcznski 1955). After leaving LSE Tad went to work in the financial sector and did not publish further in academic journals – giving him . . . one of the profession's highest ratios of fame to published works. (2001, 614)[8]

Harry's papers from the *Review* are full of thanks from authors for whom he had taken a lot of trouble – Ivor Pearce, Wilfrid Beckerman, G. C. Archibald, and E. J. Mishan. Perhaps the most typical was one from Hal Myint (Box 32, *Review of Economic Studies*, undated but surrounding correspondence with Ursula Hicks dates it to August 1954): "I want to thank you for your two sets of comments on my paper [1954–5] which have been very helpful. I also begin to appreciate why you have been described by Robertson as 'that noted inquisitor'!"(Robertson 1953–4).

Some of Harry's editorial tasks required considerable discretion. The most notable was his handling of Joan Robinson's "The Production Function and the Theory of Capital" (1953–4). The article had been circulating in draft on both sides of the Atlantic before it arrived at the *Review*. Robert Solow's comment to Harry was:

How about a recent mimeographed paper by Joan Robinson on capital theory? I wish I could understand a word of it, since Paul [Samuelson] and I have been working at what I think is a related problem. But it remains impenetrable. (Box 32, Review of Economic Studies, 26 August 1953)

Ursula Hicks's reaction was not encouraging

Now for the big problem. I had not thought Joan would land this on us. We have had several copies around in Oxford for some time and have discussed it in the internal Nuffield [College] seminar. But so far neither John nor I have studied it really carefully. So far my impression is that all this was settled ages ago by Wicksell and Gustave Akerman. Nicky must remember all that. At LSE we discussed it all very carefully in the 30^s, but at Cambridge at that stage it was impossible to interest anyone in capital theory. If you and Nicky can make Joan withdraw some of the quite ridiculously rude and patronising phrases that she uses I suppose that she will do herself more harm than us if we publish it. (Box 32, *Review of Economic Studies*, 25 March 1953)

Harry sent the paper to A. D. Scott, who replied with a letter and a series of notes on 4 April. Scott saw some good points in the capital theory of the paper, though he was critical of the details. Harry then drafted a note for

---

[8] The Rybczynski theorem describes the relationship between factor endowments and output at full employment. In a two-factor, two-good world, greater supply of one factor raised the output of the good intensive in that factor and reduced the output of the other good.

the author, which he circulated to Scott and Kaldor before sending it off.[9] On reading the draft, Scott remarked:

You've certainly been neck-deep in this!

I think your comments . . . hit the nail on the head. Had she addressed herself to this problem from the outset, she would have achieved unity and reader co-operation.

The problem of obtaining real revision is probably too delicate to be successful. . . . I don't envy your rôle, but many thanks for bringing me in. (Box 55, Joan Robinson, 10 April 1953)

Of the ensuing correspondence, virtually nothing survives in Harry's papers, as Joan Robinson revised her paper several times, first in draft and then in proof. In the last case:

You will observe (1) that I have changed the title [from "A Reconsideration of the Theory of Value"]. I hope this doesn't make a lot of bother with the table of contents etc. (2) I have cut out the section on M.P. [marginal productivity] of capital. It seemed to irritate everybody without adding anything to the argument. I have now written a note on M.P. which I shall publish elsewhere. I think it is much clearer than the omitted section. (Box 32, Review of Economic Studies, no date but the surrounding letters date from September 1953)

Further changes appear to have followed from David Champernowne before the paper finally appeared in February 1954, an issue later than originally planned.[10]

The younger economists involved with the *Review of Economic Studies* overlapped with the Oxford–Cambridge–London seminar's regulars. W. M. Corden remembered his first encounter with Harry in one seminar:

In 1954 I made my first-ever presentation of my work, to the Oxford–London–Cambridge seminar for graduate students. I presented a complicated theoretical story about the effects of growth on trade, using diagrams. At intervals, I would stop and ask, 'Is that clear?' The plump man at the back would nod, more and more quickly. Obviously, I concluded, I was going too slowly. My presentation seemed to be clear and obvious to him and to others, as soon as I opened my mouth. That was when I first met Harry. At the end of the seminar it became clear to *me* that only two people, John Black and Harry, *had* actually understood what I was talking about. One of the features of my story was the rather simple and surprising "Rybczynski theorem", not then published, but with which I was familiar because Tad Rybczynski was my fellow LSE student. A year later, the same year that Tad's paper came out, Harry's classic article "Economic Expansion and International Trade" was published. It prominently incorporated the Rybczynski theorem. More importantly, it contained a (for me) classic footnote: "The writer first encountered the argument

---

[9] Harry's comments are in Box 33, Writing 1953.
[10] There is nothing in Joan Robinson's papers on this episode.

in a paper read by W. M. Corden. . . . " That was the first time anybody had referred to me in print."[11] (2001, 645)

There was also the Association of University Teachers of Economics whose annual meetings Harry attended from 1949 onwards. His involvement in these groups, his passion for attending seminars, and his skills and energy as an editor meant that Harry soon took on a position of leadership amongst British economists who were making their reputations in the postwar period. Richard Lipsey remembered that

although Harry was only five years older than myself, he was a whole generation apart from me and my contemporaries. Because he skipped much of the graduate education that we undertook and because he was such a prodigious writer, the gap between him and us was much more than our age differences would suggest. Harry was already a fellow of King's College Cambridge when I graduated with my BA and by the time I took my first academic job he had published more than 21 articles. So to us he was a towering figure from another generation, not a near contemporary. (2001, 611)

In a world where there was a lot of serious social drinking, Harry was also becoming "a legend for his capacity – a status symbol that was extremely important in establishing one's place in the pecking order" (information from David Laidler).

Canadian Reviewer

As a Canadian abroad, Harry was seen as a natural reviewer of books on Canadian subjects and was soon asked to review not only for the *Economic Journal* but also for the *Canadian Journal of Economics and Political Science*, then edited by the Toronto Department. At an early stage, Harold Innis wrote to him:

I did want to write and congratulate you on the numerous distinctions which have fallen your way and also to say how much I approve of your reviews of Canadian books. As you know, the scholarly community in Canada is very small and it is very difficult to get a critical review of works by Canadians on Canada. You can do a first class service by maintaining a critical standard on Canadian books as is indicated by your reviews which I have read. This may mean unpopularity of a short run character but ultimately it will be to the credit of all concerned. [University of Toronto Archives, Innis Papers, B72-0025/009(04), 16 February 1951]

Harry replied:

Many thanks for your kindness in writing to me on the subject of my reviews of Canadian books. I have always tried to bear in mind what you taught me about

---

[11] Harry's note located the November 1954 seminar in Cambridge (*ITEG*, n.79).

the dangers to scholarship of a narrow academic community, and to keep my eyes on the unmentioned things and the unmentioned questions – also to avoid the aura of mutual congratulation which prevents an intimate group from realising and attempting to correct its own deficiencies. As to the unpopularity you mentioned, I have already felt its indications, though at this distance it is amusing rather than harrowing.

I might add that the Cambridge community is not totally unlike the Canadian in respect of provincialism, though it does differ in the viciousness of its mutual criticism. [University of Toronto Archives, Innis Papers, B72-0025/009(05), 20 April 1951]

A good example of "unpopularity" was brewing. In August 1950 in the *Canadian Journal* Harry had reviewed Warren James's *Wartime Economic Co-operation: A Study of Relations between Canada and the United States* (1949), which had been published under the auspices of the Canadian Institute of International Affairs. He complained its usefulness was limited by its Canadian civil service perspective, which highlighted administrative matters and minimised underlying economic forces. He also criticised the book's uncritical acceptance of the official Canadian economic interpretation of events. The effect was "to reduce the positive conclusions of the study to something dangerously like a closed circle of self-congratulation" and to reduce the value of what otherwise was "an extremely scholarly and useful book" (1950b, 438).

On 11 May 1951 A. F. W. Plumptre, now in the Department of Finance, sent Harry a note "Mr Johnson on Mr James and the Limitations of Government Economists." He had submitted it to the *Canadian Journal*, where it appeared in November 1951. The note was a rather injured defence of James's subject matter and his discretion, concluding with the difficulties faced by overworked officials who wished to write on such subjects. Innis was "amused" and suggested that "all this scandal can be discussed when we meet," as Innis was coming to Cambridge in July [University of Toronto Archives, Innis Papers, B72-0025/009(05), to HGJ, 30 May 1951].[12]

Harry replied to Plumptre on 16 May, saying he hoped the *Canadian Journal* would publish the note, but he would not comment on it unless asked to by the editors. Privately he was more damning.

Phrases that spring to mind re Plumptre
the sycophancy of the Canadian intellectual confronted by a government official – pandering gelded literature
Plumptre: significant that he should think of political censorship – I don't give a damn about it....

---

[12] Innis and his son Hugh visited Cambridge on 21 July (University of Toronto Archives, Innis Papers, B72-0025/006(10), to H. Innis, 18 July 1951). Harry put them up in King's.

significant that he should attack the 'academic' – always a term of abuse in my native land, and many others where men love power more than truth

significant that he should appeal to the personal difficulties of Dr. James – nature of Canadian academic life

Since I am living in a country where my career doesn't depend on pandering to the Civil Service.

I don't object to such stuff on relations of controlling groups – but want objective study.

Must accept without question crumbs tossed from the official table – what can you do?

Always an entertaining sight: the senior Civil Service springing to the defense of its young. (Box 44, Correspondence 1949–56)

Canadian Interlude

After the Innis visit, Harry's next contact with Toronto was with Vincent Bladen, who had just returned from an International Economic Association conference at Talloires – on the teaching of economics. Bladen had talked to Austin Robinson who had told him that Harry would have a term's leave due to him after Michaelmas 1951. After a conversation with Innis, who was dean of the Graduate School as well as head of the Department of Political Economy, Bladen wrote:

I have good reason to believe that we could arrange for you to be invited by the School of Graduate Studies to come to Toronto to lecture in the Department of Political Economy next year. I think they would offer $1000 per month for two months (possibly $2\frac{1}{2}$).... What I need to find out – to get the wheels rolling – is whether you would be available for October and November (and possibly half of December) or alternatively for Jan. Feb. & part or all of March. (Box 54, Toronto 1952, 24 September 1951)

Harry replied on 10 October that the letter was "a surprise and a delight" and that "the prospective terms are very handsome."[13] Although he couldn't make a definite commitment just yet, having drawn heavily on his credit with Austin Robinson, the chair of the Faculty Board, over his review of Meade's *The Balance of Payments* (see discussion in Chapter 6), he thought he would come for both the summer and fall of 1952. The only question was what he should teach [University of Toronto Archives, Department of Political Economy Records, A65-0005/001/10(001)]. By 14 November he

---

[13] He added in a postscript to the letter "I really think this is a wonderful invitation, and hope I'll be worth it."

had, however, received assurances that if he applied for leave from Cambridge his application would be successful.

The next stage saw Innis appear again.

I am now writing to you in another capacity, that of President of the American Economic Association, to ask whether it would be possible for you to give a paper at the meetings in Chicago at the end of the year. I would like to have you select a topic of significant interest and to present a paper on it with other papers subordinate to it.... In brief I would like to play you up as a star performer presenting a crucial paper. (Box 54, Toronto 1952, to HGJ, 7 January 1952)

Harry accepted immediately, offering a paper on "Recent Developments in British Monetary Policy." Innis proceeded to organise a session that included papers by Henry Wallich on American developments and Mabel Timlin on Canadian, with Lloyd Mints as a commentator (Box 54, Toronto 1952, HGJ to Innis, 12 January 1952; Innis to HGJ, 7 February and 15 March 1952),

At the same time, after consulting G. A. Elliott, William Hood, and Stefan Stykolt, Bladen tried to organise Harry's teaching at the University of Toronto – a graduate course on international trade that Elliott would complete after Harry left, a series of formal lectures on British banking "where you could use your Harvard thesis project" and "a series of popular – though still serious – lectures on the present state and prospects of the U.K. Economy" (Box 54, Toronto 1952, Bladen to HGJ, 15 January 1952). Harry was happy with the first two suggestions but on the third he was

a bit nervous about giving serious popular lectures on the position and prospects of the British economy, as this is not a subject on which I am much of an expert, and it involves a tremendous amount of material. I don't suppose it will hurt me; it's just that I would prefer to lecture on something on which I have done a lot of work already, and would consequently prefer a shorter to a longer series on the topic. Probably these fears will melt away when I find myself in front of an eager audience; at the moment, I feel this would be the hardest part to prepare for, and incline to fight shy of it – so perhaps you shouldn't take me too seriously. [University of Toronto Archives, Department of Political Economy Records, A65-0005/001(087), HGJ to Vincent Bladen, 11 February 1952]

Bladen's response was accommodating: the third set of lectures disappeared as a requirement, only to be reinstated by Harry, presumably after he arrived, for there is no documentary record.

Harry, Liz, and two children (a daughter Karen had been born in October 1951) sailed for Quebec on 25 June 1952. In Canada they based themselves at his mother's house in Streetsville, a small town just west of Toronto, although they spent much of the summer visiting Liz's parents in Ottawa and at the cottage on Georgian Bay that Harry's parents had bought after the war. Harry's parents had sold Spruce Ridges for suburban subdivision in April 1951 and moved to Streetsville. Harry's father, who had been in poor health for a couple of years died at home on 22 January 1952. Harry and Liz borrowed a British car for their time in Canada. Harry was not impressed.

The writer, who drove a British car in Canada for six months, was assured by owners and garage mechanics alike that the higher costs of repairs and maintenance more than outweighed the saving on gasoline, so that a British car is more expensive to operate than an American – an opinion which in this case proved sadly true. ("Canada: A Lost Opportunity," 1954a, 16)

Harry's time in Toronto was productive. He renewed old acquaintances with people such as William Hood and Stefan Stykolt. He made new friends such as J. R. N. Wolfe, an Oxford graduate who had come to Toronto and later became professor of Political Economy in Edinburgh. He also did a fair bit of work, most notably his American Economic Association paper "Recent Developments in British Monetary Policy" (1953a), "Equilibrium Growth in an International Economy" (1953b), and his public lectures *The Overloaded Economy*, which were published by University of Toronto Press in 1952. The delivery of the lectures was complicated by Harry's coming down with pneumonia. Stefan Stykolt read the first one for him on 22 October and the second and third were postponed until late November.

The main theme of Harry's lectures was that

the economic tasks which the United Kingdom has been expected to perform have been consistently up to and beyond the capacity of the country's economic system. Consequently the economy has been unable to perform all the tasks satisfactorily, and the efforts to do so have kept it in a state of constant strain which has made it extremely vulnerable to sudden shocks . . . and led to a series of economic crises. (1952c, 3)

He used his first lecture to set the problem out in a general way, and in his second and third looked at postwar sterling crises and the attrition of the welfare state.

Harry argued that the economy had been set five postwar tasks: restoring external balance, paying for defence, improving social welfare, providing a rising standard of living, and increasing production. Achievement of these goals had been constrained by certain socioeconomic and institutional factors: the commitment to full employment, the maintenance of freedom in job choice and collective bargaining, and the philosophy of the welfare state and income redistribution. Of these constraints, full employment was probably the least important, while the major effects of the latter two had been an unwillingness to use the price system to allocate resources and an inevitable reversion to controls, moral suasion, or taxation. The overloading had meant that none of the tasks had been performed satisfactorily, that the economy had been in a state of continuous strain where minor interruptions could have major consequences and had become more vulnerable to shocks that produced economic crises, that the authorities had been prone to use physical controls, or the threat of such controls and that changes in the objectives or methods of economic policy had become almost impossible. Moreover, there had been a persistent moral strain arising from "the frustration of hopes and expectations of improvement in personal economic welfare" and the government's heavy reliance on appeals to patriotism and self-restraint in the conduct of economic policy. "All in all," as he put it, "the British economy has been drawing heavily on its cultural capital – the British traditions of honesty, responsibility, patriotism, and respect for lawful authority – and the strain has begun to show" (1952c, 12).

The second lecture was largely a narrative of postwar balance of payments crises. The common thread in the narrative was the low level of Britain's external reserves; the overloading of the economy, which had diverted goods from exports and attracted imports, as well as raising the rate of inflation; and the arrangements Britain had made with her sterling-area partners, the dollar shortage, and the deterioration in Britain's terms of trade. Harry saw this last phenomenon as "a long-term problem reflecting the pressure of growing world population on natural resources" and "as the major cause of the British balance-of-payments problem." Moreover, he thought that the deterioration in the terms of trade would continue with the result that "she is bound to be poorer than she has been in the past" with important implications for the welfare state, overseas defense commitments, and the level of British overseas investment (1952c, 32). Such a vision was not new in Cambridge: Keynes had held similar views in the 1920s; Dennis Robertson continued to hold them in the 1950s. However, by the late 1950s, they had fallen out of fashion.

As for the welfare state, Harry took as its defining characteristics the investment in the human resources of the community, especially in medicine and education; the existence of guaranteed minimum standards as of right; providing a standard of service at the level of the best the community can afford; and stabilising the cost of living through subsidies and controls. He noted the falling real value of benefits, user charges appearing in the National Health Service, serious overcrowding in schools, declining standards in public housing, and reduction of cost-of-living subsidies. In the future he thought that there would be a further transition from the principle of benefit-by-right to the requirements of efficiency by means testing, and he worried, rather surprisingly (or presciently) given the then current baby boom, about the burden of pensions for an aging population.

Between Harry's first and second lectures Innis died. He had been seriously ill during the final stages of his Royal Commission on Transportation in the summer and fall of 1950, but he seemed to recover his old vigour and enthusiasm during his trip to Europe in the summer of 1951 which had included a visit to Cambridge. The severe winter of 1951–2, "with steady cold, lowering skies and quantities of snow"(Creighton 1957, 143), coupled with a lengthy transit strike, which meant walking to and from work, exhausted him. Moreover, he developed a pain in his back, which forced him to his bed. He tried to carry on through March and early April but to no avail. In April he was in hospital and on 14 May he underwent surgery. It was cancer. Surgery checked the disease, and there was a period of recovery until late August, when he became desperately ill again. He died early in the morning of 8 November 1952.

Innis's death took the edge off Harry's American Economic Association debut in Chicago. The presidential address, scheduled for 28 December became a memorial with papers by his colleagues Vincent Bladen and W. T. Easterbrook and by J. H. Willits of the Rockefeller Foundation. Innis's eldest son Donald read a fragment of and talked about the address that his father had been unable to complete. After the meetings, Harry returned to Toronto before proceeding, with a detour to New Haven, to New York to sail back to England.

After his return Harry took Canadian topics as a possible subject for talks to student societies at Aberystwyth, Birmingham, and LSE. He tried to get his Aberystwyth paper, "Canada and the Commonwealth," published, circulating it and his LSE paper, "Canada in the Atlantic Economy," for comment, not only in Britain but to Canadian friends such as William Lawson at the Bank of Canada and R. N. MacIntosh at the Bank of Nova Scotia. Eventually, with Richard Sayers's encouragement, he prepared an article for the *Three Banks Review*. The article, "Canada: A Lost Opportunity," was concerned with the postwar development of Anglo-Canadian trade and the reasons why Britain continued to run a bilateral trade deficit with Canada despite British official emphasis on increasing exports to and reducing imports from the dollar area and despite boom conditions in the Canadian market to which British manufacturers had preferential access. On the import side it was clear that a number of British imports of Canadian foodstuffs – cheese, bacon, fish, and apples – had fallen markedly, but Britain had become more dependent than previously on Canadian wheat and flour, forest products, and nonferrous metals. On the export side, however, "with few exceptions, British exports have failed by a wide margin to keep pace with Canadian demand" (1954c, 15). Harry questioned the standard Canadian explanation for this failure: "that British exporters had not been trying sufficiently hard, that they had failed to study the requirements and conditions of the Canadian market, and had been unwilling to meet competition on price, quality and delivery specifications"(15). He argued that the Canadian market was a difficult market for British exporters for several reasons: the demand for producers' goods and capital equipment for developmental projects that relied on American finance and American-trained technicians and engineers; the influence of the American media and large-scale tourism on mass tastes, which left British consumer goods catering to minority or snob tastes; the regional nature of the Canadian market, which meant higher start-up costs, particularly in the case of consumers durables such as Harry's borrowed car with their requirements for after-sales service, availability of parts, and rapid repair. He then considered whether Britain might redeem herself in the future. He could conceive of Britain substituting Soviet-bloc wheat and forest products for Canadian, but on the export side he was pessimistic:

Britain's failure to assert herself in the Canadian market during the flush of the post-war boom has permitted American exporters to entrench themselves to an extent that would be difficult to counteract. . . . Britain had missed an opportunity to capitalise on the absence of German competition, which is now beginning to emerge. (20)

Harry's article brought a long letter from A. F. W. Plumptre. He was disturbed by

the underlying assumption, cropping up at various points, that in some sense there "ought" to be bilateral balance between any pair of countries, such as the United Kingdom and Canada, and that if a bilateral balance is not struck, one party or the other ought to do something about it. (Box 44, Correspondence 1949–56, to HGJ, 25 August 1954)

This bilateral emphasis had led Harry to the view that Canada was a contributor to the dollar problem – a view Plumptre strongly questioned. Harry vigorously defended himself on "the view you impute to me, a view which of course Canadian government economists have been detecting and attacking everywhere since I was an undergraduate at Toronto." He defended his view that Canada had contributed to the dollar problem and remarked that "I don't think that what I said in the article implied enough blame to require the barrage of praise [of Canadian policy] in yours – so far as I remember,

I didn't argue that Canadian policy had been ungenerous" (Box 44, Correspondence 1949–56, to A. F. W. Plumptre, 16 September 1954). Again Canadian sensitivities had been aroused.

Harry's nationality also put him occasionally in odd positions. In the fall of 1954, as a part of the movement that eventuated in the European Economic Community, there was a meeting in London called the Council of Westminster with delegations from most European states and overseas countries with close relations to them. Canada wanted to be present, but to do so on the cheap; so it cast about for potential delegates from Canadians already in the United Kingdom and settled on Robert Clark, a University of British Columbia economist then on leave in Manchester; Richard Lipsey, a second-year graduate student at LSE; and Harry.[14] Suitably briefed by the High Commission, where Harry met Lipsey and Clark for the first time, they did their duty. Lipsey remembers making an intervention, but there is no record of Harry's doing so (Lipsey, 2000, 118).

Harry, the Apostle

There was a final new link for Harry as a don. After he became a fellow of King's, Harry was recruited by another King's fellow, the economic historian Eric Hobsbawm (2002, 189), to the Cambridge Conversazione Society, commonly known as the Apostles. The Society had begun life in 1829 when George Tomlinson, later Bishop of Gibraltar, with eleven others founded a discussion group in St. John's. Its existence and membership were not secret, for it was just one of many small undergraduate discussion societies whose existence was of no importance to anyone but their members. The Society became important in Cambridge intellectual life because of its longevity and, after its obscure beginnings, the intellectual importance of many of its members. A significant proportion of the Victorian reformers who laid the foundations for the modern, centralised, science-based Cambridge were members – Henry Sidgwick, Frederick Maurice, Henry Jackson, Richard Jebb, and F. W. Maitland. The dominance of its members in Cambridge philosophy is also remarkable – Henry Sidgwick, Frederick Maurice, James Ward, Alfred North Whitehead, J. E. McTaggart, Bertrand Russell, G. E. Moore, Ludwig Wittgenstein, Frank Ramsey, and Richard Braithwaite. The list of economists may be shorter, but it includes Ralph Hawtrey, Maynard Keynes, Gerald Shove, and Dennis Robertson.

---

[14] New Zealand did the same thing, with the result that one of its delegates was Bill Phillips from LSE.

The transformation of the Society from a group of Johnians to one so eminent that its membership and activities became secret from the 1850s onwards was largely the work of Frederick Maurice and John Sterling, who toughened its intellectual discipline while widening its range of concerns. The Society's business became "to make its members study and think on all matter except Mathematics and Classics *professionally* considered"[15] and to impose no restrictions on such thought other than rationality and sincerity (Allen 1978, 13). As Henry Sidgwick put it in an often-quoted passage:

> I can only describe it as the spirit of the pursuit of truth with absolute devotion and unreserve by a group of intimate friends, who were perfectly frank with each other, and indulged in any amount of humorous sarcasm and playful banter, and yet each respected the other and when he discourses tries to learn from him and see what he sees. Absolute candour was the only duty the tradition of the Society enforced. No consistency was demanded with opinions previously held – truth as we saw it then and there was what we had to enforce and maintain, and there was no proposition so well established that an Apostle had not the right to deny or question, if he did so sincerely and not from love of paradox. The gravest subjects were continually debated but the gravity of treatment, as I have said, was not imposed, though sincerity was. In fact it was rather a point of the apostolic mind to understand how much suggestion and instruction may derive from what is in form a jest – even in dealing with the gravest matters. (Sidgwick and Sidgwick 1906, 34–5)

Of course not every paper reached Sidgwick's serious ideal, but the Society proved an important supplement – and counterweight – to the norms of university life.

With the ideals came a more formal routine. Members of the Society were the "brethren." They were expected to attend every meeting when in Cambridge in term. Members who could not meet these requirements – membership was for life – "took wings" and became "angels"; they could still attend any meetings they wished and take part in the discussions. Members met annually for "the Dinner" – usually in London. Angels played an important role as advisers, especially over the selection of new members. The world of the Society was "real"; the world outside was "phenomenal." Prospective members or "embryos" were subject to the scrutiny of active members and perhaps one or two angels, normally without the individual knowing. If elected – and election required unanimity – the new member was inducted in a ceremony called "birth" and his sponsor was sometimes referred to as his "father." The records of the Society – membership, topics

---

[15] In the 1850s these were the only two Triposes – classics having only arrived in 1854.

discussed and voted on, as well as some papers – were (and are) held in the Ark.

The routine for a meeting was straightforward. In Harry's time, members met on Sunday evenings in the rooms of the paper-giver or moderator, who read his paper, on a topic agreed at the previous meeting, from the hearthrug. The others present drew lots to determine the order of speaking and proceeded in turn to discuss points raised by the moderator, or others not raised. At the end of the discussion, a question would be put to the vote. From the mid-nineteenth century, the question could not bear an obvious relationship to the topic discussed, although it normally bore some relationship to the evening's conversation. Once the question was formulated and written down in a record book, votes took the form of members signing in agreement, disagreement, or abstention. Refreshments followed before those present decided on the topic for the next meeting and drew lots for next week's moderator. Occasionally papers went unprepared but the member in default might pay the price of entertaining those present to dinner and the basis for discussion might then be an old paper from the Ark. The rituals and slang remained constant for over a century.[16]

When Harry was elected, the active older members were Noel Annan and Eric Hobsbawm, both fellows of King's. The younger members in Harry's time were Neil Ascherson, Christopher Bennett, Mark Boxer, Ronald Bryden, Christopher Foster, Richard Layard, Karl Miller, and Jonathan Miller – all Kingsmen except for the Millers.

Six of Harry's papers for the Society survive, as well as a copy of his 1971 presidential address at the Dinner. The Cambridge papers – "People Who Live in Glass Houses Don't Have To" (November 1951); "Is the *Times* Crossword a Good Thing?" (1952); "Procrastination – Thief or Ali Baba" (1953); "When Do I Take My Wife to the Movies" (1953); "Socialism and the Rise of Religion" (1955); and "Unenthusiasm as a Way of Life" (1955) – along with his published "The Economics of Undertaking" (1951e) and "The Private Eye of Mickey Spillane" (1954a), both of which show a lighter side of Harry.

The glass houses paper was itself serious – an examination of the problem of ideology, especially in the social sciences – an issue raised by Gunnar Myrdal's 1951 Marshall Lectures, which themselves had led Harry into a dispute with Joan Robinson on value-free economics and also by his review of James Meade's *The Balance of Payments* (see discussion in Chapter 6), to

---

[16] The sources for the above have been Sidgwick and Sidgwick (1906), Harrod (1951), Allen (1978), Levy (1979), Moggridge (1992), and Hobsbawm (2002).

which he referred in the paper.[17] He was particularly concerned with the
appropriate means of overcoming ideological bias, making a strong plea that
instead of admitting one's biases one should aim at arriving at truth that
does not involve ideology.

In conclusion, I should like to relate my paper to its title. The fact that we are all
subject to our own ideologies means that we all live in glass houses. While we are
free to throw stones at other's houses, all we can achieve by doing so is to aggravate
the housing shortage. I have argued that there is no way by which we can rearrange
the glass or redesign the houses so as to make them unbreakable; but we can, by
suitable tests, discover materials that will not break under the impact of neighbourly
stones. Consequently, I conclude that people who live in glass houses don't have to.
(Box 33, Writing 1951)

The *Times* crossword paper was written as a substitute for a more serious
philosophical paper, which had not come to pass because "I have been
deeply involved in contemplation of the cosmic ramifications of a ½% rise
in Bank rate."[18] Harry reported that he had been a "healthy amateur of
crossword puzzles," "prepared to have a go at any crossword published by
any newspaper" until

I found to my regret one cannot take The Times Crossword Puzzle in one's stride.
One's intellectual pride is involved; one feels more and more deeply the shame
of the last literary reference, the ignominy of the unsolved anagram, the Freudian
implications of the misinterpreted clue. One hopes to do better, and at that point
all is lost.

As a result, he decided to examine the function of the crossword for the
individual and for society. For the individual "it is a test of good English
public school and university education – a sort of daily pocket Tripos."
But that raised the further question of what was being tested – a flexible
and enquiring mind or a store of knowledge and a set pattern of mental
gymnastics. He suspected the latter "since the conventions of the crossword
lend themselves . . . to the exploitation of a corpus of common knowledge
and the repetition of the same old mental tricks." This led him to suspect
that the social function of the *Times* crossword "is a constant reminder to
the relatively small band of those capable of attempting it that they have

[17] Myrdal's lectures on "The Political Element in Economic Theory" were delivered on 23
February, 26 February and 2 March 1951. The argument with Joan Robinson began on
12 March and continued until 20 March (Box 55, Joan Robinson).

[18] As Harry's first draft of his paper for the Oxford symposium reached Oxford on 12 February
and was receiving comment from Ronald Henderson the same day, it is likely that the paper
was given on 10 February 1952. See Box 33, New Monetary Policy, from D. Worswick,
12 February 1952 and from Ronald Henderson, 12 February 1952.

a common background, common education, common standards to keep up." As to whether or not it was a good thing – "Personally, I think it a good thing, *if* everyone who is capable is taught in school how to do it" (Box 33, Writing 1952). Later in life the ability to do the *Times* crossword would be taken as an index of Harry's recovery from his first stroke (see discussion in Chapter 16).

The autobiographical procrastination paper, written at the end of the 1952–3 academic year concerned itself not with "simple procrastination . . . putting off doing something in order to do nothing in particular . . . a kind of procrastination with which . . . I am relatively unfamiliar" but with "complex procrastination . . . putting off doing something in order to do something else." He argued that there were advantages to this kind of procrastination as a way of life – not only matters of taste (it gives a certain zest for life) but also efficiency

[O]ne's efficiency in performance is, I believe, often increased by taking on rather more than one could conceivably manage to get through, the pressure of other jobs egging one on to do more than one thought one could. I think this is particularly true of mental work. . . . I find myself rather stimulated than fatigued by the thought that I have more to do than I can manage. (Box 33, Writing 1953)

"When Do I Take My Wife to the Movies" was actually about democratic decision making – the possible divisiveness of stating positions strongly as against the possible inefficiencies of being prepared to go along with the general consensus. Hence the question "which is the better course of action – when I suggest a trip to the movies to my wife, should I tell her I'd like to see the thriller, or should I tell her I'd like to see the movie I think she would like to see?" (Box 33, Writing 1953).

In "Socialism and the Rise of Religion," Harry was concerned with the possible explanations of the recent rise in religious activity, both in the reception accorded evangelists such as Billy Graham and the increased intellectual respectability of religious discussion. He argued that at a social level it might have something to do with the decline of Britain's position in international affairs, which had been accompanied by a greater emphasis on national institutions and on the British way of life – notably the monarchy and the established church. At an individual level, relative British decline had reduced the attractiveness of interest in politics and economic affairs. The connection was heightened by the realisation that 1930s and wartime optimism about the ease of and benefits of social engineering had been misplaced. "In short, I shall reverse Tawney's thesis and argue that socialism (in the broad sense) has fostered the rise of religion in the post war period, both as a substitute for the limitations of socialism as a humanist faith and as a reaction against it" (Box 34, Writing 1955).

In "Unenthusiasm," as in "Procrastination," Harry was again examining his own behaviour.

The inspiration of this paper was an after-dinner incident some nights back, when our brother Layard suddenly asked me whether I thought the War on Want was a good thing.[19] Not having the faintest idea who the belligerents were, I answered 'no', or more likely a donnish 'probably not' – a conclusion which I was obliged to defend in ever-widening circles of discourse for the rest of the evening. . . . What struck me most about the incident when, I reflected on it later, was my capacity for unenthusiasm – the strength and stability of my propensity to say no, when yes is the answer expected. As so often happens in these cases of self-revelation I was driven to investigate the rationale of my behaviour.

He then argued that unenthusiasm had a lot to be said for it as far as reacting to new ideas, leaving aside the nature of the new ideas themselves. Unenthusiasm was probably more efficient as a technique of learning, of digesting new ideas and integrating them with the old, given one's limited mental capacity and adaptability.

The argument of unenthusiasm is that it recognised explicitly the limitation of time and capacity to examine and absorb new ideas, and embodied this recognition in a technique for testing at each step the worthwhileness of further commitment of energy in this direction, namely by placing the onus of proof on the idea or its proponents, and allowing the commitment to be determined by the ability of the idea to stand up to objections. Further, the method of proceeding by the formation of objections permits the [testing] of implications of the new in terms of the reorganization the old which it requires to be worked out *pari passu* with the progression towards acceptance. Whether the new idea is a failure or success, the disorganisation of the normal operating routines of the mind is kept to a minimum.

Moreover, "unenthusiasm may be a socially useful sieve, selecting those changes which are advances for implementation and economising on social experiment" (Box 34, Writing 1955).

In his paper "Procrastination – Thief or Ali Baba?" Harry had noted:

I had hoped to produce a penetrating analysis of my favourite modern novelist, Mickey Spillane, relating his fiction and now overworked discovery that the most effective plot for a thriller is to have one pure and upright character in the jungle of crooks, perverts, and bitches turn out to be the mastermind behind the crime, to the cowboy and vigilante tradition, to the tactics of Senator McCarthy and the mass-mind which makes such tactics pay off, to the difference between

---

[19] War on Want was (and is) a British charity founded in 1951 concerned with poverty and injustice in the third world.

American and British attitudes to government and concepts of democracy and to the difficulties of Anglo-American understanding, On the more literary plane, I thought there would be plenty of elbow-room, without calling in Freud, for a fruitful contrast between the lascivious voyeurism of Spillane's heroes' sex lives – 'she stood there in a negligee you could see through – she was a real blonde' – and his detective's almost invariable practice of capitalising a loved one by shooting her in self-defence – 'How could you?' she said – 'It was easy', I replied – and the feudal chivalry which cloys the work of Damon Runyon and Raymond Chandler, a survival of victorian sexual ethics typifying the more photogenic aspects of American courtship.

The Mickey Spillane paper took over all of the text that had been in "Procrastination" and filled out that paper's prospectus. Thus on the motif of personal vengeance, he continued:

In this philosophy of the personal administration of justice, Spillane's heroes merely reflect . . . an important aspect of the American attitude to the problems of law and order which has no significant counterpart in this country. This is the frontier tradition of rough and ready justice administered individually by the six-gun citizens of the wild west or the mining camp and collectively by the vigilante committee or the lynch mob. Though the conditions which created it have largely disappeared, the cowboy ethic of civilian exercise of the judiciary functions remains an active part of contemporary attitudes; and its survival explains some otherwise puzzling features of the American way of life. In particular it sheds some light on the successful career of the currently lamented Senator McCarthy. For the cowboy ethic implies the acceptance of two principles of law alien to the British tradition. One is that public opinion can define crimes and punishments lying outside the official code and beyond the scope of law enforcement. The other is that the citizen who undertakes to administer the unofficial code is a public benefactor whose methods are condoned if the results are satisfactory to public opinion.

The prose may be Johnsonian but the sweep is more characteristic of Harold Innis. He uses Spillane to comment on other aspects of American life from courtship customs to probable contemporary American opinion on respected community figures

His surprise ending generally hinges on the disclosure that some respected member of the community – the banker, the psychiatrist, the wealthy philanthropist, the reform politician – is really a master criminal, trading viciously on human weakness. For such disclosures to carry conviction, the idea that an apparently decent person can turn out to be a foul pest must be a credible one. The fact that Spillane counts on his readers to accept the idea obviously reflects something of the climate of opinion in contemporary America. While it is a necessary corollary of the cowboy ethos, its transference into a basic attitude could lead to utter social disorganisation. (1954a)

North America Again

During 1953–4 Milton Friedman was a visiting fellow of Gonville and Caius College. Over twenty years later Harry would write: "I still recall with shame the deliberate rudeness with which you were cold-shouldered by my colleagues at Cambridge during your year there" (Hoover Institution, Friedman Papers, Box 28, Folder 33, from HGJ, 14 October 1976). He also reported meeting Friedman as "a traumatic intellectual experience for myself and the only two other Cantabrigians who were willing to expose themselves to the moral risks involved and which ultimately brought me as a pilgrim to Chicago" (1972i, 277).[20]

Friedman was impressed by Harry. As early as 23 October he was writing to T. W. Schultz, his chair about prospective appointments mentioning

> another name that the department ought to keep in mind in considering its long run plans; namely Harry Johnson, now here at Cambridge, but originally a Canadian. Of the various younger people I have met around here, he impresses me by all odds the best and most promising, and as of the moment I would unhesitatingly rate him above Tobin. As you know his specialty has been money . . . but he has been doing some work in international trade. (Regenstein Library, University of Chicago, Department of Economics Records, Box 42, Folder 10, Prospective Appointments)

He wrote again on 29 March 1954 "to strongly press on you Harry Johnson of Toronto, who is the one new person I have come to know here who really impressed me" (ibid.). Friedman's opportunity came when Northwestern was looking for possible appointments at both senior and junior levels. He reported to Schultz on 14 April that he had tried two senior visitors, Nicholas Kaldor and Richard Kahn, without success, but as regards juniors

> Johnson seemed to me clearly the best of the rest, so that our self-interest and my duty as an agent coincided. I have checked with him, indicating that any Northwestern arrangement could probably be combined with a quarter at Chicago. He expressed real interest and thought that he could be available. It seemed to me that the Chicago half attracted him more than the Northwestern half, but that may be only wishful thinking or the fact that he was talking to me. I think it would be splendid all around if such an arrangement could be made. (Ibid.)

The Chicago part of the arrangement fell through. But the result was an invitation to visit Northwestern during the spring quarter (April–June) to teach the graduate course in international trade theory, to lead a series of

---

[20] The two are not known.

faculty/graduate student seminars, and to give two or three lectures to a wider audience. With support from the Rockefeller Foundation, Northwestern offered $3,500 for the three months, plus $1,500 for expenses. Later in the year, Stanford offered him teaching – international economics and money and banking – over ten weeks, putting another $2,200 into the pot, to which he would be able to add anything he made from speaker's honoraria.[21] Harry blanched at the thought of two lectures a day over the 10 weeks – the equivalent of $2\frac{1}{2}$ years lecturing at Cambridge – but accepted when he was reassured by Lorie Tarshis, a visitor to Cambridge from Stanford in 1954–5, that they wouldn't have to be up to the same standard as his Cambridge lectures (Box 43, Northwestern 1955, HGJ to K. Arrow, 15 November 1954).

The family sailed from England on the S.S. *United States* on 17 March 1955. Liz and the children went on to Canada to see parents and friends. Between Harry's arrival in New York on the 22nd and reaching Evanston on the 25th, he visited Johns Hopkins on the 23rd where he gave an early version of "The Transfer Problem and Exchange Stability" – his bread and butter paper for American seminars – and made a lightning visit to MIT to see Paul Samuelson. The family's arrival from Canada was delayed until late April because Ragnar had a tonsillectomy in Canada, but Harry reported "batching it quite comfortably . . . in a large house with TV, automatic washing machine, big frig, etc." (Silberston Papers, to Aubrey Silberston, postmarked 21 April 1955).

Once at Northwestern, Harry, with the advice of savvy students and colleagues, equipped himself with a big dark green Buick for $200 (Reuber and Scott 1977, 672; Elizabeth Simpson, 26 July 2005). The car proved useful for visits to nearby universities, such as Iowa State where Harry and Peter Bauer, another Northwestern visitor, opened a discussion on "Some Aspects of Economic Growth (in the light of British Experience)." There were also visits to Carnegie Institute of Technology in Pittsburgh, Vanderbilt University in Nashville, and, on the way back out of the country in September, MIT. Naturally he appeared in Chicago. The "Transfer Problem" (1955) served as his staple paper, but as he worked it up, he offered a preliminary version of "The Revival of Monetary Policy in Great Britain" (1956c) as a supplement, an offer that Vanderbilt accepted.

---

[21] Harry could claim his Cambridge stipend in full provided that he could demonstrate that any emoluments he earned in America, less expenses, did not leave him materially better off than he would have been had he remained in Cambridge.

The Buick took them west first along Route 66 towards Stanford. After the Stanford teaching, it took them up the west coast and back across the Canadian Rockies and prairies to Ontario, where there was a brief reunion with families, before they drove on to Cambridge where Harry gave a paper at MIT and they left the car as a wedding present for English friends on a Fulbright. Harry, Liz, and the children sailed from New York on the S.S. *United States* on September 30.

SIX

Cambridge Economist

On 14 and 15 July 1949 at 6 P.M. Harry gave two lectures on "The Significance of Lord Keynes" to members of a Ministry of Education course in commerce and related subjects meeting in Sidney Sussex College. Thus began a long series of talks on Keynes and Keynesian economics to various audiences over the next 17 years, the last being "The Shadow of Keynes," which appeared after his death in 1977. In his first lecture, Harry dealt with "The Keynesian Theory"; in the second, "An Evaluation of the Keynesian Approach." At the start of the first lecture, he remarked:

I might describe myself as a third-generation Keynesian – Keynesian, in that I am convinced, as many economists are not, of the usefulness of the approach originated by Lord Keynes, and the importance of the problems with which his analysis deals; third-generation, in both the time at which I came to the study of the theory and my attitude towards it. I have neither the passionate conviction of revealed truth of the first generation, with its tendency towards bibliolatry, hero-worship, and intolerance towards critical points of view; nor the pioneering enthusiasm of the second generation, acknowledging the limitations of Keynes' book but not of his analysis, and assuming that the "General Theory" is the starting point of economic wisdom. I regard Keynes' "General Theory" as an extension rather than a replacement of previously existing knowledge, a book which omits not only some of the answers but also some of the questions; and I believe that further progress requires a synthesis of the Keynesian analysis with the general corpus of economic theory. (Box 32, Writing 1949, 3)

The introduction may have sounded eclectic and conciliatory, but the presentation that followed was an orthodox presentation of both 45° Keynesianism and the more sophisticated IS-LM version, to which he added aggregate supply and employment functions. The more sophisticated model, he claimed, demonstrated the possibility of unemployment equilibrium – one that did not depend on an assumption of rigid money wages. He ran through what he regarded as the standard criticisms, making the most of the

126

limitations of the theory as a theory of prices, of its inappropriateness for the study of cycles and growth, and of the static oversimplification of Keynes's treatment of consumption. The Keynesian emphasis on full employment had he argued 'serious, even dangerous limitations', not so much because full employment as a fact involves various kinds of economic wastes, but because full employment as a definition of policy involved "a mistaken diagnosis of the British economic problem" (Lecture 2, 16) – "the change in Britain's world trade position with the rise of the United States and Germany, and the industrialisation of formerly agricultural countries" (15) – the theme he returned to in *The Overloaded Economy* (1952c) (see discussion in Chapter 5).

After the event, Harry showed his lectures to Dennis Robertson. Robertson who had "extreme admiration for their compactness and lucidity of exposition," naturally disagreed with many of the conclusions:

Of course it *does* seem to me that what you say on II, 12–13 about the unsuitability of the apparatus for the analysis of cyclical changes and the evanescence of the various functions makes a bigger hole than you admit in the validity of the concept of 'unemployment equilibrium' (I, 18), in the value of the alleged 'exact and quantitative formulation' of the forces at work (II, 17) and above all in the claim that the rigidity of wage rates is not vital to the whole caboodle (I, 4; II, 3–4). I think your whole-hearted backing of this last claim is the real surprise in the paper, – my own view (as you will know from the QJE article) [1950] having hardened considerably in the opposite direction. (Box 32, Writing 1949, 23 May 1950)

Robertson's note had another subject as well.

I wonder if you would have time to read during the summer my 12 summer term lectures, – over which I took some trouble last vacation? They are all pretty fully written out (jokes and all) and (for me) pretty legible.

Robertson's willingness to discuss their differences bore fruit the next term, when in an attempt to elucidate the issues of the liquidity preference/loanable funds debate that had preoccupied Cambridge economics for some time (above p. 63), Harry wrote out an extended commentary on Robertson's "Mr. Keynes and the Rate of Interest" (1940, chapter I). Once he had completed a draft, he gave copies to Joan Robinson, Kenneth Berrill, and Robertson – sending Robertson a substantial revision following Joan Robinson's comments. Robertson replied on 14 December 1950 with, for him, a long letter and a thirteen-page note. Discussion with Robertson and some revision of their original pieces continued the next term – it was agreed by Robertson that taking stock of where they had got to "might be a suitable religious exercise for Good Friday!" (Box 33, Notes on DHR, 17

March 1951).[1] Eventually it was agreed that the interchange, with an editorial introduction, would appear in the *Review of Economic Studies* under the title "Some Cambridge Controversies in Monetary Theory" (1951–2). Throughout the discussion Harry was careful to maintain the emphasis on theory: He would not worry about practical matters, which were left to his writings on monetary policy.

One can also learn his views on the Cambridge controversies at the time, from the introduction to a paper "Current Controversies in Cambridge Interest Theory," a variant of his *Review of Economic Studies* paper, which he read to the Economics Club of University of Birmingham on 21 February 1951 (Box 33, Writing 1951).

In giving this paper the title 'Current Controversies in Cambridge Interest Theory' I may perhaps have been a trifle misleading. Such a title might suggest that Cambridge is bursting with new ideas on the subject, new ideas which are being hotly debated and which will eventually lead to progress being made in the theory of interest. This, unfortunately, is not the case: instead, Cambridge is still debating the old issues of the 1930s, the controversy over liquidity preference versus loanable funds. . . .

Outside Cambridge, I think it is fair to say, these issues have largely lost their heat: in large part the two approaches have been reconciled in a more general approach to the theory of interest, with matters of controversy being reduced to differences in technique, emphasis, or factual assumption. Inside Cambridge, however, the debate goes on in its old form.

Just why this should be so is an extremely interesting question. . . . Fundamentally it is a matter of the personalities involved. The contrast between the personalities of the two protagonists in the original debate, Keynes and Robertson, both Cambridge men and close personal friends for a long time, was itself sufficient to ensure that the controversy on the theoretical plane would be charged with personal feeling. On the one hand there was Robertson, the lifelong scholar, imbued with a deep sense of the continuity of intellectual progress and the responsibility of the scholar to the sources of his ideas; always conscious of his debt to his teachers . . . always anxious to repay them with more than adequate interest by disguising the true originality of his own contributions; but always conscious in his own heart of the value of his contributions, and of the hard thought and scholarship that went into them. On the other hand was Keynes, the brilliant dilettante, . . . impatient by temperament and intellectual outlook with the weight of received authority . . . , apt to overgeneralise his case and over-emphasise his differences with economists of the past in order to call attention to his own policy recommendations. . . .

The personal nature of the controversy of the thirties has been carried on into the forties and fifties, past the death of Keynes himself, by Keynes's disciples – people who were the younger generation of the thirties, and who have added to the controversy the iconoclasm of youth and the perpetual war between the generations, sometimes

---

[1] For Harry the major revisions occurred in the discussion of Section VIII "Increased Thrift and the Rate of Interest." For Robertson, the revisions involved both a more complete exposition of his views in a few places and a reduction in the acerbity of his comments.

forgetting in the delight of debate that as time passes they themselves are becoming the older generation. Robertson also has his supporters; but they are either members of the unconvinced older generation, too senior to carry the debate into fresh fields, or applied economists, not particularly interested in monetary theory, but hostile to the personalities or politics of the Keynesians; none of them are in the class, in monetary theory, with the Keynesians or with Robertson himself. The preservation of old controversies is also facilitated by the peculiar nature of Cambridge academic life, with its intimate society and the College system which cuts sharp across the Faculties; loyalty to College is as important as loyalty to Faculty, and to some extent the theoretical controversy can be interpreted as an internecine war between King's and Trinity, John's and Caius.[2]

The perpetuation of this kind of controversy, however stultifying it may be for the progress of economics, is always great fun for the participants.... But it is not fun for the student who has to find his way through the tactical manoeuvres of controversy to the economic truth either as an undergraduate at Cambridge or as a reader of the writings of the Cambridge economists.... The result is a great waste of student manhours.

Thus his later memoirs in the 1970s of Cambridge in the 1950s were consistent with his 1951 opinion, if not with the state of affairs in 1945–6 (see discussion in Chapter 3).

Monetary Economics

When Harry left Harvard in 1948, he had intended, as he said in his Ramsey-Berry application (see discussion in Chapter 5), to do his thesis on the chancellor of the exchequer's attempt to reduce the long-term rate of interest to $2\frac{1}{2}$ percent in 1946–7. He had worked at this and gone some way in collecting statistics and background material. In January 1950, he reported to G. A. Elliott that "I am giving first priority to my Harvard thesis which has to do with the Dalton cheaper money policy" [University of Toronto Archives, Department of Political Economy Records, A76-0025/034(01), 20 January 1950]. Yet at his first meeting of the Association of University Teachers of Economics (AUTE) he had found that "three others were already engaged in studies of cheap money, one of whom was in process of submitting a completed thesis to a Midlands university." However, as he told Alvin Hansen,

I have become interested in British joint-stock banking, a subject on which very little research has been done since the beginning of the war ... and I feel that a study of changes in British banking in the period 1930 to 1950 would offer more scope

---

[2] Trinity was Robertson's college. The Johnians were Jan Graaff and Robin Matthews; those at Gonville and Caius were Stanley Dennison, Robertson's political lieutenant in Cambridge, and Peter Bauer.

for original work, and at the same time be of more general usefulness. [Houghton Library, Harvard University, Hansen Papers, HUG(FP) 3.11 A. H., Hansen Correspondence 1926–1959, File 1951, HGJ to A. H. Hansen, 24 May 1951]

Accordingly, he asked for permission to change his topic, enclosing the first fruits of his work in the area, "Some Economic Implications of Secular Changes in Bank Assets and Liabilities in Great Britain," already scheduled for publication in the *Economic Journal* in September (1951a).[3] Permission was granted (Box 54, Toronto Correspondence 1952, from A. H. Hansen, 29 May 1951).

The statistical work at the beginning of the *EJ* article highlighted four important changes: the large-scale expansion in deposits, both absolutely and relative to national income; the massive increase in the liquidity of the banking system; the increase in the public debt held by the banking system; and the decrease in the proportion of bank credit extended to the private sector, partly as a result of a secular fall in its demand for bank loans. These changes had been even more extreme immediately after the war, but a return to the prewar state of affairs was unlikely. Harry argued that it was necessary to examine the implications of these changes for commercial banking, for monetary policy, and for the framework of economic policy. The first was that

[c]hronic defective demand does not seem to be an economic problem in this country for a long time to come. Rather the full employment problem is likely to continue to be a problem of inflationary pressure; and in this context . . . the effect of secular banking trends is to complicate rather than ease the problems of economic policy. (1951a, 556)

The second was that "greater cyclical stability of the money supply" would ease the problem of countercyclical policy, though the effects of such stability were not something "to which any great quantitative significance can reasonably be attached." He expected these developments implied "that overall economic policy will rely on budgetary measures, buttressed with some degree of direct controls, rather than on monetary measures" (1951a, 555). He thought traditional methods of monetary control were unlikely to be applied in the near future because the increased role of government in the economy and the increased proportion of government debt in the total would make changes in interest rates a much less attractive method of control than in the past; "the short-term rate of interest has ceased to be

---

[3] A companion piece of statistical work was "Clearing Bank Holdings of Public Debt, 1930–50" (1951b).

regarded as a very important policy variable" and the "generally accepted view is that the interest-elasticity of investment is rather low, the inference being that variations in long-term interest rates are unlikely to be a very effective means of economic control" (1951a, 554).

In summary, the implications of changes in bank assets and liabilities for monetary policy are that the money supply in future will likely be a passive result rather than an active determinant of other developments, that monetary policy in its traditional form is unlikely in the future to be an important element in economic policy; and that such monetary control as there is will probably be selective rather than general. (1951a, 555)

More speculatively the developments might have implications for interest rate theory: Given "interest rates are now highly artificial phenomena," "the pursuit of a theory of the relation between the long and short rates is not a rewarding task" (1951a, 561). The presuppositions of classical interest theories, most notably that the rate of interest bore some relationship to real forces, were unlikely to hold (1951a, 557–8).

Harry's timing in entering practical British monetary discussions was impeccable. He put his marker down early in what would become a new game, in this case just before the revival of monetary policy in Britain after a long period of pegged interest rates and reliance on direct controls on credit allocations – all in a context of continued inflation.

Harry's next discussion of monetary policy followed its revival. The general election of 25 October 1951 produced a Conservative government. The Bank of England and the Treasury expected to make a move on monetary policy, as part of a deflationary policy to deal with a balance-of-payments crisis as soon as the new administration was in place (Howson 1993, 310). On 7 November 1951, Bank rate rose from 2 to $2\frac{1}{2}$ percent, its first rise (except for the opening two months of World War II) since 1932. At the same time, the Treasury ceased pegging the Treasury bill rate and offered £1,000 million $1\frac{3}{4}$ percent Special Funding Stock maturing on 14 November 1952, 1953, and 1954 in exchange for Treasury bills with less than 60 days to run, thus drastically reducing the liquidity of the banking system. These initial moves were supplemented early in December by a stiffening of the chancellor's instructions to the Capital Issues Committee, whose consent was necessary to make new issues of securities, new instructions to the clearing banks on their policy on advances, and a Board of Trade order, effective 1 February 1952, fixing minimum deposits and maximum repayment periods for consumer durables bought on hire purchase (the instalment plan). Then on Budget Day, 11 March 1952, Bank rate rose to 4 percent.

David Worswick, editor of the *Bulletin* of the Oxford University Institute of Statistics, organised a symposium. He commissioned two papers for the April/May 1952 issue – from Harry Johnson and Charles Kennedy – "to describe the backgrounds of the new monetary policy and to raise the most important issues of technique and policy involved" (1952a, 117). The papers were sent to contributors – including Frank Paish, Richard Kahn, Thomas Balogh, John Hicks, and Dennis Robertson – for comment and for "any other points which they thought would be worthy of discussion." In August 1952 the *Bulletin* left room for another round of comments including some from the United States, before giving Harry the last word.

Harry's first contribution, as well as providing a straightforward account of what had transpired, made some attempt at evaluation. He was sceptical as to the efficacy of the new monetary measures. As he put it, "the moderate raising of short interest rates . . . could in itself have had very little influence on contracting credit," since it did not substantially reduce the profitability of the banks of shifting from bills to advances and the rate increase on advances of only $\frac{1}{2}$ percent would not significantly reduce demand. He emphasised the unorthodoxy of the funding operation, which threw the emphasis on gilt-edged rates as determining the cost of cash and relied on a liquidity ratio to control the volume of bank credit. He also raised the issue of the desirability of the new policy as a method of controlling bank advances.

> While there might be a case for the rationing of credit by price – and the case for orthodox measures is usually conducted in these terms – that case is largely irrelevant;[4] and there is no good reason to presume that the results of credit rationing by the banks correspond either to the equilibrium of a competitive market or (more important) to the national interest. (1952a, 129)

There were alternatives available to raising Bank rate, namely directions under the Bank of England Act 1946 to impose a liquidity ratio of 40 percent and to restrict advances.

As far as one can tell from the surviving records, Harry had not discussed [with Dennis Robertson] before publication either his *Economic Journal* or his Oxford *Bulletin* piece, though the "secret seminar" had heard a version of the former. Once his *Bulletin* contribution was in print, Robertson complimented Harry on his "lucid and useful narrative" (some quibbles on details), but Harry's suggestions as to what should have been done raised real hackles.

---

[4] [original footnote] It is also open to the objection that the ability to pay high interest rates is not necessarily a proof of the superior social desirability of the project to be financed.

Mr Johnson's remarkable erudition and ingenious mind will stand him in good stead when he becomes the first manager of Branch X of the United Bank of the British (?or Canadian) Soviet Socialist Republic; and long, in that capacity, may he succeed in keeping intact his head upon his broad shoulders. But meanwhile I do not think his advice will be of much service to those who are seeking to re-invigorate, with due regard to the changes in climate over the last twenty years, a wholly different system.

Hubert Henderson had a word for it all.... The word was "silly-clever".[5] (1952, 156)

Robertson's remarks drew J. R. Hicks's ire.

It is, I suppose, inevitable that a Restoration should produce a re-alignment of forces; different people take it in different ways. I myself, and I think Mr Johnson and Mr Kennedy also, are mere *ralliés*; we are prepared to give the new régime a chance to see what it can do, but we do not want, or expect, to put the clock back to 1640 or 1789. Professor Robertson, however, whom one had thought to be a moderate man, discloses himself in the unexpected guise of an *ultra*. Bank Rate is hallowed with the oil of Rheims, and anathemas are hurled at poor Uzzahs like Mr Johnson who with the best of intentions are trying to make the Ark of the Lord ride smoothly upon its chariot. (1952, 268)

Harry also defended himself in August:

My purpose in suggesting them was to provoke rational discussion of the technical problems and possibilities of British monetary policy, as a corrective to the *mystique* of Bank Rate and "orthodoxy" which revived so rapidly after November.... It was perhaps inevitable that my "could" has been translated into "should", my suggestions have become "policy recommendations", and I have become something of an Aunt Sally for anti-planners; I should at any rate like to express my gratitude to Professor Hicks for his generous interpretation of my intentions. (1952b, 302)

He also argued powerfully against setting monetary policy and controls as alternatives:

Set up in such general terms, the argument can only lead to an affirmation of personal preferences as between the imperfections of monetary restraint and the imperfections of controls. This solution, while in the best traditions of welfare economics, seems to me an unsatisfactory one for two reasons. In the first place, it tends to foster an unhealthy confusion of means and ends, with some economists recommending monetary policy because they would prefer a free enterprise economy and others recommending controls because they would prefer a different system – regardless of the situation facing the policy-makers, or of the extent to which the community shares their preferences for one or other social system. In the second place it tends to promote the false impression that monetary policy and controls, as policy instruments, are strictly substitutes for one another.

[5] Henderson died in February 1952.

A more useful approach ... is to regard monetary policy and direct controls as both substitutes and complements. (1952b, 305)

During his Cambridge years, Harry returned to discuss British monetary policy on three occasions – at the American Economic Association meetings in Chicago in December 1952 as arranged by Harold Innis (1953a), at the meetings of the AUTE in Sheffield in January 1954, and in the *Three Banks Review* in 1956. On all these, there are comments from Dennis Robertson – all supportive and less acerbic than on the symposium paper.

The American Economic Association paper, "Recent Developments in British Monetary Policy," was a straightforward recapitulation of what had passed since the increase in Bank rate that had occurred just over a year before it was delivered. With more evidence available as to techniques and effects, Harry could strengthen the points he made earlier – points on which he had been criticised by both Dennis Robertson and E. Victor Morgan, who had regarded the forced funding of November 1951 as exceptional, only to see it repeated a year later, with the authorities' explicit intention to reduce the liquidity ratio down to 30 percent. In evaluating the new developments, he emphasised how historically unorthodox they were as compared with prewar practice, their not being a substitute for other methods of credit control – "the general effect of the revival of quantitative credit control has been to furnish an iron glove to fit the velvet hand of qualitative controls" (1953a, 26) – although they had, by shaking loose the rigid structure of market rates characteristic of the period since 1939, prepared the way for a genuine return to quantitative methods if the authorities so desired. At this stage, although he still found it difficult to draw general conclusions, he was prepared to suggest that "recent British experience probably supports the view that monetary restriction can have a significant effect on economic activity without requiring a substantial rise in interest rates" (1953a, 26) – a position he had taken the previous August. Perhaps the most significant change was one of language: instead of talking of controlling bank credit or bank advances, he talked in terms of "restoration of control over the money supply" (1953a, 21) hardly the usual British Keynesian language.[6]

The AUTE paper, "Some General Aspects of Monetary Policy" (Box 33, Writing 1953), delivered on 4 January 1954, was deliberately provocative. Perhaps from a longer term perspective the most interesting section of the paper was its second, where he started with the premise that "the post-war

---

[6] Speaking of language, Harry was able to meet Dennis Robertson's one criticism and substitute "the general British philosophy of government intervention" on page 26 for "the general British philosophy of centralised economic planning."

experience which has led to the revival of monetary policy emphasizes certain shortcomings of the Keynesian analysis" (8), which were worth examining even though "there can be no possibility of dismissing Keynesian theory as a temporary aberration of the 1930s" (9).

He also made what he regarded as "the obvious point"

that the Keynesian prejudice against monetary policy . . . is less the work of Keynes himself . . . than of some of his critics, and even more of those of his followers who did not share his expressed desire to save free enterprise from itself. (9)

As he summarised his argument:

[T]he Keynesian theory tends to understate the scope for monetary policy, by imparting a spurious impression of precision and stability to the determination of income in the short run; while the theory of liquidity preference – which incidentally illustrates many of the disadvantages of the two-dimensional Marshallian tradition – is too narrowly conceived to provide an adequate approach to the theory of how monetary policy works. (12)

No wonder Robertson could say that he had read it "with interest, and a great deal of agreement, especially (as you would expect) with the second section" (Box 44, Correspondence 1949–56, 21 January 1954). However, Harry did *not* make great claims for monetary policy.

I have not argued for monetary policy as a means of aggregative control over effective demand, because I believe that such control can be secured more effectively by fiscal policy. This brings me to my general conception of the role of monetary policy in economic policy. The advantages of monetary policy, to my mind, lie in its flexibility and suitability for making rapid minor adjustments – particularly contractionary adjustments – rather than its power to enforce major adjustments of effective demand. The modern arguments for the effectiveness of monetary policy are, I think, chiefly arguments for a short-term effectiveness rather than a long-term effectiveness, or, to put it another way, they concentrate the influence of Bank rate on stock decisions rather than on flow decisions. (15)

Early in February 1956, Harry wrote "Some Reflections on the Revival of Monetary Policy in Britain." He showed it to Alan Day, Jack Wiseman (who passed it on to Richard Sayers), and Dennis Robertson. Sayers accepted it for publication in the *Three Banks Review*. At the time it was widely read. The article did not register significant changes in view from 1954, or even 1953, although one might see some retrogression in his identifying the view that the quantity of money is the key policy variable with the view that the total volume of bank credit rather than bank advances was the important factor – a misunderstanding that he proceeded to dismiss on the ground that borrowers on bank advances did not have the access to alternative sources of finance available to those who sell securities to the banks (1956c, 16–17).

> To summarise a rather extensive argument, the influence of monetary policy and the argument for using it, seem to rest chiefly on its effectiveness in controlling stockholding, and possibly also on its influence on short-term capital movements; its long-run influence on fixed investment is doubtful. It is best conceived as a short-run instrument for influencing stock decisions rather than flow decisions; and is more appropriately used for trimming effective demand temporarily than for setting its level. (1956c, 18)

The paper, however, did introduce a new theme to his writing: "the major long-term monetary problem of the British economy, the tendency for British wages and prices to increase more rapidly than those of Britain's international competitors" (1956d, 19). Although he identified long-term inflation as a monetary problem, he did not see monetary policy as playing an important role in its solution:

> [E]xperience suggests that substantial unemployment would be required to prevent wages from increasing at an inflationary rate. Given the narrow limits set by current opinion as to what constitute a tolerable margin of unemployment, this means that neither monetary policy nor alterative methods of controlling aggregate demand offer much prospect of solution. (1956c, 19)

He thought that none of the other possible solutions proposed would work, given that "such methods attempt to solve the economic problem by ignoring the economic forces that produce it" (1956c, 20). The only solution seemed to be "to stagger on as we have been doing" hoping that the absence of a need to devote large resources to defence and to meet an adverse shift in the terms of trade would allow increasing productivity to raise real incomes, allowing for "the necessary condition for a workable 'national wage-policy' – the possibility of substantial non-inflationary wage increases" (1956c, 20).

Robertson regarded the paper as "a really solid contribution to the debate" and continued "I don't believe we differ greatly in analysis. But I'm not much soothed by your promise of the jam of a little unemployment for tomorrow. . . . That particular jam gets *harder* to manufacture the nearer we get to the next election day!" (Box 43, Writing 1956, 13 February 1956).

The vague hope for a national wage-policy as the ultimate solution was not linked to what David Laidler (1984, 596) called "a rather ill-defined cost-push explanation of inflation based on the failure of real income to rise." As Harry set out the argument in *Granta* in an article "On British Crises" in April 1956:

[T]he source of chronic inflation, then, is to be found in a chronic tendency towards putting excessive demands on the capacity of the economy. Why has this been the case with the British economy since the war? The answer lies in the coincidence of the victory of what may be broadly described as socialist ideas on domestic and foreign economic policy with a relative decline in the ability of the British economy to supply the resources required to give effect to these ideas and the survival of other ideas with which they have been uneasily combined. (1956b, 6)

Parts of the argument echoed "*The Overloaded Economy*," Harry's autumn 1952 Toronto lectures. The adoption of the welfare state, the commitment to full employment, the commitment to assist in the economic development of backward countries, and the desire to maintain Britain's political and economic position in the world (including a commitment to heavy defence expenditure and the reestablishment of Britain's position in trade and finance) all implied a reduction in the proportion of output available for individual consumption. Unless the public was reconciled to this by an acceptance of the social philosophy underlying the policies or there was a substantial rise in the output available to allow for these policies, inflation was inevitable. Neither development came to pass: Britain retained "the philosophy of personal capitalism and of capitalistic institutions, particularly collective bargaining," and economic developments (the effects of the war itself and the postwar deterioration of the terms of trade) meant that additional productive capacity was not available to meet the additional demands. This explanation was sociopolitical (the sort that Harry would decry in later life) rather than simply cost-push, although one might concede that the implications of "frustrated desires for higher living standards" for trade union behaviour would look like cost-push.

This sort of explanation of inflation did not sit well with another aspect of Harry's later Cambridge thinking. Here I refer to a paper delivered in September 1954 but not published until 1957, "The Determination of the General Level of Wage Rates." That paper, as well as being extremely critical of Keynesian theory, stated flatly:

The conclusion which emerges from the argument is the rather obvious one that the level of money wages is a proper subject for economic analysis, unless we are to reject the assumption that wage-earners (and other economic units) are in some sense economically rational and that the level of money wages will be governed by the quantity of money, though not in the simple way postulated by classical monetary theory in its unsophisticated form. (1957f, 35)

In 1954, he thought that the practical applicability of the conclusion was limited by the absence of a theory of the rate at which wages change and the traditional belief that the quantity of money was an autonomous variable – in the modern economy the money supply was a matter of government policy and it and the wage-price level were jointly determined by government policy. That still left a gap between his more formal and his more popular discussions.

The gap was perhaps made larger by the refusal of the Department of Applied Economics to fund the project with which he had returned from Chicago and Stanford in 1955, the development of money supply statistics for the United Kingdom (see discussion in Chapter 7). Harry related its origins:

> I went to Stanford for the summer.... I taught a course on money from Shaw's book [1950]. Being at that time a Cambridge Keynesian of the most arrogant sort, I chafed under the obligation of understanding how money supply statistics are created – enough to teach the course.... But some sense of the importance of the subject must have rubbed off on me, for I went back to the U.K. with a project for constructing a U.K. money supply series – only to be told by Brian Reddaway...that the results would not be worth the £500 I estimated it would cost to do properly. (1975n, 299)

Harry also discussed Keynesian economics in general terms in the summer of 1956 in one of five lectures that he delivered in Karachi in July, "Monetary Theory and Keynesian Economics." The lecture was not published until 1958 and was not widely available until he republished it in *Money, Trade, and Economic Growth* in 1962. The lecture notes for this, as for the other papers survive (Box 43), and these have the very strong criticisms of Keynesian doctrine whose distinctive features were noted by David Laidler (1984, 597–8), although Laidler was working from the slightly revised 1962 version – that Keynesian economics was a special case of classical economics and that Keynesian economics had serious weaknesses as a theory of prices. In the lecture Harry made reference to the trend back towards considering the quantity theory in the work of A. J. Brown, whose *The Great Inflation* he had reviewed in the *Economic Journal* (1956a) and also explicitly to Milton Friedman, whose *Studies in the Quantity Theory of Money* with its essay "The Quantity Theory of Money: A Restatement" appeared in 1956 but whose ideas could have been known to Harry when he was in Chicago in the spring of 1955, if not even earlier. Thus it is likely that "Harry Johnson's first large step away from orthodox Cambridge Keynesianism" was taken not in Manchester, as David Laidler (1984, 398) claims, but in Cambridge. But then there is also the question as to whether, given the influence of his

Harvard training, he was ever, despite his own later self-identification, "an orthodox Cambridge Keynesian."

The Balance of Payments

There is a second area of economics in which Harry had developed a distinctive profile before he left Cambridge. By the summer of 1956, both in lectures and in publications, Harry had developed most of the material that would appear in "Towards a General Theory of the Balance of Payments" initially published in *International Trade and Economic Growth* (1958) but presaged in the *Pakistan Economic Journal* (1958d) and the *Indian Journal of Economics* (1956e).[7] Nineteen fifty-six also saw the publication of "The Transfer Problem and Exchange Stability," which joined the "General Theory" article in the American Economic Association's *Readings in International Economics* (1968). Over and above these two papers, there was Harry's 1951 review of James Meade's *The Balance of Payments* – a review that cost him Meade's LSE chair in international economics and drove him to Chicago in 1959.

That Harry should have been asked to do the review at all is interesting: He had published one article dealing with the subject matter of Meade's book (1950c), thus making him what he often complained of later – one of those "often unfamiliar Cambridge names [that] dominated the reviews section of the [*Economic*] *Journal*" (*Shadow*, 154). Harry had already appeared fourteen times as a reviewer for the *EJ*. However, this time it was not just a review but a substantial review article.

Once the article was written, it was widely circulated and commented on – not merely by the editors of the *Economic Journal* and those whom they or Harry may have consulted. In Oxford Thomas Balogh saw a copy (Box 33); at LSE not only Harry's friends but James Meade and Lionel Robbins saw copies, and it appears to have been the talk of the senior common room well before it was published in December 1951. As Alan Peacock reported on 8 November:

Robbins announced in stentorian tones at lunch the other day that he thought that you must have some personal antipathy to J. E. M. Ralph [Turvey] and I rose to your defence but of course Lionel is uncrushable. I think you have convinced James about the balance of payments definitions, by the way.[8] I think it is time he paid

---

[7] The Pakistan lecture was delivered in July 1956; the Indian paper was dated "Manchester, July 1956." Harry left England on 6 July.

[8] Meade had distinguished between the "actual" deficit or surplus on the balance of payments and the "potential" deficit or surplus, which he defined in terms of the amount of

the price of not reading the literature (an Oxford characteristic, I think, judging by Little's article in the same journal [1951] and the efforts of our mutual friend [Peter] Wiles [1950]). I pointed out to him before that his scheme for the reform of inheritance taxes in 'Planning and the Price Mechanism' is potted Rignano [1925] and Dalton [1920]. But this latest effort is much more serious and I don't think the Americans will be pleased. I think that you are fundamentally right on both counts, the methodological and the analytical, but I am doubtful if you will convince the high-ups in L.S.E. who are more sensitive than I thought. (Box 44, Correspondence 1949–56)

Far more than sensitive – Robbins took serious offence. He did not speak to Harry again until Arnold Harberger's wedding in London on 15 March 1958, by which time he had almost finished preventing Harry's receiving a chair at LSE (see discussion in Chapter 7).

But the LSE reaction was rather late in the day. Almost a month earlier, when writing to Vincent Bladen about a possible visit to Toronto (see Chapter 5), Harry wrote:

I cannot as yet make a definite commitment, for the following reason: I have just at the moment been drawing very strongly on my credit with Austin Robinson, since I have written an extremely critical review of James Meade's new book and Austin is assuming a great responsibility for me in undertaking to accept it for the Economic Journal. [University of Toronto Archives, Department of Political Economy Records, A65-005/001(10), 10 October 1951]

Roy Harrod, Austin Robinson's coeditor, had his own strong views of the book, which he had reviewed favourably (and anonymously) for the *Times Literary Supplement* (7 September 1951, 562). Harry had been unhappy with the *TLS* review and had written the editor taking issue with the reviewer's remarks on devaluation and the terms of trade, on the place of Meade's book in the literature, and on the criticism of the absence of dynamics in the book. Harrod replied vigorously through Kathleen M. Dowding, the *TLS*'s assistant editor (Box 44, Correspondence 1949–56, to HGJ, 8 October 1952). As Austin Robinson wrote Harrod on 24 October

Your comments on James Meade's book make me more than ever anxious to make sure that Harry Johnson's review is within the bounds of decent controversy. It is

accommodating finance necessary to prevent exchange depreciation without any exchange controls, imposition of import controls, or other restrictions on the demand for foreign exchange. Harry had argued instead in favour of working in terms of the actual deficit because thinking in terms of potential deficits was "by nature ideological in the sense that they measure disequilibrium by reference to some abstract situation which . . . is presented as the ideal" (1951c, 814); that it made calculations of disequilibria more difficult, and that it "by its very nature almost excludes further analysis" (1951c, 815).

certainly critical. I don't want to stop him being that. But I am anxious that controversy should be good-tempered and that is the one thing I am anxious to ensure about this. (British Library of Political and Economic Science, Royal Economic Society Archives, RES6/2/111)

When the page proofs arrived, he wrote to Harry:

I am having a great deal of difficulty over your review of James Meade. Harrod has reacted violently, and pleads with me to withdraw the review, allow the book itself to be reviewed by someone else, and encourage you to rewrite parts of the article on the Taxonomic Approach to be published sometime next autumn.

I need not say that I dissent from this very strongly. I believe that what you have to say is, in most respects, important and deserves to be said. I shall not, therefore, willingly surrender to RFH's pleas. On the other hand I cannot ignore his views in total. And I find it the more difficult to ignore his views because, now that I see in cold print some of the things that were affording me misgivings before, I feel utterly miserable myself about them. I do not think that you have yourself taken in the full violence of the language in which you appear to be attacking Meade. This is, in my view, incomparably the most violent attack that has been made on any writer in my time as editor of the E.J.[9] But I myself believe that it conveys quite a wrong impression, or at least an impression that you ought to avoid conveying. If you are going to accuse someone (as everyone who reads this believes you to be doing) of faking results to accord with political bias, it is extraordinarily important that you should yourself appear utterly free of bias, and that you should pitch your criticism in a low key so that the reader regards you as judicial and unbiased. The review as it stands gives a strong impression of white-hot political fury on your part – of bias being assailed by opposing bias. I believe that impression is utterly contrary to the impression that you had been intending to convey – an impression of grave judicial indignation that an honest thinker should allow himself to be betrayed. I am myself quite prepared to go to the wall for this review, if you on your part are prepared to accept a certain number of changes which will have the effect of toning down the stridency of some of your more damnatory passages. I myself believe that the cumulative effect that you are anxious to create would be enhanced rather than reduced by the changes.

I have been very carefully through the review, and have pencilled in the margins the changes that would make me happy. If you are prepared to accept them, I am prepared to tell Harrod that I will insist on this going in – and Harrod will, I feel sure, concur if he knows that these more extreme passages have gone – though he will of course still disagree with very much. If you do not feel yourself able to accept them, then I think I cannot resist Harrod's plea, at least to the extent of holding it out of the issue. (Box 33, Meade Balance of Payments, 4 November 1951)

Robinson asked for six changes, two of which had been suggested by Richard Kahn, whom he had consulted before writing the letter. Robinson also

---

[9] He had become review editor in 1934.

suggested that if necessary they should meet. He reported to Harrod on 8 November:

He did in fact do everything to meet me and has, I think, behaved remarkably well over the whole thing. He has rewritten many of the passages that I had indicated in his own words and somewhat differently from my draft amendments. (British Library of Political and Economic Science, Royal Economic Society Archives, RES 6/2/111)

Harry may have been prepared to make the few changes requested, because he had taken to heart some earlier advice from Richard Stone, who had found the "article really excellent":

I hope you will not allow the article to be tampered with on account of the author's feelings. The reason is that your main point goes too deep for tampering to be of any use. Meade, who is a great friend of mine, is a liberal: rational and incorruptible above everything. It is a sad fact of life that such people are often ideologically biased though it is the last thing in the world they would want to be. (Box 33, Meade Balance of Payments, n.d.)

Stone gave an example:

I was a bit taken aback when, during the discussion of Morgan and Corlett's paper at the RSS [Royal Statistical Society] last summer [1951], Meade warmly supported the paper, the details of which he claimed not to understand, on the grounds that it gave relatively large foreign trade elasticities despite the fact that on the authors' admission the confidence regions of their estimates were large or infinite and they clearly did not consider their exercise a success. (Box 33, Meade Balance of Payments, n.d.)

In other words, Meade was welcoming the supposed evidence of large elasticities because it favoured the use of the price mechanism to remedy balance-of-payments imbalances.

Meade's book attempted to integrate two strands of theoretical innovations from the 1930s, Keynesian theory and the revival of general equilibrium theory as epitomised in Hicks's *Value and Capital* (1939), and to extend the theory of the balance of payments beyond its concentration on the balance of trade or the balance on current account to the overall balance of payments by including international capital movements. The core of the book was a policy model where the objectives were internal and external balance and the available instruments were income adjustments (fiscal or monetary policy) and price adjustments (exchange rate changes or price and wage flexibility). With that model, the focus shifted from the positive analysis of the effects of policy changes to the normative analysis of the policy changes needed to meet certain normative targets.

Harry's review recognised Meade's achievement:

> The most important feature of Professor Meade's approach . . . is that . . . this model is both comprehensive and extremely flexible. It includes all the relevant variables, allows for the influence of both price and income variations, and is capable of analysing the effects of all the important types of spontaneous changes. Even though most of Professor Meade's analytical results have been obtained by other writers employing particular models of which his is the general case, the conception of the model must be regarded as a notable act of creative synthesis. (1951c, 816)

Harry's review criticised Meade's book at several levels. The most important was Meade's willingness to draw important policy conclusions from qualitative theorising. As he put it

> Professor Meade has made an impressive attempt to develop a theory of international economic policy. The reviewer does not, however, believe that much assistance could be rendered to practical economic policy by further development along the lines he has laid down. The opinion is based on two general considerations.
>
> The first of these is the nature of economic theory itself, which, as Professor Meade and most other economists use it is essentially taxonomic, a method of classifying the universe of possible cases. It is possible, by pure theory, to specify the direction or sign of influence of one variable on another in a limited number of cases; but the problems in which most theorists are interested require the specification of the direction of effects operating in opposite directions, and this in turn requires a specification of the magnitudes as well as the signs of the influences. For such problems, all that theory can do is to specify some (measurable) quantity on which the outcome will depend.
>
> To determine the outcome in any particular case, however, it is necessary to measure the quantity. . . .
>
> Once this is admitted, it follows immediately that the role of economic theory in the solution of practical problems is extremely limited: the important (and more difficult) part of the task becomes the problem of measurement, however it is performed. Furthermore, beyond a certain point economic theory may easily become a handicap rather than a help; this is because the taxonomic approach is subject to two distinct forms of bias. The first is that, in order to keep the number of possible classifications within manageable bounds, and their distinguishing characteristics readily understandable, the theorist is strongly tempted to simplify the problems to the point at which his results cannot be applied at all easily to practical problems. . . . Second, in order to choose among the impossible number of alternatives with which even a relatively simple analytical problem confronts him, the theorist is strongly tempted to eliminate some of the cases by prejudicing the result of measurements he does and perhaps could not make, either by illegitimately assuming that a number of qualitative statements can be added up to a quantitative fact, or by postulating an ideal world in which only the cases he discusses will exist. This temptation is particularly dangerous when questions of economic policy are involved, because the desire for simplicity may be reinforced by personal preferences in prompting the exclusion of particular cases. (1951c, 826–8)

Harry was not criticising taxonomy: He was criticising how Meade went from taxonomy to policy recommendations without quantifying some or all of the parameters to reduce the possible number of outcomes. Meade had substituted qualitative considerations for quantitative – a procedure that Harry regarded as illegitimate and dangerous. For example, Harry made quite a point of Meade's attempts to establish a central empirical assumption that normally the sum of the elasticities of international demand will be greater than unity – a proposition central to Meade's choice that favoured price-level adjustments to controls (1951c, 820; see also 826).

Meade took Harry's critique seriously. "This review ... has been a chief factor in moderating certain claims for the method which I should have previously made and which I would regard as excessive," although "Mr Johnson's complete condemnation of the method seems to me misplaced" (1955, vii–viii). Indeed "an important pitfall in Chapter XVII was avoided by reading the admirable taxonomic classification of possible cases contained in H. G. Johnson's 'Optimum Tariffs and Retaliation'" (1955, x). As he put his revised position:

Taxonomy plus a modicum of awareness of, and experience in, affairs of the real world would probably be able to take one a very long way if one only had to deal with what in the present volume are called the "utopian" solutions of problems in economic policy. In those circumstances the number of categories of possible solutions about which one could not make fairly reliable realistic assumptions would be limited.... But when allowance is made for the necessity of making what are called in the present volume choices between "second best" policies ... then the number of possible relevant categories becomes so large that detailed factual study of each separate case becomes much more important.

... The best course would seem to be to undertake general taxonomic analysis as an exercise in looking for important factors and important relationships, and then to turn to the study of particular problems, making what use one can of econometric studies, from case studies, and from the feel of the market. Perhaps for a long time economic policy in the final count must remain more of an art than a science. (1955, viii–ix)

Later Harry was fair and generous to Meade, most notably in "James Meade's Contributions to Economics," which he wrote in the fall of 1973 for the Committee for the Nobel Memorial Prize in Economic Science. It was published by the committee after Meade shared the prize with Bertil Ohlin in 1977. In his appreciation of Meade for the committee, Harry stated that he was "in close agreement with the modified position on the issue stated by Meade ... [in] the 'Preface' to *Trade and Welfare*" (1978b, 70).

In addition to his methodological complaints, Harry had detailed criticisms to make of Meade's book. As noted earlier, he criticised Meade's concept of balance-of-payments disequilibrium in terms that are now common to the profession. He also was unhappy with Meade's basic model, which differed from the existing literature of Keynesian international economics in defining the marginal propensity to import with reference to domestic expenditure rather than to income – another case where the profession chose not to follow Meade. He also had a number of detailed complaints about Meade's development of his model at crucial points.

Robert Mundell has suggested that Meade was underappreciated by his 1950s reviewers.

> There is no question in my mind that the reviews of the work published in the 1950s did not do justice to it or realise its significance as a major treatise in economics. This is only partly because of defects of organisation and presentation. . . . I should attribute its tepid reception rather to the state of confusion of the science in the early 1950s and the lack of sensible criteria by which merit could be separated from chaff. (1968, 113 n.3)

This is a rather odd remark as regards Harry, who reviewed all three volumes of Meade referred to in Mundell's comment between 1951 and 1956[10] and who reprinted the comment as "worth noting" in his Nobel evaluation of Meade (1978b, 71, n.1). It is not clear what new criteria of chaff detection appeared after 1956, unless it was the presence of Mundell himself. Nor, given that Harry's comments have stood the test of time, do they seem mistaken. For although Meade did make a major contribution to theory, he was open to attack over his attempts to apply it to economic policy – criticisms he deserved and accepted. One might still dislike the *balance* of Harry's review: The praise is buried, and the criticism is relentless. However, as Harry's own work on the balance of payments would show, certain of Meade's insights were essential to what followed.

I turn now to two other contributions concerning the balance of payments, both dating from Cambridge – "The Transfer Problem and Exchange Stability" and "Towards a General Theory of the Balance of Payments." I deal despite its date with the latter first: it can be taken as a part of Cambridge. As Harry put it:

> This chapter embodies ideas developed in lecture courses in Cambridge and elsewhere; part of the argument is reproduced in an earlier paper "Sketch of a Generalization of Keynesian Balance of Payments Theory," *The Indian Journal of Economics*, XXVII, no. 44 July 1956, 49–56. (*ITEG*, 153 n.1)

---

[10] In addition to *The Balance of Payments* and *Trade and Welfare*, the Mundell comment referred to the *Geometry of International Trade*. The comment was not in the original version of "International Disequilibrium and the Adjustment Process" (1967).

He might have added his July 1956 Karachi lecture "The Balance of Payments" (1958d) for it is clear from his lecture notes that the article follows his lecture faithfully and that the revisions for publication in *Money, Trade, and Economic Growth* were trivial. It is also clear from the typed copies that remain that he had worked through the analysis for his lectures in International Monetary Theory, which he gave in Cambridge and L.S.E. in 1954–5 and 1955–6 – lectures attended in 1955–6 by Robert Mundell (Box 34, International Monetary Theory Lectures).

The purpose of the "general theory" was "to synthesize and generalize the work of... [James Meade, Jan Tinbergen, and Sidney Alexander], and to use their approach to clarify certain aspects of the policy problem" (*ITEG*, 154). The creative act of synthesis was to use Tinbergen and Alexander to generalise notions initially in Meade. As Harry put it, Meade had highlighted the policy problem of conflict between the goals of full employment and balance-of-payments equilibrium and the ways of resolving it, while Tinbergen was concerned with the more general problem of multiple policy goals and multiple policy instruments – the conclusion of both being that for each policy objective a separate policy instrument was required. Alexander's contribution was to formulate the problem of maintaining internal balance in a more fruitful way than Meade, who had habitually assumed that the government would follow appropriate policies.

At the centre of Harry's presentation, assuming that there was an official exchange authority prepared to operate in the exchange market with official reserves to defend a fixed exchange rate, was an accounting identity: The balance of payments is the difference between aggregate receipts from and payments to foreigners by residents. A deficit on the balance of payments thus implied an excess of residents' aggregate payments over their receipts. This had been the starting point of Alexander's "absorption approach." The excess of payments over receipts implied either that residents were running down their cash balances as they purchased foreign exchange from the authorities or, alternatively, that residents' cash balances were being replenished by the authorities' open-market operations. In the first case, where the deficit is financed by residents' dishoarding, it would be self-correcting over time, although the authorities might be forced to act earlier if their stock of international reserves was small relative to the domestic money supply. In the second case, there would be no corrective process at work until the authorities' loss of reserves forced a change in policy. Hence "balance of payments deficits and difficulties are essentially monetary phenomena" (*ITEG*, 157).

Harry proceeded to note that the aggregate decisions leading to a balance-of-payments deficit could be of two kinds: a "stock" decision to change the composition of the community's assets by substituting other assets for domestic money, or a "flow" decision to spend in excess of current receipts. The stock deficit was inherently temporary, whereas a flow deficit was not. The former did not imply a real worsening of a country's situation, but the latter could.

Dealing with the stock deficit implied discouraging either the substitution of stocks of goods for domestic currency or the substitution of securities for domestic currency. In either case, Harry saw three alternatives – credit restriction, devaluation or controls. In the context of the 1950s, for Harry the "evaluation of the policy alternative... [suggested] the use of controls rather than price-system methods" (*ITEG*, 160) – for the former provided greater certainty of effect and the avoidance of repercussions on the flow equilibrium of the economy.

To deal with flow deficits, the authorities had to change their policies, particularly as such deficits might be weakening the country's international capital position. To concentrate on the central policy problem, Harry focused on the current account (excluding official reserve flows), a situation where the balance-of-payments deficit represented an excess of real expenditure over income. Instead of moving to discuss expenditure-reducing or output-increasing ways of dealing with the deficit (i.e., policies that dealt with the effects of actions), he suggested that the concentration should be on expenditure-reducing or expenditure-switching policies.

The usual candidates for expenditure reductions were monetary restrictions, budgetary tightening, or an intensification of direct controls, the first two of which would reduce inflationary pressure but might increase unemployment. Expenditure-switching policies were either general (devaluation) or selective (trade controls). But whether selective or general, expenditure-switching policies, which sought to reduce the deficit by switching expenditure from foreign to domestic goods, required for their success the availability of extra output necessary to satisfy the increased demand for domestic goods. His discussion then centred on the sources of the additional output required to meet the demand induced by the expenditure switching. If there were unemployed resources, the switching policy might increase output and employment, although one could conceive of more complicated cases.[11] If

---

[11] He anticipated, from the discussion of his "transfer problem" paper that the market for at least one commodity was not in unstable equilibrium, that the country's output was not a "Giffen case" in world consumption.

the economy was fully employed, on the other hand, real expenditure would have to be reduced to "make room" for increased demand, although the inflationary effects of the switching policy in full employment conditions might result in some expenditure reductions. The argument went on to allow for the complexities of individual cases and of the appropriate circumstances for the use of controls rather than devaluation, but the formal analytical basis of the paper had been laid. Congratulated by Jan Graaff on the paper, Harry replied, "I am fairly proud of that, as I felt I pulled together a number of strands of thought into a comprehensive framework accessible to an undergraduate" (Box 51, Correspondence to 1964, D–G, 19 April 1961).

"Towards a General Theory of the Balance of Payments" was later treated as a "basic article" in the development of the monetary theory of the balance of payments. Given its date, this "suggests that Johnson's geneology of the Chicago monetary approach . . . was unduly modest" (Polak 2002, 27; see also Chapter 13).

The transfer problem loomed large in the literature of twentieth-century economics both because international economic relations have concerned transfers of various kinds – reparations, bursts of foreign investment, the accrual of increased income from oil price increases – and because each new wave of theorising such as international Keynesianism was applied to the problem. In all cases the transfer of capital from one country to another meant that there must be a net export of goods and services to match the amount of the long-term financial transaction, or, to put it another way, if country A was going to transfer capital to country B it must generate a current account surplus, which was matched by a current account deficit in B. In the twentieth-century literature, the mechanics of the capital transfer were analysed in both classical and Keynesian terms. In the former, which assumed full employment, perfectly competitive markets with flexible prices, and a fixed exchange rate, the question at issue was whether the transferring country could generate a large enough current account surplus to effect the transfer without suffering a deterioration in its terms of trade. In the latter, with elastic supplies of labour and commodities and a fixed price level, the question was whether or not the transfer could be effected without further changes in the level of income or the exchange rate.[12] There was a subsidiary question as to whether the adjustment in the terms of trade or the exchange rate would tend to restore equilibrium and whether the improvement could be large enough to meet the relevant surplus or deficit. This second part of

---

[12] Or, to put it another way, will the financing and disposal of the transfer in the two countries equal, fall short of, or exceed the amount of the transfer, or, again, whether the transfer is effected, undereffected, or overeffected.

the analysis was really a question about the stability of the exchange market when it was subject to a shock equivalent to the over- or undereffected transfer.

The standard classical caricature of the transfer problem was that the transfer would be under-effected and the terms of trade would turn against the country undertaking the transfer. A particularly pessimistic example of such a view had been Keynes's March 1929 discussion of Germany's ability to pay reparations – a view that was challenged by Bertil Ohlin and others in subsequent issues of the *Economic Journal*. In the Keynesian literature developed after the publication of the *General Theory*, particularly by Lloyd Metzler (1942) and Fritz Machlup (1943), the developing consensus conceded that "it all depends," but tended to be more optimistic than Keynes in 1929.

In his paper (1956e) Harry compared the classical and Keynesian models. He found that there was no presumption for the terms of trade to turn one way or another in the classical: It all depended on the preferences of the receiving or transferring country. Transfer costs or impediments to trade would further complicate the analysis. The same (it all depends) was true in the Keynesian case, but the presumption was, unlike the Metzler–Machlup case, that the transfer would normally be undereffected. He then moved to the second part of the story: Under what conditions, if the transfer was under- or overeffected, would the disequilibrium in the balance of payments be removed? In the classical case, the exchange market would be stable if the sum of the price elasticities for imports in the countries concerned was greater than unity – the famous Marshall–Lerner condition for devaluation to improve the trade balance. In the Keynesian case, the sum of the price elasticities for imports had to be equivalent to unity plus the sum of the marginal propensities to import in the two countries.

The Theory of International Trade

Harry's paper on the transfer problem furnishes a link to his work in the theory of international trade, where he was also extremely active. Here he did what most economists do, namely take an existing problem and improve the profession's understanding of it, but in Harry's case the improvement in understanding was substantial. Harry described his analysis as having

two major functions, both of which are comprised in the scientific objective of simplicity of generalization. The first is to push the application of known and tested techniques into new areas, thus extending the range of the analytical apparatus built up by the labours of successive economic theorists. The second is to review the existing literature with the double object of verifying the accuracy of accepted conclusions and synthesizing the methods and results of previous writers into a simpler, more readily usable analysis. (*ITEG*, 9)

This was "unenthusiasm" as a way of professional life (see discussion in Chapter 5). At the same time, however, there was a certain nihilism in Harry's work. As Richard Lipsey put it:

Harry's work on pure trade in the 1950s . . . consisted of a series of case studies in which an extremely ingenious and subtle mind found exceptions to virtually all of the qualitative "laws" of international economics with which he was presented. (1978, S37)

What was the source of this nihilism, which was not apparent in his undergraduate or postgraduate courses? My suspicion is that it was a product of his Cambridge experience after 1949 and contemporary welfare economics, particularly the work of Jan Graaff. Graaff was a fellow faculty member who submitted a doctoral dissertation on welfare economics in 1951 before leaving the profession. A group of Graaff's friends persuaded him to allow the publication of his thesis in an unrevised form provided that they saw it through the press. It appeared from Cambridge University Press in 1958 under the title *Theoretical Welfare Economics*.

The book was an examination of the formal theory of welfare economics and its limitations. The limitations, in fact, proved to be so severe that Graaff concluded

I do feel that the greatest contribution economics is likely to make to human welfare, broadly conceived, is through positive studies – through contributing to our understanding of how the economic system actually works in practice – rather than through normative welfare theory itself. . . .

No doubt many professional economists are reluctant to abdicate what they may like to regard as their traditional prescriptive role and are unhappy at becoming mere purveyors of information. If they are, it is up to them to show how welfare economics can be set up upon a basis which is reasonably satisfactory – or can be made to yield conclusions with which a significant number of men are likely to concur. (1958, 170–1)

When it came to specific injunctions such as marginal cost pricing,

the conditions which have to be met before it is correct (from a welfare standpoint) to set price equal to marginal cost in a particular industry are so restrictive that they are unlikely to be satisfied in practice. The survival of the marginal cost pricing principle is probably no more than an indication of the extent to which the majority of professional economists are ignorant of the assumptions required for its validity.... I suggest that the only price a public enterprise or nationalised industry can be expected to set is what we may as well call a *just price*. (154–5)

Graaff was not alone: Amartya Sen remarked of the work of Graaff and others:

Nihilism has been the dominant note in a number of studies of welfare economics bearing, as Baumol [1965, 2] puts it, "an ill concealed resemblance to obituary notices." (1970, 58)

However, the direct Cambridge influence would probably been have been stronger on Harry. Given these attitudes and the subject matter of international trade theory, the nihilism is not surprising.

In the years after World War II, there was considerable talk of a dollar shortage. The manifestation of the shortage was persistent balance-of-payments deficits with the United States – deficits that could with hindsight be traced back to the interwar period. However, rather than being seen as the result of a series of particular historical circumstances, economists' explanations of the shortage tended to assume a more general theoretical origin stemming from deep-seated structural forces – a secular tendency towards greater stagnation in the United States than elsewhere; low elasticities of demand and supply in international trade; the greater dependence of the rest of the world on the United States than vice versa; an international demonstration effect encouraging non-Americans to try to live beyond their means; more rapid innovation and growth of productivity in the United States than elsewhere, and so on. The notion had become sufficiently common currency at the end of the war for Maynard Keynes to devote his last paper to debunk the notion – a version of which Harry had heard and commented on in his first meeting of the Political Economy Club in February 1946 (see discussion in Chapter 3). The first books and serious articles on the problem began to appear at the end of the 1940s, and the flow continued for a decade with economists such as Thomas Balogh, Charles Kindleberger, Roy Harrod, John Henry Williams, and Donald MacDougall all making contributions to its explanation. John Hicks devoted his "Inaugural Lecture" as Drummond Professor of Political Economy at Oxford to the problem (1953).

In his Cambridge period, Harry devoted two major articles to the subject: "Increasing Productivity, Income-Price Trends and the Trade Balance" (1954d) and "Economic Expansion and International Trade" (1955). The latter, based on three lectures delivered in Manchester in December 1954, not only secured a second invitation to fill the Manchester chair in Economic Theory but was also "the Johnson article that has had the biggest impact on trade theory" (Corden 1984, 569), where "Harry probably came as close as he ever did in the real theory of trade to being seminal" (Lipsey 1978, S39).

In his first paper he considered "one theoretical explanation of the dollar shortage," which attributed it to the effects of the rapid increase in American productivity in lowering the money prices of American goods relative to the prices of goods produced elsewhere." He reached several conclusions. First,

[i]t is necessary to recognize that increasing productivity affects the American trade balance in two ways, and not just one as this theory implies. In addition to its effects on relative prices of American and foreign goods, increasing productivity raises American real income and therefore – unless American imports are inferior goods in American consumption – increases American demand for imports.... Consequently, in so far as proponents of this theory emphasize the high rate of increase of American productivity *per se*, rather than its alleged effects on relative prices, their analysis is misleading or wrong. (*ITEG*, 114–15)

Second,

with regard to the effect of increasing American productivity on the relative price of American and foreign goods, the assumption that relatively falling American prices turn the trade balance of the United States in its favour necessarily implies that the elasticities of international demand are high enough for a devaluation against the dollar to improve the trade balance of the rest of the world with the United States. (*ITEG*, 115)

Third,

[n]othing in the argument presented here ... contradicts the proposition that productivity and price trends in the world economy may lead to a chronic dollar shortage of the type described. Indeed, our analysis points to a number of factors which may contribute to this result. (*ITEG*, 115)

As usual, anything can happen: One needs quantitative restrictions on the values of the parameters to make predictions.

The Manchester "Economic Expansion" lectures, which appeared in a very compressed form in the *Manchester School* and were further revised for *International Trade and Economic Growth*, sought to generalise and extend the earlier case. The world consisted of two countries Mancunia, which exported manufactures, the income elasticity of demand for which was greater than one, and Agraria, which exported foodstuffs with an income elasticity of demand of less than one. In the first two sections of the paper, labour, capital, and technology were immobile. In part I there was complete specialisation in the production of one good in each economy; in part II there was incomplete specialisation. Agriculture was labour intensive and subject to diminishing returns to scale. Part III relaxed the complete immobility assumption. The concerns of the analysis were two: (i) whether a particular sort of economic expansion will increase the demand for imports by less or more than proportionately to the rise in output; (ii) under what conditions will the adverse terms of trade required to maintain equilibrium outweigh the rise in output and lead to a fall in income.

In part I, the analysis opened with Mancunia growing and Agraria static. Growth in Mancunia would turn the terms of trade against it, and the extent of that shift will determine how the benefit of that growth is distributed internationally. Given the rate of growth of Mancunia, the rate of deterioration of the terms of trade would be higher the higher its marginal propensity to spend on food and the greater the price elasticity of world demand for manufactures. One could conceive of a situation in which greater satiation in the demand for manufactures would lead to an increasingly rapid deterioration in Mancunia's terms of trade, eventually reaching a point at which further growth would actually reduce its real income, but one could conceive of other possibilities.

In part II, the analysis became more complex with five possible causes of expansion.[13] The effects of each type of expansion were measured for each country in terms of its effects on production, consumption, and overall for each country. The analysis allowed for five types of trade effects: neutral, pro-trade biased, ultra-pro-trade biased, anti-trade biased, and ultra-anti-trade biased. What was being measured was whether the supply of exportables increased in proportion to output, in more than proportion to the rise in output, reduced the supply of importables absolutely, increased the supply of exportables less than importables in proportion to the rise in output, or reduced the supply of exportables absolutely. The analysis was dense and detailed but extremely rich with fifteen possible net effects. The general conclusions were

that expansion will tend to increase Mancunia's demand for imports and reduce Agraria's demand for imports, except possibly when *either* expansion is due to technical progress which is not proceeding much more rapidly in industry than in agriculture, *or* expansion is due to population growth and agriculture is subject to

[13] (i)   technical progress
         a) classical (in industry only)
         b) equal
  (ii)   capital accumulation
 (iii) population increase
         a) slightly diminishing returns
         b) strongly diminishing returns

slightly diminishing returns. Apart from these last two cases, expansion in either country will tend to turn the terms of trade against Mancunia and in favour of Agraria. (*ITEG*, 83)

The final section, relaxing the factor immobility assumption of the first two parts, looked in turn at technology transfers, migration, and capital flows. The analysis is concerned with

the difference it would make to a country's (specifically Mancunia's) international trade position if advances in technical knowledge in that country were communicated and applied to the other country as well, if capital were invested abroad instead of at home or if labour emigrated instead of remaining at home. (*ITEG*, 84)

This reduced the complications but allowed comparison with the previous results. Again the analysis is extraordinarily rich and complex, making one wonder how much the listeners to this verbal presentation (there were no diagrams and only one table) took in at the time. Fortunately, Harry summarised the trade and growth literature in "Economic Development and International Trade" (1959c) "leaving behind the verbal density and excessive taxonomy of the earlier article" and adding "some neat diagrams" (Corden 1984, 570).

Before leaving Harry's Cambridge contributions to international economics, I should look at his optimum tariff articles. In the interwar period, the imposition of tariffs by Great Britain, the American programme of reciprocal trade agreements, and other tariff changes led to a revival of interest in the use of tariffs as a bargaining weapon. A number of classic articles by Paul Samuelson, Nicholas Kaldor, and others were concerned with the implications of national attempts to improve economic welfare by imposing tariffs. Their culmination was Tibor Scitovsky's "A Reconsideration of the Theory of Tariffs" (1942), which demonstrated that the imposition of tariffs by one country increases the probability that retaliatory tariffs would improve welfare in the other; nonetheless, the result of all countries following the same policy would be a reduction in welfare.

After the war, optimum tariff articles became something of a Cambridge Keynesian cottage industry with contributions from Joan Robinson, Richard Kahn, and Jan Graaff – the last extending into the theory of the optimum tariff structure. In this context, Harry wrote "Optimum Welfare and Maximum Revenue Tariffs" (1951d). There he set out to do three things: to develop alternative forms of the optimum welfare tariff formula;[14] to develop a formula for the maximum revenue tariff and to determine that "the optimum

[14] Harry had assistance from Jan Graaff with this section of the article.

revenue tariff will be at least as high as, and generally higher than, the optimum welfare tariff" (1951d, 33); and to draw some possible implications of the last proposition for tariff policy.

The purpose of "Optimum Tariffs and Retaliation" (1954b) was ostensibly "to re-assert the proposition that a country *may* gain by imposing a tariff even if other countries retaliate; and to determine the conditions under which it *will* gain in a special group of cases" (*ITEG*, 31). The original assertion was made by Kaldor in a 1940 note in *Economica*. Harry restated the theory of optimum tariffs in the context of a two-country, two-commodity exchange model where the retaliation for any tariff change takes the form of an optimum tariff on the assumption that the other country's tariff remains unchanged. The analysis was thorough and his reworking of the Scitovsky results proved that all would not lose.

Whatever the final equilibrium point, one country *must* lose under tariffs as compared with free trade; since gain depends on obtaining an improvement in the terms of trade sufficient to outweigh the loss of trade volume, and this is impossible for both countries simultaneously; and both countries *may* lose . . . ; but it is not necessarily true that both will lose. (*ITEG*, 46).

Harry could even demonstrate the *possibility* of one country being better off under optimum tariffs than under free trade, even if it was impossible to state the condition "in terms of simple and objectively assessable concepts" (*ITEG*, 47). However there was one special case where it was possible to establish the required conditions, which he demonstrated with an ingenious numerical example:

As an example, if the elasticity of country I's demand for imports were 2.0, country I would be better off under tariffs than under free trade if the elasticity of country II's demand were 1.5 or less; both countries would be worse off if the elasticity of country II's demand lay between 1.6 and 2.8 inclusive; while country II would be better off under tariffs than under free trade if (country I's elasticity remaining at 2.0) its elasticity of demand for imports were 2.9 or greater. (1954b, 152)

When he came to revise the paper in 1957 for inclusion in *International Trade and Economic Growth*, he was able to take advantage of a forthcoming article in the *Review of Economic Studies* by W. M. Gorman, "Tariffs, Retaliation and the Elasticity of Demand for Imports," to deal with four special cases and get a result:

Taken together, the special cases . . . suggest that the scope for one country to benefit from optimum tariff retaliation is greater the more internationally traded goods are luxuries in the country of destination, and the likelihood of a country actually gaining is greater the more its exports are a luxury in world consumption and the higher is the elasticity of import demand relative to the foreign elasticity; but if both elasticities are low, the country may gain even though its demand for imports is less elastic than the other country's. (*ITEG*, 54–5)

His conclusion remained the same. It was particularly nihilistic.

The implication,[15] as in so many problems in the theory of international economic policy, is that the answer depends on the circumstances of the case, and that anyone who asserts that one conclusion is universally valid is making an explicit assumption about the facts which ought to be explicitly defended – if it can be. (*ITEG*, 55)

With the increased use of game theory in international trade theory, this 1954 paper has come to be seen as pioneering in that direction (Brander 1995, 1398; Staiger 1995, 1512).

Leaving from Cambridge

Harry enjoyed Cambridge and its opportunities, but there was almost always an undertone of dissatisfaction. To some extent this was a reflection of his insecurity. Offers or talk of offers from outside were reassuring. However, there were also economic pressures, especially when the arrival of children (Ragnar in 1949 and Karen in 1951) and the inflation following the devaluation of sterling in September 1949 and the outbreak of the Korean War in June 1950 put pressure on what once might have been a generous salary. There was also intellectual isolation.

When he first arrived in Cambridge, he commented on Thomas Balogh's observation in conversation on the dullness of Cambridge as compared with Harvard

There is something in this, I think – the War left a large gap, in terms of both people and research, and since then much time has been taken up with government business. . . . Richard Stone's Department of Applied Economics has been the only active element in economic research. (Box 44, Correspondence 1949–56, HGJ to A. H. Hansen, 18 March 1949)

Later in the year, things began to improve.

Cambridge is returning to something like normal academic pursuits. We have several new lecturers and assistant lecturers, and a longer lecture list. Kaldor has finally

[15] [Original footnote] "A further implication . . . which is too obvious to deserve elaboration is that optimum tariff theory is not a very useful approach to the explanation of tariff history. Contrast Scitovszky."

come back,[16] but he is lecturing from his pre-war lecture notes as yet. We have a junior faculty seminar in operation which helps stimulate research and altogether we have become more brisk and alert than when I first arrived. [University of Toronto Archives, Department of Political Economy Records, A76-0025/034(01), to G. A. Eliott, 20 January 1950]

In a letter to Innis in which he reported that he had "after much thought" turned down the offer of an assistant professorship at Harvard and that he had "more than a dozen notes and articles either published or in process of publication in the last two years," he commented:

I find the supervision system here makes it difficult to work effectively, since one is always being interrupted for teaching. We also have a number of seminars, and as I have become interested in econometrics I go to two a week – not to mention unofficial meetings with members of the faculty which takes up time. I am also bothered by the rising cost of living, which obliges me to take up outside activities such as book reviewing for the Economist; fortunately in England one can do this thing at a high enough level not to make it a waste of time. [University of Toronto Archives, Department of Political Economy Records, A76-0025/009(05), to H. A. Innis, 20 April 1951]

Later in the year, referring to his forthcoming visit to Toronto, he wrote to Vincent Bladen:

I am looking forward very much to coming back to work among my sometime colleagues and friends, both from a personal desire to renew contacts and from a need for a change from the English and Cambridge atmosphere. One needs a fresh group of people and a fresh set of problems to make continued progress. [University of Toronto Archives, Department of Political Economy Records, A65-005/001(10), to V. W. Bladen, 14 November 1951]

The next spring he was gossiping with James Tobin (Box 32, 29 March 1952) about a possible move to Nuffield College, Oxford, which Tobin said "sounds good." Indeed, after consulting with John Hicks in May, he went so far as to apply for the fellowship, but subsequently withdrew his application (Box 54, Bank Structure Draft, to J. R. Hicks, 6 October 1952).

Meanwhile, there was a chair in economic theory open at Manchester. R. M. Goodwin had turned it down in the spring of 1952. Harry was offered it the next year, but declined. Early in 1954 he was approached about joining the Economic Section of the Treasury under Robert Hall. According to Hall, "He would like to come but is not free at present" [Robbins Papers, Staff

---

[16] He had left LSE (which had been in Cambridge during the war) in 1947 for the United Nations Economic Commission for Europe and returned to academic life in England as a fellow of King's and university lecturer in economics in 1949.

(1950–7) File II, Robert Hall to Lionel Robbins, 11 May 1954]. He was offered the Manchester chair again at the end of 1954 after his trade and growth lectures.[17] This time he took it with effect from April 1956, which would allow him to take a term's leave from Cambridge to visit Northwestern and Stanford. James Tobin remarked on the result that

> any congratulations regarding the chair at Manchester should go to Manchester and to [Arthur] Lewis. Does this irrevocably tie you to England. I ask because the grapevine tells me that there is a good chance you would be offered, were you interested, a permanent post at Harvard. Harvard needs someone in money and banking, fiscal policy and employment theory, now that Hansen and Williams retire. Harvard isn't Yale, but it would be pleasant to have you in Cambridge, New England. (Box 44, Correspondence 1949–56,17 January 1954)

At the time his appointment took effect, he was the youngest professor of economics in the United Kingdom.[18]

Harry later reported his dissatisfaction with Cambridge as one reason for his departure for Manchester:

> I became increasingly dissatisfied with Cambridge – my colleagues seemed stuck in dead monetary controversies, or immersed in growth models with little relevance to the real world. I was getting intellectual stimulation from my students and from American visitors. I therefore decided to accept the Manchester offer when it was renewed. (1969 Autobiographical Notes, 9)

There is some contemporary evidence to support this retrospective comment. On 20 June 1955, while Harry was in America, Robin Marris wrote:

> Rumours have got back to Cambridge, no doubt exaggerated and distorted, that in the Provinces you let it be known that the main reason why you are taking this job is that you are fed up with Cambridge and that it is too cliquy and you are unwillingly forced to take sides. This has not caused amusement. As a rather indiscreet chap myself I know exactly how one comes to say these things, but watch it chum. (Box 44, Correspondence 1949–66)

There was also another factor at work. His prospects for advancement in Cambridge were at best bleak. The last reader appointed had been Nicholas Kaldor, who had obtained the post at the age of 44. Joan Robinson had been a few months younger when she got hers in 1947. If Harry were to be as high a flier as they were, it would be 1967 before he would find preferment, and

---

[17] In his 1969 Autobiographical Notes (99), Harry states that he gave these lectures during the 1953–4 academic year. He also mistakenly states that he gave two rather than three lectures and that these "established me as a trade theorist."

[18] Data from the *Commonwealth Universities Yearbook, 1958*, which reflected the position in 1957, and *Who's Who*.

there were indications that he was regarded as technically very good but not as original. Manchester would give him an opportunity to make his mark.

To judge from the surviving correspondence, among his contemporaries in Cambridge, Harry was closest to Jan Graaff. With him Harry organised a self-teaching group to work their way through Samuelson's *Foundations of Economic Analysis* (*Shadow*, 98; Samuelson 1998, 1378). His relations with the older generation were mixed. He regularly sent pieces to D. H. Robertson and regularly got comments in return. Among the next generation, Richard Kahn was aloof and reserved and in many ways uninterested. Joan Robinson was preoccupied with ploughing her own furrow and not interested in Harry's work unless it related to hers. Richard Stone was more forthcoming and supportive, as we have seen. Kaldor was stimulating and cooperative, but always competitive. Harry and Brian Reddaway never really hit it off. Thus, with the exception of Robertson and Stone, Harry's later recollection that "I received no assistance whatsoever from my seniors in the Faculty, and especially those in my own College, in the way of comments on my early professional papers" (*Shadow*, 97–8) rings true. One must also remember, however, the enabling role played by Austin Robinson in terms of opportunities, but he was not a stimulus or a critic.

Later, when Richard Lipsey was considering coming to King's as a fellow and asked for advice, Harry summed up his experience:

It is on the professional side that you will have the real trouble. . . . To take first things first, you may find that you are under-estimating the teaching load. . . . Again, since everything funnels through the faculty board, and since Cambridge does not have much in the way of graduates anyway (and these go straight to the thesis) you might find yourself without students to talk to, unless you went to the trouble of collecting them yourself. This was the most discouraging thing to me, and one which drove me to theory more than anything else; in King's, Nicky preempted the graduates in his own seminar, and I got only odd balls to supervise aside from that.

I would also be suspicious of the idea that the D. A. E. is lying there with all its facilities ready for use. It is not so easy as that, because the Director, Reddaway, is pretty well determined not to pay for any research that does not give answers he can predict before he starts. . . . The chief problem I had was over my Economica paper on money supply [1959a]; Reddaway turned it down flat when I mentioned it to him many years ago, and that sort of killed my interest.[19] . . .

Summing up . . . in terms of career, I think you would gain by going there; but you would have to fight harder than you think to get access to the facilities and help you want. My own experience was that I never got any genuine help when I needed it, only pats on the back when I had solved my problems; and I often didn't see

[19] He did the work when he got to Manchester "where as professor I had a little money to waste on fractious frivolity" (1976n, 299).

colleagues for weeks or months on end. On the other hand it was possible to arrange private self-teaching groups and we did a lot of that.

The main thing you have to realise is that in Cambridge every man is his own entrepreneur. On the other hand, everyone is shielded from everyone else's intrusion by his ability to retreat into his own college and stay there. (Box 31, Correspondence to 1963 H–L, to R. G. Lipsey, 12 February 1960)

SEVEN

Manchester

The department Harry joined in April 1956 was large: It had twenty-two members – economists, economic historians, and statisticians.[1] It had a distinguished history: Its undergraduate commerce degree had been far more successful than the more loudly trumpeted but less rigorous one at Birmingham (Tribe 1993, 185); its distinguished faculty had made important contributions to the subject and to British public life – one need only think of William Stanley Jevons, A. W. Flux, S. J. Chapman, and C. F. Bickerdike of the pre-1914 era or John Hicks, John Jewkes, Harry Campion, Henry Clay, and T. S. Ashton from the interwar department; and it had an important research tradition with a separate research unit dating from the interwar period, which had been able to attract promising researchers early in their careers. Harry's new professorial colleagues included one future Nobel Laureate, W. Arthur Lewis, and Ely Devons, a distinguished applied economist. The quality of his juniors was also high – most of the lecturers and assistant lecturers would retire from chairs – something not all that common in 1950s departments, despite British and overseas university expansion in the 1960s. However, the department's economics programmes were relatively small, and much of its teaching served other programmes such as commerce. It offered a BA, MA, and PhD in economics, but in 1955–6 there had been only thirteen BAs, five MAs, and three PhDs awarded.

The University of Manchester was smaller than Cambridge, with a full-time enrolment of less than 5,000 if one excluded the rather anomalous Faculty of Technology which for four decades would become part of a separate institution only to merge with the university in 2004. It had a distinguished record of scholarship in the sciences – with Nobel Prizes to show for it such as Ernest Rutherford, Lawrence Bragg, and P. M. S. Blackett – and in the

---

[1] There was also a separate agricultural economics group of seven.

humanities – whose faculty had included Sir Lewis Namier and Dorothy Emmet – and, at the time Harry arrived was providing strong leadership in areas such as computing (F. C. Williams who had brought Alan Turing to Manchester) and radio astronomy (Bernard Lovell).

But it was not Cambridge. Like the city, the university's buildings were soot-encrusted and bleak.[2] "[T]he dense fogs, industrial filth and bronchitic sub-climate ... depressed newcomers"(Pullen 2000, 4). It was "intolerably smoky" (Kermode 1995, 208). In Harry's case, even though the Johnsons lived out on the Cheshire fringe at Cheadle, the northernmost outpost of the home counties, which was more salubrious[3] and had the advantage of good train connections to London, the climate combined with his history of pneumonia and bronchitis helped him to quit smoking.[4] The straw that broke the camel's back was *Life* magazine's lurid pictures of a smoker's lungs which he encountered on his July 1956 flight to Karachi. He quit, cold turkey. The pangs of withdrawal were tempered by his fascination with the East. Without cigarettes he took up more seriously a childhood hobby, small-scale wood carving, to see him through the interminable academic meetings and give him a sense of having accomplished something. Just before he left Manchester, between 24 June and 24 July 1959, he mounted "Pocket Pieces" an exhibition of fifty-five of his carvings at Gibb's Bookshop (Plate 6). Harry regarded the exhibition as "very successful ... though mostly because we have given the thing a 'giving up smoking' angle" (Perkins Library, Duke University, Baumol Papers, to W. J. Baumol, 6 July 1959). The exhibition got him appearances on both radio and television, as well as mentions in four newspapers. It also solved the packing problem for America, as the whole show was bought up by friends and other attenders who eagerly paid one or two pounds each (Elizabeth Simpson, 26 July 2005).

---

[2] When the main University building was cleaned in the early 1970s everyone was astonished to discover that it had bright coloured tiles rather than black slate on the roof. Pevsner (1969, 309–10) does not mention the Waterhouse roof; Clare Hartwell (2001, 112) provides photographs of the tiles.

[3] David Laidler recalls in 1970 one could "leave our house in Bramhall – about 2 miles south of Cheadle – in broad daylight and bright sunshine, and have to turn on the headlights as one crossed the Mersey at Stockport or approached Didsbury."

[4] One need only remember his hospitalisation in 1945 and his pneumonia in Toronto in 1952. Later, as he told Stephanie Edge, a former student, in 1966: "I always found that the approach of Christmas was the absolute low point of the English academic year. ... For at least three years ... before I went to Manchester, I spent at least a week prostrate in bed, unable to talk through loss of voice" (Box 56, Correspondence 1964–6, A–L, 21 February 1966).

In 1954 he also managed to combine bronchitis and examining (Box 33, Review of Economic Studies, from Ursula Hicks, 12 June 1954).

Most of the university was concentrated west of the Oxford Road "a noisy thoroughfare and tramway, dangerous to tangle with in the infamous Manchester fogs" (Pullen 2000, 65). However, the university had started to cross the divide. The department of economics, which shared the superannuated 1881 Girls' High School in Dover Street with the rest of the Faculty of Economic and Social Studies, as well as education, music, and law, was on the east side of Oxford Road. There the university lived cheek-by-jowl with the locals: Dover Street was in the red light district. The faculty was surrounded by terraces of two-up two-down houses with the associated shops, factories, and churches. It was deprived inner-city squalor, much of which would be swept away in the university's expansion in the sciences and replaced with nondescript products of the 1950s and 1960 and early 1970s. But the terraces of Ardwick, immediately adjacent to Dover Street survived until the early 1970s, so the view from the windows remained "pure Lowry" until then (information from David Laidler). When Lionel Brett surveyed civic university architecture for the *Architectural Review* in 1957, Manchester had four buildings, "most of its programme to date," singled out for criticism: They were "the monumental record of the failure of nerve in academic patronage, envelopes of red brick and stone enveloping an entirely vacuous concept of who, what and where a university is" (Pullen 2000, 68–9). And it continued. Nikolaus Pevsner wrote a decade later

Manchester University has been timid, and there are more buildings to be marvelled at for their reactionary style or their readiness to be just utilitarian than buildings to be praised. (1969, 54–5)

Architecturally, it is a sad record. If the University of Liverpool has asked too many architects to design their buildings and the result is a lack of unity, the University of Manchester has shown too little initiative, too easy a sense of satisfaction, and the result is lack of architectural interest.... Manchester University has too much that is just run of the mill. This is the justification for the following perambulation giving for many buildings no more than architect and date. (1969, 310)

The second statement has been carried over in large part to the later Pevsner Guides (Hartwell 2001, 107; Hartwell, Hyde, and Pevsner 2004, 425).

According to Frank Kermode, who came to Manchester as professor of English in 1958,

[t]he university had a kind of grim friendliness and a justified assurance of its own value, at a time when the metropolitan claims of Manchester were weakening but still pretty strong.... The mood of the place was always to oppose the south, and the university had, or professed, no inferiority feelings about the ancient universities; if bright people came to Manchester, sharpened their talents, and left for Oxbridge, that was their business, and they might well come to repent their foolishness in

leaving a serious place for institutions that devoted themselves to feasts and gaudies. (1995, 205)

The students too differed from those at Cambridge. They were over-whelmingly the products of grammar schools financed by local education authorities; whereas in Cambridge they were most likely to come from pub-lic [private] schools or the 175 quasi-independent direct grant schools, who received grants direct from the national government to admit by competi-tive examination up to half of their pupils whose fees were paid directly to the schools, the remainder being private fee-payers (Halsey 1992, 78).[5] They were two and a half to three times as likely to come from families of manual workers than their Cambridge counterparts (Halsey and Trow 1971, 73). Once they entered the university they would enjoy fewer amenities. They would also receive smaller state grants than Cambridge students – £225 as compared with £325 (74). There was less space in halls of residence than in Cambridge colleges (or for that matter other provincial universities), and it was generally of lower quality (Pullen 2000, 80). Given that the majority of Manchester students came from Lancashire and Cheshire, many chose to live at home rather than in halls of residence or lodgings, which were in short supply in the 1950s. By the early 1960s, even though new halls of residence had been built and the availability of digs exceeded the demand, a quarter of the student population lived at home (115). The university's attitude towards students also differed:

Until the early 1960s proof of attendance at lectures rather than seminars was consid-ered necessary to satisfy educational authorities that the grants they paid were being properly used, and that a student's work and attendance were adequate. Attendance lists were circulated for signature at lectures, although it was easy to falsify them. (57)

In economics, the lecturing was of high standard, but the availability, and quality, of seminars was variable, and there were few opportunities for essay writing and discussion – much less advice on academic or personal problems (60, 62).

Nor was the university like Cambridge in its governance. The department was the basic unit of the system. Within departments, life revolved around the professors, all of whom were normally treated as equals – the term head of department being rare – who organised the affairs of the unit.

---

[5] Many of the direct grant schools were old, established day grammar schools noted for their high academic standards such as those in Manchester, Bristol, and Bradford.

Professors were at liberty to call staff meetings and consult with them if they would, but were under no constitutional obligation to do so, and not bound to regard expressions of opinion by such meetings as tying their hands. (9)

Professors might have some power and responsibility, not to mention some status in the community, but they were not allowed much freedom by the central administration – the vice chancellor, registrar, treasurer, librarian, chancellor, and chair of the council.

To most people then in high authority it seemed undesirable that academics should be required to be businessmen or administrators on a large scale, to raise funds, manage budgets or wade through heavy paperwork other than examination scripts. They should devote themselves to the things they did best, leaving the world of action and affairs to other, more worldly beings, like a medieval religious community entrusting the defence of their monastery and estates to lay protectors. (11)

The senior administrators who counted were largely Mancunians who had grown up in the university. The members of the governing oligarchy transacted business by word of mouth. They were visible and they were available. Given his Apostles' paper (recall discussion in Chapter 5), Harry would have been amused at some of their habits:

The Registrar, the Bursar and the Librarian would generally repair to Staff House between half-past ten and eleven o'clock of a morning, do the *Times* crossword jointly with one of them acting as scribe, and make themselves available to discussion with anyone from any part of the University who cared to approach them. The great men of the University were also on display at lunch time, for the oak-panelled dining room of Staff House contained a high table on a dais, where the senior administrators and the professors sat; the high table waitresses went to the front of the queue to ensure that their charges were promptly served, in advance of the lesser beings below the salt. Only professors of exceptionally liberal outlook ... would defy convention by choosing to eat with their junior colleagues and friends. (19–20)

According to contemporaries, including Harry, Ely Devons was able to operate very successfully within this system (24). W. J. M. Mackenzie, the professor of government, wrote of Devons:

Manchester University meant a great deal to him symbolically; indeed it was in its symbolic form one of the few things he treated with deference. The quirks of university politics gave him as much sport as those of Whitehall politics,[6] and he was in no sense the leader of a reform caucus. But he thought naturally in university terms, not simply in those of discipline or department; and his voice, quiet but insistent, carried great weight in many different spheres of university life. (quoted in Cairncross 1970, 22–3)

---

[6] He had spent his war in the Ministry of Aircraft Production.

Others found it bewildering. Charles Carter, later a vice chancellor himself, who came in 1959 as Stanley Jevons Professor to succeed Arthur Lewis recalled:

I think there were faults in Manchester. Maybe a problem of size or of structure. To start with, there was the Faculty of Economic and Social Studies which really consisted of warring departments. ... Manchester was very difficult to get hold of. This was true of the University as a whole. I mean it rapidly became apparent that the machinery of the University and the Senate[7] and all that had absolutely no connection with what actually happened. Everything was cut and dried before it got to the Senate. Where it was cut and dried nobody knew! But it was. And it was true in the Department that there was a lack of sense of community. We were a lot of individuals beavering away ... and we didn't exploit our advantages anything like to the extent we should have done. (Tribe 1997, 151)

During Harry's Manchester period, Arthur Lewis was away, initially on research leave and then as adviser to the president of Ghana. Ely Devons, the other professor of economics was dean of the Faculty of Economic and Social Studies, a post he had held since 1949. Of Devons, Alec Cairncross wrote:

To those who did not know him personally he was not a particular significant figure. ... But to those who did know him how different the impression he conveyed! Few more formidable in debate on public affairs; few more intellectually stimulating; not given to writing easily but always in command of the relevant facts; never willing to bow to received opinion without question or to accept that what actually went on must be what everyone assumed to go on; and yet possessed with an acute and firm judgment rooted in common sense. He loved debating and was given to paradox and skittishness. ... Behind it all there was a rare integrity which gave him at times the air of a prophet. (1970, 1)

The other professorial colleagues who put their stamp on the faculty were Max Gluckman, the professor of social anthropology; W. J. M. Mackenzie, the professor of government; and Michael Polanyi, the physical chemist who had been given a chair in social science. Dorothy Emmet, the philosopher, also took an active part in the faculty's intellectual life. As a group, the seniors believed in the unity of the social sciences, and they were not afraid to cross disciplinary boundaries or attend each others' seminars outside their disciplines – to everyone's mutual benefit. One of the exemplars of cross-disciplinarity was *Closed Systems and Open Minds: The Limits of Naivety in Social Anthropology*, published in 1964. It consisted of a series of essays written during 1958–9. The main concern of the essays was what was common in

---

[7] Consisting until 1963 of only professors.

the methods and analyses of social anthropologists and what related them to or distinguished them from other social scientists. The enterprise was such that Gluckman and Devons together contributed both an introduction and a concluding commentary to the essays. Harry was thanked in the introduction of the finally published book for his constructive criticism of the papers.

Harry, like many arriving from elsewhere to take over a department, which he did in effect given Lewis's leave and Devons's deanship, found adjustment to the chair difficult. After he left Manchester, his former colleague, Jack Johnston, the econometrician who had just been appointed to Ely Devons's chair after the latter's departure for the London School of Economics, enquired about the advisability of moving to the University of British Columbia. Harry naturally provided advice, but he also offered some autobiographical recollections:

Now as to you. I imagine you are going through the hard part of your promotion right now; not just the hangover from being an irresponsible participant observer in someone else's culture to being a responsible citizen of your own, but the whole business of making the dual adjustment of promotion from acted on to chief actor in a hierarchy. You have to fit yourself into the framework left by your predecessors, and at the same time establish your authority with your colleagues at your new level and over those of your old level. It takes time for both and it takes hundreds of almost insignificant acts and decisions, each of which is a strain and an irritation. It took me well into my second year to come to grips with Arthur and Ely, especially the absent one, and to sort out what I needed to take a stand on and what I was prepared to compromise on. There are all sorts of precedents you haven't heard of, considerations that everyone else but you knows of, things that are someone's pet project, etc. you just have to grow into the tradition and the folklore by experience. As to former colleagues, I was lucky to come from outside completely, but there was still a long period of nervousness about how far I was violating past personal relations formed when I was a lecturer like everybody else. That you have to grow into too. And the hardest part is at the beginning, because they are all trying to reassure themselves against the prospect of uncomfortable or demanding change by reiterating all the time how things have always been done, and what was said about a problem in the past, etc....

When I came over here, I was on the same ship as Frankie Hahn.... I told him what I think is true, that if Chicago had come after me in my third year at Manchester instead of the second, I should have stayed there; by that time I had things going the way I wanted to, had worked out relations with Ely, Bill [Mackenzie] and Max [Gluckman], and had participated in enough appointments to feel that it was my Department.

One further point – I stalled Chicago off for that extra year, because I wanted to feel that I had made something of the Chair before I left.

This is turning out to be more about me than you. (Box 31, Correspondence to 1963 Unsorted, 2 December 1959)

Frank Kermode who had one other professorial colleague recalled a similar experience:

In those days…the person arriving to take command of a strange department could rarely expect an unqualified welcome from colleagues who believed themselves, and not without reason, to be at least equally well qualified for the job, and he needed plenty of tact and self-assurance …. Moreover, I didn't understand that malice…can be for others a perfectly usual way of responding to the challenges of private and professional life. Anyway, it was some time before the older hands consented to treat me as something better than an imprudent interloper. (1995, 206)

At Manchester, Harry's main teaching responsibilities involved the introductory principles of economics course and a final year course in monetary theory. Fragments of notes for the former survive. The notes for the latter do not, which is unfortunate in tracing the evolution of Harry's views. This teaching load left him with lots of time for writing, despite his administrative responsibilities.

Manchester's research tradition, plus the available funding, made it possible to attract good research fellows and associates to Manchester. Notable amongst those Harry attracted was Christopher Foster, a Kingsman who had taken firsts in Part I history and Part II economics and spent 1957–9 in Manchester as Hallsworth Research Fellow before going on to Oxford and a distinguished career as a transport and urban economist. There was also S. F. Kaliski, a Canadian who had been a research worker and a graduate student in the Department of Applied Economics in Cambridge before going to Manchester in 1958–9 and then on to Carleton University in Ottawa and Queen's University in Kingston. Finally there was Laurie Hunter, an Oxford doctoral candidate finishing a dissertation on John Stuart Mill during his year as a research associate in Manchester. After military service Hunter became a postdoctoral fellow at Chicago where his interests shifted to labour economics, which he pursued at Glasgow where he became professor of applied economics in 1969.

The faculty seminars were of a high standard. Harry remembered the Devons–Lewis staff seminar as "the most devastatingly critical forum in the country into which a careless economist could wander" (1968c, 13). But the other seminars were as lively. Richard Rose recalled the faculty seminar:

The atmosphere was exciting, and the action fast. A seminar held in a street where Friedrich Engels had kept a mistress and surrounded by two up, two down houses (one of which was the birth place of David Lloyd George) was not a place for small talk, or exquisite analyses of trivia. It was the major league and each presenter of a paper was pushed to explore a chosen topic as far as it could be driven.... There were also informal seminars, described as "discussions held in various environments, some of them not very academic."[8] (1999, 475)

Harry found the interdisciplinarity of Manchester very stimulating. It was in this setting that he first encountered John Kenneth Galbraith's *The Affluent Society* (1958). The book was a best-seller, much to the chagrin of Galbraith's economist colleagues. It struck a chord, particularly among the liberally inclined, and helped shape political discussions and agendas for the better part of a decade.

Galbraith argued that economics had been shaped in a world where poverty was the norm for the populace. Conjoined to that poverty were an inequality in the distribution of income and an insecurity in the receipt of income. The obvious solution was to increase output to mitigate the inadequacy, inequality, and insecurity, but efficiency in the use of resources and the need for capital accumulation placed severe constraints on attempts to mitigate insecurity and inequality.

Production, inequality, and insecurity, the problems of the nineteenth century, were no longer the problems of the twentieth century, Galbraith argued. Technological progress and the modern organisation of the economy had solved the problems of production; rising incomes had reduced inequality, made it less obvious, and reduced its sting; and rising incomes plus increased social consciousness had reduced the problem of instability. But affluence had its own problems. The insistence on the priority of production had left attitudes inimical to sensible social and economic policy: The cult of efficiency produced opposition to measures to reduce income insecurity and with the emphasis on private consumption, strong opposition to the provision of public services and public consumption financed by taxation. Affluence plus the priority of private consumption produced a world where high-powered advertising and other forms of persuasion encouraged individuals to enter the rat race to acquire the means to buy the goods that producers dreamt up for them.

Harry reviewed *The Affluent Society* in *The Spectator* for 19 September 1958. He thought it "an exceptionally provocative book" and "exceptionally witty." However he thought it had problems:

Few people would dispute that Americans as a nation have more money than they know what to do with; but equally few would argue that other countries have reached

[8] Rose's quotation came from W. J. M. Mackenzie's *Politics and Social Science* (1967).

a comparable state of economic saturation. Nor is it obvious, since all 'superior' wants have to be taught, that extra production even in the United States is otiose. One feels that Professor Galbraith is over-generalising from a sample limited in both time and space, and this, together with his excessively self-conscious iconoclasm, makes it difficult to accept the parallel with Tawney's classic [*The Acquisitive Society* (1920)] solicited by the book's title. (1958h, 381)

But Harry was stimulated. He discussed the issues with his Manchester colleagues, and before he left for America he appears to have settled on the "opulent society" as his working phrase – opulence having echoes of Adam Smith – and sketched out his ideas. He did not have a venue until he agreed to give a paper at the annual meetings of the Canadian Political Science Association in Kingston on 10 June 1960.[9] Other papers, embodying other influences, would follow. The result was a powerful series of papers which would culminate in Harry's inaugural lecture at LSE in October 1967 (see discussion in Chapter 9).

During Harry's tenure at Manchester, the economics group split into subdepartments of economics, economic history, and economic statistics – whose smallness and relative isolation caused difficulties later as Charles Carter suggested. The split lasted until 1995, when the sections other than economic history were reunited. Harry extended the academic connections of his colleagues. Manchester became part of the Cambridge-Oxford-London joint seminar. Regular links were established with the University of Liverpool, which also joined the seminar. He added two pedagogical activities to the Manchester program. The first was a seminar run jointly with Brian Chapman, a political scientist, open to all MA students in the faculty. At the time the MA was by dissertation, and the seminar gave them an opportunity to talk about their research and its difficulties.[10] The second was an Easter "reading party" in the Lake District. Ely and Harry between them were the movers of this project, which took some faculty and honours students to Ruskin's old home on Lake Coniston for a five-day period "with the mornings given over to a mixture of informal seminars and discussions, the afternoons to recreation, and the evenings to darts, drink and talk in the congenial Lake District pubs"(Jack Johnston to author, 20 January 2001).

---

[9] "I am at last going to put 'The Political Economy of Opulence' into Print" (Box 31, Correspondence to 1964, A–L, to John Knapp, 23 May 1960).
[10] A course-work MA did not come until after Harry had left.

Christopher Foster, who came to Manchester in 1957, spent his first months there living with the Johnsons before marrying and becoming a neighbour. He found Harry very demanding of his time in the evenings, which were characterised by long discussions of economics and gossip lubricated by whisky. He finally stopped going when his new wife put her foot down. By this stage Harry was beginning to drink too heavily, not to incapacitation but, perhaps, to provide enough isolation for intellectual achievement. His drinking and the necessity of running a car meant that his professorial salary was never enough, and he again took outside jobs such as regular reviewing for the *Spectator* in 1958–9. Nonetheless,

as a result of never earning more than the equivalent of U.S. $7000 a year, heavily taxed, and with a family to support, I had been unable to accumulate any capital whatsoever, and my children were approaching an age at which money would become useful to improve their educational opportunities. (1969 Autobiographical Notes, 11)

Asian Encounter

The move to Manchester coincided with Harry's first visit to Asia. He had almost gone in 1953 when he had been asked if he would fly out to Bangkok for two months (August and September) to write the chapter dealing with monetary problems and price developments since the war for the next economic survey of the United Nations Economic Commission for Asia and the Far East (Box 44, Correspondence 1949–56, Gisele Padbieski to HGJ, 14 July 1953). He was interested, but complications started to emerge. P. S. Lakanathan, the executive secretary of the commission asked Harry if he could manage four months; Harry who had just had leave the previous year said no.[11] Lakanathan tried for three and received the same answer. Annoyed, since he had already been to London to arrange a visa and a flight, Harry terminated the negotiations on 24 July.

The 1956 invitation came from the International Economic Association, in other words, Austin Robinson, who was its secretary. The centrepiece of the expedition was to be a South-East Asia refresher course in economics at the University of Malaya in Singapore. The external participants – Harry, Dudley Seers from Oxford, and J. J. Spengler from Duke – assisted by local faculty and staff from local and regional agencies would offer a series of

---

[11] Even if he could get leave, he did not want to impose on Nicholas Kaldor who would have to take over his college teaching.

courses between 26 July and 7 September. Before the start of the Singapore course, Harry and Karl Kaysen from Harvard would offer an advanced refresher course in Karachi Pakistan from 10 to 22 July.

In Karachi, Harry was to offer lectures on monetary theory and Keynesian economics, banking and monetary policy, comparative costs and commercial policy, the balance of payments and economic adjustment, and planning, the market, and economic development. The papers that formed the basis of these lectures appeared in the *Pakistan Economic Journal* for June 1958 and, with the exception of the rather dated banking paper, in *Money, Trade and Economic Growth* (1962f), where they proved invaluable reading for a generation of undergraduates (including the author). Kaysen's lectures covered price theory, welfare economics, aggregate dynamic models, and problems of economic development.

In Singapore Harry offered a course on international trade (which also covered the balance of payments) and joined Sir Sydney Caine, the vice chancellor of the University of Malaya, and T. H. Silcox, the professor of economics at the university, in offering a course on fiscal policy in less-developed countries.

Initially Harry had difficulties in getting permission from his new employer to be away, but once over that hurdle planning proceeded. There was some tension between those on the ground, particularly Professor Silcox, and those in England, Harry and Austin Robinson, over the balance between theory and its applications. The English side emphasised the importance of general theoretical training, especially given the wide variety of applications of interest to the participants who were drawn from universities and government offices across South East Asia, and the overwhelming comparative advantage of people such as Harry in teaching theory. As Harry had sole control of the course, his international economics was pitched at the level he deemed appropriate. The reading list included Meade's *The Balance of Payments, Trade and Welfare, The Theory of Customs Unions*, and *Problems of Economic Union*, as well as Harry's "Optimum Tariffs and Retaliation" and "Increasing Productivity, Income-Price Trends, and the Trade Balance." Silcox put up some resistance: After all, he had to design a programme that would be worthwhile for institutions in the participating countries to release and pay for their personnel. However, he accepted Harry's suggestion that a course in rural development planning be dropped as overspecialised and agreed with Harry's suggested replacement, a course with more general principles such as fiscal policy. Harry also recognised the need for some "window dressing" for Silcox's letter did "much to clarify my understanding of the problem you are up against, which has some similarity with problems I have encountered before in working in Canada" (i.e., at St. Francis Xavier) (Box 32, Singapore, to Silcox, 10 May 1956). In spite of the fact that he had "never done any formal work in the fiscal field," he agreed to give a series of lectures on general problems.

In collaboration with Joyce Baird, Austin Robinson's assistant, Harry began organising his first long-distance journey by air. He would leave London at 01.45 on 7 July and arrive in Rome at 05.15. He would then have a day in Rome for sightseeing before meeting Kaysen and picking up the BOAC flight for Karachi at 00.10 hours on 8 July, arriving, after stops at Nicosia, Damascus, Baghdad, and Bahrain, at 9 local time that night. After Karachi, he would fly on to Singapore via Columbo, where he had a layover. On the way back he stopped at Bangkok, Rangoon (where he and Spengler gave lectures), Calcutta, Benares, Delhi (where he took a side-trip to Agra to see the Taj Mahal), and Bombay before flying to Manchester where he arrived on 25 September.

Harry fell in love with Asia. He sent the family excited postcards "and came back with a suitcase filled like a Santa Claus pack – Thai records, Malay sarongs, Burmese tote bags, Indian cobras, Chinese carved horses and fish and so on" (Elizabeth Simpson, 26 July 2005). He returned to Karachi two years later and then regularly during the 1960s,[12] although, over time, his base of operations shifted from Singapore to Pakistan and Japan (1969 Autobiographical Notes, 9).

While Harry was in Karachi, Kaysen told him that the Harvard PhD regulations had changed so that it was now possible to obtain a degree on the basis of previous publications. Harry leapt at the opportunity. He put together the essays involved in *International Trade and Economic Growth* and in the summer of 1957, with six weeks at the Merrill Center for Economics at Southampton on Long Island,[13] managed to obtain an oral examination in August with James Duesenberry, Paul Samuelson, and Franco Modigliani as his examiners.

International Economics

Harry's years in Manchester overlapped the founding of the European Economic Community, (EEC). At the beginning of June 1955, the foreign

---

[12] In 1966 between moving from Chicago to London, he took the whole family with him around the world in two months to India, Pakistan, Thailand, Singapore, and Japan.

[13] He was away from England from 27 June to 1 September. He had leave of absence from Manchester, from 8 July to 16 August.

ministers of Belgium, France, Germany, Italy, Luxembourg, and the Netherlands meeting at Messina appointed a preparatory commission to meet in
Brussels under the chairmanship of Paul Henri Spaak to consider extensions
of sectoral integration already achieved along the lines of the European Coal
and Steel Community, including the possibility of a common market. Britain
was invited to join in the discussions and a representative attended meetings until November 1955. The Spaak Committee reported in March 1956
favouring the formation of a common market. In November 1956 Britain
proposed a free trade area designed to include the six but without a common
external tariff or a common agricultural policy. In March 1957 the six signed
the Treaty of Rome, though negotiations continued on the free trade area
proposals from August, until they finally collapsed on 14 November 1958.
The response of those outside the EEC was the Stockholm Convention of
July 1959 and the "outer seven" or the European Free Trade Association,
ratified in November 1959.

Harry provided eight papers relevant to the ongoing discussions, three
of which were theoretical. The theoretical pieces were "The Economic Theory of Customs Unions" delivered to the second 1958 Pakistan refresher
course at Murree and published in the *Pakistan Economic Journal* (1960b),
"Discriminatory Tariff Reduction: A Marshallian Analysis" and "Marshallian Analysis of Discriminatory Tariff Reduction: An Extension," published
in the *Indian Journal of Economics* (1957b and 1958k). The applied pieces
included two contributions to an Oxford symposium – one in February
1957 (1957a), and a second (1960a) written in August 1959 as the original
symposium with a few additional papers went off for publication as a book
edited by David Worswick, *The Free Trade Proposals* (1960). In addition there
were two general discussions of the issues (1957c and 1958j) and, unusually
for Harry, a statistical attempt to estimate the gains from freer trade with
Europe (1958i) – "an important and much-cited article" (Corden 1984, 576)
which was one of the first calculations of its type.

The pioneers of theoretical discussion of customs unions were Jacob Viner
(*The Customs Union Issue*, 1950) and James Meade (*Trade and Welfare*, 1955
and *The Theory of Customs Unions*, 1956). Meade's contribution, building
on earlier work by Marcus Fleming, developed the theory of the second
best, later restated and generalised under Harry's influence by Lipsey and
Lancaster (see discussion in Chapter 5). One speaks of the second best in
the case of customs unions because in a customs union only tariffs facing
your union partners are reduced. Trade barriers with the rest of the world
may increase, decrease, or remain unchanged depending on the union's
arrangements for external protection. Harry's major contribution to the

discussion came in his Murree survey. As was often the case, his paper had a simplicity and clarity of exposition that made it ideal for teaching. Harry's analysis departed from the earlier literature where the discussion of the trade-creating and trade-diverting aspects of a customs union had concentrated on the effects of the changes in production – changes in consumption yielding extra trade being dealt with separately. From the beginning of his discussions of the issue in February 1957 through to the general theoretical statement in "The Economic Theory of Customs Unions," Harry looked at both consumption and production effects when talking of trade creation and trade diversion.

Harry's analysis began from the fact that a customs union involves the elimination of tariffs on goods from partner sources but not from foreign sources. This should lead to domestic production of goods identical with those produced abroad being reduced or eliminated, with the good now being imported from the partner country, and of increased consumption of low-cost partner substitutes for domestic goods. This trade creation has two sorts of economic gain: a saving on the real resource costs of goods previously produced domestically and now imported and, with substitution of lower-cost for higher-cost means of satisfying wants, an increase in consumers' surplus. However, the elimination of tariffs for partner-produced goods while maintaining tariffs on goods from the rest of the world also opens up the possibility of trade diversion – the shift in the source of imports from low-cost foreign to higher-cost partner sources. This has two causes: a shift in the production of identical goods to higher-cost partner sources and the substitution of higher-cost partner goods for lower-cost foreign goods suitable for satisfying the same needs. Further gains or losses could come from economies of scale – a case foreshadowed by Viner but more clearly raised by Harry – and from changes in the terms of trade.

His February 1957 piece, "The Criteria of Economic Advantage," followed the common Oxford symposium format of a comment stimulated by a position paper, in this case a paper by John Black attempting to set out the statistical magnitudes relevant to the discussion. Harry concerned himself with what would be necessary to calculate the long-term effects of an European Economic Community–Free Trade Area including Britain, leaving the transitional effects to one side. He did not believe that market enlargement would bring significant economies of scale. In part, this was because the former national markets with their own language, customs, and distribution systems would offset the same opportunities for mass distribution in a more homogeneous market, but it was also because he found it hard to believe that economies of scale could not be exploited in an economy of 50 million well-off consumers with substantial additional overseas markets. As he put it in a May 1957 lecture in Edinburgh,

the evidence of unexploited economies of scale within the United Kingdom market – as evidenced by the lack of standardisation of electrical connections and voltages, the small scale of retailing, and so on – suggests that it is not mere numbers but the heterogeneous nature of the market which is the obstacle; and I am not convinced that the aggregation of European countries into one by the removal of tariff barriers, without more fundamental changes, will do much to change the situation. (1957c, 272)

Nor did he believe that the terms of trade effects would be significant. He admitted that calculating these would be extremely difficult as they were so dependent "on the reaction of other countries' trade policies as well as other complex reactions," and suggested that concern should centre on measuring the possible consumption and production effects. But he did not attempt a detailed calculation.

In his Edinburgh lecture, which made his notion of production and consumption effects clearer (1957c, 273–5), he was prepared to hazard several guesses.

Judging by the fondness of United Kingdom residents for Continental travel and Continental goods, there is a strong likelihood of trade creation through the consumption effect. That there is substantial scope for saving through production effects is evidenced by the fact that, in spite of tariffs, about £91 million of "machinery and transport equipment" was imported into the United Kingdom from OEEC countries in 1956. (1957c, 275)

He provided other examples, optical goods, clocks and watches, textiles and clothing, and chemicals. He was worried about the possibilities of trade diversion, not from Commonwealth sources, but from the United States, but he suggested that the result would be a net gain – even if he could not estimate its magnitude.

He was, however, soon to have a shot at an estimate. The stimulus was a study by the Economist Intelligence Unit, *Britain and Europe: A Study of the Effects on British Manufacturing Industry of a Free Trade Area and the Common Market*, which appeared in December 1957. The volume provided estimates of trade between Britain and Europe, with and without a free trade area, for 1970 for eight major industries and of trade quantities for another five, which could easily be translated into trade values. In 1955 the thirteen industries accounted for about 50 percent of British exports to and 25 percent of imports from Europe. From these, on certain assumptions, he found it possible to estimate the gain that would result from the free trade area on both the export and import sides – £62 million to £92 million per year on the export side and £31 million on the import side, or for the economy as a whole £125 million to £400 million and £100 million, respectively – a total gain of £225 million or one percent of 1970 prospective (GNP).

Harry's final contribution to these discussions might be regarded as his parting shot from Manchester. He finished "The Common Market: The Economists' Reactions" in late August 1959 before he sailed for America from Liverpool on 2 September.

On receiving the article, David Worswick remarked:

It reminds me of a telegram which Michael Foot once sent to Alan Taylor before one of their television free speech discussions, 'Nothing above the belt. Mike.' This kind of symposium almost invites the psychic and the Gestalt, but I think your comments in a wider context are very fair. (Box 26, Writing 1959, Chicago, 25 August 1959)

Harry replied on 26 August: "The great temptation to aiming below the belt is that there is so much to aim at. Anyway, I am glad that you think it is (probably) fair – it is about time I left the country, I guess."

The paper had two parts. The first was a postscript to "The Gains from Freer Trade with Europe," in which he emphasised that a more refined set of calculations would probably result in a measure of gain of a similar order of magnitude. The grounds here were that the process involved multiplying small numbers by small numbers with the inevitable result that their product would be small – a principle later enshrined as Harberger's principle named after Harry's future Chicago colleague.

The second was a reflection on British economists' reaction to the whole discussion. He found that

by-and-large economists accepted, or at least did not actively challenge, both the Government's offensively Anglo-centric definition of the problem as one of obtaining the maximum gains from trade with Europe at the minimum sacrifice of other British interests, and its vulnerable belief that Britain stood to lose a great deal economically from the establishment of a Common Market without a surrounding Free Trade Area. (1960a, 137–8)

There was a very narrow, very British definition of the possible meaning of economic cooperation – freedom of trade not freedom of factor movements or the coordination of economic policies and institutions – and irritation that, for example, the French might have a different conception.

There was also a commonality to the contributors' assessments of the effects of the Free Trade Area Scheme:

[A]ll contributors, faced with the problem of evaluating a scheme whose effects would be far-reaching changes in economic structure of a sort easy enough to predict in direction but extremely difficult to predict in magnitude, were under a strong inducement either to exaggerate the relevance of the knowledge they were sure of, or to form and use judgments as to the magnitudes of various economic effects based necessarily on sheer speculation. (1960a, 138)

In the arguments deployed

Two such characteristics are particularly noteworthy: the tendency to use descriptive statistics as if they were arguments, and the use of what might be described as Gestalt, analogue, and psychic methods of arriving at quantitative appraisals of economic significance.

The plain truth is that facts are only facts; for predicting the effects of economic changes they cannot take the place of relationships between economic variables; and for evaluating economic performance, they cannot be their own criteria.

By the use of Gestalt, analogue, and psychic methods of arriving at quantitative appraisals of economic significance, I refer to methods which justify a judgment as to the magnitude of a complex change to oneself without necessarily justifying, or even explaining, it to anyone else. . . . What is objectionable is guesswork which produces a final conclusion without either reducing the area within which the guesswork is necessary as far as possible, or defining as clearly as possible the nature of the guess and the factors considered in making it. Such guesswork has the undesirable effect of implying that one man's guess is as good as another and that there is no great need to try and reduce the area of ignorance. (1960a, 140–2)

He was accusing most of the British profession of behaving as he had accused Meade of behaving (although Meade was not involved in this case), using qualitative judgements for quantitative arguments, which he had criticised in 1951. In the process he wickedly characterised some of the symposium's contributors.

Dr. Balogh, his emotions as usual more obvious than his conclusions, provided his familiar complicated problem play, with Germany instead of the United States this time appearing as the villain of the piece.

Mr Worswick in his privileged position of herald to the tournament, demonstrated the weak spots in his contributors' armour with point, blade or flat of his sword as occasion offered, without engaging anyone in actual combat.

Professor Kahn began with an introspective tour of an unusually subtle psyche and ended by reiterating his well-known discovery that a regional bloc can obtain terms-of-trade benefits from discrimination against the outside world. So delighted was he with this thought that he apparently forgot that in the Viner analysis trade diversion is a cause of loss, not gain; in fact the region gains on its terms of trade to the extent that trade diversion does *not* take place. (1960a, 138)

It was an entertaining prelude to his criticisms of the practices of British economics that would appear over the next two decades.

As well as his work on customs unions, Harry's Manchester period saw him produce three articles "that represent his principal contributions to mainstream H-O-S theory" (Corden 1984, 572).

The first, "Factor Endowments, International Trade and Factor Prices" (1957d), was in Harry's words "a systematisation of one branch of the theory of comparative costs ... into a simpler, more readily usable analysis" (*ITEG*, 9–10). He took the standard Heckscher–Ohlin–Samuelson two-country, two-factor, two-commodity model and used 'a diagrammatic representation of the technological side of the economy, developed from one originated by R. F. Harrod," to clarify the analysis, and allowing for factor reversals, to come to general conclusions.[14] As might be expected, they were nihilistic

First, it is not necessarily true that a country will export the commodity which uses relatively intensively the factor with which it is relatively heavily endowed.... Second, it is not necessarily true that a country will export the commodity which uses relatively more of the factor which would be relatively cheaper in the absence of trade.... Thirdly the proposition that trade will tend to equalise factor prices, and will in fact do so if both countries continue to produce both goods is valid only on [certain conditions].... Thus the conclusions of the Heckscher–Ohlin model depend not only on the assumption of competition, absence of trade barriers, constant returns to scale, and so forth, but also on an empirical assumption about the nature of technology or the degree of variation in the factor endowments of the two countries. (*ITEG*, 28–9)

Moreover, if he could upset many generalisations with such a simple model, that was "a virtue rather than a defect in an argument whose purpose is to show how little can be said"(*ITEG*, 18 n.3)

The second and third contributions, which he consolidated into one paper when he came to reprint them in *Aspects of the Theory of Tariffs* (*ATT*; 1971),[15] appeared in the *Manchester School* as "International Trade, Income Distribution and the Offer Curve" (1959b) and "Income Distribution, the Offer Curve and the Effects of Tariffs" (1960g). As he put it in 1971, they were "an attempt to construct a truly general, though simplified,

[14] Harrod had presented the representation in a paper delivered to the AUTE in January 1957. Harry's use of Harrod's diagram caused Harrod some annoyance, as he had not yet written the article in which he hoped to use it (British Library of Political and Economic Science, Royal Economic Society Archives. RES 6/2/111, HGJ to Harrod, 17 May and 17 June 1957; Harrod to HGJ, 6 and 26 June 1957; Harrod to E. A. G. Robinson, 6 and 26 June 1957).

[15] Where it was called "International Trade, Income Distribution, the Offer Curve and the Effects of Tariffs."

model of trade and tariff theory incorporating the distribution of income" (*ATT*, x). As usual it was not merely a work of consolidation. The second article incorporated a series of cases discovered by Abba Lerner, Lloyd Metzler, and Harry's former Cambridge "student" Jagdish Bhagwati, which pointed to the unexpected effects of tariffs on the terms of trade, domestic prices, and factor incomes.[16] The major innovation in the paper was the derivation of offer curves not from a unique community indifference map that does not change but from the behaviour of two types of factor owners – labourers and capitalists – each with its own community indifference map. This allowed for the consideration of the effects of income distribution on trade and trade on income distribution. Allowing for the effects of changes in income distribution on demand made the analysis more complex.

An increase in the relative price of the imported good has in addition to the usual income and substitution effects, the effect of shifting domestic production towards producing more of that good and less of the export good, and re-distributing income towards the factor used intensively in producing that good, thus altering the weights of the preference systems of the two factors in determining aggregate demand for the goods. While the income, substitution, and production effects of the price increases will tend to reduce the quantity demanded, the redistribution effect may work in either direction.... [T]he re-distribution effect may outweigh the other effects over a certain range of the offer curve so that the quantity of imports demanded increases as the price rises and decreases as their relative price falls.... It is even possible that as the price of the imported good falls, the redistribution effect will convert the country from an importer into an exporter of the good concerned.... The re-distribution effect therefore introduces new possibilities of instability and multiple equilibria not suggested by the standard offer curve analysis. (*ATT*, 249–50)

It also produced some rather exotic offer-curve geometry.

The third paper investigated the implications for the model for the conclusions of the standard theory of tariffs. With normal, elastic offer curves on both sides, with a tariff,

the external price of imports must fall and the internal price rise; so that the price and earned income of the factor used relatively intensively in producing importable goods must rise, and the price and earned income of the factor used relatively intensively in producing exportable goods must fall.

---

[16] Harry did not, however, regard Bhagwati as his student. As he reminded him in 1974: "But you are too flattering in calling me your teacher: you may remember our first real encounter intellectually, at the P[olitical] E[conomy] Club, when I learned a lot from your paper on the geometry of trade and growth; and we got on pretty soon to joint papers" (Box 40, Correspondence 1971–7, A–B, 27 June 1974). Harry's reference was to the dedication in Bhagwati and T. N. Srinivasen 1975.

However, if one or other of the offer curves is inelastic

> this conclusion does not necessarily hold. If the domestic offer curve is "inelastic" the demand for imports may increase and turn the terms of trade against the country as a result of the tariff. . . . If the foreign offer curve is "inelastic" the terms of trade may improve so much that the domestic price of imports falls, production of imports falls, and income is redistributed towards the factor used relatively intensively in producing exportables. (*ATT*, 223–4)

Nor do these complications end the story. Although in all cases but the last the imposition of a tariff tends to increase the real earnings of the factor used most intensively in the protected industry and reduce the real earnings of the factor used in the export industry, one has to take into account the disposition of the proceeds of the tariff on the real disposable incomes of those involved. Once one does that, the normal conclusion that the factor used relatively intensively in the production of imports would enjoy an unambiguous increase in real wages still holds, but the factor used relatively intensively in the export industry may gain more from its share of the tariff proceeds and be better off and even in some circumstances raise its relative share as compared with the factor used relatively intensively in the protected industry.

Monetary Economics

In the course of his first Budget speech on 9 April 1957, the chancellor of the exchequer, Peter Thorneycroft, announced the appointment of a committee on the working of the monetary system. According to the formal Treasury Minute, dated 3 May, the committee was "to enquire into the working of the monetary and credit system and to make recommendations." Chaired by Lord Radcliffe, it included two economists, Richard Sayers and Alec Cairncross. The committee's report was signed on 30 July 1959 and it appeared on 30 August, just in time to give Harry some shipboard reading on his way to the United States. The existence of the committee informed most of Harry's writings on monetary affairs in Manchester.

Inevitably, the appointment of the committee spurred the editor of the *Bulletin* of the Oxford University Institute of Statistics to organise another symposium. "The Money and Credit System," which appeared in November 1957, with the normal position paper, this time "Monetary Control and Economic Policy" by G. R. Ross. Comments came from Ralph Hawtrey, I. M. D. Little, J. C. R. Dow, Thomas Wilson, Paul Streeten, Thomas Balogh,

J. R. Sargent, H. F. Lydall, Edward Nevin, and E. Victor Morgan, as well as Harry.

His contribution, "Bank Rate Reform and the Improvement of Monetary Statistics" (1957e) touched on most of the issues that would be embodied in his written and oral evidence to the committee. By the time he met the Radcliffe Committee on 7 October 1958, he had also read "British Monetary Statistics" (1959a) to a joint meeting of the Manchester Statistical Society and the Royal Statistical Society, although the paper would not appear in *Economica* until February 1959. Indeed "the urge to make some propaganda in this direction is, quite frankly, the underlying motivation for this paper" (1959a, 3). The paper was the result of a process, which started in his earlier work on British banking and continued in his experience of teaching E. S. Shaw's money and banking course at Stanford in the summer of 1955. After failing to find money in Cambridge to support the project, as a professor in Manchester, he had access to funds and with the assistance of Alison Martin produced series for the U.K. money supply. These admittedly imperfect series suggested that the existing statistics were not good indicators of short-term changes in the money stock. He also found producing the statistics helped him. As he told the committee,

I think that until one comes to the preparation of statistics one often does not define one's ideas very clearly. The definition and collection of relevant statistics is itself an educational process, as I found myself in collecting statistics on money supply in this country. (1960j, Question 10,594)

His appeal for better statistics went beyond figures for the money supply and the underlying balance sheet information. He also suggested (1957e, 345) better indicators of the velocity of circulation and statistics on unused overdraft facilities.

His emphasis on better statistics was, however, part of a larger programme – of making the whole policy process more open and, to use a later word, transparent. He told the committee that, as an academic economist "one feels that whereas one can talk to the Treasury people without any great difficulty, talking to bankers is an experiment rather than a habit" (1960j, Question 10,607). Moreover, the language in which monetary policy was discussed was "metaphysical and imprecise," "emotive and obscure," compared to the "quantitative," "prosaic" language used for discussion of other aspects of economic policy (1960i, para. 8). What he wanted was both more adequate official explanation of what monetary policy was intended to achieve and the provision of adequate materials for outsiders to evaluate policy. Both would promote informed discussion and analysis of the issues. Both would also require the authorities to be clearer in their own minds as to what the current situation was and, given their goals, which policy changes were called for. Less secretiveness, aloofness and obscurantism on the part of the Bank of England might reduce what Harry regarded as "a latent hostility to monetary policy and those responsible for it, especially on the part of the younger economists" (1960i, para. 5). The greater openness and clarity that Harry hoped for now seem far from revolutionary – improved statistics and a quarterly economic bulletin – but they were at the time. As he put his hopes, using the September 1957 balance-of-payments-crisis measures which took Bank rate to 7 percent for the first time since 1920–1,[17]

> I would look for a twofold approach on this: that at the time when they took that sort of crisis action they should give an explanation of why they were taking it, but that in the quarterly or annual publication they should look back over the experience, trace the developments that led up to it and explain the decision and also, I hope, try to envisage the consequences as far as they could. (1960j, Question 10,601)

The argument for greater transparency at the Bank was but a part of Harry's position: There was also the question whether changes in Bank rate, surrounded as they were with such mystery and myth, were the most appropriate way to conduct monetary policy. In this area, however, Harry's views were evolving. In the Oxford symposium his suggestions were different from, and less well thought through than, those in his presentation to Radcliffe. In the symposium he raised three questions: whether instead of initially fixing the price of bank credit, the Bank should not start with an attempt to control the quantity of credit though open-market operations, possibly in longer-dated securities and perhaps accompanied by a more flexible Bank rate on the Canadian model;[18] whether, given changed postwar circumstances (specifically a commitment to full employment and high marginal rates of tax on profits) the range of possible movements in

---

[17] When Bank rate went to 7 percent, there were allegations that there had been improper prior disclosure of information. In response the government set up a Tribunal of Enquiry, which reported in December 1957. The oral evidence presented to the tribunal appeared at the same time. The Manchester Faculty held a series of interdisciplinary seminars on it which resulted in "The Bank Rate Tribunal: A Symposium," *Manchester School*, 27 (January 1959), 1–51. The evidence to the tribunal confirmed all of Harry's prejudices about central bankers, but it also emphasised the statistical void in which the decision was made and the limited role of economists. See in particular Ely Devons's contribution to the symposium (3–7).

[18] The Bank of Canada rate was "automatically" set at $1/4$ percent above the average weekly tender on 91-day treasury bills.

Bank rate might have to be wider than before the war; and whether the conventional credit control operating on lending through the availability of cash and "a modicum of ear-stroking" might be better replaced by one that emphasised selective controls on particular forms of lending (1957e, 342). When it came to the Radcliffe committee, the emphasis had sharply shifted. Selective, direct controls were only mentioned in passing (1960i, para. 11) in his memorandum and not at all in the evidence. Instead the emphasis was on the desirability of a shift to open-market operations as the initiating centrepiece of monetary policy followed by accommodating movements, where necessary, of Bank rate. The vehicle for open-market operations would not be bills of exchange or treasury bills but longer term gilt-edged securities, which he believed "would be more effective both in restricting bank credit and influencing other institutional lenders in the same direction" (1960i, para. 16). He also recommended the replacement of the 30 percent liquid assets ratio for banks with a lower *but variable* cash reserve requirement – accompanied by the imposition of similar obligations on competing deposit-accepting institutions, in particular building societies and hire purchase companies (1960i, paras. 20–1).

When it came to Harry's oral evidence to the committee, the bulk of the discussion centred on his proposal for greater emphasis on open-market operations. The committee's concerns probably partially reflected official preoccupations with funding the floating debt to ensure that there were few enough treasury bills about to make the 30 percent liquidity ratio bite and the need to sell new debt to cover new borrowing by the central government, local authorities, and nationalised industries, coupled with the Bank of England's belief that it could not sell bonds on a falling market because investors would expect bond prices to continue to fall and thus incur capital losses. Harry's proposals might also imply greater volatility in long rates, and thus implied higher long-term rates than under the old régime. Harry replied that he was not prepared to make a judgement on volatility (1960j, Question 10,624). On the level of rates, he thought that

[t]here might be an increase in the average cost of financing the Government but I think that this would be small compared to the other effects. After all, if one's sole concern was to finance the Government at the least possible cost one would run monetary policy quite differently. One has to accept that some problems with the cost of Government debt are the price one pays for using it as an instrument of monetary policy. (1960j, Question 10,625)

The final aspect of monetary policy Harry dealt with during his Manchester period was inflation. Leaving aside one review that adds nothing to the main thread of the story, one is left with one article, a contribution to the June 1958 issue of the *Scottish Journal of Political Economy* symposium on wage policy and inflation (1958b). Harry's paper, "Two Schools of Thought on Wage Inflation," was largely a commentary on the views of others, but he set out his own views clearly. He was inclined to the view that inflation was predominantly a result of excess demand, although he emphasised that one of the effects of a prolonged period of wage inflation was the tendency for it to set up its own momentum through indexation. However, he did not believe that inflation of the postwar British sort had done any demonstrably serious damage or that it held out the prospect of catastrophic hyperinflation. Rather

the argument against inflation in Britain is . . . that the gradual erosion of the value of money entails a host of unfairness – some cumulative and some temporary, but all irritating – between different members of the community, and makes more complicated and frustrating the task of economic calculation for all concerned including the Government itself.

How much weight should be attached to this argument is a difficult problem in the making of value judgements to which neither the convenience of a decent salaried existence nor the habit of thinking of the working class in R.S.P.C.A.[19] terms is a fair guide. But it is at least arguable that neither the desperate need for more employment nor the need in the 1940s for more production is the appropriate standard for the present situation, and that the country can probably now afford to trade some loss of output and employment for greater stability of prices. (1958b, 151)

He was uncertain about the costs of restraint, but he thought that the view that 3 percent was probably enough was rather an optimistic view of the level of unemployment necessary to stop wage inflation. He thought that the machinery of collective bargaining needed some improvement but that such an improvement might come from an environment of constrained demand (1958b, 153). Again, these views differed from those of 1954, but it is not clear what the source of the change was. One suspects that it was less Manchester than the slow change in opinion outside certain Labour circles and Keynesian Cambridge that had come to accept slightly more unemployment as a price worth paying for price stability.

Moving to Chicago

Chicago had maintained an interest in Harry after his 1955 visit to Northwestern. The department had been rebuilding after losing key members in

---

[19] Royal Society for the Prevention of Cruelty to Animals.

the late 1940s, but after the loss of Tjalling Koopmans, Jacob Marschak, and Frederick Harbison, the retirement of Frank Knight, and the illness of Lloyd Metzler, it needed to hire outside at a senior level "to attract talent and make clear that we were in business" (Regenstein Library, University of Chicago, Box 74, President's Papers 1952–60, Folder 2, Economics Department 1955–58, T. W. Schultz, A Program to Rebuild the Department of Economics, 1956). The university's response was encouraging and during the next year the department began to consider candidates. On 9 April 1957 the department met to discuss a major appointment for W. Arthur Lewis.[20] The minutes noted: "In general there was a consensus of a kind that can best be described by saying that no one amongst those present expressed an objection to his appointment." They also reported that the "chief alternative" to Lewis was Harry. A vote on the relative ranking or priority of approach to the two men found that six of the thirteen present favoured Harry, five favoured Lewis (Regenstein Library, University of Chicago, Department of Economics Records, Box 41, Folder 2).

On 14 May Milton Friedman sent Harry a proposal concerning the Cambridge Economic Handbooks of which Friedman had become coeditor with Claude Guillebaud in 1956:

The gap ... that seemed to me most obvious and urgent when I reviewed the Series, was that it contains no book on income and employment theory, something of a paradox in view of the fact that the Series was initiated by Keynes. I am most anxious, therefore, to have Chicago redress the balance of Cambridge as soon and as effectively as possible. In writing Guillebaud about this, I said that you seemed to me the ideal author for the book. . . .

The time seems to me now most opportune for a really important contribution in this area. The controversies have largely declined and there seems to me now a very large area of agreement, at least on the theoretical level. Yet it seems to me to have been no authoritative statement of the present position on the subject which is accessible to either the ordinary but not specialized economist or the educated layman. The volume I would hope for in the Cambridge Series would be one which would do just this. I think there is a real opportunity here, and I feel also that you have just the right qualifications to seize it. Guillebaud's one doubt was that you might have a tendency to be too technical for the purpose, but I assured him that you were master enough of the technique so that you could rise above it. Unless I am mistaken, what is called for here is partly a creative as well as an expositional task. We are all in agreement in a sense, and yet we are by no means clear what it is we are in agreement about – to what extent it is a question of new wine in old bottles, and to what extent of old wine in new bottles.

---

[20] This incident is not discussed in Robert Tignor's 2005 biography of Lewis.

I certainly hope very much that you will feel challenged by the task and will want to undertake it. I would personally feel that the assumption of the editorship had been more than worthwhile if it could result in a volume by you in this area that would occupy the place with respect to this range of subject matter that Robertson's *Money* has occupied in its field for so long. (Box 43, Miscellaneous Correspondence E–H)

The letter was a further indication of how he was regarded in Chicago. There is no sign that he ever started the project.

On 28 May the Chicago department met again to discuss the possible appointment of Lewis and Johnson. At the end, "[a] motion was passed unanimously authorizing the chairman to proceed to negotiate the appointment of Harry Johnson to a major tenure post in the Department" (Regensetein Library, University of Chicago, Department of Economic Records, Box 41, Folder 2).

While Harry was at the Merrill Centre in July 1957 working up *International Trade and Economic Growth* as his Harvard PhD thesis, D. Gale Johnson visited and sounded him out as to the possibility of moving to Chicago. Harry responded favourably, although saying that if he accepted he would not be able to come immediately. Thereafter, Arnold Harberger appears to have been his main contact, and later champion, in the department, although others did play supporting roles. Harberger wrote on 30 July 1957:

We are all hoping strongly that you will decide to come to Chicago. I am very proud of the department and of the way it is organized. It is one of the few places where the members really interact, and operate on the principles that a) every significant disagreement can be reduced to errors in logic, questions of empirical fact, or differences in premises and that b) colleagues really *should* do this. Think about it and you'll see that these principles can't effectively be applied where colleagues basically don't respect each other's ability; and think too about the few places in the world where they are applied. To my mind Chicago is almost unique in this regard. I think it is probably the most stimulating department going – and I think its distinction in this regard stems purely from the tradition of getting arguments honestly into the open and partly from the fact that there simply is no dead wood in the group.

I am sure that if you decide to come, you'll never regret it. I'm not much for writing letters, so in view of the fact that I'll probably be able to talk at length with you in England, I won't ramble on and on. Why don't you, though, drop me a line here – especially if there are any questions in your mind about the dept. at Chicago, the life there, etc. (Box 43, Miscellaneous Correspondence E–H)

Harberger wrote again on 9 August answering Harry's queries about teaching loads, medical insurance, retirement, and group life insurance arrangements. Harberger's presence in England in 1958 at LSE and Cambridge certainly helped matters.

Harry received other enquiries. Toronto tried in the summer of 1957, when Harry's mother congratulated him on turning them down – the offer was "*too small*" (Box 31, Correspondence to 1963, Unsorted, 15 October 1957). However, Harry told Vincent Bladen that he would not be able to leave Manchester until Arthur Lewis returned from Ghana and he promised "not to close with any American University without giving you a chance to see what you can do" (University of Toronto Archives, Department of Political Economy Records, A65-0005/0001, 16 October 1957). Bladen wrote about possible terms on 17 February. Johns Hopkins also inquired about an appointment in March 1958.

Harry was interested in Chicago, but he did not rush into negotiations. He had discussions with Carl Shoup about a Ford Foundation visiting professorship at Columbia, and, after discussions at Manchester with the vice chancellor (William Mansfield Cooper) and his colleagues, told Shoup on 15 January 1958 that he was prepared to come in 1960–1. Columbia replied on 22 January that they would be willing to have him then, but when Harry wrote again on 10 March, he declined the Columbia offer.

The reason for the delay and the change of heart . . . is that I have pretty well decided to move to the U.S.A., and in that event I should have to break off my commitment to you in fairness to my new university.

As I have not yet committed myself, and as negotiations might break down, I would be grateful if you would treat this letter as strictly confidential. (Box 41, Correspondence to 1963, Unsorted)

In the interval, Harberger had been in Manchester on 29 and 30 January.

Chicago still did not have Harry completely in the bag. He was approached in February by Stanford and Princeton, who made very attractive offers. Chicago responded with an improved offer. He was also still getting letters from possible Chicago colleagues. To one, from Lloyd Metzler, he replied on 11 April:

Thank you for your two letters. The first was both generous and helpful in giving me an idea of what life is like in Chicago for the minority opinion; I would like you to know that your presence there is an important attraction – I have been a fan of yours since I read your work and heard you speak at the AEA in 1947.[21] (Box 31, Correspondence to 1963, Unsorted)

---

[21] At the meeting in Atlantic City in January 1947 when Metzler was a discussant in a session on Domestic and International Equilibrium on 24 January. The other letter, which is the one that survives, pursued a loose end from a 1955 discussion over the transfer problem.

There was another factor in the background. Dennis Robertson retired from the Professorship of Political Economy in Cambridge in 1957. James Meade was elected to succeed him, thus opening the LSE chair in commerce with special reference to international trade. However, with Lionel Robbins at the helm, LSE's wheels turned slowly and deliberately. The School had no immediate teaching needs in international economics that couldn't be covered by A. C. L. Day and Helen Makower, and graduate supervision was not an immediate problem. Moreover, to Robbins it was more important that they filled Hayek's chair, the Tooke Professorship in Economics and Statistics, so that LSE could retain W. A. H. Phillips. That appointment had the advantage of being uncontroversial. Replacing Meade, moreover, presented problems. Some members of the School's staff might be considered to have claims. As well there were outsiders to consider, including Harry. In a mid-September 1957 paper setting out the whole position, Lionel Robbins provided his view of Harry:

Johnson. I mention him because I know some members of our profession think him to be eligible. I have indeed heard his name mentioned as a desirable choice by one of the juniors at the School. I have no doubt that he is a clever fellow and I can conceive that in years to come we may want to have him. But I definitely do not want him now. His articles, though showing obvious power, seem to me to lack a sense of direction and his practical judgment to be definitely poor. And it is a relevant circumstance that, when he deputised for Alan Day while the latter was at the Treasury, he was certainly not a success as a teacher. I know that Meade, who was responsible for inviting him, was worried about this.[22] In any case, I cannot think that he is as good as at least four of our Readers and I should be very sorry indeed to appoint such a man over their heads. (Robbins Papers, Staff, File II, 1950–7, "Notes on the Vacant Chairs in Economics," 17 September 1957, circulated on 23 September to the professors of economics for discussion when they met the Director early in term to discuss vacancies).

Robbins's preferred strategy was to leave the chair vacant for eighteen months to two years in the hope that his favoured internal candidate, A. C. L. Day, could grow up to it, but he was prepared to consider an outsider senior to Harry, namely Alec Cairncross.

Robbins was correct that the junior members of staff might hold different views. However, it is indicative of the gap between the professors and the young that Robbins had only heard Harry's name from one, for he had probably not talked to any others about the issue. By this time Harry was the undisputed leader of the younger generation of serious economists

---

[22] See Chapter 5 for Meade's comments.

outside Cambridge. Moreover, his possible appointment was associated with expectations that Harry would become an advocate for all the changes the younger people desired – more mathematics in the curriculum, more attention to graduate work, and so forth. According to Richard Lipsey, "the LSE junior staff whom I knew had a short list containing only one name, H. G. Johnson" (1978, S41 n.14).

On 3 February 1958 Robbins wrote a personal letter to Ely Devons sounding him out as to his availability for the chair. Devons was interested, and arrangements for an election proceeded. Devons was formally offered the chair on 18 April. He formally accepted the offer on 23 April and told the vice chancellor of Manchester that he would go to LSE from 1 April 1959 (Devons Papers, D. W. Logan to E. Devons, 18 April 1958; S. Caine to E. Devons, 25 April 1958; E. Devons to S. Caine, 29 April 1958). Robbins was pleased: "The flags are definitely out in Houghton Street" (Robbins Papers, LSE Staff File III, 1958–61, to Ely Devons, 1 May 1958). Devons's appointment was announced in the *Manchester Guardian* on 30 April; it did not make the *Times* until 5 May. According to Lipsey, "many of the full professors were surprised that the less-senior staff thought it a scandal that Harry was not appointed" (1978, S43 n.14).

Harry was happy for his colleague but, given Devons's expertise,[23] outraged "that the British academic establishment could apparently decide appointments on what seemed to him irrelevant grounds" rather than on competence in the field (S43 n.14). Lipsey remembered:

Harry happened to be in London when (or very soon after) he found out that he had been passed over. The three of us went out for one of the famous Harberger-Johnson drinking bouts with which I was just barely able to keep up. One of my memories of that evening is of a cab refusing to pick us up at 4 A.M. on some London street corner – I guess we seemed too disreputable for the cabby. My more important memory is of Al working on Harry, relentlessly saying that, as Harry was not appreciated in England, it was time for him to move to Chicago. (2001, 616)

He was also annoyed that when he mentioned going to Chicago to the vice chancellor of Manchester there was no attempt to persuade him to stay, even though that was typically Mancunian. In his 1969 Autobiographical Notes,

---

[23] At the time of his appointment to LSE, Devons had published three articles on international trade (1951, 1952, and 1954). As Harry put it in an obituary notice (1968c), Devons "felt no deep involvement in international economics," yet Robbins thought that the chair could be defined to make it "a field in which … [Devons's] special qualifications would be deployed with quite peculiar advantage" [Robbins Papers, Staff File III (1958–61), to Ely Devons, 3 February 1958].

he mentioned the Meade chair and stated that "had I been offered it I would have felt obliged to take it out of loyalty to my friends at L.S.E., and my concern over the state of economics in Britain."

By 10 May, Harry was writing Friedman, thanking him for an earlier letter (unfortunately lost)

which played its part in my decision to accept Chicago's offer, I don't agree with your view that the British intellectual climate has been inhibiting me – rather the reverse – but we can argue about that some other time. (Hoover Institution, Friedman Papers, Box 28, Folder 33)

He also told Richard Kahn of his impending move to Chicago on 12 May (King's College, Cambridge, Kahn 13/48A). Later in the month letters of congratulation started to arrive from Vincent Bladen (21 May 1958) and Charles Tibout of Northwestern (Box 31, Correspondence to 1963, Unsorted, 30 May 1958).

In his 1969 Autobiographical Notes Harry stated that

I decided to go to Chicago for two reasons. The first was that it was increasingly clear that English economics was stuck in a groove, largely because of its conquest by Keynesian economics and its politicization in favour of Labour party socialism, and that the only progress in the subject that was being made was occurring in the United States. . . . The second was that it was already apparent that fiscal and balance-of-payments pressures on the government were forcing it into policies it has increasingly pursued since, of starving the university system of funds and forcing it to emphasise teaching and administration rather than research. (10–11)

In the 1974 Self-Evaluation, the notion of Britain becoming an academic backwater was also mentioned, as was "that the British academic system offered little stimulus and time for scientific work as compared with the American" (9).

But although the 1969 and 1974 memoirs tell part of the story of Harry's decision to move to America, its timing seems to have a lot to do with developments at LSE. Indeed, one might go even further, for if, as is likely, Ely Devons had consulted Harry during "his considerable heart-searchings over abandoning what he has created in social science in Manchester" (Johnson 1968c) between Robbins's first approach and the decision to let the formal proceedings begin, the announcement of his decision to Shoup on 10 March fits very well into the tale. Moreover, the later comments about the British intellectual climate do not mesh well with the statement to Friedman.

But then, Harry later said that "my days in Manchester were probably the happiest in my life, professionally speaking" (*Shadow*, 150)

Harry's was the third economics professor resignation at Manchester in a month. Arthur Lewis had also resigned to become principal of the University College of the West Indies. As a result, Harry's resignation did not take effect until after the 1958–9 academic year.

EIGHT

Chicago

It was in Chicago in the 1950s that I first learned to understand this most un-English conception [the research university] through appreciative acquaintance with that beleaguered academic square mile in which the probability on any given day of an exciting conversation was, and possibly still is, greater than in any other place that I have known.[1]

(Halsey 1992, 39–40)

At the time Harry came to Chicago, the university and the surrounding community had just passed a low point. During his last years as chancellor, differences between Robert Hutchins and the faculty over the organisation of the undergraduate curriculum and the standards of hiring and promotion at the undergraduate College, where, according to William McNeill (1991, 147), "in some quarters writing scholarly books and articles was taken as a sign that the individual in question had betrayed the College and the ideal of general education," had led to several departures and a weakening of some departments in the graduate divisions. After Hutchins's departure in 1950, his successor, Lawrence Kimpton, had to restore the university's financial position. This required cutbacks: Those with outside offers were encouraged to depart, as many did to the expanding University of California system, while junior contracts were allowed to expire (McNeill 1991, 166). Only later in the decade did the University begin to repair the damage.

At the same time the physical environment around the university had deteriorated. The immediate neighbourhood was known as Hyde Park. Hyde Park was "a sort of village in the city" where much of the staff and most of the faculty lived and walked to work.

---

[1] Halsey was in Chicago in 1959–60.

A good many members of the University stayed in the neighbourhood for weeks on end – working, sleeping, shopping and socialising in the immediate vicinity. On some blocks, faculty and other University employees constituted a clear majority and they often knew one another, at least slightly, both as neighbours and in their professional capacity at the University. This created a network of acquaintanceship that undergirded and enlarged the more strictly professional contacts that occurred on campus and made the University community far more coherent that it could otherwise have been.[2] (McNeill 1991, 137)

Hyde Park's problem was its location. It is on Chicago's South Side, home of the city's largest black neighbourhood, which started at 12th Street and extended southwards. As new migrants moved into the South Side, densities rose and black middle-class families tried to get out by moving further south into previously all white neighbourhoods – neighbourhoods segregated "by fiercely maintained custom and, in many cases, also by force of law through 'restrictive covenants' that barred blacks from buying houses" (Leman 1992, 63). The pressure intensified as the black population rose from 277,731 in 1940 to 812,637 in 1960 (Hirsch 1983, 17). At the same time, Chicago's dwelling stock, which had fallen in the 1930s, rose slowly, and much of that expansion occurred in the suburbs. The housing market was a dual one: Blacks paid substantially higher rents than whites.[3] As a result, with strong pressure on whites moving out of areas on the fringe of the old black belt to sell to blacks, market forces were working for racial succession, overwhelming restrictive covenants. The effect of market forces was strengthened when restrictive covenants were ruled illegal by the Supreme Court in 1948.

Bounded by Lake Michigan on the east, Hyde Park was being approached from both the north and the west by the expanding ghetto. It was ripe for succession: Much of the housing stock could be easily subdivided; some of the stock was already in bad shape; and dilapidation was spreading. So long as Hutchins was chancellor, there was no community action to preserve middle-class occupancy or to organise the local community. The university was a large local landowner, but it did not have a clear policy that had support from the administration, faculty, and students.

In 1949 the Hyde Park–Kenwood Community Conference (the conference), concerned with the area between 42nd and 59th Streets, was formed.[4] Initially it had problems with the local community organisations with which

---

[2] The neighbourhood was mixed, with a substantial white-collar and professional population which was about 40 percent Jewish (Abrahamson 1959, 7).

[3] According to Hirsch (1983, 29), 15 to 50 percent more in the 1940s and 10 to 25 percent more in 1960.

[4] Kenwood is the neighbourhood immediately to the north of Hyde Park.

the university had been involved (the Hyde Park Planning Association and Woodlawn, Inc.) for these had supported restrictive covenants and the policies of the university's business office had kept blacks from the immediate vicinity of the university (Hirsch 1983, 145). The conference intended to deal creatively with the prospect of an influx of blacks. It was integrationist, but it wanted to maintain standards by stopping blight and enforcing zoning and building regulations and rules about trash, vermin, and safety. It also worked to obtain new and improved services such as schools, lighting, and parks. Its liberalism lost it some powerful business supporters.

In 1952 the university established the South East Chicago Commission (the commission), through which it attempted to preserve "an economically upgraded and predominantly white neighbourhood" (Hirsch 1983, 137). The conference slowly transformed itself into the vehicle to secure public support for the commission, which was essential for what followed; because its espousal of an integrated community, its local activities and its creation of an atmosphere of change, slowed white out-migration and gave the university time to marshall resources.

It was the university, in its role as property owner, that was in the front lines in the battle to preserve the area as "desirable." The university shouldered the main burden of local self-defense, made the difficult decisions it felt had to be made, exposed itself to the criticism its position naturally attracted. The university, as the institution with the most to lose and the power to assure its own survival, thus afforded its neighbours the luxury of their liberalism. (Hirsch 1983, 138)

The commission had the resources and connections to obtain the necessary legislation, for the slum clearance regime was unsuitable for much of the neighbourhood. The result, approved in 1958, was three projects: a redevelopment plus mixed use and shopping project in one of the most blighted areas; the South West Hyde Park Neighborhood Redevelopment Corporation to conduct renewal activities to the west of the campus; and an urban renewal plan for the entire community. The whole process, unlike those in other neighbourhoods facing the same pressures, involved a willingness to tolerate a significant black presence in the community

It would . . . be more accurate to conceive of this integration of Hyde Park as a necessary by-product of its renewal rather than the purpose behind it. . . . By the mid-1950s, the question was not whether there would be any blacks in Hyde Park but whether there would be any whites. The maintenance of a white presence around the University of Chicago subsequently meant, by definition, integration. . . . This willingness [to tolerate], carefully cultivated by the HPKCC, gave the community the resilience and the time it needed to respond to the challenge without being overwhelmed. In acting in what it perceived to be its own defense, the university employed no half measures, refused to compromise its self-defined interests, and permitted others the satisfaction of participating in a 'noble experiment'. (Hirsch 1983, 169–70)

The result was a middle-class, socially mixed neighbourhood, which continues to thrive.

Chicago Economics

So much for the neighbourhood, what of the institution? The university had always been predominantly a graduate institution – and it became more so when the divisions with the established departments lost responsibility for undergraduate general education to the undergraduate College in 1931 and then ceased dealing with undergraduates at all in 1942. This specialisation shaped the ethos of the departments.

At Chicago, diligent teaching, service in university administration, great distinction – even fame – in government service are at best partial substitutes for continuing research productivity. (Reder 1982, 2)

Or, as George Stigler put it, "Chicago is not a good university in which to retire from scholarship" (1988, 45). Another, recalling the camaraderie, the willingness to share problems, drafts and sharp criticisms, remarked "I never knew a professor could become lonesome until I left Chicago" (46). Ernest Sirluck found similar activity in English

Virtually everyone in the department from established scholar to neophyte, was actively at work on some project intended for publication, usually with much shorter planned deadlines than prevailed in Toronto; the result was a livelier, more intense environment. It was also inevitably more competitive. . . . This competitiveness led to tension and some sharp oppositions as junior members competed for tenure, the middle ranks for promotion, seniors for influence, and all ranks for salary, but I thought the price worth paying for the greater intensity. (1996, 170)

The Chicago School of Economics has carried different meanings for different scholars. In Harry's case, when he was in Manchester corresponding with Robert Mundell, who had been to his lectures at LSE in 1955–6, the phrase meant Milton Friedman and the quantity theory (Box 31, Correspondence to 1963, Unsorted, to HGJ, 2 October 1956; to Mundell, 9 October 1956). The term usually had broader connotations. In the 1930s and 1940s the role of economic theory in the department was strengthened by a shift in the focus of the field courses and the comprehensive examinations. Both became method rather than problem oriented, and price theory came to play an important role. Success in either depended more and more on the candidate's ability to apply the relevant price theory – or as Harry put it to Jagdish Bhagwati and Amartya Sen, to "understand economic theory as a problem-solving tool" (Box 56, Correspondence 1964–6, A–L, 18 January 1966).

At the centre of most accounts of the modern Chicago school have been four individuals, Jacob Viner, who left the department in 1945 for Princeton, and three postwar figures, Milton Friedman, Allen Wallis, and George Stigler – all in some sense students of Frank Knight, although only Stigler did a dissertation under him. The three were not reunited in Chicago until 1958, when Stigler returned from Columbia to join Wallis in the business school. All three were

extremely good expositors and very effective advocates. . . . Their skill and energy, coupled with Knight's prestigious support, made them an effective and cohesive group – at the University of Chicago and elsewhere – in promoting their common ideas. (Reder 1982, 8)

At the centre of their long-term influence was the structure of the Chicago PhD programme as it evolved since the early 1930s. The admissions policy of the Chicago department had always been lenient. Two examinations, one in price theory and one in monetary economics, were the department's filter, and the courses leading to them were essential preparation. The success rates in these courses was normally around 50 percent. The teaching of the first of these, Economics 301, was the prerogative of the "big guns" of the department and was successively associated with Jacob Viner, Milton Friedman, Arnold Harberger, and, later, Gary Becker – all stern task-masters exposing inappropriate questions or wrong answers "without concern for the feelings of the inept offender":

Together with the preparation for the qualifying examination, the Ph.D. theory courses constitute an acculturation process lasting one or two years whose end result is an economist with the Chicago style of thought. . . . To obtain a Chicago Ph.D. one must learn to do certain specific and fairly difficult things quite well, and the learning process inculcates distinctive habits of thought. (Reder 1982, 9)

The late 1940s and 1950s brought another innovation, the workshop or research group with its emphasis on the collaborative exploration of problems using new research methods and training graduate students. Its origins probably lay with the Cowles Commission, which had moved to Chicago in 1939. The workshop, with its echoes of graduate training in the natural sciences, became the normal method for training PhD students. By the mid-1950s workshops existed in the fields of doctoral specialisation – money and banking, agricultural economics, public finance, labour, economic development, and the economics of consumption (Emmett 1998, 145–7). According to Yoram Barzel (2000, 226), "[t]he workshop was a great innovation for writing dissertations, its main advantage being the 'socializing' of the writing process."

One final characteristic of student and faculty life in the department was the intensity of economic discussions. Shop was the normal subject of conversation, even at parties, to a greater extent than amongst economists elsewhere. As Yoram Barzel remembered the years when Harry arrived:

The intellectual atmosphere at Chicago was electrifying; the economics faculty was free of deadwood and did virtually no consulting. Small talk occurred, of course, but it occupied only a small fraction of our time, the rest of which was relentlessly overtaken by economics. Already then, in Chicago, "economics" meant nearly everything. . . . The atmosphere of total involvement was contagious. You couldn't spend two minutes in the company of most graduate students without hearing about the marginal cost of something. . . . In Israel, I had seldom taken part in course discussions, but I became quite aggressive in the classroom immediately after arriving at Chicago, an unplanned, but quick adjustment to the Chicago style. (2000, 225)

Dan Usher also remembered:

The economics department of the University of Chicago was a place where things were really happening, where the frontiers of knowledge were being pushed back in a big way. . . . It was a heady time to be a student of economics. You can often judge the tone of a place by its afternoon tea time or coffee hour. At Chicago in those days, the faculty and the graduate students assembled every day in the faculty lounge to discuss, to analyze and to argue. There was, as I remember, no respite and little gossip. Economics was too important. (2000, 286–7)

Richard Norgaard, who was at Chicago for course work in 1969–70 had similar memories.

There were cultural shocks, but Chicago was very much in the oral tradition. You could argue your point. People were expected to listen to your argument and go back and forth; it was extremely intellectually stimulating. . . . [T]he core theory courses were not that mathematical. It was really about whether you could understand the basic logic and be able to use it. Basic logic is fun, so I did enjoy it, but it did get a little heavy; I'd go to parties and people would be drinking and still talking economics. They talked about economics day and night. Harry Johnson was amazing. He was totally plastered most of the time I saw him in Chicago, but he could still argue economics. That part was depressing. (Collander, Holt, and Rosser 2004, 217)

Throughout the discussion the emphasis has been on the department, a relatively small group of people, without undergraduate teaching responsibilities, who worked in the same place (in this case one floor of the Social Science Building) and largely lived in the surrounding community, and who had a shared vision of graduate education. Zvi Griliches, one of Harry's colleagues during his first decade in Chicago, who later went to Harvard, caught it nicely.

I must say when I came [to Harvard] I missed Chicago very dearly. Because Chicago was a department, and Harvard was not. It was just a collection of people doing their own thing. . . . It was not really together. I remember, having come from Chicago . . . I spent quite a bit of time in the first couple of years feeling out, feeling I wasn't in until it became clear to me that there was no in. (Krueger and Taylor 2000, 179)

The dominant feature of Chicago training became what Reder calls "Tight Prior Equilibrium" theory (TP), which was

rooted in the hypothesis that decision makers allocate the resources under their control so there is no alternative allocation such that any one decision maker could have his expected utility increased without a reduction occurring in the expected utility of one other decision maker. (Reder 1982, 11)

This in itself is the well-known definition of Pareto optimality. Chicago economists associated this with a model yielding testable hypotheses by assuming that market participants and markets behaved in certain ways: All participants were price takers, treating the prices at which they bought and sold as independent of the quantities they transacted; that the prices at which they agreed to deal were market clearing prices consistent with optimisation by all; that information was traded like any other commodity; and that neither monopoly nor government action significantly affected relative prices. Of course, disturbances could occur, but in the Chicago view "one may treat observed prices and quantities as good approximations to their long-run competitive equilibrium values. . . . the 'good approximation assumption'" (12).

Hard use of the good approximation assumption is a hallmark of Chicago applied research; but the assumption is not tested directly. . . . [T]he Chicago style is to treat it as a maintained hypothesis and apply it, using the resulting research findings as a test of TP. (12–13)

If the results were inconsistent with the implications of standard price theory, the Chicago reaction was not to alter the theory but to reexamine the data or redefine or augment the variables. Similarly, Chicago-trained TP theorists were likely to protect basic theory by discrediting or playing down reports of irrational or inefficient behaviour or to treat reports of alleged monopoly with scepticism (and if they were confirmed to treat the phenomena as transitory and relatively limited in impact).

Generally, Chicago economists have been regarded as antistatist. To some extent this followed from TP, which centred on the private disposition of resources by individuals but allowed them to use agents even though these would reduce the gains to individuals. On this view, the government was an agent that was very difficult to control and therefore probably inefficient at achieving individuals' goals. Such a view did not, however, go as far as normative antistatism, which regarded providing government officials with control of resources as wrong, even if this might accomplish some social purpose faithfully and efficiently. Such normative antistatism has been associated with many of Chicago's leading figures who have been members of the Mount Pelerin Society, founded at a conference organised by Friedrich Hayek in April 1947. Knight, Friedman, and Stigler were founder-members and Wallis was treasurer from 1948–54 (Hartwell 1995, 45–6, 66).

Settling In

This milieu the Johnsons entered in September 1959. Harry was in some senses a deliberate outsider: to the locals he was a Keynesian – a threatening term if there ever was one for TP-trained economists. The Keynesian consumption function, which was not derivable by the aggregation of the consumption behaviour of individuals, challenged the basic model, as also did the suggestion that money wages, if not rigid, did not follow their long-term equilibrium values. In effect, TP implied rejection of an autonomous enterprise called macroeconomics. But Harry was in Chicago to replace Lloyd Metzler, a brilliant Keynesian of the 1940s, who was in his prime "one of the half dozen leading economists in the world" (Samuelson 1986, 359) but whose creativity and drive had been impaired by surgery to remove a brain tumour. That Harry was so recognised was clear in Friedman's 1957 invitation to undertake a Cambridge Economic Handbook on income and employment theory (see discussion in Chapter 7).

When they arrived in Chicago the Johnsons moved into a third-floor apartment at 5757 South Kenwood Avenue, a block from the university's Laboratory School where both of the children were enrolled[5] and about as close to the Department of Economics as one could get. The apartment building, built about 1910, had big rooms, big closets, big halls, and a maid's room and bath, which was immediately commandeered by Karen. As the top flat, its balcony looked out over the trees to Lake Michigan, six blocks away.

---

[5] Milton and Rose Friedman (1998, 200) emphasised the role of the neighbourhood and the links established through having children at the Laboratory School.

The previous tenants, separating after twenty-five years of marriage, sold the contents of the apartment to the Johnsons for $800, which turned out to be a godsend as their English furniture scheduled to arrive in October did not arrive until 17 December, just as Harry's mother arrived for the Christmas holiday (British Library of Political and Economic Science, Royal Economic Society Archives, RES 9/7/3, Elizabeth Johnson to Jane Thistlethwaite, 8 January 1960).

Liz reported enjoying life and finding it only too easy to fit in:

> The neighbourhood just around the university . . . has all the good characteristics of a small town (familiar faces, feeling of belonging) without, so far as I can see now, any of the bad ones, because it is part of a big city. . . . The nice things to me that I mentally said goodbye to when I left England are all very present here – people of all colours, all shades of the rainbow, to look at and listen to in the streets and stores . . . and eccentric characters – people are every bit as nutty in Hyde Park as in the correspondence columns of The Times. . . .
>
> The people you meet live highly organised lives and the women are very active do-gooders. . . .
>
> The children have taken to school like ducks to water. . . . Writing Christmas cards made both of them very sad, though. This is a much bigger change for them than for Harry and me and they cannot feel as we do that they can come back, although Ragnar makes plans. (British Library of Political and Economic Science, Royal Economic Society Archives, RES 9/7/3, to Jane Thistlethwaite, 8 January 1960)

Harry seems to have found settling in more difficult. As he told B. R. Williams, "Talking of adjustment problems, I have plenty" (Box 31, Correspondence to 1963, S–Z, 3 November 1959). He had no teaching commitments for his first year and, as he told his former Manchester colleague John Knapp, could "spend my year travelling around the country giving lectures for vast sums of money" (Box 31, Correspondence to 1963, H–L, 25 May 1960). But as he told W. J. M. Mackenzie at the end of the year:

> When I look back on the first year I have spent in Chicago, I find it hard to discern any achievement to justify a year off teaching. But I have got around a lot and got to understand a bit of how the place works. Manchester is a triumph of organizing genius compared to this university. (Box 31, Correspondence to 1963, M-R, 30 June 1960)

He was unhappy with the lack of secretarial support as compared with Manchester. He told his former student, Samuel Brittan, then at the *Financial Times*:

> Please excuse the typing, which I do myself, in this capital-intensive, labour-short country I get one-eighth of a secretary to myself, but a first-class reconditioned

typewriter and typewriter table in my office. (Box 31, Correspondence to 1963, A–C, 2 February 1960)

He took an active role in the professional life of the department. He became a member of the money and banking workshop run by Milton Friedman. According to Allan Hynes:

Milton . . . ran a tight ship. Papers had to be circulated a week in advance and it was assumed that they had been read. The papers were not presented but discussed. This to a large extent involved Friedman going through the paper line by line commenting both on the quality of the economics and the writing – apparently neither as a rule were very satisfactory. Harry would sit in the middle of the conference table, take out his current wood carving, and begin to work. Wood chips would pile up and periodically be swept to the floor. When things were slow, Harry would take a bit of snuff, but he would make only an occasional comment. This was not a particularly supportive environment. (2001, 625)

Harry also took an active part in the social life of the department and the university – perhaps too active for Liz's taste – even going so far as to join the faculty's baseball team for Saturday games against the graduate students.[6] He got involved in regular poker evenings initiated by A. C. Harberger and Larry Sjaastad, with the other regulars including Martin Bailey, John Hause, Allan Hynes, and Ralph Winter. "This was not high-powered gambling; the game was really an excuse to drink beer, gossip, drink beer, tell stories, and drink beer" (Hynes 2001, 625). It was a department with a core of well-seasoned drinkers with whom Harry could more than hold his own: At parties Harry normally drank scotch 'in about the same quantities as others . . . [drank] beer and soft drinks' (625). David Laidler remembered that in 1962 "I discovered that drink could be very much a part of the Chicago economist's way of life too. Indeed, I was a good year into my first appointment at Berkeley before I realised that economists' parties were not always intended to be events at which everybody got a bit drunk, as a preliminary to offering frank criticism of everyone else's work" (2000, 331).

Once Harry started teaching he found his days so full that he and Liz began to get up at 6 A.M. to work before breakfast, "Chicago hours" as Liz called them (British Library of Political and Economic Science, Royal Economic Society Archives, RES 9/7/3, to Jane Thistlethwaite, 13 December 1960). But

---

[6] Liz remarked "already after three months here our calendar is in the same state as after three years in Manchester. This, plus avoiding getting involved in the women's organizations, are my problems" (British Library of Political and Economic Science, Royal Economic Society Archives, RES 9/7/3, to Jane Thistlethwaite, 8 January 1960).

Harry was dissatisfied. When Jan Graaff wrote him from Cambridge, where he was spending three weeks, Harry replied:

It was good to receive your letter from Cambridge, especially as it came at a time when I was feeling depressed with my American environment. I am sorry we are not still in England, so that we could have seen you on your visit there. All things considered though, I am not sorry to have left Cambridge precisely because it changes so little: but Manchester was fun after the first year, more so than here. On the other hand, the Department here is active and very professional, and I feel that I have benefitted professionally from the change. Sooner or later I shall have to adopt the path of positive economics, which you forecasted as the way ahead in the last chapter of your book.[7] (Box 31, Correspondence to 1963, D–G, 10 April 1961)

As for his view of family life in Chicago, he found it, as he told Graaff "pleasant enough on the whole but not very rich."

Chicago meant more travelling than Manchester did. At first Harry enjoyed it – remarking to Jan Graaff in 1961, "I'm off to London. Air travel is marvellous" (Box 31, Correspondence to 1963, D–G, 18 August 1961). Earlier in the year, however, he reported its down-side to John Heath: "I have been very busy going here and there and giving stupid talks on this and that" (Box 31, Correspondence to 1963, H–J, 4 May 1961). And it got even more intense. In June 1964, Liz reported to Judith Masterman in Cambridge that May she had "a trip to Washington with my husband (whom it seems I can only see these days by driving to an airport or leaving Chicago)" (British Library of Political and Economic Science, Royal Economic Society Archives, RES 9/7/5, 2 June 1964).

Conflict

Some of Harry's difficulties in the transition to Chicago arose from his own behaviour. He and Jagdish Bhagwati published a joint paper in the *Economic Journal* for March 1960, "Notes on Some Controversies in the Theory

---

[7] Graaff (1958, 170) had written: "I do feel very strongly that the greatest contribution economics is likely to make to human welfare, broadly conceived, is through *positive* studies – through contributing to our understanding of how the economic system actually works in practice – rather than through normative welfare theory itself.

"If positive economics can provide people with an understanding of the various far-reaching indirect effects of particular policies, it will probably also provide them with the basis for drawing welfare conclusions for themselves and according to their own lights. In my view the job of the economist is not to try to reach welfare conclusions for others, but rather to make available the positive knowledge – the information and the understanding – on the basis of which laymen (and economists themselves out of office hours) can pass value judgements."

of International Trade" (1961c). The last section of the paper, which, according to Bhagwati (1977, 224) "was almost wholly Harry's contribution," dealt with Marshall's theorem concerning the stability of international equilibrium. At the end of that section, Harry added a footnote, almost a page long, which dealt with Friedman's assertion and Egon Sohmen's alleged proof that equilibrium is necessarily enclosed by stable equilibrium points in an unstable foreign-exchange market. In referring to Sohmen's contribution Harry continued:

[T]hese sentences illustrate the extent to which *non sequitur* and *ignoratio elenchi* can be accepted as valid argument if the conclusion purportedly reached is of sufficient propaganda value. (1960c, 93)

Bhagwati later recollected that

[W]hat astonished Harry and me was that, at Chicago, Milton Friedman was up in arms. Oddly, Friedman considered the footnote to be an unprofessional piece of writing, and also to constitute unwarranted bullying by Harry of a lesser economist. Unfortunately, he would not keep these notions to himself and to Harry. This style of skirmishing was entirely novel to both of us and left Harry acutely embarrassed and uncomfortable.[8] (1977, 224)

Friedman's grievance to Sohmen ended up in the files of the *Economic Journal*:

Until I received your letter with its enclosed comment, I had not looked at the Bhagwati and Johnson piece. Your letter led me to do so and I was profoundly shocked by what I found. I have told Johnson so, that he ought to be ashamed of himself and that he owes you a public apology. (British Library of Political and Economic Science, Royal Economic Society Archives, RES 6/1/451, quoted in E. Sohmen to R. F. Harrod, 4 June 1960)

When the controversy between Sohmen on the one side and Johnson and Bhagwati on the other finally wound down in the *Economic Journal* for June 1961, they allowed in a footnote that "[w]e should not perhaps have used the word 'propaganda' in this connection, however, since to some casual readers of our footnote it seems to have conveyed an implication of deliberate deceit

---

[8] Bhagwati may have been more astonished than Harry, for when talking of publication dates with Roy Harrod, Harry had written "I should be sorry to see it delayed as late as June 1960 for one particular reason which is that Bhagwati and I will both be at the University of Chicago this coming year and the last part of the article is a pretty hard-hitting criticism of some strongly-held Chicago views. I should like the article to appear before he has left Chicago." (British Library of Political and Economic Science, Royal Economic Society Archives, RES 6/2/111, HGJ to Harrod, 26 June 1959).

which was in no way intended" (427). That was hardly "a public apology"; nor would Friedman have been pleased at being called a "casual reader."

Certainly the incident rankled with Harry. But there were other irritations. Edward Shils remembered

I first met him [Harry] not long after he had come to the University of Chicago. . . . He was not entirely at home at the University of Chicago, where the rough and tumble of discussions in the economics department . . . was not what he liked. He was thinking of throwing up his post at . . . Chicago and accepting a very attractive invitation to Johns Hopkins. He wanted my advice. (Shils 1977, 87)

The invitation may have come later (see below) but the feeling was real. It even carried over into his 1969 Autobiographical Notes when he spoke of the department "pretty much dominated by Milton Friedman" as "a tough environment, especially for someone accustomed to the English traditions of the reasonable compromise between conflicting points of view" (11). Later, he referred to needing his first year in Chicago without teaching "to get used to and become a part of the prevailing intellectual brutality" (Box 39, Correspondence 1972–7, P–T, to Merton J. Peck, 1 April 1971).

Some of his grounds for unhappiness with the department surfaced in a speech he gave to the Chicago graduate student Political Economy Club at a cocktail party on 28 October 1960, "A Keynesian's Impression of Chicago." He reported that "at least in some quarters in Chicago" a Keynesian meant something different from what he had always taken it to mean. In Chicago

A Keynesian . . . is a weak and spineless creature, who blindly follows the master along the path of error, refusing to modify or develop the system of thought Keynes started, or to test it in any way, or to consider the allegedly conclusive evidence thrust before his nose by Chicago economists.

He noted that this was not his first look at Chicago. He had had contact with Chicago theory through the work of Veblen and Knight, which he had read in Toronto in 1946–7 under the guidance of his teachers – one of whom had been a pupil of Veblen's.[9] He had then come across Chicago again at Harvard where he had read the work of Oscar Lange and Lloyd Metzler as they developed Keynesian theory and integrated it with general equilibrium theory.[10] At the time he was also aware

that there existed in Chicago a lonely group of theorists so devoted in principle to free enterprise that they wanted to reconstruct the world in the image of perfect

---

[9] He was thinking of Innis, who had actually been a student of Knight's and done his PhD dissertation under Chester Wright.

[10] He had also read both in Hood's seminar in Toronto in 1946–7.

competition, with government reduced to the single function of exchanging cash for consols or consols for cash as the needs of price stability might dictate.

Finally, before he left Manchester he had come to know a Chicago where testing hypotheses and particularly interesting questions seemed promising. He had observed it from the safety of suburban Evanston, where he was most impressed by "the missionary zeal of the place and the theological character of its discussions." He reported that

seminars in those days were very similar to Buffalo Bill's Wild West Show: the stagecoach of economic orthodoxy would drive out into the arena; it would be attacked by a yelling mob of pagan Indians; on the verge of its capture Buffalo Bill would charge out to the rescue with pistols blazing, long golden hair streaming in the breeze, followed by his cowboys (Buffalo Bill always has the fastest horse); and the Indians who were not slaughtered would gallop off in confusion pursued by the cowboys while Buffalo Bill solicitously helped the fair occupant of the coach to step out. Sometimes the visiting speaker rode in the coach but usually he was one of the Indians – it was more fun for the cowboys that way.

He continued:

I have referred to three main themes or motifs of Chicago economics as it appeared to me from outside Chicago – speculation about the nature and quality of capitalism as a human society, together with a sceptical questioning of the relevance of formal economic theory to this problem; the theological interpretation of the theory of static equilibrium; and the insistence of testing theory by statistical means. So far as the first of these is concerned, it is abundantly clear to me that this manifestation of Chicago's originality in economics is now totally dead – whether by suicide or murder I cannot say, though I have my suspicions. . . . I think this indifference, or even hostility towards, social speculation is a great pity. . . .

In contrast . . . the second motif . . . is very much in evidence. Chicago is probably the only department in the country, with the possible exception of some Southern universities, where the principle of marginal productivity is still regarded as a manifestation of divine justice. . . . I have heard it said that Chicago is the only department in the country where a Ph.D. is a joint degree in economics and theology, but this is an unfair exaggeration. It is also unfair to maintain that there is a unanimity of opinion on matters of economic principle at Chicago. . . . A high degree of unanimity there certainly is. . . . But one senses a certain pressure to conformity underlying the unanimity, a certain self-searching to make sure the principles of free enterprise are being properly applied at all times, and a certain anxiety to be the first to attack a new idea and root out any possible heresy. One senses this especially in the products of the system, the Chicago Ph.D.s who can usually be distinguished from other universities' Ph.D.s by a certain grim and joyless earnestness of expression and an inability to laugh at intellectual jokes.

Thirdly, there is the empirical work on hypothesis-testing. It is on this last that Chicago's claims to professional prestige mainly, and quite justifiably, rests. One can have some reservations about this too; the work tends to be restricted to a rather narrow range of problems, and to be dominated by the objective of proving either that the price system is efficient or that the government is not . . . and it is not altogether obvious that the only possible way to find out how the economy works is to sit for two years in a cellar behind a calculating machine. (Box 25, Writing 1960)

Such blunt speaking caused a stir.[11] Some bewildered graduate students shuffled up to Friedman and asked if they should have been amused. They shouldn't have been. Members of the minority approved. Anthony Downs congratulated him on "outstanding . . . wit, candor and trenchancy" (Box 25, Writing 1960, 3 November 1960). Jacob Mincer called it " [a] fair hit – and that includes fair in the sense of even-handed and generous." But Mincer mentioned that his colleagues were piqued, although he couldn't decide if it was Harry's reference to Chicago's statistical testing or to joylessness (Box 31, Correspondence to 1963, Unsorted, no date). The next spring, Joan Robinson, visiting Chicago, reported to Richard Kahn that Harry had "caused such grave offense that he was more or less sent to Coventry." She continued, "Unfortunately he has never been keen on my stuff so that he does not feel as happy to have my backing as he might. There is nothing to do in this horrid city except argue" (King's College, Cambridge, Kahn Papers, RFK 13/90/6/219, 21 April 1961). Almost a week later she reported him "subdued and hopeless" (King's College, Cambridge, RFK 13/90/6/215 27 April 1961).[12] According to Alvin Marty, who was visiting Chicago at the time, Harry was concerned that he might have to leave Chicago because life in the department had become so unpleasant (Interview 10 October 2004).

[11] He also raised similar issues when discussing C. Wright Mills's *The Sociological Imagination* with G. C. Archibald: "I found him stimulating because he wants to get on to work on problems with some social relevance which seems to me more and more the shortcoming of the Chicago approach and because he puts the emphasis on work and not on the methodological discussion. I don't think I would go so far as to deny the usefulness of any methodological discussion, but it can quickly turn into a way of ignoring people's work without trying to match it. In Chicago it often amounts to defining as important only those problems which your particular technique will cope with, and this seems to me a bad thing" (Box 31, Correspondence to 1963, A–C, 23 November 1960).

[12] Liz reported to Jane Thistlethwaite on Joan's visit: "We've been pretty busy with Joan Robinson's 10 day visit to Chicago. She found the place disconcertingly unresponsive – as they were sure to be to a left-wing economist – and went on to discover that Northwestern (where all the students are out big for Barry Goldwater!) was much more responsive. While it was a pleasure to have her here, it was also pretty dismal for her to see the place reacting so true to form – although her visit does seem to have started some subversion among the students under the surface which didn't appear at the time – a few of the thoughtful ones are now voicing some resentment against the glib characters who keep shooting off the local line" (British Library of Political and Economic Science, Royal Economic Society Archives, RES 9/7/3, 7 May 1961).

In the spring of 1961, Harry was reporting to Charles Carter that "I am doing fairly well here, not that I have settled in. I edit the *Journal of Political Economy* and give classes that I like – but how long that will last I don't know" (British Library of Political and Economic Science, Royal Economic Society Archives, RES 6/2/111, 7 April 1961). In the autumn he was more enthusiastic, reporting to Carl Christ:

Things are going along at Chicago pretty much as ever though the influx of something like four new young people may restore some zip to the place that was lacking last year. We made an offer to Bob [Fogel], but quite predictably failed to interest him. I got interested in the Committee for the Comparative Study of New Nations, which introduces me to some of the anthropologists and sociologists and broadens my cocktail party conversation just a bit. (Box 31, Correspondence to 1963, A–C, 20 October 1961)

Within months there was a brief flurry of interest in possibly moving. As Harry reported to A. C. Harberger:

I have been besieged by Toronto, Berkeley, Northwestern . . . and Michigan State. Berkeley couldn't reach to my current price. Chicago has topped Toronto, if one does not allow for the six-month Canadian academic year; I have not finally said no to Toronto – I happened to be there, and insisted on seeing the President and giving him an idea of what he would have to do to interest me. I don't think he will want to do it, which means we will be colleagues next year.

   . . . I can't yet say that I have decided to stay, but the chances of my deciding to go look small at the moment.[13] (Box 31, Correspondence to 1963, H–L, 14 March 1962)

Harry's estimate was correct. And not surprisingly, as Ernest Sirluck, who was coming from Chicago to Toronto as dean of the Graduate School and had been asked to try to bring Harry back with him, reported the whole incident:

Johnson came to discuss his [offer] with me. It was for barely more than his Chicago salary, but his main concern was that, as in previous offers it had made to him, Toronto didn't seem to have any specific reason for hiring him in particular: "they just want to add some laurels to their reputation." I told him of [President] Bissell's intention to build up Toronto's key departments, and he replied that, if Bissell personally would convince him that a serious strengthening of economics was in prospect he'd consider the offer. I wrote to Bissell, a visit was arranged. It did not go well. [Dean] Bladen and Tom Easterbrook, the department chairman, made it clear that they would not make the kinds of changes that would enable Johnson to

---

[13] According to R. B. Heflebower, Harry had "turned down Toronto's fancy offer because Chicago liberally overmatched it" (Duke University, Clower Papers, Box 2, R. B. Heflebower to R. W. Clower, 13 March 1962).

effect serious improvement in the department, and his interview with Bissell was unhappy. Johnson told me that he'd given Bissell "an earful," and Bissell likened Johnson to "an eastern potentate." (1996, 217)

It was the last time Toronto attempted to hire him. There matters rested for a time. The following year there was a brief flurry of interest from Johns Hopkins (Box 31, Carl Christ to HGJ, 24 May 1963). The next inquiry would be more successful.

A Joint Appointment at LSE

When Ely Devons arrived at LSE, he quickly realised what had gone wrong over the appointment of Meade's successor in 1957–8. He began to mend fences and became instrumental in bringing in new blood to revive the School's prospects. He also changed the title of his chair (Johnson 1968c). At the end of 1962, Devons reported to Harry that LSE had applied to the University of London to invite him over to lecture for two to three weeks "sometime next [academic] year" and to warn him that a formal invitation would be coming some months later. Finally it was agreed that Harry would give a series of five lectures in January and February 1964. At the time, the LSE chair in economics which had been held since 1929 by Lionel Robbins was vacant.[14] The vacant chair may have been in the background to the School's invitation, for at the end of a letter of 23 October 1963 on another subject there was a casual P.S. "Any chance of our being able to attract you now or in a couple of years?" (Box 31, Correspondence to 1963, D–G), which drew the following reply from Harry on 5 November: "Chair at LSE – I am occasionally tempted, I must say, but I don't want to raise any false hopes. I'll see you in January–February anyway" (Box 31, Correspondence to 1963, D–G). Two months later A. W. H. Phillips added to the brew:

When we last met we thought that one or two influential persons here might not be in favour of the suggestion we were discussing. I find that this was wrong; they do in fact support the idea. I thought I should let you know this, since there will probably be an early opportunity for a decision. (Box 36, Correspondence 1964–6, M–Z, 9 January 1964)

Harry duly gave his lectures on the standard theory of tariffs, arguments for protection, the cost of protection, the theory of the tariff structure, and

---

[14] In 1961, when Robbins became chairman of the Financial Times, the University of London had refused to allow him to be a part-time chair holder and thus forced him to vacate it.

tariffs and economic development, which he planned to turn into a book for Allen and Unwin.

The file then remained silent until May 1964. Then the usually well-informed Harberger, on leave at the Catholic University of Chile, reported:

> I hear from the Grape Vine that London is again trying to persuade you to go there. I sincerely hope that you will stay with us in Chicago. For my money, your coming to Chicago was the best thing that has happened to our Department in the time that I have been there. (Box 56, Correspondence 1964–6, A–L, 19 May 1964)

Harberger was afraid that LSE would reduce Harry's productivity. If he stayed at Chicago he could do as much for public policy and probably still produce more. A little over a fortnight later Zvi Griliches wrote from Jerusalem:

> I am surprised and distressed to hear that you are seriously considering LSE again. I'd hate to see you go just when we were beginning to make some progress at Chicago.
>
> God knows Chicago is no Eden. It has its problems, but surely LSE is not better. I presume you are much better informed than I on this matter, but when I spent a few days at LSE in December I came away quite depressed. There is no real graduate program there, there are no first rate young guys on the faculty . . . and there is no prospect of improvement. . . . I can see that there might be a challenge in trying to improve matters there, after all, they can't get much worse, but the long term prospects for the place are not encouraging. In Yiddish we say 'Why put a healthy head into a sick bed?' If you had decided to move to Harvard, or even Berkeley or Toronto – I would have been distressed but I'd understand – this just doesn't make sense. Six-seven years ago the LSE chair would have meant something – today it seems a little too late. (Box 56, Correspondence 1964–6, A–L, 7 June 1964)

But he was too late. On 12 June, Richard Lipsey was writing that

> I have just heard from London that the agreement has apparently been settled for you to go to the L. S. E. London is, by all reports, in a state of jubilation. I am personally extremely pleased and write you at this juncture to offer my best wishes for the undoubted success of this adventure. Your presence in London will no doubt add to our staff and other troubles at Colchester.[15] (Box 56, Correspondence 1964–6, A–L)

Harry replied "I think it will be fun" (23 June).

The Appointments Committee reported to the Standing Committee on 23 June that Harry would be willing to come to take Robbins's chair. The Standing Committee approved and appointed its representatives to the University Board of Advisers, which met on 17 July. The university formally offered him the chair from 1 October 1966 at an annual salary of £4,750 plus

---

[15] Lipsey had gone to the University of Essex as one of the five founding professors in 1964. He was the only LSE economist to leave a chair to go to a new university.

London allowance. Harry accepted on 5 August.[16] The press was informed on 20 August (LSE, Personal File). Harry also agreed to give ten lectures in macroeconomics, plus classes and seminars for MSc students, in the course of two visits of a month in the Michaelmas term 1965 and two weeks in the Lent term of 1966.

In the fall of 1965, Arnold Harberger took over as chair of the Chicago department. He had been deeply distressed by Harry's planned departure. Now he began to try to devise a set of arrangements that would make it possible for Harry to maintain a connection with Chicago. There were precedents for joint appointments at Chicago: Edward Shils, for example, held his Chicago chair simultaneously with one at University College, London, and later a Fellowship at King's College, Cambridge. The key to the solution in Harry's case lay in the fact that there were no lectures at LSE during the Easter Term as students prepared for examinations. During his November 1965 visit to LSE, Harry told the professors of economics that he wished to combine his LSE appointment with one at Chicago, spending the first two terms at LSE and returning for two to three weeks in the third term for examining and maintaining contact with supervisees. He would, however, spend all three terms of 1966–7 at the School. The joint arrangement would be for five years in the first instance. The professors of economics approved of the arrangement because they "all felt we would like to have you for ourselves – but we agreed that the proposed arrangement was the next best thing" (Box 36, Correspondence 1964–6, M–Z, from B. Yamey, 5 December 1965). The proposal went forward to the director for approval in January. Once approved within the School, it went on to the university where it ran into difficulties in the form of Vice Chancellor Sir Douglas Logan who had been involved in the Robbins case and wrote on 24 March 1966:

I very much dislike the arrangement suggested in your letter which seems to me to cut right across our general principle that Professors should hold full-time appointments in the University of London. (HGJ, LSE, Personal File)

Logan thought it would be "very difficult to get the Academic Council [which had voted against a part-time arrangement for Lionel Robbins] to agree to this proposal" and suggested that LSE go ahead without the

---

[16] Harry chose 1966 because it let Ragnar finish high school in Chicago. This turned out to be unfortunate, as Ragnar, who "was the most anxious of us all to return to the United Kingdom," found "the struggle to re-establish himself in a different educational system than he had become used to ... very difficult" (British Library of Political and Economic Science, Royal Economic Society Archives, RES 9/7/5, Elizabeth Johnson to Judith Masterman, 2 June 1963; Box 41, Correspondence 1968, HGJ to D. O. Judd, 11 April 1968).

formal approval of the University with "the minimum of publicity . . . given to the proposed arrangement." Thus, in the end, Harry's formal LSE appointment remained unchanged, but he was allowed to go to Chicago on a leave-without-pay basis that reduced his London salary by £750.[17] However, it gave him a substantial Chicago salary, which given the existing tax arrangements was very attractive. As Harry would later explain:

> I have been financially able to devote myself to academic activity at the School . . . by working each year at the equivalent of a full teaching year at the School and a full teaching year in Chicago. I have been able to meet my London expenses partly by transmitting foreign income (and paying British taxes on it) and partly by reducing my London expenses by living abroad and working there part of the year. To do this, I pay American tax on all my income, and take as a tax credit the taxes paid to the British government on the British income. The offsetting effects of the higher British tax rates and the lower income total to which they apply mean that my total income taxes are about the same . . . as I would pay if my income were not subject to British income tax. (LSE, Personal File, letter to the Director, 22 May 1976)

The new arrangement entailed a very strenuous teaching load.

The die was cast. Harry and Liz sold the house they had built in 1962–3 at 5628 South Dorchester to Arnold Zellner in May 1966. In future, they would rent an apartment in Chicago at 5825 South Dorchester. Their London base would be a rented flat at 91 Bedford Court Mansions, just west of the British Museum and within walking distance of LSE.

---

[17] At the time the joint London–Chicago appointment was being finalised, the Graduate School of International Studies in Geneva tried to arrange a joint appointment for Harry. He turned it down (Box 56, Correspondence 1964–6, A–L, from Gerard Curzon, 22 February 1966; to Gerard Curzon, 18 April 1966). It was revived later (see discussion in Chapter 16).

NINE

Canada, Economic Nationalism, and Opulence, 1957–1966

When I moved in 1959 from the University of Manchester to the University of Chicago, I had no expectation of becoming involved in public discussion of Canadian economic policy issues. . . . That I have since become involved in analysis and criticism of Canadian economic policy has largely been the consequence of the dramatic reversal of Canada's economic fortunes since 1957–8 and of a sense of responsibility to put my professional knowledge at the disposal of my countrymen if invited to do so.

Canadian Quandary (CQ), vi

In his Autobiographical Notes of 1969 he claimed that when he went to Chicago

I had not intended to take any interest in Canadian economic problems, but I got started down that primrose path by an invitation to prepare a paper on trade policy for the Kingston Conference of liberally-minded people in September 1960. (13)

But he had been commenting on Canadian affairs for some years (see discussion in Chapter 5). Moreover, given the subject of his concerns after 1959 and the centrality of Walter Gordon to them, it makes sense to go back to Manchester and, as he did in his 1974 Self-Evaluation (10), begin with his review of the *Preliminary Report* of the Royal Commission on Canada's Economic Prospects chaired by Walter Gordon, which appeared in the *Canadian Journal of Economics and Political Science* in February 1958. The arguments of his review presaged many of his subsequent criticisms.

[The Commission] also feels that . . . legislation to control monopolies should be "restudied" to take account of the view of "some reasonable people" that concentration and agreement are desirable under Canadian conditions.

These transcriptions of interested opinion serve as a prelude to a section on commercial policy which is a model of under-developed economic thinking, really requiring a review of its own. The Commission apparently believes that the fact

213

that "there is no satisfactory way of measuring... the true cost of the Canadian tariff in economic terms" (p. 72), is an excuse for not trying.... It then asserts an erroneous proposition that unwillingness on the part of other countries to reduce trade barriers makes it sensible to hold the tariff line at the present level....

Problems connected with the investment of foreign capital in Canada are discussed in Section 14, the most controversial in the report.... Such investment, though beneficial to growth, has two alleged disadvantages.... The Commission wants more foreign capital to be invested in bonds and mortgages, and the rest to be associated with Canadian capital. Its reason is that "many Canadians are worried about such a large measure of economic decision-making being in the hands of non-residents or in the hands of Canadian companies controlled by non-residents" (p. 89).

The Commission provides no convincing arguments in support of this attitude, and several against it, but alarmed lest xenophobia lead to extreme action in the future it states three objectives for the operation of foreign concerns doing business in Canada....

In view of the fact that the Commission provides no concrete evidence of misbehaviour by foreign subsidiaries, only vague fears for the future and an unspecified possibility of extreme action... it is difficult to see in the Commission's argument anything more than another attempt to blackmail successful alien risk-takers into paying tribute to unenterprising but powerful local capitalists as the price for controlling the mob.

... [T]he report is unsatisfying but not exciting. It is disappointing to find a report which professes faith in the flexible market economy so uneven in its understanding of how the market system works, so prone to accept the existence of problems put forward by interested parties, and so willing to cope with the problems it sees by putting someone in charge of issuing permits. (*CQ*, 7–10)

After his review and before his arrival in Chicago, Harry took part in one other discussion of Canadian economic policy. The Canadian Institute of International Affairs held an annual study conference as a part of the annual meetings of Canada's learned societies. The June 1959 conference, held at Queen's University, Kingston, had "Canada's Foreign Trade Problems" as its theme. Harry attended as a guest. Afterwards, he reported on the roundtable, providing some preliminary impressions of Canada's trade policy problems and a brief observation on the central issue they raised (1960d). The central problem "was the conflict in Canadian thinking between the economic considerations favouring closer economic integration between Canada and the United States and the political fear of American domination and the loss of Canadian national identity"(*CQ*, 78). A long series of future papers would explore this and related questions.

The first opportunity after his arrival in Chicago came in September 1960, and again in Kingston. The origins lay in Canadian politics. In June 1957 the federal Liberal Party, which had been in power since 1935, won just 105 of the 265 seats in the House of Commons. The government of Louis St. Laurent resigned and John Diefenbaker formed a minority Progressive Conservative government with 112 seats. The next February, just over two weeks after Lester Pearson was elected leader of the Liberals, Diefenbaker called a snap election in response to a maladroit Liberal parliamentary manoeuvre. The Progressive Conservatives won 208 seats to the Liberals 49.

The process of rebuilding the Liberals began soon afterwards. One aspect of this rebuilding involved restocking the party with ideas. When they had last been out of power, Vincent Massey organised a summer school at Port Hope in 1933. This time Pearson approached Mitchell Sharp, a former deputy minister of trade and commerce who was now in private business. Sharp raised the funds and with a group of Toronto business and academic friends, including R. M. MacIntosh and Stefan Stykolt, planned the programme. The Kingston Conference, 6–10 September, covered ten topics – defence; external economic policy; growth, stability and the problem of unemployment; social security; organised labour; agriculture; urban development; and values and cultural heritage. Each topic was introduced by a speaker (in the case of social security more than one) who provided a paper circulated in advance. Each paper was commented upon by preselected commentators before being thrown open for exhaustive discussion. At the suggestion of Stefan Stykolt, Harry was asked to produce the paper on external economic policy. His commentators were R. M. Fowler and R. B. Macpherson.

The original plan had been to limit attendance to 50 "thinkers" but, in the end, the organisers found it difficult to keep numbers down to about 200. With one exception, no member of Parliament was on the programme as a speaker. Of the 196 who turned up, 48 were later named to senior appointments in the Liberal administration after the party's return to power in 1963 (English 1992, 218).

Harry opened the discussion on the morning of Wednesday 7 September. The previous afternoon, the conference had heard a paper by Michael Barkway on "How Independent Can We Be" with Walter Gordon, Harry Wolfson, and Harry's former colleague William Hood, as commentators: "Gordon," according to Harry, "helped me out . . . by stating four reasons why integration with the United States is a bad idea. I must confess that those reasons confirm my view that this is a very good idea" (*CQ*, 119). The afternoon's discussion had also considered a proposal present in both the Cordon Commission's *Preliminary* and *Final Report* "for manipulating the tax laws," as Harry put it, "in order to foist Canadians into the shareholding and directorships of American corporations." Harry saw "that what was at work is not so much the noble spirit of Canadian independence, as the small, smug mind and large, larcenous hands of Bay Street"(*CQ*, 114–15).[1] Harry's paper took as its main recommendation that "Canada should aim at some sort of economic integration with the United States." His favourite recommendation was for reciprocal free trade with the United States in the form of a free trade area – a proposal that came to fruition in 1989. His more minimal aims centred on a substantial reform of the Canadian tariff, whose costs to the Canadian economy following J. H. Young's *Canadian Commercial Policy* (a study for the Gordon Commission), which he estimated at 3.5 to 4.5 percent of gross national expenditure net of indirect taxes, or adding in its effects on government expenditure and distributors' margins $4^1/_3$ percent of national income. At the root of his argument for closer integration was the growing regionalism of world trade, symbolised by the formation of the European Economic Community and the European Free Trade Association, and the increasing concentration of Canadian trade in the United States. In correspondence soon afterwards, he also said that he favoured the American link because contemporary British proposals for increasing trade with Canada were not serious and "that the effects of joining either of the two European organisations would probably involve a greater sacrifice of Canadian sovereignty than an economic union with the United States" (Box 31, Correspondence to 1963, A–L, to Clarence Barber, 12 December 1960). Noting in passing that loss of national identity had not been an argument used against economic integration in Europe, he did not think that increased trade, or large-scale participation of foreign capital in Canadian economic development, posed a threat to Canadian independence or Canadians' national identity. "More integration, in my mind, means a richer and more prosperous Canada; and nobody is as independent as the man who can afford to pick up his own cheques" (*CQ*, 120).

Harry noted at the time to S. F. Kaliski that he was "too liberal for the Liberals" (Box 31, Correspondence to 1963, A–L, 29 August 1960). His ideas were indeed at odds with contemporary thinking in the Liberal Party – whose economic agenda was increasingly associated with the views of Walter Gordon who was responsible for reorganising the party, the chair of its policy committee and, eventually, minister of finance when the Liberals returned to power. As far as one can tell, Harry's paper fell rather flat. More of a stir was caused by another speaker recently resident in Manchester, Tom Kent, a former editor of the *Manchester Guardian* and *The Economist*, who had come to Canada in 1954 to edit the *Winnipeg Free Press*. Kent's paper

---

[1] Bay Street is the main street of Toronto's financial district and was then the site of the Toronto Stock Exchange.

called for a substantial expansion of the Canadian welfare state to include medical care, enhanced old age assistance and aid to education – some of which Harry would pick up in his discussions of opulence. The Liberals, in particular Walter Gordon, would provide Harry with many bases for future criticism.

Yet Harry's proposal had important long-run effects for the chair of the Royal Commission on the Economic Union and Development Prospects for Canada (1985), Donald Macdonald. A former supporter of Walter Gordon's policies, he attributed his conversion to its central recommendation of a free trade agreement with the United States in part to Harry's influence.

I have to tell you that just within the last year I read a monograph that I had not read in years . . . a speech given by Harry Johnson . . . in which he argued for Canada opening up its markets and taking a chance with the competition, which I'm sure I rejected at the time. But it seems to me now, twenty-three years on, that Harry Johnson . . . was proven right in the end. But I would not have agreed with him much of the time when I was younger. (Inwood 2005, 248)

Harry returned to the issue of Canadian nationalism in a 1961 speech at the University of Western Ontario (1961d). He found preparing the speech more difficult than he expected, for, as he told Kildaire Dobbs, he had problems with cultural nationalism.

The trouble is that I have fallen so far out of sympathy with it that I don't know enough about it to make the most telling points. I am writing to you as a man in the centre of things to ask for some literary and artistic activities in Canada. In particular, have you any writings of your own or any easily remembered references on this subject. This is a tall order, but perhaps you have something succinct to which you can refer me. I can be insulting about economics and politics without having to struggle, but culture takes a little homework. (Box 31, Correspondence to 1963, A–L, 2 March 1961)

Dobbs's reply, if he did reply, has not survived. He does not seem to have provided any useful ammunition, for Harry's paper concentrated on economic and political issues, and he remained detached from Canadian culture in the broader sense and was always relatively uninterested in culture in the narrower sense.

Harry began with a confession that recent Canadian nationalism disturbed him because it

seems to me to appeal to and to reinforce the most undesirable features of the Canadian character . . . not only the mean and underhanded anti-Americanism which serves many Canadians as an excuse for failure to accomplish anything worthy of national pride, but also . . . the small-town pettiness of outlook. . . . Canadian nationalism . . . has been diverting Canada into a narrow and garbage-cluttered cul-de-sac. (*CQ*, 11–12)

He had no difficulty with the notion of a distinctive Canadian identity. Nor did he question the fact that Canada was an independent country – even on occasions when Canada's best interests involved supporting American policies. He did not see Canadian independence being impaired by the consumption of American types of goods or by the pursuit of American ways of life – after all these were associated with growing opulence. It wasn't clear to him that "forcing people to buy Canadian goods and magazines instead of American" would make much difference: "Canadian producers would simply produce the same sort of goods, and probably not as well" (13). Nor was he prepared to accept that closer economic relations with the United States through trade and investment would lead to America's absorbing Canada, which seemed "to assume a degree of economic determinism in politics going far beyond anything the facts of history would warrant" (14).

It was in anti-Americanism that "the Canadian talent for genteel hypocrisy comes to its finest flower" (16).

It is this two-faced character of anti-Americanism in Canada – the desire to enjoy the emotional jag of indulging in hatred, envy and greed while maintaining the pretence that one is being very restrained and reasonable and that Americans not only should not be offended but should in fact approve – that I find particularly repugnant to me as a Canadian. It seems to be a characteristic which distinguishes Canadian anti-Americanism, to its discredit, from anti-Americanism elsewhere . . . and paradoxically . . . it seems to confirm what it seeks to deny, the similarity of Canadians to Americans, for this desire to be loved in spite of one's obnoxious behaviour is a deeply ingrained American characteristic. (16)

He then criticised the measures advocated by economic nationalists: increased industrial protection and provision for Canadian management and ownership of American enterprises in Canada. On the first, he could turn the guns of standard economic theory; on the second he witheringly noted: "It is hard to understand how one will become master in one's house by becoming a dividend-receiver or major-domo in someone else's house" (18–19).

He concluded by developing a theme that would grow stronger in ensuing papers: that the advocacy of protectionism and Canadianisation by nationalists had diverted attention from the fact that the depressed condition of the Canadian economy was the result of misguided policies pursued by the federal government and the Bank of Canada. Nationalists had helped Canadians evade a searching discussion of such policies – a discussion that became more animated between the paper's delivery and its publication by the Coyne affair – the attempt by the government of Canada to sack James Coyne, the governor of the Bank of Canada, ostensibly on the grounds that he had allowed his board of directors to grant him a generous pension increase without consulting the minister of finance.[2] However the real ground for Coyne's removal was disagreement over the governor's tight money policy coupled with the government's refusal to accept publicly responsibility for the conduct of monetary policy, and his public speeches advocating a more restrictive fiscal policy than the government was pursuing. When asked by the minister of finance to resign, Coyne refused. The government responded with a bill declaring the office vacant. This passed the House of Commons but was defeated in the Liberal-dominated, appointed Senate after Coyne had his "day in court." Coyne resigned on 13 July. On 20 July the minister of finance announced that there would be a Royal Commission of Banking and Finance; that would provide Harry with some summer employment the next year.

Harry had two Canadian opportunities in 1962 to comment on these events and the reversal of Canadian monetary and fiscal policy that followed Coyne's resignation – the Plaunt Lectures at Carleton University, *Canada in a Changing World Economy* (1962c) (15 and 17 February 1962), and "Canada in a Changing World" (1962d), a lecture to the Canadian Club of Toronto (5 November 1962). By the time of his Toronto lecture, the authorities had ended the régime of floating exchange rates, which had been in place since 1950 and undergone a speculative exchange crisis when markets doubted the appropriateness of the new pegged rate – a crisis that produced an austerity programme. His analysis was straightforward: He placed the origins of Canada's difficulties directly on the policy of monetary restriction by the Bank of Canada, which had significantly lengthened the average term to maturity of the national debt in the 1958 Conversion Loan. Monetary deflation, at a time of declining demand for Canadian exports owing to a recession in the United States, raised interest rates, which raised the value of the Canadian dollar. High domestic interest rates also encouraged foreign borrowing by Canadian governments and industries and, by making Canadian assets cheaper, increased foreign investment in Canada. Higher unemployment

---

[2] Even before Harry delivered his paper, twenty-nine academic economists – a quarter to a third of the national total – had signed a letter to the Minister of Finance asking him "to alter the management of the Bank of Canada" because the reasoning of the governor's public statements "does not appear . . . to approach that level of confidence which is a foundation for successful central bank policy" (Gordon 1961, vi). The original letter had been drafted by Harry Eastman and Stefan Stykolt.

and lower tax receipts also pushed the federal budget into deficit, further increasing the upward pressure on interest rates. In the process, the slowing down of economic growth was blamed on any number of symptoms – increased competition from foreign firms, low productivity, foreign investment, the federal deficit – which brought calls for symptom-specific remedies rather than calls for the reversal of the restrictive monetary policy.

The Conversion Loan had also meant the end of Highbrow Investments, a vehicle devised by R. M. MacIntosh for Harry and Stefan Stykolt to make money in the Canadian bond market. Funded in Harry's case with some spare cash after his 1955 leave, it had successfully speculated on a fall in interest rates and risen in value from $5,000 to $30,000. Emboldened by their success, they bet again on falling interest rates and heavily leveraged themselves with the result that the rising rates surrounding the Conversion wiped them out. Eventually, after Harry's death MacIntosh paid Liz $10,000 that he had earned over twenty years trying to recover from the fiasco.

The resignation of Governor Coyne had brought about a reversal of monetary policy. At the same time, fiscal policy was loosened. These would have reduced the Canadian dollar, but the depreciation was exacerbated by the minister of finance's attempt to "talk down" the exchange rate. Markets reacted adversely, and there was further depreciation followed by a decision to peg the rate and, given the lack of confidence, a crisis. Harry continued:

Unfortunately, one of the universal characteristics of intelligent and educated public opinion – a characteristic accentuated in Canada by the national urge to be thought responsible and sound by one's fellow citizens, and aggravated by the legacy of masochism implanted in our culture by the Scottish influence – is that it never faces basic problems or recognizes basic causes. Instead it devotes its ingenuity to the prescription of recondite remedies for superficial problems. (*CQ*, 26)

Avoiding the appropriate solution, a return to a floating rate accompanied by fiscal and/or monetary expansion, left "a boundless opportunity to all forms of economic quackery," which, he suggested, came in two varieties: economic gadgetry – "a limitless array of devices for achieving by indirect and dubious means the same effects as would be achieved by . . . devaluation" – and imitative magic – "the process of looking at other countries with currently more successful records . . . discerning some institutional difference . . . and recommending the transplantation of the relevant institution . . . regardless of how it came to be established . . . or what makes it work" (28).

Setting the problem up explicitly in this way strengthened Harry's polemical hand: He could still castigate protectionists and economic nationalists as before, but their often self-interested solutions to Canada's problems took on the appearance of even greater intellectual error.

Harry had an opportunity to comment on a piece of "economic gadgetry" when the editor, John Dales, asked him on 7 December 1961 to review for the *Canadian Journal of Economics and Political Science* the *Report* of the Canadian Royal Commission on the Automobile Industry. The Royal Commission consisted of one commissioner, Harry's former teacher and sometime colleague Vincent Bladen, and a secretary, Elizabeth Leitch of the Department of Trade and Commerce. Bladen had been appointed in August 1960 "to enquire into and report upon the situation of and prospects for the industries in Canada producing motor vehicles and parts therefor . . . and report upon: (a) the present and prospective competitive position of the Canadian automobile industry . . . ; (b) the relations between companies producing motor vehicles and parts in Canada and parents, subsidiary or affiliated companies in other countries . . . ; (c) the special problems and competitive position of the industries in Canada producing parts for motor vehicles . . . ; (d) the ability of the Canadian industry to produce and dis- tribute economically the various types of motor vehicles demanded or likely to be demanded by Canadian consumers; and (e) measures that could be taken to improve the ability of such industries to provide employment."[3] Production in the industry had peaked in 1953 with 481,000 units of which 60,000 had been exported; by 1960 output had declined to 396,000 units and exports had fallen to 23,000 while imports had trebled to 180,000 units.

Despite being dean of the Faculty of Arts and Science at Toronto and maintaining a one-course decanal teaching load, Bladen worked quickly. His *Report* was signed on 14 April 1961 and released at the time of the 1961 budget, which had provided some relief to the industry.

It took Harry some time to get down to the review, which he wrote between 5 and 8 January 1963; it appeared in May (1963a). The review was devastatingly critical of the *Report*'s level of argument. Bladen had rejected free trade on the following grounds:

The decision was taken long ago to manufacture automobiles in Canada. Today, many thousands of workers and considerable capital are committed to the industry. Considering the state of development which the automobile industry had achieved in Canada, it would be socially impossible to adopt any policy which might lead to its drastic contraction. (*Report*, 48)

---

[3] Royal Commission on the Automotive Industry, *Report*, Ottawa: Queen's Printer, 1961, Appendix 1.

Harry commented:

Some day, someone should write an essay on the concept of responsibility in public life; suffice it to remark here that the implied doctrine that no mistakes should ever be admitted, and no errors ever corrected, if anyone might be hurt thereby is an exceedingly poor basis for intelligent policy-making ... and a perfect recipe for the preservation and augmentation of economic inefficiency and the strangulation of economic growth. (*CQ*, 135)

When Bladen rejected increased tariffs on the grounds that "there is a point beyond which the cost of having an automobile industry in Canada would be so high as to be intolerable to the consumer" (*Report*, 48), Harry commented: "Political tolerability, like responsibility is a concept that relieves the economist of the necessity for facing any hard choices" (*CQ*, 135). He continued:

With the social irresponsibility of lower tariffs and the political irresponsibility of higher tariffs as his guides, an economic expert can arrive anywhere, and travel more quickly for being unimpeded by his professional baggage. (135)

At the heart of Bladen's proposals for the industry was a scheme for increased protection. Supplementing this was a series of proposals to lighten the tax burden on the industry and improve its competitive position against imports from Britain of cars and potential imports of parts for assembly in Canada. Previously British cars and parts had been allowed into Canada free of duty under imperial preference while the content regulations for Canadian manufacturers had been cast in terms of "commonwealth" rather than "Canadian" content. Harry was critical of the economic analysis underlying these proposals, as well as the notions of equity involved

if that concept is defined in a sufficiently Pickwickian sense, to mean that it is inequitable for the British automobile producers to enjoy imperial preference on automobiles now that they have learned to produce and market automobiles efficiently enough to be able to use the preference. (138)

At the time Bladen reported, the Canadian tariff protected both the assembly of vehicles and the production of vehicle parts in Canada – the former through a tariff on imports of completed vehicles, the latter through a tariff on parts of a class and kind made in Canada and by free entry for parts of a class or kind not made in Canada, with free entry being conditional on a minimum proportion of the factor cost of production being incurred within the Commonwealth. Bladen's extended content plan extended duty-free entry to all parts and to completed vehicles contingent only on the content requirement; it envisaged classifying parts produced in Canada as "Canadian content" if they were embodied in vehicles produced outside

Canada for sale in third countries or sold anywhere as replacements; it recommended a change in the base for the content calculation, and revised the schedules relating content to the volume of production.

At the most general level, Harry criticised Bladen's proposal for failing to take any account of the cost of the scheme to Canadians as taxpayers while trumpeting possible reductions in prices to Canadians as consumers. He noted that an illustrative table of the *Report* (Table VIII of Appendix VI) suggested that an increase in domestic production of $41 million would involve a loss of $28.3 million in duty collected. He also criticised the export subsidy element in the scheme, which was "perhaps one of the most ingenious devices for evading the rules of G.A.T.T. yet invented" (*CQ*, 144). On the basis of a later publication by Dean Bladen, he estimated the rate of subsidy of the order of 58.2 percent. (145). But he wondered whether the plan would work as intended, as its heavy discrimination against large-scale manufacturers and in favour of the small might militate against the large-scale manufacturers maintaining their market share and gaining the economies of scale necessary to reduce prices. This was particularly likely, Harry thought, as the *Report* seemed to assume either that large-scale manufacturers earned excess profits, which could be squeezed, or that the industry's oligopolistic structure had inhibited the exploitation of economies of scale. If it did not work as intended, one might get small-scale manufacturers replacing large-scale manufacturers, raising unit costs and reducing the Canadian content of Canadian consumption. There were also criticisms in the details. However, the tenor of the review was regret that "the Royal Commissioner . . . chose to plump for . . . gadgetry" when "the trained economist ought to have known enough to stand firmly for direct resort of appropriate policies, and to resist the temptation to lend his talents to the fabrication of economic gadgetry" (152).

Bladen's reaction to Harry's review and related pieces is unknown. He devoted considerable space in his memoirs *Bladen on Bladen* (1978) to the making of the report and some to events subsequent to its publication. He did not mention Harry's review. He sent Harry copies of later reports such as his report for the Association of Universities and Colleges of Canada on the financial problems of higher education and his report on the financing of the performing arts in Canada; Harry introduced Bladen when he gave the first Innis Lecture to the Canadian Economics Association in June 1975. The author can remember Bladen being tickled pink and distributing copies to his colleagues when Harry dedicated *Technology and Economic Interdependence* (1975i) "to Vincent Bladen who made me an economic theorist." The same volume also recommended Bladen's *Introduction to Political Economy* as "an introduction for lay readers that is well written and good on policy problems" (172).

The Bladen Plan was never implemented as a package. The recommended repeal of the special excise tax on automobiles happened in the 1961 Budget introduced on the day of the *Report*'s publication. In November 1962 a Duty Remission Programme started with an order-in-council permitting the recovery of duty on imported automatic transmissions and some engines to the extent that firms increased their exports of Canadian-made parts over the previous year, extended in November 1963 to cover all imported vehicles and most parts. Protests from American parts manufacturers led the U.S. Treasury to consider whether the Canadian Programme constituted a bounty under the U.S. Tariff Act of 1930, which required the imposition of countervailing duties, which would have undone the Programme. The resulting discussions between Canadian and American officials led to the U.S.–Canadian Automotive Trade Agreement of 16 January 1965, which meant effective free trade in automobiles and original equipment parts between Canadian and American manufacturers. The agreement remained in place until struck down by the World Trade Organisation in 2001.

Harry had other opportunities to address the issues raised in the Bladen *Report*. The first came in reply to Neil B. MacDonald, special financial studies coordinator at Ford of Canada and an undergraduate contemporary of Harry's at Victoria College where he read English. MacDonald thought that his alternative illustrative model to that provided in Harry's review more accurately reflected the considerations involved in parent company/subsidiary discussions over the location of production and provided more support for the Bladen commission's conclusions (1963). Harry demurred (1963e).

The second opportunity came when Harry was a visiting professor at the University of Western Ontario. He was encouraged by Grant Reuber and Ron Wonnacott to write up the results of his seminar discussion of the October 1962 and November 1963 changes in Canadian tariff policy on automobiles for publication in the Western Business School's journal *Business Quarterly* (1964b). In the resulting article he doubted the effectiveness of the policy as a method of increasing the efficiency of Canadian industry and argued that the government, like Bladen, seemed to be unaware of the protectionist nature of its policy and the costs it would impose on the Canadian taxpayer. Moreover, the costs were borne in an odd quest.

If the policy works as intended, the Canadian taxpayer will in effect be paying the import duties levied by the American government on the additional exports;

one cannot refrain from the observation that the Canadian government's vociferous insistence on its right to pay import duties is an exceedingly strange way of demonstrating Canada's sovereignty and independence from the United States. (1964b, 45)

He noted the policy differed from Bladen's proposals in several respects – extending the subsidisation to vehicle exports, not revising the existing system of content protection, offering duty remission only on incremental exports, and targeting the programme much more specifically at the big American companies. He found the American focus ironic.

In effect, the new policy seeks to convert the American companies with manufacturing facilities in Canada into dumping agents for Canadian parts exports, and the result is likely to be both increased dependence of the Canadian parts producers on the American companies and further organisation of Canadian parts production facilities by the American parent companies or their subsidiaries. Strange indeed are the paths to national independence! (53)

The last of Harry's pre-1966 commentaries on Canadian economic nationalism was not to a Canadian audience but in a lecture at the London School of Economics where Harry had been invited to give five lectures on the theory of tariffs in January and early February 1964.[4] On 3 February he gave a lecture entitled "Problems of Canadian Economic Policy," which he subsequently offered to a Canadian journal, *The Commentator*, edited by Paul Fox. He also sent copies to other friends and was surprised by the reactions he got.

John Dales and Scott Gordon both replied on 28 April (Box 56, Correspondence 1964–6, A–L). John Dales wrote:

This is the only paper of yours that I have ever read that I think is definitely off base. I think you must have been far too angry when you wrote it, and that your anger has played you false. I don't intend to criticise it in detail, but . . .
(a) p. 15 Tariff as price of Canadian independence. This is the sort of sloppy Canadian misidentification that you yourself have often exposed. . . . You *mustn't* align your self with your enemies. . . .
(c) Your 'history' bottom of p. 9. This example of your 'history' reminds me of the worst examples of my 'theory'! Enough said.

Scott Gordon wrote:

I am rather disturbed by your London lecture – all the more so because I agree with the general picture you present of the Canadian scene and the identification you make of the source of our difficulties; all the more so because it is written in

---

[4] For more on this visit, see Chapter 8.

terms that harmonise with my own moods of rage and despair at our economic and political situation. It disturbs me because I have serious doubts as to whether it can work towards persuading Canadians to recognise our mistakes of interpretation and policy. It is, in a way, too honest for that. It is a cri de coeur, a kicking of the bastards, but it will, I fear, accomplish little but resentment. H. L. Menchen [sic] would have starved in Canada. I don't know how economists of cosmopolitan sentiments may best exercise an influence here at the present time. . . . I have run over almost the whole range myself in the past few years and I feel it's been like mumbling into a high wind. Your influence in Canada now is higher than that of any living economist, in or out of the country, and I would be very disturbed to see it diminished – which, in my unhappy view, would be the result of publishing your lecture as it stands.

In reply to Scott Gordon (6 May 1964) Harry remarked that at the original lecture "the Canadians in the audience reacted as you feared – at least one went to the High Commissioner to demand that I be silenced." Harry reported Dales's and Gordon's reaction to Paul Fox who had tentatively accepted the article and that "Liz points out that (a) some expressions may be libellous, (b) that it is noticeably more bitchy to Walter Gordon than to Coyne and Bladen" (Box 56, Correspondence 1964–6, A–L, 19 May 1964). He also reported to John Dales (4 May 1964) that Richard Lipsey thought it should be published "outside Canada, and with the offensive phrases removed." The upshot was that the lecture was not published in Canada. Harry had some Canadian supporters, particularly R. M. Fowler of the Canadian Pulp and Paper Association, who had been his commentator at Kingston:

It is an excellent lecture and I hope you publish it. I do not see why you fear it may be 'too inflammatory'. As far as my knowledge goes, it is accurate and deals with matters of some public importance. Of course, you will not endear yourself to Walter Gordon or to the senior civil servants, but I haven't detected in them any overwhelming enthusiasm for your views . . . , so you have little to lose in that area of popularity. (Box 56, Correspondence 1964–6 A–L, 20 May 1964)

Anthony Scott was also supportive.

The lecture was not suppressed: Harry was not one to let manuscripts lie fallow. It appeared in *Lloyds Bank Review* (1964d), to whom Ely Devons had sent a copy, *Challenge* (June 1964), to whom Harry had sent a copy, and in a collection of essays Harry edited, *Economic Nationalism in Old and New States* (1967), of which more later in this chapter.

The article drew together all of Harry's previous criticisms of Canadian economic policy and brought them up to date to include the Liberals' disastrous first budget with its later-withdrawn-as-unworkable tax on foreign takeovers and its ineffective attempt to encourage Canadian ownership through adjustments in the nonresident withholding tax on dividends and the tendency in that and the succeeding budget to tinker indirectly with unemployment rather than take deliberate steps to increase aggregate demand. Thus the message was not new. What was new was the demonising, especially in the LSE lecture, of "the particular contribution to nationalist economic policy ideas of three individuals who have together shaped Canadian economic policy" – James Coyne, Walter Gordon, and Vincent Bladen. Coupled with this was the anger in the tone.

It is essential to realize that Canada represents the losing side in the American revolution. The central part of the country – the Province of Ontario – was settled by embittered Tory refugees from the United States, many of whom had been deprived of their property and arrived in Canada practically destitute. Ever since, the tradition of disdain for and fear of the Americans which they brought with them had had – owing to their superior education and social status – a disproportionate influence on Canadian thinking about the United States. . . . The greater facility of communication between the United States and Canada, together with the flood of European immigrants [in the post-1945 period] was also eroding the parochialism of the dominant – and in my view anachronistic – British culture and fostering a more cosmopolitan way of life, a development scornfully and inaccurately described by Canadian intellectuals as "American cultural penetration."[5] (1964e, 29–30)

When finally published, the lecture had been toned down. Two examples will suffice – the italicised material disappeared between the typescript of the lecture and the version published in *Lloyds Bank Review* while the material in square brackets was added.

This policy was adopted by the [then] Governor of the Bank of Canada, it seems, partly out of an unwarranted terror of inflation, and partly out of an *egomaniac* [strong] conviction that it was the Governor's personal responsibility to arouse the country to the need for nationalistic economic policies. *Both the contemporary monetary policy and the Governor's writings and speeches in defence of it made no economic sense, but they were approved by many among the public and tolerated by the Government of a disastrously long period, because* the view expressed by the Governor conformed to the nationalistic, and strongly anti-American, sentiment that had been gathering strength during the post-war boom. (1964d, 26)

This concern found its expression in the Report of the Royal Commission on Canada's Economic Prospects set up in 1955 with Walter Gordon [then a wealthy Toronto accountant] as Chairman, *one of whose purposes was to launch Mr. Gordon on his political career in the Liberal Party. Mr. Gordon is a man of substantial wealth by Canadian standards, and was then a senior partner in an important Toronto firm of chartered accountants with interests in industrial consulting.* Without intending any disrespect to Mr. Gordon, whose conduct and ideas have consistently displayed that

---

[5] In the LSE lecture the sentence continued "a phrase with significant Freudian overtones."

sense of public responsibility that is characteristic of the best among the owners of *inherited wealth* [considerable property], it is fair to say that the Gordon Report's ideas on economic policy *are exactly what might be expected of a man of his* [reflect faithfully those held by many with his kind of] background. (29)

There was also the excision of a page-long attack on the senior Canadian economic civil service, which had included charges of producing misleading statistics, of downplaying of actual levels of unemployment, of the virtual rupturing of relations between economists at the Bank of Canada and those elsewhere in Ottawa, and, of course, of numerous cases of bad advice over Coyne and Walter Gordon's first budget.

Above all, there has been the unwillingness or inability of a trained economic civil service, which had only been too willing to take the credit for the success of free enterprise principles in fostering the boom of the 1950s and to lecture their English and European counterparts on the evils of government intervention and planning, to teach their political masters the elementary principles of economic policy in an open economy, and their eagerness to retreat into *dirigisme* at the first symptoms of economic adversity. (Box 25, Writing 1964 I)

Harry's harsh treatment of the Bladen *Report* was somewhat bewildering. His later linking of Bladen with James Coyne and Walter Gordon was simply bizarre. This is particularly the case when in later years Harry would begin to grapple with imperfect competition theories of trade, which were very much related to the auto pact, direct investment, and the international transfer of technology. In his Wicksell Lectures and related work, he would be at the interface of trade and industrial organisation. He saw the need to take imperfect competition into a more general model. But he did not find the time to do it. It was left to a still younger generation of international economist – Paul Krugman, Elhanan Helpman, and Avinash Dixit – to make the transition.

Economic Nationalism

The ultimate destination of the LSE lecture, *Economic Nationalism in Old and New States* (1967 ed.), reflected a coming together of several interests. Harry joined the Committee for the Comparative Study of New Nations (CCSNN) when it was formed in the fall of 1961. He was looking for interdisciplinary stimuli outside the economics department and its normal collaborators at Chicago, the School of Business and the Law School. The committee provided him with the sort of bracing, cross-disciplinary stimulus he had encountered at Manchester. Members of the committee met regularly to discuss their research – their approaches, problems, and findings – and to give the meetings some structure, each year organised a seminar, chaired by one of its members, with an agreed theme. In the first two years

the seminar discussed general concepts relating to the political, social, economic and cultural problems of the new nations: representatives of the various disciplines presented their key ideas for discussion with their colleagues and from this discussion emerged a common understanding of mutual interests and problems. Next, the seminar turned to the study of the economics of development, pooling the insights of the various disciplines and the rigor of economic theory in a discussion that ranged far beyond the bounds of conventional economics and achieving a better understanding of the problems of economic dualism, of central planning, and of political and social obstacles to economic development. (Box 25, Writing 1964 I, What the Committee Has Done)

The committee also sponsored a graduate course, An Introduction to the Study of New States.

Edward Shils remembered Harry and the Committee:

Year after year he came regularly to our weekly seminars. He would come in quietly, sliding his substantial bulk through the crowded reading room where we usually had coffee before settling down to business; he sometimes stood with us for a while, not speaking but looking on gravely. Sometimes he went directly into the seminar room and began to carve while waiting for the proceedings to begin.

He taught members of the committee much that they had not known before; above all he straightened out the minds of some of the members of the committee who took the then-common uncritically protective attitude towards the new states. Above all, he exemplified, week in and week out, his talent for tracing interconnections. (Shils 1991, 203–4)

In 1964–5, the theme was economic nationalism; the chair was Harry. The focus of the seminar was broader than economic nationalism in new nations: He thought that there might be something to be learned from nineteenth-century Europe's experience of nationalism and from contemporary manifestations of nationalism in more developed nations such as Canada.

Harry's contribution[6] to the seminar series was "A Theoretical Model of Economic Nationalism in New and Developing States," which, after discussing it with Peter Kenen at Bellagio in December 1964 (see discussion in Chapter 10), he sent to the *American Political Science Review* where it appeared (1965d). In preparing his paper, Harry drew on three strands

---

[6] His LSE lecture predated the seminar series, and his chapter "The Ideology of Economic Policy in New States" originated after the seminar ended as a lecture to the committee's annual graduate course, An Introduction to the Study of New States (1967 ed., vi).

in the recent literature where standard economic theory had been used to discuss unusual problems: Gary Becker's *The Economics of Discrimination* (1957), one of whose central ideas is "the taste for discrimination," a willingness to sacrifice economic gain so as to enjoy a psychological gain in avoiding contact with the group discriminated against; Albert Breton's "The Economics of Nationalism" (1964), which identified nationalism with the ownership of various types of property by nationals and regarded such ownership as a type of collective consumption good that could be created with public funds and yield a stream of utility as income; and Anthony Downs's *An Economic Theory of Democracy* (1957), an extended study of the implications of Joseph Schumpeter's insight[7] that politicians operating democratic governments were not motivated by a desire to implement certain policies or provide certain services but by the power and perquisites of office and that they used policies to attract votes to gain and maintain public office.

Harry opened his analysis with Downs's work, which emphasised the high costs of acquiring information for both politicians and the public. This led the former to rely on interest groups and lobbyists and the latter to rely on the parties' ideological statements. In well-established democracies, the party system would thus depend on the electoral system, the geographical distribution of voters' preferences, and the distribution of ideological preferences. If the distribution of ideological preferences was unimodal, a two-party system with considerable overlap in policy positions should emerge. Where democracy was less well-established, the party in power had a strong incentive to fashion a comprehensive and preclusive ideology so as to retain exclusive control of the government. The incentives for such behaviour were strong in less-developed countries, Harry suggested, because alternative job opportunities for officeholders were less good than in developed countries where the private sector offers considerable opportunities for those defeated at the polls.

Harry added another element from Downs's work: the observation that the concentration of producers' interests and the dispersion of consumers' interests will lead to politicians tending to concentrate on addressing the former. In polities where nationalism is important, this means that policy interest will concentrate on specific producer interests while spreading the costs, which may be greater than the gains, widely amongst consumers.

He then turned to the suggestive strand of analysis in Becker's work. Nationalism attaches value to having certain jobs held or property owned

---

[7] In *Capitalism, Socialism and Democracy* (1942), Chapters XXII and XXIII.

by group members rather than nonmembers. As to the forms of property that would be involved, he thought it obvious that cultural and artistic activities, and positions of authority in the political and social structure would be preferred. Bretonian nationalistic utility could also be acquired through observing property held and activities in the country by foreigners that yielded income and status – a factor of particular importance in former colonies – and through observing other nations' practices that could be emulated – national airlines, steel industries, automotive industries.

The recipients of the tangible benefits tended to be the educated, the entrepreneurially qualified, and other elite groups. Intellectuals engaged in cultural activities, and those involved in the media might use nationalism, particularly when it could be combined with linguistic differences, as a barrier to entry to foreign cultural influences. When it came to more strictly economic matters, there might be elements of nationalising confiscation as in a transfer of government jobs from foreigners to nationals,[8] but the norm was using domestic resources to produce material property or job opportunities for nationals. If the process involved nationalisation, the desire to provide more jobs and more prestigious jobs for nationals would tend, other than concentrating on industries employing a larger proportion of foreigners, to aim at industries with established, relatively static technologies that lend themselves to bureaucratisation or domestic monopolies, which could accept larger total numbers and/or lower quality nationals in place of foreigners. Alternatively, of course, one could use tariffs, tax concessions, or special privileges to promote the desired ends, even though these means were more likely to produce economic losses, although, as he noted from the Canadian experience, such policies might incidentally have the perverse effect of encouraging foreign firms to establish themselves.

One implication of this was that nationalism would tend to redistribute income towards the middle, particularly the educated middle class, although this might not mean that the poor would necessarily be worse off when both real and psychic income were taken into account. However, the probabilities of substantial redistribution were high, given the dominance of producer interests in the political process and the tendency towards one-party states with control of the local media by the party. Harry ruefully admitted that

---

[8] Whether there would be a transfer of income from foreigners to nationals or merely among nationals would depend on whether discrimination against the hiring of nationals had been present.

even this might improve long-term development prospects if "an investment in the creation of a middle class, financed by resources extracted from
the mass of the population, may be the essential preliminary to the creation
of a viable national state" (1965d, 185).

The same analysis underlay a paper published in the same month in
the *Journal of Political Economy*, "An Economic Theory of Protectionism,
Tariff Bargaining and the Formation of Customs Unions" (1965e).[9] This last
contribution from Harry's pen in this area was an ambitious paper, which he
regarded as important: "it seeks to start a whole new line of analysis" (Box 56,
Correspondence 1964–6, A–L, HGJ to J. R. Hicks, 25 January 1965). It was
an attempt to understand areas of international economic policy, which the
traditional theory of international trade regarded by definition as irrational
or noneconomic or hopelessly second best. He acknowledged some stimulus
from his former Manchester colleague John Knapp "who has persistently
posed the question why, if the reduction of tariffs is economically beneficial,
tariff negotiators always regard a tariff reduction as a concession that must
be compensated by the other party to the bargain" (*ATT*, 240). The paper
presented

> a theory capable of explaining a variety of important and observable phenomena,
> such as the nature of tariff bargaining, the commercial policies adopted by various
> countries, the conditions under which countries are willing to embark on customs
> unions, and the arguments and considerations which have weight in persuading
> countries to change their commercial policies. (239)

The paper continued in the spirit of two earlier papers, "The Cost of Protection and the Scientific Tariff" (1960e) and "Optimum Trade Intervention in
the Presence of Domestic Distortions" (1965a), in accepting the relevance
of noneconomic objectives and of governments trying to offset divergences
between private and social costs and benefits. However, it abandoned the
distinction between economic and noneconomic objectives as biasing the
discussion in favour of private consumption as the exclusive measure of
economic welfare. Instead, it distinguished between private and public consumption goods and labour real income (including private and public consumption) and real product (production of privately appropriable goods
and services). The motivating idea was to posit a "preference for "industrial
production," involving the treatment of industrial production as a collective consumption good" the quantity of which is governed by commercial

---

[9] From the footnote to that latter paper, it is clear that the *American Political Science Review*
paper was written first (*ATT*, Chapter 10, n.5).

policy.[10] With a motivating idea such as this and the rational vote-maximising politicians of "A Theoretical Model of Economic Nationalism," the predictions followed, once Harry had got over the step of why, given direct subsidies would be more efficient than tariffs, governments opt for tariffs. (The reasons given are that the revenues necessary to finance subsidies are difficult to collect; that those involved do not wish the alternative opportunity costs to be easily visible; or that "the preference for industrial production includes the specification that the country's industry must appear to be able to compete with imports without explicit government support" (*ATT*, 243). None of these, even invoking the dominance of producer interests, is that compelling on rationality grounds.) Initially, industrial production was treated as a single aggregate produced with domestic resources, but later Harry abandoned this assumption and assumed instead that industrial production comprised a variety of products in which countries had varying degrees of comparative advantage, depending on the availability of cooperating factors – natural resources, skills, technology – or market size combined with the existence of economies of scale in some industries rather than others. In both cases,

the theory implies that the degree of protection practised by the various countries will vary inversely with their net industrial export position; and that an improvement in a country's comparative advantage in industrial production as against non-industrial production will lead it to reduce its degree of protection and vice versa . . . [T]hese implications are consistent with experience – countries whose competitiveness in world markets is improving tend to move in the free trade direction, while countries whose competitiveness is deteriorating tend to move towards increased protectionism. (257–8)

The second hypothesis also proved useful in explaining tariff bargaining. The first could only explain such behaviour where countries had monopolistic or monopsonistic advantages. In a multicountry world,

there are limits to the extent of the reciprocal reductions of tariffs that can be negotiated on a most-favoured-nation basis; furthermore, these limits introduce the possibility that reciprocal preferential tariff reduction . . . will be more attractive than non-discriminatory tariff reduction, a possibility that would not exist apart from the preference for industrial protection. (261)

Thus Harry provided the basis for launching himself into the theory of customs unions, which are discriminatory reciprocal tariff reductions among

---

[10] Whether the hypothesis of "industrial production as a collective consumption good" is plausible is disputed. M. W. Corden finds it implausible among industrial countries (1984, 577). R. G. Lipsey (1978, S48) "doubts if . . . [it] will provide the whole answer."

groups of countries. It was all extraordinarily fruitful and showed how with new hypotheses about variables, such as the collective industrial good theory, could be amended to reduce the discrepancies between its results and those of actual observation.

Opulence

Canada also played another role in Harry's activities after 1959. He used Canadian occasions and Canadian audiences to develop his views on opulence. As noted in Chapter 7, his thinking on such matters went back to the publication of Galbraith's *The Affluent Society* (1958) which he had reviewed favourably but critically.

The ideal venue to try his ideas out was the 1960 meetings of the Canadian Political Science Association in Kingston. The association still included among its members not only political scientists but also sociologists, economists, and anthropologists – the same mixture of social scientists he had known at Manchester and later knew in CCSNN at Chicago. He thought his paper, "The Political Economy of Opulence" (1960h), important: He reprinted it three times in book form – something he did with only two other articles[11] – perhaps because as he put it, the paper "incorporated views reached before his exposure to the work of T. W. Schultz at Chicago on the role of the consumer as the owner of 'human capital' faced with the problems arising from economic change and uncertainty" (1974 Self Evaluation, 10). The paper sketched a more modern theory of distribution using 'the conceptual rather than the social content of the classical categories of wages, rent interest and profits' (10). With the addition of the human capital concepts the next year in an address to the Canadian Social Welfare Council on "The Social Policy of an Opulent Society," the analysis became richer. It became richer still with the addition of an economic theory of government, discussed previously, which was stimulated by the work of Downs, Becker, and Breton. The result was a powerful set of papers culminating in his inaugural lecture at LSE in October 1967, "The Economic Approach to Social Questions."

---

[11] In *Money, Trade and Economic Growth* (1962), *The Canadian Quandary* (1963), and *On Economics and Society* (1975). Another article was "Social Policy of an Opulent Society," one of the other papers in the same series. "The Keynesian Revolution and the Monetarist Counter Revolution" was reprinted four times. For all the multiple venues for articles, there appear to be only sixteen articles that he put in two or more volumes of his collected papers; ten if one excludes *Selected Essays in Monetary Economics*, which reprinted the first part of two of his earlier collections.

In the process of working out his ideas, Harry developed a number of points. First, he thought that in looking at consumer's demand it was worth reverting to Alfred Marshall's notion that "although it is man's wants in the earliest stages of his development that give rise to his activities, yet afterwards each new step upwards is to be regarded as the development of new activities giving rise to new wants, rather than of new wants giving rise to new activities" (1920, 89), and the notion associated with his retired Chicago colleague Frank Knight "that one of the basic human social characteristics is a continuing desire to improve and educate one's tastes" (*CQ*, 241). Recognition of these factors led to a reconsideration of the role of advertising, an activity decried by Galbraith and other social critics. For if wants are learned and better tastes acquired, advertising may be a socially useful means of providing consumers with new information on how to spend their high and rising incomes.[12] Its provision by the seller is natural given his resources and the incentive structure of the transaction. Modern technology renders mass, impersonal advertising possible and, following Adam Smith, Harry argued that it had the advantage of rendering economic transactions free of such extraneous influences as class, status, religion, and ethnic differentiation that affect personal contacts (291; *Wealth of Nations*, Book III, Chapter 4).

Second, with opulence the typical consumer good changed: More and more consumption took the form of the services of capital goods. In other words, consumption became more capital intensive. This increase in the capital intensity of consumption replaced the use of labour services both inside and outside the home. Indirectly, the substitution of capital for labour could take place outside the home. Harry's example here was food preparation.

Third, according to Harry, one's own time became more valuable relative to commodities. This had three effects. Individuals as they grew more opulent tended to look at nonpecuniary considerations more often in employment decisions thus affecting the supply of household labour services in response to a given wage. Individuals' enjoyment of commodities was complementary to leisure, thus providing another factor that would affect the supply of labour services in response to a given wage. Finally, individuals' leisure time itself tended to become more capital intensive. Surprisingly,

---

[12] This was neatly drawn together in "The Consumer and Madison Avenue": "All economically relevant wants are learned. Moreover, all standards of taste are learned. It is therefore arrogant and inconsistent to assume that those who have acquired their standards from general culture and advanced education can choose and pass judgments according to standards possessing independent validity, while those who have acquired their standards from social pressures and advertising can neither understand nor learn to understand the difference between good and bad taste" (1960f, 8).

however, Harry missed one aspect of the increased importance of time: the need to work harder to employ the increasingly expensive labour to service and maintain consumers' capital (assuming, as is normally the case, that productivity in the service sector rises more slowly than elsewhere yet service wages keep pace with those elsewhere), or, if labour became too expensive, to scrap and replace consumer capital more frequently.[13]

Fourth, opulence probably required a rethinking of the theory of distribution. The major impetus for change was the alteration in the nature of labour where skills were the product of capital investment in education and skills required for the specific job. This human capital view of labour became even more central in subsequent papers. For the moment, however, the emphasis was on how the traditional link between categories of income with traditional productive factors that had been the case from classical economics onwards had changed. It would be more illuminating, Harry argued, "to lump all factors together as items of capital equipment created as past investment and rendering current services to production." One could still use the concepts of the theory: They could still provide "an illuminating way of looking at the pricing of factor services."

The current price of a factor's services can be divided conceptually into two elements: the payment necessary to keep the factor in existence (or in a particular employment corresponding to the classical notion of "wages") and a surplus above that necessary payment, arising from scarcity of a factor and corresponding to the classical notion of "rent." Considered as a return on the capital investment incurred in creating the factor, the current price can be resolved analytically into interest on the capital investment and a residual corresponding to the profit or loss resulting from the entrepreneurial decision to invest capital in the specific form represented by the factor. (*CQ*, 249–50)

"The Social Policy of an Opulent Society" revealed what Harry in his inaugural lecture at LSE called "the tremendous integrative power of the concept of human capital" in understanding the labour market and the household's decision-making problems (*E&S*, 20). The individualistic economic system in an opulent society assigned important economic responsibilities to the family.

It is the basic spending unit, whose decisions determine whether increasing opulence will raise the quality of life or debase it, the income it has to spend is obtained by selling the services of its members and their property, so that its decisions in this regard determine both its income and the efficiency with which its human and

---

[13] For an illuminating discussion of time in opulent societies, which had the benefit of Harry's 1960 paper, see Linder (1970).

non-human capital is used; and it determines the amount and type of education acquired by its children, so that collectively it determines the size and quality of the stock of human capital handed on the next generation. (*CQ*, 255–6)

The family's capacity to undertake its human capital formation and utilisation functions is constrained by its small size, its ability to acquire and process information, and its ability to borrow.[14] As an income-earning unit, the family might be unable to maximise the returns from its existing human and nonhuman capital because it lacked knowledge of opportunities or the means of borrowing to move to higher income-earning opportunities. As a creator of human capital, even when schools and universities were tuition-free, the family had to decide how much in terms of foregone earnings to invest in the acquisition of skills, and it had to decide on the specific form of human capital in which to invest, the returns on which would be realised by the child over the ensuing two or more generations. The information requirements for the latter decision were immense, the possibilities of error were large, and the availability of resources to supplement those of the family militated against the bright child of poor parents while doing nothing to prevent overinvestment by the better-off parents of the less intelligent rich child.

The family's ability to support itself rested on its ability to sell the services of its human capital both present and prospective. The risks of interruptions to the stream of income were nonnegligible, especially because its human capital was specialised and because more and more consumption required the acquisition of consumer durables paid for by claims against future income. There were the risks of change that lie at the heart of opulence and the risks of short-term fluctuations in income and employment – as well as personal risks, which were in principle insurable (sickness, accident, and old age). Harry thought that the starting point for social policy in an opulent society should be to recognise the limitations households face in the accumulation and deployment of human capital and to overcome them.

Harry also had a Galbraithian side. Opulence was accompanied by metropolitan agglomeration, which required the provision of communal services on which the quality of life depended. The provision of such services required finance, and Harry believed that there was a bias towards the underprovision of such services because the certain sacrifice of income was

---

[14] It was also constrained by its inability to deal in human capital with the same freedom it can deal in nonhuman capital: It could not, for example, sell children to someone who will invest in their education.

accompanied by less easily appreciated appropriation of such services. The same difficulties affected the collective prevention or control of some of the external effects of urbanisation – noise, air and water pollution, insecurity of person and property.

In framing social policy for the opulent society, Harry emphasised four principles. The first was that individuals needed assistance in making the most of the opportunities provided by opulence, in particular education (possibly supplemented by grants to offset the income foregone for the less well-off); information, welfare, and counselling services to enable individuals to manage their affairs; and a realisation that the demands an opulent society made on individuals were such that 'those who . . . are unable to meet these demands ought not to be treated simply as contemptible failures, but should be treated as casualties of the struggle for progress' (*CQ*, 263). The second was the recognition that rising living standards involved improved communal services and amenities as well as environmental enhancement. The third was that society should bear the economic risks that it creates for families. Here he was advocating a reversal of the traditional social insurance principle: Families in opulent societies could bear the costs of short-term unemployment or minor illnesses, but they could not provide against events that destroyed human capital (technical change) or impaired an individual's ability to sell services (severe illness or depressed business conditions). The fourth was that society should apply the same principles of rational calculation, innovation, and exploitation that were so fruitful in its productive system to social policies. The suggested changes invariably involved the financing of individuals in higher education – reforms that took on a new edge when he began to worry about the international circulation of human capital – and increasingly as time went on the organisation of higher education and its control by academics.

At this stage, Harry's policy predilections were more often than not interventionist and left-of-centre. There was one aspect of the opulent society where he was remarkably prescient. In 1965, in "Economics and Politics of Opulence," he wrote:

The growth of the knowledge, rationality and responsibility of the average opulent citizen raises the question whether the present allocation of responsibilities between the public and the private sector of the economy is socially optimal or whether a substantial proportion of the functions now performed by governments should be transferred back to the private sector. The position of the modern conservative is that they should be so returned to private responsibility; and there is enough foundation for this view in the nature of the opulent society for conservatism to exercise an appeal amongst sections of the population that cannot be dismissed as simply reactionary or politically illiterate. . . . [I]t is highly probable that the future politics of the opulent society will centre on the proper division of responsibility between the individual citizens and their government. (1965g, 326)

Canada – Postscript

During his LSE years and afterwards Harry was less intensively involved in Canada and its affairs than he had been after his move to Chicago. He maintained an interest in the development of the economics profession in Canada and continued to operate as a placement office/adviser to many departments. However his efforts centred more on the University of Western Ontario, which under Grant Reuber and Clark Leith developed claims to international distinction in several areas of economics.

He also continued to use Canadian occasions for some of his more speculative papers. One need only think of his "Economic Theory and Contemporary Society," a lecture at the University of Toronto in November 1967, which developed themes touched on in his earlier "opulence" papers as well as his LSE inaugural lecture, "The Economic Approach to Social Questions," all of which he collected together in *On Economics and Society*. He also used the Canadian convention of having honorary degree recipients address convocation to present thoughtful papers such as "The Progressive Society" (St. F. X. Archives, RG 30-4/22/11-12, 1965).

Inevitably, he continued to comment on Canadian affairs as a reviewer, speaker, or honorary degree recipient. He was almost invariably critical, but on one occasion, in a submission to the American Commission on International Trade and Investment, he attempted to sympathetically explain Canadian peculiarities and obsessions to an American audience while discussing "The Special Economic Relationship between the United States and Canada."

By 1970, he had sufficient material to contemplate a successor to *The Canadian Quandary* with the working title "The Canadian Character: Is Nationalism Enough?" It would have included, his 1961 "Problems of Canadian Nationalism" (*CQ*, Chapter 2), retitled "Canadian Nationalism: The Garbage in the Alley"; his controversial 1964 LSE lecture "Economic Nationalism in Canadian Policy"; and his 1965 "Theoretical Model of Economic Nationalism in New and Developing States," a running commentary on the development of Canadian thinking and policy concerning foreign ownership. It would also have included under the rubric Canada and Contemporary Society, his "Economics and Politics of Opulence," "Economic Theory and Contemporary Society," and "The Progressive Society." It naturally would have included commentary on Canadian macroeconomic policy, particularly the return to flexible exchange rates in May 1970.

In the end, he did not proceed with the project, perhaps because he didn't have enough material and ended with padding it out with such pieces as "Canadian Contributions to the Discipline of Economics since 1945," his centennial contribution to the meetings of the Canadian Economics Association (1968i), and his "Federal Government Support of Basic Research" (1964c). Nor did he try to write an introduction.

In the early 1970s the issue of Quebec's separation from Canada became live. At least for a time Harry thought that there might be something in it. As he told Rodrigue Trembley of the University of Montreal in November 1972:

> On Sunday evening I expressed myself as favouring a separate French-Canadian state. I am fairly strongly in favour of that. First I think that Quebec is economically a viable basis for a nation state. . . . Second I do not think that French Canadians can become fully mature citizens of the world so long as they define their objective in terms of a struggle for power with the English Canadians . . . the French-Canadian vs English-Canadian framework seems to me to divert Canadian attention from what Canada has that is distinctly Canadian, and also to prevent Canada from being as useful to the modern world as it could be. (Box 52, Correspondence 1971–7, P–T, 27 November)

The only general discussion of the range of issues he had tackled in *The Canadian Quandary* turned out to be his last published contribution on Canadian affairs, a preface to a paperback edition of the book written while he was in Kiel in June 1976. That preface made gloomy reading. "[T]he Canadian decision to return to fixed exchange rates in 1962 . . . turned out to be a ghastly error" (iv). The decision to refloat the Canadian dollar in 1970, which "might have been used to pursue genuine independence of Canadian action and policy," instead showed the authorities going "even further into a perverse policy of permitting even more inflation and using traditional monetary policy less effectively in fighting it than had been true of American economic policy" (iv).

> [T]he behaviour and pronouncements of the Bank of Canada . . . have conveyed the impression, even to the most timid academic mind, of an institution trying to do a job it does not understand by using tools it does not now know either how to select or how to manipulate. (v)

Nor had trade policy moved in the direction he had advocated in 1960. His original proposal for Canadian-American free trade, which had evolved into the North Atlantic Free Trade Area (see discussion in Chapter 15) "eventually became one of the casualties of the war in Vietnam, which made crucial sectors of both Canadian and British opinion hostile to the political implications of an arrangement . . . that economically offered great attractions" (viii). Moreover, "the emphasis of Canadian nationalism shifted from economic arguments concerning alleged economic misbehaviour by American subsidiaries in Canada to political, anti-American and anti-capitalist system arguments"(vii). The result was a continuation of what he had called gadgetry in the 1960s (see earlier discussion in this chapter) or what he now called mercantilism, which resulted in "a proliferation of both enforced and unenforceable restrictions on the freedom of competition that achieves no clear-cut objective but shackles the economy into impotent economic inefficiency" (vii). It also produced the unedifying, to Harry, attempts at "Canadianization" of Canadian universities and intellectual life in general.

He was even unhappy with his "opulence" essays, which

on re-reading seem excessively optimistic to the point of euphoria . . . because they ignore a possibility that has since become a real problem: that . . . [those who] desire to modify the principles of competition in order to achieve a more just society will form a coalition with the interest of the government and its bureaucracy in extending the government's share of national economic resources and its power of regulation of the citizen's activities, to create a cumulative and irreversible trend towards a fully regulated and bureaucratized society. (ix)

If one needed confirmation of this "ponderous and pretentious note" on which he had concluded his preface, argued Harry, look at the Canadian government's introduction of an incomes policy in 1975 and

the Prime Minister of Canada . . . lecturing the citizens on their obligation to restrain their greed for the national good. When government begins to lecture the people on their duties to the government, compulsion to do that duty is the next logical step. (ix–x)

TEN

Chicago

Money, Trade, and Development

Money

During his first year in Chicago Harry received two invitations that were firmly to establish him as a more important figure in monetary economics. The first was from Paul Samuelson, president-elect of the American Economic Association:

I should like to invite you to give a substantial paper, if you have some suitable topic in mind.... No particular topics occur to me beyond the one I mentioned earlier.[1] A provocative discussion of monetary policies here and there might be suitable. The issues connected with a low and high pressure economy might also suggest themselves. Or perhaps you have some unified research that you would like to report on. (Box 31, Correspondence to 1963, S–Z, from P. A. Samuelson, 29 January 1960)

In his 1969 and 1974 memoirs Harry reported that Samuelson suggested the topic on which he eventually spoke in St. Louis, "The General Theory After Twenty-Five Years." If Samuelson did so no record survives. The second was an invitation from B. F. Haley, the managing editor of the *American Economic Review*, to prepare one of the Rockefeller Foundation–financed surveys of economic theory jointly sponsored by the American Economic Association (AEA) and the Royal Economic Society. His topic would be "Monetary Theory and Policy" (Box 25, AEA Survey, from B. F. Haley, 3 March 1960). Harry hesitated before replying. In particular he wanted to know what his teaching responsibilities would be at Chicago during the 1960–1 academic year. When it transpired that he would be teaching money and banking rather than international trade and that he could spend the

---

[1] "a slashing and well-thought-out attack on what passes for the current theory of economic development."

summer of 1961 doing the bulk of the reading and writing, he accepted
(Box 25, AEA Survey, to B. F. Haley, 5 April 1960). The second invitation
had unintended consequences: "Unfortunately for the author, it established
an authoritative status that has obliged him to continue to survey recent
developments in monetary theory for specialist conferences at indiscreetly
frequent intervals" (1974 Self-Assessment, 19).

The St. Louis lecture had a number of distinguishing features. It continued (see discussion in Chapter 6) Harry's practice of distinguishing between
"the economics of Keynes" and "Keynesian economics" – a distinction he
highlighted particularly in his discussion of the policy implications of the
General Theory (*MTEG*, 144–7). The distinction also came out in his discussion of liquidity preferences versus loanable funds with its reference to
"the prolonged defence in the English literature of the proposition that an
increase in the propensity to save lowers the interest rate by reducing the
level of income is a credit to . . . ingenuity rather than . . . scientific spirit"
(134). He saw severe weaknesses in the *General Theory*. "Keynes drastically
over-generalized a particularly bad depression which was made worse by
errors of economic policy" (143). The "consumption function is nowhere
as simple as Keynes made it out to be and unemployment equilibrium is a
special case of dynamic disequilibrium and anyway not the chronic problem
of modern capitalism" (143–4). "Keynes made the analysis of the demand
for money explicitly a branch of capital theory, whereas the role of money as
a form of wealth-holding had been left implicit in the neo-classical analysis"
but "his theory of the demand for money is . . . misleadingly presented, very
confused and, as a theory of the demand for money in capital theory terms,
seriously incomplete" (135). However, he concluded

The contribution of the *General Theory* to modern economics is certainly not
Keynes's specific model of income determination. . . . Rather the contribution lies
in the general nature of Keynes's approach to the problem of income and employment. In the first place, he concentrated attention on the expenditure-income and
income-expenditure relationships which are much easier to understand and apply
than the quantity theory relationship and which provides, in the multiplier analysis, a key to dynamic processes of change. In the second place, he provided a
useful macro-economic general equilibrium model for the analysis of a monetary
economy. . . . Finally, what is most important for scientific economics . . . he set out
his theory in a model in which the important variables and relationships are specified
in a form suitable for statistical measurement and testing. The stimulation given by
the *General Theory* to the construction and testing of aggregative models may well
prove to be Keynes's chief contribution to economics in the longer perspective of
historical judgment, since the application of capital rather than income concepts to
monetary theory may well produce better and more reliable results, and the present

predominance of the income-expenditure approach prove to be a transitional stage in the analysis of economic behaviour. (144)

Harry's criticisms of Keynesians took two main tacks. First, they turned "a theory in which money is important... into the theory that money is unimportant." Part of the explanation was a hardening of certain of Keynes's conclusions into rigid dogmas in the hands of his disciples and partly in the fact that "Keynesians have tended to be politically left of centre, a position associated with a distrust of central bankers – particularly in England" (145). Second, as a result, the Keynesians ran into problems in dealing with "the dominant post-war policy problem of inflation" where "the Keynesian approach... has tended to degenerate into a confused and often obstructive eclecticism," which "virtually assume[s] away the possibility of controlling inflation by monetary means." (145–6).[2]

The St. Louis lecture, when eventually reprinted in *Money, Trade and Economic Growth* (1962f), brought a new phrase into the economic literature – "bastard Keynesian." Reviewing the book in the *Economic Journal* for September 1962, Joan Robinson accused Harry of not knowing what he was talking about.

Unfortunately he was just the wrong age to make such an appraisal. A younger man would have felt obliged to do some research to find out the orthodox theory that Keynes was attacking; an older man would himself have once been submitted to it. Professor Johnson, who grew up amid the controversies surrounding the *General Theory*, thinks he knows what it was all about, but actually he does not discuss the changes which Keynes' theory made in economic thought that he is confusing it with his own bastard progeny. (1965, 100)

The review went on to discuss the bastard Keynesians' criticisms of Keynes.

Harry's survey of "Monetary Theory and Policy" (1962b) took longer to prepare than expected. Instead of having it ready for the March 1962 issue of the *American Economic Review*, he reported to Bernard Haley:

I have got buried in an unusual amount of editorial work on the Journal [*JPE*] and other administrative responsibilities around Chicago, and this has made it difficult

---

[2] In his 'Harry G. Johnson as a Chronicler of the Keynesian Revolution: His Search for a Non-Revolutionary Account' (2000, 676–7), Robert W. Dimand correctly notes that there are differences between the version published in the *American Economic Review* in May 1961 and the version published in *Money, Trade and Economic Growth* (but not *On Economics and Society*). In addition to his providing full bibliographical references, Harry also added to the text on pages 2 (two changes), 6, and 8, as well as making a correction on page 15. In the cases where Dimand cites the revised paper, the text is identical to that originally printed in the *American Economic Review*. This is important because the impression created by Dimand's citation procedures is that the *Money, Trade and Economic Growth* version was more critical of his former Cambridge colleagues than the original.

for me to sort out the issues . . . as clearly as I would like to. (Box 25, AEA Survey, 8 November 1961)

He asked to be allowed to submit it after the end of the year.

It was February before he sent the paper off to Haley. Haley sent the piece off to John Gurley and Edward Shaw, the authors of *Money in a Theory of Finance* (1960), as well as Don Patinkin, the author of *Money, Interest and Prices* (1956). Both sets of reviewers turned the piece around within days of receipt. All were enthusiastic, Patinkin commenting:

My general reaction to the manuscript is very good. What I particularly liked was Harry's emphasis in Sections II [The Demand for Money and the Velocity of Circulation] and III [The Supply of Money, Monetary Control and Monetary Dynamics] on the frontiers of the work being done. He has really carried off a *tour de force* in showing the reader the ferment of the thinking during these past five years: the great majority of his references are to this period! So the article is far more a dynamic picture of where things are moving, than a static one of where they were: and this obviously makes it much more valuable. (Box 25, AEA Survey, Patinkin to Haley, 8 March 1962)

The reviewers inevitably had criticisms, especially as their work had been at the centre of much of the discussion. Patinkin, although he "tried to maintain the fine distinction between *commenting* on Harry's manuscript and *replying* to it" found himself indulging in what he called "preventative polemics." When it came to dealing with the comments, partly because of lack of time – the article went to press on 21 March and he had been sent Gurley and Shaw's comments on 28 February and Patinkin's on 9 March – Harry "eventually decided to do very little about them" (Box 25, AEA Survey, to B. F. Haley, 7 and 14 March 1962). He did give the comments careful thought however and in his correspondence gave an inclination of his principles of selection in preparing the survey. For example, when he was taxed on not including A. J. Meigs's Chicago thesis, eventually published as *Free Reserve and the Money Supply* (University of Chicago Press, 1962), he replied:

I have not missed Meigs. I am fully aware of his contribution. But it is still an unpublished dissertation. . . . I felt that references to our unpublished Ph.D. theses are only too common in the literature emanating from this place, and that many other schools could boast of good theses of whose existence I am unaware. I specifically indicated that I was referring to published work, to show that I know there is good work in existence. . . . If you think Meigs' thesis deserves a mention, I shall be only too happy to advertise the home team. But I think it would lead to justified accusations of bias to mention unpublished Chicago Ph.D.s while excluding articles published, say, in the AER. (Box 25, AEA Survey, to B. F. Haley, 7 March 1962)

There was also criticism of his underplaying the work of the Yale school, to which he replied:

This is a point that bothered me in the writing. The trouble is that Tobin's teaching and research direction are reflected only in a smattering of articles by him; I have mentioned, I think, almost all of these articles. But I do not think that a survey article can appropriately deal with oral traditions or dittoed working papers. I am sorry about this, because I think that Tobin is an important figure in the field, but I don't see that a graduate student or out-of-touch professional can simply be given this information, without being told what Tobin has been doing. I don't think it fair to give a lot of space to unpublished work when I have to ignore so much worthy published material. (Ibid.)

On Gurley and Shaw, he concluded:

Anyway, I am pleased that Gurley and Show are enthusiastic about the general lines of the article. I have gained some confidence from the fact that Friedman, Modigliani, and Gurley and Shaw all disagree with my final paragraphs on neutrality, each because my argument does not agree with their own theory – Friedman believes that the distinction between human and non-human capital is fundamental to capital theory because the former is not marketed; Modigliani believes that it is fundamental because human capital has a limited life; Gurley and Shaw on the other hand believe that the differing liquidity characteristics of different assets are more important than the human-non-human distinction. If nobody agrees, presumably the argument is not biased in anyone's favour. (Ibid.)

In organising his 1962 survey, Harry remarked that "most of recent theory and research on money can be classified either as application and extension of Keynesian ideas or as counter-revolutionary attack on them" (*EME*, 16). Nonetheless, he organised his survey by research topic rather than by the issues Keynes had raised. He would follow the alternative form of organisation in the summer of 1963 when he repeated the survey exercise for a lecture in Argentina (*EME*, Chapter 2).

In his discussions with Haley, Harry remarked that he had "resisted a lot of pressure of various kinds to make the survey a statement of the current position of the Chicago school" (Box 25, AEA Survey, to B. F. Haley, 7 March 1962). Even if he successfully did so, however, he had to deal with it. If he regarded Keynes's great weakness as his "neglect of the influence of capital on behaviour" (*MTEG*, 147)

Friedman's application to monetary theory of the basic principles of capital theory – that income is the yield on capital and capital the present value of income – is probably the most important development in monetary theory since Keynes' *General Theory*. (*EME*, 33)

Naturally, he praised the postwar consumption-function literature associated with Friedman, Modigliani, and others for the same reasons. Similarly he praised "the approach to monetary dynamics that has been emerging in the past few years, from both 'Keynesian' and 'quantity' theorists, as an outgrowth of the formulation of monetary theory as part of the general theory of asset holding" citing Friedman in the company of Tobin, Cagan, and Brunner from the last of whom he drew a lengthy quotation (*EME*, 50). Nonetheless, although Friedman started his discussion of the demand for money "from the fundamentals of capital theory," Harry thought that "in its final form Friedman's demand function for money is hard to distinguish from a modern Keynesian formulation" (*EME*, 32), and he certainly put Friedman in a theoretical tradition that started with Keynes.

He returned to Friedman on the demand for money in his 1963 Argentine survey (95) and again in his review of Friedman and Schwartz's *A Monetary History of the United States, 1867–1960* (1963) (1965f). The latter is the more interesting because of his critical discussion of Friedman's empirical work as Friedman tried to distinguish his approach from the Keynesian tradition as Harry conceived it. One gets a flavour of it in the following:

The interdependence between the book and the statistical studies, which are not yet available but whose broad outlines are known, imposes a serious handicap on the reader and reviewer – the inability to make an independent evaluation of the reported findings – a handicap that familiarity with Professor Friedman's style of operations leads one to suspect is not entirely unintentional. The origins of the book in a much larger research endeavour also accounts in part for a characteristic that many readers are likely to find exasperating, namely a strong propensity not to spell out the theoretical model explicitly. . . . This propensity, however, is also characteristic of Professor Friedman, as is the book's general theoretical approach which entails the use of extremely simple naive models . . . supplemented by more elaborate theoretical and statistical analysis to the extent required by the concrete problem at hand. (1965f, 388–9)

Later on, after he had discussed the *Monetary History* as history, Harry turned to "the validity of Professor Friedman's 'permanent income' formulation of the demand for money." The relevant test is set up over the postwar period. If the demand for money depends, as Friedman argues, "only on expected income and prices and not on interest rates" velocity should have fallen, but in fact it rose (395). Harry's discussion of Friedman and Schwartz's Chapter 12, which was devoted to the issue was very critical of "an instructive example of the art of winning an argument by establishing the form the debate must take" (1965f, 395). The result of their strategy was summarised neatly: "Occam's Razor is a useful principle, but there is no need to cut the throat of empirical research with it" (395). The episode left Harry worried:

Professor Friedman's attachment to the permanent income formulation of the demand for money and his resistance to allowing interest rates any important influence on velocity, in spite of good theoretical reasons and a great deal of empirical evidence attesting to such an influence, is itself a rather perplexing puzzle in the monetary history of the United States. Contemplation of this book suggests two mutually sustaining hypotheses to explain it. One relates to the methodological position... which reflects the more fundamental position that U.S. monetary behaviour must be treated as homogenous over the century on record. The other involves the recognition of the enormous simplification permitted by a velocity function independent of interest rates. If interest rates do not affect velocity monetary analysis can be divorced from analysis of the real sector.... If on the other hand interest rates do affect velocity, monetary analysis must incorporate the real sector in a general equilibrium model simultaneously explaining interest rates, velocity, real income and prices. Moreover this need for a general equilibrium model comprising the real and monetary sectors is what the Keynesian Revolution was about; hence to admit interest rates into the demand function for money is to accept the Keynesian Revolution and Keynes's attack on the quantity theory. (395–6)

Harry's attack resulted in a strong reaction from Friedman, who in 1959 had published an article reporting empirical work that failed to find a relationship between the rate of interest and the demand for money over the period 1869–1957. It was the only article to report that result. When David Laidler (1966) replicated Friedman's methods, he discovered that the original results were mistaken and that the inclusion of the rate of interest improved the predictive power of the relationship. Friedman replied to Harry first in correspondence and then in "Interest Rates and the Demand for Money" (1966). Interest rates, Friedman said, did have a role to play in the velocity function and in the essential characteristic of Keynesian monetary theory, which he took to be the liquidity trap. "Thus," as David Laidler later put it, "Friedman declined the invitation to embrace the Keynesian revolution" (1984, 602). There matters stood – for the moment.

Canadian Monetary Policy Again

Critical as he may have been of some Chicago empirical work, Harry nonetheless took it seriously. This is most clearly shown in his work with John Winder for the Canadian Royal Commission on Banking and Finance, chaired by Dana Porter – *Lags in the Effects of Monetary Policy in Canada* finished in November 1962 (1962e). The complete study was never widely available, despite attempts by Harry and Grant Reuber to get it and other commission studies published. Harry read a paper with an extended summary of his work with Winder at a seminar at Berkeley on 21 March 1963 and included it as Chapter 12 of the *Canadian Quandary*.

He also prepared another essay for the Commission "Alternative Guiding Principles for Monetary Policy in Canada," which appeared as a Princeton Study in International Finance in November 1963. On 2 January 1963 the secretary of the Royal Commission, A. H. Hampson informed the research staff that the commission had not yet decided on its own publication programme but had agreed that members of the staff could publish their own material independently (Public Archives of Canada, RG33, 53, 1-2-2, to Research Staff). Harry must have sent "Alternative Guiding Principles" to Fritz Machlup almost immediately because when Machlup accepted it, he attributed the delay to his being in Europe for almost a month and a large number of manuscripts (Hoover Institution, Machlup Papers, Box 47, Folder 2, to HGJ, 26 February 1963).

As they had only four months to work full-time on the empirical study, Johnson and Winder worked from the stock of previously available models, largely for the American Commission on Money and Credit,[3] as well as three more directly relevant Canadian pieces – Rudolph Rhomberg's use of the IMF's model of the Canadian economy subsequently published in the *Journal of Political Economy* (1964) and two studies by George Macesich, his 1958 Chicago PhD dissertation, "The Quantity Theory and the Income-Expenditure Theory in an Open Economy, 1926–58," and "Determinants of Monetary Velocity in Canada" (1962). Despite the short cuts, the summer was not long enough. In a note on commission note paper dated 1 October 1962, as well as saying that he had "little time free from the work on which I am presently engaged," Harry remarked to Don Patinkin "Unfortunately we do not even have convenient access to a library" (Perkins Library, Duke University, Patinkin Papers).[4] Harry's work for the commission dragged on until 17 December 1962 when he and John Winder were interviewed by the commissioners on their econometric study and Harry was interviewed on the subject of monetary theory and policy.

After it was all over, Harry commented to William Hood, the director of research for the commission

May I say that while the facilities were not ideal, the research staff functioned as a research team should; I do not think I have ever worked so hard or so enjoyably, nor

---

[3] Ando et al. (1963) and Friedman and Meiselman (1963).

[4] See also *Lags in the Effect of Monetary Policy in Canada*, 2. The research team worked at 55 St. Clair Avenue East in Toronto.

have I ever had a group of colleagues with whom I worked with such co-operation and mutual respect and interest. (Public Archives of Canada, RG33, 53, 1–2-2, 7 February 1963)

The Johnson–Winder study concluded that given the substantial inside lag[5] the use of monetary policy for short-term stabilisation was remarkably inefficient. However, given substantial variations in velocity, the alternative policy of adopting a fixed rule for monetary management would not have produced substantially improved results. Indeed, on occasion it would have made matters worse. As to establishing the influence of monetary policy on the Canadian economy, they concluded "that while we cannot point to any significant substantial effect of monetary policy on the Canadian economy, neither can we maintain that the influence of monetary policy is insignificant" (*CQ*, 186). They also found substantial and variable lags in the effects of monetary policy. As a result, "[t]he general conclusion we draw . . . is that the effect of monetary policy on the Canadian economy is imprecise, slow and variable; there is a relationship present but it is extremely hazy" (187). This had implications for the use of monetary policy. The authorities could accept that its operation was slow and imprecise and lower their standards of stabilisation. Alternatively, they could improve their knowledge of how policy worked and improve their instruments so that it became more efficient. Or they could rely on other policy instruments for short-term stabilisation and set monetary policy, the growth-supporting task of maintaining a stable long-term environment.

Harry's "Alternative Guiding Principles" essay explored these alternatives. Given Canada's experience with both fixed and floating exchange rates, he made it clear that the choice of an exchange rate régime would affect the choice among the alternatives as a fixed exchange rate would oblige the authorities to conduct monetary policy with reference to the balance-of-payments position, often in cooperation with other central banks. This would affect the first two alternatives since balance-of-payments considerations would probably lower the standard of stabilisation expected and cooperation with other central banks would necessarily shift the balance of monetary policy towards more traditional central bank methods and inhibit radical reform of the central bank's constitution and operating methods. A fixed exchange rate régime that required the use of monetary policy to influence international capital movements would also probably compromise attempts to use monetary policy to create a longer-term, growth-sustaining

---

[5] The lag between the emergence of a problem and the central bank doing anything about it.

environment. Floating exchange rates, on the other hand, given their function of automatically insulating the economy from changes in overseas markets, removed the problem of balancing the balance of payments and allowed a consideration of the choice among the alternatives on strictly economic grounds. Then, after discussing the alternative in more detail and looking carefully at various types of credit controls (moral suasion, controls on the chartered banks, controls on other institutions or controls on specific types of borrowing), Harry made his preferences clear – the creation of a long-term stable monetary environment under a régime of flexible exchange rates (224). On the issue of controls, he opposed extending the Bank of Canada's authority in the direction of moral suasion or controls on the liquid asset ratios of the chartered banks because he admitted

a prejudice against extension of the cental bank's authority in these directions on the grounds that it involves increased dependence on the central bank's judgment of complex economic problems, and tends to support economic concentration and monopolistic practices. (224)

The only form of control he thought might make sense was enabling the central bank to fix down payment and repayment terms for consumer instalment credit contracts – a common practice in Britain in the postwar period until they were abandoned in July 1982, largely on the grounds that the growth of personal lending not involving instalment credit arrangements had largely circumvented the control leaving nothing but an unnecessary interference with the way one set of financial intermediaries and their customers did business (Britton 1991).

Harry's work with the Porter Commission had another important effect. Among his fellow members of the commission's research staff was Grant Reuber, then at the University of Western Ontario, whom Harry had first met in Cambridge. For his study "The Objectives of Monetary Policy," written in 1962 between March and November, Reuber credited Harry as being "instrumental in giving the study its orientation" (1962, 2), which involved developing systematic analyses of the trade-off among economic objectives in the economy, of the policymakers' preference functions, and of the benefits gained by favouring one objective over another. Reuber concentrated on the policy trade-offs between inflation and unemployment and on finding the optimum inflation–unemployment combination for the Canadian economy. He thus developed "a fully articulated theoretical and empirical treatment of the Phillips curve as a policy menu, with the items priced in terms of Okun gaps and Harberger triangles" (Laidler 1997, 99).

Not only did Harry provide the orientation for Reuber's study: When it became clear that the publication arrangements for the commission's studies would be minimal, Harry, as convenor of the Chicago Money Workshop while Friedman was on leave, arranged for Reuber to give a shortened version of the study early in 1963 and he published it in the *Journal of Political Economy* in April 1964. He also played up Reuber's findings before publication in his "Survey of Theories of Inflation" (1963c; *EME*, 141–2) and afterwards (1968a; 1970h; *FEME*, Chapters 3 and 1).

Harry's work with the Porter Commission also, according to his 1974 Self-Evaluation, interested him in the question of the use of monetary policy under floating exchange rates. This had a formative influence on his subsequent work on the international monetary system and its reform, and on the theory of economic policy under fixed and flexible rates (12–13). The Report of the Porter Commission was put together during 1963. This meant it was sufficiently late for what eventually became known as the Fleming–Mundell model, still the bread and butter of undergraduate macroeconomics courses, to begin percolating into the journals.[6] Building on earlier work by James Meade – notably in the book Harry had reviewed so harshly in 1951 – and Jan Tinbergen, it developed the notion that policymakers had to relate policy targets to policy instruments and assign the most appropriate. In an open economy with international capital flows, it turned out that the assignments for monetary and fiscal policy would vary with the exchange rate régime. Such a model spoke volumes to those concerned with analysing the past experience and recommending future changes in the monetary arrangements of Canada, a country whose economic difficulties since 1957 could be attributed to such a misassignment under flexible exchange rates– a régime that had ended in a fixed exchange rate financial crisis in 1962.

---

[6] Fleming's contribution appeared in *IMF Staff Papers* in November 1962; Mundell's was delivered to the meetings of the Canadian Economic Association in June 1963 and appeared in the *Canadian Journal of Economics and Political Science* in November 1963. Initially, Harry seems to have missed Fleming's paper, for when he wrote a reference for Mundell's appointment to a visiting professorship at Chicago he referred to Mundell as "the first to enter seriously into the problem of the effectiveness of fiscal and monetary policy under fixed and flexible exchange rates, adding a new dimension – capital movements – to the existing analysis" [Box 36, Correspondence 1964–6, to Albert Rees, 8 July 1964; see also Correspondence 1964–6, to G. Curzon, 16 September 1965, and his contribution to the *International Encyclopedia of the Social Sciences* (1968j, 94)]. He first mentioned Fleming's paper in "Some Aspects of the Theory of Economic Policy in a World of Capital Mobility" (1966c), but he generally ignored it. Later he made partial amends in his foreword to Fleming's *Essays in International Economics* (1971) when he called Fleming's paper "a pioneering piece of analysis that helped stimulate research in what came to be known as the fiscal-monetary policy mix."

The nonexistence of Fleming–Mundell did not prevent economists such as Harry from talking intelligently about Canadian affairs (Chapter 9; 1952c, 36–8), but the talk was less focused than it would be with a formal model at the back of one's mind.

An indication of Harry's stature as a commentator on monetary affairs came in 1964 when his "Major Issues in Monetary and Fiscal Policies," a paper delivered to the American Banking Association's Conference of University Professors in Princeton became the first paper by an outsider ever to appear in the *Federal Reserve Bulletin* (1964h).

International Monetary Reform

Harry's move to Chicago coincided with a watershed in international monetary affairs, the beginnings of concern about the U.S. balance-of-payments deficit and associated worries about the long-term viability of the Bretton Woods fixed-exchange-rate system. The American balance of payments had actually been in overall deficit since 1950, but in conditions of dollar shortage, increases in the supply of dollars for official reserves were regarded as a godsend and had enabled the major European currencies to adopt current account convertibility at the end of 1958. Yet the large U.S. deficit of that year and the associated reductions in American gold reserves, as some monetary authorities exchanged dollars for gold, raised questions about the future of the dollar as a reserve currency, since every decline in U.S. gold reserves reduced the backing for U.S. dollar official liabilities. The demand for U.S. dollars as reserves reflected the fact that the growth in the supply of monetary gold had not kept pace with the demand for international reserves. There was a subsidiary problem that the mix in the supply of international reserve assets had not kept pace with the demand, with the result that the U.S. gold stock was falling. These circumstances triggered intense discussions of how to reform the international monetary system, which lasted for the rest of Harry's life.

This does not mean that there had not been discussions before 1958–9. Harry had cut his teeth on the issue in 1949 with his "The Case for Increasing the Price of Gold in Terms of All Commodities: A Contrary View" (1950a). Proposals to increase the supply of international liquidity by raising the price of gold had continued to appear, largely from the pen of Roy Harrod, throughout the 1950s. Harrod's was not the only voice arguing that supplies of international liquidity were inadequate. In 1952 a group appointed by the United Nations had reported just that. Rumblings continued through the decade, particularly in Britain, which, chronically short of reserves, experienced a series of balance-of-payments crises. In January 1958, Sir Oliver Franks commented:

At present the credit-creating powers of that institution [the IMF] are rigidly limited by the size of quotas; nor would an all-round increase in quotas be a suitable remedy for the situation we have in mind. There might be general advantage for the world, however, if the Fund could move in the direction of becoming a super central bank. (quoted in Machlup 1964, 40 n.41)

In May 1958 in a memorandum for the Radcliffe Committee, A. C. L. Day, the LSE economist whose lectures Harry had covered in 1954–5 and 1955–6, had proposed the transformation of the IMF into an international central bank, a proposal that the committee explored during his testimony on 1 July and subsequently endorsed in its 1959 *Report.*[7] In October 1958 Maxwell Stamp published "The Fund and the Future" in *Lloyds Bank Review*, recommending that any increase in international liquidity be tied to aid for developing countries. At the time of these discussions, the IMF was doing its own review of members' quotas with the result that an increase of quotas by a minimum of 50 percent was agreed at the annual meetings in September 1959.

However, the cat was really put among the pigeons by Robert Triffin with a series of publications beginning with "The Return to Convertibility 1926–1931 and 1958–?" and "Tomorrow's Convertibility: Aims and Means in International Monetary Policy" in the *Banca Nazionale del Lavoro Quarterly Review* for March and June 1959. Both articles formed the core of his *Gold and the Dollar Crisis* (1960). Triffin highlighted the fundamental contradiction of the gold exchange standard: The expansion of the national currency liabilities of reserve currency countries such as the United States weakened the gold backing for such liabilities and increased the likelihood of a repetition of the events that led to the run on sterling and the collapse of the interwar gold exchange standard in September 1931.[8] He pointed out that the ratio of reserves to liabilities for both Britain and the United States was already *worse* than it had been in 1931. To remedy the situation he made a series of proposals to reform the International Monetary Fund,

---

[7] Day's proposal is in "The World Liquidity Problem and the British Monetary System" (Committee on the Working of the Monetary System, 1960b, III, 71–6); his discussion with the committee (1960a, Questions 9891–977); and the committee's *Report* (1959, paras. 660, 678).

[8] Triffin had actually raised the possibility as early as 1947 in 'National Central Banking and the International Economy', *Postwar Monetary Studies*, 7, 46–81.

which would have moved it to towards becoming a world central bank. The discussion was joined in earnest.

As noted above, Harry had first discussed the international liquidity issue back in 1949–50, a time of dollar shortage rather than dollar glut. At that time, he was "highly doubtful whether the solution to the world's problem really lies in more international liquidity" (1950a, 203), was derisive in his treatment of the gold producers' self-interested case for an increase in the price of gold, and pointed out that gold appreciation on the scale then suggested "would . . . not constitute a very large contribution to the solution of the dollar shortage" (1950a, 205) and would moreover not be particularly useful from a European (or non-gold-producer's) point of view. Finally the proposal would be less efficient than Marshall aid in transferring American resources to the rest of the world.

His post-1959 discussions of the problem initially treated them as an aspect of the problems associated with sluggish Canadian (and American) economic growth from the late 1950s. It was not until 1961 that he turned his attention directly to the issues, first in a submission to and a discussion with the Subcommittee on International Exchange and Payments of the Joint Economic Committee of the U.S. Congress on International Payments Imbalances and Need for Strengthening International Financial Arrangements on 21 June 1961 (1961b) and in "International Liquidity: Problems and Plans," which he presented to the research seminar at the summer Institute for Economic Research at Queen's University in Kingston in August (1962a).

In his presentation to the Subcommittee and at Queen's he noted that given the major weakness of the existing gold exchange standard system – its reliance on a national currency to provide international reserves and its reliance on newly mined gold and faster expansion of reserve currency holdings to provide for growing liquidity needs – there were two alternative measures that could deal with both weaknesses. The first was an increase in the price of gold, which would inefficiently distribute the resulting increase in reserves providing "undeserved permanent income gains to gold producers" and reinstate a principle that all advanced countries had abandoned in their domestic affairs, namely "that the supply of money should be governed by the quantity of gold." The second was adopting a régime of flexible exchange rates for which "the theoretical case . . . is virtually incontestable" (*CQ*, 395). However, as he remarked to the subcommittee

I would be in favour of flexible exchange rates, but my feeling is that the monetary institutions and banks and traders and so on prefer fixed rates. And that being so, I would rather spend my time on how to make the system work, than on advocating a system that doesn't have much chance of being accepted. (1961b, 226)

Leaving aside unilateral steps that the United States could take to strengthen its position – removing the 25 percent reserve requirement against Federal Reserve notes and deposits and using existing credits with the IMF and its drawing rights at the IMF as international reserves – he then had to evaluate alternative proposals. Perhaps inevitably, given his evolving views about central banks and central bankers, which if anything grew stronger,[9] he did not hold out much hope for increased central bank cooperation

both because a central bank's first duty is to its own government and because it involves negotiations among autonomous powers each with its own view of the contemporary situation, views probably of a conservative nature and likely to be conflicting. . . . Reliance on central bank collaboration is . . . likely to result in break-down in a crisis. (*CQ*, 308)

Reliance on such collaboration was particularly risky in a reserve currency system

owing to the interrelation between the reserve currency role and national power in the world economy: to ask a non-reserve currency central bank to support the reserve currency is to ask it to support the policies of the reserve currency country and strengthen the international influence its reserve centre position gives it, and this it may be reluctant or unwilling to do. (308)

The fact that nonreserve currency countries would be asked to support reserve currency countries also told against some of the many plans for revision or reform of the international monetary system emerging in what became a minor growth industry in the early 1960s. In his subcommittee discussion, Harry only mentioned two such plans: one by E. M. Bernstein, a former director of research at the IMF, and one by Robert Triffin. In his Queen's paper, he cast his net more widely to include discussion of plans put forward by Maxwell Stamp and Xenophon Zoltas, the governor of the Bank of Greece. However, it was clear in both presentations that in the summer of 1962, if flexible exchange rates were ruled out, his preference was for the conversion of the IMF into an International Reserve Bank whose liabilities would, over time, come to dominate supplies of world liquidity and eventually replace gold as "the ultimate logical solution to the problem of providing adequate liquidity in a system of fixed exchange rates" (318).

---

[9] See his statement to and testimony before the Subcommittee on Domestic Finance of the Committee on Banking and Currency, House of Representatives, 25 February 1964 (1964g).

In 1962, concentrating on the AEA survey and the work for the Porter Commission, he made no further contribution to the discussion. Once Porter was out of the way he became more engaged in the issue. In 1963 his major concern was with the overvaluation of the dollar, which in comparison with the major European currencies he estimated amounted to 'anywhere between fifteen to twenty-five per cent' (326).[10] Overvaluation concerned him because it constrained American domestic macroeconomic policy, led American policymakers to try to limit its consequences by covert protection-ism and less than optimal, palliative interventions in official international transactions and put the international monetary system in a "potentially dangerous situation,"

since it means that the reserve currency country must command the confidence of the fraternity of central bankers in its currency . . . since the most potent disturber of confidence is a fear of devaluation. (334)

Later in the year, in a review in the *Review of Economics and Statistics* (1964a) of H. B. Lary's *Problems of the United States as a World Trader and Banker* and Walter Salant and others' *The United States Balance of Payments in 1968* he touched on a notion that would later become important in policy circles:

[T]here is no guarantee that policies for eliminating the U.S. deficit can be success-fully devised if the European countries are not prepared to relinquish their surpluses. This consideration in turn suggests that the international liquidity problem is related to the U.S. deficit . . . and . . . that the provision of additional international liquidity is a prerequisite to eliminating the deficit and not merely a temporally subsequent problem that will emerge gradually as the deficit is reduced. (31)

The conclusion of the article, with its view that the Europeans had polit-ical interest in the dollar's weakness, led Harry to a remarkably prescient comment as to how the overvaluation might finally work itself out.

This political approach would suggest that the difficulties of the dollar will continue until the U.S. authorities are prepared to face a showdown with Europe over the dollar's key currency role. To precipitate such a showdown, the United States would have to face Europe with a choice between an agreed devaluation of the dollar supported by central bank co-operation . . . and a suspension of the convertibility of gold. . . . Needless to say, the chances of such a showdown are extremely slight. (32)

By this stage, external events had got Harry more involved in the issue of reform. At the annual meeting of the International Monetary Fund in Washington on 2 October 1963, Douglas Dillon, the American secretary of

---

[10] An estimate was based on materials submitted to the Subcommittee on International Exchange of the Joint Economic Committee during its 1962 hearings.

the treasury, announced at a press conference the initiation of two studies on "the outlook for the functioning of the international monetary system" – one by the Group of Ten, the industrialised countries associated with the 1961 General Arrangements to Borrow, the other by the IMF.[11] In the course of the press conference, it was made clear that the Group of Ten would not hold hearings.

A later explanation of the negative answer was to the effect that the academic economists 'have had their say'.... [T]he nongovernmental economists had for years been busy spawning plans and proposals, they had not come up with any new and practical ideas, and their views were so much in disagreement with one another that their advice was practically useless to those in charge of decision-making. (Machlup and Malkiel 1964, 6)

In response, three academic economists who had been invited to the Fund Meetings, Fritz Machlup, Gottfried Haberler, and Robert Triffin, decided to organise another study by academic economists from several countries, a study specifically designed to make clear the bases of economists' disagreements in a form that would be useful to policymakers. Unlike the official studies, moreover, there would be no constraints on the problems and proposals that could be considered.

The first meeting of the economists was held in Princeton on 18–19 December 1963. Harry had been invited but was unable to attend because he was at an Organisation for Economic Cooperation and Development (OECD) seminar in Athens. This first meeting compiled and roughly classified objections to freely floating and, afterwards, to fixed exchange rates. The second meeting was held between 17 and 23 January 1964 at Villa Serbelloni at Bellagio. Harry attended. The purpose of the meeting was to enumerate the positive assumptions made by advocates of particular proposals and the reasons these advocates preferred these particular plans to others. The group managed to produce drafts on the semiautomatic gold standard, multiple currency reserves, centralisation of international reserves, and flexible exchange rates. Harry attended a third meeting held in Princeton on 21–22 March to clarify assumptions further. He was unhappy with this Princeton meeting. He believed "that the proceedings went quite contrary to the spirit in which the exercise was conceived.... [W]e spent most of our time at Princeton producing a statement which was to influence the

---

[11] The Group of Ten study directive saw ministers and central bank governors agree that "the underlying structure of the present monetary system – based on fixed exchange rates and the established price of gold – has proven its value as the foundation for present and future arrangements" (Machlup and Malkiel 1964, 5).

group of ten in the direction of the Triffin plan. All other aspects of the plan, and with them our original purpose of finding areas of disagreement, were shelved. . . . We have in fact ceased to be concerned with scientific questions, and have become concerned to influence policy" (Hoover Institution, Machlup Papers, Box 47, Folder 2, to F. Machlup, 23 March 1964). In reply, on 26 March, Machlup agreed to get the process back on track at Bellagio where they held a fourth meeting, 29 May to 6 June. After this, a copy of the group's report went to the printers on 30 June. In all, thirty-two economists had taken part in the discussions – twenty-four of whom had served on one or more drafting committees at one or more conferences. Harry was among the twenty-four. The report was published in August 1964, the same month in which the Group of Ten report appeared. The economists' report introduced a language that became common currency among commentators. Everyone spoke of the three major problems of the international monetary system as those of adjustment, international liquidity, and confidence.

Soon afterwards members of the economists' and the Group of Ten study groups attended a conference at Princeton and agreed to form a seminar to exchange views. The result was a conference at Bellagio between 17 and 22 December 1964. Further meetings of officials and academics followed in Zurich in January 1966 and Princeton in April 1966.[12] The joint meetings of practitioners and academics continued every six months or so after 1966 with an informal meeting of those involved in the annual meeting of the IMF. Harry attended his last meeting in Vienna in January 1973. The moving spirit for the meetings was Fritz Machlup – supported by William Fellner, Gottfried Haberler, and Robert Triffin. Machlup had a proclivity for elaborately programming the meetings for most of the waking hours. This meant, initially, according to Harry, "very little, if any time for free socialising among participants, especially as the Villa Serbelloni's catering arrangements were themselves very formal and tightly time-tabled" (1982, 81).

The result was that the [1964] Bellagio meetings . . . were very hard work . . . with groups of two or three desperately putting together drafts of sections of the final document in the short intervals between formal sessions and formal mealtimes and after the formal sessions ended. This effort also probably contributed to the development of durability in the network of international contacts. (1982, 81–2)

---

[12] The papers from the last two appeared as *Maintaining and Restoring Balance in International Payments* (Princeton University Press 1966); they included one contribution from Harry, "The Objectives of Economic Policy and the Mix of Fiscal and Monetary Policy under Fixed Exchange Rates" (1966b).

For the meetings of the academics and practitioners, an elaborate agenda was prepared by Machlup and the academics before the officials arrived and the academics stayed on to discuss what had transpired for a couple of days after the officials left. The officials, who normally came on to the meetings from the often difficult meetings of Working Party Three of OECD, tended to be on their guard and to behave like national representatives. Harry recalled:

This continued to be the case with the British official representatives, who, whether or not they had the intellectual resources for intelligent discussion of system issues, invariably "stone-walled" on issues of both British financial policy and of other countries' policies, and as a result came to be treated with politeness but no great respect. Some of the American officials, especially the higher-placed ones, were no better, but their views were backed by the power of action and hence treated respectfully. The Canadians had no ideas, and gradually dropped out; the Japanese may have had no ideas either, but their silence was accepted as related to their language problem. . . . The French were aloof but clearly of high intellectual quality; the Italians were also impressive. Gradually, two personalities emerged as dominant, in terms of intellectual power and toughness – Jonkeer van Lemp of The Netherlands and Otmar Emminger of the Deutsche Bundesbank, van Lemp being the tougher and Emminger more clearly the lucid intellectual. (1982, 82–3)

In the end, Harry regarded the main educational effect as being on the academics rather than the officials, as under the pressure of events the latter's thinking developed more quickly and more boldly. The meetings gave the academics the opportunity to write about a succession of problems, which established their credibility as experts. They also fostered the development of national subnetworks that were, for example, willing to cosign letters to the *New York Times*. The mixed background of the academic group, many of whom had countries of citizenship different from their birth, or citizenship different from their countries of current residence, and the often wide international experience of those of single birth citizenship and residence meant that theirs was a cosmopolitanism of outlook and concern, which meant a lot to Harry (1982, 83–5).[13]

International Trade

During his Chicago period, Harry's contributions to international trade theory fell into two parts. The first, consisting of articles that reflected projects

---

[13] In addition to Harry's there is a memoir by Fritz Machlup in Folder 1 of Box 113 of his papers at the Hoover Institution, which also contains more complete records of the meetings through to March 1977 in Basle.

he had conceived or undertaken while he was still at Manchester appeared in 1960 and 1961. These "late Manchester" papers, if we may call them that, were also unusual in that in two of them he had a collaborator, Jagdish Bahgwati, who had first encountered Harry as a Cambridge undergraduate (1954–6) before going to MIT and Nuffield College, Oxford. Bhagwati was originally to accompany Harry to Chicago as a postdoctoral fellow, but instead visited during the spring quarter of 1960 and then went on with Harry to the Institute for Economic Research at Queen's for the summer. The second series of articles followed on after a period during which Harry did relatively little work in trade theory and concentrated instead on monetary economics and matters Canadian. When he was free from his obligations to the Porter Commission, he turned back to the field, first with his review of the Bladen proposals for the Canadian automobile industry (see discussion in Chapter 9), which raised the question of tariff structure, and then with a lecture on optimal trade intervention in the presence of domestic distortions – the beginning of an interest on trade policy and economic development, which would culminate in *Economic Policies Towards Less Developed Countries* (1967e).

An important landmark along the way was the set of five lectures which he gave at LSE in January/February 1964. These covered the standard theory of tariffs, arguments for protection, the costs of protection, the theory of tariff structure, and tariffs and economic development. Originally, Harry had intended to combine the lectures as delivered into a book, *Aspects of the Theory of Tariffs*, but this project was overtaken by events, and the book of that title which appeared in 1971 was significantly different from the one for which he had signed a contract in 1964. For a time in 1970, Harry thought of reviving the LSE lectures as a book and even raised the matter with Charles Furth at Allen and Unwin with whom he was also discussing the collection of papers actually published as *Aspects of the Theory of Tariffs*:

> Just a day or so ago, I came across the material intended for the [1964] book, which has been stored in my Chicago apartment, and found it was fairly fully written out, and while dated by its references to 1964 still full of relevant material and perhaps distinguished by more of my personal style of speech and thought than comes through in my writing for a professional audience. I think that with a week or so of work I could translate it into a publishable product, or at least one that would have been publishable easily in 1966.
>
> The question is whether it would be worth doing it. The result would be a short parallel to the book now under preparation, written generally at a lower and looser level than the material in the bigger book, running to perhaps 120 pages.... An excuse could be that I would dedicate it to the memory of Ely Devons. (Box 31, Correspondence with Allen and Unwin, to Charles Furth, 27 April 1970)

The first two later Manchester papers – "International Trade, Income Distribution and the Offer Curve" (1959b) and "Income Distribution, the Offer Curve and the Effects of Tariffs" (1960g) have already been discussed under Manchester (see discussion in Chapter 7). The second paper with Bhagwati, "A Generalised Theory of the Effects of Tariffs on the Terms of Trade" (1961f) relaxed the restrictive assumptions normally employed in such discussions to show that through a variety of unexpected effects on spending, tariffs could worsen the terms of trade by reducing the demand for imports. This article "together with the 1959 and 1960 articles, tidied up this whole body of theory in which income distribution is affected by changes in relative prices and, in turn, through effects on demand, influences the final equilibrium" (Corden 1984, 573).

The first paper with Bhagwati (1960c), the article that caused all the difficulties with Milton Friedman (see discussion in Chapter 8) saw them combine forces to reexamine four disputed problems in the theory of international trade, three of them arising in the work of Marshall and the fourth in that of F. Y. Edgeworth. The paper had brewed in their separate lives as trade theorists until they decided to combine their talents.

The remaining late Manchester paper, "The Cost of Protection and the Scientific Tariff" (1960e), was one of Harry's most important trade papers, which presaged a number of later contributions that helped to tighten the links between the theory and practice of trade policy. The article was in two parts: The first part developed in a rigorous fashion a cost of protection theory in a multigood general equilibrium framework. In dealing with these costs on the production and consumption sides, Harry demonstrated Harberger's law: "if you multiply enough small fractions together you can forget about the answer" (*ATT*, xi). To be specific, as Harry put it

The consumption cost of protection is likely to be a small proportion of national expenditure because its calculation involves multiplying together for each commodity four fractions, of which one is $\frac{1}{2}$ and the others are likely to be substantially under $\frac{1}{2}$. (*ATT*, 205)

Similar results also probably held true for the production side. However, these results had interesting implications as he later put it: "the proposition that the cost of protection is likely to be small has had to be interpreted carefully to avoid the implication that tariffs do not matter" (1974 Self-Evaluation, 16). Harry himself fell into that trap in the initial argument when he concluded the first section of his article as follows:

The probability that the consumption and production costs of protection will be small – and that the total will be still smaller when allowance is made for the terms of trade benefit it may procure for the country – has an important general implication.

For, if the cost of protection is a small proportion of the level of national income at any point in time and if the protectionists happen to be correct in their claim that protection increases an economy's rate of growth, the increase does not have to be very great for its effect in raising national income to counter the reduction due to the cost of protection within relatively few years. (206–8)

Taking an example where protection reduced the level of national income by 5 percent from the free trade level but raised the average rate of growth from $2\frac{1}{2}$ to 3 percent per annum, it would take $10\frac{1}{2}$ years for national income to regain its free trade level and would be growing more rapidly than under free trade. As growth rate improvements of this magnitude were commonly tossed around in the age of John F. Kennedy and Harold Wilson, the use of such examples was dangerous. However, his guess that "the effect of alternative commercial policies on the rate of growth may well be the quantitatively significant issue in the free trade versus protection debate" (208) has turned out to be wide of the mark.

The second part of the article, "the scientific tariff," worked out the minimum cost tariff structures to meet various noneconomic objectives such as national self-sufficiency and independence, diversification, industrialisation or agriculturalisation, military preparedness, or international bargaining strength. In it he concluded that

The variety of scientific tariff structures implicit in different arguments for protection points to what is probably the fundamental problem in giving concrete content to the notion – the difficulty of reconciling conflicting objectives of protection in a single scientific tariff structure. (218)

Harry returned to "the costs of protection and self-sufficiency" in a 1965 article of that title (1965h). There he attempted to calculate the welfare changes resulting from tariffs in relatively simple models into which a wide variety of parameter values were substituted. On this basis he concluded that

both the gains from international trade and the cost of protection are likely to be relatively small in large advanced industrial countries owing to their relatively flexible economic structures, probably high elasticities of substitution among the goods on which consumption is concentrated, and relatively low dependence on trade, while they are likely to be appreciably larger, relative to maximum potential income in the smaller and less developed countries, whose economies tend to show opposite characteristics. (*ATT*, 236)

This time, however, he was more cautious in drawing the implications:

This does not imply . . . that the income sacrificed by protectionist policies is negligible. On the contrary, it may be very substantial, when measured against the appropriate standard of cost in terms of additional resources or time of obtaining an increase in real income comparable to what could be obtained from trade lib-eralisation. (The increase of one-third [as the maximum possible gain in utility by changing from self-sufficiency to free trade] . . . corresponds to an investment equal to a year's national income with a marginal capital/output ratio of 3 and to nearly ten year's growth at an annually compounded rate of 3 percent.) (236–7)

The other 1965 paper "Optimal Trade Interventions in the Presence of Domestic Distortions" was "one of Harry's major works – even more so that his 'cost of protection' paper [1960e]" (Corden 1984, 575). It had a curious history that shows Harry's tendency to hide his light under a bushel. Orig-inally a March 1963 lecture at the Claremont Colleges, it was submitted to and rejected by the *Review of Economic Studies* before he offered it to the *Indian Economic Review*, then in the process of trying to become more visi-ble with Jagdish Bhagwati and Amartya Sen as editors – only to be rescued and finally also published in a *festschrift* in honour of Gottfried Haberler – again not the most prominent of venues for important papers. Richard Lipsey remarked that

the substance of this long, carefully reasoned article deserves to be in the textbooks alongside the fallacious first-best arguments for tariffs. This would help counter the widespread belief that tariffs are a sensible second-best reaction to a wide set of domestic distortions that cannot be removed directly. (1978, S45)

Harry summarised its major points:

The purpose of this paper is to explain and elaborate on two propositions concerning arguments for protection derived from the existence or alleged existence of domestic distortions. The first proposition is that such distortions do not logically lead to the recommendation of protection in the sense of taxes on international trade; instead, they lead to the recommendation of other forms of government intervention which do not discriminate between domestic and international trade and which differ according to the nature of the distortion they are intended to correct. The second proposition is that if protection is adopted as a means of correcting domestic distor-tions, not only will the result be that economic welfare will fall short of the maximum attainable, but that economic welfare may be reduced below what it would be under a policy of free trade. These two propositions can be combined in the proposition that the only valid argument for protection as a means of maximising economic welfare is the optimum tariff argument; all other arguments for protection of this kind are in principle arguments for some form of government intervention in the domestic economy, and lead to the recommendation of protection only when supplemented by practical considerations that render the appropriate form of intervention infea-sible, and empirical evidence that protection will in fact increase economic welfare. (*ATT*, 119–20)

The final Chicago period paper was a June 1964 lecture "The Theory of Tariff Structure with Special Reference to World Trade and Development"

(1965b) published by the Graduate Institute of International Studies in Geneva – another "obscure" place, which Harry soon rather regretted "as the ideas deserve more circulation" (Box 56, Correspondence 1954–6, A–L, HGJ to J. Bhagwati, 27 October 1964). Indeed, he unsuccessfully tried to place it more visibly, given what he thought was an immanent paper from Max Corden (Box 66, Correspondence 1964–6, A–L, to G. Curzon, 21 July and 3 December 1964).

Corden's paper, "The Structure of a Tariff System and the Effective Protection Rate" (1966), had its own history.

The first version of this paper was rejected by the *Economic Journal*, but Harry Johnson . . . encouraged me to submit a revised version to the *Journal of Political Economy* . . . and it had an immediate impact. It really generated a large literature. . . . For several years there was a world wide boom in the calculation of effective rates. (Corden 2000, 232)

It was the possible publication of Corden's paper in the *Economic Journal* that had made Harry try to remove his from the Institute. When the *Journal* rejected Cordon's paper, the matter of moving Harry's became moot, although reprints went into the Committee for the Comparative Study of New States reprint series.

The correspondence with Corden on his *JPE* paper also shows Harry as the effective editor.[14]

The more general problem I have is with the level at which the article is pitched – more specifically, the various levels between which it wanders. . . . I must ask you to select a level of audience and stick to it. Specifically for the J. P. E. you should assume that you are writing for people who teach international trade, though not necessarily very well, and then you need to tell them what the theoretical issues are.

For this purpose, I think you need to do something like the following . . . (Box 56, Correspondence 1964–6, A–L, 3 December 1965)

Harry's own paper was "the first theoretical exploration of effective protection" (Corden 1971, 248). The notion of effective protection had obviously been in the minds of businessmen and tariffmakers for a long time. It starts from the fact that production is not normally vertically integrated and that internationally traded inputs may be subject to taxes and subsidies. The question then arises whether a tariff on a good protects the value

---

[14] For Harry's nurturing of the paper and maximising its impact by making it the lead article in the June 1966 issue of the *JPE*, see also the related correspondence in Box 56, Correspondence 1964–6, A–L, to HGJ, 9 September 1965; to Corden, 14 October 1965; to HJG, 21 October 1965 (two letters); to Corden, 3 December 1965; to HGJ, 10 September 1965; to Corden, 4 January 1966; to HGJ, 10 January 1966.

added in the production of the good or whether that protection extends to its inputs. Building on earlier work by Clarence Barber and Max Corden, a Harvard doctoral dissertation by William Travis and his own examination of the Bladen Plan, and taking advantage of ongoing empirical work by Giorgio Basevi, his graduate student at Chicago,[15] Harry proceeded to explore the theory and its implications for both developed and developing countries. Later Harry would popularise and make piecemeal additions to the theory, but it was Max Corden who made most of the running with the theory and consolidated it, beginning with his June 1966 article. Harry made extensive use of the concept in his *Economic Policies for Less Developed Countries*, which gave him opportunities to do more calculations and sort through the various implications of the theory.

In December 1964, Harry was able to sum up his views on international economic problems when he delivered the K. E. Norris Memorial Lectures at Sir George Williams (now Concordia) University in Montreal. The lectures were subsequently published by the Canadian Trade Committee in Montreal and, after Sir John Hicks read them, by Oxford University Press as *The World Economy at the Crossroads: A Survey of Current Problems of Money, Trade and Economic Development* (1965i) (*WEC*).

In addition to providing commentary on the evolving discussions on the shape and reform of the international monetary system, the lectures provided a vehicle for comments on the evolution of the world trading system and the Kennedy Round of bargaining negotiations under GATT, which had been under way since early 1963, and the deliberations of the United Nations Conference on Trade and Development (UNCTAD), which was in session in Geneva. As Harry was in the process of reading up to prepare a study which had been commissioned by the Brookings Institution, eventually published as *Economic Policies Towards Less Developed Countries* (*EPLDC*; 1967e), the Montreal lectures could not have been more appropriately timed.

Economic Development

Although Harry had been active in the developing countries since his 1956 visits to Karachi and Singapore, returning to Asia in 1958, 1961, and 1965, he published little on the subject until the 1960s. Nonetheless, his "Planning and the Market in Economic Development" (1958f), a lecture from the 1956 Karachi series, which he republished in *Money, Trade and Economic Growth*,

---

[15] He had also touched on the issue and used Basevi's work in "Tariffs and Economic Development" (1964e).

represented a benchmark. The lecture made a strong case for the market as the instrument of choice for economic development, partially "because the market figures relatively little in the literature of economic development and the theoretical analysis which economics has developed in relation to the market is often overlooked or disregarded" (*MTEG*, 153). In it he also raised a theme that he would touch on again and again.

> To a large extent, "the economic development of underdeveloped countries" is a second-best policy, in which gifts of capital and technical training by advanced to underdeveloped countries are in compensation for the unwillingness of the former to consider the alternative way of improving the labour to resources ratio, the movement of the labour to the resources. The fact that development is a second-best policy in this respect may impose severe limitations on its efficiency and rapidity. (162)

He began to shift his interests and his energies towards development after his arrival in Chicago, although at first his membership of the new nations committee was its only manifestation (see discussion in Chapter 9). More signs came in 1964 with the publication of "Tariffs and Economic Development: Some Theoretical Issues" in the first issue of the *Journal of Development Studies* (1964e) and his willingness in the fall of 1964 to take on the organisation of the new nations committee's seminar programme (see discussion in Chapter 9). Nineteen sixty-four also saw the conception of a grander project, which eventuated in *Economic Policies Towards Less Developed Countries*. The origins of the project lay in the experience of the United States at the meeting of the United Nations Conference on Trade and Development, which met in Geneva, from March to June 1964. As Harry put it in his Montreal lectures:

> For the United States, which arrived for the Conference ill-prepared, and relied for guidance, as it is only too inclined to do, on a few highly moralistic and vaguely defined principles – notably the principle of non-discrimination and the immorality of price-fixing agreements – together with the assumption that because it knows its motives are pure other nations will trust its judgment and excuse it from making any firm commitments, the Conference was a traumatic experience. Not only were the Communist *bloc* countries present and egging on the developing countries, but the European countries . . . were in important respects more sympathetic than the United States to the developing countries' point of view, while the French . . . actively opposed the U.S. point of view. The result was that the United States was virtually isolated as a minority of one. (*WEC*, 93)

In order to increase public discussion during the preparations for the next meeting of the Conference scheduled for 1967, the Brookings Institution commissioned Harry to survey the main issues in the United States' relationship with the developing countries and explore the main policy alternatives.

Harry read up for the project over the fall, winter, and spring of 1964–5, wrote his report in six weeks in the summer of 1965 and revised it in the light of the comments made by individuals and participants at two conferences that discussed his draft in December 1965 and March 1966 before sending his final draft off to the editors at Brookings in April.

The book was "a tour de force", his most successful venture in '"spreading economic literacy"' (Corden 1984, 584). In his 1974 Self-Evaluation Harry claimed it

marshalled the major new ideas in international trade theory in an analysis of the trade policy issues raised by the 1964 Conference . . . especially the proposal for preferences for developing country exports of manufactured goods. (18)

It did more than that. It surveyed a much broader literature, fitted it into a coherent framework and presented it in a clear, balanced literary way. He did not shirk difficulties but presented them clearly. The discussion was densely thorough. As one reviewer put it: "[T]he argument is carried on at a relentless pace; one wonders how many of the policy-makers at whom the book is in part, at any rate, aimed will be able to keep up with it" (Prest 1968, 209). In his discussion of the issues, he was regarded "as virtually embodying the neoclassical tradition in economics" while "his specific comments on the LDCs show him as an acute and astute observer, wise though at times sharp and acerbic in his judgments" (Harberger and Wall 1984, 621–2).

As in his 1956 Karachi lecture, his emphasis was on improving and strengthening the market system. In his view the international economic system produced strong pressures for the diffusion of development through the rising demand in the developed world for primary products and, given the relative immobility of labour, a growing comparative advantage in the developing world for the production of labour-intensive goods. These pressures could be blunted by unfavourable environmental conditions such as population pressures, which restrained or nullified the raising of incomes through primary product exports, or unfavourable factor proportions, which resulted in too small a domestic market, or traditional social arrangements, which inhibited the diffusion of appropriate skills and attitudes through education.

In addition to these unfavourable factors, both the LDCs and the developed countries often pursued policies that inhibited or even reversed the pressures for diffusion. In his survey, replete with specific estimates where available, Harry was scathing. The LDCs' nationalism, which derived economic objectives by imitation and emulation and envisaged development in terms of the ownership and control of certain types of modern property rather than in raising incomes, was dysfunctional. Development was inhibited by deficiencies in competitive organisation and belief in the superiority of planning or socialism; bureaucratic controls combined with an absence of decision-making skills;[16] a tendency to discriminate against agriculture by raising the cost of inputs through import substitution while controlling output prices to benefit urban workers; a penchant for import-substituting industrialisation which raised domestic costs above world costs and reduced competition and efficiency; and hostility towards private foreign investment, particularly to international corporations in the extractive and mass-production, technically advanced manufacturing sectors, which offered possibilities of integration into their global operations.

The developed countries were inefficient aid-givers, preferring soft loans to grants and bilateral, project-based aid tied to multilateral programmatic aid. They produced barriers to LDCs' commodity exports through their own agricultural policies (including the disposal of surplus commodities on concessionary terms),[17] inhibited export earnings though taxes on non-competitive products such as coffee, cocoa, and bananas, not to mention tariff and nontariff barriers on imports of manufactures, particularly textiles. At one point, he summarised the position in terms familiar to readers of his 1956 lecture:

The developed countries prevent the people of the less developed countries from personal participation in their opulence through immigration and at the same time impede them from absentee participation in it through international trade; in this set of circumstances foreign aid on a massive scale appears less like generosity than compensation for injury. (*EPLDC*, 108)

The developed countries' immigration policies discriminated less against, or even actively encouraged, migration by educated and professionally trained people, with the result, he suspected, that the United States gained substantially from such immigration, an issue he discussed extensively in other fora (see discussion in Chapter 15).

He then turned to possible changes in policy within existing arrangements – increasing levels of aid, the untying of aid, the internationalisation

---

[16] Although Harry added his own blooper when he wrote: "Licensing substitutes the administrative mechanism of detailed quantitative decisions by civil servants who lack the economic training that would be necessary to make these decisions as efficiently as the market could" (*EPLDC*, 69).

[17] In the process he utilised and extended the work of R. H. Snape on the effects of protection in the world sugar industry (1963) to suggest that free trade in sugar would have raised imports from the LDCs by $897 million and released $482 million for development purposes (*EPLDC*, 87–8).

of aid, increasing foreign investment, and increasing export opportunities for LDCs within the GATT framework. As usual, the discussion could be brutally frank.

Thus, if the other developed countries (and particularly the Common Market countries) refuse to cooperate with the United States in the negotiation of tariff reductions for the benefit of less developed countries, and if the United States prefers to adhere to its traditional trade policy principle of non-discrimination and to act within the existing GATT framework, but desires to open export opportunities to the less developed countries, it could easily do so . . . It could unilaterally reduce its tariffs on products of special interest to the less developed countries and in so doing exploit the opportunity for product discrimination allowed by the most-favoured-nation principle by concentrating its tariff reductions on those products in which the other developed countries have the least comparative advantage – choosing, for example, the products on which those countries impose high tariffs. (*EPLDC*, 134–5)

His twenty-seven-line footnote provided the good second-best grounds for such a strategy, which was deliberately designed to help the LDCs, while imposing losses on noncooperating developed countries.

Having surveyed the situation and the prospects for change within the existing arrangements, Harry turned for 100 pages to three possible reforms: changes in the arrangements for trade in primary products; tariff-preferences for the LDCs' exports of manufactures to the developed world; and reform of the international monetary system. Each had received consideration at Geneva, and each had spawned sets of proposals allegedly designed to nurture the growth of the LDCs.

Harry was generally unhappy with proposals for changing the arrangements for trade in primary products. His unhappiness stemmed from his belief in some cases that there was some uncertainty as to the existence of the problem that the changed arrangements were supposed to address, while in others that the changed arrangements would not efficiently address a problem that existed. Thus, as well as following other economists in disputing the allegation that the terms of trade showed a long-term tendency to turn against primary producers, he also accepted contemporary work that suggested that instability of quantities rather than instability of prices seemed to be the most pressing problem for primary producing countries. This meant that attempts to stabilise primary product prices through buffer stocks, output controls, or other arrangements were unlikely to contribute much to the improvement in the welfare of LDCs, especially when one took into account the costs of running such schemes and their limited possible coverage. Nor did he see such schemes as effective ways of redistributing income from the developed world to the less developed world. As he put it:

Once one begins to think seriously about commodity arrangements as a means of increasing external resources, one is forcibly struck by their inefficiency as a means of taxing the richer countries to raise resources for the development of the poorer countries and inevitably drawn to the consideration of more efficient methods of international taxation. (262)

Even compensatory financing schemes for smoothing fluctuations in the export earnings of less-developed primary producers would make only a limited contribution to stabilisation. Whether that contribution would be worth its cost would depend on the value placed on stabilisation – "a matter on which economists can offer no adequate guidance" (152)

Harry was more attracted by a proposal for LDC exports of manufactures to receive preferential treatment in developed country markets. Political/administrative arguments against the scheme were, on balance, inconclusive, while the economic arguments were quite powerful, given high rates of effective protection on developing country manufactures or on further processed raw materials in developed country markets. But he did not support infant-industry preferences.

[E]ven when infant-industry conditions exist – an empirical issue concerning which the ratio of unsupported assertion to empirical evidence is probably unequalled in any other field of economics – these conditions do not locally lead to the recommendation of a tariff. . . . The . . . resort to infant-industry tariffs appears as a second-best policy. Correspondingly, the recommendation of tariff preferences from developed countries, with their inefficiencies appears as a third-best policy recommendation. (183–4)

Nonetheless, he proceeded to give the preference proposal more serious consideration. Inevitably, the results were not unambiguous – it was international trade theory after all. Despite all the difficulties he could see with preference proposal, he argued that

contrary to superficial appearances, preferences might be an extremely powerful tool for stimulating the industrial development in the less developed countries, the reasons being largely inherent in the recently developed theory of effective protection. Given the emphasis placed by the less developed countries on their need for such preferences and the possibility that the formation and policies of the European Common Market will block further progress after the Kennedy Round towards trade liberalization along traditional GATT lines, the possibilities of using trade preferences to promote development deserve serious consideration. (204–5)

He emphasised the need for more research since the relevant conceptual framework was extremely new and the empirical work difficult. He suggested that this investigation should be accompanied by a parallel examination of

what factors account for the inability of less developed countries, and specifically of the "developing" countries that already produce manufactures for the home market, to export in competition with the developed countries in spite of their comparative advantage in availability of materials and low-wage labour. . . . Chapter II suggested that a major part of the explanation is to be found in the import-substitution and currency-overvaluation policies typically pursued by . . . less developed countries and that the cost disadvantages resulting from these policies may frequently be far greater than the competitive advantage that could be conferred by preferences from the developed countries. If this suggestion is confirmed . . . it would imply that neither preferences nor non-discriminatory tariff reductions wold help the less developed countries unless they were prepared to make major changes in their . . . policies. Thus, the developed countries could legitimately insist on such policy changes . . . as a condition for trade concessions. (206)

Harry then turned to reform proposals for the international monetary system. He proceeded in two stages: (i) the general interest of the less developed countries in a properly functioning international monetary system and the current problems of international monetary reform, and (ii) proposals to *link* international monetary reform with the provision of increased development assistance to the less developed countries, in particular the Hart–Kaldor–Tinbergen scheme for a commodity reserve currency.

The discussion of the first set of issues followed familiar lines, with an added twist: The LDCs would benefit from a smoothly functioning international monetary system because balance-of-payments reasons for inefficient aid practices or trade-inhibiting quantitative restrictions would be less compelling, and, more importantly, the openness of the international economy would allow more efficient diffusion of the forces favouring development. He also noted the specific interest of the less developed countries in a system that expanded supplies of international liquidity at a rate great enough to produce an inflationary bias in the world economy.

This is because . . . some moderate upward trend of prices in a developed country induced by demand pressure facilitates the reallocation of resources and the mobility of labour and because the promotion of planned economic development in the less developed countries tends to generate inflationary price movements which tend to cancel out their ability to export unless offset by price increases in the developed countries to which they export. (217)

On the link schemes that proposed to channel the real savings involved in the growth of international reserves directly to the less developed countries in the form of capital assistance, he noted the desired result might not come to pass. In the development business the right hand normally knew what the left hand was doing, and if international monetary schemes resulted in giving more aid than developed countries thought desirable, there would likely be reductions in other forms of aid. If there were no international central bank, but some sort of secondary reserve asset, the potential flows through the link would be smaller and more erratic. All of this was, however, but a prelude to his discussion of the Hart–Kaldor–Tinbergen scheme. This was to convert the IMF into a world central bank whose liabilities over a modest fiduciary issue would be backed by gold and warehouse receipts for a bundle to commodities whose value would be stabilised in terms of gold by the Fund's open-market operations. He was not convinced by the authors' argument that the plan would of itself promote world economic growth, which, he suggested assumed "a naive Keynesian model of the world economy." He continued:

If the developed countries used monetary and fiscal policy to maintain full employment adjusting their exchange rates as necessary to maintain international equilibrium the [alleged] asymmetry and its retarding effects on economic growth would not arise. The solution to the authors' problem is therefore to establish a properly functioning international monetary system, not necessarily to adopt their scheme. (232–3)

He also pointed to a number of practical objections. The scheme would stabilise the average money prices of the commodities involved, which was by no means equivalent to stabilising the average purchasing power of those commodities in terms of manufactured goods or the average money or real incomes of the producers or the export earnings of the producing countries. Open-market operations in the fixed ratios comprising the bundles could destabilise the prices of particular commodities important to particular countries. Given its concentration on the money prices of commodities, it would do little to counteract the alleged long-term tendency of the terms of trade to turn against primary producers. Finally, the scheme, with its annual additions to its stocks, its need to store stocks, and its dealing costs (especially in turning over its stocks of perishables), would be extremely expensive to operate and yet only a small fraction of those costs would benefit less developed countries through greater export earnings.

Moreover the scheme was open to the usual objections to a commodity reserve standard. Grafting such a scheme onto an international gold standard while leaving domestic credit creation in national hands "is not truly a reform of the monetary standard but a scheme for price support of the commodities included coupled with a cyclical deficit-surplus fiscal policy mediated through the commodity stocks" (235–6). The stabilisation of commodities accounting for only a small part of world output and unrepresentative of that output, coupled with differential rates of technical progress and the accidents of resource discoveries would probably destabilise the general price level, perhaps by more than had been the case under the classical gold standard. The small share of the commodities in total output, as well as their limited elasticities of supply and demand, would mean the automatic stabilising effects of the standard were likely to be small and long in coming.

In view of all these considerations, and especially of the plan's inefficiency in achieving worthwhile objective and the deliberate reversal of the historical evolution from the gold standard to intelligent monetary management, the . . . plan appears to offer little to recommend it as a solution to the problems of international monetary reform. Less developed countries and their sympathisers would be better advised to press for as liberal a credit-based international monetary system as can be achieved, preferably an internationally controlled world central bank. (236)

In his final chapter, as well as making a powerful plea for more empirical research on many of the issues raised in his study, Harry emphasised that the United States faced a number of choices. What it could not continue to do was

to follow protectionist policies for itself, while using the language and concepts of the free-trade position to deny that these policies injure the less developed countries whose economic development it has pledged itself to promote, and to reject their proposals for improvement of their trading opportunities. (241)

He recorded his preference for the United States continuing to act within the GATT framework but to take a number of steps to demonstrate the strength of its commitment to development. In particular, the United States should cease to use tariffs and other protectionist devices to shield domestic producers from increased competition, make its intent clear by pledging not to introduce any new quotas or import restrictions and not to raise any tariffs on goods where the less developed countries had or might in future have developed an export trade with the United States, and reinforce that commitment by adopting a programme for phasing out the Cotton Textile Arrangement (later called the Multifibre Agreement, which did not disappear until the end of 2004). He also recommended that the United States commit itself to untying aid as it relaxed its intervention in response to balance-of-payments improvements, and that it remit any increase in prices caused by tying as a grant.[18] He also proposed a review by experts of the effects of American tariff policy and its consistency with the country's domestic and international policy objectives.

With *Economic Policies* in press, Harry was ready to move to London. He was there briefly in late June and early July before taking the family on a two-month trip around the world.

---

[18] He acknowledged in a footnote that "the prospect for an early improvement...looks extremely bleak" and reiterated his 1964 *Review of Economics and Statistics* remarks about a show-down with Europe that might involve the suspension of gold convertibility for the dollar (*EPLDC*, 243 n.1; this chapter).

ELEVEN

LSE

The School Harry joined in 1966 was rather different from the one he had encountered in the mid-1950s. Up to the 1963–4 academic year, the School's policy had been to cap undergraduate numbers while allowing graduate numbers to drift slowly upwards. In 1963–4, in response to the October 1963 Robbins Report on higher education, which was accepted immediately by the Macmillan government, the School proposed to increase its undergraduate numbers by 20 percent by 1967 (with half of this increase to occur in 1964–5), while letting graduate numbers increase as before. The overall effect of the 1963–4 plans would be to increase regular full-time student numbers from the 2,450 of October 1963 to about 3,000 in October 1967.

Greater student numbers meant an expanded faculty. Between 1963 and 1967 staff numbers rose more rapidly than student numbers with the result that the student–staff ratio improved from 11.1:1 to 9.7:1 (Kidd 1969, 4; Dahrendorf 1995, 429). In absolute terms, staff numbers were three-quarters larger than they had been when Harry lectured at LSE in 1955–6.[1]

The expansion at the School was a reflection of the expansion in the university system as a whole, which had grown by 40 percent in the six years before the Robbins Report and would grow another 50 percent in the succeeding four years. The expansion was accompanied by the founding of new universities – East Anglia, Essex, Kent, Lancaster, Stirling, Sussex, Warwick, and York – and the conversion of some former colleges to universities – Bath, Bradford, Brunel, City, Loughborough, Salford, Strathclyde, and Surrey. The expansion required staff and drained mainly nonprofessorial talent away from the existing universities. At LSE, for example, this meant losing

---

[1] Student numbers had risen by 41 percent over the same period.

Richard Lipsey and later G. C. Archibald to Essex[2] and Jack Wiseman to join Alan Peacock at York. America, of course, still had its attractions – Kelvin Lancaster left for Johns Hopkins – as did the world of affairs – Ralph Turvey left for the Electricity Council. Replacing the departed or even hiring at the entry level was difficult. Expansion made the job market very tight – a tightness heightened by an expanding demand for economists in government. The number of university teaching posts in economics rose by 60 percent between 1964 and 1968, while the number of professional economists employed by government rose six and a half times. Overall, demand from these two sources went from 422.5 to 839.5 (Booth and Coats 1978, Tables 4 and 5). Of course the number of higher degrees awarded was expanding, from 139 in 1963–4 to 281 in 1966–7, but a significant proportion of these degrees went to foreigners who were not normally a part of the U.K. labour market. In any case, the expansion in the numbers of university and government posts for economists over the period, 417, loomed large in relation to the flow of advanced degree recipients, most of whom were in master's programmes.[3] Not surprisingly, salaries were not bad, and the long-term relative decline in academic salaries was stayed, at least for a time.

While LSE and the university system expanded, other forces were also at work. After considerable post-Robbins debate, LSE decided to remain on the crowded, expensive central London site it had occupied since 1901 (Dahrendorf 1995, 433–6). A concomitant of that decision, in many minds, was the expansion of graduate teaching at the School – an enterprise that Harry had been hired to lead in the case of economics. At the time Harry was hired, it looked as if this shift in emphasis had the support of the University Grants Committee (UGC) (Director's Report 1964/65, 54). However, from the time of Harry's arrival, government policy embarked on another tack: In the quinquennium 1967–72 the UGC informed the University of London that it had "not felt able to make provision for a further swing from undergraduate to postgraduate work in Social Studies at the London School of Economics" (Director's Report 1967/68, 51). A further complication in the plans for the expansion of graduate studies was the introduction of a senior (professors + readers + senior lecturers)/junior (lecturers and assistant

---

[2] The departure of Lipsey and Archibald led to the collapse of the LSE seminar on Methodology, Measurement and Testing which had played an important role in the life of the School's economists since the mid-1950s. The demise of M^2T meant a strengthening of older attitudes towards method in the School which came to annoy Harry. See pp. 329–30.

[3] Moreover, these figures ignore the demand for staff from the newly created polytechnics. By the early 1970s, the whole UK system was producing 100 PhDs in economics per year.

lecturers) staffing ratio of 35 percent for all universities. The proportion at LSE at the time of the announcement was 45 percent. This did not bode well for future replacements as senior faculty retired. The School was, however, able to win recognition of its special situation and to avoid the most damaging consequences (Director's Report, 1967/68, 52).

According to the LSE Calendar, when Harry arrived at the School he had forty-eight economist colleagues. Of these, ten were professors, eight were readers, and four were senior lecturers. The senior faculty had a very "applied" air about it: the only theorist among the professors was A. W. H. Phillips, although there was more strength in theory among the readers. Moreover, some of the most distinguished senior faculty, such as Richard Sayers and Henry Phelps Brown were nearing retirement, and death and changing interests would deprive the School of Ely Devons in 1967 and A. W. H. Phillips in 1968. On the other hand, Frank Hahn and Terence Gorman were scheduled to arrive in October 1967. More new senior faculty would arrive later. At the lower end of the ranks, there were a number of newly hired assistant lecturers, often without advanced degrees, and recently promoted lecturers on whom the future strength of the School would depend. Developing procedures and raising standards for hiring and tenure at a time when market conditions favoured the seller of academic services would be difficult, particularly as university expansion was not confined to the United Kingdom.

All universities have their peculiarities, but LSE was more peculiar than most. First, it was part of the larger University of London whose approval was required for senior appointments and such things as degree regulations. Second,

[t]he School's written constitution was that of a company limited by guarantee of the beginning of the century; since that time it had gone substantially unrevised. Its sketchy outlines had been filled in by conventions and understandings, but they had not always been reduced to writing and were sometimes difficult to ascertain with precision. (Kidd 1969, 5)

If this difficulty affected the School's senior civil servant until his departure to Oxford in 1967, the position was more opaque to faculty and students. Nominally, the supreme body was the largely self-perpetuating Court of Governors, numbering eighty, which long ago had delegated most of its powers to a Standing Committee of about a dozen, including three professorial governors and the director. The director's primary function "but a largely unrecognised function . . . was to hold the School together" (Kidd 1969, 5). It was up to him, as chair of most school committees, to shape and form the consensus and move the institution forward. Shaping that consensus meant consultation with various academic persons and bodies, who were slowly gaining the power of decision. But that process of transfer, quiet and gradual, often without explicit recognition, could be a source of difficulties, as the governors who still held legal authority came to have less and less knowledge and legitimacy in the eyes of those over whom they exercised that authority. Nor were the lower levels of what is now called governance much more helpful: the Academic Board, made up of all who held School appointments, was a talking shop/town meeting and its General Purposes Committee, elected by caste (five professors, four readers or senior lecturers, and four lecturers or assistant lecturers) rather than by discipline frequently did not reflect opinion within the institution. The student body was excluded from governance.

In 1962 the School saw the beginnings of formal departmentalism with the creation of convenors for various disciplinary groups, including the economists. However, the choice of title was revealing, "person who arranges meeting of committee, etc.,"[4] for it was not a label that suggested that the incumbent had substantial power as might have been the case if he had been called head or chair. Moreover, in personnel matters the convenor had little influence. Appointments were normally in the hands of the Appointments Committee consisting of all professors in the school. In 1962 it spawned a standing subcommittee consisting of the director and eight professors. For senior appointments, the Appointments Committee chose one lay governor and two professors to sit with the director on the Board of Advisors, which advised the Senate of the University of London on the appointment. For other academic posts, decisions were made by selection subcommittees, each consisting of the director, two or more professors from the discipline concerned and one or two from related disciplines. The recommendations of these committees required the approval of the governors. The arrangements for appointments also covered promotions and tenure, which effectively came with appointment to a lectureship. As salary scales were related to years of service in rank, there was no procedure by which units could reward merit or penalise idleness among lecturers other than by initiating a process for dismissal, which was, in a word, extreme, although it was invoked during "the troubles" of 1968–9.

The convenor for economics who was responsible for attracting Harry to LSE was Ely Devons. But Devons became ill in September 1965, had surgery in October when he was given a year to live, and, except for short intervals,

---

[4] *Concise Oxford Dictionary*, 6th ed., 1976.

was an invalid until he died on 28 December 1967, aged 54. Devons was succeeded as convenor by Basil Yamey, an industrial economist, who held the post until 1969; Dennis Sargan, an econometrician held the post from 1969 to 1972; and finally A. C. L. Day took over the responsibilities. According to Harry's obituary notice, Devons "did much to reform and democratise the Department's administrative structure" and was also largely responsible for instituting one-year MSc degrees in economics and econometrics. Of Devons, Harry remarked,

[p]erhaps his greatest contribution was to inspire his colleagues, and especially those recently appointed to professorships from outside the School, with his own vision of the potentialities of the School as an international centre for economics teaching and research. (1968c, 13)

Harry enjoyed working with LSE's graduate students. Unlike Chicago students, they were not aiming for a PhD and a professional career; they "were often merely spending a year of post-B.A. study in an exciting location while making up their minds what to do with themselves" (1974 Memoir IV, 23). This made them less interesting professionally than their Chicago contemporaries but often more interesting as individuals. Harry found that he

had to be fairly brusque in rationing out my time. Students often fail to understand that even though a theoretical difficulty is new to them, it isn't new to you after you have explained it to several dozen students previously; or that part of the teacher's job is to write letters of recommendation, and that he doesn't need a personal explanation of what and where Harvard University is but he does need the standard recommendation form with the name and address of the graduate admissions officer, dean or department chairman as the case may be, and his secretary is quite capable of putting it on his desk for immediate attention. The one thing I had to watch out for was the standard pest who lies in wait and traps many an inexperienced young instructor: the graduate student who hasn't the faintest idea of what research he wants to do, but believes that if he can waste your afternoon by asking a question, listening to your answer, telling you that you don't really understand the question or he hasn't made himself clear, formulating another question, listening to your answer, formulating still another question, and wearing out your patience and leaving you both utterly confused about where you have got to, [or whether] he has advanced a giant step in his research. My solution to that menace is to insist on a written statement of his problem; if he can't state it clearly enough to write it out, you can't hope to solve it. (1974 Memoir IV, 25)

With his LSE appointment, Harry's international travelling, which had seri-ously started in 1956 became legendary. He found it "rather wearying, but on the whole enjoyable and certainly stimulating." In 1969, he described a typical year:

[F]irst week of October to mid-December teaching at LSE. In this period there will be one or two visits to Continental Universities, several to British universities, perhaps a conference in the United States; week between Christmas and New Year's, the A.E.A. meetings; after that a week in Pakistan at the Institute of Development Economics and another somewhere in the Pacific conferring on Pacific trade and development problems; mid-January to mid-March, LSE teaching and visits to European and British universities, possibly another transatlantic conference; last two weeks of March, a week's conference on the international monetary problem; first of April to Chicago to teach there, with visits to Canadian and American universities for seminars, to Washington to give testimony to Congressional Committees or to consult with the Government, and with one return to England in April for the annual meetings of the Association of University Teachers of Economics, of which I am currently Chairman. About the first week of June teaching ends for the Quarter, and I go to the meetings of the Canadian Economics Association, return to mark my Chicago exams, then go to London to mark the examinations there, possibly going on to somewhere in Europe for another international monetary conference. Then back to Chicago for the summer, except possibly for a conference in North America or Europe. The Chicago quarter finishes at the end of August. September may be spent on either continent, depending on what conferences I have been invited to. This September I shall be touring Australia. (1969 Autobiographical Notes, 15–16)

He became even more peripatetic as the years passed: in May 1970 he wrote that he normally flew twice a week and made 12 transatlantic flights and one trip to Asia per annum (Box 27, Manuscripts 1970, "How Airlines Could Improve Their Service?" 30 May, written on United Airlines stationery).

Just before Harry arrived at LSE, he delivered his presidential address to the Canadian Political Science Association, "The Social Sciences in the Age of Opulence" (1966a). It was the last presidential address to the combined association. One of Harry's accomplishments as president had been the dissolution of the association into disciplinary associations for economists and political scientists.[5] In his address he talked about graduate education as he saw it; how graduate education differed from the current Anglo-Canadian notion, which, with an emphasis on the primacy of undergraduate instruction, made graduate teaching "a part-time, amateur occupation of the teacher of undergraduates"(436). Graduate instruction, he argued, must be "far more labour-intensive and intellect-intensive than undergraduate education" (436) and oriented towards techniques and problems. These differences raised questions as to whether the organisation of higher education might see efficiency gains from institutions specialising in either type,

---

[5] The anthropologists and sociologists had left earlier in the 1960s to form their own association.

as had been occurring de facto as well as explicitly in the United States, and whether graduate education should be differentiated to produce different streams of students for different career paths. Harry's tentative answer to both questions was "Yes," but the graduate/undergraduate specialisation question concerned him more. He turned to institutions:

> A graduate department requires three things: a good graduate faculty, meaning a team of scholars capable of original contributions to the development of the subject and actively engaged in some sector of frontier research; a departmental atmosphere encouraging the graduate faculty to devote a sufficient part of its time to the teaching of graduate students; and a flow of graduate students good enough to teach each other under the stimulation of good instruction and as a result call forth the best teaching efforts of the faculty. (437–8)

In developing such centres, he worried about the inefficiencies of excessive competition in Canada and toyed with the alternatives – national centres for graduate study on the model of the Australian National University or self-selection on the American model of Chicago, Harvard, Princeton, and Yale, which "have devoted tremendous intellectual and financial efforts to the search for superior talent and the provision of academic facilities consonant with the evolving requirements of excellence in the social sciences" (439).

He also discussed the problems of research, in particular the widespread use of contract research by governments. Contract research had its advantages in "propagating the idea that the social scientist can make an important contribution to social policy by applying the tools of his trade . . . [and] drawing social scientists into the performance of better designed and more urgently timed research projects than they would have undertaken if left to themselves." Such research taught "that research can be planned to a timetable and executed as a part of normal professional life, rather than being a vaguely structured activity to which one gets around when one can find the free time for it" (439). However,

> contract research involves the consumption of intellectual capital rather than investment in the formation of such capital – and there are many unfortunate examples of contract researchers who have sought to live on an intellectual overdraft and gone bankrupt in the process. (439)

Although he appreciated the advantages of such research he strongly argued for increased funding for independent research on topics not of immediate practical concern.

The importance of Harry's presidential address as background to his LSE years cannot be overestimated. It outlined his agenda – and when things did not go well, it gave an edge to his reflections on his experience. He would also, in his penultimate year at LSE, bring his subsequent experience to bear in refining his views on the whole question of graduate education in economics through his review of Ontario graduate programmes in economics and his "Uneasy Case for Universal Graduate Programmes in Economics" (1973d) – of which more later.

The Troubles – I

When Harry arrived at the School in October 1966, "the troubles" were about to begin. Their foundations had been laid earlier. Expansion had produced problems: the School's buildings, never spacious, were overcrowded. Library seats were at a premium, as were reading materials. Larger numbers brought more formality, more bureaucracy, and less sense of a wider community as individuals retreated into their disciplines. Governance became a matter for discussion. It became one in an era of change: The American civil rights movement showed how direct action could influence the course of events; worries about nuclear weapons, particularly after the Cuban missile crisis, gave the Campaign for Nuclear Disarmament a new lease on life; the war in Vietnam expanded and took on worldwide dimensions; apartheid, for which South Africa had been expelled from the Commonwealth in 1961, was a source of moral outrage for many; the white minority government of Rhodesia's unilateral declaration of independence from Britain in November 1965 kept the issues of race relations at the boil.

The occasion that sparked the initial difficulties was the appointment of a new director to replace Sir Sydney Caine, who at the end of the 1964–5 session had announced his intention to retire in July 1967. The selection process that followed had been more formal and consultative than ever before. A committee of governors and five professors from the Academic Board began to trawl for possible candidates in October 1965. Its first trawl and an elaborate consideration of the results did not produce a director. When it met again in April/May 1966, it considered two new candidates, one of whom, Walter Adams, quickly accepted the post. Adams had connections with the School that went back to 1938 when he had become its secretary, the senior administrative post. Since 1955 he had been principal of the University College of Rhodesia and Nyassaland in Salisbury. With the Rhodesian white minority settlers' unilateral declaration of independence (UDI) from Britain, Adams had been in the thick of things.

At the time Adams's appointment was announced, LSE students had been preoccupied with Rhodesia for most of the previous year. The student leadership had also been somewhat concerned with students' lack of involvement in the running of the School. They realised, however, that governance by itself would only become a "big issue" if tied to some important external event that would light the long fuse (Dahrendorf 1995, 444–5).

In October 1966, the Socialist Society, refounded the previous year by those disillusioned with the Labour Party,[6] published *L.S.E.'s New Director – A Report on Walter Adams*, the product of a summer's labour by two of its members. The pamphlet concluded that "Adams . . . is not a suitable person to be placed in charge of any centre of higher education" (Dahrendorf 1995, 448). The thrust of the pamphlet was that his unsuitability was demonstrated by his unreadiness to oppose Rhodesia's UDI outright and his general attitudes towards racial discrimination. The evidence for these conclusions was interviews with some lecturers from the University College who had been arrested the previous year, as well as some students, and in part upon certain public documents, which the authors used selectively (Kidd 1969, 18–19). When the pamphlet was published, the president of the LSE students' union wrote the chair of the governors, Lord Bridges, enclosing a copy and asking about the truth of the allegations against Adams, about how much had been known of them at the time of his appointment, and about whether there was now a case for reconsidering the decision. Bridges, a former Secretary to the Cabinet and Permanent Secretary to the Treasury, replied that it was impossible for him to engage in a public debate on the merits of an appointment. Moreover, given the confidential nature of the advice received and of the proceedings of the selection committee, he was not at liberty to answer the president's question other than to say that "the pamphlet cannot be accepted as a complete, or as an accurate account of the matters with which it deals" (Kidd 1969, 20). Before this exchange of letters was complete, the students' union met and asked its president to ask Adams to reply to certain public criticisms of his behaviour. It also stated that if it regarded the reply as unsatisfactory it would oppose Adams's appointment. The chairman of the governors cabled Adams not to communicate with the union. Then "on the advice of a small group of members of the academic staff" (Kidd 1968, 21), Bridges wrote to *The Times* explaining why the School was making no formal reply to the pamphlet and also praising Adams.

Bridges's letter put the union and its president, David Adelstein, in a quandary. As a result of events in the 1930s involving, among others,

---

[6] The Socialist Society had been quite active in the late 1950s after receiving a big boost from the combined effects of the Suez adventure and the Soviet suppression of the Hungarian revolution.

Harold Laski, the Court had issued a regulation precluding members of the School, both staff and students, from using its name and address without the director's permission when sending resolutions or letters to the press. In 1955 the rules for staff and students were separated, and in 1958 the director was authorised to give general permission for staff to use the name of the School in letters to the press. But the 1930s rule for students still stood; so that when Adelstein produced a draft letter from the School as president of the students' union he was refused permission to send it but was told that if he wrote as a private individual from a private address there would be no need for permission. The union, advised by two junior members of the law department, disputed the director's interpretation of the rules and instructed Adelstein to write the letter to *The Times* in his official capacity.

The School promptly instituted disciplinary proceedings. As Dahrendorf relates, "a substantive difference was turned into a dispute about authority and its use, coupled, to make matters worse, with a question of the right to express views freely" (1995, 450). And it got worse. Correspondence in the press mushroomed, with the director as one of the participants. The Board of Discipline, which was to hear the case against Adelstein, had not met for fifteen years and its composition presented a problem, as it would have normally included both Bridges and the director. Bridges stood down, but the presence of the director, whose order was at issue, raised questions of natural justice. The board met on 21 November and found that Adelstein had been in breach of the School's regulations but had acted in good faith. His mistake "was an error in judgement" (Dahrendorf 1995, 450). No penalty was imposed.

The result left the students claiming victory. The School was deeply divided: After a meeting of the Academic Board, which had ended in a published resolution of support for the Adams appointment and the School's procedures, the director noted that if he had asked two simple questions – "Do you like the Adams appointment?" and "Were you 'entirely happy' with the selection procedure?" – a majority would have said "No" to both. Militancy was very much in the air. The Adams question resurfaced at the beginning of the next term. As Dahrendorf related: "[A]gain substance slipped away and issues of authority came to the fore, which changed the mood, united the disunited and led to trouble" (1995, 451–2). The director banned a student meeting about the Adams affair. The students' union reacted and there was an occupation of the Old Theatre during which a porter died from heart failure. The director instituted an enquiry, and the School again began disciplinary procedures. The hearing dragged on for 3½ weeks – weeks during which the students' union was in turmoil – before

Adelstein and the chair of the Graduate Association were found guilty of disobeying the director in letting the banned meeting take place in the Old Theatre and were suspended until the end of the summer term. This provoked a boycott of lectures and a sit-in. The Standing Committee of the Court of Governors heard an appeal and reduced the sentences; a subsequent settlement saw the penalties suspended. As Harry summed up the affair: "Unfortunately, we have imported the student sit-in – but we lack an administration capable of coping with it" (Box 32, Correspondence Various, to Milton Friedman, 22 March 1967). The seeds were thus sown for later difficulties, which, after a quiet year, burst into bloom in 1968–9. By then, Walter Adams was director and Lionel Robbins was chairman of the Court of Governors.

Reform

When Harry arrived at LSE, there were two graduate degree programmes in economics – the MSc and the PhD. The former, as a taught one-year degree, was a recent creation and consisted of four papers or examinations – two compulsory papers in economic theory and in quantitative methods and two optional papers, normally chosen from the fields delineated by particular professors or (rarely) readers. These arrangements seemed appropriate for an MSc that was conceived as a topping-up or fourth-year arrangement for British undergraduates, but to Harry its professional utility was questionable. The PhD operated as elsewhere in Britain on the standard "master–apprentice" model in which the aspiring candidate attached himself to a supervisor willing to take on the topic proposed by the student. At the time, there were no mechanisms to support graduate students doing dissertations: The young-staff-and-graduate-student seminars of the previous decades such as the famous Robbins seminar, which had nurtured important work in welfare economics and monetary theory in the 1940s and 1950s, or the Sayers seminar on monetary institutions had either disappeared or become the teaching vehicles for the options in the MSc. As well, in the University of London there was no machinery for setting standards at the doctoral level: The system of external examiners was somewhat compromised, given that the second (internal) examiner was the student's supervisor. There was also still the ambiguous position of the PhD in the British job market in the 1960s, which meant that it was "a sop for second-rate foreigners" (1974 Memoir IV, 22). In the late Bernard Corry's view, if you couldn't get a job in less time than it took to complete a British PhD, there was something wrong with you, and once you had a job, why bother with the PhD.

Harry's first graduate initiative concerned the organisation of MSc teaching in the theory paper. On arrival in 1966, he found that he could not begin his MSc lectures for four weeks while his students attended crash courses in mathematics and statistics. The LSE summer term was normally free of lectures to allow revision for examinations; this meant that the effective teaching time was reduced to just over a term and a half and heavily concentrated in the Lent term. Given the scarcity of books and journals and library space – not to mention the principles of good pedagogy – this did not make sense.

Harry's proposed solution was to move the crash courses to September with provision for an examination for those who thought themselves adequately qualified. He related what happened next in his 1974 memoir.

Everyone agreed that this suggestion was eminently sensible, but everyone was sure that it was impossible to arrange because someone else wouldn't co-operate – what I soon came to think of as the English genius for preventing things from happening without actually stopping them. Laboriously I checked it out. The Social Science Research Council would not pay the English students their maintenance grants for the extra month: in fact the other subjects had twelve-month courses, they thought ours rather short and they would pay without a murmur. The catering officer couldn't provide meals: in fact he was overjoyed at the prospect of an extra seventy-five meals a day in a slack month. My specialist colleagues wouldn't teach the course in September: in fact, when I said I would personally guarantee that their teaching load would be correspondingly reduced during the regular term, they were overjoyed to have extra time for seminars and self-improvement activities in the busy season. The students wouldn't come: I talked to a large sample, and they took the natural view that if they had to do the work anyway, they would like to get it out of the way before the regular year started. We made the change; it worked like a charm and has been introduced in other one-year masters' programmes in other countries.

But even then there were problems as "one year when the Convenor, without consulting me, decided to cancel it … because he thought the teachers might like to go to a three-day econometrics conference being held that September" (1974 Memoir IV, 12–13).[7]

The next reform concerned the MSc degree itself. Here the proposed change was to move from two to three compulsory papers and one optional paper from the old "two-and-two" format. The three compulsory

---

[7] Most probably the Second World Econometric Congress, which was held in Cambridge from 8–14 September 1970.

papers would be macroeconomics, microeconomics (each with a mathematical question), and quantitative methods. To improve the quantitative methods paper, Harry proposed adding an element of econometrics, and in the case of the mathematical component of the macro- and
microeconomics papers proposed less emphasis on straight manipula-
tion and more on solving and interpreting simple general equilibrium
systems.

The proposal had to go to a departmental meeting for approval. This
meant that among those voting would be individuals who did no graduate teaching and of those who did teach graduates there would be few
who had teaching experience outside LSE. Nonetheless, he thought he
had approval. However, final approval would have to wait until the next
academic year. Then difficulties arising from Harry's peripatetic existence
kicked in, in this case the first part of his month in Toronto as Centennial Professor in October and November 1967. While he was away, the
department looked at the proposal and sent it back for reconsideration,
according to Harry, as a result of objections by two staff members, one
of whom insisted that his own specialty be the core of value theory and
thus essential, and the other, a nongraduate teacher who managed to persuade enough individuals that, his remarks to the contrary, there must
be some good reason against it (1974 Memoir IV, 14–15). Harry was
furious:

I came back from Toronto angry enough to resign, and saying so, whereupon they
made apologetic noises and the opposition caved in.
It was a Pyrrhic victory, though, because thereafter a number of my colleagues
were out to sabotage the programme at any chance that offered. (1974 Memoir
IV, 15)

The issues varied. He spent one autumn "fighting off a professional colleague who insisted that students be free to take any courses they wanted
to." Another bone of contention arose over offering courses on issues that
might be "hot" and thus give students an edge in the job market. There
was no problem with subjects where his colleagues were active in research
such as the economics of education or urban economics. The arrival of
Michio Morshima at the School from Osaka University via the University
of Essex in 1970 enabled Harry to play to the radicals and introduce an
option "Marx in the Light of Contemporary Economics" (Morshima 1973,
viii) – a move unpopular in other LSE departments. The real problem came
when he proposed outsiders such as Alexander Swoboda of the Graduate Institute of International Studies in Geneva to lecture on international

monetary economics or Melvyn Krauss from Amsterdam to lecture on European economic integration.[8]

Instant resentment came from staff members neither competent nor interested in the subjects, who took the view that if regular staff members weren't interested in teaching a subject it should not be available to students. And it was impossible to persuade economists who regularly taught the economics of overhead costs and the welfare economics of extended choice that it was more economical and academically efficient to hire an expert in a narrow and transitorily scientifically lively subject only while interest lasted . . . than to add him to the permanent staff in the hope he would keep the subject alive for forty years. (1974 Memoir IV, 17)

Swoboda and Krauss did come, but the experiment ended after 1971–2.

Harry's interventions with the PhD programme were more limited. He tried to strengthen the supervision system by introducing three-person committees. The second was to introduce a graduate workshop in Economic Research from 1970–1, which he ran with Alan Walters and Jim Thomas. He also ran a seminar in "Monetary Economics: Theory and Testing" with Roger Alford. He thought these efforts a failure in the context of LSE

since most of the Ph.D. registrations were mere declarations of intent by people who already had teaching jobs in polytechnics or rubber-stamp exercises by people who wanted a certificate for work already done and paid for by some government or other, neither of whom would bother to attend a research seminar. . . . This was extremely disheartening, because a graduate school that produces no presentable offspring in the form of successful academics is merely a scientific eunuch. (1974 Memoir IV, 22)

Harry was also determined to improve faculty standards for hiring and tenure. In economics, as in most other subjects, the North American and English models of hiring differed. On both sides of the Atlantic universities advertised vacancies, but there the similarities ended. In North America the centrepiece of the hiring season, then as now, was the annual meetings of the Allied Social Science Associations of which the American Economic Association is a component. These meetings then occurred between Christmas and New Year.[9] They had the usual academic sessions – indeed multiple sessions – and social functions, but they also played an important role in the job market. Before the meetings, all those on the job market for that year had their curricula vitae and references circulated to the departments in which they

[8] The School had a specialist in the former field, A. C. L. Day, but, according to Harry, "he refused to offer it at the graduate level because he didn't have the time to get up the (rather limited) mathematics it employed" (1974 Memoir IV, 16).
[9] Now they occur early in January.

were interested. These departments used members attending the academic sessions, supplemented by those sent especially for the purpose, to interview potential job candidates. These interviews, supplemented in many cases by drafts of parts of dissertations, provided the basis for departments' invitations for job visits, which involve interviews with prospective colleagues and the presentation of research results. The market moved quickly: In most years it was over for good candidates by the beginning of March.

In Britain, by contrast, job candidates made formal application to their chosen institutions' appointments committees, who, after taking references, invited a short list of candidates for interview (normally all of them on a single day) and made their decisions. The job candidate normally had no contact with other prospective colleagues until after he/she accepted the job offered. Moreover, in this system there were not the tight timelines of the American régime.

Harry suspected that tenure standards had been too low in the recent past for an institution with the School's ambitions. With the post-Robbins boom in hiring, "which has obliged the School – and every university – to hire any qualified body that was even slightly warm" (1974 Memoir IV, 18), it was essential that the School should impose high standards on the post-Robbins bulge, particularly if the unsuccessful candidates could be replaced with newly qualified PhDs from American graduate schools. These had attracted an increasing number of British and Commonwealth students and were beginning to produce an oversupply of PhDs. At the same time, the manpower needs of the Vietnam War were making the United States a less attractive place to pursue a career: Holders of green cards were obliged upon receipt to register for the draft, and in 1966 faculty deferments began to be cancelled (Laidler 2000, 334). But central to the attraction of the graduates of American programmes was being able to interview candidates at the American meetings and to get offers out as early as the School's North American competitors.

Harry took up the story:

For a while – that is, while Basil Yamey was Convenor – we succeeded. We got rid of most of the dead saplings (they were too immature to be called wood) . . . and partly because I went to the AEA meetings at my own expense and could find some colleagues also going, we were able to have candidates interviewed by two staff members in satisfaction of the School's rules, while . . . [the Convenor] took care to get the committee work out of the way for the offers to be competitively dated.

But all that organisational effort changed with the next Convenor. The committee work was allowed to slide, so that the selection committee's careful ranking of the candidates left us with a list of people who already had accepted good jobs elsewhere, and we were left with a crop of new staff each year that had been culled from our own students and whatever else had come on the market at a late stage, usually people no one would have considered *a priori* as a potential colleague.[10]

It is a difficult and demeaning situation to be in, attempting to run a graduate school with pretensions to quality on the basis of a staff hired by someone else off the nearest street corner. (1974 Memoir IV, 19)

The Troubles – II

Harry's attempts at reform were complicated by another outbreak of "troubles" at the School in 1968–9. Despite student restiveness elsewhere in Britain, the United States (Columbia and the Democratic Convention in Chicago), and Western Europe (most dramatically in Paris), 1967–8 had been "quiet" at LSE. Walter Adams had arrived and settled in. Lord Bridges, who had chaired the Court of Governors since 1957, had been succeeded by Lionel Robbins, now almost 70, whose commitment to the School was total. Attempts to reform governance since 1966 had come to naught except that the General Purposes Committee of the Academic Board had coopted four student members of the union.

The second round of "the troubles" began with a student-union motion, debated but not passed, that the union provide "sanctuary, medical aid and political discussion" for participants in a national demonstration against the war in Vietnam scheduled for Saturday 27 October 1968. In response, the director posted a notice on behalf of the governors closing the School on the evening of 26 October and all day on 27 October, even to academic staff, except to those who had his permission to enter. The students reacted immediately with an occupation that lasted all weekend, cleaning up before they left on the Sunday evening. Four days after the occupation, the governors issued a statement saying that the unauthorised occupation had done "grave damage to the reputation of the School" and declaring that

[s]ince threats have already been made that future operations of a similar kind may be attempted . . . we declare that we shall regard the organisation of such attempts

---

[10] For confirmation of these developments see Harry's 24 July 1971 letter to the Director in Box 48, LSE concerning that 'the lack of entrepreneurial talent of the present Convenor, in the matter of new appointments, has set us back pretty disastrously . . . by losing first-class new appointments and leaving us with the dregs of our own hangers-on'.

and participation in them by members of the School as grave offences liable to the severest penalties. . . .

Moreover, they continued:

We have considered the position of certain junior members of the staff who are alleged to have encouraged and participated in the unauthorised occupation. On this occasion, having regard to the immaturity of those concerned, we take the view that the process whereby staff in clear breach of contract can be dismissed need not be invoked. But we declare that any future attempt on the part of staff, senior or junior, to encourage or participate in action on the part of students likely to endanger the integrity and orderly conduct of the School could be regarded as misconduct warranting the termination of contract. (Hoch and Schoenbach 1969, 26)

Inevitably, opinion in the School, both staff and student, was divided. Robbins was very much hands-on and generally favoured taking a hard line with those who disrupted the School's activities. The director was isolated: Robbins "thought little of him" and told a colleague that his support for Adams's appointment as director had been "a major error of judgement"; the Academic Board "tended to set him aside" (Dahrendorf 1995, 462). There was no real focus of moderate academic opinion as there was in many other universities in the same circumstances. Initially matters drifted. There was an attempt to disrupt Oration Day in November, where the speaker was Hugh Trevor-Roper, whose apparent support for the Greek colonels' régime irked the left, but it failed. January saw renewed agitation over Rhodesia and South Africa and included a teach-in where the director appeared once. Only slowly did attention centre on "the gates," which the School authorities, without consulting anyone, had started installing the previous summer. Their purpose should have been obvious – to restrict access to certain parts of the School. It was only after Robbins admitted such when he addressed the students' union in January that they became "the issue" (Dahrendorf 1995, 465). Immediately afterwards, the union passed an emergency motion that the gates be removed in seven days or the students would do so themselves. On 24 January the gates were attacked. Later that evening, the director declared the School closed indefinitely and called in the police.

While the School was closed, there were attempts to maintain some degree of normality. Classes were held elsewhere: Harry, for example, continued his MSc macroeconomics lectures, appropriately enough, from a stool in the bar at Passfield Hall, an LSE residence. At the time, he told Arthur Seldon of the Institute of Economic Affairs: "The closure of the School and our efforts to do our teaching in various halls of residence have cut down my performance efficiency by about 50 per cent" (Hoover Institution, Institute of Economic Affairs Papers, Box 272, Folder HP46, 14 February 1969). However to some of his MSc students it seemed more efficient teaching in a two-hour block from 9 to 11 on Tuesday mornings than in two one-hour blocks on Tuesday and Thursday. But, once closed, there was the problem of how to reopen the School. The court raised the ante by sending notices to three members of staff that they would be subject to disciplinary proceedings. One of these, Laurence Harris, taught macroeconomics with Harry. In Harris's case, the finding of the special committee set up to recommend to the Standing Committee of the Court of Governors was that he had been guilty of misconduct but that it was not serious enough to warrant dismissal. Harry, who had initially been a great Harris fan, making enquiries on his behalf for visiting positions in the United States and including two of Harris's papers in his 1970–1 reading list for macroeconomics and monetary theory, was later bitter about his conduct because he thought, rightly or wrongly, that Harris had behaved unprofessionally as a teacher, as well as not publishing (Box 56, Correspondence 1964–6, A–L, to David Laidler, 1 December 1965; *MMT*, 200, 204; 1974 Memoir IV, 28–9).[11] The School also took out injunctions against thirteen persons involved in the gates incident, preventing them from entering LSE. Ultimately the standing committee of the governors decided to reopen the School on 19 February, but it emphasised that the disciplinary proceedings and the injunctions would continue and that

If there is further disruption of the orderly working of the School, whether by sit-in, occupation, intimidation, attacks on individual students or members of staff, serious interruptions of lectures or classes, or by any other form of direct action, then the School will be declared closed and grant awarding bodies will be notified. (Hoch and Schoenbach 1969, 117)

Had the Academic Board been in control, the disciplinary actions might have been dropped. Instead the other two lecturers had their contracts terminated on the recommendation of their special committees and their dismissal was upheld on appeal. Four students were eventually found guilty in the courts. Two of the foreign students, one of whom was Paul Hoch, were deported.

Although lectures and classes resumed, disruptions continued. Colin Crouch called the result "virtual chaos" (1970, 94).

Lectures were boycotted, lecturers were verbally and at times physically attacked; the reinstated gates were damaged; metal glue was used to block doors all over the School; stink and smoke bombs were dropped into meetings; . . . the Senior Common Room was occupied on several occasions; Lord Robbins's portrait was

---

[11] However, Harris resigned his lectureship when it became clear that he would not be awarded tenure.

taken down; false fire alarms were set off; deliveries to the Senior Common Room and the refectory were "blacked". (Dahrendorf 1995, 470)

Some of Harry's MSc students thought (and think) that Crouch was exaggerating. Inevitably, the troubles became grist to the mills of those who wanted to reduce support to universities and the social sciences in general.

Harry believed that the troubles "did incalculable damage" to LSE, both immediately and for several years afterwards. In May 1960 he wrote Donald Tyerman, a former editor of *The Economist*:

The academic mind, unfortunately, always tries to avoid taking a stand on hard issues; instead, it prefers to wait for a confrontation of views to develop and then shows its superiority by finding justice on both sides. There is an old American story that fits: a negro preacher and his wife are out walking one Sunday, when along comes a bear; the preacher makes it up the nearest tree, leaving his wife to cope with the bear; she puts up a good fight, but the preacher is conscious that the bear may very likely win; so he keeps shouting "Go it, wife! Go it, bear!"

My main fear about the School is that the serious young scholars, on whose devotion to their work and willingness to accept little money in return for the privilege of being on our staff the future of the School depends, will get fed up with the interruption of their work that the present mess involves, and depart, leaving us only with juniors who put politics ahead of performance and seniors whose days of scientific contribution are long past. [Robbins Papers, Letters (Personal) 1968–9]

Later he commented on student disruption:

I had the good luck of seeing it properly handled at Chicago, and the bad luck of seeing it handled falteringly (but in the end, thanks to Robbins, with principled decisiveness) at the L.S.E. I was, as a graduate teacher in economics, not much affected directly by it in either place. The only lesson I learned from it, which I scarcely needed, was the utter stupidity, or worse, sheer dishonesty, of academics who assume that the taxpayer and their political representatives will happily go on ladling out vast sums of money to support a leisured class of self-important loud-mouthed idlers who have nothing better to do than destroy the disciplined pursuit and dissemination of knowledge that is the only social justification for giving them leisured privilege in the first place. (1974 Memoir IV, 30)

The "troubles" also gave Harry occasions to examine the "economics of student protest" both in his November 1967 inaugural lecture (1968a)[12] and in an article under the same title published in *New Society* the week after

---

[12] Harry's treatment of the issue in his Inaugural Lecture appeared in the version originally published in *Economica* (February 1968, 12–14) but it does not appear in the version later reprinted in *On Economics and Society*.

the weekend occupation of the School in October 1968 (1968f). At the heart of the difficulties, he argued, were a number of longer-term processes – the democratisation of higher education, the assumption by governments of a greater responsibility for financing it, the increasing bureaucratisation of universities, and the spread of affluence.

The democratisation of higher education meant that such education was no longer the preserve of those preparing for membership in the political, economic, and social elite. Democratisation reduced the value of a university degree: "[I]t has become increasingly a hunting licence rather than a meal ticket in the competition for elite jobs" (1968f, 64). Democratisation also reduced the incentives for faculty to concentrate on teaching rather than research. However, neither side fully understood the processes at work; so students felt themselves short-changed, and faculty felt themselves subject to excessive demands. These gaps between perceptions and reality were heightened by government attempts at cheeseparing – keeping close control of student grants, underspending on university facilities, and holding down university salaries. Low grants, in the face of high urban rents, meant long daily journeys for students in urban universities and a tendency to identify further with those less well off. Bureaucratisation with its common pay scales for academic staff, age-related increments, and early granting of tenure encouraged teachers to minimise academic effort and maximise outside earnings and, given that the only way to increase one's income was to get promoted, normally at another institution, put a premium on research rather than teaching. Bureaucratisation also meant that resource allocation, largely by committees of senior academics, was not always transparent and extremely difficult to change, which increased the frustration and discontent of students, as well as the junior staff who often identified with them. Finally affluence increased the value of time, but the universities' bureaucratisation did not allow this to be reflected in teaching programmes or instructional methods.

At LSE, with its central location and high costs of local expansion, Harry argued these tendencies were exacerbated. Overcrowding was worse in the "public" parts of the buildings and was aggravated by lengthy commuting, which led many students to maximise the time spent in the School on the days they came in. The high costs of living in London further encouraged faculty to maximise outside earnings and minimise the time spent in the School, further frustrating the expectations of students for advice and counsel and for opportunities to participate in decisions about the affairs of the School. In his inaugural lecture, he suggested that the School's location made it increasingly uneconomic as a centre for undergraduate studies.

Disappointment

He returned to these issues when the School began planning for the next funding quinquennium, 1972–7, in the fall of 1969. When the economists met to discuss their needs, the larger question of the long-term future shape of the School reemerged. Harry, having touched on the issues in his inaugural, was asked to initiate the discussion. After the discussion, the economists agreed that the consideration of the long-run shape of the School should be kept separate from their quinquennial submission, but also, at the suggestion of Frank Hahn, that Harry should set out his views, as modified by his colleagues' arguments, for circulation to the group. They could then indicate assent, suggest changes in wording, or dissociate themselves from the document, which, suitably revised, would go to the convenor for transmission to the director as the personal views of a group of economists. The final document was supported by twenty of the fifty teaching staff in economics.[13]

The conclusion of Harry's paper was that LSE should become a predominantly graduate institution. The bases for this conclusion were both negative arguments against its being a centre for undergraduate education in the social sciences and positive arguments in its advantages over other institutions at the graduate level. The economic arguments against using costly space in central London for undergraduate education were the need for students and faculty to travel considerable distances from the School to affordable housing, the consequential effects of travel on students' studying, and the need for supplementary income-earning activities on the part of faculty, which reduced their academic activity and thus standards. He also argued that LSE undergraduates' lack of exposure to students in the humanities and sciences was educationally harmful. The positive advantages for graduate work at the School were bibliographical (the British Library of Political and Economic Science and other libraries, such as the British Library, in the neighbourhood), locational (closeness to the City, the law courts, government officials, etc.), and reputational (a diminishing asset, given the economic pressures facing faculty and because the undergraduate teaching efforts associated with the current arrangements inhibited research).

Harry acknowledged that the transition to an entirely graduate institution would pose problems. He argued that with advance planning and careful arrangements for the transition, it was possible. The problems to be

---

[13] The numbers supporting Harry's document come from A. C. L. Day, 'The Future of the LSE – Some Economic Considerations', 1 January 1970 in Box 48.

addressed were the creation of a faculty capable and experienced enough to teach graduates – which would involve considerable effort in the selection and training, a comprehensive reevaluation of the existing faculty and changes in the criteria for tenure. The School would also have to employ a higher proportion of senior faculty, which would put it in conflict with University Grant Committee staffing ratios and, perhaps, nationally agreed salary scales. As he put it:

A good graduate school cannot be run on the basis of a predominance of young men and women who have yet to publish their first article; nor can it be run on the basis of more senior people who, having devoted themselves to scientific activities in their youth, have discovered that the social and financial returns of the continued pursuit of academic excellence are meagre by comparison with the returns to involvement in political and other affairs in London and on the national scene. The School would have to collect a staff of people senior and able enough to command the respect of students and the outside world, and it would have to pay them enough, relative to their age and circumstances, to ensure that they kept working on the advancement of their particular branch of social science. (Box 48, "The Future of the London School of Economics and Political Science," December 1969, 4)

The School would also have to increase the supply of graduate students by offering adequate financial packages and reduce the attraction to the School of less-well-prepared students enticed by its low fees. Finally, it would have to convince the government that a changed educational policy geared to producing qualified university teachers would support its proposed expansion of the university system.

When Harry submitted his paper, he was not optimistic. 'I doubt if I'll get anywhere with this,' he told G. C. Archibald at the end of December (Box 48, LSE, 30 December 1969). He drew a hostile reaction from A. C. L. Day in a paper, "The Future of the LSE – Some Economic Considerations," which Harry found "poorly thought out and rather strange." As he summarized the paper:

Day's "some economic considerations" are not considerations of the problems facing the School, but pseudo-economic defences of the status quo, based on the valid but empty assumption that whatever now exists must satisfy somebody. (Box 48, Comments on Alan Day's 'The Future of the L.S.E. – Some Economic Considerations', February 1970)

LSE opinion supported further graduate expansion, but support for a wholly graduate school was limited. When the School's submission to the University of London emerged, it foresaw no increase in student numbers and an increase of graduate students within that total from 41 percent to 50 percent.

The quinquennial settlement was announced on 11 January 1973 (i.e., well into its first year), and it was not until June 1973 that LSE knew the details of its fate – 3,382 full-time-equivalent students of which 43.8 percent would be postgraduates. Moreover, within that régime the finance available per student would be 2 percent less than in the previous quinquennium. The School found the proposed postgraduate numbers "unacceptable" (Director's Report 1972–73, 62) but it was left to later years to discuss changes. Significantly, the proportion of postgraduates remained stuck at 45 percent for the next twenty years (Dahrendorf 1995, 439–40). At the same time, inflation was beginning to take its toll on the School's finances. Government grants, responsible for 80 percent of the School's income, were normally supplemented in full for salary rises, but the School was at risk for half the remainder – no small matter as inflation rose towards its peak of over 24 percent in 1974–5.

By 1971–2 Harry's health began to give way. Years of very heavy drinking were taking their toll. His temper, always a problem, became much shorter, and the resulting explosions became verbally more violent. He became more morose. He became forgetful. Bad temper and forgetfulness reduced his effectiveness, especially among those who did not know him well, in making changes at LSE or in British economics. He was also more depressed about the progress of reform at LSE. As he put it in "Some Notes on the Ontario University System for Caves and Hicks";

I think we [LSE] have a good M.Sc. course and that a student who has taken it has an edge on his rivals when he gets to a first class graduate school, but he is not going to be a good economist if he stays with us and does not go to a first class graduate school. (Box 27, Manuscripts 1972–3, 2 September 1972)

His depression reflected the lack of progress in building the graduate programme at LSE. It also reflected his comment to Alexander Swoboda: "I am going to have to take a tighter hold on that place [LSE] – every minute I'm not watching the place started to fall apart" (Box 41, Commitments Completed 1971, to Swoboda, 26 July 1971).

If he needed further proof, it came in February 1972. By then, Harry had agreed to spend the time he would have spent at LSE in 1972–3 as Irving Fisher Visiting Professor at Yale. This raised the question as to who would teach his macroeconomics course. On 9 February, the day Harry was to visit Warwick to give a paper, the committee responsible for teaching arrangements for the MSc asked him to approach John Williamson who then taught there (Box 53, Correspondence 1971–7, T–Z, from John Williamson, 10 February 1972; to John Williamson, 29 February 1972). After talking with

Williamson, Harry seems to have had second thoughts. In his 1974 Memoir, he claimed that a subcommittee of his colleagues

calmly overruled my proposal for a stand-in . . . and proposed a favourite of theirs whom I knew was completely out of sympathy with the field as I taught it and in fact proposed to make his course by criticising my published lecture notes at length. (1974 Memoir IV, 19–20)

Harry called a meeting of the professors of economics for early the next week and put his resignation on the table. Before the meeting he also approached David Laidler about teaching the course and David suggested that as he shared the course in Manchester with Michael Parkin it would make sense for the two of them to do the same at LSE. This would maintain continuity in the course, an important factor given that students were allowed to sit the examinations twice.

In his notes for the meeting, Harry recalled that he had threatened resignation in 1967 over his colleagues' rejection of the proposed reforms of the MSc now in place. He told his colleagues that in the last two years he had turned down offers of "very lucrative" chairs, not involving administrative work of the sort he did at the School, at Harvard, Yale, Princeton, and Pennsylvania, as well as the offer of the chairmanship at Chicago. He was under strong pressure to return full-time to Chicago. Nonetheless, he would prefer to say at LSE.

But there is no point at all in my staying here, if my colleagues do not approve of what I am trying to do with the graduate school and persist in assuming that their casual judgments on the issues I have to think seriously about are superior to mine and are binding on me. Frankly, I know no other university where I could go where I would be treated with the contempt I have experienced here and no other place where democratic modesty in making a proposal would be automatically interpreted as a sign of incompetence in one's job. (Box 63, Manuscripts 1972, "Resignation Statement, Feb. 13")

He asked for "a vote of confidence in the way I have run the graduate school and in my authority to continue to run it." He also made suggestions, open to negotiation and discussion, for a reorganisation of the administration of the department. In particular, he proposed a separation of the graduate from the undergraduate administration with the former not being a mere "side-play of undergraduate administration" – a convenor of graduate work, effectively a chair for all who taught in the MSc programme, who would be responsible in collaboration with his colleagues for all post-MSc research degree candidates. The purpose of the proposal, he said, was to ensure that decisions would be taken by those actively concerned with graduate teaching. The graduate convenor would also have a budget of his own to hire people to teach special courses and would also have an ex officio say in the appointment of new staff. The net effect of the proposal would be to remove the constraints that Harry thought he had been working under.

Harry got his vote of confidence. The Williamson proposal was withdrawn on 16 February. David Laidler and Michael Parkin taught the course, leaving Williamson to help out with international monetary economics (Box 53, Correspondence 1971–7, T–Z, to John Williamson, 16 and 29 February 1972; from J. Williamson, 28 February 1972).[14]

The 1974 memoir is thus broadly consistent with the surviving documentation. It is true that in the late 1960s and early 1970s Harry "had gone off" John Williamson, perhaps for not very good reasons – Williamson favoured entry to the Common Market, a subject on which he had a very acrimonious discussion with Harry on the BBC,[15] and as an ex-Treasury civil servant would be regarded by Harry as having sold out to the establishment. Williamson also reviewed Harry's macroeconomics lecture notes in the *Economic Journal* for September 1972. The review was critical. He was not enamoured with what he called "The Gladiatorial Approach to Economic Theory" (1063), was extremely critical of the standard of production for which he blamed Harry as not being "prepared to invest considerable trouble and effort in editing what his scribes produce" (1063), and was critical of several details. Some of this may have been communicated to Harry during his conversation with Williamson on 9 February. That timing would fit the *Journal*'s production schedules.

The proposal for the reorganisation of the administration of the graduate programme did not go through, although Harry was given the title of chairman of the graduate programme. At least one colleague began

circulating to the School the story that I had demanded dictatorial powers over the graduate programme, and telling all his friends that he was firmly convinced that I was on the verge of a nervous breakdown. That conviction, in the mouth of his

---

[14] The LSE made their arrangements with Laidler and Parkin once Harry was out of the country. The stipend initially offered barely covered the train fare from Manchester. Laidler phoned Harry in Chicago and, as Laidler later put it, 'the trajectory became orbital and then some'. The next offer was much improved and accepted. Because of Harry's stroke, Laidler and Parkin ended up teaching the course for two years.

[15] On another occasion, when they were recording a discussion of the issues for the secondary school market, Harry had raised questions about the political arguments for joining the EEC and was met by Williamson's remark that Harry 'was after all only a Canadian'. That brought a lengthy, heated response from Harry, a collapse by Williamson and a re-taping of the interview 'this time without any nonsense about the political ignorance of colonials' (1974 Memoir III, 3–4).

friend the Oxford Professor . . . became the assurance that I was 'finished', which is a gleeful Oxford euphemism that I was as good as dead, physically as well as mentally, and therefore of no account. (1974 Memoir IV, 20–1)

In 1971 Walter Adams's appointment as director of LSE was extended until September 1974. Soon afterwards, the School began preparing for the succession by establishing a selection committee for the next director. Lionel Robbins was in the chair. Harry was appointed to the committee on the nomination of the Academic Board.[16] On his letter of appointment, he wrote "NOTE BIG COMMITMENT'(Box 52, Correspondence 1971–7, P–T, from Lionel Robbins, 1 November 1971). The commitment did turn out to be large. It was not until 18 September 1973 that Ralf Dahrendorf, then a member of the European Commission in Brussels, was elected director. It was, according to *The Times* the next morning "An Original and Welcome Appointment." However, for Harry on leave at Yale, with "so many trips back to the LSE for meetings of the Committee . . . and another in prospect" he was "feeling the financial pinch of responsibility" and took up Robbins's offer of help with his expenses (Box 52, Correspondence 1971–7, P–T, to Lionel Robbins, 18 May 1973). At that stage he was worried "that the School fail by default to preserve itself in the next ten years, which I see as a really desperate problem" and was worried about "What to do?"

Earlier, after the selection committee's first meeting on 9 March 1972, Harry had set down his thoughts on the directorship. They were "expressed badly, partly because I am not used to an electric typewriter and partly because I am not accustomed to thinking in terms of competing institutions" (Robbins Papers, Selection Committee to Appoint Director, to Lionel Robbins, 11 March 1972). In the letter, he recounted some of his long-standing concerns about the school.

We are not a going concern . . . though we have the potential of becoming one. Instead, we are a school that once was great, in a number of different fields, but is in extremely grave danger of slipping into becoming just one of a large number of nonentitious second or third rate metropolitan undergraduate teaching establishments. . . . Another caretaker [appointment] would end the School, except as the caretaker of a good library and a reputable place for visitors to be associated with in an attractive location, i.e. London.

I think we have a chance of rebuilding the School as an academic centre in the social sciences. But we will have to work very hard at it, because, contrary to the 1930s, we face all sorts of competition, most of it with more money to spend than we have.

---

[16] The other professorial members of the committee were Bernard Donoughue, Ernest Gellner, Leonard Schapiro, and Basil Yamey.

In rebuilding itself as a centre of the social sciences, LSE had two advantages. "The first is that it was once good, seminally lively and important on the world scene." This gave it credibility – something that new institutions didn't have. Harry had seen other old institutions – Toronto, Harvard, and Queen's – revitalise themselves "very quickly because their historical reputation enabled them to recruit good people from the upstart universities." In economics, the School also had the advantage that "Cambridge has made some ludicrous appointments and is ensuring its own ineffectiveness." However, Oxford had realised its "pretty undistinguished" record of appointments and had started to build itself up. If LSE acted quickly enough there was hope.

The second major advantage for LSE was Britain's forthcoming entry into the Common Market. With Britain in "the School will be the obvious centre in the United Kingdom for people from the Continent to come to."

We could become *the* centre for the advanced study of the social sciences for the whole of Europe. But to do so we have to think of ourselves as a world centre. . . . [W]e should be aiming . . . to establish ourselves as the social science centre of Europe, good enough not only to attract Europeans by offering them education as good as they could get in America, but still better enough to offer Americans the opportunity to learn things they cannot get in their own university system.

To do this the School would have to do something about its low salaries and the "pusyllannimity [sic] of our major review procedures."

The need for additional resources led Harry to run a risk with Robbins and turn to the about-to-begin LSE library appeal, chaired by him, to raise funds to purchase Strand House, W. H. Smith's London warehouse, which was adjacent to LSE, as the new home of the British Library of Political and Economic Science.

I can understand the concern about the Library; but a library constitutes no claim to academic excellence. I almost never use the library myself; in my field, I rely on attendance at conferences, and on receipt of preliminary drafts of papers by my colleagues, to keep me up to date; if I relied on the library, I would be at least two years behind what was going on and therefore doomed to be obsolete. I think myself that the School would have been better advised to launch an appeal for funds to enable it to pay salaries good enough to command the presence of talented people from all over the world, and to escape from the present Treasury-dominated position that no academic can ever be worth as much as a civil servant. . . . The library appeal . . . is a pure waste of our prestige on behalf of the government. The prestige ought to have been used, on behalf of the School, to build it up in independence of the government.

The two did not get an immediate opportunity to discuss Harry's letter. Robbins replied on 23 March (Robbins Papers, Selection Committee to Appoint Director). He agreed that the appointment of a caretaker would be "most unfortunate." He shared Harry's view that the School should become more of a graduate institution and that "we should move much further in that direction than most of our colleagues are willing to do," and he agreed with an effort to make the School "a centre of social science studies in the Common Market." Of course he disagreed on the library appeal versus a general appeal.

I can see that in some branches of economics and other subjects taught at the School the Library is not the centre of the picture, and I respect, although I don't share your feelings about priorities *sub specie aeterrnitatis*, but believe me Harry, at this moment there would not be a celluloid cat's chance in hell of an appeal for general funds, whereas with the Library with Government backing, there is at least a fifty/fifty change of pulling it off.[17]

Once that is done it will be up to you or some other person to inaugurate another general appeal and it may be that our public relations will be good enough by then to have some degree of success. But at present . . . the opportunity of raising a sufficiently large capital sum to do anything of the kind you have in mind is just not on.

Further Thoughts on Graduate Education

Harry's eminence in the profession and his Canadian origins made it inevitable that when the Council of Ontario Universities, faced with a burgeoning demand for graduate programmes from institutions that had recently gained university status or had substantially increased their student numbers, decided to do a discipline-by-discipline review of existing and proposed programmes in the province, it approached him to do economics. The call came in January 1972. Harry accepted a month later. He was to work as one of three – the other two being Richard Caves of Harvard University and Henry Hicks, the president of Dalhousie University. Over sixteen days in July and August 1972, in twos and threes, the group visited eleven universities. Harry visited all the universities bar one – the University of Windsor. He took the lead in devising processes and procedures, as well as in drafting the report, which was submitted in February 1973.

---

[17] The library appeal was for £1.8 million to purchase Strand House and £600,000 for its conversion. The University Grants Committee and the University of London were to commit £2,850,000.

Before drafting the report, largely on the basis of his experience, Harry drafted a paper, "The Uneasy Case for Universal Graduate Programmes in Economics" (1973d), which appeared in *Minerva* as well as in the final Report (43–53). He was challenging the view "written into the British conception of the university" "that good undergraduate teaching requires the presence of some sort of graduate programme leading up to the PhD"(1973d, 263). He did not deny that research fed back into teaching and vice versa; what he denied was the principle that both needed to be done by the same individuals in the same institution. Indeed, as he put it:

There are, on the contrary, good reasons to believe that properly conducted graduate instruction at an adequate level will neither feed back directly into the undergraduate teaching of a department . . . nor be efficient unless based on an informal or formal separation of the department into the primarily or exclusively graduate-level and undergraduate-level teachers. (1973d, 264)

The reasons for taking this position were threefold: (1) graduate students who had decided to take a professional, postgraduate degree in a subject were a different breed from undergraduates; (2) graduate teaching was more exhausting than undergraduate teaching and required a very different balance of knowledge; and (3) the substantial economies of scale in graduate teaching made for concentration of such teaching in departments where there was more than one specialist per field and several specialists in cognate fields. One of the advantages of concentration was that there would be enough graduate students in each cohort to learn from each other, yet too many to allow for the formation of an effort-reducing cartel. Such an arrangement made even more sense when there was a fairly well-agreed specification of what good graduate training involved – something that had become widely agreed in economics in the postwar period.

When it came to the Ontario programmes, Harry and his colleagues had to put some empirical content into his more general discussion. It became clear that the significant economies of scale came in the production of PhDs – in their discussion they posited minimum student intakes at twelve per annum for MAs, compared with twenty for PhDs – and they regarded these as perhaps underestimates, given the quality of Ontario graduate students in economics as compared with "some of the world-famous universities of the north-east coast of the United States" (Report, 90–1). Some indication of the quality-of-students problem of Ontario universities were their lower admission standards and their very low yield or completion rates when compared with Harvard, Yale, and Chicago (Report, 91–2). Yet, when it came to cases, Harry and his colleagues faced a dilemma: The one department with enrolments large enough to reap the scale economies, the University of Toronto, had a long tradition of "incredibly inefficient administration, very lax and inconsistent promotion standards . . . and a general atmosphere of anarchy" (Report, 93). The committee hoped recent signs of improvement in the department would carry the day, but they hedged their bets. Although they recommended the termination of two "paper PhD programmes" (Report, 96, 135), they were prepared to allow three other suboptimally sized programmes to continue. But they did not countenance any further programmes beyond a joint initiative between economists and political scientists for a joint MA and PhD in public policy at Toronto that would utilise existing resources. Something finally emerged from that proposal in 2006.

The committee attributed the problems at Toronto to the jointness of the Department of Political Economy, where the presence of a large contingent of political scientists had retarded the modernisation of the programme in economics and the enforcement of rigorous standards. The large group of economic historians had complicated matters by insisting on a less quantitatively oriented programme than required for economics, despite the recent cliometric revolution. The committee recommended that the University of Toronto actively consider the establishment of separate departments of economics and political science – something that happened on 1 September 1982.

By the time he had finished the Ontario review, Harry had come to have more radical ideas about "how to achieve efficiency in a large university system with limited resources for graduate training" (1974 Memoir IV, 35). He presented these in a discussion at the 1973 Warwick meeting of the Association of University Teachers of Economics. Edith Penrose, chair of the Social Science Research Council's (SSRC) economics committee, encouraged him to write them out for public discussion. He did so, and while in London in April attending a Brookings conference on trade policy, he left a copy with the council official who had been at the AUTE discussion and another, courtesy copy for Robin Matthews, the council's chair. The result was a letter from Matthews inviting him to the council's annual conference in Exeter in July to initiate discussion of the topic, and if he came to speak, not to publish his paper until after the conference "when you will have had the opportunity of hearing the views there expressed." Matthews also suggested Harry had the case of economics too much in mind and noted there were substantial differences between economics and the other social sciences and even larger differences between economics and the humanities (Box 49, SSRC, from Robin Matthews, 19 April 1973). Harry agreed to postpone publication, but, eventually, hearing no more about the conference he sent his paper to *The Times Higher Education Supplement* (THES), where it appeared on 13 July (1973e), the first day of the conference. Although there was also some comment in the same issue by Maurice Kogan, the commentary was not wholly critical. Nonetheless, the episode bothered Harry for he referred to it again in correspondence with the editor of the *THES* after he resigned from LSE (Box 39, Correspondence 1971–7, I–O, to Brian MacArthur, 12 and 27 June 1974; from Brian MacArthur, 18 June 1974)

The conference began with the SSRC announcing its policy decisions *before* the discussions began. Harry was annoyed. His annoyance turned to outrage when he found that his "session Chairman had never heard of me before but that he told me that I had not been as outrageous as he had been told to expect" (1974 Memoir IV, 36–7). David Laidler drove back from Exeter to Heathrow in a rented Volkswagen Beetle with Harry at the helm. "Every roundabout is etched in my memory!" Not surprisingly, when there were delays in reimbursing his airfare, there was another, bad-tempered row.

Given that Harry believed that the general subsidisation of graduate work represented a regressive transfer from the general public to the student or the employer of educated labour, he favoured a fee schedule that reflected tuition and faculty costs and a system of student loans for those who lacked the means to pay the fees. However, as he thought that such a régime was unlikely to prove acceptable to public opinion, he attempted to devise a compromise. This involved raising fees towards the full costs of graduate education – preferably for all students but at a minimum for foreign students. However, he would restrict graduate student grants to students enrolled in taught master's programmes, which he thought should be concentrated in fewer institutions to gain economies of scale. Students taking master's degrees by dissertation or PhD degrees would not be subsidised because "it is doubtful whether the research training [involved] is useful apart from the specific types of employment in which either the employer or the employee rather than the state could be reasonably be expected to pay for it." As most dissertation degree candidates were aiming at academic careers where continued research was expected and where ample time for research was available, he could see no case for public support. If academics needed highly skilled research-degree candidates for their own research, they should fund them from their own research grants, rather than treat research assistance as a by-product of student grants. Harry's proposals sank without a trace: He never revived them.

TWELVE

Professional Life – Largely British

For Harry, LSE economics was part of several British networks. He resumed his connection with the Association of University Teachers of Economics and in a contest with Richard Lipsey was elected president for three years in 1968.[1] By virtue of his LSE position, he joined the Council of the Royal Economic Society. He also joined the Council (and later the Executive Committee) of the National Institute for Economic and Social Research. In 1968 he became a member of the London Political Economy Club, founded in 1821 with Robert Malthus, David Ricardo, and James Mill among its original members. He became involved in the making of science policy when he joined the Council on Science Policy in 1968.

With these connections, Harry tried to shape his profession's response to changing circumstances and opportunities. Some of his initiatives reflected his American and Canadian experience in discussions of public policy, where he thought there were lessons that could be learned; others reflected the changing English economics profession in a world of expanding enrolments and new universities, for the "typical situation of young people just starting out" in the profession had changed markedly in less than 20 years.

[W]hen I started my career in Cambridge, there were very few significant economics departments in the country; most of these were fairly large in numbers; and the proportion of junior to senior faculty was fairly low. Hence young people could establish their reputations by personal contact with their senior colleagues and become recognized in advance of any major publications; and they could readily obtain assistance, advice and comments on their work from their seniors. Now . . . there are many departments of economics; many of the newer ones are very small;

---

[1] After a further three years on the executive committee as past president, the AUTE executive unanimously agreed that Harry should be asked to serve for another three years (Box 39, Correspondence 1971–7, J–P, from Edward Nevin, 17 April 1974; to Edward Nevin, 1 May 1974).

307

and the proportion of young economists is very much higher, especially in the new departments, where the professors themselves are often "young" in the professionally relevant sense. (British Library of Political and Economic Science, Royal Economic Society Archives, RES 2/1/9, Memorandum for Circulation to the Council of the Royal Economic Society, 1971)

As the profession was becoming larger and more dispersed, it was also becoming more specialised – "narrowly focused on specific problems, constituents of a larger group of problems, and on the application of a great deal of mathematical, statistical and econometric expertise in their solution" (ibid.). This triple process of expansion, diffusion, and specialisation emphasised for Harry the need for ways of improving communication and mutual support for the young academic economist.

The Money Study Group

One networking initiative, the study group, came to play an important role in the lives of British economists in subdisciplines well removed from Harry's – econometrics, monetary history, post-Keynesian economics. The first such group was the Money Study Group. It grew out of a conference organised by a former LSE colleague, David Croome, held at Hove in Sussex in November 1969, to mark the tenth anniversary of the publication of the *Report* of the Radcliffe Committee on the Working of the Monetary System. The conference, for which Harry provided one of his surveys of developments in monetary economics (1970h), was a success. A number of the participants believed with Harry that the establishment of an interuniversity study group would accelerate the development and consolidation of empirical research in monetary economics in Britain. They formed a committee whose members were David Laidler (Manchester), Marcus Miller (LSE), Robert Nobay (National Institute), Michael Parkin (Essex), and Alan Walters (LSE). They asked Harry to chair it. The Money Study Group was formally established on 20 January 1970 when, appropriately enough, Harry delivered an inaugural survey lecture to the committee and invited guests. The group launched an appeal for funds, which it discussed at a meeting on 6 April 1970 during the annual conference of the AUTE. The appeal for funds was only partly successful: In the end it was the assistance of the Social Science Research Council obtained through the efforts of David Worswick and Catherine Cunningham that got the regular seminar programme of the group well off the ground, though company and financial sector support proved invaluable in funding what became a series of annual conferences, the first at Sheffield in September 1970, the second at Bournemouth in 1972, and then Oxford in

1973, 1974, and 1975. The group also held conferences on particular topics: "The Current Inflation" (February 1971), the Bank of England's consultative document "Competition and Credit Control" (June 1971), Sir John Hicks (July 1972), and West German Monetary Developments (July 1974).[2] It also produced a very useful *Readings in British Monetary Economics* edited by Harry and a committee of the group (1972l).

The seminar programme provided a regular forum for the presentation of ongoing research. It attempted to bring together academics often relatively isolated in their various departments. The group experimented with a mix of whole-day seminars on topics of broader interest – reports of the two SSRC-funded research programmes in monetary economics at LSE (see in Chapter 13) and Manchester, or Bank of England research on money income and causality and the stability of monetary relationships following the introduction of Competition and Credit Control – and those that allowed an exchange of ideas on individuals' work-in-progress. As the series of seminars developed, preceded as they came to be by what after 1973 was a "beginning of term" conference at Merton College, Oxford, British monetary economists developed an esprit de corps and found themselves, and their graduate students, not just less isolated but integrated into the international network of monetary economists. Because of Harry's yeoman work as entrepreneur, organiser, and editor, the group survived his departure from England in 1974, as well as the departures of David Laidler and Michael Parkin to Canada in 1975. Indeed it continues as the Money, Macro and Finance Group with purposes, programmes, and financial arrangements remarkably similar to those of 1970.[3] A Canadian successor organisation also flourishes.

The meetings of the Money Study Group also showed another side of Harry – his emphasis on professional behaviour. An after-dinner discussion by Harry and Nicholas Kaldor was scheduled on the second evening of the Bournemouth Conference in February 1972, held in the middle of a coal miners' strike and therefore often by candlelight. The Kaldor–Johnson session was recorded with the intention of including it in the published proceedings. However, when Kaldor received a transcript of his talk from Robert Nobay in July, he claimed that he had no knowledge "that this talk of mine was tape recorded nor that you had had any intention of publishing

---

[2] The 1974 Oxford Conference honoured James Meade.

[3] ESRC, Regard, 2003. The only difference is that its publishing programme now only publishes selected papers from its annual conferences – a sensible development, given that its Thirty-Fifth Annual Conference had over 100 papers (*Royal Economic Society Newsletter*, October 2003, 9–10).

it or indeed the paper presented at the study group." He refused permission to publish any of the talk (Box 39, Correspondence 1971–7, J–P, to A. R. Nobay, 8 July 1972). He later apologised to Harry, repeating what he had told Nobay about recording and possibly publishing and adding

[W]hen I saw the record I was quite convinced that it is not the sort of thing that I would like to see published under my name. Also there was no proper discussion, & no "reply" on my part, at the end. (Box 39, Correspondence 1971–7, J–P, from N. Kaldor, 25 August 1972)

Harry's annoyed draft of a reply to Kaldor, which he did not send, is of interest both as regards his views on professional behaviour and his long-standing underlying respect for Kaldor.

Dear Nicky,
I thank you for your note explaining your refusal to allow your remarks at the Bournemouth Conference of the Money Study Group to be published. I am sorry that you are unprepared to allow them to be published, because we had hoped that the volume would represent current controversy and research in Britain, and show economists in other countries that we are not such an intellectual backwater in economics as they quite justifiably assume from the virtually complete absence of published contributions by eminent people to the development of economic science.

I am also sorry that you should have offered the explanation you have offered: I would never myself take such a condescending attitude towards a group of serious economists as to offer them remarks that I had thought out so little, or that I intruded so much as unsupported verbal propaganda that I would be ashamed to sign my name to them in cold print.

As to the question of your having been denied the right of reply, the major reason for that was your own fault. If you had stopped after the first half hour, you would have left me with a difficult task and yourself with a reputation as a serious economic theorist. Instead you rambled on for another half hour, plus or minus, and I had to cut my remarks very short to prevent the audience getting bored beyond impatience. You have done this to me, or to other people, before, to my knowledge; it was, and still remains, the Germanic style of economic discussion, in which the Professor is the great man and anyone else is there simply to demonstrate the greatness – hence your insistence on the right to reply to any criticism, regardless of how much time your own discourse has consumed. That is not the style of contemporary economics, in which the audience is not composed of students and ignorant laymen but of people actively engaged in theory and research who have come to hear an eminent professional in the hopes of hearing new ideas, or of hearing old ones defended by fresh arguments based on the literature, not simply of being reassured by a rehearsal of old arguments. From that point of view, your performance was pretty disastrous from the point of view of the Keynesian cause. The young people who still have their name to make in our profession do not want to be told that whatever effort they put in you are still the final arbiter of truth, even if you put in no more than making a few notes on the train down and spend more of your time with reading or listening to their papers. Instead, they are looking to you for guidance to new ideas that they can work on that will enable them to excel their contemporaries in producing new theories and new research. If you fail them, by treating such an occasion lightly and not producing your best – even if adapted to the circumstances of an after-dinner address instead of a journal paper – you leave your side of the debate condemned to dependence on third-rate people to deploy second-rate ideas. The fact that you, having delivered the second-rate ideas, refuse to publish them for the condescending or trivial reasons you have chosen, deprives your followers even of the minimal guidance you could have given them.

I hope you will realize that I am writing to you as a former and grateful student rather than as an adversary. I learned a lot of economics from you, first as a reader of your early works, which were brilliant, then as a junior colleague at King's, where your writing of *An Expenditure Tax* [1955] made me think about a lot of basic issues that nothing in my previous training had made me realise were basic. As an adversary, nothing would suit me better than to have made the kind of appearance that you made at Bournemouth – a smug, self-satisfied, prosperous, old professor whose arguments could easily be punctured by a second-rate mind like myself who had spent twenty-five years of hard work in following and attempting to master the literature and whose main concern was to provide some sort of motivation for other second-rate or third-rate minds to work on the subject instead of merely repeating the pronouncements of their intellectual superiors. As a friend and admirer in my youth, I do not like to see you set yourself up as an easy target for second-rate minds to despise. You made it too easy; and I think that is bad for the profession. A good economist should not coast by virtue of his having obtained a Professorship. He should instead take the Professorship as an obligation to prove that he deserves it.

Scholarly Publishing

Another initiative, started in Chicago but carried over to the LSE years and expanded saw Harry involved in two substantial publishing projects – the Aldine Treatises in Modern Economics, which he edited, and the Gray-Mills Lectures in Economics, where he was involved as a risk-taking entrepreneur as well as a stimulator of manuscripts, two of them his own.

Both series, in Harry's view, were designed to fill gaps in the existing communications networks for economists. Without the treatise – "something above the level of a textbook but more comprehensive than the usual monograph, containing a full scale presentation of a subject that is unified by the logical organisation of a first-class mind [–] ... students do not have access to the considered judgment of the best scholars on the work of their contemporaries and on the most promising lines of further development, except through a fortunate choice of graduate school, and ... teachers and researchers in the majority of universities are likely to be out of touch with what is going on in their fields" (Box 47, Aldine, to F. Modigliani,

15 December 1964)[4] The lectures were designed to fill another gap: keeping up with one's subject and contributing to its advance left no time for the writing of textbooks – "the medium through which advances of knowledge are diffused from the major research centres to students and their teachers in other university institutions concerned primarily with teaching" (*MMT*, 1). Harry thought that published lecture notes might prove a useful compromise. Moreover, lecture notes were more compact than textbooks and allowed the reader to see how the lecturer saw his subject's highlights in a way that was impossible in the more measured, more comprehensive textbook.

For the Aldine series, Harry spent considerable time approaching authors and, once their manuscripts appeared in draft, editing them not only for readability and possible errors but also for the appropriate level of difficulty. Much of the resulting comments were inevitably on the manuscripts themselves which were returned to their authors, but occasionally in the correspondence one gets a sense of the effort involved. With Martin Bronfenbrenner's *Income Distribution Theory* (1969) he read the first fourteen chapters in late September 1967, posting them back from London, Chicago, and Rio de Janeiro. He was unhappy with several aspects of the book – an overdone "strong tendency to refer to Marxist theory and concepts wherever vaguely relevant"; "a random-striking propensity to convey the pith of an argument in a terse phrase culled from such languages as French, German and Latin"; a "notabl lack of good education in macro-theory." Yet, he concluded a letter written at 2:20 A.M. between Rio and London, "Bronfenbrenner is just the kind of risk we thought he would be, but our concept of the series was designed to get guys like that to produce books and he's doing it" (Box 31, Aldine, to A. Morin, 30 September 1967). Nor was Bronfenbrenner unhappy with the criticisms, writing Harry about his follow-up letter "in which you seek to mollify certain criticisms which I must not yet have seen. (The ones I have seen I find quite reasonable, even in the small percentage of cases where I think they are mistaken.)" (Box 31, Aldine, to HGJ, 9 October 1967).

To judge by the surviving correspondence, Harry seems to have worked hardest on the early volumes of the series. Thus in a letter to Robert Wesner (Box 31, 18 September 1970) he reported that he hadn't read Telser's *Competition, Collusion and Game Theory* (1972) even though it was in press.

---

[4] Aldine was a small Chicago publisher whose directors included Milton Friedman and the sociologist Philip Hauser. Its moving spirit was Alexander Morin, a Harvard PhD in economics who had been managing editor of University of Chicago Press from 1952–1959.

However, with respect to Albert Breton's *The Economic Theory of Represen-tative Government* (1974), he reported to Robert Wesner

I have been working with Breton on the book since he started it, not for Aldine but because he is a protegé of mine for whose originality I have a great deal of respect. I have just read what is intended as a final draft, and very nearly is . . . (Box 31, Aldine, to Robert Wesner, 12 March 1972).

Breton's was the seventh and last treatise he and Aldine did together. However, after his stroke he wrote to Alex Morin (Box 31, Aldine, 12 February 1974) of "lessons we've got from the last round":

(1) Young coming men are a waste of our time – once they think about starting [a treatise] their careers have moved on. We should do our hard recruiting from people like Ray Mikesell, who love to write big books or people like Burkhart [sic] and Mincer, who see an important chance of it. . . . Old men like Shoup are a problem too, the fields have been moving too fast for them and their devotees are too few to give us a lot of good reviews. In short what we should aim for is Associate Professors with tenure and settled for five years ahead.[5]

The lecture series resulted in six volumes, including Harry's LSE lectures on *Macroeconomics and Monetary Theory* (1971d) and his Chicago lectures on *The Theory of Income Distribution* (1973h). There was a related sympo-sium volume edited by Keith Cowling. Gray-Mills published its last volume in 1974. Hamish Gray (Mills was a dentist), the firm's managing director and a former student of Harry's, may have been reasonably good at getting things done, but he was less good at keeping his affairs and that of the firm separate. Early on, Harry referred to Gray-Mills as "an active if somewhat shady firm" (Box 58, Aldine, to R. Wesner, 12 March 1972). Eventually, Gray "went berserk and pretty well run [sic] Gray-Mills into bankruptcy" as Harry told David Laidler (Box 39, Correspondence 1971–7, I–O, 30 January 1976). Gray and Mills both promised Harry they would borrow against other assets and both defaulted on their commitments (Box 39, Correspondence 1971–7, I–O, to A. R. Nobay, 29 October 1975). The only asset of the firm was its stock of books which were sold to Blackwell's in 1976 for £13,600 (Box 39, Correspondence 1971–7, I–O, from A. R. Nobay, 1 April 1976). Blackwell intended to continue to sell the titles and to reissue them under a new imprint, Parkgate, along with new titles such as James Tobin's lectures in macroeconomics (Box 58, Miscellaneous Notes and Correspondence,

---

[5] Mikesell was the author of the first treatise *The Economics of Foreign Aid* (1968); Jesse Burkhead and Jerry Mincer, the authors of *Public Expenditure* (1971); Carl Shoup, of *Public Finance* (1969).

J. K. D. Feather to J. Tobin, 27 May 1976). Such new volumes never appeared; nor were the older ones reprinted. In August 1976 Robert Nobay, who had been managing much of Harry's English affairs since his stroke, estimated that Harry's own losses on the enterprise amounted to £5,400 (Box 39, Correspondence 1971–7, I–O, to HGJ, undated but internal evidence suggests August 1976).

Thus ended two experiments, the second of which looked sufficiently attractive for Aldine to think of doing its own series of Aldine Lectures (Box 58, Aldine, Morin to HGJ, 5 February 1973). Aldine itself ran into financial difficulties. After a failed attempt to sell itself to another Chicago publisher, it became a division of Walter de Gruyter in 1978. Transaction Publishers acquired Aldine de Gruyter in June 2004.

Public Policy Research – Science and Trade

Harry's first public contact with the "economics of science" came in 1964. Early that year the OECD asked him to be an examiner of French science policy. All that survives from this experience, is his "Notes and Impressions formed During the OECD Examination of Science Policy in France, March 8–14 1964" (Box 9). Later on he became a member of the Daddario Committee of the U.S. National Academy of Sciences undertaking an ad hoc enquiry for the Committee on Science and Astronautics of the House of Representatives on basic research and national goals. As he commented, the area of science policy was a new one for him and he was "rather daunted by the complexity of the issues" (Box 53, Green Box, "Some Reflections on Leadership," 16 July 1964). His approach to the issues reflected the state of the art in the economics profession: Science produced a thing called knowledge. The relationship between the two might be linear and there was a sharp distinction between basic and applied research. His stance was questioning, sceptical, and critical – in a word "unenthusiastic" (see discussion in Chapter 5). When asked if leadership in basic scientific research was necessary for leadership in applied research, his answer was "No, there was no necessary connection." He could even see circumstances in which there might be a conflict between leadership in basic science and technological leadership. As for the argument that it was "the obligation or the privilege of the United States to support basic scientific research as a means of exercising leadership in the progress towards a higher form of civilisation" (1964c, 504), he remarked

Most of the contemporary "scientific culture" argument for government support of basic scientific research is to put it ... in the class of economically functionless activity. The argument that individuals with a talent for such research should be supported by society . . . differs little from arguments formerly advanced in support of the rights of owners of landed property to a leisured existence, and is accompanied by a similar assumption of superior social worth of the privileged individuals over common men. Again, insistence on the obligation of society to support the pursuit of scientific knowledge for its own sake differs little from the historically earlier insistence on the obligation of society to support the pursuit of religious truth, an obligation accompanied by a similarly unspecific and problematical payoff in the distant future. (505)

Clearly if the public decided "scientific culture" was desirable, it should be supported, but it was a form of consumption expenditure in competition with other uses of funds such as the relief of poverty, aid to less-developed countries, or increased consumption by taxpayers. Weighing the evidence in favour of the alternatives was, however, the responsibility of politicians. It was not clear, moreover, that American leadership in other areas such as social policy might not do more for the image of the United States as the society of the future than scientific leadership.

When it came to economic arguments for supporting basic research, Harry argued that one had to go further than simply say that it was important for economic growth. In a market economy one had to make the case that the market, if left to itself, would allocate too few resources to research in general or basic research. This seemed to be the case. But this only took the argument one stage further to the questions of whether existing supplements to the market were adequate and whether the allocation of resources was reasonably efficient. At this stage Harry could only pose questions, given the state of the economics literature on the subject.

Just how difficult it was to formulate questions and to discover answers became clearer once Harry became a member of the British Council for Scientific Policy, a body set up in January 1965 "to advise the Secretary of State for Education and Science in the exercise of his responsibility for the formation and execution of Government science policy." The council consisted of fifteen members from industry, universities, and government research establishments. It was attended by assessors from the University Grants Committee and the four natural science research councils (the chair of the Social Science Research Council was added in 1969). Much of the council's work was concerned with making the case for expenditure on science coming under the Department of Education and Science and with allocating the "science budget" of some £200 million between the research councils, the Natural History Museum, the Royal Society, and the Royal Society of Edinburgh, though it could concern itself with more general questions of science policy including the economic benefits of research. Harry joined meetings of the council on 8 July 1968. He then proceeded to miss five meetings, only returning on 6 December when the council discussed "An Attempt to Quantify the Benefits of Academic Research in Science and Technology" by A. V. Cohen and I. C. R. Byatt.[6] His irregular attendance continued throughout his term, which ended in June 1971 when he was succeeded by Frank Hahn: in a good year he might attend one in three meetings. The council itself disappeared soon afterwards in a reorganisation of the institutions of British science policy.

One result of the Cohen and Byatt paper, which was revised as "An Attempt to Quantify the Economic Benefits of Scientific Research" in January 1969, was a Working Party on Economic Benefits, which Harry chaired. Its terms of reference were

[t]o consider possible methods of quantifying the economic benefits of scientific research; to advise what studies might be commissioned for this purpose; and to report from time to time to the Council for Scientific Policy.

In addition to Harry, it consisted of two members of the council and the secretary and later the director of the Programmes Analysis Unit of the Department of Education and Science. Cohen and Byatt were the initial secretaries to the working party. It first met on 18 March to discuss publication of the revised paper (which appeared as *Science Policy Studies, No 4* from the Stationery Office in 1969) and to discuss possible follow-on studies of particular scientific discoveries and possible authors for these. It met twice more in 1969 to commission two feasibility studies – the Programmes Analysis Unit added a third from its own resources – and to discuss their results. The working party commissioned three further studies from groups at the University of Manchester over the next three years; the Programmes Analysis Unit offered a fourth. Two meetings in 1970 were involved in supervising the work at Manchester, discussing the results and preparing an interim report that was considered by the council at its 22 January 1971 meeting. The council asked for a final report by the end of 1971. The working party met only once in each of 1971 and 1972, this last meeting to discuss the factual part of its final report, dated 22 June 1972. It never met again, and the report was never completed.

Harry's experience with the council and its working party was chastening. As he put it:

---

[6] Cohen was scientific secretary to the council; Byatt was senior economic adviser to the Department of Education and Science.

First, on the scientific side, the accumulation of knowledge does not proceed linearly from basic discoveries to applications so that one cannot really answer the question, "Would the expenditure of a little more research money at some point in time have brought forward in time the economic and social benefits?" Secondly, on the economic side, I should have realised from price theory, but somehow failed to, the benefits of intellectual advance do not appear anywhere in the price system, or appear very imperfectly. . . . Hence it appears virtually impossible to establish any empirical basis for science policy decisions. (1971i, 545)

As a result, all he could conclude from the present state of the art was that

how far the organised pursuit of knowledge in the form of science as it exists today can be credited with responsibility for the economic basis of contemporary civilisation, and how far society gains from public support of science, remain open questions. (1972k, 18)

Subsequent decades have served to show that proper framing of the questions has become even more complex than Harry thought, with the result that the answers are, if anything, more elusive.[7]

While Harry was at Chicago, he had been involved with the Private Planning Association of Canada, in particular the Canadian-American Committee, which it organised jointly with the National Planning Association of the United States. The Private Planning Association had been founded in 1958 "for the purpose of undertaking independent and objective studies of Canadian problems and policies, mainly in the field of economic affairs, and of Canada's relationships with other countries." Its committees met twice a year to consider current issues and commission academic studies. Occasionally they were more entrepreneurial, publishing Harry's *The World Economy at the Crossroads* when the university at which he delivered the lectures lacked a ready means of disseminating them.

In May 1966 the Canadian-American Committee released a pamphlet, "A New Trade Strategy for Canada and the United States," which proposed a North Atlantic Free Trade Area of Canada, the United States, the United Kingdom, and her European Free Trade Association partners. After this, the Private Planning Association's publication programme got more ambitious: In its series Canada and the Atlantic Economy, it published (in association with University of Toronto Press) eighteen studies of aspects of Atlantic relationships by authors such as Harry, Richard Caves, Grant Reuber, R. A. Shearer, John Young, and Paul Wonnacott. In North America the Private Planning Association was not alone in producing such policy-related

---

[7] For the current state of play, see Mirowski and Sent (eds., 2002).

materials – witness the Brookings Institution for which Harry had just written *Economic Policies for Less Developed Countries.*

When Harry returned to England in 1966, he readily fitted into a nascent British trade policy network. The catalyst for this network was Hugh Corbet, an Australian journalist aged 28 then working on *The Times.* After Harry's LSE appointment was announced, Corbet invited him to join a nonparty Foreign Affairs Club. Harry agreed on 27 July 1965. From this group sprang the Atlantic Trade Study and the Trade Policy Research Centre.

At the time Harry became involved again in the British discussion of trade policy, particularly relating to Europe, he knew that the earlier 1950s discussions "had turned up a number of crucial and researchable questions that had not been researched, and on which no research was done after the ... [larger European Free Trade Area] scheme had crashed" (1974 Memoir III, 1). Moreover, he was unhappy with the quality of policy research available from the existing British sources:

One sign of this that puzzled me for a long time was that, aside from the National Institute for Economic and Social Research – a short-run forecasting enterprise safely in the hands of Oxford economists devoted to full employment and an incomes policy – all the economic and political research institutes I came across were under the direction of a former journalist with an Oxford B.A. in Politics, Philosophy and Economics [with] no research experience whatever, people who identified research with interviewing top people and misunderstanding a random collection of published statistics.

One of the most successful of these intellectual entrepreneurs Andrew Shonfield (Royal Institute of International Affairs, and for a time Chairman of the Social Science Research Council) I had known earlier through a Third Programme review of his book on *British Economic Policy Since the War* [1958] which made a powerful case for stimulating investment on the basis of an elementary confusion of the output-to-capital ratio with the net rate of return on new investment.[8] He ran true to form ... on ... occasions on which I observed him thereafter. One involved one of those R.I.I.A. study groups founded on the belief that an important book can be produced by a rapporteur listening to the conversation over sherry and dinner of miscellaneous popular experts meeting weekly over a year or so. (1974 Memoir III, 3–4)

The atmosphere of contemporary economic policy discussion was not helped by the attitudes of the press. It was "excessively prone to assess news values and present the news according to its judgment of what is currently politically acceptable or unacceptable ... [and] it has not hesitated to interpret the news according to its views of the desirable direction of policy." It had

[8] The broadcast 'Growth without Tears' was on 14 June 1958. A copy of the script is in Box 26, Writing 1958.

also "typically assumed an omniscience on complex questions of economic fact with respect to which scientific research results are either non-existent, controversial or contrary to the press's own assertions" (1969i, 11).

In these circumstances,

I felt that Britain should develop policy research at the academic level I was used to in North America – it was just not good enough to have economists like Roy Harrod pose this policy question in terms of how many British automobile firms would survive competition in a European market and guess at the answer. I knew how to do it: there were many British and European economists who had relevant experience on particular facets of the subject, were casting about for some way of applying their experience, and could be induced for a relatively modest lump-sum payment to write it up into an essay directed at our policy problem and delivered by a deadline, provided we guaranteed to let them publish any unfavourable results they found. We were in fact very successful and produced a high quality series of manuscripts ultimately collected by topic into a series of books. (1974 Memoir III, 1–2)

The Atlantic Trade Study was founded in 1966 to produce a series of studies on world economic affairs. Before it became The Free Trade Association Trust in 1972, it had published eighteen volumes by authors such as Hans Liesner, Max Steuer, Tim Josling, Roy Harrod, and David Wall. "[T]hanks to Corbet's ingenuity as a builder, we were able to use the Atlantic Trade Study organisation as a springboard for the Trade Policy Research Centre" (1974 Memoir III, 3). The centre was founded in 1968 as an independent research organisation that acted as the Atlantic Trade Study's agent. Corbet became the centre's first full-time director; Harry, chairman of the Advisory Board and director of studies. They attracted a strong board (or council after 1970) which included Roy Harrod, Richard Lipsey, Max Corden, James Meade, Maxwell Stamp, and Eric Wyndam White,[9] with funding by subscriptions, donations, and grants from the Ford, Rockefeller, and Nuffield Foundations, as well as the Leverhulme Trust.

Although the Centre sponsored seminars and dinner meetings, the heart of its activities was its research and publications programme, which produced short staff papers of ten to twenty pages as well as longer essays. Many of these found their way into larger collective volumes (ten between 1969 and 1974). Initially the focus of the centre's interests was Atlanticist; after Britain joined the EEC in 1973, it became more European, with a council that came to have a significant contingent from the Graduate Centre of International Studies in Geneva but still multilateral. Later expansion saw it open offices

---

[9] The first director of GATT.

in New York and Washington. Naturally, it maintained close links with the Private Planning Association of Canada and its American counterpart.

During his association with the centre, which given his later connection with the Graduate Institute in Geneva survived Harry's departure from LSE in 1974, he worked hard for its ends. Some indication of his labours are the two books he edited for the centre, one he coedited, and one he wrote between 1969 and 1976 – not to mention the introductions he provided for others' volumes. At least one volume never came to fruition, a joint centre–Brookings volume, tentatively entitled *International Negotiations and Non-Tariff Barriers* that he was to have edited with Stanley Metzger. It was listed as "about to be published" in the 1974–5 schedule of the centre. The centre continued to thrive after Harry's death, but it ran into financial difficulties in the late 1980s and lost control of its journal *The World Economy* in 1989. Its last monographs appeared in 1992.

Professional Associations

The AUTE was another possible networking institution ripe for Harry's attention. It had been founded after meetings in 1924 and 1925 "with a view particularly to the discussion of methods of teaching and of other topics of common interest in economics and kindred subjects" (H.P. 1925, 154). Its membership was heavily concentrated outside Oxbridge, and its annual conferences, which began in Birmingham in January 1926, were an important unifying force. However, its conference proceedings were not published, and its institutional presence moved with its chair.

One possible source of support for the AUTE in changing times was the Royal Economic Society, which, according to Harry, had been "primarily a journal-publishing society, with side interests in publications in the history of economic thought." Given its relative wealth and its international reputation as the national association of British economists, it was the "only body capable of taking the lead in establishing new arrangements that would serve the interests of British economists over, say, the next quarter century" (Box 52, Correspondence 1971–7, P–T, Future of the Royal Economic Society, 11 November 1969). The relationship of the society to the profession had two dimensions – the *Economic Journal* on the one hand and further services that the society could provide for its members on the other.

Once a member of its council in 1968, Harry became involved in the affairs of the society as a member of a committee charged with finding a replacement for Austin Robinson as secretary. At an early point of its proceedings, Harry worried about the future of the society:

It seems to me that the Royal Economic Society has for a long time run the risk of becoming a club for a small group of senior men in the profession out of touch with the majority of economists in the country because of their very eminence and taking decisions based on experience of twenty or so years ago and out of touch with the current situation. We now have forty universities in the country, and a tremendous number of economists in both business and government. This situation raises many problems, which the Society has only begun to study and come to terms with. I do not want to discuss these in this letter, but it does seem to me that the Council has not been prepared to think boldly and rationally about them. (British Library of Political and Economic Science, Royal Economic Society Archives, RES 4/4/2, to Sir Alec Cairncross, 10 June 1969)

He went on to discuss the notion of the ideal secretary and the idea of the society's moving its offices from Cambridge.

The committee met without Harry on 3 July. They discussed the functions of the secretary and possible candidates. Charles Carter, the current editor of the *Economic Journal*, was their first choice if he was prepared to take the job. The committee met again with Harry present on 28 October and, after discussion, agreed to appoint Carter as secretary-general. This left the editorship of the *Journal* vacant and there was

a lengthy discussion on the Editorship in which Professor Johnson urged strongly that it would be a mistake to select a group of Editors from Cambridge, although he would not object to the association of two or more principal editors, one of whom might be from Cambridge. Lord Robbins took much the same line. (British Library of Political and Economic Science, Royal Economic Society Archives, RES4/4/2, Meeting of the Committee on the Secretaryship, 28 October 1969)

When the council met to approve Carter's appointment on 7 November, it handed the task of selecting the editors to the same committee. At this stage, Alec Cairncross summed up the situation to Lionel Robbins:

No-one has yet come up with a better idea than that we should ask Brian Reddaway to take on the job with such co-operation and help as he and we think desirable either in Cambridge or elsewhere. As would be clear from Harry Johnson's interventions, there will be considerable suspicion in the profession that we are turning the editorship into a Cambridge prerogative if we do as has been suggested; invite Brian Reddaway to be Editor in Chief and three other Cambridge economists to act as Assistant Editors. The fact, however, is that Cambridge is in a much stronger position than anywhere else except possibly London to provide the necessary leadership. There doesn't seem to me to be a great deal to be said for seeking to associate with Brian an economist from elsewhere, mainly in the interests of allaying suspicion about Cambridge empire building. (British Library of Political and Economic Science, Royal Economic Society Archives, RES 4/4/2, Cairncross to Robbins, 7 November 1969)

Robbins replied on 13 November that he was "not enthusiastic about Reddaway" even if it was "a respectable appointment" and continued

But I do think that there is a great substance in Harry Johnson's attitude: I am sure there will be real discontent if so much power resides exclusively in Cambridge. I hasten to say that I think that the same objection would apply to placing the editorship in the hands of an LSE man and his associates. . . . Before our meeting I had no idea of Harry's feeling in this matter. But the very fact that he, who is on the whole so well balanced a chap and so catholic in his sympathies, should think like this gives me to see a red light. (British Library of Political and Economic Science, Royal Economic Society Archives, RES 4/4/2)

It was at this stage that Harry circulated his "The Future of the Royal Economic Society." There he argued that the problem of the *Journal* was the Oxbridge orientation of its editors – one need only think of the succession of senior editors (Edgeworth, Keynes, Harrod, C. F. Carter) or their assistants (Edgeworth, D. H. Macgregor, E. A. G. Robinson, R. C. O. Matthews) – and the power of the editor in determining what got published.[10] In the future, Harry believed, the editors should be able to come from anywhere and that for decisions on articles, aided by referees' reports, the editor-in-chief should have the assistance of a representative editorial board. Moreover, if the editors could come from anywhere, it made sense that the society's main office should be in London.[11] If this were so, among the facilities the society could provide would include "some sort of meeting place and reading room." It could also supply office space for organisations such as the AUTE and develop a common "directory" of British economists along the lines of the regularly updated Directory of the American Economic Association. He also suggested that a selection of papers from the AUTE's annual conference be published as a supplement to the *Economic Journal*. Harry's proposals met with resistance. After its meetings on 17 November and 10 December, the committee on the editorship produced an editorial team of Reddaway assisted by his Cambridge colleagues David Champernowne and Phyllis Deane. All that came out of Harry's first initiative was a Committee on New Activities, of which Harry was a member; this met once on 10 December (immediately after deciding on the editors) and supported the AUTE initiative and attempts through a conference secretary to organise specialist conferences and an information secretary to improve flows of information.

---

[10] Carter had left Cambridge for a chair in Belfast and then a chair in Manchester before becoming the vice-chancellor of the University of Lancaster. On Keynes as editor from 1912 to 1945, see Moggridge (1990). Refereeing, extremely rare and idiosyncratic under Keynes and still rare under Harrod, only started to become the norm under Carter.

[11] As had been the case before 1934, Harry showed no inkling of knowing this.

Nothing came of the proposed *Economic Journal* supplement for some years. Instead, initially with financial support from the Royal Economic Society, the AUTE began publishing its proceedings in separate volumes. The arrangement was unstable as different publishers took on the volume in years that were financially challenging: Between 1973 and 1980 Longmans, Manchester University Press, Blackwell, Cambridge University Press, and Croom Helm were involved.[12]

In a separate move in 1971, Harry supported an attempt, unsuccessful at first, for the Royal Economic Society to underwrite the cost of setting up an index service for working papers – a course he recommended because of the role that working papers played in knitting together networks of younger colleagues by helping them form professional identities and obtain assistance and advice, linking together small specialist groups and providing prepublication dissemination for new ideas in a world where publication lags were becoming longer and longer.

When the 1969 editors' terms came up for reconsideration in 1974 Harry was made a member of the selection committee, along with Sir Donald MacDougall, Charles Carter, Robin Matthews, and Alan Prest, all of whom were appointed by name rather than office. When he was appointed, Harry wrote Charles Carter (with a copy to Alan Prest):

I have one major problem in discussing the matter, which I ought to mention in confidence. I've edited or assisted with journals for nearly 25 years – Review of Economic Studies, Manchester School, Journal of Political Economy, Economica, now the J. P. E. again half-yearly (with George Stigler) – and have been on the board of the A.E.R., J.I.E. and J.M.C.B., and consultant one way or another for a lot of others. I think I've done well, particularly with the first three, for the latter two of which I was sole editor; and I think I have always kept my own interests in economics out of the editing, as regards economic ideology, though not as regards standards of what is useful and important scientific work as distinct from theoretical curiosa or persuasive non-scientific essays. I think I could handle the E.J., at not too much extra cost, despite my commitment to teach half-year in Chicago (which would of course have to be broken as regards the J.P.E.); and my stroke is being steadily overcome on the physical side and reduced physical mobility together with a new teetotal way of life are likely to mean more time for sedentary scholarly work. However, I know full well that I am persona non grata with and highly suspect to a lot of people who "count," and I would not want to take on a commitment that I would regard as

---

[12] It was appropriate that when the publisher Croom Helm decided to sponsor an annual lectureship at the AUTE conference, the association decided to call it the Harry Johnson Lecture. Martin Bronfenbrenner gave the first Harry Johnson Lecture to the AUTE at the University of York in 1978. The lecture continued until the year 2000, despite the demise of the AUTE and Croom Helm.

a matter of responsibility to the British profession imposing considerable cost on me, if it were regarded by others as a matter of personal aggrandizement (which it would not be) and had the effect of causing or contributing to dissension among the profession.

My own practice for the J.P.E. . . . is that the majority of articles deserve only a quick editor's opinion saying that they are unsuitable for the journal, either inherently (with a reason) or by virtue of subject (with a recommendation of another journal if one suggests itself as potentially more interested). Submission is a screening process; editorial and referee time should be reserved for articles that promise eventual publication in the journal. The editor should be willing and able to provide the opinion mentioned, however, as a part of his responsibility as editor, without needing the moral support of referees. There are, after all, lots of other journals for a disgruntled author to appeal to. (Box 38, Correspondence, Economic Journal, 23 January, 1974)

At the end of his January letter, Harry noted that he hoped to be well enough for the first meeting of the search committee on 7 March. He was. The first meeting considered a long list of names of possible editors suggested by members of the council and others, on the assumption that the present editors did not wish to continue and decided to ask the editors some general questions about their organisation. A second meeting followed in June. Harry was not present. At this stage Nicholas Kaldor, the new president of the society, joined the committee. He suggested that the present editors might after all be prepared to continue beyond their present terms and that Francis Cripps, who had not been proposed by anyone in March, would be a suitable replacement for Professor Champernowne if he did not wish to continue. The committee agreed to ask the present editors about their willingness to continue. There was no agreement to approach Cripps, who had already blotted his copybook with Harry with his remarks on his resignation from LSE (see discussion in Chapter 16).

In the ensuing correspondence, it became clear that Reddaway was prepared to stay on until December 1978 but Champernowne was unwilling to stay beyond June 1976. In the course of the summer there was correspondence among committee members about two possible senior names with Cambridge affiliations, which received support but were dropped when Kaldor objected to both. In September, Reddaway suggested that he should approach Cripps informally as a possible third article editor. He was asked not to do so, as the committee had not agreed to the Cripps proposal. Nonetheless he did so and subsequently wrote that he would be prepared to work with Cripps and that Champernowne might be prepared to continue with Cripps.

That put the cat amongst the pigeons. The secretary-general (Carter) and the treasurer (Prest) stated their desire to resign their offices from 31 December. Their grounds were the conduct of the search for a new editor, particularly the roles of the president and one of the current editors. They also raised a new issue: The removal of the society's accounts from Cambridge had resulted in the discovery that the society had substantial unrecorded debts on its publication account, which together with the future intentions of those responsible for the edition of the *Collected Writings of John Maynard Keynes* had grave financial implications for the society.[13]

The ensuing meeting of the council saw a final attempt to add Cripps to the editorial team. It failed, and a new subcommittee was charged with recommending editors for the period beginning in January 1976. The other result was the appointment of a "special committee" with Lionel Robbins and Alec Cairncross as joint chairs to review the future administration of the society, the future editorship of the *Economic Journal*, and the financial situation and arrangements of the society.

The ructions within the society certainly fuelled Harry's strong anti-Cambridge feelings. They also allowed him to renew his campaign for the society to become a national society, with its officers and council elected by postal ballot and for the editorship to become a position of responsibility to the profession as a whole. He argued that, given the recent past, the next editorial team should exclude anyone from Cambridge. He also argued that the society should get out of the "history of thought publications business," except as an occasional source of grants to support research and publication in the history of thought (Box 52, Correspondence 1971–7, P–T, to T. M. Rybczynski, 17 December 1974).

By this stage Harry's reactions to anything associated with Cambridge had become almost irrational. When the *Economic Journal* ceased to use Macmillan, its publishers since 1891, and transferred to Cambridge University Press, the press touted the change with a circular that proclaimed "A New Journal from Cambridge." Harry complained to Alice Prior:

Apart from myself, who have inside knowledge, a number of my colleagues have been disturbed by the fact that the editorial arrangements for the *Economic Journal* have

---

[13] Work on the edition had started in 1954. The first volumes, edited by Elizabeth Johnson, appeared in 1971. By 1974 fourteen volumes were in print and a further dozen were projected. The society acted as its own publisher and paid Macmillan a royalty for distributing the volumes; consequently, the stocks of these volumes represented a substantial investment.

been the subject of considerable controversy. In particular, though the *Economic Journal* announces itself as a national society journal, the faculty at Cambridge seem determined to keep control of the editorship itself and in particular to insist on the appointment of quite unqualified people in defiance of the procedure officially adopted by the Royal Economic Society for the selection of the present editors.

In view of all this, it would seem to us only honest to make it clear in your publicity whether the *Economic Journal* is a Cambridge Journal or really a national economics society journal. (British Library of Political and Economic Science, Royal Economic Society Archive, RES 7/2/9, to Alice Prior, 15 April 1975)

Harry's letter was passed on to Phyllis Deane, the managing editor, on 28 April. Brian Reddaway tried to get Lionel Robbins to assist, but Robbins noted: "I am afraid I am not my brother's keeper as far as this particular brother is concerned and I cannot guarantee that anything I say will moderate these occasional outbursts" (British Library of Political and Economic Science, Royal Economic Society Archives, RES 7/2/9, Robbins to Reddaway, 6 May 1975). It was left to Phyllis Deane to rebuke Harry, saying:

In writing this about an internal argument within the Council of the Royal Economic Society to a publisher with which it is in a purely commercial relationship you seem to me to have been bent simply on making mischief. I cannot imagine what useful purpose you expected your letter to serve. (Box 52, Correspondence 1971–7, P–T, to HGJ, 26 May 1975)

Harry was unrepentant.

The results of the special committee, over and above an increase in subscriptions and the prices of society publications, were a reorganisation of the governance of the society with a small executive committee placed in charge of day-to-day business. The Keynes edition received its own supervisory committee, as well as the general financial rule that new volumes would be printed (or old volumes reprinted) only if previous receipts covered printing costs. The edition of thirty volumes was completed in 1989. The editorial arrangements saw the retirement of the existing editorial team in the course of 1975–6 and its replacement by a new managing editor and chief articles editor, J. S. Flemming of Nuffield College, Oxford, advised by an editorial board and a new review editor, Donald Winch of the University of Sussex.[14] The administration became London-based.

Further changes followed. The society became the *national* society of economists. From 1982 the society and the AUTE jointly sponsored an annual conference, selected papers from which would appear as a separate

[14] The results of the Special Committee's deliberations were reported in "Current Topics" in the *Economic Journal* for September and December 1975 (85, 628–9, 996–7, 909–10).

conference papers supplement to the *Economic Journal* (["Current Topics," *Economic Journal,* XCII (December 1982), 1078]). The joint conferences continued until 1989. Thereafter, the AUTE disappeared and the conference became simply the Royal Economic Society Conference. In 1990 the society published its first register of members. The society's newsletter provides regular information to the profession on a full range of matters of interest and the council and officers of the society are elected by postal ballot rather than by a thinly attended annual meeting. With the millennium, the editorial board of the *Economic Journal* became international.

National Styles in Economics

Harry's years at LSE sharpened his views about the differences in the practice of economics in different national settings. This sharpness was particularly visible in his explicitly autobiographical writings at the end of his LSE period.

For Harry, the shift in the orientation of economics away from political economy towards what he called economic science had gone furthest in the United States.[15] Although he could see specific post-1945 historical reasons for the research frontier of economic science being in the United States, he saw the most important reasons for the shift in orientation in American academic traditions. The American professorate was more self-contained, with entry strictly governed by academic standards. Moreover, the United States had a long tradition of organised graduate programmes whose content adapted to developments in the subject and that could support students. As well, the pragmatism of American society was more congenial to the techniques and research-oriented trends in the discipline.

Certain aspects of American society also affected the way developments played out. The profession was not politicised. Economists were treated as independent experts. There were always enough experts available, given the size of the American profession, to serve governments of all stripes. Moreover most of the public fora for economic advice were structured to emphasise economic expertise and to maintain professional standards.[16]

---

[15] The most accessible of Harry's writings on the subject are in Part III of *Economics and Society.*

[16] Harry disliked the hands-on policy-making experience for economists. As he put it: "[T]he most potentially dangerous corrupting influence on economic science is actual participation in the policy-decision process, since such participation confuses the sense of scientific integrity and objectivity in the need to achieve politically acceptable compromises, and turns the object of activity from scholarly understanding and inquiry to achieving effective influence on policy-making. (Very few indeed of economists who have served on the

American conditions and practices also fostered high professional standards. The relative social isolation of American academics produced a stronger commitment to the subject than elsewhere as well as a commitment to good teaching and research. Standards were enforced through the tenure and promotion system, as well as by the mobility that rewarded success in a world where pay was related to performance. In addition, the fact that most people taught at a less prestigious institution than the one from which they received their PhD resulted in a continuous attempt by scholars to prove to the world at large that they were better than their own institution's rank in the subject might imply. The diversity of the United States also meant that there was a wide range of sources of research funding available, both private and public.

With the rise of economic science had come a different research style. Economics became more portable: The new generation, qualified by formal graduate instruction and a PhD at a different university from that of their first degree, proceeded to take their first jobs in a third. The professional discipline became the professional environment, and the norm for behaviour became continuous involvement in research and publication. The research and publication orientation and the emphasis on portable qualifications meant that the tenure and promotion process became one of "publish or perish"; the locus of decision making became the department; the structure of programmes emphasised courses focused on the "core" of the discipline as generally recognised.

This new model, which Harry strongly supported, replaced the older, single-scholar apprenticeship régime, which had emphasised relatively limited postgraduate training and a long programme of research not necessarily centred on publication, undertaken in a single university with intervals of amateur and unpaid administration.

Later (1977e) he added to the American picture by noting that McCarthyism had also played a role in the process. Although universities were generally successful in maintaining academic freedom, the experience discouraged philosophical speculation and encouraged more research on the American economy. At the same time, economics became "harder," more "natural scientific" as it emphasised mathematicisation, formal techniques, and statistical testing. The process produced professional narrowness when embodied in PhD programmes, but it also produced an ability to deal dispassionately with emotionally charged issues.

Council of Economic Advisers have returned quietly and happily to the calm of academic life.)" (*E&S*, 142).

Britain and Canada were different. In England "economics . . . [was] converted from a scientific subject into a species of political necromancy." The economist "lost his role as an independent citizen distinguished by his scholarly knowledge" (*E&S*, 134–5). At the heart of the problem was the centralisation of much of British educational, intellectual, and political life. Oxbridge was dominant in educating the political elite, the senior civil service, and the shapers of opinion in a unitary state whose political, cultural, and intellectual centre was London. Yet this centralised system at the academic level was characterised by a lack of formal graduate training or of a real emphasis on research as the basis for professional success. At best a master's degree was the entry qualification for academic life:

> [P]ossession of a Ph.D. by those who would make their careers in . . . [Britain] (in university or elsewhere) frequently . . . [denoted] insufficient competence, personal charm, or quickness of wit, to achieve academic appointment without one (though often the Ph.D. is necessary to enable the student from a backward country to break into the charmed concentric circles of British academic life). (*E&S*, 179)

Added to the centralisation were the effects of a system where salaries were age-related and where standards of tenure and promotion saw research "as a minimal requirement" and "service . . . rivals, and sometimes takes priority over, research performance as a criterion" (*E&S*, 135). Moreover, the relative decline of the don's status to that of, say, the civil servant meant that outside paying commitments were more necessary and further reduced the already weak incentive to devote effort to one's academic activities.[17]

Harry thought that British economics had another characteristic, derived, he thought, from the Oxford tutorial and the Cambridge supervision systems – "a teacher proves his academic quality by his ability to find fault with the published work of others" (*E&S*, 135). Not only did this inhibit publication – in case one was criticised – but it also affected the form of publication. As he put it in his 1974 Memoir (IV, 26–7):

> [A] number of the junior staff took the view . . . that in so far as they deigned to publish the ideal consisted in nit-picking the pelts of the eminent economists elsewhere. I quickly came to recognise the nit-picking style of the L.S.E. graduate's approach to economics: never ask what makes superior economic sense, instead look for a cranny in the logic or a slight shift of assumptions that will make the conclusion not quite watertight, then shout the news from the housetops; 'the emperor has no clothes'. Far more devastatingly I realised that much of the L.S.E. work that I had regarded as good in the past had been precisely of this character, though of superior

---

17 See also the earlier material in Chapter 11 on the economics of student protest and the future of LSE.

quality – like the Lipsey discovery of a trade-diverting welfare-increasing customs union, and the Morton–Makower dissection of the proposition that a customs union is more likely to be more beneficial the more similar in economic structure the partners are (both of which involved nit-picking the great trade theorist Jacob Viner), and one section of the Archibald–Lipsey article on Lange and Patinkin that parades a mathematical *curiosum* in which the quantity equation is not inconsistent with Say's Law.[18,19]

He then proceeded to provide an example from the issues of *Economica* from his own LSE period:

My irritation was aroused particularly ... by an article by Mishan and Desai [sic] that had just appeared in *Economica*, which had all the trappings of thoroughly pretentious bad work [Mishan and Needleman 1966]. It started by quoting a statement by a Cabinet Minister to the effect that immigration was beneficial to the economy and the balance of payments, made a major scientific issue of the question, performed a lot of calculations, and produced with the surprise of a magician finding a rabbit in his top hat the result that immigration had an adverse effect for a long period after it took place. Anyone with a grain of common sense could have put in a sentence the point, if one assumes as they did that immigrants have to be provided with houses, schools, and hospitals to the level enjoyed by the existing population, it will take them years to earn enough to repay the capital investment; but no such sentence occurred in the article. (1974 Memoir IV, 27)

According to Harry, the Oxbridge tradition "which involves training economists primarily for the civil service or politics and only secondarily for academic careers" (*E&S*, 135), produced a polarisation in the profession between left and right that had its origins in the Keynesian revolution of the interwar period. Economics in both ancient universities had been controlled by the left since 1945 and, given their cultural and academic dominance, set the impression of economics as a political subject – an impression maintained "by the practice of applying political criteria to the assessment of scientific ability and achievement." One result of this was to enhance the position of mathematical economics in Britain

because mathematical economics is a way of appearing to do economics without actually doing anything controversial or committing oneself to belief in what one is

---

[18] The references are to Lipsey (1957), Makower and Morton (1953), and Lipsey and Archibald (1958).

[19] Or, as he put it in print: "One is tempted to remark with regard to the L.S.E. tradition of that part of at least the postwar II period, that its besetting sin was to wait for some upstart like Viner or Patinkin to work out a solution to a real problem and then assail him with the deficiencies of his own logic; fortunately the process was rarely applied to the giants of the L.S.E. itself, and the young eventually discovered the attractions of Friedman's positive economics" (1972e, 728).

doing. Cambridge turned to mathematical economics when concentration on real economics became blocked by Cambridge politics. Mathematical economics was compatible with either avoiding right-wing or accepting left-wing political commitment. In the same sort of way the rise of mathematical economics in the United States reflected the pressures for conformity of the McCarthy period and after.... British mathematical economics may well remain world-eminent – by becoming the equivalent of classical scholarship in the mandarin system of selection for the Chinese civil service. (1974 Memoir IV, 7–8)

The British system of research support tended to reinforce "desultory and dull work on unimportant problems" (*E&S*, 136). Academics were regarded as intellectually and socially inferior to civil servants. Humdrum, mundane work for government was the norm, with the better academics providing rationalisations for government decisions or bright ideas for future use. Research money was available in "austere amounts" for socially useful applied projects and in larger amounts for applied projects demonstrably useful to government, such as the forecasting models of one of Harry's many British *bêtes noires*, the National Institute for Economic and Social Research, "which is essentially an indirect branch of government and produces virtually no economic research worthy of the name" (*E&S*, 136). As he concluded:

Britain has completely lost the reputation it established in the 1930s as the world centre for the serious study of economics, and its only hope of regaining its repute lies in the small group of its economists who belong to the American-based world community of highly qualified and research-oriented scholars. (*E&S*, 136)

As usual Canada was in an intermediate position. Society still had a colonial attitude to academics, who had an uneasy place in the national culture. Its economists had been well trained at American graduate schools

but of these a large number regard acquiring a Ph.D. as an initiation rite into adulthood of an extremely painful kind that does not have to be repeated, while those who have acquired the scientific research orientation find it has little payoff once they return to Canada. (*E&S*, 137)

The root of the problem lay in the slack tenure and promotion criteria where age and university service counted too much and in the absence of competition for high-profile individuals. Part of the problem lay with the government's demand for economists, which respected the technical training of the MA-holder or the all-but-dissertation (ABD) PhD candidate but regarded the PhD holder as "an awkward item to digest into the civil service apparatus" (*E&S*, 179). One result was a tendency for the ABD to become the standard of graduate aspiration and of academic appointment, making it difficult for universities to raise standards.

Nonetheless, research, often of high quality, got done. The practice of governments treating academic economists as hired professionals meant a steady demand for research from Royal Commissions or government departments, often with the right or even guarantee of publication and with sustained supervision and opportunities for association with other researchers. These supervised opportunities were often superior to those available in economists' home or graduate departments. But government support came at a price: Not only did it tend to consume rather than create intellectual capital, as Harry had noted in 1966 (see discussion in Chapter 11), but its dominance tended to set the standards for support from other agencies that supported research and diverted attention from theoretical or curiosity-driven research, "thus making the Canadian profession less independent and less interesting to economists in other countries than it could be" (*E&S*, 180).

It also had two specific deleterious effects on Canadian economics. It led to a "tendency of Canadian theorists to become competent combat troops in intellectual wars whose strategy is planned in other countries." It also led to another tendency that raised Harry's hackles

the temptation to Canadian academics with either insufficient professional competence by present standards or a taste for easy popularity among the masses to take the easy route of imitating and regurgitating the unscholarly and rabble-rousing pseudointellectual outpourings of their opposite numbers in foreign countries. . . . It would be extremely difficult to discern from the shallow and frequently near-psychotic writings of some Canadians employed in otherwise reputable economics departments, on such subjects as American investment in Canada and the destruction of pollution of the environment, that serious Canadian economics scholars have achieved world-wide professional recognition for their contributions to the economics of resource utilisation and of the multinational corporation. (*E&S*, 180)

THIRTEEN

Money and Inflation

My own scientific work, so far as the English end of it was concerned, lay in the field of monetary economics. My interests at Chicago had been in international trade theory, but the L.S.E. was well stocked, body-wise if not brain-wise, with teachers in that area, whereas no-one in Britain seemed aware of the 'monetarist counter revolution' that had been going on in the United States and in the scientifically active academic world generally and it seemed important to me that our own students should be instructed in post-*General Theory* developments and controversies.

1974 Memoir IV, 31

Hence the centrality to Harry of his MSc macroeconomics lectures at the School, eventually published as *Macroeconomics and Monetary Theory* (*MMT*, 1971d). However, there were a number of other strands in Harry's involvement in macroeconomics after 1966. As a result of his earlier concerns with money and economic growth and British worries about competition in banking, he got involved in discussions of efficiency in banking where he had a major effect on opinion. He continued to concern himself with the problem of inflation. He also tried to place Friedman's monetarism in some longer term perspective. Finally, under the stimulus of contemporary problems and theorising among his Chicago colleagues and students, he redeveloped a major interest in money and the balance of payments where he had made a pioneering contribution, "Towards a General Theory of the Balance of Payments," in the 1950s.

After 1966 Harry's thinking was in transition. The results would become clear in 1972 and 1973 with the publication of his first papers on the monetary approach to the balance of payments and his October 1971 de Vries Lectures *Inflation and the Monetarist Controversy* (*IMC*, 1972j). But during that period there was, as he admitted in his preface to his LSE lectures, a certain schizophrenia in his writings as he considered and reconsidered the changing face of monetary theory and his own place in it (*MMT*, iii).

In the same paragraph of the preface to his LSE lectures, Harry referred to Axel Leijonhufvud's *On Keynesian Economics and the Economics of Keynes: A Study in Monetary Theory* (1968). Leijonhufvud argued that Keynesian economics, especially as developed by Keynes's American followers and by the econometricians and forecasters, was quite different from Keynes's own macroeconomics, which was "deeply rooted in the preceding quantity theory tradition" (*MMT*, iii–iv).

Harry was very taken with the book. He put it on his reading list for his LSE lectures before publication as "a critical study of modern trends in macroeconomics" and a "stimulating complement" to more orthodox approaches. Harry arranged for Leijonhufvud to give two lectures on "Keynes and the Classics" at LSE in March 1969, which were subsequently published by the Institute of Economic Affairs (1969).[1] He also reviewed Leijonhufvud's book in *Encounter* (1970i).

Although he had some doubts as to "how far Leijonhufvud's re-reading of Keynes . . . [was] snatching at straws in order to prevent the breaking of the camel's back and to retain the beast as a working member of the caravan of progress" (*FEME*, 72), he accepted Leijonhufvud's basic misinterpretation hypothesis. He repeated it in his 1970 Ely Lecture, "The Keynesian Revolution and the Monetarist Counter-Revolution" (*Shadow*, 190), his preface to his LSE lecture notes (*MMT*, iv), his de Vries Lectures (*IMC*, 2) and many of his post-1971 papers where he rethought the evolution of monetary theory and Keynes's place in it, culminating in his 1976 Innis Lecture, "Keynes's *General Theory*: Revolution or War of Independence," where he also noted "that English Keynesianism, at the popular and policy level, is a creation of Oxford and not of Cambridge" – an echo of Leijonhufvud (*Shadow*, 242).

British Banking

Harry's renewed involvement in British monetary affairs and its longer term consequences was serendipitous. It originated before his return to England when in June 1966 the government asked the Prices and Incomes Board to investigate the system and level of the banks' charges to their customers in the light of their current levels of profits and dividends. As was usual in many of its references, the board turned to outside specialists – in this case The Economists' Advisory Group, a number of academic economists organised to take advantage of the money becoming available for private economic

---

[1] The fee for the Institute's Occasional Paper, arranged by Harry, was sufficient to cover Leijonhufvud's airfare and living expenses (Hoover Institution, Institute of Economic Affairs Papers, Box 99, Folder OP 30, "Keynes and the Classics," HGJ to Ralph Harris, 27 November 1968; HGJ to M. Mann, 15 January 1969).

advice. The chair of the board, Aubrey Jones, a former conservative minister as well as a governor and honorary fellow of LSE, was unhappy with the result and consulted Harry. On reading the report by E. Victor Morgan, Harry was stimulated. On 1 February 1967, he wrote some "Notes on a Proposed Research Project of the Welfare Loss from the Present Regulation of Interest Rates Paid on Charges by the Banking System" (Box 60, Manuscripts 1967). He followed this up with a four-page letter and eleven pages of detailed comments, characteristically written during a transatlantic flight.

> I agree that this is a very conservative and unimaginative document, on the whole. The reason is partly that the author is too responsible a citizen to contemplate questioning the present system of rigging the Treasury Bill market for the benefit of the Treasury and the Bank of England, and partly that, being a monetary economist, he asks a monetary economist's questions, which questions are superficial and misleading. (Box 60, Manuscripts 1967)

According to Harry, the letter resulted in an invitation to lunch with Jones and a fruitful discussion. It also resulted in a short "Note on the Required Cash and Liquidity Ratios as an Implicit Tax on the Clearing Banks," written on 27 April 1967 and presented to his LSE colleagues, one of whom, Brian Griffiths, "took it up and became an academic expert on it" (Griffiths 1970; 1974 Memoir IV, 32). Soon after this, on 27 May 1967, the Prices and Incomes Board report on bank charges appeared. Harry reviewed it favourably on 9 July – although chiding the board for its faint-heartedness and its failure to push its analysis to its logical conclusions – in *The Bankers' Magazine*. By this stage his fundamental position was clear.

> On grounds of economic efficiency ... what is required is to eliminate the special taxes on financial intermediation by banks, whether imposed by monetary regulations or by private monopolistic charging practices. In principle this would require not only the introduction of competition among the banks (eliminating private monopoly taxation), but also, and perhaps with much more significant quantitative effect, the termination of direct controls on bank assets, minimum liquid asset ratios, Special Deposits and cash reserve ratios, and the payment of a market rate of interest on Bankers' Deposits at the Bank of England. None of these changes would be inconsistent with the maintenance of effective powers of monetary control, since open market operations alone could perform the tasks of monetary management. (1967b, 66)

Nor was this the end of things. In January 1968 he prepared a major paper "Problems of Efficiency in Monetary Management" (1968e).[2] The paper was originally used for a lecture in Bonn and appeared first in *Kredit und Kapital*.

---

[2] In September 1973 he claimed that the paper was written in January 1967 (Box 39, Correspondence 1971–7, J–P, to Robert Nobay, 14 September). In his 1974 Memoir IV (32), Harry

It later formed part of a lecture at the University of Surrey and several other places before it appeared in the *Journal of Political Economy*.

The *JPE* paper drew together three bodies of literature – that concerned with the structural efficiency of the banking system "in the ordinary economic sense of the... system considered as an industry whose primary function... is to provide the means of payment for the economy"; that on optimal stabilisation policy; and that on "efficiency in secular economic policy... the choice of the desired level and trend over time of the major macroeconomic variables that reflect the economy's performance"(1968e, 972). It allowed Harry to bring together his recent contributions to British banking discussions, recent work by others on the use of stabilisation policy and his own work on money and growth models, as well as the still burgeoning literature on the possibility of a trade-off between inflation and unemployment as suggested by the Phillips curve, which for the purposes of this article he presumed to exist. It was a classic example of Harry's synthetic and expository powers that he could suggestively pull together material from several bodies of literature in twenty pages – and then add to it.

A related paper (1969d) got Harry involved in the optimum quantity of money literature to which Milton Friedman would also make a contribution in 1969.[3] Harry situated his contribution firmly in the literature of the role of money in a growing economy and its contribution to welfare, to which he had made a contribution in 1966 which, after criticism from James Tobin and suggestions from Alvin Marty and Milton Friedman, he had revised for his *Essays in Monetary Economics*. At least one observer found Harry's contribution "sets out all the essential results while managing to be the most readable paper on the subject" (Laidler 1984, 605). To Harry the welfare analysis was significant as a component to the case for a more competitive banking system and as a possible source of insights into possible reforms to the international monetary system, matters he had touched on in his 1968 *JPE* paper.

Money, Inflation, and Keynesian Economics

To follow the evolution of Harry's views while at LSE on the appropriate ways to treat inflation in theory and policy, we need a benchmark. Fortunately,

claimed he "wrote the paper in a day." The handwritten manuscript (Box 60, Manuscripts 1968) says it was written "Jan 17–28 off and on."

[3] The Friedman contribution is the title essay in Friedman 1969. Harry was somewhat unhappy with Friedman's contribution as he made clear in a survey later in 1969 (1970h), his unhappiness reflecting in part the difference in their publishing styles (*FEME*, 43; see also discussion in Chapter 17).

we can take a survey given in a lecture in Buenos Aires in the summer of 1963. There he had discussed the Keynesian and the monetarist theories of inflation as well as recent work on the Phillips curve, the relationship between the rate of unemployment and the rate of change in money wages discovered by his LSE colleague (Phillips 1958). He was uncomfortable with several aspects of Keynesian theory, most notably the absence of a theory of wage determination in Keynes's own work and the tendency for his successors to make arbitrary assumptions about wage and price behaviour and to ignore the fact that this behaviour would depend on expectations of the future as the inflationary process got under way, as well as assuming that their models were independent of the monetary environment. This meant they implicitly assumed that a permissive monetary policy would continue and avoided the need to consider how spending would be financed and how rising money incomes would affect the demand for money. In contrast, he argued that the quantity theory assumed

that in an inflation the economy becomes accustomed to the expectation of continued inflation, so that the processes of determining wages and prices are fundamentally real processes and not arbitrary processes determined exogenously. (*EME*, 122)

In this scheme of things, there was a stable demand for money in real terms and the rate of inflation represented the cost of holding real balances and affected the demand for the same. However, at this stage, he saw ambiguity in the evidence:

So far as substantial inflations are concerned, the evidence seems to favour the quantity theory approach over the Keynesian approach. For the mild type of inflation typical of the United States and other advanced countries, the approach has not proved nearly so useful. The theory implies the existence of a stable demand function for money in which the expected rate of inflation appears as an argument; but while many researchers have established the existence of satisfactorily stable demand functions, the expected rate of price change has not appeared as a significant determinant of the quantity demanded. (*EME*, 126)

As for the Phillips curve, he found it "new and very interesting." It substituted "an empirical relationship . . . for . . . vague literary and judgmental arguments." But he acknowledged "serious doubts" as to its applicability to policy. It was a statistical description resting on a simple model with little traditional theory behind it, and he doubted whether it would hold its shape "if an attempt were made by economic policy to pin the economy down to a point on it" (*EME*, 132–3). But he was attracted by the possibility of a trade-off between inflation and unemployment and cited the work of

Grant Reuber for the Porter Commission, which he had influenced and later published in the *JPE* (see discussion in Chapter 10).

He returned to the issue in his introduction to the second edition of *Essays in Monetary Economics* in May 1969, at the November 1969 conference at Hove marking the tenth anniversary of the Radcliffe *Report*, and in his 1969–70 LSE macroeconomics lectures. By then Edmund Phelps and Milton Friedman had both attacked the Phillips curve for ignoring the role of expectations in the wage-setting process. If inflation was fully anticipated in wage and price fixing, there was no permanent trade-off between unemployment and inflation. If the coefficient of the expected rate of inflation on wages was unity, the trade-off vanished and only one rate of unemployment, the "natural rate," was consistent with a constant rate of inflation.[4] At the same time, there had been further doubts about the "curve" as "an arbitrary and illegitimate linkage of the behaviour of the labour market under conditions of approximately full employment and of mass unemployment" (*FEME*, 46). In the introduction, he argued that the evidence suggested that the lags in the adjustments of expectations to experience were "sufficiently long for policy-makers safely to disregard them" (*EME*, 2nd ed., x). In the Hove paper he reported results from "a rather obscure source" where empirical evidence by Robert Solow "strongly" supported other evidence by Phillip Cagan that "[did] not refute" a coefficient for expected inflation well below unity (*FEME*, 47). Thus the trade-off appeared to be still alive if less favourable. His 1969–70 lectures followed his Hove paper but with more supporting evidence. In general the discussion was more "Keynesian" or Phillipsian. He developed the Solow model where people were rational and adjusted to inflation but subject to an element of money illusion that implied the existence of a long-run Phillips curve with some trade-off. He added a model by Albert Rees where there was a range of permanent unemployment rates given the transaction costs of adjusting real wage rates under inflationary conditions. In this situation one obtained a long-run Phillips curve with some trade-off (*MMT*, 159–61). He remained attached to that model in his "Comments on Inflation" in a November 1972 conference organised by Robert Mundell at the University of Waterloo (1975d, 149–51), where he concluded

The general conclusion to be drawn from all this is that . . . economists would be better advised to invest more economics in what was originally and remains a very crude model of the inflation unemployment problem. (151)

[4] E. S. Phelps, "Phillips Curves, Expectations of Inflation and Optimal Unemployment Over Time," *Economica* 24 (August 1967), 254–81; M. Friedman. "The Role of Monetary Policy," *American Economic Review*, 58 (March 1968), 1–17.

In 1970 and 1971 Harry wrote relatively little on inflation because he was more preoccupied with the international monetary system and its disintegration and, incidentally, with the early stages of the monetary approach to the balance of payments, which would carry the discussion of inflation in a new direction. One can see the transitional nature of his position in his introductory comment to *The Current Inflation*, the Money Study Group conference held in London on 22 February 1971.[5] In these comments Harry made three points. First, the apparent inability of large econometric models to deal with inflation might reflect the fact that levels of output and employment are the really important items for governments and firms to forecast. If this was the case, "the implication is that inflation is by no means as serious an economic problem ... as the conventional wisdom proclaims" (1971f, x). Second, the recent disintegration of the Phillips curve in Britain might reflect, or imply, that what the unions in Britain were after was

the increase in *real* wages that experience ... [had] taught them that they should be able to get given the normal rise in productivity, rather than the increase in *money* wages past experience has taught them they can get with a given level of overall pressure of demand for labour. (x)

Finally, British economists might have made a serious mistake in trying to explain British inflation by purely domestic factors, but they had been lucky in that neither domestic policies nor world events had brought external inflationary pressures into Britain.

By the fall of 1971 the transition had proceeded further. In the first of his de Vries Lectures, *Inflation and the Monetarist Controversy* (*IMC*) given in Amsterdam on 5 and 6 October, he announced that the monetarist position

that the real economy is inherently fairly stable, but can be destabilised by monetary developments, which therefore need to be controlled as far as possible by intelligent monetary policy ... seems to me the only alternative consistent with the facts (as distinct from the myths) of historical experience. (*IMC*, 7)

He reported that he had

arrived at this judgement, not by dogmatic conviction, but out of growing dissatisfaction with the explanatory power of the theories and the empirical results in which I was instructed during my youth at the two centres of the [Keynesian] revolution. (7)

---

[5] The first version of the monetary approach to the balance of payments was given in Geneva on 5 February but it was substantially revised and extended before publication (see discussion later in this chapter).

He spent much of the remainder of this lecture making the argument that recent work on the costs of inflation and the role of money in growth models had resulted "in a strong case for stability in the trend of prices . . . but a very weak case . . . for the pursuit of a zero price trend (price stability) as a major goal of economic policy" (35–6).

In his second lecture he turned to the theory of inflation, noting that

the accepted theory of inflation and of anti-inflationary policy up until the Keynesian revolution was firmly based on the quantity theory of money. The Keynesian revolution, at least in the English-language countries, destroyed the intellectual credentials of that approach – which has only painfully and slowly been restored to academic respectability in the past fifteen years and especially in the last five – and created an intellectual vacuum that had to be filled by new construction when inflation again became a problem during and after the Second World War. (*IMC*, 51)

Since the early postwar period, Keynesian theory "produced only one significant contribution to monetary analysis – the Phillips curve" (58), but that empirical rather than theoretical relationship had become increasingly suspect for three reasons. The first was that it was a statistical artifact linking incompatible periods of full employment and depression. The second was that the theory behind the Phillips curve was "about the crudest and least sophisticated possible explanation of the dynamics of economic models" where price adjustment was dominated by excess demand and supply in one market, the labour market, irrespective of developments in other markets, and that a single theory could comprehend real and relative price adjustments that were assumed identical. Finally, the relationship seemed "to have broken down completely in the face of the inflationary facts of the past two years or so" (59).[6] Then after mentioning the postwar revival of the quantity theory approach through the work of Friedman and his students, with the recent supporting leadership of Allan Meltzer and Karl Brunner, he described the rise of monetarism, its "staged" (61) empirical victory over Keynesianism and Friedman's use of the 1968 AEA presidential address to restate the essence of his critique: Monetary policy can control monetary magnitudes and not real magnitudes, which are determined by the

---

[6] Nonetheless, he was still prepared, as he was earlier at the Money Study Group's Hove Conference and a year later in a paper delivered to a seminar at the University of Waterloo, to commend recent attempts to enrich the model. However, by August 1974 he was telling D. F. Gordon: "I've changed my mind a lot on the Phillips curve. I now think that it was an unjustified steal from mathematical dynamics, with the implicit and money-removing assumption of a fixed stock of commodity money, or alternatively of nominal money, and it got its appeal because it was the first econometrics since the consumption function that seemed to tell us something important" (Box 51, Correspondence 1972–7, 13 August).

real forces operating in the economy. However, he thought that monetarism would be only briefly triumphant. Monetarists exaggerated the potency of monetary restraint as a means of stopping inflation in terms of the amount and duration of unemployment. It was not that monetarism was wrong but the political process attached a low cost to inflation and a high cost to unemployment. The result had been theoretical and empirical counterattacks. But, although monetarism was important, "the particular formulation of the monetarist position embodied in the past works of Milton Friedman is not in fact tolerably consistent with the empirical evidence." Moreover,

at the level of abstract monetary theory, Friedman has recently attempted to fill the gap in the empirical applicability of the quantity theory left by his restatement of that theory as a theory of the demand for money, with no implications as to the relative magnitudes of the effect of monetary impulses on money prices and real quantities of output, with results that in my judgment come very close to returning monetary theory to the position reached in Franco Modigliani's classic article of 1944. (66–7)

In other words, he might have said, "This is where I came in."

In his conclusion he made it clear that he had not become a monetarist of the Friedman variety:

The results [of recent work] . . . should be to free both Keynesians and Friedmanians from the obligations of loyalty to what they believe their master's words . . . and to permit monetary theorists to concentrate on the full range of diverse individual insights into monetary phenomena on the understanding of the pressing problems that confront us – which concern the short-run dynamics of an economic system in which money has an undeniable long-run determining influence. (67)

On 29 April 1973, Harry sat down to write a paper for a volume of *Essays on John Maynard Keynes* (1975) that Keynes's nephew Milo Keynes was preparing for Cambridge University Press. Harry's "Keynes and British Economics" accepted Keynes as an important figure in the history of economics, but his take differed from before.

Had the policy-makers of the 1930s really understood what was occurring in the international monetary system and their own part in it, or had the economists of the time understood it (as they could have done by developing available monetary theory) and explained it effectively, the great depression of the 1930s would have been nipped in the bud and the *General Theory* either not written, or perceived as one eccentric English economist's rationalization of his local problems. (*Shadow*, 207)

But monetary economists, including the Keynes of *A Treatise on Money*, although concerned with the shorter-term problem of the "conditions of monetary equilibrium," maintained the traditional assumption of full employment that they had used in discussion of the longer term – the assumption successfully challenged in the *General Theory*, whose

> importance from the long-range point of view of the development of economics... lies not in its refutation of a classical "orthodoxy" but in its application of capital theory to the theory of the demand for money and the stimulus it provided to study the dynamics of price and quantity adjustments to changes in aggregate demand. (*Shadow*, 212)

Harry's de Vries Lectures marked the end of his contributions to traditional macroeconomics, as he devoted more of his time to the monetary approach to the balance of payments. He did, however, provide one survey article for a Money Study Group conference in 1973 (1974f) and wrote a substantial paper with Robert Nobay (1977f) where he extended some of his comments in his de Vries Lectures and his contribution to Milo Keynes's volume, in addition to a brief (1976g) note on Thomas Mayer's article "The Structure of Monetarism." In the first, he repeated his de Vries Lecture comments about Friedman's monetary theorising (1974f, 219), while in the second he quoted with approval Franco Modigliani's 1976 suspicion that monetarism was an "appeal for turning back the clock 40 years" (1977f, 470).

What he was trying to do, particularly in the *Journal of Economic Literature* piece with Nobay, was to get some historical perspective on contemporary theoretical discussions, as well as his own theoretical position, and to situate them in terms of an interwar discussion which had included Robertson, Hayek, the Swedes, and the Keynes of *A Treatise on Money*, before the publication of *The General Theory* sent discussions off in another direction. This was not the first time that he had brought an historical perspective to his surveys – that had always been one of their strengths – but the attempt here was more provocative. There was a similar attempt at perspective in his June 1976 Innis Lecture to the Canadian Economics Association, "Keynes's *General Theory*: Revolution or War of Independence?" (1976i), but it had the added twist of looking more closely at the evolution of "Keynesian economics" in all its varieties over the previous forty years. The conclusion in the lecture was, not surprisingly given his piece in the 1975 Milo Keynes collection, that Keynes's change had been a war of independence rather than simply a revolutionary change of personnel at the top.

> [I]n the long perspective of the development of monetary theory... the so-called Keynesian Revolution has to be viewed as the third stage of the evolution of the theory of a monetary (and capitalist) economy. (*Shadow*, 236)

In its first stage, the classical economists elucidated "the nature of the economic system as a coherent, interdependent system that tended towards an equilibrium of price and quantity variables" (*Shadow*, 236–7). In that system the chief function of monetary theory was to demonstrate the neutrality of money – the purpose of the quantity theory. In the second stage monetary economists "shifted from demonstrating the neutrality of money to investigating the conditions under which money would be neutral – . . . the conditions of monetary equilibrium" (*Shadow*, 237). This line of thinking was stopped by the success of the Keynesian revolution and only began to be recovered in the later 1960s. Keynes's contribution in the *General Theory* then became the replacement of a price-adjustment mechanism with a quantity-adjustment mechanism, a narrower contribution than the one he had suggested in 1973. However, Keynes's removal from professional action by a heart condition in 1937 left the way open for a different enterprise, which obliterated Keynes's alternative "war of independence." In this other endeavour money came not to matter, and the original Keynesian model became crystallized in the IS–LM formulation of Hicks and Hansen. This stage culminated in the "Keynesian synthesis," which accepted full employment as a policy objective as well as the Keynesian model, but admitted that the notion of "unemployment equilibrium" rested on either an approximation of wage rigidity or some other "peculiar and not seriously defensible behavioral assumptions" (*Shadow*, 243).

Over the ensuing decades, the work of Tobin, Patinkin, and Friedman consolidated and extended "the new theoretical approaches and insights provided by Keynes the monetary theorist" (*Shadow*, 243). This consolidation and synthesis with the insights of Keynes's predecessors had been succeeded by a period of questioning of the usefulness of both the Keynesian and the monetarist approaches. This had produced a number of responses, the Cambridge, post-Keynesian one being that

the spirit of revolution . . . needs to be revived by a denunciation of the bastards and a return to the pure principles and noble spirit of the original revolution (as remembered, reconstructed or invented by the saved survivors and elect descendants of the disciples).[7] (*Shadow*, 248)

---

[7] Incidentally in this paper Harry forgot (*Shadow*, 246n) that the term "bastard Keynesian" dated not from a Joan Robinson paper of 1975, "What Has Become of the Keynesian Revolution?" but rather from its original source of her review of his own *Money, Trade and Economic Growth*, in particular his "The General Theory after Twenty-Five Years," in the *Economic Journal* for September 1962 (see discussion in Chapter 10).

Obviously, Harry did not endorse this approach, He thought that the *General Theory*

> involved a process of looking past the models and the problems of pure theory to the real world to which theory claimed to be a scientific guide, recognizing a glaring gap between the assumptions and hypothetical economy of the models and the actual behaviour of the models and the actual behaviour of the real world, and attempting to remedy the deficiency by redesigning the machinery of theory while thriftily cannibalizing those component parts that remained useful. (*Shadow*, 248)

The present discontents of monetary economics required more such attempts to define problems as they really were and trying to solve them.

Revolution and Counterrevolution

In 1970, as president-elect of the American Economic Association, James Tobin invited Harry to give the Association's Richard T. Ely Lecture. They agreed on the topic, "The Keynesian Revolution and the Monetarist Counter-Revolution" (1971a), a subject Harry had been thinking about for some years even though "the actual writing took only a few days" (Box 38, Journal of International Economics, to J. Bhagwati, 26 March 1971; see also Encounter, to M. Lasky, 12 January 1971). He gave a preliminary version of the lecture, under the title "The Monetarist Revolution" on 7 April 1970 at the AUTE meetings in Belfast (Leeson 2000, 747). What he was concerned with in the lecture were "the social and intellectual conditions that make a revolution or counter-revolution possible" in economics (*FEME*, 66). In particular he was concerned with the rate of diffusion of the two revolutions. In tackling this question he found it useful

> to adopt the "as if" approach of positive economics, as espoused by the chief protagonist of the monetarist counter-revolution, Milton Friedman, and to ask: suppose I wanted to start a counter-revolution against the Keynesian revolution in monetary theory, how would I go about it – and specifically, what could I learn about the technique from the revolution itself? To pose the question in this way is, of course, to fly in the face of currently accepted professional ethics, according to which purely scientific considerations and not political considerations are presumed to motivate scientific work; but I can claim the protection of the "as if" methodology against any implication of a slur on individual character or a denigration of scientific work. (52–3)

He proceeded to set out what was needed in terms of the objective social situation in which the new theory was proposed and the characteristics of the new theory. As for the first, one needed an established orthodoxy that was inconsistent with contemporary reality yet sufficiently confident of its explanatory power to try to explain reality and expose its own difficulties. To displace this old orthodoxy, the new theory would have to offer a convincing explanation of the difficulties and offer a set of policy prescriptions based on that explanation. But to win intellectual acceptance and policy success, it would have five characteristics. First, it would have to attack a central proposition of the old orthodoxy. Second, although it had to appear new, it had to absorb as much as possible of the nondisputed aspects of the old theory. Third, the

new theory had to be so difficult to understand that senior academic colleagues would find it neither easy nor worthwhile to study, so that they would waste their efforts on peripheral issues, and so offer themselves as easy marks for the criticism by their younger and hungrier colleagues. At the same time, the new theory had to appear both intellectually difficult to challenge the intellectual interest of younger colleagues and students, but actually easy enough for them to master adequately with a sufficient investment of intellectual endeavour. (55)

Fourth, it had to offer a new methodology, which was more appealing than those currently available. Finally, it had to offer important empirical relationships for testing.

He argued that by the mid-1950s Keynesianism had become an orthodoxy as ripe for attack as "classical economics" had been for Keynes and his followers in the 1930s. But to mount a counterrevolution one would have to find an important social problem that orthodoxy could not solve and to develop a counterrevolutionary theory that could be academically successful. In Harry's view the first stage was to emphasise inflation as the problem. In this the counterrevolutionaries had mixed success, though they were aided by the Keynesians overreaching themselves when they tried to deal with inflation by Keynesian means. They were also aided by the professionalisation of economics which made it "increasingly possible for an issue to be deemed scientifically interesting and worthy of investigation even if the general public displays no visible interest in it" (60). The other pillars of the counterrevolution were defending the proposition that money does matter; stating the quantity theory of money as a generalisation of Keynes's theory of liquidity preference on a more sophisticated basis and emphasising the Fisherine distinction between real and nominal rates of interest and relating them to the expected rate of inflation; invoking the methodology of positive economics and emphasising "the crucial relationships that permit one to predict something large from something small, regardless of the intervening chain of causation . . . [offering] liberation to the small-scale intellectual"; and providing in the demand for money "an empirical relationship, suitable for determined estimation by the budding econometrician" (62). However the counterrevolution had to go one stage further and establish an intellectual continuity with the past that had been disrupted by the original revolution. In part this involved "the invention of a University of Chicago oral tradition that was alleged to have preserved understanding of the fundamental truth among a small band of the initiated during the dark years of the Keynesian despotism" (64). But, he continued, citing the work of Don Patinkin:

There was no lonely light constantly burning in a secret shrine on the Midway, encouraging the faithful to assemble in waiting for the day when the truth could safely be revealed to the masses; that candle was made, and not merely lit, only when the light had a chance of penetrating far and wide and attracting new converts to the old time religion. (65)

He also, using Patinkin, criticised the monetarists'

careful combing of the obiter dicta of the great neoclassical quantity theorists for bits of evidence that showed recognition (or could be interpreted to show recognition) of the fact that to hold money involves a choice between holding money and holding wealth in other forms. (64)

He accused Friedman of "scholarly chicanery"(65).[8]

Friedman was outraged, but when offered a chance to comment on Harry's lecture when it was reprinted in *Encounter*, he declined, noting that "I am strongly tempted to comment not so much with respect to the substantive issues as to what I think is a serious misstatement about the oral tradition of Chicago" (Box 38, Encounter, Friedman to M. Lasky, 16 April 1971). He did take a passing shot at Harry in a reply to Patinkin's discussion of his "A Theoretical Framework for Monetary Analysis" (1969b) – "Friedman on the Quantity Theory and Keynesian Economics" (1972) – as well as his "The Chicago Tradition, the Quantity Theory and Friedman" (1969) when he referred to "the even more misleading discussion of that tradition by Harry Johnson in his Ely Lecture" (1972, 907). In an early draft of his

---

[8] When he first read Patinkin's 1969 piece on Friedman, which he referred to as a "hatchet job," he referred Patinkin to a 1963 *Public Finance* review of *Capitalism and Freedom* by Hugh Folk, which mentioned Friedman's "inexhaustible store of hypothetical history." He continued, "You have shown him to be a crook and I accept that, but I can't help thinking he has been not only clever but also useful" (Duke University, Patinkin Papers, 27 September 1969). Folk had two references to Friedman and history, referring to his "secret stores of historical truth" and his "[d]rawing on his wealth of hypothetical history" (1963, 207, 208). Harry had written for an offprint of the review (Box 56, Correspondence 1964–6, A–L, to Hugh Folk, 22 April 1964).

reply, he called Harry's Ely Lecture a "libel," but he reluctantly removed the term on the advice of Robert Clower (among others) (Box 38, from R. A. Gordon, 28 January 1972; Clower Papers, Box 4, M. Friedman to R. W. Clower, 15 March 1972). Clower himself remarked that Harry's

> rather juvenile interpretation might best be regarded as a bit of high spirits dictated by his desire to appear more independent of your influence than some of his friends suspect (I should call them his enemies, I guess!). (Duke University, Clower Papers, Box 4, R. W. Clower to M. Friedman, 5 April 1972)[9]

The Monetary Approach

As already noted, from 1971 a new strand of analysis began to appear in Harry's work, first in lectures and later in publications: the monetary approach to the balance of payments. Its coming had been presaged for a year or two. In an after-dinner speech at Monash University on 16 September 1969, he had noted that "work has only just begun on the development of a neo-quantity theory approach to the policy problems of an open economy and the international monetary system" (1971g, 8–9).[10] In his 1969–70 LSE lectures he concluded with a discussion of "the monetary standard and international monetary theory" that included a brief discussion of a "monetary approach to devaluation," which assumed a high degree of substitutability between goods produced in different countries and which yielded different results from the "traditional theory" (*MMT*, 182–4).[11] The new theory's first public appearance was in a lecture in Geneva in February 1971. The paper purporting to be that lecture[12] was actually written some months later. As

---

[9] The earlier and subsequent literature has been brought together with an essay reassessing the debate by Robert Leeson (2003).

[10] The only reference to the literature at that point was to Robert Mundell's paper "Real Gold, Dollars and Paper Gold" delivered at the 1968 meetings of the American Economic Association (1969).

[11] The only reference to the literature in the reading list was to S. J. Prais, "Some Mathematical Notes on the Quantity Theory of Money in an Open Economy"(1961), which he and Jacob Frenkel would later refer to as one of the "significant but at the time unappreciated contributions to the revival and refinement of the monetary approach" in "a short-lived burst of theoretical interest at the International Monetary Fund" – a statement that was inaccurate (IMF 1977; Polak 2002).

[12] "The Monetary Approach to Balance of Payments Theory" first appeared in *Further Essays in Monetary Economics* (1972). It later appeared in M. B. Connolly and A. K. Swoboda (eds.), *International Economics: The Geneva Essays* (1973) and in *The Monetary Approach to the Balance of Payments* (1976).

Harry told Alexander Swoboda (Box 41, Commitments Completed, 1971, 26 July 1971)

The text of the lecture I gave in Geneva last February is now at last in the process of being typed. I hope to be able to send it to you this week. I rewrote it more or less completely, and I think it is now much more useful – in fact, I think I could use the general approach for a lot more problems, such as the optimal provision of SDRs.

The ideas were also floated at conferences in Paris in March, Bergedorf in June, and Kingston in July. In the autumn they got another airing in his de Vries Lecture, "The Monetarist Approach to Stabilisation Policy in an Open Economy," with due acknowledgement of the Dutch contributions to the theory, most notably in Robert Mundell's work at the IMF under Jacques Polak (*IMC* 84).[13]

The coincidence of his writing his first monetary approach paper and his Ely Lecture highlights an aspect of this new development that differed from Harry's previous work. This time, he seemed to want to make his own mark and firmly stake his claim to fame. His 1958 "A General Theory of the Balance of Payments" (see discussion in Chapter 6) became the "basic article" for the revival of the new approach (*MABP*, 10). With the monetary approach came the International Monetary Research Programme at LSE – the first large-scale grant-supported theoretical and empirical programme of research that Harry had ever mounted. Parallel to the programme at LSE, with Alexander Swoboda as his co-investigator, he and his Chicago colleagues and students prepared two related volumes of papers, both edited with Jacob Frenkel, *The Monetary Approach to the Balance of Payments* (1976j) and *The Economics of Exchange Rates* (1978c). He also, much more so than in the past, made repeated attempts to spread the word in various fora with simplified versions of the approach: "The Monetary Approach to the Balance of Payments: A Diagrammatic Analysis" (1975c), "Money and the Balance of Payments" (1976b), "Elasticity, Absorption, Keynesian Multiplier, Keynesian Policy and Monetarist Approaches to Devaluation Theory: A Simple Geometric Exposition" (1976e), "The Monetary Approach to the Balance of Payments Theory and Policy: Explanation and Policy Implications" (1977g), and "The Monetary Approach to the Balance of Payments: A Non-Technical Guide" (1977h) (the last carefully arranged to appear alongside Frank Hahn's review of the first Frenkel and Johnson volume in the *Journal of International Economics*).

[13] Harry's original proposed title to Jan Tinbergen for that lecture had been "Monetary Aspects of Balance of Payments Theory and Policy" (Box 41, Commitments Completed 1971, 27 June 1971).

Moreover, in this case as in no other, he, or rather his chief lieutenant, Jacob Frenkel, sought to give the new approach an historical pedigree – one that stretched back to Isaac Gervaise (1720) and moved forward in the writings of, among others, Richard Cantillon, David Hume, David Ricardo, John Stuart Mill, J. Laurence Lauchlin, Knut Wicksell, Ralph Hawtrey, and the early Keynes.[14] The message was clear: balance-of-payments theory was returning to tried and true ways after the diversions and excitements of the Keynesian revolution and, incidentally, the international economic disintegration of the interwar period – a line of argument not dissimilar to the Friedman attribution of a Chicago lineage to his revival of the quantity theory of money that Harry had derided in his Ely Lecture.[15]

Recall from the Ely Lecture that for Harry a successful counterrevolution required "an important social problem that the established orthodoxy is incapable of dealing with" and a theory that had "the requisite characteristics to be academically and professionally successful in replacing the previous revolutionary theory" (*FEME*, 56). The theory had to attack a central proposition of the existing orthodoxy; it had to appear to be new; it had to be difficult to understand; it had to offer a methodology more appealing than that currently available; and it had to provide new and crucial empirical relationships for testing.

In the case of the monetary approach, the major claim was that as the balance of payments was a monetary phenomenon, balance-of-payments imbalances should be analysed using the tools of monetary theory rather than those of trade theory. As he put it in the LSE application to SSRC for funding for his large-scale International Monetary Research Programme:

The main ideas on which the approach rests are that payments imbalances are the outcome of a stock-adjustment process between actual and desired stocks of real cash balances (or more generally financial and real assets) and that the impact of payments imbalances on the domestic monetary system is the driving force in

---

[14] In addition to their joint piece (Frenkel and Johnson 1976j), there were also Frenkel's "A Monetary Approach to the Exchange Rate: Doctrinal Aspects and Empirical Evidence," *Scandinavian Journal of Economics*, 78 (May 1976), 200–23; "Adjustment Mechanisms and the Monetary Approach to the Balance of Payments: A Doctrinal Perspective" in E. M. Classen and P. Salin (eds.), *Recent Issues in International Monetary Economics*, Amsterdam: North Holland, 1976, 29–48.

[15] The emphasis on Hume brought a critical study of Frenkel and Johnson by Dieter Fausten (1979), which concluded that "the manifest dissimilarities in analytical detail between Humean and contemporary monetary approaches serve to the serious student of balance of payments analysis as an uncomfortable reminder of the scathing irony with which Johnson . . . appraised the verisimilitude of the parallel claim, made on behalf of monetarism, to orthodox content and sanction"(672).

the adjustment process under fixed exchange rates. A natural by-product of this type of analysis is the emphasis put on the rate of domestic credit expansion as a main determinant of payments imbalances and of the effectiveness of exchange rate changes.

In developing the new approach, its proponents made a number of new assumptions – of "a high (often perfect) degree of substitutability in consumption of goods produced in various countries, of full employment, and in a dynamic context, of exogenously given growth rates and full adjustment of expected to actual equilibrium rates of inflation." There was also, as John Helliwell and Peter Jonson noted, a switch from "the search for and exposition of more complete theoretical models to the use of a highly simplified version of the monetary approach to the balance of payments" (1977, S82n).

The new theory was also difficult, for he claimed it

represents a transfer to the international monetary area of sophisticated concepts and techniques of analysis developed initially in closed-economy monetary theory, particularly by Lange and Patinkin, on the basis of Hicksian general equilibrium analysis, and involving what may be called Walrasian "tâtonnement" dynamics in contrast to the multiplier concepts of post-Keynesian balance-of-payments theory, as well as a preference for the recently popular analytical framework of equilibrium growth models. . . . In consequence, the student reared in the traditional Keynesian international monetary theory has to master a great deal of unfamiliar analysis before he can get to grips with the new approach and its differences from and common ground with the Keynesian approach. (1975c, 220–1)

The new approach naturally needed empirical testing. There had to be tests of the economic structure implied by the model, for example the validity of the assumption of a world price level and a world level of interest rates, which were tackled in the work of Genberg and McCloskey and Zecher in *The Monetary Approach to the Balance of Payments*. There were also attempts to construct and fit models of particular economies – one of the "most ambitious" being the large LSE programme using state-of-the-art econometric techniques for "a model of the U.K. economy incorporating the U.K. financial sector and using econometric techniques for translating discontinuous time observations into a continuous time of economic reality" (1977h, 264). Then, of course, there was the doctrinal-historical pedigree mentioned earlier.

The approach "explained" a number of contemporary economic problems: the unexpectedly long, drawn out and difficult adjustment of the British economy to the devaluation of sterling in November 1967, the similar experience of the United States after the Nixon measures of August 1971, and the origins of the worldwide inflation of the late 1960s and early

1970s. It also produced a number of paradoxes: that the 1960s preoccupation with a possible shortage of international liquidity was "an exact inversion of the real problem of the system" (*IMC*, 86); that the new reserve assets, such as the SDR, "would simply accelerate the pace of world inflation" (87); that under fixed exchange rates countries' attempts to reduce inflation through fiscal and monetary restraint will "wind up with the worst of all possible results, unabated inflation combined with unemployment of men and productive capacity" (88).

Harry and his collaborators were "adversarial" in tone when discussing the new approach (Helliwell 1968, S63). Harry 'departed from the more judicious and sceptical approach to various theories of his earlier years' (Corden, 2004). John Helliwell (1978, S64n) commented on "the extent to which an air of controversy is built up by reference to un-named detractors who are said to have made extreme counterclaims" and the "departure from the well-referenced and careful academic style that is usually a hallmark of Harry Johnson's exposition of balance-of-payments issues" – a remark directed explicitly at the unreferenced introductory section of the Frenkel and Johnson paper in *The Monetary Approach*, with its discussion of unnamed critics and red herrings and "so much stress ... placed ... on the extent to which the monetary approach differs from what is described without much supporting detail as the traditional approach" (1978, S64).

Harry had high hopes for the new approach that "will alter the whole course of development of the subject" (Box 47, Allen and Unwin, to C. Furth, 4 September 1973). It certainly made a splash: A 1978 survey listed 121 relevant publications (Kreinin and Officer 1978), most of which had appeared since Harry's 1971 lecture. The approach became part of the literature and fodder, therefore, for textbooks – usually with explicit warnings about its usefulness in analysing economic problems (Krugman and Obstfeld 2000, 524–5; Kenen 2000a, Chapter 17; Kreinin, 2002, Chapter 15; Yarborough and Yarborough 2002, 540–70).

In many respects Harry was unlucky with the monetary approach. His health broke down in 1972–3. At the meetings of the American Economic Association in Toronto in December 1972 he came down with an acute case of jaundice and was hospitalised for several weeks. Then on 16 October 1973 in Venice he suffered a stroke. He was not back in London until early November where he remained in University College Hospital until the turn of the year.

And there were unexpected developments in the international monetary system. The original discussions, the Frenkel–Johnson volume and the Johnson–Swoboda proposal to SSRC all took place as the Bretton Woods system collapsed into a world of floating exchange rates. This collapse meant that the puzzle the approach was intended to explain – balance-of-payments imbalances – ceased to be the centre of concern. Instead analysts were set the task of explaining the behaviour of floating exchange rates, which was something that the approach could in principle do. But it took time to readjust: The successor Frenkel and Johnson volume, *The Economics of Exchange Rates*, did not appear until 1978, although many of the papers it contained were first presented at a conference on "Flexible Exchange Rates and Stabilization Policy" held in Stockholm in the summer of 1975 – a conference Harry did not attend.

The collapse of Bretton Woods meant that as far as the LSE monetary research programme was concerned "we were stuck with a project design one stage behind where the action now lay and where we could and would have been if we had written off Britain and devoted the same planning efforts to a Continent-based project" (1974 Memoir IV, 35). Harry was annoyed that SSRC had not informed him until mid-May 1973 that the application had been successful and that he was then warned not to spend any money (even for advertisements) until official approval came from LSE in mid-June.[16] This made it difficult to recruit personnel. Moreover, as he told Robin Matthews:

I was a lot more interested in it [the research programme] last year when it was fresh than I will be by the time, having already sweated out one year of waiting, I sweat out another six months to a year of trying to find staff and get the thing going. By the time we get going, the international monetary system will probably have been substantially changed – it is already obvious that the research interest of the future should be floating exchange rates with special reference to capital movements. (Box 49, SSRC, 5 July 1973)

Nor did his problems end with the SSRC – there were difficulties with LSE, particularly over released time for LSE staff members Malcolm Knight and Clifford Wymer (Box 49, International Monetary Research Programme, from Alan Day, 6 July 1973; to Walter Adams, 11 July 1973) and space for the non-LSE staff participants, who at one stage looked likely to be offered space in Wardour Street, a half hour's walk from the School (Box 39, International

---

[16] In his original application he had put 1 May 1973 as his starting date for research before which he would have selected and hired with "preliminary contracts (pending a final decision on the SSRC grant)." Even then, however, he had remarked that "it will probably not be possible to staff the project fully before September in view of the grant decision date." In the end the programme did not begin until 1 October 1973 (Box 51, Geneva Institute General, short summary of application for £76,535 over 3 years).

Monetary Research Programme, from Lois Rogers, 4 June 1973). David Laidler, who led the SSRC visitation to LSE on the project remembers

there were times . . . when I felt as if there had been a role-reversal between LSE and SSRC reps. whereby we assumed the task of convincing them that Harry's application was worth supporting. Walter Adams seemed particularly sceptical, and when he was asked explicitly about the availability of offices for staff and visitors should it receive funding, he declared himself unable to promise anything. (Communication to author, 27 December 2004)

Moreover, many of Harry's LSE colleagues were unsympathetic. Robert Nobay whom he unsuccessfully tried to recruit from Southampton reported that "I was getting a fair amount of negative feedback from my LSE friends and acquaintances to realise that my role on the project could turn out to be a little counter-productive" (Box 39, International Monetary Research Programme, 16 May 1973). In the end Harry

got three good people from around the U.K., and one of my Chicago students who was interested in taking a year off from there and starting his Ph.D. We also had as unofficial assistants, Peter Jonson from Australia and Henry Kierzkowski from Queen's University in Canada. (1974 Memoir IV, 39)

Publishing *The Monetary Approach*

There also had been delays and problems with the collection of theoretical and empirical papers on the monetary approach from his colleagues and students in Chicago that Harry put together with Jacob Frenkel. Harry had first raised the possibility of a "symposium on The Monetary Approach to Balance of Payments Theory" in a handwritten letter to Charles Furth of Allen and Unwin in January 1972. Furth was not overly enthusiastic.

The symposium . . . sounds interesting and important, but we are getting rather too many symposia (resulting from all those conferences) and we are frightened at the awful prices we are having to put on books nowadays. (Box 47, Allen and Unwin, 25 January 1972)

Furth wanted to know more about the book's length before he made a formal commitment. Nothing further happened until Harry's sabbatical at Yale, when he and Jacob Frenkel put the book together although they had not yet asked for permission to publish from the contributors (Box 39, Correspondence 1974–7, I–O, to R. Mundell, 30 August 1973). They then tried University of Chicago Press as a possible publisher. Chicago received a favourable report from A. C. Harberger but decided it did not want edited collections of essays (Box 47, Allen and Unwin, to Charles Furth, 4 September

1973). In September 1973 Harry raised the matter again with Allen and Unwin, promising a manuscript by mid-October. Allen and Unwin accepted but were still unhappy with symposia and as a result offered a profit-sharing rather than a royalty contract (Box 47, Allen and Unwin, from C. Furth, 17 September, 11 October, and 15 December 1973).[17] By the time Harry received the contract, he had suffered his stroke in Venice. There were delays in getting him back to London for medical care and months before he was back in action with either the LSE programme or anything else.

Harry's stroke meant his resignation from LSE, as "it made me realise that I was wasting my time thanklessly on a lone battle against British academic ineptitude" (Box 47, Allen and Unwin, to C. Firth, 13 June 1974). His resignation meant the end of any administrative involvement in the LSE programme – though that had effectively ceased with his stroke, when Clifford Wymer "responded ably and effectively" to the "administrative burden, and the irritations of arguing with the School" (1974 Memoir IV, 39). However, as David Laidler reported after a SSRC site visit: "It seems to be running very well indeed, but there are questions about how much enthusiasm there is outside the programme but within the School for the work that is being done" (Box 39, Correspondence 1974–7, J–P, 18 July 1974). Harry remained in intellectual contact with the programme, but his paper on his involvement, which he gave to a May 1976 Conference designed to showcase its achievements, "Money in the Open Economy: A Historical and Analytical Survey" (Box 8), suggested "that he still felt uneasy about the empirical aspects of research" (Helliwell 1978, S82). Harry was still working on the proceedings of that conference when he suffered his 1977 stroke (Box 49, SSRC, to Ian Miller, 27 January 1977). As Clifford Wymer's health failed about the same time, the volume was never completed.

The first book with Jacob Frenkel finally appeared in 1976. The process of publication so enraged Harry that he virtually ended his relationship of almost twenty years with Allen and Unwin. There were probably faults on both sides, but the major villain of the piece was the rapid escalation of publishing costs in Britain as inflation soared to over 25 percent per annum in 1975 – compounded by Allen and Unwin's difficulties in finding a co-publisher to share some of the composition costs and thus help to keep

---

[17] "In that it is a profit (but not a loss) sharing contract, it reflects the increasing difficult[y] which we, apparently like Chicago University Press, have in selling collections of papers, simply because there are too many of them on the market nowadays and the good suffer with the bad" (11 October 1973).

down the U.K. price. The preface had been dated May 1974. In January 1975 Harry tried to hurry Allen and Unwin along:

We are particularly annoyed about this delay because we have known all along that the International Monetary Fund was planning to publish a collection of its staff members' contributions in this area, including recent empirical work, which they can do on a larger scale than we can. They have the advantage of their own press with short printing delay, and it turns out that their book will have the same title as ours. (Box 47, Allen and Unwin, to Michael Holdsworth, 2 January 1975)

By March 1975, Charles Furth was thoroughly depressed:

The thing has gone so cold and one is so depressed that we should be happy to turn it in and hand over all the editorial work to somebody else, presumably a university press in the circumstances, unless there is a hope of a more or less equal sharing of the burden on what is an Anglo-American book with an American publisher. (Box 47, Allen and Unwin, 3 March)

Harry was enraged. As he told David Morgan:

I must say that I am pretty fed up with Allen & Unwin. I and a colleague have a contract for a book on a hot subject, a new theory of the balance of payments that is sweeping the civilized world. The book contains some classic articles on the subject, and some pioneering empirical work done here in Chicago. The demand is there – among other things, at a recent Midwest meeting, a colleague who wanted to put it on a reading list for fifty graduate students asked about it. The contract was signed a year and a half ago; now it is being suggested that we take the book away and start all over again with another publisher. I do not see why I should even bother to discuss any work I might do in the future with a firm whose word is so untrustworthy. (Box 47, Allen and Unwin, 7 April 1975).

Allen and Unwin did publish the book, and before the IMF's collection, but that did not improve matters. It was the firm's refusal to supply a review copy to the *Journal of International Economics* (whose editor was in the United States) for a review by Frank Hahn that produced the final explosion.

Frankly, your firm could not have done me any worse service, if your sole job in life were to prevent my major work in international economics in the last ten years, and the work of my junior colleagues, from receiving any professional recognition whatever. You managed to delay publication for a year and a half, in spite of repeated promises of publication dates that were invariably broken. You put a price on the book that will ensure that no students, and very few libraries will buy it, though many of my colleagues in various countries have expressed a desire to use the book as a course textbook. And now your Miss Brady has managed . . . to ruin a very carefully worked out plan, that has cost me a great deal of effort, to salvage something from the wreckage by getting the only official journal in the field to give the book a big splash with a review by Prof. Hahn of Cambridge and an accompanying article by myself. (Box 47, Allen and Unwin, to M. Holdsworth, 1 April 1976)

He thus temporarily terminated his relations with the firm,[18] telling Holdsworth that he would tell everyone at conferences that "Allen and Unwin is a hopelessly incompetent publisher and that no economist can afford to do business with them."

Compared to the problems with Allen and Unwin, one would have thought that the *Journal of International Economics* package of a review and an introductory essay by Harry would be relatively straightforward. However, it wasn't.

Difficulties began over the possible reviewer. Jagdish Bhagwati had chosen Frank Hahn. Harry responded (Box 40, Correspondence 1972–7, to Bhagwati, 6 May 1974):

I am unhappy about that because I have reports of his behaviour as a journal referee, where he could not be relied on to read the article before he specified how it should be re-written or rejected, and because I was horrified by what he did in his review of Milton's *Optimum Quantity of Money*. . . . I hope he will not accept the invitation, because our book is not intended to meet the standards of Hahn and his handful of mathematical theorists but to introduce and illustrate an approach that seeks to meet the needs of the policy analyst and policy-maker.[19]

However, Hahn agreed to do the review. But Harry had severe difficulties with his own article as well. He completed his first draft in November 1974 and sent it off. Bhagwati did not deal with the submission until April 1975. When he finally replied, Harry drafted a reply (Box 58, Journal Publication Pending):

Then you wrote me that you didn't like it, and asked me to write another, whose sole purpose would be to advertise the contributions of your prospective new colleague Dornbusch.

This is the first time I have encountered any journal editor who thought that by commissioning an article he obliges the commissionee to devote his time to producing drafts of articles which the editor in question is not only free to reject out of hand if anything in the article does not please him, but to keep on writing drafts on non-subjects dictated by the editor until the editor takes a shine to publish one.

---

[18] Allen and Unwin did bring out *Selected Essays in Monetary Economics*, a selection of essays from two previous collections they had published, for which Harry provided a preface dated January 1977.

[19] Hahn's review of Friedman is reproduced in his *Equilibrium and Macroeconomics* (1984, 258–82), as is his review of Harry (237–58). It is rather dismissive (see especially pp. 254 and 258).

You also sent me your annotations on the first part of the article. It is absolutely clear from the annotation that you had decided in advance that you were going to dislike the article and refuse to publish it and to that end you were prepared deliberately to misread the article to whatever extent was necessary to support your determined a priori prejudice against it, a prejudice which seems to be in connection with a hallucination in your own mind about something called Chicago.

He did not send the draft letter. Instead, he revised the paper and sent it off to Bhagwati in December 1975. But never one to waste his writing, Harry had already sent the original *Journal of International Economics* piece off to Marcus Miller at *Economica*, noting:

I should tell you that the article was originally scheduled for another journal, but was rejected by the editor who had commissioned it, not on any substantive critical grounds but because (this is confidential of course) he wanted it slanted to advertise the work of a particular young economist. (Box 58, Journal Publication Pending, 6 November 1975)

Economica accepted the article on 31 March 1976, but suggested certain revisions, in particular an alteration of the balance between sections II and III to reduce the space devoted to non-monetary theories and to add more detail to the exposition of his own approach (Box 58, Journal Publication Pending, from M. A. M. Smith, 31 March 1976). Harry sent a revised version on 21 May, received further suggestions from Ray Richardson on 25 August 1976, and redrafted the article to meet them in a letter of 1 October.[20]

Meanwhile, except for an acknowledgment on 3 January, which said that the paper was going to referees, he heard nothing from Bhagwati. However, the acknowledgement was odd, asking Harry

to delete the line about the paper appearing in the same issue of the *JIE* as Hahn's review of the Frenkel-Johnson book; I had merely conveyed to you what I might do rather than what I will definitely do, and in any case it is not proper to refer to a review of a book which, to the best of my knowledge, has not appeared and to an author of a review which that author may well decide against writing on seeing the book. (Box 58, Journal Publication Pending)

Bhagwati did not send any comments until 16 September 1976 when he wrote, enclosing a referee's report, and making suggestions that he believed would cut the paper down by "about 10–12 pages" and asking

---

[20] The finally published version contained a warm comment on his treatment by *Economica*:

"I am extremely grateful to the Editors and referees of *Economica*, and particularly Ray Richardson as their correspondent, for many thoughtful suggestions designed to simplify and amplify the exposition of this paper." (217)

for a revised version of "no more than 20 pages," which he would publish with the Hahn review when that came in (Box 58, Journal Publication
Pending).

Harry replied that he was "utterly astounded" by Bhagwati's letter. He
rehearsed his view of the history of the article with the *Journal*, including
his unsent letter. He offered, to save something from the mess, to revise
the article, "to the extent of virtually eliminating the introduction" and
meeting the substantive points in a footnote and one reference, but he
would do no more, for he found the referee's notes "quite incompetent."
Otherwise Bhagwati could take the article as revised, or leave it (Box 58,
Journal Publication Pending, to Bhagwati, 5 October 1976).

The correspondence continued for another couple of rounds. The article
appeared posthumously in August 1977, the same month as the *Economica*
article.

The monetary approach had the advantages of analytical power and simplicity. Central to the relatively simple models was a number of assumptions,
in particular that there were no factor-market rigidities so that money wages
could adjust to keep real wages at the full employment level; that there were
no barriers to capital movements so that for risk-neutral investors interest
parity obtained; and that the prices of domestic and foreign goods were
linked by purchasing-power parity. These assumptions ran up against the
problems of the real world. To take the last assumption first, for example, since then there have been numerous tests of purchasing-power parity.
Tests of the law of one price among particular commodities have found that
outside a small range of homogeneous goods such as gold, short-run international arbitrage has a limited effect in equalising prices in goods markets.
This being the case, tests based on aggregate price data reject purchasing-
power parity as a short-run phenomenon. However, for a number of years
even long-run convergence of the real exchange rate towards purchasing-
power parity was hard to find, and when scholars started to find some it
was very slow and uncertain (Taylor and Taylor 2004). Similarly the tests
of uncovered interest parity are also mixed, with the result that assuming
either interest or purchasing-power parity is not a good approximation to
reality. Moreover, the problems with purchasing-power parity imply that
changes in relative prices are important and must be explained if exchange
rate behaviour is to be explained. Similarly the absence of uncovered interest parity implies that changes in the supplies of different assets working
through current account imbalances may be important. Nonetheless, as
David Laidler puts it:

On the other hand, the long run in economic life is not just a series of short runs. Rather, "long run" refers to underlying trends that, though always present, are sometimes obscured by shorter-run fluctuations. It is one of the great strengths of the monetary approach that it forces us to pay attention to such trends, because coherent and sustainable economic policy cannot be designed without reference to them. (1990, 133)

FOURTEEN

The International Monetary System

As we saw in Chapter 10, before Harry went to LSE he had been actively involved in discussions of the problems and prospects of the international monetary system. During his LSE period the Bretton Woods system collapsed after a series of crises and began to evolve into the system we know. Major developments since his death have been the liberalisation of international capital flows and the achievement of monetary union among members of the European Union, the creation of the European Central Bank, and the introduction of the Euro.

The month before Harry joined LSE, he attended a conference in Chicago. The conception of the conference, if one believes the published proceedings, was jointly his and Robert Mundell's (Mundell and Swoboda 1969, ix, 394). Later Harry attributed its origins to Mundell alone (1982, 86). The organisation of the conference departed markedly from that of the series of Bellagio meetings discussed in Chapter 10. First, it concentrated on theoretical problems rather than on monetary reform, although the problems discussed had emerged in the context of the consideration of systemic reform. Second, in choosing paper-givers and discussants, the emphasis was on younger members of the profession, with older members, such as Gottfried Haberler, Roy Harrod, Fritz Machlup, Walter Salant, and Harry himself, serving as session chairs. As a result, "the papers incorporated much more serious new thinking than is characteristic of a conference dominated by seniority" (1982, 86). The young had a chance to shine and display their technical virtuosity, and their shared appreciation of technical skills allowed the development of strong international relationships. The upshot was a network of young international monetary specialists, which spawned further links as those involved repeated the Johnson–Mundell experiment. The centres of the new groups were the University of Paris–Dauphine, the Graduate Institute of International Studies in Geneva, the Institute of International Economic Studies in

Stockholm, and, of course, Chicago. There were also links when they turned to international economy matters with the Money Study Group and the annual Konstanz Seminar run by Karl Brunner and Allan Meltzer. The networks raised standards of understanding, analysis, and writing and helped to develop an internationally oriented European profession. Of course, all the "problems" raised did not turn out to be fruitful: Harry believed that one "dead end" was the theory of optimum currency areas (Mundell and Swoboda eds. 1969, 395; Swoboda ed. 1973, 85), which had also "been perverted to the service of an anti-American European nationalism of a somewhat repulsive kind" (Johnson 1982, 88).[1] At the end of his life Harry predicted that the new networks would prevent the development of the long-standing divergences in view and understanding that had made the original Bellagio meetings so necessary (1982, 88).

Although its origins were earlier, the beginning of the final unravelling of the Bretton Woods system came with the devaluation of sterling from $2.80 to $2.40 announced on 18 November 1967, after a long string of lesser sterling crises dating back to the Labour Party's coming to power in November 1964. The devaluation of sterling coincided with a shift in the overall balance of supply and demand in the international gold market to a position where industrial and long-term hoarding demand exceeded new production and Russian sales. Central banks were no longer supporting the price but keeping it down, which led to speculation that the long-standing American balance of payments deficit would lead to a devaluation of the dollar and a rise in the price of gold above $35.00. The result was a rush to purchase gold while the remaining members of the London gold pool sold it to maintain its official price, thus draining official gold stocks.[2] On 17 March 1968 the gold rush led to the end of the pool and the establishment of a two-tier gold price: central banks could exchange gold among themselves at $35.00 per ounce, while private individuals would do so at the market price.[3] The next "shock"

---

[1] It was one of the two areas of innovation cited when Mundell received the Nobel Memorial Prize in Economics in 1999 [*Scandinavian Journal of Economics* 102 (2), 192].

[2] The members were Belgium, Germany, Italy, the Netherlands, Switzerland, the United Kingdom, and the United States; France had ceased to be a member in June 1967.

[3] At the time, the agreement among central bankers not to buy gold was intended to force South Africa to sell its current output in the private market and thus push the price to $35 or lower. This was not the forlorn hope it seemed, for long-term hoarding demand included a growing element of speculation, which might, if disappointed in its expectations, result in a reduction in private demand. In the end, however, the private market price stayed above $35, and South Africa came to an agreement with the United States on 23 December 1969 on the circumstances in which it might sell gold to the International Monetary Fund at the official price (de Vries 1976, 412).

to the system came from the French "events" of May 1968 where social unrest, initially among students, led to widespread strikes (at their peak ten million workers were out). The position was "sorted out" with substantial wage increases (hourly wages rose by 11 percent) and reductions in the work week, thus weakening France's international competitive position. There was substantial capital flight from France, particularly to Germany, which had been running balance-of payments surpluses from the early 1960s despite a small revaluation in 1961. The speculation on a mark revaluation or French devaluation was so intense that the major European exchanges were forced to close on 20 November 1968. Neither country changed its exchange rate at the time: the franc was not devalued until 10 August 1969 when it fell 11.1 percent and the mark was not revalued until 26 October 1969 when, after a period of floating, the par value rose by 9.29 percent.

Against this backcloth of turmoil, the British balance of payments, which at the time of devaluation had been expected to improve quite quickly, did so very slowly, with each new international hiccup putting more pressure on sterling – and frequently resulting in yet another set of deflationary "crisis measures" by the British government. It was not until late 1969 that there was a marked improvement in the British position and the balance of payments moved into surplus allowing Britain to rebuild her reserves and repay her short-term indebtedness.

Harry's commentaries on these and subsequent events took a variety of forms – articles in the press, speeches to bankers and interested laypersons, public lectures, and contributions to more narrowly professional discussions. In his commentaries he normally set his immediate concerns within some broader historical perspective. As he moved towards his monetary approach to the balance of payments, which shifted his perspective on events markedly away from his previous position as well as that of many of his contemporaries, there arose a marked disjuncture between his "private" and his "public" views, as he refrained from public pronouncements that were congruent with his new theoretical position. He seems to have wanted to wait until the basis for his new position was available in print. The gap was most noticeable in his initial comments on the 15 August 1971 American suspension of gold convertibility for central banks. In public he retained the lines of argument he had used over the previous few years, despite the fact that his contemporaneous theoretical analysis, revealed in his February 1971 Geneva lecture as substantially revised in July and his September 1971 writings in Vienna, produced conclusions sharply at variance with his public positions.[4]

---

[4] See, for example, the third of his de Vries lectures and the "Crisis '71: On the Cards since 1968" (later reprinted in *Further Essays in Monetary Economics* as "The International

Before the Monetary Approach

In his post-1966 discussions of international monetary affairs, Harry took what had become the normal academic, "Bellagio view" of the gold exchange standard–Bretton Woods system with its three fundamental problems – liquidity, confidence, and adjustment. The liquidity problem was the result of the failure of the International Monetary Fund to increase its quotas in the face of declining supplies of new monetary gold as world inflation and a fixed nominal price of gold increased the nonmonetary demand for gold and reduced supplies as mining became less profitable and the use of gold for nonmonetary purposes became more attractive. In consequence, the long-term tendency to hold higher yielding foreign currencies as a substitute for gold had received a fillip. The postwar currency of choice for such reserve holdings was the dollar.[5] But the resulting rise in official dollar liabilities took place against falling (or at best constant) U.S. gold reserves, thus calling into question the ultimate convertibility of dollars into gold – the confidence problem. The existence of this problem had been pointed out by Robert Triffin in 1959 and the devising of plans to solve it had been a growth industry for economists in the ensuing years. After 1963 governments had got themselves involved as well with the result that at the International Monetary Fund's annual meetings in Rio de Janeiro in September 1967 an outline scheme for Special Drawing Rights received approval.

According to Harry, the SDR scheme

represented a major step towards the replacement of gold by an international credit money . . . just as gold had been replaced domestically by paper currency and bank-deposit money managed by the national central bank. (1968b)

The problem was that events had already overtaken the slow process of international monetary reform. The two-tier gold market was at best a stopgap.

In a series of papers in 1968 and 1969 Harry began to explore the options available. His retrospective judgement written at the end of August 1969 was that

[t]he prospective role of gold in the international monetary system is in an important sense the crux of the international monetary problem. Unfortunately, the problem is difficult to analyse, because it lends itself to differing and conflicting analytical

---

Monetary Crisis of 1971: September 1971"), both of which were written while he was a visiting professor in Vienna.

[5] Sterling was also a significant reserve currency, but the value of sterling balances outstanding, initially the result of Britain's management of sterling in the 1930s and her overseas financial policy during the Second World War, did not rise in the postwar period. In the aftermath of the 1967 devaluation, arrangements for the liquidation of the balances were put in place at Basle in 1968.

logics, and the key problem for the analyst is to determine which of the contending logics is most likely to prevail as the system evolves in the future. The determination of this question is itself difficult because as time passes and new monetary crises arise and are resolved, the evidence of the chief actors in the system points now in one direction and now in another. Faced with this difficulty, most analysts nail their colours to the mast of one system of analytical logic and absorb the evidence of evolving experience in the arguments in favour of their own position and against the positions of rivals. Indeed, anyone who attempts to read current developments for clues as to the direction in which the cat is likely to jump, and to develop the implications of the relevant logic, is likely to expose himself both to the charge of logical inconsistency and the appearance of consistently erroneous prediction.[6]

The logics that Harry explored during 1969 were raising the price of gold (the gold standard logic), an international central bank, the dollar standard, and flexible exchange rates. Either of the last two, he recognised, might lead to what he and others had talked of "at least five years ago" (1964a), a unilateral American suspension of convertibility that would leave other participants with the option of pegging to the existing dollar exchange rate, appreciating to a new peg, or floating (1969c).[7,8]

Initially, given the slowness of devising, approving, and implementing SDRs, plus his own doubts about the value of SDRs that would be issued, and given the Europeans' new potential veto over the process and recipients' possible unwillingness to use the new asset with an explicit gold guarantee where the future price of gold was uncertain, Harry spent considerable time considering the pros and cons of raising the price of gold.[9] The purpose would be to gain "a breathing space for the ultimate logical step of demonetisation."

This alternative might not be all that bad, when contrasted with the policies of drifting improvisation that have characterised the evolution of the international monetary system since the establishment of the International Monetary Fund. . . . It would at least have the advantage of mitigating the excessive dependence of the survival of the system on privately negotiated cooperation among the central bankers, which is one of the most politically objectionable features of the system. (1969a, 18)

---

[6] "The Future of Gold, If Any: Remonetization vs. Demonetization" (1970a). The quotations are from Harry's manuscript version written 28 August 1969. A footnote to the third sentence referred to R. F. Harrod, Jacques Rueff, Robert Triffin, Gottfried Haberler, and C. P. Kindleberger. A footnote to the last sentence ran "C. P. Kindleberger has recently chided me (in correspondence) for appearing in various recent writings to favour respectively the S.D.R. solution, a rise in the price of gold and flexible exchange rates."

[7] He also allowed under this case a joint European float against the dollar.

[8] The paper was written on 7 October 1968 for delivery in Geneva on 30 October.

[9] Initially he thought the market price of gold might fall below $35.00. He revised his views after the further crisis of November 1968 (1969c, 124).

Moreover, after examining R. F. Harrod's long-standing arguments for raising the price of gold, he became even more sympathetic (1970b). As he put
it in a lecture in Calgary in May 1969:

> But most of the economic arguments against it are really very weak.... The poten-
> tially inflationary consequences of a rise in the price of existing gold reserves could
> readily be avoided by sterilising the paper profits; nations that lost because they had
> agreed to hold dollars rather than gold could be compensated; the "gift" to Russia
> and South Africa entailed by the higher gold price would be trivial compared with
> the benefits; and the waste of resources entailed in the physical production of money
> that could be created by the stroke of the pen would be negligible.[10] (1969f, 8)

In these circumstances, if central bankers could not be brought quickly
enough to the view that gold should be replaced by internationally created liquidity, as he had told the American Economic Association on 30
December 1968,

> the refusal of ... [academics and officials] to consider the possibility of solving the
> international liquidity problem by raising the price of gold ... may well turn out to
> have been a Canute-like exercise in impotent vanity. (1969g, 344)

His preferred arrangement was "the development of an internationally
provided and controlled credit money" – that is, his second option. Such an
arrangement would mark the logical end of a process that had been under
way domestically and internationally for more than a century, and there were
certainly strong economic arguments in its favour. But the more he thought
about it, the more unlikely such an outcome seemed. It would require far
more collaboration than heretofore. As he put it in his *Economie Appliquée*
paper:

> [T]he crucial question it raises is whether the major countries are prepared to follow
> the economic logic of monetary efficiency at the expense of surrendering national
> sovereignty in an important area of economic policy. (1970a, 7)

The third option was an explicit dollar standard – the word "explicit" was
important because Harry argued that from March 1968 the world had been
on a de facto dollar standard. The dollar standard had from the beginning
been the default option for the system – an option open to the United
States who could unilaterally suspend gold convertibility for central banks.
Initially, Harry worried about the consequences of such an action. He saw
parallels with the years after 1931:

[10] He would add, moreover, an argument that he picked up from Harrod, "the ultimate
beneficiaries of the incidental 'gift' to South Africa might well be the blacks rather than the
whites" (1970a, 7).

[T]he results of so doing would probably be a period of exchange rate flexibility, international monetary disturbance, and increasing restriction of trade and payments, ending with a return to fixed rates pegged on gold at a higher price.[11] (1969g, 348)

Nonetheless, fears

that the international monetary disorder of this kind would give rise to a world depression on the scale of the 1930s . . . seem almost certainly unjustified, since full employment is now a major policy objective and governments have learned the use of the policy instruments required to achieve it. Moreover, given full employment, the welfare costs of trade and payments restrictions are unlikely to be intolerably great. (1970b, 215 n.6)

By September 1968 he was still more sanguine about this possibility. Although it would be "anathema, at least intellectually, in many parts of the world," the de facto position since March 1968 was a dollar standard and "every month that passes . . . helps to consolidate the de facto position" (1970c, 115). The same process made a rise in the price of gold less likely: "In short . . . it seems fairly safe to prophesy that gold will be demonetised rather than remonetised in the course of time" (1970a, 11).

The fourth and final alternative system was floating exchange rates. Harry had supported floating rates before, but he returned to advocate them in an article in *The Times* in December 1968, in an article in *The Spectator* in April 1969, and in his influential contribution to a Hobart Paper (1969h). The "case" was not a case for flexible exchange rates for everyone: It was a case for "the major countries, . . . [whose] currencies derive their usefulness from the great diversity of goods, services and assets available in the national economy, into which they can be directly converted" (*FEME*, 206). The currencies of small and narrowly specialised countries were not useful in this sense. Such countries would gain on balance by pegging to the currency of a major country with whom they traded extensively or to whom they looked for capital investment. Thus,

under a flexible exchange rate system most countries would probably peg their currency to one or another major currency, so that most international trade and investment would in practice be conducted under fixed rates conditions, and uncertainty would attach only to changes in the exchange rates among a few major currencies or currency blocs (most probably, a U.S. dollar bloc, a European bloc and sterling, though in the event sterling might be included in one of the other blocs). (*FEME*, 210–11)

[11] See also (1969c, 109) written 24 January 1969 and (1969f, 8)

Thus the argument for flexible exchange rates was not an argument that provided an alternative to other proposals to increase international liquidity. It was a way of at least to some extent solving the balance-of-payments adjustment problem among major currencies and of allowing for differing policy preferences for, say, combinations of employment and inflation. At its heart, however, the argument for flexible exchange rates was that if the exchange rate was left free automatically to ensure external equilibrium, countries would be left free to use policy instruments for internal balance, while at the same time allowing the maximum freedom of international transactions. Or as he put it the other way around, the case for floating rates between currency areas was primarily a negative one. International mobility of goods and services, as well as factors of production, was not high enough to provide the advantages of rigidly fixed rates by enlarging currency areas. At the same time, there were no internationally effective policies available to compensate regions suffering the effects of economic change. There were also no centralised arrangements for monetary control across pegged exchange rate areas, and currency areas could resist integrative pressures by using barriers to international transactions. Finally there was no balance-of-payments adjustment mechanism under the Bretton Woods system.

Harry defended flexible exchange rates against the usual charges that they would result in exchange rate instability, reduce foreign trade, encourage destabilising speculation, or promote inflation by governments no longer subject to balance-of-payments discipline. He disposed of these criticisms clearly and carefully. Thus, on the first he wrote:

This allegation ignores the crucial point that a rate free to move under the influence of changes in demand and supply is not forced to move erratically but will only move in response to such changes in demand and supply – including changes in governmental policies – and normally will move only slowly and predictably. Abnormally rapid and erratic movements will occur only in response to sharp and unexpected changes in circumstances, and such changes in a fixed exchange rate system would produce an equally or more uncertainty-creating policy changes in the form of devaluation, deflation or the imposition of new controls on trade and payments. (*FEME*, 213)

As for the second, "trends in exchange rates should normally be slow and pre-dictable" (*FEME*, 213), and if traders wished to hedge, they could use forward markets that would develop in response to that demand. On the third, "the historical record provides no convincing supporting evidence" and more-over "speculators who engage in genuinely destabilising speculation . . . will consistently lose money," although he judiciously allowed for the counterex-ample of clever professional speculators leading amateurs into destabilising speculation to make money from them (*FEME*, 214). As for the discipline argument, "the record since the Second World War speaks poorly for the anti-inflationary discipline of fixed exchange rates" and under flexible rates the consequences of inflationary policies would be much more immediately apparent in exchange rate movements (*FEME*, 215–16). Nor would flexible exchange rates be inflationary in the sense that random depreciations would provoke wage and price increases that would validate the newly depreciated rate. Such wage and price behaviour was much more likely with abrupt changes in fixed exchange rates.

> Under a flexible-rate system, exchange rate adjustments would occur gradually, and would be less likely to require drastic revision of wage- and price-setting decisions, especially as any general trend of the exchange rate and prices would tend to be taken into account in the accompanying calculations of unions and employers. (*FEME*, 216)

"The Case for Flexible Exchange Rates, 1969" was widely reprinted and its arguments have not lost their relevance. The collapse of the Bretton Woods system in March 1973 inaugurated a new era of floating rates among major currencies. This post–Bretton Woods régime of floating rates continues to the present outside Western Europe where European Monetary Union was inaugurated in 1999 after thirty years of discussion and twenty years of experiment. Harry did revisit flexible exchange rates after the move to general floating. I shall pick up that discussion later in this chapter.

At the end of 1969 Harry did not see any urgency in solving the problems of the international monetary system. In a retrospective look at *The World Economy at the Crossroads* for a Japanese audience, dated 4 December, he thought that "the confidence problem has been more or less removed . . . by the recognition on the part of the central bankers that they must keep the system afloat" and that the "liquidity problem has been taken care of by the invention of the SDRs." Even the adjustment problem, outside the United States, had been more successfully dealt with than had seemed likely five years earlier. The remaining problem was the American balance-of-payments deficit, which was currently suppressed by tight money. Once the deficit reemerged, there would be pressure on the Europeans to revalue – "a step that they will be extremely reluctant to take, though they will probably be forced to take it sooner or later . . . since the Americans have the power and the will to force the rest of the world to adjust to them rather than vice versa." The Americans would also "insist on their objective of demonstrating that the dollar and not gold is the basis of the international monetary system" (Box 32, Miscellaneous Notes). However,

[t]owards the end of the decade [the 1970s], private demand for gold is likely to have overtaken supply and established a firm free market price above the $35 mark, with a rising trend. But by that time Special Drawing Rights should be firmly enough established as an alternative to dollars to permit the price of gold to be marked up as a trivial measure of accommodation to the central banks to retain some holding of gold as a hedge against political uncertainties. (1969k)

Nineteen-seventy was a relatively quiet year on the international monetary scene. The only event of note was the Canadian decision on 31 May to let the Canadian dollar float rather than inflate in the face of a current account surplus and substantial capital inflows. Harry welcomed the float in a piece in the *International Currency Review* (1970d) hoping that Canada would not be persuaded to resume a pegged exchange rate. He was not optimistic.

However, Canada continued to float. She was joined by Germany and the Netherlands on 10 May 1971 after massive capital inflows disrupted European markets, forcing closures in Austria, Belgium, Germany, the Netherlands, Portugal, and Switzerland. The disruption in markets reflected the swing in the American balance of payments into substantial deficit, including the first trade deficit since 1893. There was renewed talk of the dollar being overvalued and of the need for a change in the exchange rate for the dollar, but there was disagreement over who should take the initiative and over what form any changes should take. In July and August a more massive movement out of dollars began. A number of central banks presented U.S. dollars for conversion into gold. On 6 August the Joint Economic Committee of Congress issued a report, which, since it did not believe that a rise in the price of gold from $35 was appropriate and since other countries were reluctant to appreciate their exchange rates, concluded that a change in exchange rates could only come by breaking the link with gold. The report not surprisingly brought more requests for conversions. On Sunday 15 August President Nixon announced a "New Economic Program," which on the external side ended dollar convertibility for foreign monetary authorities, and imposed an import surcharge of 10 percent. Nixon's announcement closed the world's exchange markets; they remained closed for the rest of the week, disrupting many holidays. When they reopened on 23 August, most industrial countries in Europe, as well as Britain and Japan, had floating rates – some with substantial official intervention to limit their appreciation against the dollar. Negotiations among members of the Group of Ten continued until 18 December, when after a meeting their finance ministers and central bank governors at the Smithsonian Institution in Washington produced an agreement. The Nixon administration agreed to ask Congress to increase the price of gold to $38. France and Britain left their par values in terms of gold unchanged, thus appreciating their currencies against the dollar by 8.57 percent. Sweden and Italy appreciated by less, while Germany and Japan appreciated by 13.58 and 16.68 percent, respectively. Canada continued to float. For those agreeing to new rates, the range of permissible fluctuation was widened to $2\frac{1}{4}$ percent. There was a call for further discussions on reforming the international monetary system.

Afterwards

As noted in the previous section, at the time of the 1971 financial crisis, Harry's theoretical views were in transition but none of his more scholarly expressions of these changes had been published. This probably explains why his first response "Crisis '71: On the Cards since 1968," which he wrote in Vienna in September, bore few traces of his new thinking. He discussed the evolution of events through 1971 in terms of the now standard triad of confidence, liquidity, and adjustment, with the partial solution of the liquidity problem through the Special Drawing Rights case in the familiar foreigners' reserve-demand model of the determinants of the American balance-of-payments deficit. The only new element in his story was the claim that he and others in the United States "had been advocating for approximately a decade that the United States should take the action on the international monetary front that President Nixon has taken" (*FEME*, 353) – which was really stretching the historical record. At the same time he thought the overall Nixon policy package was "somewhat infantile" – a phrase he also used for the initial European responses – and worried about a possible descent into general trade warfare as a result of the import surcharge (357).

When the Smithsonian Agreement came in December, he continued in the same vein. He was concerned with the short-to-medium-term viability of the new exchange rate régime and, despite the somewhat hopeful sign of the somewhat wider band of fluctuation, concluded that "the prospect of repeated international monetary crisis still looms before us" (360). Nonetheless he assured his readers that "international monetary crisis . . . should not be identified with international economic collapse" and continued:

So long as governments and their publics remain cognizant of the central lesson of the Keynesian revolution, that mass unemployment is an unnecessary and policy-avoidable evil, the international monetary crisis will not be allowed to produce the kind of world economic disaster that the world's central bankers allowed it to produce early in the 1930s. (360)

The new year brought a series of papers, which teased out the implications of the new monetary approach for the analysis of the events leading up to the 1971 crisis and drew implications for future international monetary reform. Instead of allowing that the application of weaker versions of the monetary approach might help in understanding current events (343–4), he began to take a much harder line, which had the effect of highlighting the paradoxical implications of the monetary approach as he tried to lay the foundations for his own counterrevolution. Gone were the possibilities that there might be imperfect substitutability between traded goods (other than commodities) and assets

National economies are, to a good first approximation, now linked together in a single market for manufactures and primary products... [and] national capital markets can be regarded as linked together in a single international capital market. (1972a, 15)

With these two first approximations, "it makes sense to consider inflation as a world phenomenon" against which the only avoiding strategy "is to combine anti-inflationary domestic policies with a floating (upward) exchange rate" (15–16). The two first assumptions played an important role in his story. In the single goods market, in a world of fixed exchange rates, "prices and wages in individual countries will tend to adjust directly to world market levels for prices and comparative efficiency wages without the need for either excess demand... or prior movements of international reserves" (17). With the single capital market assumption, to support the higher level of wages and prices

the extra money required does not have to be obtained through a balance of payments surplus... but it may instead be created through domestic credit expansion.... In short, adjustment of domestic prices and wages to world inflation does not require a prior export surplus or monetary inflow; and the monetary flows that actually occur will be determined by domestic credit policy, rather than being an independent causal factor. (18)

Moreover, in this view of the world, there was no shortage of international liquidity. The newly created Special Drawing Rights would fuel inflation, a point he had already made in Bergedorf the previous May (1972b).[12]

Later contributions teased out further insights Harry derived from his new framework. "Secular Inflation and the International Monetary System" was a March 1972 rewriting of a November 1971 conference comment

---

[12] "Problems of Stabilization Policy in an Integrated World Economy" in H. Giersch (ed., 1972), reprinted in *FEME*.

(1973b).[13] There he began to criticise the prevailing Triffinesque view of the gold exchange standard as "inherently unstable" and tending to a collapse in a confidence crisis, which would be destructive of international liquidity. He argued there was an opposite possible source of instability arising from inflation in the reserve-currency country – a result of the reserve currency being so strong that

> its officials can ignore or deliberately defy the problem of maintaining foreign confidence in the currency, . . . [while] foreign monetary officials having their hands tied by the recognition that they stand to lose more than the reserve currency country by provoking or allowing a crisis of confidence in its currency to develop [can do nothing].

He reformulated the reserve-currency problem, introducing in the process a term that would later become part of the economist's language.

> A reserve currency system can work satisfactorily for the non-reserve countries . . . if the monetary and other policies of the reserve currency country are such as to ensure reasonable stability of prices in that country. . . . The stability of the price-level of the reserve currency country provides an anchor or point of reference for exchange rate changes by others. If on the other hand the reserve currency country follows strongly deflationary policies . . . or strongly inflationary policies . . . the stable reference point for other countries' policies is lost, the anchor drags, and the other countries have either to drift with the inflationary or deflationary tides, or to keep lengthening or shortening the anchor chain. (1973b, 512)

He then embarked on an exposition of his new approach acknowledging that although it had its roots in Hume, "[t]he controversy over the monetarist approach is too recent to have a readily available literature" (515 n.4).[14]

Subsequent papers and lectures, while embodying his monetary perspective, began to look at the emergence, operation, and demise of the Bretton Woods system in a longer term, historical perspective.[15] This is not to say that

[13] The comment had originally been directed at a paper by Robert Mundell at a Universities–National Bureau of Economic Research Conference on Secular Inflation held on 5 and 6 November 1971. After the conference, the organising committee "released [Mundell] from . . . [the] commitment to write a paper for this conference," thus depriving Harry's comment of its basis. Accordingly it was agreed to take up his offer of a paper on the secular implications of inflation for the international monetary system. Harry promised to finish it before January 1972 (Box 39, Correspondence 1971–7, J–P, to HGJ, 26 November 1971; from HGJ, 9 December 1971).

[14] At this point he referred to L. A. Dicks-Mireaux's contribution to *The Current Inflation* and the May 1971 Paris discussion among himself, Asser Lindbeck, Fritz Machlup, and Stephen Marris – "World Inflation" in Claassen and Salin (eds., 1972).

[15] In particular, see (1972f), (1972i), and (1973a).

Harry had lacked such a perspective before: It was now far more noticeable. As he put it in his Gilbert Lecture to the University of Rochester:

It is a fundamental principle of my own personal approach to economics that broad historical perspective is more enlightening than concentration on the technical detail of current events, and also easier to communicate to anyone other than government officials who love trees but hate woods. (1973a, 12)

The historical perspective included economics itself, not just Hume, who had been revived as a part of the monetary approach, but also John Henry Williams whose "key currency" approach to post–World War II monetary reconstruction was favourably contrasted to

the fictional form beloved by the United States of equality of nations and therefore of currencies though . . . the United States took care to represent the then actual structure of political power in the structure of management and voting power in the institution created on this fictional basis. (1972f, 6)

In these papers he revived the problems of the Bretton Woods system of the 1960s – confidence, liquidity, adjustment – but recast them as "the problems of the pre-existing system with which the Bretton Woods plans were intended to deal." To the initial three, he first added "the problem of deflationary bias" (11), and then replaced the deflationary bias problem with "persistent bad behaviour by one nation" and mercantilism (1973a, 15–17; 1972i, 286–9).

Generally speaking, the confidence, liquidity, and adjustment problems retained their 1960s forms, except in the case of confidence/or liquidity cases in the sense of the problem of reserve currencies, where he argued the architects of Bretton Woods ignored it because they did not expect it to arise given the existence of supplementary credit arrangements and the provision for a uniform increase in the price of gold.[16] The deflationary bias case of the *Three Banks Review* (1972f) paper found itself under the liquidity problem in the May 1972 Simons and Gilbert Lectures (1972i, 1973a), where it was argued that the architects of Bretton Woods believed that there was "a chronic tendency for international liquidity to be inadequate and to require increases greater than nature would provide" (1973a, 16) – a position certainly clear in the thinking of Keynes. The "persistently bad behaviour by others" notion was, of course, the view taken by many European and American economists, though not by Keynes, of the chronic American tendency to run a surplus in its balance of payments "and suck gold out of the system into the inaccessible

---

[16] This strikes me as an odd way to proceed, given that Keynes's Clearing Union proposal had explicitly provided for no further expansion of the then dollar or sterling areas. See, for example, *JMK* (XXV, 127, 183).

caverns of Fort Knox" (16).[17] Mercantilism represented the rise of trade interventions, exchange controls and devaluations of the 1930s.

Each particular problem had its appropriate Bretton Woods provision – or supplementary provision in GATT in the case of trade restrictions. Yet, despite these provisions the problems occurred, as in the case of "persistently bad behaviour" in a different (inflationary rather than deflationary) form. Mercantilism took the form of refusing to appreciate undervalued currencies.[18] The results of these recurrences were the difficulties of the 1960s, the attempts to patch up or partially reform the system, and the eventual crisis of 1971. Since Harry did not believe that the 1971 exchange rate realignments had solved any of the underlying problems, he did not expect the arrangements that had emerged from the Smithsonian discussions to last, especially given the Nixon administration's desire for reelection in 1972. His preferred improvement was greater exchange rate flexibility, especially as the alternative was greater restrictions on world trade and payments.

The Smithsonian arrangements lasted less than fifteen months. Just over six months in, on 23 June 1972, Britain floated sterling rather than take steps to defend the rate in the face of a large balance-of-payments deficit and expansionary domestic policy. Throughout 1972, Germany coped with large capital inflows, attempting to reduce them with various controls. On 23 January 1973, in the face of large capital inflows, Switzerland floated her exchange rate. February saw a renewal of the crisis with the yen floating on 9 February, a new package for a de facto dollar devaluation along with an end to American capital controls, and a continued American refusal to intervene in exchange markets. The resulting, perhaps surprising, calm lasted only a few days. At the beginning of March, a new crisis swept financial markets. By mid-month the fixed exchange-rate régime had disappeared with Canada, Switzerland, Japan, the United States, and six members of the EEC including France and Germany all floating. Bretton Woods was dead.

Between the final collapse of Bretton Woods and his departure from LSE, Harry wrote relatively little on international reform. There was a brief speech to the International Monetary Conference of the American Bankers Association in June 1972; a Stamp Memorial Lecture, "The Problem of International Monetary Reform," supposed to be delivered on 22 November 1973, but, given his stroke, only published; and a Trade Policy Research

---

[17] Harry would later cite chapter and verse for this view, specifically from Lary (1943), which he had first read in Cambridge in 1945–6 (1972i, n.410).

[18] "[T]he new economic policy was motivated by the U.S. mercantilist belief that this country has a natural right to be a net exporter of technologically advanced goods"(1972i, 290).

Centre discussion paper, "Neglected Principles in the Discussions on World Monetary Reform," later revised as "General Principles for World Monetary Reform" in a Centre volume edited by Hugh Corbet and Robert Jackson (1974).[19] The first showed little sympathy for central bankers. Harry was interested in their current difficulties for two reasons:

> The first is that there is always the faint hope that if the central banks suffer deeply enough and long enough from things going wrong, they might learn something about how to do their job better. This is a faint hope....
>
> Second, there is a somewhat less faint hope that if the central bankers keep on acting as they have been acting we shall never have a fundamental reform of the international monetary system ... and the world will become used to floating exchange rates, the system that the majority of academics of scientific integrity have always recommended. (1973f, 4)

The major contemporary worry of this paper, as well as the Trade Policy Research Centre one, was that the devaluation of the dollar had been too large, either because of a panic reaction in 1973 after getting it right in 1971 or because of a deliberate American attempt in 1973 to get the rate change officials really wanted with the result that "European countries will have to adjust ... to a period of chronic dollar shortage like the one that prevailed in the early post-war period" (1974d, 157; 1973f, 7)

The Stamp Lecture was wider ranging. Its historical perspective was that of the May 1972 public lectures – the Gilbert in Rochester and the Simons in Chicago. It had its moments of humour: the Smithsonian agreement may have been as President Nixon said "the greatest monetary agreement in the history of the world ... since it was the first time Continental Europe had ever agreed to anything significant in the international monetary field" (1974c, 15). At this stage he expected that some sort of world monetary reform would eventually arrive and that the reform would involve fixed exchange rates based on a new international reserve asset with provision for more adjustability in exchange rates and some form of link between liquidity creation and aid to less developed countries. However, he concluded:

> Whether it will be crisis proof and viable in the long run is a question on which I incline to pessimism – I expect the cast will complete the rehearsals but I don't expect the play to run for more than a few weeks – because ... experience seems to me to prove that the adjustable peg concept was itself the crucial factor in the downfall of the first I.M.F. monetary empire. (21–2)

---

[19] The paper was probably written in April 1974.

In the interim the world would continue to float, a situation he approved of, and he concluded with a brief defence of floating rates against what he regarded as unfounded criticisms. In the end, of course, floating continued, as did Harry's defence of the regime.

After 1974, although he was more concerned with selling the monetary approach, Harry continued to comment on current developments in international monetary affairs, in particular the world's experience with floating exchange rates. Generally speaking he thought that the floating rate system had "worked broadly as it should have" (1975h, 205) and that it had been "extremely useful and effective in coping with the international disequilibrium of the early middle 1970s" (1975a, 34). In dealing with criticisms, he initially concentrated on three: that "market exchange rate movements . . . are regarded as having been excessively large and erratic"; that they "have not resulted in less inflation . . . but rather produced more inflation than before"; and that "forward markets for more than a few currencies have failed to develop . . . and the result has been a constriction of transactions" (1975b, 9–10).[20] On the last point he made the predictable reply that such facilities will develop if there are market incentives (i.e., enough interested transactors), for it to be worthwhile to provide them. On the inflation point, he argued that higher inflation was a transitional problem that reflected the momentum built up by national failures to stop it, the momentum of previous events on wage and price formation, the closely synchronised nature of national upswings in 1973 with their implications for primary product prices, and the oil price shock. On the first point, the relative size of fluctuations, he questioned the bases of such statements given the uncertainties caused by the oil embargo and the difficulties of gauging the severity of monetary restraint in the circumstances. He suggested that if one looked at trade-weighted exchange rates with major trading partners such as Canada and Japan, experience differed from that of Western European exchange rates, and that in the short run at least, exchange rates would be dominated by stock demand and supply rather than flows. Market expectations in the light of available information would have led one to expect "considerable and rapid changes in relative currency prices to occur" (13)

He was still dealing with the issues in his final public lecture in New Delhi on 7 January 1977. He warned about falling victim to the "straw-man"

---

[20] The same criticisms were dealt with in his Horowitz Lectures, *Money, Balance-of-Payments Theory, and the International Monetary Problem* (1977d), which were given immediately before the paper cited.

or post-hoc-ergo-propter-hoc fallacies, before turning to the issues of exceptional and excessive exchange-rate volatility, where he thought that there had been a decline since mid-1975, especially if one excluded the pound and the Italian lira. His other arguments were basically unchanged, although he was more colourful about European currencies:

The German mark has become the lynch-pin of the effort to maintain a common European currency on the so-called "snake in the tunnel" analogy – and the chief problem has been that, given sharp divergences of European inflation rates and policy, the policy has only been kept working by changing both the dimensions of the tunnel and the pieces of the snake that will have to be fitted inside it. Guessing about whether, when the snake's head starts to rise, the tunnel roof will be raised to allow it to stretch its neck, or the floor will be raised to keep the rest of the body close to its head, or an awkward chunk of belly will simply be cast out of the tunnel for a while, gives plenty of opportunity for speculation and apparently arbitrary exchange rate movements of the European exchange rates against others. (1977b, 9)

He also spent more time developing the stock-flow distinction he had raised earlier and admitted that not making that distinction had been "a serious error in the traditional argument," albeit one that the "emerging new 'monetary approach to flexible exchange rates'" could deal with and stressed that short-run disequilibria between relative prices and expectations could persist "for a substantial number of months, perhaps for more than a year" (10–12). In other words, Harry's views were evolving, even if, with hindsight, they look rather "naive" – a phrase used by Richard Cooper with reference to Harry's "The Case for Flexible Exchange Rates, 1969." But Cooper's paper, which, in the end, takes no account of Harry's subsequent views, uses arguments about the increasing importance of financial transactions in determining exchange rates as an explanation of the failure of the view that exchange rate movements would reflect inflation differentials (1999).

FIFTEEN

Harry's "Wicksell Period"

In the years before he went to LSE, Harry financed some of his activities through a grant from the Rockefeller Foundation. The topic of the research was very general – international trade and technical change. The major expenditure under the grant was for a research assistant, Herbert G. Grubel. Most of Harry's own work on tariff structures, effective protection, economic nationalism, and protectionism has already been discussed. However one of the last topics Harry touched on was the international migration of highly skilled people, which he had first addressed in "The Economics of the Brain Drain" at the sixth Seminar in Canadian–American Economic Relations at the University of Windsor in 1964, a paper which he reprinted in *Minerva* (1965c). Harry encouraged Grubel and Anthony Scott, who was visiting Chicago as Lilly Fellow in 1965 to collaborate on such questions, and the result for them was a series of papers and eventually a monograph.

Although he continued to contribute to other areas of international trade theory during his LSE period, Harry's thinking took on a new twist – one so distinctive that Max Corden called it "Harry's 'Wicksell Period'" (1984, 580). The reference is to his Wicksell Lectures delivered in Stockholm in March 1968, *Comparative Cost and Commercial Policy Theory for a Developing World Economy* (1968h). Harry described the orientation of his 'Wicksell Period' to his chair, A. C. Harberger, in June 1968:

I am presently engaged on a major project which will take some years. It is more an effort at improving my own ability to teach relevant economics to my students, and express it in my writings on current topics of theory and policy, than something that will result in a major research monograph or series of monographs.

Briefly, the project is an attempt to work out a dynamic theory of international trade, based on an understanding of the role of technological superiority and inferiority in the causation of international exchange. The theory of international trade has traditionally been static, in the sense of assuming given supplies of factors of production and a given technology. It is easy enough to extend this theory to the case where technologies differ among countries providing one is willing to take these differences as given exogenously. But what I want to do is to develop a theory of why technologies differ, and what factors make for persistent differences in the quality of technology among countries. This leads me into about every aspect of social life one can think of – the economics of research and development expenditure, the economics of education systems, the economics of the administration of natural resources, and ultimately the whole problem of human motivation and the dynamics of social change.

I have attempted to provide answers to these questions, based on my understanding of the current state of economic theory in my Wicksell Lectures, delivered last March in Stockholm. In those I have used everything that the combined work of the University of Chicago Department of Economics has turned up in these various fields of research. But I regard that as just a starting point for an endeavour at understanding which I hope will advance several frontiers in economic knowledge simultaneously. I should add that the results of this work should be useful in throwing light on a number of contemporary problems – especially the economics of the brain drain, the economics of direct foreign investment of capital by large corporations and the so-called problem of the technological gap, about which the Europeans have been so concerned in the past three years or so. (Box 41, Correspondence, 1968, 6 June)

In 1972, in a letter to Charles Furth of Allen and Unwin proposing a new volume of "various pieces of mine written mostly since I went to London" under the working title *Essays in Dynamic Trade Theory: The Migration of People, Technology and Enterprise,* he noted that his Wicksell Lectures "contain some of my best thought" (Box 47, Allen and Unwin, 2 May 1972). The book proposal came to nothing, but in addition to his 1968 lectures the proposed volume would have included fourteen items on the brain drain, technology, and the international corporation.

By the time Harry made this proposal, he also had in prospect a related volume, *Technology and Economic Interdependence* (1975i). He had signed a contract for this book, then called "Technology, Time and Investment," in March 1970, as a part of a series *World Economic Issues* that would be edited by Hugh Corbet for the Trade Policy Research Centre. Progress on the book was slow. In the summer of 1972, Mohsin Kahn, one of Harry's LSE graduate students, worked to edit previous journal contributions into a form more suitable for a "popular" discussion. Corbet estimated that he needed another 20,000 words from Harry and he provided extensive guidance for what was wanted (Box 53, Trade Policy Research Centre, 10 November 1972). But Harry didn't get on with it. In July 1973 he told Corbet from Chicago (Box 53, Trade Policy Research Centre, 9 July): "I must get to that soon. But I've had other time-consuming calls on my time, including a new course here."

Harry's stroke halted any further progress during 1973. His subsequent progress with the book was one of the marks of his recovery, and a revised typescript reached London from Chicago on 16 May 1974 (Box 47, Macmillan, from Corbet, 21 May). At this stage Harry was calling the book "Technology and Economic Integration," but Corbet reported:

> By some lapse of memory, I seem to have renamed the book some time ago, referring to it as Technology and Economic Interdependence in advance publicity. Since "interdependence" sounds less academic than "integration" I hope you have no objection.

Further collaborative fine-tuning occurred over the summer of 1974 before the book went to press at the beginning of October.

After the publication of *Technology and Economic Interdependence*, Harry made one more substantive contribution to this line of discussion in a June 1976 paper to a Stockholm symposium on *The International Allocation of Economic Activity* – "Technology, Technical Progress and the International Allocation of Economic Activity" (1977a).

The Lectures and the Papers

The Wicksell Lectures announced an attempt to move away from orthodox static theories of trade to take into account the "new" theories of trade that had been developed in the course of the 1960s and to take account of international movements of skilled labour (the brain drain as it was, and still is, often called), the international corporation, and the then much discussed technological gap between the United States and Western Europe.[1]

To tackle these problems he started from the generalised approach to capital accumulation, which he had developed for a May 1963 OECD study group on "The Residual Factor and Economic Growth" and reprinted in *The Canadian Quandary*, in which accumulation included not only human and physical capital but also the productive knowledge to combine the factors of production. Accumulation occurred unevenly across countries, with "developed" countries having accumulated and established mechanisms for maintaining and increasing large stocks of capital. Different stocks of capital and different institutions lead to a variety of processes through which knowledge and skills were diffused and transferred in the international economy. It was not a rigorous analysis. Harry's intention "to produce a grand dynamic

---

[1] Harry summarised the lectures in "The Theory of International Trade," a paper delivered to the Third Congress of the International Economic Association in Montreal in September 1968 (1969l).

Heckscher–Ohlin model with the original factors – labour and nature – combined with capital in all its forms" ran ahead of his ability to tie down parts of the model. He was proud of the lectures and obviously wanted to work further in this area, but he never really had the time or the energy to do this and everything else (Corden 1984, 580).

He did, however, sketch in pieces. The first was his paper on "Some Economic Aspects of the Brain Drain" (1967d), which later formed the basis of Chapter 6 of *Technology and Economic Interdependence*. Harry had first looked at the subject in the Canadian context for a 1964 University of Windsor conference. The 1967 paper, itself an extension of a paper for an August 1967 conference in Lausanne, comprehensively surveyed the issues as they related to Canada, the United States, Britain, and the developing world. It demolished what he thought were unsound arguments and picked up the important aspects of the problem.

Harry began the paper by noting that the term "brain drain" was a nationalist concept that visualised welfare purely in terms of the residents of a state or a region and ignored both those who leave it and the residents of the rest of the world. He took a different tack:

> I adopt a cosmopolitan liberal position, and regard nationalism as one of the less pleasant mental vices in which mankind indulges itself, or as one of the characteristics of childish immaturity out of which I hope the people of the world will ultimately grow. . . . I start with the assumption that the international circulation of human capital is a beneficial process, since it reflects the free choice of the individuals who choose to migrate. (1967d, 379–80)

His main concern was to see if there were cases where migration might result in an economic loss to the world as a whole or where it was likely to result in an uncompensated loss on those remaining in the country of emigration. In the first case, there could only be a loss if the relation between private incomes in the two countries under consideration was inverse to the relationship between the possible alternative contributions to social output. He could conceive of such situations – a more redistributive system of taxation and expenditure in the country of emigration than that of immigration or an equivalent holding down of the incomes of potential educated migrants in the pursuit of income redistribution. He could also conceive of possible externalities that would cause private and social returns to diverge. He thought that such inversions of private and social returns were unlikely in the case of migration among developed countries. With respect to possible losses to less developed countries in cases of migration to the developed countries, he remained sceptical that they were likely to be more than insignificant.

As for policy reactions to potential losses, Harry believed that the one associated with the "gift" element in the international transfer of taxable capacity was the most easily dealt with through the repayment of either the costs of the education obtained in the sending country or the costs of education plus possible likely redistributive tax payments. Of course there was a simple solution – financing higher education by loans rather than grants,[2] allowing interest on the loans as a deduction for income tax purposes; and if any further obligation over and above interest was involved, an interest surcharge was always possible. Other compensation schemes were possible in theory but unlikely to work in practice.

In October 1968 Harry attended a Universities–National Bureau of Economic Research conference on *The Technology Factor in International Trade* (Vernon ed. 1970). He provided the lead-off paper, which reflected his Wicksell Lectures. Before publishing it, however, he revised it to reflect the conference's proceedings. The paper "The State of Theory in Relation to the Empirical Analysis" (1970e) emphasised the gap that had grown up between the traditional static theory of trade and the recent literature on trade and technology. It was a plea for a reconstruction of traditional trade theory to take account of the pervasive effects of monopolistic competition – "to translate monopolistic competition concepts into forms relevant for general equilibrium analysis" (15). At the time, he was challenged by his discussant, Jagdish Bhagwati, to state "what precisely is the manner in which we can begin to reconstruct our theories" (24). At that stage he had hunches but not precision. It was left to a younger generation of trade theorists, notably Paul Krugman, Elhana Helpman, and Avinash Dixit, to make the theoretical transition.

Discussions of the international corporation grew richer during the years when Harry was a contributor, and the theory of the reasons for multinational activity, to which Harry contributed, grew even richer in the hands of others. Harry's classic second Wicksell paper was, characteristically, published in two places in 1970.[3] Central to the discussion was the notion that multinationals were engaged in the creation and transmission of productive knowledge. But

if the need for recompensing those who make investments in the development of new knowledge is accepted, it does not necessarily follow that recompense through

---

2 This was his preferred solution for Canada (Box 56, Correspondence 1964–6, A–L, to Vincent Bladen, 26 June 1964).
3 [Kindleberger (ed.) 1970] and [McDougall and Snape (eds.) 1970]. As the latter paper is "revised," I cite it here (1970g).

monopoly profits on the use of that knowledge is the ideal arrangement for the host country. (1970g, 88)

In these circumstances, it might make more sense to think of different rules, particularly for less developed countries. Hence having carefully followed the Canadian debates on the issue for years and having recently touched on the issue in the less developed countries, he began to examine various proposals for restricting inward investment. He could think of only one first-best argument for restrictions – an optimum tax on international capital movements analogous to an optimum tariff. He was dismissive.

Undoubtedly there is an optimum tax on technological transfers or on inward investment as a mixture of capital flow and technological transplant, waiting to be analysed by a mathematical trade theorist. However it does not seem worth dwelling on this point, both because it is an obvious one and because it is hard to believe that actual national policies are governed sufficiently closely by considerations of this kind. (90–1)

He turned to the presumptive gains from inward investment. Technical progress was assumed to be a good thing, but if the return on superior technology was fully absorbed by the investor and if prices to consumers and of factors remained unchanged, there would be no direct benefit to the host country other than the quantitatively important benefit arising from the right under double-tax agreements of the host government to tax the earnings of foreign firms – earnings that would reflect both the returns on capital and on specialised knowledge. Otherwise, residents would gain only if the benefits of superior technology were passed on in lower prices or higher factor earnings. Even here, however, he could think of possible perverse results. If the failure of the foreign investor to capture the whole of his returns affected the general level of factor prices rather than the prices of the particular factors employed or lower prices for consumers, foreign investment in the more capital-intensive sector of the economy would raise the returns to capital and reduce the wages of labour.

The general conclusion Harry drew was that "inward foreign investment cannot harm and may confer substantial advantages" on the host country (94). Arguments against the freedom of direct investment must be either noneconomic or those that produce restrictions as second- or third-best policies with uncertain effects. He examined these in turn, taking national defence as the classic noneconomic argument and infant industry, socially undesirable goods, balance of payments and monopoly as possible second-best arguments. Sorting through these arguments and the related policy possibilities, Harry tried to be fair but his conclusion said it all.

[I]t is evident that with sufficient analysis one can construct cases in which there is a second-best argument for restriction of inward foreign direct investment. The fundamental problem is that, as with all second-best arguments, determination of the conditions under which a second-best policy activity actually results in an improvement of social welfare requires detailed theoretical and empirical investigation by a first-best economist. Unfortunately policy is generally formulated by fourth-best economists and administered by third-best economists. (101)

The third of the Wicksell papers was "A New View of the Infant Industry Argument" (1970f). The theme was by now familiar:

[T]he essential nature of the infant industry argument is now clear. What is involved is an investment in a process of acquisition of knowledge which is socially profitable but privately unprofitable because the private investor cannot appropriate the whole of the social return from his investment. (61)

If produced knowledge were private and inseparable from some natural economic unit such as a firm, the social and private return would normally coincide and there would be no "infant-industry" case for official intervention. He proceeded to explore possible cases for intervention. Some fell to the ground immediately. For example, general training of labour, which is transferable to other employers, would normally fall outside the possible cases because it would be possible to write contracts so that the individuals bearing the costs of the training could reap the benefits. Linkages of the production of inputs to the sale of outputs could be internalised by changes in ownership (vertical integration) or by appropriately drafted contracts to internalise the full extent of the returns. The case for infant-industry protection rested on knowledge being inherently a public good in character. Such knowledge could not be patented or protected by law and convention as a commercial secret, thus making the private appropriation of the social returns from knowledge creation possible. In other words, the social gain must be either privately unappropriable or only partially privately appropriable and there would be the possibility of privately uncapturable increases in consumer and producers surplus.

The final Wicksell-period paper was his June 1976 "Technology, Technical Progress and the International Allocation of Economic Activity" (1977a). Here he was thinking in long-term macroeconomic terms, emphasising his long historical perspective by beginning his discussion with a model of a nomadic society. As he put it:

The macroeconomic approach is concerned . . . with the process of technical change itself, as a process of maximising response to opportunities for profitable technical change on the one hand, and the costs of producing technical progress on the other, a process whose operation may be stimulated or inhibited by governmental policies . . . but whose long-run trends condition, rather than are conditioned by, governmental and social institutions. (315)

He emphasised the path dependence of any particular historical distribution of economic activity. Moreover factor flows divorced, at least in part, the international distribution of labour and capital equipment and the distribution of the production of goods and services from the distribution of total population and its consumption. As well, in his scheme, "technological levels, and differences in them, and changes in differences, can no longer be taken as exogenous or exogenously changeable" (322). In this perspective even "the nation state is itself a transient mode of human socio-political organisation" (322). It was all very stimulating – too stimulating for his discussants or other members of the symposium to come to terms with. But what else would one expect from what one reviewer called "a Toynbee-scale, very very long run macro model of the world economy" (Black 1978, 850). One wonders what Harry would have done with the ideas had he lived and had taken the time to think things through. One would like to be optimistic and think that something would have emerged, but the near decade between his Wicksell Lectures and his death did not move things far forward on this front

Technology and Economic Interdependence drew many strands together. He discussed the economics of science policy, technology as a factor in international trade, the role of the multinational corporation in development, and the economics of the brain drain, and added a recent paper on economic growth and the environment (1973g). An implicit theme of the book was that

efforts or proposals to guide and control the progress of technology by national policies of intervention in domestic industry, and intervention in international trade and investment, are likely to be poorly conceived, ineptly administered, inefficient in achieving the results desired and, in the process, injurious to economic progress, efficiency and welfare. (151–2)

He associated this theme with the mood of international economic relations until the mid-1960s, after which European resentment at American direct investment, the evolution of the Common Agricultural Policy, and Britain's new attempts to join Europe and America's abnegation of international economic leadership had resulted in international economic fragmentation – what he also called the rise of "the new mercantilism," the title of his Presidential address to Section F of the British Association for the Advancement of Science in August 1973 (1974b). I have already touched on some of these changes in talking about the international monetary system, but I have not looked to any extent at Harry's views on trade policy issues.

Going into Europe?

During Harry's time at LSE, the shape of Britain's future trading arrangements was a perennial issue. Britain had applied for membership to the EEC in July 1961, only for the application to be vetoed by President de Gaulle in January 1963. In the interim the Kennedy administration had succeeded in getting Congress to pass the Trade Expansion Act of 1962. This legislation had been predicated on Britain's 1961 application being successful and empowered the administration to negotiate what would have been a free trade area in major industrial products. Under the dominant supplier authority in the act, the administration could negotiate the complete elimination of tariffs on product groups where the EEC and the United States conducted 80 percent or more of free-world trade. The rejection of Britain's EEC bid meant that the Kennedy Round of negotiations, which opened in May 1963, had to fall back to offering a maximum of a 50 percent reduction in tariffs across the board. The difficult and protracted negotiations did not end until June 1967. Just before their conclusion, on 2 May 1967, Britain formally applied again for membership to the EEC.

It is against this background, as well as the activities of the Trade Policy Research Centre, that one can trace Harry's discussion of trade policy both for Britain and the world economy. Between 1966 and 1970, his energies were directed to the case for what came to be called the Multilateral Free Trade Association (MFTA) option – the North Atlantic Free Trade Area with possible additions raised by the Canadian–American Committee of the Private Planning Association of Canada and the National Planning Association of the United States in its May 1966, "A New Trade Strategy for Canada and the United States." In Harry's view this sort of proposal was initially "the most obvious positive alternative to [British] membership in the Common Market" (1967a). After the November 1967 French veto of Britain's second EEC application (which remained "on the table"), the MFTA came to be regarded as the most feasible way of maintaining the postwar momentum towards freer trade. True it lacked the political appeal of a British entry into Europe, but it had "the appeal of being consistent with the national objective

of various prospective members and therefore conceivably of being nego-
tiable"(1969j, 211–12). Then, as Britain's revived attempt to get into Europe
looked more and more likely to be successful, Harry moved into strong
opposition to British entry into the EEC. The final stage of this campaign
was the letters to *The Times* exercise, which he organised with Nicholas
Kaldor. When the letters appeared on 22 October 1971, just before Parliament voted on the entry, they revealed a deeply divided profession – albeit
one that was no more deeply divided than it had been over protection versus
free trade in a series of articles in and letters to *The Times* in 1903.[4]

The MFTA proposal appeared before the results of the Kennedy Round or
Britain's second application to join the Common Market were known. The
case that Harry made for the association naturally varied with the circumstances – and the late 1960s were not short of dramatic events. Nonetheless, it
is probably best to take one of Harry's pieces as the core of the argument, his
paper of 26 February 1969 to the Manchester Statistical Society, as printed
in the *Manchester School* (1969j).

The proposal for a MFTA involving Canada, the United States, Britain, and
her fellow EFTA members was regarded by its proponents as the logical successor to the Kennedy Round. It was the logical successor because the other
alternatives – another round of GATT negotiations or sectoral negotiations
for freer trade along the lines of the European Coal and Steel Community
or the Canada/U.S. automobile agreement – did not look promising. In the
Kennedy Round, the traditional GATT procedures that everyone had to fall
back on after de Gaulle's 1963 veto had proved extremely gruelling to the
negotiators as any new attempts at general formulations inevitably reverted
back to the item-by-item bargaining. Moreover, there was no consensus
among the industrialised countries on what might be a new overarching
initiative for a new set of GATT negotiations. In addition, the GATT process
did not serve the developing world well: Their competitive labour-intensive
exports of manufactures tended to be excluded from the negotiations by
political pressures within the developed countries. Although the sectoral

---

[4] Between 15 June and 10 August, W. A. Hewins, the former Director of LSE who had just
resigned to become secretary of the Tariff Reform Commission, published anonymously
ten articles on the fiscal question. In response, fourteen economists published "Professors
of Economics and the Tariff Question" on 15 August. The "manifesto" was organised by
Edgeworth and signed by six professors of political economy (Bastable, Edgeworth, Gonner,
Marshall, Nicholson, and Smart), one former professor turned politician (Courtney), and
seven other teachers of the subject (Bowley, Cannan, Phelps, Pigou, Sanger, W. R. Scott,
and Armitage-Smith). After publication, controversy rumbled on for a few weeks, with
critical letters from L. L. Price, Foxwell, and Palgrave.

approach looked more promising in that it reduced the negotiating problem to one between the leading countries concerned with any industry and
was capable of tackling both tariff and nontariff barriers simultaneously, it
proved difficult to create self-contained segments of trade for the purposes of
negotiation. Moreover such negotiations among developed countries were
unlikely to result in substantial benefits for less developed countries. In
fact they were more likely to increase discrimination against trade with less
developed countries.

The MFTA approach had several advantages. It did not require all the
leading industrial countries to agree on the desirability of universal free
trade before the negotiations started. It would also be easier to deal with the
problems of developing countries under such a régime: The free trade association could easily provide for unilateral free entry for developing countries'
exports of manufactures subject to market disruption safeguards. Moreover, although the free trade area would initially be confined to industrial
products, agreement on policies for temperate zone agriculture would be
necessary to pave the way for predominantly agricultural countries joining
and thus allowing in the long run for free trade in agricultural products.

When it came to assessing the case for Britain's going into Europe, instead
of taking the bright side as he was inclined to with MFTA, Harry tended
to emphasise worst-case scenarios. The greater regionalism and greater
problems for temperate zone agriculture resulting from the expansion of
the Common Agricultural Policy might have "disastrous" consequences for
international trading relationships.

The Americans, beleaguered by the combination of an overvalued currency and
the resulting import competition, the concentration of import competition on
politically-sensitive, labour-intensive and regionally-concentrated industries, and
growing official trade union protests against the "export of American jobs" implicit
in direct foreign investment by large U.S. corporations have rapidly been retreating
into a protectionist and isolationist mood. . . . Britain's acceptance of an agricultural
policy that explicitly benefited European farmers at the expense of American agricultural exports might be the last straw. The United States might well give way to
internal protectionist pressures, and in the course of doing so espouse a regionalist
approach to international trading relationships that would have the effect of pinning
Britain even more firmly into a European dependent status rather than a world-wide
trading role. (1971c, 169)

Similarly he painted a very bleak picture of Britain in an integrated Europe:

If one envisages Europe as eventually becoming a fully integrated economy like the
United States, Britain's position is that of an offshore island or a peripheral coastal
region such as New England. . . . The costs of competing from the periphery . . . will

be substantial, and they will be aggravated by the commitment to a common currency, since Britain apparently has a chronic tendency to excessive inflation. . . . Add to this the fiscal burdens of the EEC, which will have to come out of the standard of living of the average British citizen and the real costs of supporting British agriculture at the levels of prices set by the Common Agricultural Policy, and there becomes a strong possibility that British firms and the British working force will begin to drift towards locations on the Continent.

. . . [O]ne can readily envisage a gradual coalescence of the British population into a single conglomeration centred on London and its environs, with a decaying hinterland exporting workers to the Continent and educated people to the London metropolis. (166–7)

He used strong language and powerful rhetoric, but Harry could see no case for Britain entering Europe: "The obvious economic benefits of Britain joining . . . are negligible and the obvious economic costs are large" (1971b, 218).

It was against this background that Harry became interested in polling economists' opinions:

Nicky Kaldor, who originated the idea, undoubtedly expected a resounding no vote, but I had no particular expectations; my intent was a different one, to provide some demonstration that there were a lot of economists outside the big three and to both test and advertise the role of the AUTE as opposited [sic] to the R. E. S.[5]

Originally, the idea was a triumvirate, the third being R. C. O. Matthews of Oxford, the purpose being to have the sponsorship of the three as a means of avoiding exactly what happened – votes directed against Kaldor and me. Matthews declined because he had just been made Chairman of S. S. R. C. and didn't want to embarrass the Government that had just appointed him. (There is a moral there for you.) I suspected that Nicky wouldn't get his no vote – I had to stop him from whipping in his friends. The form of the referendum was dictated by Nicky's knowledge (and I agreed) that anything more precise would induce economists to quibble about the particular argument and not the conclusion. (Box 51, Correspondence 1971–7, to Terence Hutchison, 9 August 1976)

The texts of the letters were as follows:

The undersigned, being full-time teaching officers in economics in British universities, believe that the economic effects of joining the Common Market, taking both the short and long-term effects into account are more likely to be unfavourable [favourable] than favourable [unfavourable] to Britain. (1972g, 316 n.1)

The drafts were distributed through the local branches of the AUTE, given that the intention was to have a clear-cut definition of "an economist"

---

[5] The "big three" meant Cambridge, LSE, and Oxford. On the AUTE and RES, see discussion in Chapter 12.

and that only the AUTE could reach the British profession. When the two letters appeared on 22 October, 142 signatories were of the opinion that the economic effects would be favourable; 154 thought them likely to be unfavourable.[6] When all the letters were eventually in, 154 (including 41 professors and 4 readers) were prepared to sign the letter that they thought the effects would be favourable, and 157 (including 24 professors and 5 readers) were of the opposite opinion. If one included those who were prepared to express an opinion but not sign either letter 222 were on the favourable side, 196 on the unfavourable side, and 99 were undecided. If one looked at particular universities, Cambridge produced a large margin against, Oxford was narrowly against, and LSE was 17 to 12 in favour. In the rest of England, Southampton, Bristol, Leicester, and Manchester produced large unfavourable majorities, while Exeter, Newcastle, Sheffield, and York produced large majorities on the other side. The Scots saw favourable results (53 to 21), as did the Irish (8 to 4), but Welsh opinion produced a dead heat. It was all rather difficult to explain. Kahn and Johnson (1972g) tried two hypotheses whereby "people in remote places take their opinions from newspapers and television broadcasts, both of which tended to favour entry" and "an 'establishment' opinion based on London and the older universities, and its opposition to entry as a threat to its independence in governing the country" (317–22).

Harry was later taken to task by Terence Hutchison on these hypotheses which "completely contradicted the claims, on which the exercise was based, about 'professionalisation' and about economists being 'better qualified than other people to make up their minds on the economic issues'" (1976, 142). Kaldor and Johnson's original letter to the economists had said

It would be very important to know, from the point of view of the British public, where the professional economists of Britain stand on this issue. Everybody agrees that the question is a complex one and that economists are better qualified than other people to make up their minds on the economic issues one way or another. (Hutchison, 1976, 140)

Kaldor and Johnson's claims had been supported by a survey of economists by Samuel Brittan in which an overwhelming majority of those questioned agreed that the effects of joining the Common Market on real per capita

---

[6] When reporting the results in *Economica* with his student Mohsin Kahn, Harry used the more emotive terms "in favour of entry" and "against" (1972g).

income was a matter on which economists could offer a professional opinion (1973, 60, 102).[7]

In a reply to Hutchison, part of which I have already quoted, Harry claimed that Hutchison had misrepresented him as being "a campaigner against the common market" and stated that his objective "always was to get some economics applied to questions of trade policy." He tried to defend the hypotheses of the Johnson/Kahn paper by arguing "that economists by and large have made economics so abstract that it frees them for any kind of politics they want." He also grumbled that "virtually all of those whom you have named have contributed nothing to pure theory" – an odd grumble given that in addition to Kaldor and himself, the economists named in Hutchison's text were Wilfrid Beckerman, A. C. L. Day, Frank Hahn, and Peter Oppenheimer – small beer compared to the 517 replies that were the subject of the Johnson–Kahn article. All in all, the final Common Market debate was not Harry's finest hour.

Once the decision was taken in favour of entry (entry formally occurred in January 1973), Harry's commentary was relatively limited. Most of it was concerned with possible European monetary arrangements that had started to wend their way through the European Monetary System to the European Central Bank and the Euro that we know today. He was not enamoured of the prospect.

In my admittedly jaundiced view, the proposal to establish a common currency represents only the most recent phase of the continued efforts of the Brussels bureaucracy of the European Economic Communities . . . to force even further integration on countries which are no longer convinced of its political necessity. (1973i, 86–7)

In Harry's view the prime impetus towards monetary union lay with the difficulties exchange rate changes produced for the managers of the Common Agricultural Policy. The origins of the pressure towards union also lay in the dollar-induced inflation of the late 1960s and the consequent need of European countries to think of their collective rather than their

---

[7] Brittan's questionnaire was sent out to his sample in the autumn of 1971 (1973, 9). One should note that his sample differed from the Kaldor–Johnson questionnaire – he asked only 250 economists, of whom 117 responded. He had excluded holders of chairs in the ancient universities and "economists working in very specialised applications away from the mainstream of both general theory and public policy." Of the 117 who replied, 44 were identifiable academics, 37 were government economists, and 21 were business economists; 15 fell into a category that couldn't be ascertained. The proportion of identifiable replies in each class was parallel to the number of questionnaires sent out (9–19).

individual relationships with the dollar. The early discussions of the subject, which stalled more general discussions of international monetary reform, had played a significant role in precipitating the collapse of the Bretton Woods system. He thought the realisation of monetary union was probably "a pious hope" (1974d, 157).

SIXTEEN

Stroke and After

Harry's health began to break down in 1972. Years of very heavy drinking were taking their toll. He found his temper more difficult to control, even in letters some time after the event. On 11 August he complained to Don Patinkin of feeling "overconferenced" and that going to such events had become a "habit" (Box 40, Correspondence 1972–7).[1] He was also becoming forgetful: He invited Ruth Towse to a LSE Higher Education Research Unit party and then stood her up. As he later reported to Mark Blaug, Ruth's husband:

My invitation was genuine; the stand-up was the first phase of an illness that obviously became a lot worse before, I hope and trust, I got through the worst of it. (Box 40, Correspondence 1972–7, 20 June 1974)

At least he had leave from his LSE terms in 1972–3 to look forward to. He had been teaching year-round since 1966 and been without any leave since 1959–60, his first year at Chicago. He spent his leave at Yale as Irving Fisher Professor with no formal teaching duties but with an obligation of residence in New Haven. He did teach an undergraduate course in the theory of international monetary economics, which did not go well in its lecture format and became a seminar (Box 37, Yale Course 1972). He also grew a beard. He had colleagues, but New Haven was not Hyde Park or LSE and he was thrown more on his own resources and company.

The end of term took him to the Allied Social Science Association meetings in Toronto. He was elected a fellow of the Econometric Society. For the American Economic Association meetings there he had organised an invited

[1] Even in that letter, he couldn't help commenting on the value of conferences: "[T]he Conference has become our post-doctoral seminar, and can be especially valuable in bringing young people from small countries who often get discouraged about the worthwhileness of doing academic research in the hostile pragmatic wilderness."

lecture by Richard Kahn on the afternoon of Friday 29 December. The subject was to be "The International Monetary System" and Harry was to be in the chair. However he could not act as he came down with an acute case of jaundice and was hospitalised in Toronto Western Hospital.[2] Hospitalisation meant that he also did not attend a Royal Economic Society Conference of 3–6 January 1973 on international monetary problems at Ditchley Park near Oxford or a meeting of the Selection Committee for the next LSE director on 10 January. In hospital he was told to take it easy for the next three months.

He left Toronto only on 22 January, when he flew to Vienna for a meeting of the Bellagio Group. Afterwards, he remarked to Fritz Machlup:

The Vienna Conference appears to have been very well received by those attending. But it seems as usual we discussed with less urgency than turns out to be desirable. (Box 41, Commitments Completed 1973–4, 13 February 1973)

As he wrote, the Bretton Woods system was collapsing; the second devaluation of the dollar had been announced late the previous evening.

Once back in New Haven, Harry obeyed his doctor's orders about taking it easy, "leading a very quiet life temporarily" (Box 51, Correspondence 1971–7, C–G, to Victoria Curzon, 16 February 1973). He spent five days in February drafting the report on Ontario graduate economics programmes and a day on 18 February visiting Richard Caves at Harvard to discuss it. This allowed him to go on to Amherst the next day to lecture on "Cambridge in the 1950s"(1974a), but, with the exception of visits to London for a meeting of the Selection Committee for a director on 7 March, to an honorary degree and conference celebrating the opening of the Social Sciences Centre at the University of Western Ontario on 21–24 March (1974e), and to Princeton to act as a panellist on the subject "What we need to know?" for Peter Kenen's refresher conference on "International Trade and Finance: Frontiers for Research" (1975) later in the month, he avoided the conference circuit or any other public lectures until April. He also gave up alcohol, no mean feat given his intake.

From the beginning of April, as well as carrying his usual Chicago teaching load, he became more active. Although he did not attend a LSE Selection Committee meeting on 4 April, he attended a Brookings Conference on

---

[2] Nonetheless, while in hospital he drafted his contribution for Brinley Thomas's *festschrift*, "A Formal Analysis of Some Brinley Thomas Problems Concerning the International Migration of Capital and Labour"(1976a), presenting a copy to his specialist Irwin Hilliard, who seemed somewhat bemused by the gift (Box 41, Commitments Completed 1973–4, from I. Hilliard, 5 February 1973).

World Trade Policy at Maidenhead from 6 to 9 April where he gave a paper on "The Probable Effects of Free Trade on Individual Countries" (1975j) and acted as a discussant for Herbert Giersch's "Free Trade for Higher Employment and Price-Level Stability." He also attended the annual conference of the AUTE at the University of Warwick. He was in London for a meeting of the LSE Selection Committee on 8 May. Ten days later he was back in Europe for a conference of the German Association of Research Institutes at Bad Homberg, where he spoke on "The Optimum Solution for the Adjustment Problem" (1974d). He saw his Toronto doctor again on 1 June. But he was still rationing himself somewhat: For the first time since 1960, he did not go to the Canadian professional meetings. Nonetheless, he was in Europe again for the International Monetary Conference sponsored by the American Bankers Association in Paris, 5–8 June, the Per Jacobsson Lecture at the University of Basle on 16 June, what proved to be the final LSE Selection Committee meeting on 26 June, and the 4th Konstanz Seminar on Monetary Theory and Policy on 27–29 June. He was back again to speak to the SSRC conference at Exeter on graduate student support on 18 July and the British Association for the Advancement of Science meetings at Canterbury, giving the presidential address on "Mercantilism: Past, Present and Future" (1974b) on 20 August. Thereafter he scaled back his travelling until he returned to London and LSE in October. But he was still busy. On 27 October 1972 in a postscript to a letter to Erik Lundberg, Harry had remarked, "While I am thinking about the matter you might consider awarding a joint [Nobel Memorial] Prize sometime to J. E. Meade of the U.K. and Trevor Swan of Australia for their work on the theory of international economic policy" (Box 39, Correspondence 1971–7, I–P). He spent much of September 1973 responding to a request from the Nobel Committee for an assessment of Meade's contributions to economics (1978b). By the time Meade's prize was announced in October 1977, Harry was dead.

The LSE term got under way. On 16 October during a conference in Venice, he suffered a stroke. He was rushed to the Opesdale Civile Reuniti in the Campo SS Giovanni e Paolo, where tests indicated that he also had hepatitis. The stroke affected his left side, leaving it initially "completely frozen." When he regained consciousness,

he remembered what he had read about strokes and their dangers. He knew all about the potential damage that might result from a stroke and he was fearful. He started counting, up to ten and back to one and felt very happy about his performance. (Jacob Frenkel, Harry Johnson Memorial Meeting, 4 February 1978, 18–19)

He asked Jacob Frenkel for some mathematical notes that had been the basis for an already published article. Frenkel was bewildered at anyone wanting old mathematical proofs after a stroke, but Harry later explained that

he asked for the mathematical notes and was asking himself "can I redo what I did before." It was . . . the joyful moment of his life when he realised he could in fact find a mistake in the appendix. (Jacob Frenkel, Harry G. Johnson Memorial Meeting, 4 February 1978, 19)

Within a week of the stroke

he was already back at economics. There was a pile of new books by his bedside, and a writing pad and a pencil at his right hand. Speaking with difficulty, he said, with a diffident smile, as if craving my understanding, "I still have to work." (Shils 1977, 88)

About the same time, Clifford Wymer reported to Russell Boyer, who was coming to work on the LSE project, "His speech and mental activity seem to be normal, but he is not yet mobile" (Box 49, International Monetary Research Programme, 25 October 1973). It was not until 3 November that he was moved back to London to the private wing of University College Hospital. In an undated manuscript note (Box 31, Manuscripts 1973–4) written about this time he thought he had been

very lucky. My speech seems only slightly affected, not noticeably to other than me and my doctor. My brain seems ok – I've been correcting proof etc., and drafting a preface to a conference volume.[3] My composition is slow and tiring but the sentences and paragraphs do come. I've also got to walking with a three-footed cane, and am slowly getting more confidence. I still have an ankle, hip and left arm as strange sleeping partners, but things are slowly getting better even in the remote departments.

He told Melvin Krauss more on 23 November:

What I've had is a stroke, but it is mild as such things go. That is, my diction seems fairly well under control, and my brains are functioning fairly well. (My test is the Times and Sunday Times and Observer crossword puzzles – I'm not near top solving capacity but I'm getting some of them.) I have also been writing letters and correcting proofs of articles.

Physically, I have one side (arm pretty completely, leg about half) paralysed, but I've been progressing. I can walk with a 3-legged stick, and there is evidence of very slow and tiny but definite improvement. I feel pretty hopeful, though it will take a long time. I also find that the narrowing of my physical scope is helping me define work priorities for the next few years. (Box 39, Correspondence 1971–7, I–O)

---

[3] *The New Mercantilism*, the proceedings of the 1973 Canterbury meeting of Section F of the British Association, whose thirteen-page introduction is dated November 1973.

By 11 December he was reporting to his London publisher Charles Furth that

I . . . am well enough advanced to see occasional professional or business colleagues. . . . [But] I have to programme visits both because I have a rather exhausting physiotherapy programme and because a lot of well-meaning friends don't realise that much as I love them the carrying of a conversation is not effortless. (Box 47, Allen and Unwin)

The same day, he committed himself to attending a conference at Stanford on 18–20 April marking the retirement of Edward Shaw, even if he couldn't promise to deliver a paper by the New Year (Box 39, Correspondence 1971–7, I–O, to R. McKinnon). In the event, he went to the conference as a discussant (1976n).

The new year saw him at home in London, with physiotherapy sessions at University College Hospital as his only outings. He estimated he would not be back at work "for at least another two months" and that the hepatitis would leave him "subject to easy exhaustion for about a year," but he sounded optimistic.

No one knows how much further recovery physically can be expected, but so far improvements continue at the standard glacial pace or better, and I might in time come close to full recovery – at least as close as a sedentary academic needs. Anyway, I can handle all my usual commitments except the lectures and physical office work. (Box 52, Correspondence 1971–7, O–T, to David Smith, 8 January 1974)

Two days later he told Vincent Bladen:

Unfortunately my left arm, due to a childhood operation, will probably always be a source of bother – it does virtually nothing, except spend most of its time aching in an irritating way. But my general health has probably been improved both by the enforced rest I have undergone . . . and by a visible loss of excessive weight. But I'm still at least as tubby as when I first appeared in your class back in 1939! (University of Toronto Archives, Bladen Papers, B74–0073/001, to Vincent Bladen, 10 January 1974)

By the end of the month (Box 51, Correspondence 1971–7, C–G, 29 January) he could tell Rudiger Dornbush that he was "able to start picking up where I left off last autumn." He was also working over the past. 13 February saw him writing "Harry Johnson's Contributions to Economics: An Evaluation by Himself," an odd document, compared with his other memoirs, as it was written in the third person as if someone else was evaluating his career for a prize. Its origins lay in Gerard Curzon's telling him that he had been nominated for the Nobel Prize and remarking that "the only person who could properly assess his output in support of a recommendation was himself" (Elizabeth Simpson, 26 July 2005). When he reported working on the "memoir" to William Hood just over a week later, he also remarked 'I don't know how bad I was, but I'm nearly back in business now, at least intellectually"(Box 52, Correspondence 1971–7, P–T, 22 February).

At the beginning of March he attended the first meeting of the search committee for editors of the *Economic Journal* (see discussion in Chapter 12). At the end of March he made his first conference appearance since October when he gave a contribution, "The Future of Floating Rates" (1975h), at a panel discussion at the Université de Paris–Dauphine. On 3 April he applied to LSE for a leave of absence until September. On 5 April he was back in Chicago, where he was lecturing on "Dynamic Models of Growth, Inflation and Cycles." On 18 April he made it to Stanford for the Shaw Conference on Money and Finance in Economic Development. At the end of the month he was in Ottawa for a Senate Committee on Foreign Affairs discussion of Canada's relationship with the United States. On 6–7 May he was in Washington for an American Enterprise Institute conference on Worldwide Inflation and chaired an afternoon session on the first day with papers by David Meiselman and James Duesenberry. After the conference, he reported to Ronald Bodkin that "I'm okay, full of beans, working less but more effectively, I think, than before and growing in physical strength" (Box 40, Correspondence 1971–7, A–B, 8 May). Before his stroke Harry was ambidextrous but always carved with his dominant left hand. Now, as he told W. R. Allen:

My only problem, aside from locomotion, is that I have no left hand and have had to resort to unsatisfactory mechanical aids to continue with my wood carving. This is particularly irritating because I have got interested again in making puzzles which require exact dimensions.[4] (Box 40, Correspondence 1971–7, A–B, 15 May 1974)

Resignation

There was still the problem of what to do about LSE. In February 1973 the professors of economics had voted to extend the School's Chicago arrangement with Harry for another five years, but nothing further had apparently been done, for the academic secretary raised the issue again at the end of February 1974. Harry himself brooded about the issue during the winter.

---

[4] He had a small vise attached to his desk and tried carving with his right hand but he had to be satisfied with less ambitious projects – animal silhouettes fabricated with an electric saw and Elmer's glue or small figures modelled in plasticine (Elizabeth Simpson, 26 July 2005).

He was egged on by Christopher Archibald, who had left England for the University of British Columbia in 1970 after leaving LSE for a chair at the University of Essex in 1967.

We are, of course, agreed in our diagnosis of the School. I feel that I left only just in time, if not indeed a bit too late.... Do you really believe that your commitment to Ely [Devons] is still binding? You must know best, but I'd have thought that it is rubbed out by events neither of you could foresee or control, particularly your health. Can you really plan to continue to commute? If the LSE is going on in the old way, is there any point? In one respect it is hopeless: Govt. controls salaries, and the moonlighting will continue. In another, it dug its own grave years ago: the decision should have been *either* to leave town *or* not to be an undergraduate school (or, if to be, select and very small) but we know what was done. I wonder what you'd do if you had your druthers? (Box 40, Correspondence 1971–7, A–B, 10 February)

Later in the year Harry recalled:

I had plenty of time that miserable winter to think about the future. I'd had eight years of British university life going steadily downhill all the way, among colleagues who believed that a decision postponed or the discovery of an administrative impossibility constituted a major contribution to scientific progress, and I was pretty fed up. However, there was still the possibility that the L.S.E., or part of it, could build up a position in Europe through our contacts with the live centres there, and that the new Director-Elect of the School, Ralf Dahrendorf, would be the man to halt the School's descent into urban university non-entity. (1974 Memoir IV, 39)

The new, minority Labour Government's Budget of 26 March 1974 proposed tax changes for those who worked and earned income outside the United Kingdom that would have made Harry considerably worse off. The crucial proposal concerned the tax treatment of overseas earnings. In the past, only those remitted to the United Kingdom were subject to tax. The new proposal would subject to tax 90 percent of the income earned and received abroad even when it was not remitted, with fairly strict limits on the expenses incurred overseas that could be claimed against tax. This took the heart out of the favourable tax arrangements that Harry had enjoyed since 1966 (see the discussion in Chapter 8).

Under the new tax proposals and with the same main activities, I would still have to pay income taxes to the U.S. government, and I would be able to deduct only a fraction of what I would have to pay the U.K. government, both because U.K. marginal tax rates are so much higher and because British definitions of legitimate business expenses for academic workers exclude certain kinds of expenses that in the United States and elsewhere are accepted as necessary costs of membership in the academic community. (LSE, Personal File, letter to the Director, 22 May 1974)

Moreover, the mood of the times was redistributive: Income tax rates rose, especially for those on higher incomes, and a Green Paper on an annual wealth tax was promised for the summer. Although the proposals on overseas earnings did not become law (they were removed from the Finance Bill as it made its way through Parliament), they gave Harry grounds for resignation. His letter of resignation to the director, dated 22 May 1974, did not mention his health.[5] It was instead a recapitulation of his disappointments and fears.

As you remember, I accepted appointment at the School in 1966, on the understanding that I would take charge of what was expected to be a rapidly expanding graduate programme. In fact, virtually since my arrival the possibilities have been consistently narrowed by changes and new developments in government policy. The tendency has been accentuated by the inability of the School to arrive at any coherent view of its future role in the academic world, and a consequent tendency to delay agreement on action until the possibility of action has already been foreclosed.

The prospects look even bleaker for the future, in terms both of the development of graduate work and of the economic position and rewards of academic careers in England. I have invested eight years of low pay . . . and of much hard work in graduate training organisation and administration, much of which courted the continual danger of being casually undone by majority vote of those present during my absence or by administrative decisions taken without regard for their academic consequences. I am not attracted by the prospect of another stint of the same experience.

I had reconciled myself to staying at the School, and shifting my interests toward the development of economics on a European-wide basis; but the events of the last year have made that prospect uncertain and unattractive. First, there is the doubt about whether Britain will remain in the European Community, at least whether there will be a Community in any significant sense.[6] Second it is clear that the standards of living of senior academic personnel (to the extent that their salaries are their main means of subsistence and correspondingly their teaching and research are their main activities) will be reduced through both increased taxation and control of pay scales, as a part of Government policy for dealing with inflation. Third, the demands of the government for economists and the convention that the government has priority over academic work will make the maintenance of academic standards at the School more difficult that it has already done. (LSE, Personal File)

---

[5] In a letter to Charles Furth (Box 47, 13 June), he wrote: "My health is now pretty good. It had nothing to do with my decision, except that the stroke made me realise that I was wasting my time thanklessly on a lone battle against British academic ineptitude."

[6] Labour was not enamoured of the European Community. In the election manifesto for 1973, the party had promised a referendum on the continuation of British membership. After the election, the party and the Labour government were divided on the issue, and the Cabinet did not reach a decision to recommend continued membership until 18 March 1975. The subsequent referendum on 5 June 1975 saw 67.2 percent of those voting in favour of retaining membership.

He went on to the tax proposals themselves and the prospect of a wealth tax.

Harry later recalled that "[m]y resignation provoked quite a stir, and the stir helped to convince me that my decision was right" (1974 Memoir IV, 40). Lionel Robbins, in the course of an LSE reception for 300 alumni in Washington referred to Harry's resignation and stated that the chancellor of the exchequer, Dennis Healey "is a menace to academic freedom" and continued : "That ex-Communist! I wonder how soon it will be before he tries to stop the English from leaving their own country" (*Evening Standard*, 19 June 1974, 21). The stir was heightened by a comment from Francis Cripps, one of Nicholas Kaldor's acolytes in Cambridge who was soon to be at the centre of the row over the editorship of the *Economic Journal* (see discussion in Chapter 12). Cripps was quoted in the *Times Higher Education Supplement* (7 June 1974, back page); "Professor Johnson is a very wealthy man. He has written a large number of books and articles. It is not clear why he is worried about tax." Harry was incensed and wrote the president of the Royal Economic Society, with copies to all members of the council. The purpose of the letter was to let off steam, for it is not clear what he expected the society to do about the "instance of deliberate lying, intentionally injurious to my professional and personal reputation by a British economist" (King's College, Cambridge, Kaldor Papers, NK3/30/124, to Sir Donald MacDougall, 1 July 1974). Certainly when he sent a copy of the letter to Kaldor he made it clear that he expected Kaldor to do nothing about it (King's College, Cambridge, Kaldor Papers, 3/30/124, 31 July 1974), although he threatened to "crystallize and circulate my evaluation of the implications concerning the character and reputability of British academic economics among my professional friends in the rest of the academic economic world." The correspondence with Kaldor rumbled on through a couple of bad-tempered rounds, which satisfied neither of them, least of all Harry, whose correspondence on the subject continued well into the autumn (Box 40, Correspondence 1971–7, A–B, from C. Archibald, 29 November 1974).

Harry's resignation seems to have affected his younger colleagues most. Ray Richardson wrote on 18 June:

I was not surprised that you left the School but I was saddened. Perhaps I have never expressed my thanks for all your help to me but may I say that I feel very considerable gratitude for your support, your willingness to give advice & your making the School such a lively place. (Box 52, Correspondence 1971–7, P–T)

Nicholas Barr wrote on 30 June:

I was very sad to hear of your resignation. Doubtless you will have heard, and will continue to do so, what a loss it is to the School and the Department. But I feel it much more personally. I shall miss you, not just for all the help and advice you gave me, though that will be irreplaceable, but also because of the loss of your bearded presence at the end of the corridor.

Also I associate you inextricably with my M.Sc. year [1966–7], which was one of the happiest of my life – and I know this was true also for other[s] in the "gang." . . . In some ways it seems like the end of an era which started off in those now rather far off happy days. (Box 40, Correspondence 1971–7, A–B)

Harry was touched by such letters. He replied to Richardson on 28 June:

I have always tried to help my colleagues especially the younger ones, without trying to impose my own views on them because I regard scholarship as a cooperative adventure and not a zero-sum game, and I have lots to learn myself from the way other people conceive of problems. I am sorry in many ways to be leaving LSE, as I had hopes that our School would again become a real centre of economics, with . . . people like yourself who had more education and more time than a senior man can dispose of doing the new work, and people like myself contributing experience and judgment about how to make the results most effective and relevant. But the British environment has come to put so much financial pressure on the older academic, particularly in London, that it becomes very hard to continue a real concern with the development of the subject in one's own and junior colleagues' hands, and if one can't do that, the whole thing loses its interest and excitement. (Box 52, Correspondence 1971–7, P–T)

He added a postscript: "I learnt long ago that if factors are immobile, their earnings are taxable; if they are mobile the consumer has to pay; but to prove mobility, someone has to move, not just threaten to."

Harry admitted that his leaving the school was "the end of an era," which grieved him. True, he hoped "that the new one will be good too though different" (Box 40, Correspondence 1971–7, A–B, to N. Barr, 8 July 1974). But Chicago had made him Charles L. Grey Distinguished Service Professor of Economics,[7] and, as he told Barr,

we are busy building up what we hope will be the strongest international economics group in the whole world, between the Economics Department and the Business School, and I'd like to train a few promising professional economists for a change, instead of having to send them away from the School to be trained at the Ph.D. level at some other place. (8 July 1974)

He was also rebuilding other links. He agreed to go to Queen's University as Skelton–Clark Visiting Professor for January–March 1975. As well, the Graduate School of International Studies at Geneva, which had tried to attract him in 1966 (see discussion in Chapter 8), offered him a position for the January–March quarter in subsequent years. He was to teach a seminar

---

[7] His predecessor had been Richard P. McKeon, a classicist and historian.

and a class for graduate students each week for a salary of 30,000 Swiss francs, half in the form of expenses (Box 51, Correspondence 1971–7, C–G, Jacques Freymond to HGJ, 10 July 1974).

Tentatively, he began to travel again – to the Pacific Trade and Development Conference in Mexico City, 15–20 July, where he read "Technological Change and Comparative Advantage: An Advanced Country's Viewpoint" (1975o), and the International Economic Association's Congress in Budapest, 19–24 August, where he acted as chairman of Working Group C on "Industrial Policy: Location, Technology, Multinational Firms, Competition and the Integration of Product Markets" and reported on its deliberations on Saturday 24 August (1976m), before going on to London to clear out his LSE office and sort out his affairs there. When travelling he needed someone, normally Liz, to accompany him, and his health was still sufficiently fragile that the slightest upset, such as a case of Montezuma's revenge in Mexico City, could put him into hospital.

The events of 1973–4 had shaken him deeply. This is clear from the long autobiographical essays of the summer of 1974 – twenty-six pages on his undergraduate education in Toronto on 5 July, twenty-eight pages on his experiences at St. Francis Xavier, dated 5 and 21 August, and the forty-page segment of the autobiographical memoir relating to the School, dated 3 September, plus a brief memoir of London policy circles dated 21 August. The memoir writing was useful therapy. He could also be amused by the oddities of behaviour, even his own. In December 1974 he took out a $300 life subscription for the Econometric Society, at a time when the annual dues were $25, with the comment to the society "that my life expectancy is likely to give you a net profit on the . . . transaction" (Box 31, Miscellaneous Correspondence, 11 December 1974). But he departed from London on a lighter note with "America: Land of Opportunity," which he wrote on 16 September: It appeared on 30 October under a better title, "Me and My Brain Drain" (1974g).

Resuming Activity

The fall and winter of 1974–5 were quiet. In the fall he taught International Monetary Economics for the last time: In the next two years it would be called Monetary Aspects of International Trade, a throwback to Haberler's course at Harvard (see discussion in Chapter 4). He attended the meetings of the Eastern Economic Association in Albany in October, where on 26 October he chaired the panel and contributed to the discussion with Jacob Frenkel and Rudiger Dornbusch on "Current Problems of International Finance" by recycling the contribution that he had made in Paris in March (1975h), and went to two conferences at the end of November – one on world-wide inflation organised by the Brookings Institution (20–22 November) (1977k) and the other on the abrogation of the gold clause at the University of Miami Law School (24–26 November)(1976p) both as a discussant. His winter term at Queen's was broken only for a one-day conference in Washington on 27 January, where he spoke on "Quadrilateral Perspectives on Security, Inflation and the World Financial Structure"(1975m), and a visit to McMaster University in Hamilton on 14 March for a lecture and seminar.

From April of 1975 he was more active, even though he was giving a course in Chicago on General Equilibrium Theory, based on his textbook with Melvin Krauss (1974h). Indeed it seemed from this point onwards that travel was the best therapy and absorber of his restless energy. He took part in a Midwestern Economics Association Panel on "What's Wrong with Graduate Education in Economics" and gave the C. Woody Thompson Memorial Lecture on "Equity and Economic Theory" (1975e) on 4 April. April also saw him, accompanied this time by his daughter Karen, in Rio de Janeiro to give the Vargas Lecture, "An Overview of the World Crisis and International Trade" (1975f). At the end of the month he lectured at the University of Puerto Rico on "The Monetary Approach to Balance of Payments Theory"(1976b). In May he was in Israel to give the Horowitz Lectures at Hebrew University of Jerusalem (5 May) and Tel Aviv University (8 May) on "Money, Balance-of-Payments Theory, and the International Monetary Problem"(1977d). On 15–16 May he was at an inflation conference at Miami University at Oxford, Ohio, with a paper on "World Inflation and the International Monetary System" (1975k). At the beginning of June, he was in Edmonton, Alberta, to introduce the first Innis Lecture of the Canadian Economics Association given by his former teacher Vincent Bladen. Then at the end of the month, it was the Fifth Konstanz Conference before he moved on with Liz to an International Economic Association Conference on the Organization and Retrieval of Economic Knowledge in Kiel (6–13 July) where he presented a paper on "Learning and Libraries: Academic Economics as a Profession"(1975l), before returning to Miami to lecture to Arthur Anderson's Partners Development Program between 21 and 29 July. The next month saw him, with Karen as his helper, summing up in Helsinki at a conference on the monetary mechanism in open economies (4–9 August),[8] in Kingston, Ontario, at a Canadian Monetary Research

---

[8] But he still had to watch his activities. In summing up, he reported: "I missed Friday afternoon because I can't cope with a consistent 14-hour day of Finnish Conference and hospitality."

Conference (17–20 August), in Toronto to chair a symposium on "Macro-economic Models and Policy" at the Econometric Society's World Congress (20–22 August) (1976r) before he headed off to New Zealand for the Seventh Pacific Trade and Development Conference in Auckland (25–28 August) where he did his usual job of summing up the discussions despite the fact that he had not been present for the first day.[9] He spent most of September giving lectures and seminars as Commonwealth Visiting Professor at all six of New Zealand's universities before he and Liz went to Papua, New Guinea, for a holiday visit to Ragnar and his wife Jessica in the mountain village where they were doing anthropological field work, returning to Chicago on 5 October.[10] During the fall, while teaching Monetary Aspects of International Trade, he restricted himself to seminars and conferences in London, Ontario ["Keynes, Cambridge and the General Theory"(1978a)], Ottawa ("Unemployment and Inflation"), Washington ("Money and the Balance of Payments" and "Reform in the International Monetary System"), and the University of Alabama ("Money and the Balance of Payments" and "Goods, Money and Securities in the Adjustment Process"). The year ended with a talk on "Reform in the International Monetary System" to the Monetary Economics Society at LSE on 5 December, during his visit to sort out the problems related to the collapse of Gray-Mills (see discussion in Chapter 12).

In 1976 he followed the model of 1975 even though this was his first teaching term at the Graduate Institute for International Studies. He managed the trip from Chicago on his own (Box 51, Correspondence 1971–7, C–G, to G. C. Harcourt, 27 January 1976). Except for a three-day visit to Mexico City in February where he gave the first of several bicentenary talks on the *Wealth of Nations* and lectured on international monetary reform, he had no other commitments until March, which saw him in Freiburg for a lecture on "The Monetary Approach to the Balance of Payments"

[9] He had been promised a careful record of the proceedings by rapporteurs which would be available to him on arrival, but the papers were distributed too late for him to read them and the record-keeping was inadequate."Dealing with the first day has been like a problem in detection: I began with the discussion record, then got some of the official commentators' notes. It was like reconstructing 'Hamlet' by starting with Rosenkranz and Guildenstern, then making what one could of the words of Polonious and Fortinbras, but never reading Hamlet's part or seeing the final script; or like building a house by starting with installing the roof, then putting up the walls, and finally guessing at the foundations. What I offer is very much inference about a past civilisation from its archeological remains" (Box 35, Writings 1975).

[10] His topics for his New Zealand lectures were varied, including "The Monetary Approach to the Balance of Payments," "Stagflation," "The Transfer Problem: A Different Approach," "Inequality and Efficiency," "Man and His Environment," "World Inflation and the International Monetary System," and "The British Disease."

(8 March), as well as at home in Geneva for a Trade Policy Research Centre Conference paper on "Trade Negotiations and the New International Monetary System" (1977c) (11 March). After Geneva, he gave a repeat of the 11 March paper in San Francisco at the end of March, and then papers to conferences in Rochester ["The New International Economic Order" (1978g)], Washington ("International Monetary Problems"), and London (the introductory paper "Money in the Open Economy: A Historical and Analytical Survey" for the International Monetary Research Program's progress-report conference in April). May saw more lectures in Victoria, British Columbia ["Foreign Ownership and Economic Policy" (1976s)], and Cambridge, Massachusetts ["Commodities: Less Developed Countries' Demands and Developed Countries Response" (1977i)]. In June it was first to the Canadian Economics Association's meetings in Quebec City where he delivered the second Innis Lecture, "Keynes's *General Theory*: Revolution or Declaration of Independence" (1976i), and then a British North American Committee meeting in Bournemouth, a Nobel Committee Symposium in Stockholm, where he talked on "Technology, Technical Progress and the International Allocation of Economic Activity" (see discussion in Chapter 15; 1977a), a Trade Policy Research Centre conference at Bellagio (1977c), and finally again Kiel, where he was awarded the Bernhard-Harms Prize. In this role he delivered a lecture on "Aspects of Patents and Licences as Stimuli to Innovation" (1976h) and also gave three other lectures – "Technology and Comparative Advantage," "International Commodity Policy and the Integration of the Developing Countries in the World Economy," and "The Effects of Monetary Policy on Economic Activity and the Question of Monetary Indicators." The month ended with a meeting of the electors to the Nuffield Readership in International Economics at Oxford where Christopher Bliss was elected to succeed Max Corden.

The frantic pace continued. He gave a paper "Monetary Theory and the Balance of Payments" to a conference on monetary research in Kingston, Ontario, on 5 July, then attended the Eighth Pacific Trade and Development Conference at Pattaya, Thailand, 11–16 July, and went on a "pretty exhausting" ten-day tour with up to four performances per day (Box 41, Commitments Completed 1976, to L. J. Robock, 11 August 1976), for the United States Information Agency in Sydney, Canberra, Melbourne, and Wellington before he rested in French Indonesia. August, however, was quiet with only the American Economic Association meetings, where he delivered a paper on "The American Tradition in Economics" (1977j).[11]

---

[11] The meetings in August were a brief experiment to separate the job market from the intellectual aspects of the December meetings.

In the autumn of 1976 Harry was on the move in his old style. September opened with a conference sponsored by the Liberty Fund on unemployment and social security at Simon Fraser University in Vancouver. Two days later he was in Montevideo to give three lectures sponsored by the central bank of Uruguay.[12] At the end of the month, he went to the University of South Carolina to give the paper, "The American Tradition in Economics," which he had delivered at the American Economic Association in August. October opened with "The New International Economic Order" (1978g), the Woodward Court Lecture at the University of Chicago. On 15 October he gave a paper on "The Individual and the State: Some Contemporary Problems" as part of the University of Ohio's Adam Smith bicentennial lecture series (1978h). A week later he repeated the Ohio lecture at the University of Colorado before flying to Tokyo via San Francisco on his own to take part in the centenary symposium of *Niehon Keizei Shimbun* with a paper on "The North–South Issue" (1978f). While in Tokyo he also gave "The New International Economic Order" as a public lecture. He flew from Tokyo via New York and San Juan to Martinique to take part in a University of Paris–Dauphine Conference on International Monetary Research. Jacob Frenkel later recalled:

> In San Juan we missed our connection, and it was clear that we were going to stay in the airport for the rest of the night and that Harry's paper, which was scheduled for presentation on the following morning would have to be rescheduled. The conversation, of course, was about economics, with Harry leading the discussion about Air France and its monopoly power and about the proper social policies that were called for. Eventually, Larry [Sjaastad] arranged for a room in the airport hotel. Harry, who at the time was not a healthy man, refused to go to the room until he was promised that there were two beds in the room so that the rest of us could all take turns. (Harry G. Johnson Memorial Meeting, 19–20)

Less than a week later, on 12–13 November he took part in a conference on the role of international professional associations in international affairs at the University of Pennsylvania, where he read a paper on "Networks of Economists and their Role in International Monetary Reform" (1982), a discussion of the roles of the Bellagio Group and a series of overlapping groups of academic economists that grew out of a conference on the international monetary system in Chicago in 1966 (see discussion in Chapters 10 and 14).[13] There was then a quiet spell, including two weeks in London, before he was off to India as a guest of the Indian Chamber of Commerce in

---

[12] The lectures were entitled "The Monetary Approach to the Balance of Payments," "Problems of Stabilisation," and "Inflation as a Kind of Taxation."

[13] The Martinique conference was part of the second network. Harry's papers record him offering "a short paper" for that which was concerned with "the role of relative size for the

Bombay, Delhi, and Calcutta, to deliver a lecture on "Contemporary Problems of Industrialisation of Less Developed Countries." On 5 January he gave two seminars in New Delhi on "Commodities: Less Developed Countries' Demands and Developed Countries' Responses"(1977i) and "General Observations on Trends in International Economic Relations." The visit concluded with the V. K. Ramaswami Memorial Lecture at the Delhi School of Economics on 7 January on "World Inflation, International Monetary Reform and the Less Developed Countries"(1977b). The previous eleven months had seen him visit fifteen countries.

Harry's post-1973 contributions to seminars, conferences, and public lectures account for much of his published work after that date. With the usual lags between submission and publication, even with a speedy acceptance, a significant proportion of his later publications reflected work done before his stroke. Good examples are his renewed interest in the transfer problem in November 1972, which showed in his contribution to the *festschrift* in honour of Lloyd Metzler in 1974 (1974i), or his "Keynes and British Economics" written on 29 April 1973 but not appearing until 1975 in Milo Keynes's *Essays on John Maynard Keynes* (1975n).

The overall impression left by the publications of this last period is the continuity with the past – the working out of further implications of earlier initiatives or of applying similar methods to other new problems. Examples of the former are the raft of publications on the monetary approach to the balance of payments and the continuing attempt, culminating in "Monetarism: A Historic–Theoretic Perspective" (1977f) to sort out the longer term developments in monetary theory in the twentieth century. An example of the latter is his paper on libraries and the economics profession, which represented yet another angle of perception of his many discussions of academic life and politics. It also marked perhaps his most disparaging comments on the PhD.

One of the intellectually safe ways of producing a successful Ph.D. thesis . . . has been to do more elegantly and with greater generality a piece of work previously done by someone else in the same institution: if B does better than A, something for which A got the Ph.D, it is thought to be very difficult for the teachers who approved A's thesis to turn down B's thesis. This is one important reason why so many young economists who are promising at the stage of the Ph.D. are never heard of again; without someone else's shoulders to stand on, they turn out to be intellectual midgets. (1975l, 626)

formation of currency areas and the issue of asymmetry for the international monetary organisation."

Harry's later pieces are, unfortunately, marked by a yet more acerbic tone. It is hard to think of a commentary from an earlier Harry as sharp as that on C. Fred Bergsten and W. R. Cline's "Increasing Economic Interdependence: The Implications for Research":

Bergsten and Cline promise a research agenda; but what they actually offer is a shopping list prepared by a would-be master chef who is so accustomed to eating in first-class French restaurants that he does not know that established firms like General Mills, H. J. Heinz, Pepperidge Farms, and Birdseye exist to make it unnecessary for the home cook to grind his own corn, bake his own bread and wash his own potatoes. Their list shows remarkable ignorance of both theory and empirical work in the international economic field. (1976d, 162).

Or his discussion of J. R. Hicks's views in "What Is Right with Monetarism":

Sir John offers his readers no information on who "the monetarists" are, on what, if they exist, they have written – assuming they are atypically British enough to have published serious scientific analysis of policy problems – and on why (again if they exist) they are, or might be, of any relevance to serious discussion of British economic policy. Instead Sir John offers his readers what can best be likened to a ghost story, told by nanny to her little charges as a preliminary to getting them tucked away quietly and gratefully into bed. On normal nights this is an innocent and effective nanny-ish stratagem; but it is not to be recommended on the night the house burns down. . . .

Nobel Prizes, in economics as in other scientific subjects, are awarded for distinguished service to the cause of scholarship and advancements of scientific understanding, not for tilting at intellectual windmills, which may help explain why Sir John Hicks is the only native-born British economist so far honoured with the Nobel Laureate (for his contributions to pure economic theory). Of course, any serious scientist has the privilege of spending his leisure time as he likes, including tilting at any windmills his imagination transmogrifies into evil giants, in the name of the Fair Dulcinea. But it would be unfortunate in the extreme if Sir John's recreational tilting were to be interpreted by the general public as a gallant defence against a qualified and competent challenge. (1976c, 13, 17)

Fortunately, Harry declined to comment on Richard Kahn's contribution to the same discussion in *Lloyds Bank Review*.

I should explain with reference to Richard Kahn that I owe him many debts for his past kindnesses when I was just a beginner at King's College, and I would therefore prefer not to get involved in frontal conflict with him as I should have to do now that he is an apologist for left-wing policy expedients. (Box 38, Correspondence with Journals, to J. R. Winton, 17 December 1975)

Harry and Liz arrived in Geneva from New Delhi on 9 January 1977. Classes at the Institute began the next day. Harry's teaching responsibilities, as before, included a class in microeconomics and trade theory for doctoral students and diploma students specialising in international economics and a seminar with Gerard Curzon, Richard Blackhurst, and Jan Tumlir on "International Trade Issues: Theory and Practice."

The term started well. Harry and Liz worked on their joint book, *The Shadow of Keynes: Understanding Keynes, Cambridge and Keynesian Economics*, and had it ready for the publisher by the end of the month. He provided a preface for his *Selected Essays in Monetary Economics* (1978) from his two previous volumes of essays on the subject. Harry also revised his paper with Robert Nobay, "Monetarism: A Historic-Theoretic Perspective," which was to appear in the *Journal of Economic Literature* in June and began work on a paper, "Trade Theory with Minimal and Satiable Wants" for a *festschrift* for A. P. Lerner's seventy-fifth birthday.[14] On 3 February, Jacob Frenkel reported after a telephone conversation that Harry didn't feel busy enough (Box 51, Correspondence 1971–7, C–G, from P. Hume, 4 February 1977).

But on 5 February, Harry had a second stroke and was rushed to hospital. Despite Liz's reassurances to friends, the stroke was serious. Harry was in and out of a coma for the first week or so. Miraculously, the stroke caused no additional damage. But he was still seriously ill. His condition was subsequently exacerbated by "a bad reaction to medication he was receiving" and "serious trouble from his liver" (Box 51, Correspondence 1972–7, C–G, P. Hume to A. Krueger, 18 February 1977; Patinkin Papers, Elizabeth Johnson to D. Patinkin, 3 March 1977). On 28 February Liz reported to Arthur Seldon of the Institute of Economic Affairs that "he is miraculously off the danger list and making good progress" (Hoover Institution, Institute of Economic Affair Papers, Box 210, Folder "Keynes and Pseudo Keynes"). Visitors to Geneva during late February and March reported his condition was improving. After five weeks, Liz recorded in her pocket diary: "Harry walked." Typically he had been told by his doctor that he could attempt to walk down a hospital corridor but proceeded to walk down and back (Elizabeth Simpson, 26 July 2005). On 15 March, Liz told John Evans, the

---

[14] Harry had offered the first paper to Mark Perlman the previous March. Nobay had prepared the first version by incorporating a number of Harry's ideas from previously published papers which he sent both to Perlman and Harry at the beginning of January (Box 38, Journal of Economic Literature). As for the second paper, according to Jacob Frenkel (Box 58, to Max Corden, 5 August 1977), "Harry spent a lot of time and effort on his paper during his stay in Geneva, and it seems he basically completed most of the sections, except for one or two." It was not sufficiently complete, however, to make it into the *festschrift*.

president of the University of Toronto, which had offered Harry an honorary degree in its spring 1977 convocation, that

[h]e is making excellent progress in his recovery and I believe that he will be able to attend the convocation to receive the degree. But it is still too early to be sure that by June 7 he will be physically strong enough to address such a large audience – although he is eager to undertake the task and has already decided on the theme he would like to present. (Box 51, Commitments Completed 1977)

Later in March they hoped that he would be transferred from the hospital to a rehabilitation centre with pleasant views of the Alps where he could continue his recovery and undergo physical therapy. And he did move at the end of the month. There was even some talk of a discharge from hospital, although it was realised that it would still be some time before he would be fit to travel from Geneva or before he could take up correspondence and other activities. When Jacob Frenkel visited Harry after the 28–29 March meeting of the Bellagio Group in Basel, he brought another document. As he recalled:

During the last session of the conference in a spontaneous manner each participant attached his signature to a note to Harry telling him how he had been missed and wishing him a speedy recovery. I was asked to bring this note to Harry. . . . Harry was very touched; he could feel the genuine wish. For once, academic economists, Governors of Central Banks, officials of the Treasury, officials of international organizations, Americans and Europeans have all joined hands and have all spoken with one voice – wishing recovery to the person who they had all respected so much and from whom they have all learned so much. Harry, who was already very weak, smiled. It pleased him very much indeed.

They also talked shop. Harry was anxious to get back to work, worried about missing his classes, and concerned that his illness had held up the consideration of a paper for the *JPE*. A. C. Harberger, who had been in England for the AUTE meetings, also visited him during the first week of April (Box 51, Correspondence 1971–7, C–G, from P. Hume, 29 March 1977; Box 39, P. Hume to S. Kaliski, 5 April 1977; Box 47, Canterbury and Johnson, P. Hume to E. Ray Canterbury, 28 March 1977; J Frenkel, "Harry G. Johnson Memorial Meeting," 20–1).

On 13 April, however, Liz reported to Patricia Hume

HGJ is having a set-back but he is holding his own & I hope soon it is going to be another piece of past history. (Box 51, Correspondence 1971–7, C–G)

The set-back was so serious that Liz reported to President Evans, first by telegram on 28 April and then by letter on 30 April that

[o]nce again he is on the mend and we have had to realise that he will not be recovered sufficiently by June 7th to think of travelling to Toronto then. (Box 41, Commitments Completed 1977)

But even that put an optimistic gloss on it: Her diary entry for the day was: "Harry sick" (Elizabeth Simpson, 26 July 2005). This was the final turn for the worse: Harry died in Geneva at 12:30 a.m. on 9 May.

SEVENTEEN

Conclusion

For the economics profession throughout the world the third quarter of this century was an Age of Johnson. . . . It was his impact on his own profession . . . that justifies calling the era his Age.

Tobin 1978, 443–4

Tobin illustrated Harry's influence in terms of publications, citations, contributions to lectures, conferences and symposia, journal editing, and a "far flung, numerous and devoted band of students, friends and admirers" (444). He elaborated four reasons for his influence: his willingness to accommodate fellow scholars and students; his powers of exposition and synthesis informed by an almost limitless knowledge of the literature; his internationalism; and his status as a "character" in a profession with few colourful personalities. Graduate students at LSE used to refer to him as "big Harry."

In Harry we had a hero whose style of life and work and talk were worthy of a genius of poetry or art. Physically he stood out of a crowd, a large man, incorrigibly overweight, loudly and informally dressed years before the unconventional became the fashion. Only his eyes betrayed the fire of his mind. (446–7)

Harry was, as C. P. Kindleberger remarked, "one who never did anything by halves: writing, editing, eating, drinking, smoking and, after giving up smoking, whittling" (1991, 151).

His passing was marked as few are in economics. There was a notice by A. R. Prest in *The Economist*, which in those days did not normally publish obituaries. The *Canadian Journal of Economics* had a special supplement in November 1978, the most extensive notice that the Canadian Economics Association or its predecessor had taken of any economist since the four

essays on Keynes in May 1947.[1] The *Journal of Political Economy* devoted
147 pages to recording and assessing his contributions (August 1984). The
widely spread obituary notices did not include the *Economic Journal,* where
Harry had recently supported their suppression on the ground that they
"have been used . . . to play academic politics" (Box 38, Correspondence
with Journals, to Phyllis Deane, 22 February 1971).

One of the emphases of the discussions of Harry immediately after his
death and subsequently has been his relationships with the young, both
students and colleagues. It comes up time and time again in memories of day-
to-day contact – the way he was always available, always willing to comment
on drafts and to turn them around within the day on occasion, continually
encouraging students to press forward and get the relevant piece of work
done (Patinkin Papers, Harry Johnson Memorial Meeting, 10, Clement,
Memorial Meeting, 14–15). The relationships were business-like: Students
were advised to "Get in, make your point and get out" (Frenkel, Memorial
Meeting, 17; see also discussion in Chapter 12). Harry was a hard taskmaster,
for he expected students (and his colleagues) to be as committed, even as
obsessed, professionally as he was and would "go off" someone, not only
personally but also in comments to others, if they tried to have a more
balanced existence (Lipsey 2001, 615). Unfortunately, the "offness" almost
invariably got around. Zvi Griliches observed that Harry, like George Stigler
and Milton Friedman, was "so bright and did not suffer fools lightly" that as
a consequence he "rarely got the students that . . . [he] deserved" (Kreuger
and Taylor 2000, 178).

His accessibility was not restricted to students at whatever institution he
was currently associated with: He was accessible to everyone, perhaps even
too accessible. As Jagdish Bhagwati remembered:

Countless numbers of manuscripts would reach him, from aspiring students of
international economics and somehow Harry found the energy and the time to
read them carefully and to write back to the authors promptly. He continued doing
this long after he had started publishing furiously and the opportunity cost of his
time had risen astronomically: it was again a telling example of the responsibility
that invariably animated his professional behaviour. He once remarked with dry
humour, when he was staying with us and my wife asked him what he had been
doing in the early hours of the morning when we had been still asleep: "I read two

[1] Innis had received an obituary notice by Alexander Brady, a bibliography, and an evaluation,
"Innis and Economics" by W. T. Easterbrook over three issues between February and August
1953 [*Canadian Journal of Economics and Political Science,* 19 (February 1953), 87–96, (May
1953), 233–44, and (August 1953), 291–303].

manuscripts, one indifferent and the other bad; what is worse, I could have written one good paper during that time." (Bhagwati 1998, 493–4)

In the autobiographical essays collected by Roger Backhouse and Roger Middleton (2000) a quarter of the contributors refer to Harry's influence on their careers.[2]

As an editor he was assiduous in seeking out papers that had something significant to say, in improving them to increase their impact, and, where they intersected with his own work, in highlighting their importance in his surveys or his own extensions of their achievements. He described his own activities as an editor of the *JPE* where he was sole editor from 1960 to 1966 (and joint editor from 1969 to 1977) in terms that were echoed in many of his obituaries.

As editor I worked to principles I had developed in relation to . . . [*The Review of Economic Studies* and *The Manchester School*]. The JPE already had the principle of quick turn-around of manuscripts, but I accelerated this by looking over new submissions as soon as I could, and sorting out the ones that in my judgment were non-starters and returning them immediately, with advice on what other journals might be prepared to accept them (if it was junk I said so). I also refereed many of the manuscripts myself. A second principle was to give rejected authors as thorough an explanation of why their manuscripts were being rejected as was possible. This I did in very blunt language, often; the result was frequently an enraged reply, to which my rejoinder was that there were other journals. Many authors do not realize that if the referees don't understand their work, the readers won't either. A third principle was that articles should conform to the stated purposes of the journal, which were to encourage the progress of theoretical and especially empirical work; hence I looked for new ideas and problems rather than the elaboration of new mathematical models, and also discouraged mere exercises in regression analysis that did not properly formulate and test hypotheses. A fourth principle was to pay attention to the detail of articles, checking carefully for errors and eliminating the repetition of well-known analysis and lengthy recounting of the literature. In a busy profession, a crisp note is more likely to establish a good reputation than a soggy long article. A fifth principle, carried over from the *Review*, was to pay special attention to new and presumably young authors, teaching them how to organize and write their ideas and material to a professional standard. Sometimes I practically re-wrote such submissions. (1969 Autobiographical Note, 12–13)

In his 1974 Self-Evaluation (15–16) he added that he "did not hesitate to solicit articles from economists whom he judged had interesting work to report." And he was successful in making the *JPE* "in general opinion the liveliest and most influential scholarly publication in economics" (Tobin

---

[2] The individuals involved are Wilfred Beckerman, Samuel Brittan, Max Corden, Walter Eltis, Koichi Hamada, Peter Kenen, David Laidler, William Lazonick, and Richard Lipsey.

1978, 444). One must assume that he had a significant role in most of the articles in his field in the *Review of Economic Studies* and the *JPE* during his editorship. Corden provides examples, including his own work on effective protection discussed in Chapter 10 (1984, 587). According to Corden, he "had the remarkable ability to guide numerous authors in fruitful directions. He was able to see a contribution . . . in the perspective of the whole field and the scientific development . . . of the whole subject" (586–7). Even "when older, as the more impatient, sometimes irritable giant of the profession, he always had time to listen, to offer suggestions, to set his correspondents' ideas in new paths, to improve, and to encourage" (Scott 1977).

There were also the institutional contributions, notably in Britain and Canada. The British contributions include the enhancement of the role of the AUTE, which resulted in the transformation of the Royal Economic Society, the initiation of the study group, and pioneering use of academic talent in the discussion and formulation of public policy in the Trade Policy Research Centre. In Canada, in addition to acting as an informal placement officer, Harry had important long-term connections with the University of Western Ontario where he helped Grant Reuber build a first-class department and Queen's University where he worked hard on making the summer Institute for Economic Research a centre for professional development in the Canadian academic community in the 1960s. He provided important advice to the new Carleton University and support to the University of Windsor's annual Canadian–American seminars. At the AEA meetings he helped Canadian chairs in economics to find people for their growing departments. When A. E. Safarian, then chair at the University of Saskatchewan mentioned his university's relative isolation, Harry promptly came to Saskatoon to give several lectures and arranged contacts with several others to do the same. There were also links with the Pakistan Institute of Development Economics for which as a director he gave a week of lectures and research advice every year and the Pacific Trade and Development Conference of which he was a founding member.

When he travelled, he did not do so as a dignitary visiting the provinces and bringing news from the centre. He was a professional with things to discuss with other professionals. He would not only leave ideas behind, but he would also take what he had learned from his visit onto his next destination. Moreover, he would forge productive links between isolated scholars. As David Laidler remembers: "I knew all about Laurence Harris's work on money and he about mine, when I was still in Berkeley and he was in London as a result of a visit by Harry to the west coast" (27 December 2004) There was no condescension.

Yet if he was generous with his time to review the work of others, he made relatively few demands on them with his own drafts. His writings are remarkably sparse in their personal, as compared with publication, acknowledgements. *International Trade and Economic Growth* has one chapter (V) with a formal initial acknowledgement (five other acknowledgements in footnotes); *Money, Trade and Economic Growth* has none of either sort; *Essays in Monetary Economics* has one formal acknowledgement (IV) and one in the footnotes; *Aspects of the Theory of Tariffs* has four (4, 7, 13, and 15) and nine in the footnotes; *Further Essays in Monetary Economics* has none; *On Economics and Society* has none but two in footnotes. Nor was he that collaborative as an author: twenty-four scientific papers, one book, and one government report do not loom large in an output the size of his. Perhaps he did not circulate his drafts because he wanted to avoid criticism. That would be consistent with his insecurity, but it did not extend to his scientific contributions, even if he was anxious before delivering lectures. The absence of acknowledgements and collaborators could reflect his sureness of the rightness of his ideas – and his desire not to be held up.

In 1973 Roger Vaughan, a graduate student at Chicago drew a caricature of Harry, entitled "Great Moments in Economics No. 5: First graphical depiction of general equilibrium in an *n* sector model, circa 1973" (Plate 10). It showed Harry's head on the body of an octopus with pens, diagrams, whisky bottle and glass in the tentacles. He might have added a pocket knife and a snuff box.

The caricature highlights one characteristic of Harry, his busyness. It did not have to be economics, but a lot of it was economics related. The picture of Harry, pen and yellow pad in hand, scribbling through most of a long flight while consuming his bottle of duty-free scotch is standard fare in memories. So too was the account of him writing in the morning before anyone else was up or in the middle of the night. He was lucky that personal comfort didn't matter too much: He could work happily wherever he landed. According to Liz, he appreciated the rented professorial house at Northwestern – timeworn and ordinary – for its up-to-date, efficient appliances. If he wasn't writing he could be talking and carving a figure or a complicated puzzle. Of course, until 1973 he could be talking shop over many drinks, as at LSE where he held court for graduate students in the Three Tuns on Tuesday nights.

He could occasionally relax – particularly on the family island in Georgian Bay near Parry Sound where he could take the outboard and explore, island-hopping among the 30,000 islands, stopping to swim and dive into the cold clear water off the high rocks.

He was driven in several senses. He was a missionary for good economics. He was prepared to go anywhere to shed light, to find out what others were doing and together to add to the development of the discipline – Hence his experiments in communicating the subject – the Aldine treatises, the Gray–Mills lectures, the Money Study Group, and the Trade Policy Research Centre. This missionary aspect of Harry also explains his willingness to read, to comment and encourage. But he was self-driven. He pushed himself ever harder, encouraged by the technology that made travel over ever longer distances easier from his relatively leisurely first trip to the Far East in 1956, to his 1969 "typical year" with its half dozen transatlantic flights and perhaps one transpacific flight to his fifteen-country final eleven months of travelling. Even in his prime, he found travel tiring, but he enjoyed it on the whole and found it stimulating to know his professional colleagues all over the world and to pick up new ideas even before they were committed to paper, much less published. He was repeating on a global scale the practices that he had developed in Cambridge as he became the "teacher, guide, patron and guru ... [and] already a legend among the younger U.K. economists" (Harberger 1978, 57).

He was also a missionary for specialised graduate education in economics. His model for such education looked increasingly like Chicago with its emphasis on the department as the unit of organisation, although he could on occasion put in a good word for places like MIT. He was less happy with places like Harvard or Yale which

were not (and are not now) Departments of Economics in the same sense as Chicago's. . . . They were congeries of small personal departments depending from individual senior professors, to whose seminars (their main activity) transient Assistant Professors attached themselves. . . . In addition, the Chicago academic community lived mostly within a mile of the campus . . . in contrast to the far-flung suburban living patterns of Harvard, M.I.T. and Yale. (*Shadow*, 86–7).

The model department specialised in the instruction of graduate students and it rather than its individual members controlled the curriculum, which was geared to the production of technically well-trained, highly motivated economists. With Harry, at least, even in Chicago, well-trained meant, as David Laidler remembered, that "students should get to know 'the literature' and not just those bits of it that were being locally produced" (2000, 330).

In August 1973, in correspondence with a student who was complaining about Chicago economics, Harry restated his view of the place, which had strong echoes of what A. C. Harberger had told him in 1957 (see discussion in Chapter 7).

I think the Chicago mixture is the best kind of economics on offer. If I did not think so, I would be a professor at Harvard, Yale, Princeton or possibly Cambridge, England. . . . I came from Manchester to Chicago . . . because I was convinced that Chicago was going somewhere whereas no other place in England was, and the other places in the U.S. seemed too soft and too much like Cambridge, England. (I have come to recognize the excellence of M.I.T. by American and other standards.)

. . . One of the great things about Chicago to me is that one cannot relax and simply pass off personal prejudices as scientific dogma; one's colleagues and students will catch one out. . . .

I think we have the kind of scholarly community at Chicago that is usually held up as an ideal for universities. The simplest way of putting it is that I can trust my colleagues to know their fields, and not try to fool me and their fellow economists into accepting economic nonsense for political convenience. . . . Similarly, if a colleague states that there is a problem in his area of specialization, I can assume that there is a real problem, and not, as often happens elsewhere, that he is creating a problem to advertise himself. I might add that this is the only university I have worked in, as regular or visiting staff member, where this has been true, with the partial exception of Manchester; but I have indirect reasons for believing that the same is probably true of M.I.T. or Rochester, within their range of economic interests. (Box 41, Chicago School, to Gary Eriksen, 8 August 1973)

Harry had difficulties with some of his Chicago colleagues, most notably Milton Friedman. Yet, when he was in Britain, he did not let his relationship with Friedman interfere with his dissemination of important ideas emanating from the latter's work. He brought Friedman to the Sheffield Money Study Group conference and through David Laidler ensured that he had an invitation to take part in the BBC's *Controversy* show. If he had behaved otherwise, given British attitudes to Friedman and his work, the personal pay-off would have been larger. But the professional pay-off would have been smaller.

His ideal for graduate education resembled that found at Chicago. Harry attempted to produce the beginnings of something similar at LSE. There he ran into several problems. LSE may have been unusual in Britain in the relative size of its graduate school, but it was still predominantly an undergraduate institution. Moreover, despite his and his successors' attempts to increase the size of the graduate school, in the remainder of the twentieth century the proportion of graduate students did not reach the 50 percent proposed for the 1972–7 quinquennium, despite the strong incentives to admit overseas postgraduates, and remained around 45 percent (Dahrendorf 1995, 431). Houghton Street could not carry with it the ambience of Hyde Park: LSE students and faculty would forever be commuters coping with the high costs of living in London. Moreover, recent British governments of either political stripe have been even less willing than those of Harry's generation to fund higher education so "funding … remained predictable only in its decline" (Dahrendorf 1995, 512). As one Labour Minister put it at a dinner: "You cannot win. The Tories think that all university teachers are red, and Labour thinks that all university students are middle class. The coalition is unbeatable" (Dahrendorf 1995, 495). The result was, despite milking the full-fee overseas student market for what it was worth,[3] and substantial success in fund-raising and increasing research income, the School's financial position remained difficult and staff–student ratios declined dramatically. Nevertheless, in Harry's time the MSc was a success, as he acknowledged (see discussion in Chapter 11). Many of the things Harry worked for have come to pass first among the economists and later across the School: Procedures and standards for hiring and promotion went his way, as did the culture of professionalism. He might have been more successful had he not opted for the dual LSE–Chicago appointment, which certainly shortened his life, even while, as he believed, it increased his professional output. Many of the difficulties he reported with LSE seemed to be related to his absence or his assuming that his colleagues took his concerns as seriously in relation to their other ones as he did. But the fundamental transformation of LSE into a mainly graduate institution with appropriate staffing and remuneration would still have been blocked by lack of resources.

There is one aspect of Harry's discussions of how other people did economics that needs further comment: his critical discussions of English and Canadian economics as exemplified by practices at Cambridge and the University of Toronto. I am not here concerned with his views on individuals' commitment to the subject or professionalism in his sense, nor with their adherence to what he regarded as an older model of professional education, which he regarded as inefficient. Rather I am concerned with his comments on standards and politicisation. These criticisms were strongest when it came to British Keynesianism and for various reasons became his almost irrational reaction to the use of the word "Cambridge" in 1975 (see discussion in Chapter 12).

In thinking about his criticisms, I have been struck by a comment made by R. C. O. Matthews in his review of Roger Middleton's *Charlatans or Saviours?: Economists and the British Economy from Marshall to Meade* (1998). He remarked in passing on the author's use of Harry's writings, saying that he

---

[3] The School garnered a Queen's Award for Export Achievement during I. G. Patel's term as director!

takes Johnson's views too seriously and does not discount them sufficiently for animus. In his early Cambridge years, Johnson was an ardent Keynesian, a disciple of Kahn and an acid-tongued critic of the still-living Robertson. As was said of an earlier Oxbridge polemicist, "we cannot give up early beliefs . . . without some shock to the character. It made him hate what he had left . . . with the bitterness of one who had been imposed on." (2000, 189)

The quotation was from a review of the posthumous *Essays* by Mark Pattison, the nineteenth-century Oxford reformer (Sparrow 1967, 58).[4]

There is an element of truth in this, but it can be pushed too far. Harry may have run with the Cambridge Keynesians and crossed swords with Robertson from time to time, but the remarkable thing about the two is how well they got on. Unlike any other member of the "secret seminar," Harry published with Robertson a piece of textual exegesis on the *General Theory* (1955). To judge by what has survived, the correspondence between the two was the most extensive that Robertson had with his younger Cambridge colleagues who entered the profession in the postwar period. It had nothing to do with faculty politics. Moreover, some of Harry's own critical comments on the conflicts between Robertson and the Cambridge Keynesians date from as far back as 1951 (see discussion in Chapter 5).

It is true that in his later memoirs Harry exaggerated some aspects of the dispute, such as the Keynesians depriving Robertson of his well-deserved chair and forcing him to LSE as a result (*Shadow*, 139). It is also true that Harry left Cambridge because he did not want to take sides to the extent necessary for preferment (see discussion in Chapter 6). But he remained remarkably loyal to some of his Cambridge mentors such as Richard Kahn. And he watched in horror while the faculty, always a political place when appointments were concerned, did itself real damage in the 1960s and 1970s with a number of less than stellar senior appointments and was unable, with five vacancies, to make any junior appointment for more than a year because of splits among the economists on the appointments committee.

The Toronto story is different. As a young man he thought its undergraduate teaching was as good as Cambridge's (see discussion in Chapter 3). He never compared its graduate teaching with Harvard's, perhaps because Toronto's was relatively underdeveloped when he was a graduate student, but we know that at least initially he was unimpressed (see discussion in

---

[4] The quotation continued: "and has been led to commit himself to what he now feels to be absurd and contemptible, and the bitterness of this disappointment gave an edge to all his work."

Chapter 4). After his 1952 visit, he went off Toronto. It could tempt him for short periods, but he could not accept it as a base and eventually, after Vincent Bladen had failed with offers both as chair and dean, the university ceased making offers. By then, the department, still containing economists, political scientists, and commerce faculty (sociology left in 1963), was becoming unwieldy. From thirty-four members in 1959, its full-time staff had tripled by 1970 and would rise further during the next decade to reach 182 before its dissolution in 1982. There were a substantial number of departures (145 between 1970–1 and 1980–1) so that the actual number of new appointments greatly exceeded the net increase (Drummond 1983, 114, 152). The rise in the number of faculty was largely driven by undergraduate enrolments, although there were more graduate students about.[5] This sharp rise in numbers occurred during a period when the university's policies regarding tenure and promotion, never very clear, were in a state of flux. Even once formal, modern procedures were devised, it took time for them to become part of the culture (Drummond 1983, 112–13, 153–4). Procedural murkiness at a time when there were large numbers of new appointments meant variability of standards. The turbulence also affected the design of the graduate programme. The result drew Harry's ire in the ACAP report (see discussion in Chapter 11), despite the fact that he thought Toronto was recovering (see discussion in Chapter 11). The historian of the department thought that Harry was to some extent unjust, although he allowed that the graduate programme in economics was in difficulties in the 1970s (Drummond 1983, 146–9).

Harry may have been driven but he was also efficient. Once asked by Alec Cairncross how, given all the calls on his time, he ever read anything, he responded that "learning was subject to incr[easing] returns. One goes through work more quickly and with less effort as one went on" (Cairncross 1994, 341). Or as he put it in his 1969 Autobiographical Notes (15): "Also by maintaining an interest in a variety of fields, I derive considerable economies of overhead costs." He also attributed his ability to stay up to date in his chosen fields to the networks of friends and to conference-going. The same advantages flowed from his editing. Increasing returns, or more accurately learning by doing, were probably characteristic of his writing. As a young man, he found writing lectures or papers a struggle – full of crossings out and second thoughts. Later these became less common. He became more fluent, taking considerable pride in his prose, although he never managed

---

[5] The number of PhDs completed in any year did not rise above three until 1965.

the easy prose of a Maynard Keynes, who could write a complex paper for the British Cabinet from scratch in one draft over a weekend. As he always preferred a written text, easy writing was essential for the summing up with which he concluded many of the conferences he attended.

Harry took great pleasure in doing things well. He was proud to exhibit his sculptures, not only at Manchester but also at the meetings of the American Economic Association where Harry, William Baumol, and several others would have a special room "usually next to where the publishers were exhibiting." Baumol remembered:

Harry and I used to sit on opposite sides of the table, each with little pieces of wood, sit there carving chess sets or whatever. We used to bring pieces of wood to each other, with a little one-upmanship. I thought I had won one time when I brought him a piece of Monticello, because Julian Boyd, who was then on the faculty, was the head of the work on the Jefferson papers, and they were working on Monticello and replaced some of the beams. And Julian carefully brought me back some of the wood. So I thought, "There, I've got you Harry." And next time Harry came back with a piece of wood from King's College Chapel. So I lost that one. (Krueger 2001, 228)

After Chicago's initial failed foray into capital/labour substitution (see discussion in Chapter 8), Harry was very well supported. He had secretaries on both sides of the Atlantic, got manuscripts typed, letters answered, students accommodated and mothered, appointments recorded and kept – not to mention accomplish some of the minutiae of nonacademic daily life. Harry dedicated *On Economics and Society*: "In gratitude to my secretaries in Chicago and London . . . ," naming their names.

He read omnivorously if not systematically outside economics. Neither his surviving papers, nor his writings, nor the memoirs of others suggest that he had strong cultural interests. His recreational reading was detective stories and science fiction, read and discarded quickly. His comment on his month at the Institute for Advanced Studies in Vienna in September 1971 is telling.

September was spent in Vienna, a place I would recommend to no-one who does not enjoy listening to opera and plays in German, because there is no private entertainment apart from an evening or two in a public bar drinking new wine. (Box 27, Writing 1972–3, Faculty Report 1971–2)

His curiosity could be roused by a Chinese opera or Indian ragas. He was attracted to folk songs and folk singers – but he was tone deaf. He could enjoy a play, a concert, or an exhibition, but unless it was a special occasion he didn't have the time. His attitude to the arts was that of most Canadians of his generation: They were a preoccupation of a self-conscious and isolated elite. One catches this same sense in a comment on Vincent Bladen's report on the economics of the performing arts when he noted that "it seems to me that live performances are very inefficient from all sorts of points of view, and that movies and television should permit the fraction of the population in such performances to be reduced," a proposal with which Bladen disagreed "completely" (Box 40, Correspondence 1971–7, A–B, to Bladen, 16 April 1973; from Bladen, 26 April 1973). Movies and television were for Harry the equivalent of lecture transcripts in transferring quality to the hinterlands (Elizabeth Simpson, 26 July 2005).

The largest visible landmark of Harry's presence in economics was his published output. In terms of the categories in which he organised and recorded it, there were 526 professional articles, 35 books and pamphlets, more than 150 book reviews, and 27 edited books or special issues of journals. There was a significant amount of journalism, including contributions to British weeklies such as *The Spectator* and *The Listener*. Some observers could quibble over his including particular pieces in particular classes, but the sheer volume of the output makes such quibbles otiose. Other observers, most notably George Stigler, had reservations:

A reporter commented on George's article count of only 100 saying that he had just interviewed Harry Johnson, who had written 500. George's response: "Mine are all different." (Friedland 1993, 781)

There is a point in Stigler's crack, but a remarkably small one, for Harry was normally scrupulous in reporting as just one item articles that might have appeared initially in two or more places. Otherwise, there was always some differentiation, most of which was deliberate. It might also reflect the vagaries of the editorial process, as happened in his last two papers on the monetary approach to the balance of payments, which had their origin in a single paper before being transformed by the efforts of two editors in interaction with Harry (see discussion in Chapter 13).

The articles were inevitably variable in quality. In discussing one of Harry's collections of articles he regarded as most important, Max Corden remarked of *Aspects of the Theory of Tariffs*:

The reader will find several Johnsons here. There is the tight theorist, presenting arguments so briefly and in such a condensed fashion that many readers will overlook important points, or have to read the paper three or four times to grasp it. There are patches of graduate student Johnson (or economics-as-applied mathematics Johnson) exploring rigorously questions of little importance or not bothering to explain any possible relevance. There is the expositor and consolidator, writing articles that waste no time on trivia and are a teacher's dream. . . . And there is the worldly, clear-headed Johnson applying himself to questions of importance and displaying insights that genuinely illuminate one's understanding of the way the world works or should work. (1972, 727)

One way one can measure the impact of articles, other than their citations, is their reproduction in various collections of readings be they the classic American Economic Association's series or the work of academic entrepreneurs. Harry's four contributions to the Association's *Readings in International Economics* (1968) represented a high for that volume,[6] although over the two association collections in the field, Samuelson reaches the same total. Overall, 41 of Harry's papers (or just under 8 percent of the total) received such attention.[7] As for the citations, between 1970 and 1976, according to Herbert Grubel, Harry was cited on average 249 times a year. This made him the second most cited international economist after Paul Samuelson (Grubel 1980, 9). In terms of the number of publications cited, Harry came first with 59 over that period (14).

One of the most remarkable facets of the years after 1977 has been the demise of Harry's influence to the extent that if one asks contemporary graduate students about him, the response is normally a blank look. One can explain the reaction from several measures of influence. Let us return to the citation counts. In 1990 he was cited on 94 occasions; in 1995, 51; in 2000, 38; but the number has stabilised in the past few years (2003–5) in the upper 20s.

In 1973 Peter Kenen organised a conference on the theme "International Trade and Finance: Frontiers of Research." As Kenen recounted it, the origins of the conference were unusual:

Emerging from two years of university administration, I spent a year of intellectual rest and recuperation trying to catch up with my subject. Like most of us, I had already fallen behind being a full-time economist. But my plight had grown worse while I was away from the subject, and I did not have the usual excuse – that I was too busy writing to read. Eventually, I thought it best to ask for help. I organised a conference. (1975, xiii)

The conference was held in March 1973. Inevitably Harry was present, but his contribution was that of a panellist in the closing discussion on "what we need to know?" His discussion had no bibliographical references. If one looks at the volume, one finds that Harry's work was mentioned in every chapter except the one on Project Link, a large internationally linked macroeconomic model. In the bibliographies to the other eight, Harry's work appears thirty-two times. Of the references, four articles appear more

---

[6] It probably would have been higher had Harry not been one of the volume's editors.
[7] The corresponding figure for George Stigler, roughly adjusting the categories in his 1993 *JPE* bibliography to match those of Harry's, was 11 percent.

than once, meaning that there are references to twenty-six separate publications. Twenty years later, in April 1993, Kenen organised another conference at Princeton, this time on "Understanding Interdependence: The Macroeconomics of the Open Economy." This conference had substantial papers surveying and synthesising bodies of research, but fewer than the 1973 conference. Yet, in discussing a field where Harry had been active in his time, there were only three references to Harry's work – two to "Towards a General Theory of the Balance of Payments" and one to "The Case for Flexible Exchange Rates, 1969."

Textbooks tell a similar story. In his 1978 appreciation of "Harry Johnson's Contributions to the Pure Theory of International Trade," Richard Lipsey used Miltiades Chacholiades's *International Trade Theory and Policy* (1978b) – a book for which Harry wrote a foreword – as a way of measuring Harry's influence. He found forty-seven separate page citations to Harry's work with twenty-six separate items cited. The number of page citations put him fourth after Ohlin, Heckscher, and Samuelson, but he was first in the number of separate items cited. Professor Chacholiades also published *International Monetary Theory and Policy* in 1978. There Harry ranked third in the number of page citations, this time after Keynes and James Meade, but his fourteen separate publications cited again put him first. Yet, if one moves on to the 1990s and looks at the widely used *Foundations of International Macroeconomics* by Maurice Obstfeld and Kenneth Rogoff one finds only one reference to Harry, his 1955 "Economic Expansion and International Trade." There is no reference to Harry and the monetary approach to the balance of payments. The nearest one gets to Harry on the monetary approach is a piece of doctrinal history by Jacob Frenkel in the *Scandinavian Journal of Economics*, later reprinted in their jointly edited volume *The Economics of Exchange Rates: Selected Studies* (1978c). The recently published *Handbook of International Trade* (Choi and Harringa 2003) has references for nine of Harry's publications and nine index references. The top number of index references goes to R. W. Jones with thirty. Tad Rybczynski with his one publication had twenty-one index references. The only graduate-level textbook that refers to Harry on the old scale is Bhagwati, Panagariya, and Srinivasan's *Lectures on International Trade* (2nd ed. 1998) where the chapter bibliographies contain thirty-three references to twenty-five separate publications by Harry, including two with Bhagwati himself. Modern undergraduate textbooks present a picture of decline similar to most graduate texts.[8]

---

[8] Peter Kenen's *The International Economy* (4th ed. 2000a) has references to six pieces by Harry; Markusen et al.'s *International Trade: Theory and Evidence* (1995) has four; Paul

Thus far I have dealt with international economics. However, changing the focus to monetary economics would not change the dimensions of the story. If one looks at the *Handbook of Monetary Economics* (1990) there are references to Harry's work in the chapters on "Money, Inflation and Growth" (4); "The Supply of Money and the Control of National Income" (1); "Inflation: Theory and Evidence" (1); and "Monetary Policy in the Open Economy" (4). If one looks at Michael Woodford's *Interest and Prices: Foundations of a Theory of Monetary Policy* (2003), there are none. The more complete recent neglect of Harry's writings in macroeconomics as compared with international economics is also reflected in the *Social Science Citation Index*.

The decline in references is inevitable. Over time, innovations on the frontiers of a subject, if important, become well within the mainstream of the subject. They become incorporated in the common knowledge of practitioners and end up in textbooks often without their originator being acknowledged. Thus the reason for the "decline" is the progress in the field over the thirty years since his death, and it could be argued that some of this partly reflects Harry's influence. Surveys of an area by their nature should become dated as the subject advances. Given time, they may attract historians of thought who find them useful as snapshots of how developments in the discipline looked at the time to participants in them. In monetary economics, Harry was the master surveyor of his generation and his revival has started (Middleton 1998). And it may flourish, as it has for Gottfried Haberler's *Prosperity and Depression* (1937, 1939, 1941) whose early editions provide a picture of the profession's views on the eve of the publication of Keynes's *General Theory* and a chronicle of the first few years of the subsequent discussion. In its day, that of Harry's youth and preparation as an economist, Haberler was supplementary reading both for Toronto undergraduates and Harvard graduate students, not to mention a neophyte professor of economics at St. Francis Xavier. The same can be said of the commentaries on contemporary events such as the trials and tribulations of the international monetary system, which Harry wrote in the years after 1960. Such commentaries will become grist for the economic historian in search of examples of contemporary professional opinion. Harry's, with their strong sense of history and its lessons, are particularly appropriate. *Economic Policies Towards Less Developed Countries* is also a candidate.

Krugman and Maurice Obstfeld's *International Economics: Theory and Policy* (2000) has three; while Mordechai Kreinin's *International Economics: A Policy Approach* (9th ed. 2002) has none, even though it has a chapter on "The Monetary Approach to the Balance of Payments" (albeit "optional").

As the Rybczynski example strongly suggests, if an economist's name is attached to a piece of theory, the probability of recognition and citation in textbooks and elsewhere may rise. There are several examples in international economics – the Stolper–Samuelson theorem, the Swan diagram, and the Fleming–Mundell model as well as the Rybczynski theorem. Other examples not now formally named retain their association with particular individuals such as IS–LM once known as the Hicks–Hansen diagram. (Of course, one can also get names attached to theorems that were not associated with an author; the Ricardian equivalence theorem is a good example.) However, except for what R. W. Jones calls the "Harrod–Johnson diagram" (2003, 10–11), and the notion of "Johnson–Cournot–Nash equilibrium" with reference to "Optimum Tariffs and Retaliation" (Bhagwati, Panagariya, and Srinivasan 1998, 265), neither of which has resonated in the literature, Harry is not so remembered. In the former case, Harry was scrupulous in attributing Harrod's contribution to a lecture delivered to the AUTE in January 1957 (*ITEG*, 18 n.2).

But this was typical of Harry, who did not generally promote his own contributions or, for that matter, even worry too much about placing them in appropriate places where they would be noticed or given priority. There were of course exceptions (see discussion in Chapter 8 and 10), most notably the big exception of the monetary approach to the balance of payments. Here, initially at least, Harry did not try too hard to situate that contribution in the contemporary context as compared with the classics of previous generations – a practice that was quickly noted (see discussion in Chapter 13). Instead, his tendency was to situate his contribution in the evolving literature and not to claim originality even when he was being original. One of the most revealing comments on Harry's practices, if only because it drew a reaction from Harry, came from comments that Max Corden made about *Aspects of the Theory of Tariffs*.

In his review of that book, Corden (1972) discussed the contents as a whole but emphasised Harry's four most important papers on the theory of protection – "Optimum Trade Intervention in the Presence of Distortions," "The Cost of Protection and the Scientific Tariff," "An Economic Theory of Protectionism, Tariff Bargaining and the Formation of Customs Unions," and "The Theory of Tariff Structure, with Special Reference to World Trade and Development," all of which still turn up in the *Social Sciences Citation Index*. After discussing these papers, he continued:

I have stressed the originality of some of the contributions. Johnson's style of writing and his care in acknowledgements tend to give the impression that he has never had an original idea in his life, but that everything is consolidation, building on bricks laid by others and so on. He tends not to highlight what is new in his work but rather to stress continuity in the development of economic theory.

Thus he gives the impression that the main ideas of his "Optimal Trade Intervention" article comes from the Bhagwati–Ramaswami papers, but anybody comparing the two papers must find Johnson's paper a great advance. His "Cost of Protection" paper, he tells us, is based on the work of Corden, Harberger and Young, but while there is something in this, no one could find a systematic multi-commodity approach to the cost of protection (about which admittedly, I came to have some doubts) in the writings of the first two, nor a vigorous and systematic "scientific tariff" analysis in Young. His "Economic Theory of Protectionism" paper employs according to Johnson, "building blocks provided by a variety of recent contributions, notably, Downs' "economic theory of democracy, Becker's theory of discrimination and Breton's economic theory of nationalism." This is true, but the net result is something new. His pioneering Geneva effective protection paper goes well beyond the early papers by Barber and myself and the book by Travis he cites. (727)

On receiving a copy of Corden's review Harry replied:

I have always known that you like me personally but disapprove of me professionally, and this comes clearly through in the review. I do in all probability overdo the no-originality, recognition of other people's work, but, it is likely that I learned it from Dennis Robertson. But new ideas are scarce in our business; whereas we are all trained how to give formal expression to one when we see it. And I would rather be known as someone who appreciated his colleagues' originality than as one who stole their ideas and made excessive claims for originality on his own behalf. (Box 51, Correspondence 1971–7, C–G, to Max Corden, 30 July 1972)

In a more recent discussion, Allan Hynes provided another example of the same phenomenon. The two papers were Harry's "Inside Money, Outside Money, Income, Wealth and Welfare in Monetary Theory" and Milton Friedman's "The Optimum Quantity of Money." Both were published in 1969, Johnson's in the *Journal of Money Credit and Banking*, Friedman's as the title essay in his *The Optimum Quantity of Money and Other Essays*. Harry's first footnote indicated that he had read his paper to the AUTE conference in 1968 and that he had not seen Friedman's paper until after he had submitted his for publication. Friedman's paper caught the profession's attention. In part because it was by Friedman; in part it was the title for a book of essays; but it was also a reflection of a difference of presentational styles. Hynes continued:

Friedman's . . . paper provided a formal statement of the complete set of marginal conditions for Pareto optimality in a fully articulated capital model with fiduciary money and a menu of real and financial assets. This provided the basis for the well-known optimal deflation rule that Friedman saw as an institutionally viable way of paying interest on money. . . . The paper had few references to the literature, but instead motivated the analysis with references to the grand topics in the theory of money and capital: the optimal path of nominal prices, the optimal interest rate, and the optimal level and structure of capital. Friedman explicitly offered the analysis as a fundamental contribution to monetary theory.

Harry's paper had a different focus, and covered different ground. As always the paper was tightly connected to a literature. In this case, the initial problems . . . were those raised by Gurley and Shaw (1956) and Pesek and Saving (1967) relating to the contributions to social welfare provided by the introduction of money and financial assets. Harry observed that these questions had straightforward answers given by the standard concepts of economic efficiency supplemented with the theory of economic rent in the form of consumer surplus. Within this frame of reference, he clearly identified the social gains arising from a commodity money and the social gains arising from the substitution of a fiduciary money with zero marginal resource cost for a commodity money that has a positive resource cost. The analysis also provided a straightforward identification of one portion of the gains that banks (financial intermediaries in general) provide in the process of transforming illiquid assets into liquid assets, i.e. those assets that offer the services of money, however defined.

. . . The economically important differences between alternative monetary regimes, as Harry clearly demonstrated are those centring on whether money is backed by real capital, and therefore has a positive social as well as private cost, or whether money is a fiduciary issue, a paper money, not backed by real capital. As for the latter case there is the important case as to whether money services are optimally priced. The optimal quantity of money theorem emerged in Harry's analysis as part of this larger context. Any difference between money produced in the public sector and that produced in the private sector, assuming both carry the same marginal price, would be with respect to the distribution of economic rents. Harry's paper was the first paper to present a clear analysis of these problems. (2001, 630–1)

Harry was less impressed with Friedman's work, as he revealed in a footnote to his Hove survey of the state of monetary theory:

For a recent analysis leading to this conclusion, couched in quantity theory terms and rich in application of relevant capital theory see M. Friedman, *The Optimum Quantity of Money*. Besides being misleadingly titled, since the analysis refers to a growing and not a static economy, the essay is rather distracting in the pursuit of theoretical side issues suggested by past controversies and its intrusive concern for quantification of potential welfare gains which is provided only fragmentarily and inconclusively; the need for the rather embarrassing "final schizophrenic note" could have been avoided by presenting the argument more frankly as a logical exercise. (*FEME*, 43 n.1)

Part of Harry's unhappiness is a reflection of the difference between his authorial style and Friedman's. But it also reflected his belief that the appearance of *The Optimum Quantity of Money* had damaged his own ability to develop a serious audience in Britain for good monetary economics and his desire to distance himself from it. Apart from the 1970 dry run of "The Keynesian Revolution and the Monetarist Counter Revolution" in Belfast, the Hove survey was the only occasion when he criticised Friedman explicitly before a British audience.

But Harry's frame of reference was broader than most academic economists. He was concerned with contemporary society and its evolution. He took pride in his "Political Economy of Opulence" and "The Social Policy of an Opulent Society," even if he later came to think them "excessively optimistic, to the point of euphoria" (*CQ*, 2nd. ed., ix). He enjoyed speculating on the interaction of social and economic forces, its possible results, and the changes in institutions and practices that might be required to accommodate their results. He was also a social critic directing his attention to social institutions such as universities or revolting students. In doing so, he showed a fine grasp of the interactions involved. His explanations were often economic, for he tended to see political behaviour as the outcome of economic interests, and he appreciated the explanatory power of microeconomic theory. Thus

the university is a multi-product firm, important constituents of its line of products being "public goods" of one or another ill-defined kind. Both the consumers and producers of these goods have widely divergent preference functions. (*E&S*, 174)

This complexity made it impossible to apply the conventional tools of maximisation to its overall activities. There was always a temptation to do in particular measurable aspects of its activities, but to do so begged the question of what the university's function was. Inevitably he frequently extended the boundaries of economic analysis to encompass new problems, new institutions, or new forms of behaviour. As with the university he was inclined to begin with the fairly simple tools of economic analysis to the problem. The results were often illuminating even on the small scale of his four-page "The Economic Future of Sex" (1970j).

Perhaps I should leave the last word to F. A. Hayek as quoted by Theodore Schultz at the Harry G. Johnson Memorial Meeting:

The physicist who is only a physicist can be a first class physicist and a most valuable member of society. But nobody can be a great economist who is only an economist – and I am very tempted to add that an economist who is only an economist is likely to become a nuisance if not a positive danger. (2)

Harry Johnson was a great economist.

Sources

Manuscript Collections

Baumol Papers – Perkins Library, Duke University
Bladen Papers – University of Toronto Archives
Blatz Papers – Thomas Fisher Rare Book Library, University of Toronto
Clower Papers – Perkins Library, Duke University
Devons Papers – British Library of Political and Economic Science
Dobb Papers – Wren Library, Trinity College, Cambridge
Friedman Papers – Hoover Institution, Stanford University
Haberler Papers – Hoover Institution, Stanford University
Hansen Papers – Houghton Library, Harvard University
Hayek Papers – Hoover Institution, Stanford University
Innis Papers – University of Toronto Archives
Institute of Economic Affairs Papers – Hoover Institution, Stanford University
Johnson File – Archives, Jesus College, Cambridge
Johnson Files – St. Frances Xavier University Archives
Johnson Memoirs and Autobiographical Notes – Elizabeth Simpson
Johnson Papers – Regenstein Library, University of Chicago
Johnson Personal File – London School of Economics and Political Science
Kahn Papers – Modern Archive Centre, King's College, Cambridge
Kaldor Papers – Modern Archive Centre, King's College, Cambridge
Keynes Papers – Modern Archive Centre, King's College, Cambridge
MacEachen Papers – Allan MacEachen
Machlup Papers – Hoover Institution, Stanford University
Patinkin Papers – Perkins Library, Duke University
Public Archives of Canada – Royal Commission on Banking and Finance
Report of the Economics Consultants to the Advisory Committee on Academic Planning,
    Ontario Council on Graduate Studies, on Graduate Programmes in Economics
    in Ontario, Submitted February 1973, University of Toronto, School of Graduate
    Studies
Robbins Papers – Christopher Johnson
Robertson Papers – Wren Library, Trinity College, Cambridge
Joan Robinson Papers – Modern Archive Centre, King's College, Cambridge

Royal Economic Society Archives – British Library of Political and Economic Science
Shackle Papers – Cambridge University Library
Silberston Papers – Aubrey Silberston
United Kingdom, Council on Science Policy – National Archives
University of Chicago, Department of Economics – Regenstein Library, University of
 Chicago
University of Chicago, Presidents' Papers – Regenstein Library, University of Chicago
University of Toronto, Department of Political Economy Records – University of Toronto
 Archives

Books and Articles

Abrahamson, Julie 1959, *A Neighbourhood Finds Itself*, New York: Harper and Row.
Addison, Paul 1985, *After the War Is Over: A Social History of Britain, 1945–51*, London:
 Cape.
Adler, J. H. (ed.) 1967, *Capital Movements and Economic Development*, London: Mac-
 millan.
Allen, Peter 1978, *The Cambridge Apostles: The Early Years*, Cambridge: Cambridge Uni-
 versity Press.
Allen, Robert L. 1991, *Opening Doors: The Life and Work of Joseph Schumpeter*, New
 Brunswick, NJ: Transaction Publishers.
Ando, A., Brown, E. C., Solow, R. M., and Karaken, J. 1963, "Lags in Fiscal and Monetary
 Policy" in Commission on Money and Credit, *Stabilisation Policies*, Englewood
 Cliffs, NJ: Prentice Hall, 1–163.
Arnon, Arie and Young, Warren (eds.) 2002, *The Open Economy Macromodel: Past,
 Present and Future*, New York: Kluwer Academic.
Backhouse, R. and Middleton R. (eds.) 2000, *Exemplary Economists*, 2 vols., Cheltenham:
 Edward Elgar.
Barber, W. J. 1987, "The Career of Alvin H. Hansen in the 1920s and 1930s: A
 Study in Intellectual Transformation," *History of Political Economy*, 19 (Summer),
 191–205.
Barclay, Craig R. 1986, "Schematization of Autobiographical Memoirs" in D. C. Rubin
 (ed.), *Autobiographical Memory*, Cambridge: Cambridge University Press, 82–99.
Barr, Nicholas 2000, "The History of the Phillips Machine" in Leeson (ed.) 2000,
 89–114.
Bartlett, F. C. 1932, *Remembering: A Study in Experimental and Social Psychology*,
 Cambridge: Cambridge University Press.
Barzel, Yoram 2000, "Yoram Barzel" in Backhouse and Middleton (eds.) 2000, vol. I,
 221–38.
Baumol, W. J. 1965, *Welfare Economics and the Theory of the State*, Cambridge, MA:
 Harvard University Press.
Becker, Gary 1957, *The Economics of Discrimination*, Chicago: University of Chicago
 Press.
Beckerman, Wilfred 2000, "Wilfred Beckerman" in Backhouse and Middleton (eds.)
 2000, vol. II., 146–97.
Bergsten, C. Fred 1975, *Toward a New World Trade Policy*, Lexington, MA: Lexington
 Books.

Berhardt, Karl S., Fletcher, Margaret I., Johnson, Frances C., Millichamp, Dorothy A., and Northway, Mary L. (eds.) 1951, *Twenty-five Years of Child Study: The Development of the Programme and Review of the Research at the Institute of Child Study, University of Toronto, 1926–1951*, Toronto: University of Toronto Press.

Bernstein, Edward M. et al., 1976, "Reflections on Jamaica," *Essays in International Finance*, 115 (April).

Beveridge Report 1942, *Social Insurance and Allied Services*, Cmd. 6404, London: His Majesty's Stationery Office.

Bhagwati, J. 1977, "Harry G. Johnson," *Journal of International Economics*, 7, 221–9.

 1998, *A Stream of Windows: Unsettling Reflections on Trade, Immigration and Democracy*, Cambridge, MA: MIT Press.

Bhagwati, J. and Frenkel, J. 1988, "Johnson, Harry G.," in David L. Sills (eds.), *International Encyclopedia of the Social Sciences: Biographical Supplement*, vol. 18, New York: The Free Press, 351–8.

Bhagwati, J. and Srinivasen, T. N. 1975, *India*, New York: Columbia University Press.

Bhagwati, J., Panagariya, A., and Srinivasan, T. N. 1998, *Lectures on International Trade* (2nd ed.), Cambridge, MA: MIT Press.

Black, John 1978, "Review of B. Ohlin and Others," *The International Allocation of Economic Activity: Proceeding of a Nobel Symposium held at Stockholm, Economic Journal*, 88 (December), 649–50.

Bladen, Vincent 1941, *An Introduction to Political Economy*, Toronto: University of Toronto Press.

 1978, *Bladen on Bladen: Memoirs of a Political Economist*, Toronto: Scarborough College.

Blitch, C. P. 1995, *Allyn Young: The Peripatetic Economist*, Basingstoke: Macmillan.

Booth, A. E. and Coats, A. W. 1978, "The Market for Economists in Britain, 1945–75: A Preliminary Survey," *Economic Journal*, 88 (September), 436–54.

Brander, James 1995, "Strategic Trade Policy" in G. W. Grossman and K. Rogoff (eds.), *Handbook of International Economics*, vol. III, Amsterdam: North Holland, 1395–1455.

Brebner, J. B. 1945, *Scholarship for Canada: The Function of Graduate Studies*, Ottawa: Canadian Social Science Research Council.

Breton, Albert 1964, "The Economics of Nationalism," *Journal of Political Economy*, 72 (August), 376–87.

Brittan, S. 1973, *Is There an Economic Consensus?*, London: Macmillan.

 2000, "Samuel Brittan" in Backhouse and Middleton (eds.), vol. II, 271–95.

Britton, A. J. C. 1991, *Macroeconomic Policy in Britain, 1974–1987*, Cambridge: Cambridge University Press for the National Institute for Economic and Social Research.

Cairncross, Alec (ed.) 1970, *Papers on Planning and Economic Management by Ely Devons*, Manchester: Manchester University Press.

 1994, *The Wilson Years: A Treasury Diary, 1964–1969*, London: The Historians' Press.

Cameron, James D. 1996, *For the People: A History of St. Francis Xavier University*, Kingston and Montreal: McGill–Queen's University Press.

Chacholiades, M. 1978a, *International Monetary Theory and Policy*, New York: McGraw Hill.

 1978b, *International Trade Theory and Policy*, New York: McGraw Hill.

Choi, E. K. and Harringa, J. 2003, *Handbook of International Trade*, Oxford: Blackwell.

Clark, S. D. 1981, "The Contribution of H. A. Innis to Canadian Scholarship" in W. H. Melody, L. Salter, and P. Heyer (eds.), *Culture, Communication and Dependency: The Tradition of H. A. Innis*, Norwood, NJ: Ablex, 27–35.

Classen, E. and Salin, P. (eds.) 1972, *Stabilization Policies in Interdependent Economies*, Amsterdam: North Holland.

Collander, D., Holt, P. F., and Rosser, J. B. 2004, *The Changing Face of Economics: Conversations with Cutting Edge Economists*, Ann Arbor: University of Michigan Press.

Committee on the Working of the Monetary System 1959, *Report*, Cmnd. 827, London: Her Majesty's Stationery Office.

1960a, *Principal Memoranda of Evidence*, vol. III, London: Her Majesty's Stationery Office.

1960b, *Minutes of Evidence*, London: Her Majesty's Stationery Office.

Conway, Martin 1996, "Autobiographical Knowledge and Autobiographical Memory" in David C. Rubin (ed.) 1996, 67–93.

Cooper, Richard N. 1999, "Exchange Rate Choices" in Janet S. Little and Giovani P. Oliveri (eds.), *Rethinking the International Monetary System*, Boston: Federal Reserve Bank of Boston, 101–23.

Corbet, Hugh and Jackson, R. (eds.) 1974, *In Search of a New World Economic Order*, London: Croom Helm.

Corden, W. Max 1957, "The Calculation of the Cost of Protection," *Economic Record*, 33 (1), 29–51.

1966, "The Structure of a Tariff System and the Effective Protection Rate," *Journal of Political Economy*, 74 (June), 221–37.

1971, *The Theory of Protection*, Oxford: Clarendon Press.

1972, "Review of H. G. Johnson, *Aspects of the Theory of Tariffs*," *Economic Journal*, 82 (June), 698–701.

1984, "Harry Johnson's Contributions to International Trade Theory," *Journal of Political Economy*, 92 (August), 567–91.

2000, "W. Max Corden" in R. Backhouse and R. Middleton (eds.), 2000, vol. II, 224–42.

2001, "Harry's View of the Scientific Enterprise," *American Journal of Economics and Sociology*, 60 (June), 641–6.

2004, "Harry Gordon Johnson 1923–1977," *Oxford Dictionary of National Biography*, Oxford: Oxford University Press, vol. 30, 263–5.

Creighton, Donald 1957, *Harold Adams Innis: Portrait of a Scholar*, Toronto: University of Toronto Press.

Crouch, Colin 1970, *The Student Revolt*, London: The Bodley Head.

Dahrendorf, Ralf 1995, *LSE: A History of the London School of Economics and Political Science, 1895–1995*, Oxford: Oxford University Press.

Dalton, Hugh 1920, *Some Aspects of the Inequality of Incomes in Modern Communities*, London: Routledge.

Devons, Ely 1951, "Some Features of International Trade in 1950," *Three Banks Review*, 10 (June), 3–24.

1952, "Some Aspects of United Kingdom Exports," *Lloyds Bank Review*, 25 (July), 28–45.

1954, "Statistics of the United Kingdom Terms of Trade," *Manchester School*, 22 (September), 258–75.

and Gluckman, Max (eds.) 1964, *Closed Systems and Open Minds: The Limits of Naivety in Social Anthropology*, Edinburgh: Oliver and Boyd.

de Vries, Margaret 1966, *The International Monetary Fund, 1966–71: The System Under Stress*, Washington DC: The International Monetary Fund.

Dimand, Robert 2001, "Harry G. Johnson as Chronicler of the Keynesian Revolution: His Search for a Non-Revolutionary Account," *American Journal of Economics and Sociology*, 60 (July), 667–91.

Dow, J. C. R. 1965, *The Management of the British Economy, 1945–1960*, Cambridge: Cambridge University Press for the National Institute for Economic and Social Research.

Downs, Anthony 1957, *An Economic Theory of Democracy*, New York: Harper.

Draaisma, D. 2004, *Why Life Speeds Up as You Get Older: How Memory Shapes Our Past*, Cambridge: Cambridge University Press.

Drummond, Ian M. 1983, *Political Economy at the University of Toronto: A History of the Department, 1888–1982*, Toronto: Faculty of Arts and Science, University of Toronto.

Eltis, Walter 2000, "Walter Eltis" in Backhouse and Middleton (eds.) 2000, vol. II, 296–324.

Eltis, Walter, Scott, M. F. G., and Wolfe, N. (eds.) 1970, *Induction, Growth and Trade: Essays in Honour of Sir Roy Harrod*, Oxford: Clarendon Press.

Emmett, Ross. B. 1998, "Entrenching Disciplinary Competence: The Role of General Education and Graduate Study in Chicago Economics," in M. Morgan and M. Rutherford (eds.), *From Interwar Pluralism to Postwar Neoclassicism, Annual Supplement to Volume 30, History of Political Economy*, 134–50.

English, John 1992, *The Worldly Years: The Life of Lester Pearson, Volume II, 1949–1972*, Toronto: Knopf.

Evan, W. M. (ed.) 1982, *Knowledge and Power in a Global Society*, Beverley Hills, CA: Sage Publications.

Evans, E. (ed.) 1971, *Destiny or Delusion: Britain and the Common Market*, London: Gollanz.

Fausten, Dieter 1979, "The Humean Origin of the Contemporary Monetary Approach to the Balance of Payments," *Quarterly Journal of Economics*, 93 (November), 655–73.

Fleming, J. Marcus 1962, "Domestic Financial Policies Under Fixed and Under Flexible Exchange Rates," *IMF Staff Papers*, 9 (November), 369–79.

1971, *Essays in International Economics*, London: Allen and Unwin.

Folk, H. 1963, "Freedom and Welfare: Friedman on Economic Policy," *Public Finance*, 18 (3–4), 199–216.

Foster, Christopher 2001, *Lord Noel Gilroy Annan, 1916–2000: Fellow, Provost – A Memoir*, Cambridge: King's College.

Frenkel, Jacob 1976a, "A Monetary Approach to the Exchange Rate: Doctrinal Aspects and Empirical Evidence," *Scandinavian Journal of Economics*, 78 (May), 200–23.

1976b, "Adjustment Mechanisms and the Monetary Approach to the Balance of Payments: A Doctrinal Perspective" in E. M. Classin and P. Salin (eds.), *Recent Issues in International Monetary Economics*, Amsterdam: North Holland, 29–48.

Friedland, Claire 1993, "On Stigler and Stiglerisms," *Journal of Political Economy*, 101 (October), 780–3.

Friedman, Benjamin M. and Hahn, Frank H. (eds.) 1990, *Handbook of Monetary Economics*, Amsterdam: North-Holland.

Friedman, Milton (ed.) 1956, *Studies in the Quantity Theory of Money*, Chicago: University of Chicago Press.

1959, "The Demand for Money – Some Theoretical and Empirical Results," *Journal of Political Economy*, 67 (June), 327–51.

1966, "Interest Rates and the Demand for Money," *Journal of Law and Economics*, 9 (October), 71–85.

1968, "The Role of Monetary Policy," *American Economic Review*, 58 (March), 1–17.

1969a, *The Optimum Quantity of Money and Other Essays*, London: Macmillan.

1969b, "A Theoretical Framework for Monetary Analysis," *Journal of Political Economy*, 80 (April), 193–238.

1972, "Comments on the Critics," *Journal of Political Economy*, 80 (September/October), 906–50.

Friedman, Milton and Friedman, Rose 1998, *Two Lucky People: Memoirs*, Chicago: University of Chicago Press.

Friedman, Milton and Meiselman, David 1963, "The Relative Stability of Monetary Velocity and the Investment Multiplier in the United States, 1898–1958" in Commission on Money and Credit *Stabilization Policies*, Englewood Cliffs, NJ: Prentice Hall, 165–268.

Galbraith, John Kenneth 1958, *The Affluent Society*, Boston: Houghton Mifflin.

1981, *A Life in Our Times: Memories*, Boston: Houghton Mifflin.

Gehrels, H. 1957, "Customs Unions from a Single Country Viewpoint," *Review of Economic Studies*, 25 (1), 61–4.

Gibson, F. W. 1983, *Queen's University: To Serve and Yet be Free, Vol. II, 1917–1961*, Kingston and Montreal: McGill–Queen's University Press.

Gidney, R. D. 1999, *From Hope to Harris: The Reshaping of Ontario Schools*, Toronto: University of Toronto Press.

Giersch, H. (ed.) 1972, *Demand Management – Globalsteverung*, Tubingen: JCB Mohr.

Gordon, H. Scott 1961, *The Economists versus the Bank of Canada: Why Twenty-nine Professors Signed a Letter to the Minister of Finance Calling for a Drastic Reorganization of the Bank of Canada*, Toronto: Ryerson Press.

Gow, A. S. F. 1945, *Letters from Cambridge, 1929–1944*, London: Cape.

Graaff, Jan 1958, *Theoretical Welfare Economics*, Cambridge: Cambridge University Press.

Gray, Arthur and Brittain, Frederick 1979, *A History of Jesus College, Cambridge*, London: Heinemann.

Griffiths, Brian 1970, *Competition in Banking*, Hobart Paper 51, Institute of Economic Affairs.

Grubel, Herbert G. 1980, "Citation Counts for Economists Specializing in International Economics: A Tribute to the Memory of Harry G. Johnson," *Malayan Economic Review*, 25 (April), 1–18.

Gurley, J. G. and Shaw, E. S. 1956, *Money in a Theory of Finance*, Washington, DC: Brookings.

H. P. 1925, "Second Annual Conference of Teachers of Economics," *Economic Journal*, 35 (March), 153–5.

Haberler, Gottfried 1976, "Some Reminiscences," *Quarterly Journal of Economics*, 90 (February), 9–13.

Hahn, Frank 1984, *Equilibrium and Macroeconomics*, Oxford: Blackwell.

Halsey, A. H. 1992, *The Decline of Donnish Dominion: The British Academic Profession in the Twentieth Century*, Oxford: Clarendon Press.

Halsey, A. H. and Trow, M. A. 1971, *The British Academics*, London: Faber and Faber.

Hamada, Koichi 2000, "Koichi Hamada" in Backhouse and Middleton (eds.) 2000, vol. II, 332–49.

Hansen, Alvin H. 1936a, "Underemployment Equilibrium," *Yale Review*, 25 (June), 828–30.

   1936b, "Mr. Keynes on Unemployment Equilibrium," *Journal of Political Economy*, 44 (October), 667–86.

Harberger, A. C. 1978, "Harry G. Johnson (1923–1977)," *Challenge*, 21 (November/December), 56–9.

Harberger, A. C. and Wall, D. 1984, "Harry Johnson as a Development Economist," *Journal of Political Economy*, 92 (August), 616–41.

Harkness, Ross 1963, *J. E. Atkinson of the Star*, Toronto: University of Toronto Press.

Harris, L. 1969, "Professor Hicks and the Foundations of Monetary Economics," *Economica*, 36 (May), 196–208.

Harrod, R. F. 1951, *The Life of John Maynard Keynes*, London: Macmillan.

Hartwell, Clare 2001, *Manchester*, London: Penguin.

Hartwell, Clare, Hyde, Matthew, and Pevsner, Nikolans 2004, *The Buildings of England – Lancashire: Manchester and the South East*, New Haven, CT, and London: Yale University Press.

Hartwell, R. M. 1995, *A History of the Mount Pelerin Society*, Indianapolis: Liberty Fund.

Helliwell, John F. 1978, "The Balance of Payments: A Survey of Harry Johnson's Contributions," *Canadian Journal of Economics*, 11 (Supplement), S55–85.

Hicks, J. R. 1952, "Monetary Policy Again," *Bulletin of the Oxford University Institute of Statistics*, 14 (August), 268–72.

   1953, "An Inaugural Lecture," *Oxford Economic Papers*, N.S. 5 (June), 117–35.

Hirsch, Arnold R. 1983, *Making the Second Ghetto: Race and Housing in Chicago, 1940–1960*, Cambridge: Cambridge University Press.

Hobsbawm, Eric 2002, *Interesting Times: A Twentieth Century Life*, London: Allen Lane.

Hoch, Paul and Schoenbach, Vic 1969, *LSE: The Natives Are Restless, A Report on Student Power in Action*, London: Sheed and Ward.

Howson, Susan 1993, *British Monetary Policy, 1945–51*, Oxford: Clarendon Press.

Hutchison, Terrence 1976, *Knowledge and Ignorance in Economics*, Cambridge: Cambridge University Press.

Hynes, Allan 2001, "Memories and Reflections," *American Journal of Economics and Sociology*, 60 (July), 624–32.

IMF 1977, *The Monetary Approach to the Balance of Payments: A Collection of Research Papers by the Staff of the International Monetary Fund*, Washington, DC: International Monetary Fund.

Inwood, Gregory J. 2005, *Continentalizing Canada: The Policies of Legacy of the Macdonald Royal Commission*, Toronto: University of Toronto Press.

Johnson, Elizabeth 2000, "Economist – Washing Machine Fixer" in Leeson (ed.) 2000, 23.

Johnson, Frances L. 1951, "Activities and Aims of Parent Education," in Bernhardt et al. (eds.) 1951, 39–45.

Johnson, Harry G. 1944, *The Antigonish Movement: A Lecture to Students of Acadia University*, Antigonish: St. Francis Xavier University.

1948, "An Error in Ricardo's Exposition of his Theory of Rent," *Quarterly Journal of Economics*, 62 (November), 792–3.

1949, "Demand for Commodities Is Not Demand for Labour," *Economic Journal*, 59 (December), 531–6.

1950a, "The Case for Increasing the Price of Gold in Terms of Commodities: A Contrary View," *Canadian Journal of Economics and Political Science*, 16 (May) 199–209.

1950b, "Review of Warren James's *Wartime Economic Co-operation: A Study of Relations between Canada and the United States,*" *Canadian Journal of Economics and Political Science*, 16 (August), 435–8.

1950c, "Diagrammatic Analysis of Income Variation and the Balance of Payments," *Quarterly Journal of Economics*, 64 (November), 623–32.

1951a, "Some Economic Implications of Secular Changes in Bank Assets and Liabilities in Great Britain," *Economic Journal*, 61 (September), 544–61.

1951b, "Clearing Bank Holdings of Public Debt, 1930–50," *London and Cambridge Economic Service Bulletin*, 29 (November), 102–9.

1951c, "The Taxonomic Approach to Economic Policy," *Economic Journal*, 61 (December), 812–31.

1951d, "Optimum Welfare and Maximum Revenue Tariffs," *Review of Economic Studies*, 19 (1), 38–35 (reprinted in *ITEG*).

1951e, "The Economics of Undertaking," *Cambridge Journal*, 4 (January), 240–44.

1951–2," Some Cambridge Controversies in Monetary Theory," *Review of Economic Studies*, 19 (February), 90–104.

1952a, "The New Monetary Policy and the Problem of Credit Control," *Bulletin of the Oxford University Institute of Statistics*, 14 (April–May), 117–31.

1952b, "Monetary Policy Again – Concluding Comment," *Bulletin of the Oxford University Institute of Statistics*, 14 (August), 298–306.

1952c, *The Overloaded Economy*, Toronto: University of Toronto Press.

1953a, "Recent Developments in British Monetary Policy," *American Economic Review*, 43 (May), 19–26.

1953b, "Equilibrium and Growth in an International Economy," *Canadian Journal of Economics and Political Science*, 19 (November), 478–500 (reprinted in *ITEG*).

1954a, "The Private Eye of Mickey Spillane," *Granta*, 57 (15 May), 16–18.

1954b, "Optimum Tariffs and Retaliation," *Review of Economic Studies*, 21 (2), 142–53 (revised version in *ITEG*).

1954c, "Canada: A Lost Opportunity," *Three Banks Review*, 22 (June), 3–21.

1954d, "Increasing Productivity, Income–Price Trends and the Trade Balance," *Economic Journal*, 64 (September), 462–85 (reprinted in *ITEG*).

1955, "Economic Expansion and International Trade," *Manchester School*, 23 (May), 95–112 (revised version in *ITEG*).

1956a, "Review of A. J. Brown's *The Great Inflation, 1939–1951*, *Economic Journal*, 66 (March), 121–3.

1956b, "On British Crises," *Granta*, 59 (April), 5–6.

1956c, "The Revival of Monetary Policy in Great Britain," *Three Banks Review*, 30 (June), 3–20.

1956d, "The Transfer Problem and Exchange Stability," *Journal of Political Economy*, 64 (June), 212–25 (reprinted in *ITEG*).

1956e, "Sketch of a Generalisation of Keynesian Balance of Payments Theory," *Indian Journal of Economics*, 27 (July), 49–56.

1957a, "The Criteria of Economic Advantage," *Bulletin of the Oxford University Institute of Statistics*, 19 (February), 33–8.

1957b, "Discriminatory Tariff Reduction: A Marshallian Analysis," *Indian Journal of Economics*, 28 (July), 39–47 (reprinted in *MTEG*).

1957c, "The European Common Market – Risk or Opportunity?: A British View," *Weltwirtschaftliches Archiv*, 79 (2), 267–83.

1957d, "Factor Endowments, International Trade and Factor Prices," *Manchester School*, 25 (September), 270–83 (reprinted in *ITEG*).

1957e, "Bank Rate Reform and the Improvement of Monetary Statistics," *Bulletin of the Oxford University Institute of Statistics*, 19 (November), 341–5.

1957f, "The Determination of the General Level of Wage Rates" in J. T. Dunlop (ed.), *The Theory of Wage Determination*, London: Macmillan, 31–8.

1958a, "Canada's Economic Prospects," *Canadian Journal of Economics and Political Science*, 23 (February), 104–10 (reprinted in *CQ*).

1958b, "Two Schools of Thought on Wage Inflation," *Scottish Journal of Political Economy*, 5 (June), 149–53.

1958c, "Banking and Monetary Policy," *Pakistan Economic Journal*, 8 (June), 1–15.

1958d, "The Balance of Payments," *Pakistan Economic Journal*, 8 (June) 16–28 (reprinted in *MTEG*).

1958e, "Comparative Costs and Commercial Policy," *Pakistan Economic Journal*, 8 (June), 29–43 (reprinted in *MTEG*).

1958f, "Planning and the Market in Economic Development," *Pakistan Economic Journal*, 8 (June), 44–55 (reprinted in *MTEG*).

1958g, "Monetary Theory and Keynesian Economics," *Pakistan Economic Journal* 8 (June), 56–70 (reprinted in *MTEG*).

1958h, "Review of J. K. Galbraith's *The Affluent Society*," *Spectator*, 201 (19 September), 381.

1958i, "The Gains from Freer Trade with Europe: An Estimate," *Manchester School*, 26 (September), 247–55.

1958j, "The Economic Gains from Free Trade with Europe," *Three Banks Review*, 39 (September), 3–19.

1958k, "Marshallian Analysis of Discriminatory Tariff Reduction: An Extension," *Indian Journal of Economics*, 39 (October), 177–81 (reprinted in *MTEG*).

1958l, *International Trade and Economic Growth: Essays in Pure Theory*, London: Allen and Unwin (*ITEG*).

1959a, "British Monetary Statistics," *Economica*, 26 (February), 1–17.

1959b, "International Trade, Income Distribution and the Offer Curve," *Manchester School*, 27 (September), 241–60 (reprinted in *ATT*).

1959c, "Economic Development and International Trade," *Nationalokonomisk Tidschrift*, 97, Bund 5–6, 47–71 (reprinted in *MTEG*).

1960a, "The Common Market: The Economists' Reactions" in G. D. N. Worswick (ed.), *The Free Trade Proposals*, Oxford: Blackwell, 135–42.

1960b, "The Economic Theory of Customs Unions," *Pakistan Economic Journal*, 10 (March), 14–32 (reprinted in *MTEG*).

(with Jagdish Bhagwati) 1960c, "Notes on Some Controversies in the Theory of International Trade," *Economic Journal*, 78 (March), 74–93.

1960d, "Canada's Foreign Trade Problems," *International Journal*, 15 (Summer), 133–41 (reprinted in *CQ*).

1960e, "The Cost of Protection and the Scientific Tariff," *Journal of Political Economy*, 68 (August), 327–45 (reprinted in *ATT*).

1960f, "The Consumer and Madison Avenue," *Current Economic Comment*, 22 (August), 233–41.

1960g, "Income Distribution, the Offer Curve and the Effects of Tariffs," *Manchester School*, 28 (September), 327–45 (reprinted in *ATT*).

1960h, "The Political Economy of Opulence," *Canadian Journal of Economics and Political Science*, 26 (November), 552–64 (reprinted in *MTEG*, *CQ*, and *E&S*).

1960i, "Memorandum of Evidence" in Committee on the Working of the Monetary System *Principal Memoranda of Evidence*, London: Her Majesty's Stationery Office, 136–8.

1960j, "Minutes of Evidence," in Committee on the Working of the Monetary System *Minutes of Evidence*, London: Her Majesty's Stationery Office, Questions 10579–649.

1961a, "The *General Theory* after Twenty-five Years," *American Economic Review*, 51 (May), 1–17 (reprinted in *E&S*, revised version in *MTEG*).

1961b, "The International Liquidity Problem" in *International Payments Imbalances and Need for Strengthening International Financial Arrangements*: Hearings before the Subcommittee on International Exchange and Payments of the Joint Economic Committee, U.S. Congress, 16 May and 19–21 June 1969, Washington, DC: U.S. Government Printing Office, 173–5, 204–7, 241.

(with Jagdish Bhagwati) 1961c, "Notes on Some Controversies in the Theory of International Trade: A Rejoinder," *Economic Journal*, 71 (June), 427–30.

1961d, "Problems of Canadian Nationalism," *International Journal*, 16 (Summer), 238–50 (reprinted in *CQ*).

1961e, *The Social Policy of an Opulent Society*, Ottawa: Canadian Welfare Council 9 (reprinted in MTEG, CQ, and E&S).

1961f, "A Generalised Theory of the Effects of Tariffs on the Terms of Trade" (with Jagdish Bhagwati), *Oxford Economic Papers*, 13 (October), 225–53 (reprinted in *ATT*).

1962a, "International Liquidity: Problems and Plans," *Malayan Economic Review*, 7 (April), 1–19 (reprinted in *CQ*).

1962b, "Monetary Theory and Policy," *American Economic Review*, 52 (June), 335–84 (reprinted in *EME*).

1962c, *Canada in a Changing World Economy*, Toronto: University of Toronto Press.

1962d, "Canada in a Changing World," *International Journal*, 18 (Winter), 17–28 (reprinted in *CQ*).

(with J. W. L. Winder), 1962e, *Lags in the Effects of Monetary Policy in Canada*, Ottawa: Queen's Printer.

1962f, *Money Trade and Economic Growth*, London: Allen and Unwin (MTEG).

1963a, "The Bladen Plan for Increased Protection of the Canadian Automotive Industry," *Canadian Journal of Economics and Political Science*, 29 (May), 212–38 (reprinted in *CQ*, abridged in *ATT*).

1963b, "Recent Developments in Monetary Theory," *Indian Economic Review*, 6 (August), 1–28 (reprinted in *EME*).

1963c, "A Survey of Theories of Inflation," first printed in English in *EME*.

1963d, "Alternative Principles for the Use of Monetary Policy," *Princeton Essays in International Finance* 44 (November) (reprinted in *CQ* and *EME*).

1963e, "The Bladen Plan: A Reply,"*Canadian Journal of Economics and Political Science*, 29 (November), 315–18.

1963f, "Lags in the Effects of Monetary Policy in Canada," first printed in *CQ*.

1963g, *The Canadian Quandary: Economic Problems and Policies*, Toronto: McGraw Hill; 2nd ed. 1977, Toronto: McClelland and Stewart; 3rd ed. 2006, Kingston and Montreal: McGill–Queens University Press (*CQ*).

1964a, "The International Competitive Position of the United States and the Balance of Payments Prospect for 1968," *Review of Economics and Statistics*, 46 (February), 14–32.

1964b, "The New Tariff Policy for the Automotive Industry," *Business Quarterly*, 29 (Spring), 43–57.

1964c, "Federal Support of Basic Research: Some Economic Issues," *Minerva*, 3 (Summer), 500–14.

1964d, "Economic Nationalism in Canadian Policy," *Lloyds Bank Review*, 74 (October) 25–35 (reprinted in ed. 1967).

1964e, "Tariffs and Economic Development: Some Theoretical Issues," *Journal of Development Economics*, 1 (October), 3–30 (reprinted in *ATT*).

1964f, "Towards a Generalized Capital Accumulation Approach to Economic Development" in OECD *The Residual Factor in Economic Growth*, Paris: OECD, 219–25 (reprinted in *CQ*).

1964g, "Statement, the Federal Reserve System after Fifty Years," Hearings before the Subcommittee on Domestic Finance of the Committee on Banking and Currency, House of Representatives, 88th Congress, 2nd sess., 25 February 1964, 970–1020, 1023–46.

1964h, "Major Issues in Monetary and Fiscal Policies," *Federal Reserve Bulletin*, 50 (November), 1400–13 (reprinted in *EME*).

1965a, "Optimal Trade Intervention in the Presence of Domestic Distortions" in R. Baldwin et al. (eds.), *Trade, Growth and the Balance of Payments: Essays in Honor of Gottfried Haberler*, Amsterdam: North Holland (reprinted in *ATT*).

1965b, "The Theory of Tariff Structure with Special Reference to World Trade and Development" in H. G. Johnson and Peter B. Kennen, *Trade and Development*, Geneva: Librairie Droz, 9–29 (reprinted in *ATT*).

1965c, "The Economics of the Brain Drain: The Canadian Case," *Minerva*, 3 (Spring), 299–311.

1965d, "A Theoretical Model of Economic Nationalism in New and Developing States," *Political Science Quarterly*, 80 (June), 169–85 (reprinted in ed. 1967).

1965e, "An Economic Theory of Protectionism, Tariff Bargaining and the Formation of Customs Unions," *Journal of Political Economy*, 73 (June), 256–83 (reprinted in *ATT*).

1965f, "A Quantity Theorist's Monetary History of the United States," *Economic Journal*, 75 (June), 388–96.

1965g, "Economics and Politics of Opulence," *University of Toronto Quarterly*, 34 (July), 313–31.

1965h, "The Costs of Protection and Self-Sufficiency," *Quarterly Journal of Economics*, 82 (August), 356–72 (reprinted in *ATT*).

1965i, *The World Economy at the Crossroads*, Montreal: Private Planning Association of Canada; London: Oxford University Press (*WEC*).

1966a, "The Social Sciences in the Age of Opulence," *Canadian Journal of Economics and Political Science*, 32 (November), 423–42.

1966b, "The Objectives of Economic Policy and the Mix of Monetary and Fiscal Policy under Fixed Exchange Rates" in W. Fellner et al., *Maintaining and Restoring Balance in International Payments*, Princeton: Princeton University Press, 145–50 (reprinted in *FEME*).

1966c, "Some Aspects of the Theory of Economic Policy in a World of Capital Mobility," *Essays in Honour of Marco Fanno, II, Investigations in Economic Theory and Methodology*, Padua: Cedam, 345–59 (reprinted in *FEME*).

1967a, "The Atlantic Case," *New Society*, 18 May, 724.

1967b, "Economic Theory and Contemporary Society," *University of Toronto Quarterly*, 37 (July), 321–37 (reprinted in *E&S*).

1967c, "The Report on Bank Charges," *Bankers' Magazine*, 204 (August), 64–8.

1967d, "The Economics of the Brain Drain," *Pakistan Development Review*, 7 (Autumn), 379–411.

1967e, *Essays in Monetary Economics*, London: Allen and Unwin (*EME*).

1967f, *Economic Policies Towards Less Developed Countries*, London: Allen and Unwin (*EPLDC*).

(ed.) 1967, *Economic Nationalism in Old and New States*, Chicago: University of Chicago Press.

1968a, "The Economic Approach to Social Questions," *Economica*, 35 (February), 1–21 (abridged in *E&S*).

1968b, "Dethroning Gold," *The Listener*, 21 March, 334–5.

1968c, "Ely Devons: Obituary," *LSE Magazine*, 35 (June), 13.

1968d, "Economic Theory and Contemporary Society," *University of Toronto Quarterly*, 37 (July), 321–7 (reprinted in *E&S*).

1968e, "Problems of Efficiency in Monetary Management," *Journal of Political Economy*, 76 (September/October), 977–90 [as "Probleme der Effizienz der Geldpolitik," *Kredit und Kapital*, 1 (1968), 127–51].

1968f, "The Economics of Student Protest," *New Society*, 12 (7 November), 173–5.

1968g, "The Safety Valve in a Floating Exchange Rate," *The Times*, 9 December.

1968h, *Comparative Cost and Commercial Policy for a Developing World Economy*, Stockholm: Almqvist and Wicksell.

1968i, "Canadian Contributions to the Discipline of Economics since 1945," *Canadian Journal of Economics*, 1 (February), 129–46.

1968j, "International Trade Theory": in D. L. Sills (ed.), *International Encyclopedia of the Social Sciences*, vol. 8, New York: Macmillan, 83–96.

1969a, "Current International Economic Policy Issues," *Journal of Business*, 42 (January), 12–21.

1969b, "The Case for a Floating Exchange," *The Spectator*, 222 (18 April), 496–7.

1969c, "The Future of Gold and the Dollar," *Journal of World Trade Law*, 3 (March/April), 117–29.

1969d, "Inside Money, Outside Money, Income, Wealth and Welfare in Monetary Theory," *Journal of Money, Credit and Banking*, 1 (February), 30–45 (reprinted in *FEME*).

1969e, "The Decline of the International Monetary System," *The World Today*, 25 (March), 103–9.

1969f, "The International Monetary Problem: Gold, Dollars, Special Drawing Rights, Wider Bands and Crawling Pegs" in *Linking Reserve Creation and Development Assistance*, Hearings of the Subcommittee on International Trade and Payments of the Joint Economic Committee, 28 May, Washington, DC: Government Printing Office, 16–28, 59–82.

1969g, "The Gold Rush of 1968 in Retrospect and Prospect," *American Economic Review*, 59 (May), 344–8.

1969h, "The Case for Flexible Exchange Rates, 1969" in H. G. Johnson and J. E. Nash, *U.K. and Floating Exchange Rates: A Debate on the Theoretical and Practical Implications*, Hobart Paper 48, Institute of Economic Affairs, May (reprinted in *FEME*).

1969i, "Time for a Change in Trade Strategy" in H. G. Johnson (ed.), *New Trade Strategy for the World Economy*, London: Allen and Unwin, 3–18.

1969j, "Some Aspects of the Multilateral Free Trade Area Proposal," *Manchester School*, 37 (September), 189–212.

1969k, "World Economic Prospects for the 1970s," *Financial Times*, 31 December.

1969l, "The Theory of International Trade" in P. A. Samuelson (ed.), *International Economic Relations*, London: Macmillan, 55–66.

1969m, *Essays in Monetary Economics* (2nd ed.), London: Allen and Unwin (*EME, 2nd*).

1970a, "The Future of Gold, If Any: Demonetization vs Remonetization (L'Or a-t-il un avenir?)," *Économie Appliquée*, 23 (1), 129–48.

1970b, "Sir Roy Harrod on the Price of Gold" in W. Eltis, M. Fg Scott, and J. R. N. Wolfe (eds.), *Induction Growth and Trade: Essays in Honour of Sir Roy Harrod*, Oxford: Clarendon Press, 266–93.

1970c, "The International Monetary Crisis" in McDougall and Snape (eds.) 1970, 105–20.

1970d, "Canada's Floating Dollar in Historical Perspective," *International Currency Review*, 2 (July/August), 4–9.

1970e, "The State of Theory in Relation to Empirical Analysis" in R. Vernon (ed.), *The Technology Factor in International Trade*, New York: Columbia University Press, 59–76.

1970f, "A New View of the Infant Industry Argument" in McDougall and Snape (eds.), 9–21.

1970g, "The Efficiency and Welfare Implications of the International Corporation" in McDougall and Snape (eds.), 83–103 [a revised version of the paper of the same title that appeared in Kindleberger (ed.), 1970].

1970h, "Recent Developments in Monetary Theory: A Commentary" in D. R. Croome and H. G. Johnson (eds.), *Money in Britain, 1959–1969*, London: Oxford University Press, 83–114 (reprinted in *FEME*).

1970i, "Keynes and the Keynesians: Some Intellectual Legends," *Encounter*, 34 (January), 70–3 (reprinted in *FEME*).

1970j, "The Economic Future of Sex" in Stephen Clarkson (ed.), *Visions 2020: Fifty Canadians in Search of a Future*, Edmonton: M. G. Hurtig, 81–4.

1971a, "The Keynesian Revolution and the Monetarist Counter-Revolution," *American Economic Review*, 61 (May), 1–14 (reprinted in *FEME*, *E&S*, and *Shadow*).

1971b, "The Case Against," *The Spectator*, 226 (13 February), 218.

1971c, "The Implications for the World Economy" in D. Evans (ed.), *Destiny of Delusion?: Britain and the Common Market*, London: Gollancz, 164–72.

1971d, *Macroeconomics and Monetary Theory*, London: Gray-Mills (*MMT*).

1971e, "The University and Social Welfare," *Minerva*, 11 (January), 20–52 (reprinted in *E&S*).

1971f, "Introduction" in H. G. Johnson and A. R. Nobay (eds.), *The Current Inflation*, London: Macmillan vii–xi.

1971g, "Reflections on Current Trends in Economics," *Australian Economic Papers*, 10 (June), 1–11.

1971h, "Crisis '71: On the Cards since 1968," *Money Management*, (November/December), 16–18 (reprinted in *FEME*).

1971i, "Comments on Senator Grosart's Paper," *Minerva*, 9 (October), 544–7.

1971j, "Foreword" to Fleming 1971, 7–9.

1972a, "Inflation and World Trade: A "Monetarist" View," *Journal of World Trade Law*, 6 (January/February), 9–19.

1972b, "Problems of Stabilization Policy in an Integrated World Economy" in Giersch (ed.), 1972, 338–52 (reprinted in *FEME*).

1972c, "The Monetary Approach to Balance of Payments Theory," *FEME* and *MABP* (also in M. B. Connolly and A. K. Swoboda (eds.) 1973, *International Economics: The Geneva Essays*, London: Allen and Unwin, 206–24).

1972d, *Further Essays in Monetary Economics*, London: Allen and Unwin (*FEME*).

1972e, "Review of R. G. Lipsey's *The Theory of Customs Unions*," *Economic Journal*, 82 (June), 728–30.

1972f, "The Bretton Woods System, Key Currencies and the Dollar Crisis," *Three Banks Review*, 94 (June), 3–22.

(with Mohsin Kahn), 1972g, "The Common Market Questionnaire, October 1971," *Economica*, 39 (August), 316–22.

1972h, "Political Economy Aspects of International Monetary Reform," *Journal of International Economics*, 2 (September), 401–24 (reprinted in *E&S*).

1972i, "The International Monetary System and the Rule of Law," *Journal of Law and Economics*, 15 (October), 277–92.

1972j, *Inflation and the Monetarist Controversy*, Amsterdam: North Holland (*IMC*).

1972k, "Some Economic Aspects of Science," *Minerva*, 10 (January), 10–18.

(ed. with others) 1972l, Readings in British Monetory Economics, Oxford: Clarendon Press.

1973a, "The International Monetary Crisis of 1971," *Journal of Business*, 46 (January), 11–23.

1973b, "Secular Inflation and the International Monetary System," *Journal of Money, Credit and Banking*, 5 (February), 509–19.

1973c, "National Styles in Economic Research; The United States, the United Kingdom and Various European Countries," *Daedalus*, 102 (Spring), 64–74 (reprinted in *E&S*).

1973d, "The Uneasy Case for Universal Graduate Programmes in Economics," *Minerva*, 11 (April), 263–8.

1973e, "Time to Reconsider Support for Graduate Work," *Times Higher Education Supplement* (13 July), 11.

1973f, "The Problems of Central Banks in a World of Floating Rates," *Euromoney*, (July), 4–7.

1973g, *Man and His Environment*, London, New York, and Montreal: British North American Committee.

1973h, *The Theory of Income Distribution*, London: Gray-Mills.

1973i, "The Exchange Rate Question for a United Europe: Internal Flexibility and External Rigidity versus External Flexibility and Internal Rigidity" in A Swoboda (ed.) *Europe and the International Monetary System*, Leiden: A. W. Sijtoff, 81–91.

(with Richard E. Caves and Henry D. Hicks), 1973j, *Graduate Programmes in Economics in Ontario* Advisory Committee on Academic Planning, Ontario Council on Graduate Studies.

1974a, "Cambridge in the 1950s," *Encounter*, 42 (January), 28–39 (reprinted in *E&S* and *Shadow*).

1974b, "Mercantilism Past, Present and Future" in H. G. Johnson (ed.), *The New Mercantilism: Some Problems in International Trade, Investment and Money*, Oxford: Blackwell, 1–19 (reprinted in *E&S*).

1974c, *The Problem of International Monetary Reform*, London: Athlone Press.

1974d, "General Principles for World Monetary Reform" in H. Corbet and Robert Jackson (eds.), *In Search of a New World Economic Order*, London: Croom Helm, 150–68.

1974e, "The Current and Prospective State of Economics in Canada" in Thomas N. Guinsberg and Grant L. Reuber (eds.), *Perspectives on the Social Sciences in Canada*, Toronto: University of Toronto Press, 85–123 (reprinted in part in *E&S*).

1974f, "Major Issues in Monetary Economics," *Oxford Economic Papers*, 26 (July), 212–25.

1974g, "Me and My Brain Drain," *Punch*, 267 (30 October), 698–701.

1974h, *General Equilibrium Analysis: A Microeconomic Text*, London: Allen and Unwin.

1974i, "The Welfare Economics of Reversed International Transfers" in G. Horwich and P. A. Samuelson (eds.), *Trade, Stability, and Macroeconomics: Essays in Honor of Lloyd A. Metzler*, New York: Academic Press, 79–110.

1975a, "On Living without an International Monetary System," *Euromoney*, (April), 34–5.

1975b, "World Inflation and the International Monetary System," *Three Banks Review*, 107 (September), 3–22.

1975c, "The Monetary Approach to the Balance of Payments: A Diagrammatic Analysis," *Manchester School*, 18 (September), 220–74.

1975d, "Some Comments on Inflation Theory" in R. A. Mundell and B. E. von Snellenberg (eds.), *Policy Formation in an Open Economy*, vol. I, Waterloo: University of Waterloo, 19–26.

1975e, "Equity and Economic Theory," *Nebraska Journal of Economics and Business*, 14 (Summer), 3–17.

1975f, "An Overview of the World Crisis and International Trade," *Kredit und Kapital*, 8 (4), 433–49.

1975g, *On Economics and Society*, Chicago: University of Chicago Press (*E&S*).

1975h, "The Future of Floating Rates," *Weltwirtschaftliches Archiv*, 110 (Heft 2), 205–9.

1975i, *Technology and Economic Interdependence*, London: Macmillan.

1975j, "The Probable Effects of Freer Trade on Individual Countries" in C. Fred Bergsten (ed.), *Towards a New World Trade Policy: The Maidenhead Papers*, Lexington, MA: D. C. Heath, 35–47.

1975k, "World Inflation and the International Monetary System," *Three Banks Review*, 107 (September), 3–22.

1975l, "Learning and Libraries: Academic Economics as a Profession: Its Bearing on the Organisation and Retrieval of Economic Knowledge," *Minerva*, 13 (Winter), 621–32.

1975m, "Quadrangular Perspectives on Security, Inflation and the World Financial Structure" in Penelope Hartland-Thunberg (ed.), *Commissioned Papers on Inflation, Recession, Energy and the International Financial Structure*, Washington, DC: Georgetown University Centre for Strategic and International Studies, 25–62.

1975n, "Keynes and British Economics" in M. Keynes (ed.), *Essays on John Maynard Keynes*, Cambridge: Cambridge University Press, 108–22 (reprinted in *Shadow*).

1975o, "Technological Change and Comparative Advantage: An Advanced Country's Viewpoint," *Journal of World Trade Law*, 9 (January/February), 1–14.

1976a, "A Formal Analysis of Some Brinley Thomas Problems Concerning the International Migration of Capital and Labour" in H. Richards (ed.), *Population, Factor Movements and Economic Development: Studies Presented to Brinley Thomas*, Cardiff: University of Wales Press, 52–67.

1976b, "Money and the Balance of Payments," *Banca Nazionale del Lavoro Quarterly Review*, 116 (March), 3–18.

1976c, "What Is Right with Monetarism," *Lloyds Bank Review*, 120 (April), 13–17.

1976d, "Discussion of 'Increasing International Economic Interdependence: The Implications for Research,'" *American Economic Review*, 66 (May), 162.

1976e, "Elasticity, Absorption, Keynesian Multiplier, Keynesian Policy and Monetary Approaches to Devaluation Theory: A Simple Geometric Exposition," *American Economic Review*, 66 (June), 448–52.

1976f, "Scholars as Public Adversaries: The Case of Economics" in Charles Frank (ed.), *Controversies and Decisions: The Social Sciences and Public Policy*, New York: Russell Sage Foundation, 171–84 (reprinted in *E&S*).

1976g, "Comment on Mayer on Monetarism," *Kredit und Kapital*, 9 (2), 145–53.

1976h, "Aspects of Patents and Licenses as Stimuli to Innovation," *Weltwirtschaftliches Archiv*, 112 (3), 417–28.

1976i, "Keynes's *General Theory*: Revolution or War of Independence?," *Canadian Journal of Economics*, 9 (November), 580–94 (reprinted in *Shadow*).

(ed. with Jacob Frenkel) 1976j, *The Monetary Approach to the Balance of Payments*, London: Allen and Unwin (*MABP*).

(with Jacob Frenkel) 1976k, "The Monetary Approach to the Balance of Payments: Essential Concepts and Historical Origins" in *MABP*, 21–45.

1976l, "The Monetary Theory of Balance of Payments Policies" in *MABP*, 262–84.

1976m, "[Industrial Policy: Location, Technology, Multinational Firms, Competition and Integration of Product Markets:] Report on Group Discussion" in F. Machlup (ed.), *Economic Integration: Worldwide, Regional, Sectoral*, London: Macmillan, 160–2.

1976n, "Comment on Porter" in R. I. McKinnon (ed.), *Money and Finance in Economic Growth and Development: Essays in Honor or Edward S. Shaw*, New York: Marcel Dekker, 298–301.

1976o, "Economics and Long-term Forecasting" in C. Freeman, Marie Jahoda, and I. Miles (eds.), *Progress and Problems in Social Forecasting*, London: Social Science Research Council, 26–31.

1976p, "Comments" in Henry G. Manne and Roger LeRoy Miller (eds.), *Gold, Money and the Law*, Chicago: Aldine, 83–92.

1976q, "A Tribute to Homer Jones," *Journal of Monetary Economics*, 2 (November), 437–8.

1976r, "Chairman's Notes on the Symposium in Macroeconomic Models and Policy, Econometric Society World Congress, Toronto, August 22 1975" in M. D. Intriligator (ed.), *Frontiers of Quantitative Economics*, vol. 3, Amsterdam: North Holland, 756–7.

1976s, "Foreign Ownership and Economic Policy: The Perennial Problem," *Journal of Energy and Development*, 2 (Autumn), 23–9.

1977a, "Technology, Technical Progress and the International Allocation of Economic Activity" in B. Ohlin et al. (eds.), *The International Allocation of Economic Activity: Proceedings of a Nobel Symposium*, London: Macmillan.

1977b, "World Inflation, International Monetary Reform and the Less Developed Countries," *Indian Economic Review*, 12 (April), 1–14.

1977c, "Trade Negotiations and the New International Monetary System," *Commercial Policies Issues* 1, Leiden: A. W. Sijtoff for the Trade Policy Research Centre.

1977d, "Money, Balance-of-Payments Theory, and the International Monetary Problem," *Princeton Essays in International Finance*, 124 (November).

1977e, "Economics and the Radical Challenge: The Hard Social Science and the Soft Social Reality" in Joseph ben-David and Terry N. Clark (eds.), *Culture and Its Creators: Essays in Honor of Edward Shils*, Chicago: University of Chicago Press, 97–118.

(with A. R. Nobay) 1977f, "Monetarism: A Historic–Theoretic Perspective," *Journal of Economic Literature*, 15 (June), 470–85.

1977g, "The Monetary Approach to Balance of Payments Theory and Policy: Explanation and Policy Implications," *Economica*, 44 (August), 217–29.

1977h, "The Monetary Approach to the Balance of Payments: A Non-Technical Guide," *Journal of International Economics*, 7 (August), 251–68.

1977i, "Commodities: Less Developed Countries' Demands and Developed Countries' Responses" in J. Bhagwati (ed.), *The New Economic Order: The North-South Debate*, Cambridge, MA: MIT Press, 240–51.

1977j, "The American Tradition in Economics," *Nebraska Journal of Economics and Business*, 16 (Summer), 17–26.

1977k, "Comment on Salant" in Lawrence B. Krause and Walter S. Salant (eds.), *Worldwide Inflation: Theory and Recent Experience*, Washington, DC: Brookings Institution, 650–2.

1978a, "Cambridge as an Academic Environment in the Early 1930s: A Reconstruction from the Late 1940s" in D. Patinkin and J. Clark Leith (eds.), *Keynes, Cambridge and the General Theory*, London: Macmillan, 98–114 (reprinted in *Shadow*).

1978b, "James Meade's Contributions to Economics," *Scandinavian Journal of Economics*, 80 (1), 64–85.

(ed. with Jacob Frenkel) 1978c, *The Economics of Exchange Rates: Selected Studies*, Reading, MA: Addison-Wesley.

1978d, *Selected Essays in Monetary Economics*, London: Allen and Unwin (*SEME*).

(with Elizabeth Johnson) 1978e, *The Shadow of Keynes: Understanding Keynes, Cambridge and Keynesian Economics*, Chicago: University of Chicago Press (*Shadow*).

1978f, "The North–South Issue" in K. Brunner (ed.), *The First World and the Third World: Essays on the New International Economic Order*, Rochester: Centre for Research on Government Policy and Business, 94–104.

1978g, "The New International Economic Order" in K. Brunner (ed.), *The First World and the Third World: Essays on the New International Economic Order*, Rochester: Centre for Research on Government Policy and Business, 81–93.

1978h, "The Individual and the State: Some Contemporary Problems" in Fred R. Glahe (ed.), *Adam Smith and the Wealth of Nations: 1996–1976 Bicentennial Essays*, Boulder: Colorado Association University Press.

1982, "Networks of Economists and their Role in International Monetary Reform" in W. M. Evan (ed.), *Knowledge and Power in a Global Society*, Beverly Hills, CA: Sage Publications, 79–90.

Jones, R. W. 2003, "Trade Theories and Factor Intensities: An Interpretative Essay" in Choi and Harrigan (eds.) 2003, 5–31.

Kenen, P. B. (ed.) 1975, *International Trade and Finance: Frontiers for Research*, New York: Cambridge University Press.

ed. 1995, *Understanding Interdependence: The Macroeconomics of the Open Economy*, Princeton, NJ: Princeton University Press.

2000a, *The International Economy* (4th ed.), New York: Cambridge University Press.

2000b, "Peter Kenen" in Backhouse and Middleton (eds.) 2000, I, 257–77.

Kermode, Frank 1995, *Not Entitled: A Memoir*, New York: Farrar, Strauss and Giroux.

Keshen, J. 1998, "Getting it Right the Second Time Around: The Reintegration of Canadian Veterans of World War II" in Neary and Granatstein (eds.) 1998, 62–84.

Keynes, J. M. 1929, "The German Transfer Problem," *Economic Journal*, 39 (March), 1–7.

Kidd, Harry 1969, *The Trouble at LSE, 1966–67*, Oxford: Oxford University Press.

Kindleberger, C. P. (ed.) 1970, *The International Corporation*, Cambridge, MA: MIT Press.

1991, *The Life of an Economist: An Autobiography*, Oxford: Blackwell.

King's College 2006, "Indraprasad Gordhanabi Patel," *Annual Report*, Cambridge.

Kreinin, M. E. 2002, *International Economics: A Policy Approach* (9th ed.), Mason, OH: South-Western.

Kreinin, M. C. and Officer, L. H., 1978, "The Monetary Approach to the Balance of Payments: A Survey," *Princeton Studies in International Finance*, 43.

Krueger, A. B. 2001, "An Interview with William J. Baumol," *Journal of Economic Perspectives*, 15 (Summer), 211–31.

Krueger, A. B. and Taylor, T. 2000, "An Interview with Zvi Griliches," *Journal of Economic Perspectives*, 14 (Spring), 171–89.

Krugman, P. A. and Obstfeld, M. 2000, *International Economics: Theory and Policy* (5th ed.), Reading MA: Addison-Wesley.

Laidler, David 1966, "The Rate of Interest and the Demand for Money – Some Empirical Evidence," *Journal of Political Economy*, 74 (December), 545–55.

1984, "Harry Johnson as a Macroeconomist," *Journal of Political Economy*, 92 (August), 592–615.

1990, *Taking Money Seriously*, London: Philip Allen.

1997, "The Emergence of the Phillips Curve as a Policy Menu" in B. C. Eaton and R. G. Harris (eds.), *Trade, Technology and Economics: Essays in Honour of Richard G. Lipsey*, Cheltenham: Edward Elgar, 88–106.

2000, "David Laidler" in Backhouse and Middleton (eds.) 2000, vol. I, 323–53.

Lancaster, K. and Lipsey, R. G. 1956, "The General Theory of the Second Best," *Review of Economic Studies*, 24 (1), 11–52.

Lange, Oskar 1938, "The Rate of Interest and the Optimum Propensity to Consume," *Economica*, V (February 1938), 12–32.

Lary, H. B. 1943, *The United States in the World Economy: The International Transactions of the United States in the Interwar Period*, Washington, DC: Government Printing Office.

Leacy, F. H. (ed.) 1983, *Historical Statistics of Canada* (2nd ed.), Ottawa: Statistics Canada.

Leeson, Robert 2000, "Patinkin, Johnson and the Shadow of Friedman," *History of Political Economy*, 32 (Winter), 733–64.

(ed.) 2000, *A. W. H. Phillips: Collected Works in Contemporary Perspective*, Cambridge: Cambridge University Press.

2003, "From Keynes to Friedman via Mints: Resolving the Dispute over the Quantity Theory Oral Tradition," in Leeson (ed.) 2003, vol. II, 481–525.

(ed.) 2003, *Keynes, Chicago and Friedman*, 2 vols., London: Pickering & Chatto.

Leijonhufvud, Axel 1968, *On Keynesian Economics and the Economics of Keynes: A Study in Monetary Theory*, London: Oxford University Press.

1969. *Keynes and the Classics: Two Lectures*, London: Institute of Economic Affairs, Occasional Paper 30.

Leman, Nicholas 1992, *The Promised Land: The Great Black Migration and How it Changed America*, New York: Basic Books.

Lemieux, Thomas and Card, David 2001, "Education, Earnings and the 'Canadian G. I. Bill,'" *Canadian Journal of Economics*, 34 (May), 313–34.

Lemon, James 1985, *Toronto Since 1918: An Illustrated History*, Toronto: James Lorimer for the National Museum of Man.

Levy, Paul 1979, *Moore: G.E. Moore and the Cambridge Apostles*, London: Weidenfeld and Nicolson.

Linder, S. B. 1970, *The Harried Leisure Class*, New York: Columbia University Press.

Lipsey, R. G. 1957, "The Theory of Customs Unions: Trade Diversion and Welfare," *Economica*, 24 (February), 40–6.

1978, "Harry Johnson's Contributions to the Pure Theory of International Trade," *Canadian Journal of Economics*, 11 (November, Supplement), S34–S54.

2000, "Richard G. Lipsey" in Backhouse and Middleton (eds.) 2000, vol. I, 109–46.

2001, "Harry as Mentor of Young Economists," *American Journal of Economics and Sociology*, 60 (July), 611–18.

Lipsey, R. G. and Archibald, G. C. 1958, "Money and Value Theory: A Critique of Lange and Patinkin," *Review of Economic Studies*, 26 (1), 1–22.

Longawa, Vicky M. 1984, "Harry G. Johnson: A Bibliography," *Journal of Political Economy*, 92 (August), 659–711.

London School of Economics 1967–8, 'Report of the Director on the Work of the School during the Year 1964–65," *Calendar*.

1969–70, "Report of the Director on the Work of the School during the Year 1967–68," *Calendar*.

1974–75, " Report of the Director on the Work of the School during the Year 1972–73," *Calendar*.

MacDonald, Neil B. 1963, "A Comment: The Bladen Plan for Increased Protection for the Automotive Industry," *Canadian Journal of Economics and Political Science*, 24 (November), 505–15.

MacEachen, Allan J. 1997, "All These Years: Practice and Purpose in Politics" in Tom Kent (ed.), *In Pursuit of the Public Good: Essays in Honour of Allan J. MacEachen*, Montreal and Kingston: McGill–Queen's University Press, 3–20.

Macesich, George 1958, *The Quantity Theory and the Income-Expenditure Theory in an Open Economy: Canada, 1926–58*, University of Chicago, PhD dissertation.

1962, "Determinants of Monetary Velocity in Canada," *Canadian Journal of Economics and Political Science*, 28 (May), 245–54.

Machlup, F. 1943, *Foreign Trade and the National Income Multiplier*, Philadelphia: Blakiston.

1964, "Plans for Reform of the International Monetary System," *Special Papers in International Economics*, No. 3, revised, Princeton, NJ: International Finance Section.

Machlup, F. and Malkiel, B. 1964, *International Monetary Arrangements: The Problem of Choice: Report on the Deliberations of an International Study Group of 32 Economists*, Princeton, NJ: International Finance Section.

Makower, H. and Morton, G. 1953, "A Contribution to the Theory of Customs Unions," *Economic Journal*, 63 (March), 33–49.

Markusen, J. R., Melvin, J. R., Kaempfer, W. H., and Maskus, K. E. 1995, *International Trade: Theory and Evidence*, New York: McGraw-Hill.

Marsh Report 1943, *Report on Social Security for Canada*, Ottawa: The King's Printer.

Marshall, A. 1920, *Principles of Economics: An Introductory Volume* 8th ed., London: Macmillan.

Mason, Edward S. 1982, "The Harvard Department of Economics from the Beginning to World War II," *Quarterly Journal of Economics*, 97 (August), 383–433.

Matthews, R. C. O. 2000, "Review of Roger Middleton, *Charlatans or Saviours?: Economists and the British Economy from Marshall to Meade*," *Economic Journal*, 110 (February), 188–9.

McDougall, I. A. and Snape, R. N. (eds.) 1970, *Studies in International Economics: The Monash Conference Papers*, Amsterdam: North Holland.

McKenty, Neil 1967, *Mitch Hepburn*, Toronto: McClelland and Stewart.

McKillop, A. B. 1994, *Matters of Mind: The University in Ontario, 1791–1951*, Toronto: University of Toronto Press.

McNaught, Kenneth 1999, *Conscience and History: A Memoir*, Toronto: University of Toronto Press.

McNeill, William C. 1991, *Hutchins' University: A Memoir of the University of Chicago, 1929–1950*, Chicago: University of Chicago Press.

Meade, James 1951, *The Balance of Payments*, London: Oxford University Press.

1955, *Trade and Welfare*, London: Oxford University Press.

1956, *A Geometry of International Trade*, London: Allen and Unwin.

Mehrling, Perry G. 1997, *The Money Interest and the Public Interest: American Monetary Thought, 1920–1970*, Cambridge, MA: Harvard University Press.

Metzler, L. A. 1942, "Unemployment Equilibrium and International Trade," *Econometrica*, 10 (April), 97–112.

Middleton, Roger 1998, *Charlatans or Saviours?: Economists and the British Economy from Marshall to Meade*, Cheltenham: Edward Elgar.

Millichamp, Dorothy A. and Fletcher, Margaret I. 1951, "Goals and Growth of Nursery Education" in Berhardt et al. (eds.) 1951, 26–38.

Mills, Judy and Dombra, Irene 1968, *University of Toronto Doctoral Theses, 1897–1967*, Toronto: University of Toronto Press.

Mirowski, P. and Sent, E-M. (eds.) 2002, *Science Bought and Sold: Essays in the Economics of Science*, Chicago: University of Chicago Press.

Mishan, E. J. and Neeldeman, L. 1966, "Immigration, Excess Aggregate Demand and the Balance of Payments," *Economica*, 33 (May 1966), 129–47.

Modigliani, Franco 1944, "Liquidity Preference and the Theory of Interest and Money," *Econometrica*, 12 (January), 45–88.

Moggridge, D. E. (ed.) 1979a, *The Collected Writings of John Maynard Keynes, XXIX, The General Theory and After: A Supplement*, London: Macmillan.

(ed.) 1979b, *The Collected Writings of John Maynard Keynes, XXIV, The Transition to Peace*, London: Macmillan.

1990, "Keynes as Editor" in John D. Hey and Donald Winch (eds.), *A Century of Economics: 100 Years of the Royal Economic Society and the Economic Journal*, Oxford: Blackwell.

1992, *Maynard Keynes: An Economist's Biography*, London: Routledge.

2003, "Biography and the History of Economics" in W. J. Samuels, G. Biddle and J. B. Davis (eds.) *A Companion to the History of Economic Thought*, Oxford: Blackwell, 588–605.

Morgan, D. J. and Corlett, W. J. 1951, "The Influence of Price in International Trade," *Journal of the Royal Statistical Society*, 114 (3), 307–58.

Morgan, Lorne 1943, *The Permanent War or Homo the Sap*, Toronto: Workers Educational Association of Canada.

Morshima, M. 1973, *Marx's Economics: A Dual Theory of Value and Growth*, Cambridge: Cambridge University Press.

Mundell, R. A. 1963, "Capital Mobility and Stabilization Policy Under Fixed and Flexible Exchange Rates," *Canadian Journal of Economics and Political Science*, 29 (November), 475–85.

1967, "International Disequilibrium and the Adjustment Process" in J. H. Adler (ed.) 1967, 44–62

1968, *International Economics*, New York: Macmillan.

1969, "Real Gold, Dollars and Paper Gold," *American Economic Review*, 59 (May), 324–31.

and Swoboda, Alexander (eds.) 1969, *Monetary Problems of the International Economy*, Chicago: University of Chicago Press.

2002, "Notes on the Development of the International Macroeconomic Model in Arnon and Young (eds.) 2002.

Myint, Hal 1954–5, "The Gains from International Trade and Backward Countries," *Review of Economic Studies*, 22(2), 129–42.

Neary, P. and Granatstein, J. L. (eds.) 1998, *The Veterans Charter and Post-World War II Canada*, Montreal and Kingston: McGill–Queen's University Press.

Obstfeld, M. and Rogoff, K. 1996, *Foundations of International Macroeconomics*, Cambridge, MA: MIT Press.

Ohlin, Bertil, Hesselborn, Per-Ove, and Wijkiman, Per Magnus (eds.) 1977, *The International Allocation of Economic Activity: Proceedings of a Nobel Symposium*, London: Macmillan.

Oliver, Dean F. 1998, "Awaiting Return: Life in the Canadian Army's Overseas Repatriation Depots, 1945–1946" in Neary and Granatstein (eds.) 1998, 32–61.

Oliver, Peter 1975, *Public and Private Persons: The Ontario Political Culture 1914–1934*, Toronto: Clarke, Irwin & Co.

Ozga, S. A. 1955, "An Essay on the Theory of Tariffs," *Journal of Political Economy*, 63 (December), 489–99.

Parr, Joy 1999, *Domestic Goods: The Material, the Moral and the Economic in the Postwar Years*, Toronto: University of Toronto Press.

Patinkin, Don 1956, *Money, Interest and Prices*, Evanston, IL: Harper and Row (2nd ed. 1965).

1969, "The Chicago Tradition, the Quantity Theory and Friedman," *Journal of Money, Credit and Banking*, 1 (February), 46–70.

1972 "Friedman on the Quantity Theory and Keynesian Economics," *Journal of Political Economy*, 80 (September/October), 883–905.

Pesek, B. P. and Saving T. R. 1967, *Money, Wealth and Economic Theory*, New York: Macmillan.

Pevsner, Nikolaus 1969, *The Buildings of England: Lancashire I, The Industrial and Commercial South*, Harmondsworth: Penguin Books.

1970, *The Buildings of England: Cambridgeshire* (2nd ed.), Harmondsworth: Penguin Books.

Phelps, E. S. 1967, "Phillips Curves, Expectations of Inflation and Optimal Unemployment Over Time," *Economica*, 34 (August), 254–81.

Phillips, A. W. H. 1958, "The Relation between Unemployment and the Rate of Change of Money Wage Rates in the United Kingdom, 1861–1957," *Economica*, 25 (November), 283–99.

Plumptre, A. F. W. 1941, *Mobilising Canada's Resources for War*, Toronto: Macmillan.

Polak, J. J. 2002, "The Two Monetary Approaches to the Balance of Payments: Keynesian and Johnsonian" in Arnon and Young (eds.) 2002, 19–41.

Prais, S. J. 1961, "Some Mathematical Notes on the Quantity Theory of Money in an Open Economy" *IMF Staff Papers*, 8 (May), 212–26.

Prest, A. R. 1968, "Review of *Economic Policies Towards Less-Developed Countries, Economica*," 35 (May), 208–9.

1977, "Harry Johnson," *The Economist*, 14 (May), 121.

Pullen, Brian (with Michelle Abendstern) 2000, *A History of the University of Manchester, 1951–1973*, Manchester: Manchester University Press.

Reder, Melvin 1982, "Chicago Economics: Permanence and Change," *Journal of Economic Literature*, 20 (March), 1–38.

Reuber, G. L. 1962, *The Objectives of Monetary Policy*, Ottawa: Royal Commission on Banking and Finance.

    1964, "The Objectives of Canadian Monetary Policy, 1949–1961: Empirical Trade-offs and the Reaction Function of the Authorities," *Journal of Political Economy*, 72 (May), 109–32.

Reuber, G. L. and Scott, A. D. 1977, "In Memorium: Harry Gordon Johnson, 1923–1977," *Canadian Journal of Economics*, 10 (November), 671–7.

Rhomberg, R. H. 1964, "A Model of the Canadian Economy Under Fixed and Fluctuating Exchange Rates," *Journal of Political Economy*, 82 (February), 1–31.

Rignano, Eugenio 1925, *The Social Significance of Death Duties*, London: Douglas.

Roach, J. P. C. 1959, "The University of Cambridge" in J. P. C. Roach (ed.), *The Victoria County History, Cambridgeshire, III*, London: Institute of Historical Research, 150–312.

Robertson, D. H. 1940, *Essays in Monetary Theory*, London: P. S. King.

    1950, "A Revolutionists Handbook," *Quarterly Journal of Economics*, 64 (February), 1–14.

    1952, "Comments on Monetary Policy and the Crisis," *Bulletin of the Oxford University Institute of Statistics*, 14 (April–May), 154–6.

    1953–4, "More Notes on the Rate of Interest," *Review of Economic Studies*, 22 (2) 129–42.

Robertson, D. H. and Johnson, Harry G. 1955, "Keynes and Supply Functions," *Economic Journal*, 65 (September), 474–8.

Robinson, Joan 1953–4, "The Production Function and the Theory of Capital," *Review of Economic Studies*, 21 (2), 81–106.

    1962, "Review of *Money, Trade and Economic Growth, Economic Journal*," 72 (September), 690–2 (reprinted in Robinson 1965).

    1965, *Collected Economic Papers, Volume III*, Oxford: Blackwell.

Rose, Richard 1999, "William James Millar Mackenzie, 1909–1996," *Proceedings of the British Academy*, CI, 465–85.

Rosenbluth, Gideon 2001, "Harry, the Workaholic Student and Radical," *American Journal of Economics and Sociology*, 60 (July), 606–10.

Rubin, David C. (ed.) 1996, *Remembering Our Past: Studies in Autobiographical Memory*, Cambridge: Cambridge University Press.

    1996, "Introduction" in Rubin (ed.) 1996, 1–15.

Rubin, David C., Rahhal, Tamara A., and Pool Leonard W. 1998, "Things Remembered in Early Adulthood are Remembered Best," *Memory and Cognition*, 26 (10), 3–19.

Rybczynski, T. 1955, "Factor Endowment and Relative Commodity Prices," *Economica*, 22 (December), 336–41.

Salant, Walter 1976, "Hansen and the Fiscal Policy Seminar," *Quarterly Journal of Economics*, 90 (February), 14–23.

Samuelson, Paul A. 1967, "The Monopolistic Competition Revolution" in R. E. Keune (ed.), *Monopolistic Competition Theory: Studies in Impact – Essays in Honor of Edward H. Chamberlin*, New York: Wiley.

    (ed.) 1969, *International Economic Relations*, London: Macmillan.

1976, "Alvin Hansen as a Creative Economic Theorist," *Quarterly Journal of Economics*, 90 (February), 25–31.

1977, *The Collected Scientific Papers of Paul A. Samuelson, Volume IV* (eds. H. Nagatani and K. Crowley), Cambridge, MA: MIT Press.

1986, *The Collected Scientific Papers of Paul A. Samuelson, Volume V* (ed. K. Crowley), Cambridge, MA: MIT Press.

1996, "Gottfried Haberler, 1900–1995," *Economic Journal*, 106 (November), 1679–87.

1998, "How *Foundations* Came to Be," *Journal of Economic Literature*, 36 (September), 1375–86.

2001, "Harry, the Full Achiever," *American Journal of Economics and Sociology*, 60 (July), 601–6.

Saywell, John T. 1991, "'Just call me Mitch': The Life of Mitchell F. Hepburn," Toronto: University of Toronto Press.

Schumpeter, Joseph 1942, *Capitalism, Socialism and Democracy*, New York: Harper.

Scitovsky, Tibor 1942, "A Reconsideration of the Theory of Tariffs," *Review of Economic Studies*, 9 (Summer), 89–110.

Scott, A. D. 1977, "Harry Gordon Johnson, 1923–1977," *Proceedings of the Royal Society of Canada*, Series IV, 15, 79–82.

Sen, A. K. 1970, *Collective Choice and Social Welfare*, San Francisco: Holden-Day.

Shaw, Edward S. 1950, *Money, Income and Monetary Policy*, Chicago: Irwin.

Shils, Edward 1977, "Harry Johnson," *Encounter*, 49 (November), 85–9.

1991, "Harry G. Johnson, 1923–1977" in Edward Shils (ed.), *Remembering the University of Chicago*, Chicago: University of Chicago Press, 197–209.

Sidgwick, A. and Sidgwick, E. M. 1906, *Henry Sidgwick: A Memoir*, London: Macmillan

Silberston, Z. A. 1978, *Harry Johnson as a Young Man*, London: Imperial College.

Simpson, Elizabeth Johnson 2002, "How Harry Worked," *American Journal of Economics and Sociology*, 60 (July), 634–41.

Sirluck, Ernest 1996, *First Generation: An Autobiography*, Toronto: University of Toronto Press.

Snape, R. H. 1963, "Some Effects of Protection in the World Sugar Industry," *Economica*, 30 (February), 63–73.

Spafford, Shirley 2000, *No Ordinary Academics: Economics and Political Science at the University of Saskatchewan. 1910–1960*, Toronto: University of Toronto Press.

Sparrow, John 1967, *Mark Pattison and the Idea of a University*, Cambridge: Cambridge University Press.

Stacey, C. P. 1966, *Six Years of War: The Canadian Army in Canada, Britain and the Pacific*, Ottawa: The Queen's Printer.

Stacey, C. P. and Wilson, B. M. 1987, *The Half Million: The Canadians in Britain, 1939–1946*, Toronto: University of Toronto Press.

Staiger, R. W. 1995, "International Roles and Institutions for Cooperative Trade Policy" in G. W. Grossman and K Rogoff (eds.), *Handbook of International Economics*, vol. III, Amsterdam: North Holland.

Stankiewicz, W. J. (ed.), 1964, *The Living Name: A Tribute to Stefan Stykolt from Some of His Friends*, Toronto: University of Toronto Press.

Stigler, George 1988, *Memoirs of an Unrelated Economist*, New York: Basic Books.

Strong-Boag, Veronica 1982, "Intruders in the Nursery: Childcare Professionals Reshape the Years One to Five, 1020–1940" in Joy Parr (ed.), *Childhood and Family in Canadian History*, Toronto: McClelland and Stewart, 160–78, 217–23.

Swedeberg, Richard 1991, *Schumpeter: A Biography*, Princeton, NJ: Princeton University Press.

Swoboda, Alexander (ed.) 1973, *Europe and the International Monteray System*, Leiden: A. W. Sijtoff.

Taylor, Alan M. and Taylor, Mark P. 2004, "The Purchasing Power Parity Debate," *Journal of Economic Perspectives*, 18 (Fall), 115–34.

Tignor, Robert L. 2005, *W. Arthur Lewis and the Birth of Development Economics*, Princeton, NJ: Princeton University Press.

Tobin, James 1978, "Harry Gordon Johnson, 1923–1977," *Proceedings of the British Academy*, 64, 443–58.

Tribe, K. 1993, "Political Economy in the Northern Universities," in Alon Kadish and K. Tribe (eds.), *The Market for Political Economy: The Advent of Economics in British University Culture, 1850–1905*, London: Routledge, 184–226.

(ed.) 1997, *Economic Careers: Economics and Economists in Britain, 1930–1990*, London: Routledge.

Triffin, Robert 1947, "National Central Banking and the International Economy," *Postwar Monetary Studies*, vol. 7. Washington, DC: Board of Governors of the Federal Reserve System, 46–81.

1960, *Gold and the Dollar Crisis*, New Haven, CT: Yale University Press.

Twigg, John 1987, *A History of Queen's College, Cambridge, 1448–1986*, Woodbridge: The Boydell Press.

United Kingdom, Economic Social and Research Council, Regard, 2003.

Usher, Dan 2000, "Dan Usher" in Backhouse and Middleton (eds.) 2000, vol. I, 284–310.

Vernon, Raymond (ed.) 1970, *The Technology Factor in International Trade*, New York: National Bureau of Economic Research.

Volpe, R. (ed.) forthcoming, *Human Security: Reflections on the Life and Work of W. E. Blatz*, Toronto: University of Toronto Press.

Watson, Alexander John 2006, *Marginal Man: The Dark Vision of Harold Adams Innis*, Toronto: University of Toronto Press.

Weintraub, E. Roy 2005, "Autobiographical Memory and the History of Economics," *Journal of the History of Economic Thought*, 27 (March), 1–11.

Welton, Michael R. 2001, *Little Mosie from the Margaree: A Biography of Michael Moses Coady*, Toronto: Thompson Educational Publishing.

Wiles, P. J. D. 1950, "Empirical Research and Marginal Analysis," *Economic Journal*, 60 (September), 515–30.

Williams, J. H. 1920, *Argentine International Trade Under Inconvertible Paper Money, 1880–1900*, Cambridge, MA: Harvard University Press.

Williamson, John 1972, "Review of *Macroeconomics and Monetary Theory*," *Economic Journal*, 82 (September), 1062–4.

Woodford, Michael 2003, *Interest and Prices: Foundations of a Theory of Monetary Policy*, Princeton, NJ: Princeton University Press.

Worwick, David 1960, *The Free Trade Proposals*, Oxford: Blackwell.

Wright, M. J. 1983, "The Saga of William Ernest Blatz I," *CPA Section on Development Psychology Newsletter*.

1984, "The Saga of William Ernest Blatz, Part II," *CPA Section on Developmental Psychology Newsletter*.

2007, "William Ernest Blatz: The Person and his Work" in Volpe forthcoming.

Yarbrough, B. V. and Yarbrough, R. M. 2002, *The World Economy: Trade and Finance*, 6th ed., Mason, OH: South-Western.

Zweiniger-Bargielowska, Ina 2000, *Austerity in Britain: Rationing, Controls and Consumption. 1939–1953*, Oxford: Oxford University Press.

Index